A Guide to Color Reproductions

by

Margaret Bartran

Second Edition

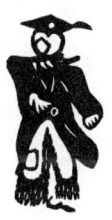

The Scarecrow Press, Inc.
Metuchen, N.J.   1971

For my mother, Clara M. Bartran

Introduction

The selection of color reproductions available for purchase in the United States today appears to have increased by about 50% since 1965.

As in the original edition, this revised Guide to Color Re- productions is intended to be a handbook for the retail print dealer. It is an attempt to organize a helpful record of the art reproductions available in the United States as of about January 1, 1969, with an unbiased approach to both the original works of art and the printing processes which reproduced them.

Artists, titles, sizes, prices and sources from catalogs of the better-known picture publishers and distributors in the United States have been arranged so that the retail picture dealer can as- certain quickly which of his many catalogs to consult for more detailed information.

The book is arranged in two sections. The first is a list of artists with their names alphabetically arranged and under each name is a list of that artist's work which has been reproduced. Next to each title are dimensions in inches with vertical measure- ment first. The largest available size of each print is listed first and smaller sizes are listed beneath in diminishing order. The next column gives a source for ordering, and the last gives the retail price for each size in U. S. currency.

Artists' names have been searched in standard indexes of artists to check accuracy of spelling, identification and standard ar- rangement.

The second section of the book, which is an Index of Titles, has been arranged in this edition to refer to both the artists' names and the item numbers of the first section.

This book is limited to information about art reproductions in sheet form commercially printed in color on paper, available in the United States at prices quoted in U. S. currency. (Prices are, of course, subject to change at the discretion of publishers and sellers.) This book is not meant to refer to any original or hand-made prints, artists' proofs, signed copies, already-framed pictures, photographs, slides, postcards, book or magazine illustrations, or those miniature reproductions which are smaller than 7 x 5 inches. It includes a few black and white subjects which are well-enough known to add to the usefulness of the book without increasing its size too much.

Some of the sources listed are publishers as well as whole-sale distributors of reproductions, some are distributors only, and a few sell prints of special subjects on a retail basis only. Most of the publishers and distributors listed here are in a position to offer the retail dealer a discount for resale. It is suggested that the prospective customer consult his local retail picture dealer to order prints for purchase.

M. B.

January, 1970

Abbreviations and Distributors' Symbols

AA
Aaron Ashley, Inc., 174 Buena Vista Ave., P. O. Box 244, Yonkers, N. Y. 10702

Ac. or AC.
Active

AJ
Arthur Jaffe, Inc., 3 E. 28th St., New York, N. Y. 10016

AK
Arthur A. Kaplan Co., Inc., 28 W. 25th St., New York, N. Y. 10010

AL
Art Lore, Inc., 28 W. 25th St., New York, N. Y. 10010

AP
Artext Prints, Inc., Westport, Conn. 06880

AR
Arthur Rothmann Fine Arts, 1123 Broadway, New York, N. Y. 10010

AS
Alfred Schiftan, Inc., 460 Park Ave., S., New York, N. Y. 10016

Attrib.
Attributed

b.
Born

B & W
Black and White

C
Circa or About

CAC
Colonial Art Co., 1336-1338 N. W. First St., Oklahoma City, Okla. 73106

CFA
Catalda Fine Arts, Inc., 15 W. 27th St., New York, N. Y. 10001

Contemp.
Contemporary or Now Living

Cv. or Canv.
Canvas-Textured Paper

d.
Died

DAC
Donald Art Co., 90 S. Ridge St., Port Chester, N. Y. 10574

Diam.	Diameter of a Circular Composition
Dr. or DR.	Drawing
ESH	Erich S. Herrmann, Inc., 3 E. 28th St., New York, N. Y. 10016
Fl.	Flourished
Gr.	Gravure
H. C.	Hand Colored
HNA	Harry N. Abrams, Inc., 6 W. 57th St., New York, N. Y. 10019
IA	International Art Publishing Co., 243 W. Congress St., Detroit, Mich. 48226
JM	Johnson Meyer Co., 850-A Brewster Ave., Redwood City, Cal.
MMA	The Museum of Modern Art, 11 W. 53rd St., New York, N. Y. 10019
NWF	National Wildlife Federation, 1412 16th St., N. W., Washington, D. C. 20036 (Retail only)
NYGS	New York Graphic Society, Ltd., Greenwich, Conn. 06830
PENN	Penn Prints, Harlem Book Co., Inc., 221 Park Ave., S., New York, N. Y. 10003
Pr.	Processed Surface, smooth lacquer or brush strokes
Ps.	Pseudonym
Res.	Resident of
RL	Rudolf Lesch Fine Arts, Inc., 225 Fifth Ave., New York, N. Y. 10010
Tr.	Translation
UNICEF	U. S. Committee for UNICEF, 331 E. 38th St., New York, N. Y. 10016 (Retail only)
UWA	UNESCO World Art Series (Order from NYGS)
W. C.	Water Color

Color Reproductions

Titles Arranged Alphabetically by Artist

ABBEY, EDWIN AUSTIN (American, 1852-1911)
1.	Castle of the Maidens	19 x 44	CAC	18. 00
2.	King Lear	20 x 46	CAC	18. 00
		11 x 27	CAC	7. 50
		c. 8 x 10	AP	. 50
3.	Richard, Duke of			
	Gloucester	22 x 45	CAC	22. 00

ABBOTT, LEMUEL FRANCIS (English, 1760-1803)
4.	Goffers at Blackheath	26-1/2 x 18	IA	25. 00
		19 x 13	IA	15. 00
		13 x 9-1/2	IA	6. 00
5.	Henry Callender	24 x 16	AA	25. 00

ABDULLAJEW
6.	Bengal Girls	20 x 16	AP	5. 00

ACKERMANN, MAX (German, 1887-)
7.	Jubilieren (Jubilation)	25-1/2 x 20	AP	10. 00

ADAM, RICHARD BENNO (German, 1873-1927)
8.	Brazilian Brig	14-1/2x22-1/2	ESH	10. 00
9.	Passenger Coach	12 x 18	PENN	1. 50
10.	William Lawrence			
	Clipper	14-1/2x22-1/2	ESH	10. 00

ADAMS, JOHN OTIS (American, 1851-1927)
11.	Hunting in Autumn	c. 7 x 9	AP	. 50

ADAMS, JOHN QUINCY (American, Res. Austria, 1874-1927)
12.	Her First Recital	21 x 24	NYGS	10. 00
		11 x 13	NYGS	3. 00

ADLER, EDMUND
13.	Yellow Bird	24 x 30	DAC	7. 50

ADRION, LUCIEN (French, 1889-)
14.	Blue Waters	24 x 30	PENN	1. 95
15.	On the Boulevard	25 x 31	CFA	12. 00
		16 x 20	CFA	5. 00
16.	Sunny Day	19 x 23	CFA	12. 00

AERTSEN, PIETER (Dutch 1508-1575)
17.	The Cook	15 x 8	IA	3. 00

AFFORTUNATI, ALDO
18.	Moonlight in Tuscany	19-1/2x27-1/2	AS	12. 00

AGAR, JOHN SAMUEL (English 1770-1835)
19.	Bury Hunt	22 x 28-1/2	AA	25. 00

AGASSE, JACQUE LAURENT (Swiss, 1767-1849)
20.	Last Journey on the			
	Road	11 x 16	CAC	12. 00

AHLERS-HESTERMAN, FRIEDRICH (Fritz) (German, 1883-
21.	River Memories	23 x 27	ESH	12.00

AIGNER, EDUARD (German, 1903-
22.	Coastline at Sete	18 x 24	ESH	12.00

AIZPIRI, Paul (French, Contemporary)
23.	Little Black Tug	22 x 30	RL	12.00
24.	Pipo	35 x 17-1/2	ESH	18.00
25.	Zani	35 x 17-1/2	ESH	18.00

ALAUX, GUSTAVE (French, 1887-
26.	Departure of the Mayflower	22 x 15	CAC	10.00

ALAUX, JEAN-PIERRE (French, Contemporary)
27.	Sunflowers	20 x 30	RL	10.00

ALBANI, FRANCESCO (Italian, 1578-1660)
28.	Dance of Cupids and Rape of Persephone	12 x 15 Oval	IA	3.00
29.	Dance of Cupids-- Detail of No. 28	11 x 15	IA	3.00
30.	Mars Jealous of Adonis	11-1/2" Diam.	AS	3.25
31.	Toilette of Venus	11-1/2" Diam.	AS	3.25

ALBERS, JOSEF (American, 1888-
32.	Homage to the Square: "With Rays"	27 x 27	NYGS	18.00

ALBERTINELLI, MARIOTTO (Italian, 1474-1515)
33.	Nativity of Christ	6 x 15	IA	3.00
34.	Visitation	15 x 10	IA	3.00

ALBO, AUGUST (Estonian, 1893-1963)
35.	Boats Ashore	12 x 30	PENN		1.50
36.	Boats Offshore	12 x 30	PENN		1.50
37.	Christ on Mount Olive	c. 8 x 10	DAC		.60
38.	Emperor Ballet (2)	15 x 6	DAC	ea.	1.50
39.	Free as the Wind	18 x 24	PENN	ea.	1.50
40.	From the Old West	24 x 18	PENN	ea.	1.50
41.	Fruit Still Life (4)	16 x 21	DAC	ea.	5.00
		10 x 14	DAC	ea.	1.75
		c. 7 x 9	DAC	ea.	1.00
42.	Guardian Angel	c. 8 x 10	DAC		.60
43.	Interiors (4)	11 x 14	DAC	ea.	2.25
44.	Dutch Door				
45.	Family Portrait				
46.	Fireside Comfort				
47.	Old Rocking Chair				
48.	Liberty Island	24 x 40	DAC		8.50
49.	Music Room	24 x 18	PENN		1.50
50.	Once Upon a Time	24 x 30	DAC		7.50
51.	Sea in Sunlight	18 x 24	PENN		1.50
52.	Seaman's Den	24 x 18	PENN		1.50
53.	Strummin Days	24 x 18	PENN		1.50
54.	Strauss Waltz	24 x 40	DAC		8.50
55.	Sunset on the Snow	24 x 40	DAC		8.50

56.	Les Sylphides	24 x 40	DAC		8. 50
57.	Tending His Flock	c. 8 x 10	DAC		. 60

ALBRECHT, Karl (German, 1862-

58.	Guardian Angel (4)	12 x 10	AS	ea.	1. 25
59.	Holy Mother	23-1/2x31-1/2	AS		12. 00

ALBRIGHT, MALVIN MARR (American, 1897-

60.	Peaceful Harbor	15-1/2 x 33	NYGS		12. 00

ALDIN, CECIL C. W. (English, 1870-1935)

61.	London Bridge	12-1/2 x 18	ESH		6. 00
62.	Night Patrol	12-1/2 x 18	ESH		6. 00
63.	Old Swan Wharf	12-1/2 x 18	ESH		6. 00
64.	Westminster Bridge	12-1/2 x 18	ESH		6. 00

ALDRICH, GEORGE AMES (American, 1872-

65.	Winter's Glory	12 x 16	CAC		3. 50

ALDRIDGE, JOHN (English Contemporary)

66.	Hayfield	18 x 26	ESH		10. 00
67.	Morning on the Grand Canal	20-1/2 x 28	ESH		12. 00

ALEX (Ps. for Jelinek, Adolf J.) (Czechoslovakian, 1890-

68.	Boy with Horse	27 x 17	CFA		15. 00
69.	Girl with Ball	28 x 17	CFA		15. 00
70.	Man with Flowers	31 x 18	CFA		15. 00
71.	Woman with Fruit	31 x 18	CFA		15. 00

ALKEN, HENRY THOMAS (English, 1784-1850)

72.	Bachelor's Hall (6)	12 x 14-1/2	AA	ea.	5. 00
73.	Flowers of the Hunt: (6)	14 x 18	CAC	ea.	42. 00
	Dandelion				
	Jonquil				
	Passion Flower				
	Pink				
	Rose				
	Sunflower				
74.	Foxhunting (4)	8 x 26	AA	ea.	10. 00
	Foxhunting (4)	11 x 16	CAC	ea.	30. 00
75.	Breaking Cover				
76.	Drawing Cover				
77.	Full Cry				
78.	Tally Ho				
79.	Partridge Shooting (4)	10 x 12	AA	ea.	6. 00
80.	Rexworthy Billiard Parlor	12 x 21	CAC		10. 00
81.	Small Hunt and Coaches (6)	7 x 9	CFA	ea.	3. 00

ALKEN-CLARK

82.	Fox Hunting (4)	11 x 14	AA	ea.	6. 00

ALKEN-SUTHERLAND

83.	Fox Hunts (4)	10 x 17	AA	ea.	7. 50

ALLEGRI, ANTONIO (See CORREGGIO)
ALLINSON, ADRIAN PAUL (English, 1890-

84.	Goat Farm	15 x 24	ESH		6. 00

ALLISON, ALEXANDER (See KURTZ and ALLISON)

ALLORI, ALESSANDRO See BRONZINO
ALLORI, CRISTOFANO (Italian, 1577-1671)
  85. Judith   14 x 11   IA   3. 00
ALMA-TADEMA, (Sir) Laurence (English, 1836-1912)
  86. Reading from Homer 14 x 29   CAC   7. 50
ALQUIST See SCHNARS-ALQUIST
ALT, JACOB (Austrian, 1789-1872)
  87. Traunsee   14 x 21   AR   10. 00
ALT, RUDOLF VON (Austrian, 1812-1905)
  88. Landscape Near
      Gastein   19 x 26-1/2 AR   15. 00
ALTAMURA, SAVERIO (Italian, 1826-1897)
  89. Good Old Time!   16 x 11 Oval IA   3. 00
ALTDORFER, ALBRECHT (German, 1480-1538)
  90. Adoration of the
      Kings   33-1/2x23-1/2 NYGS 18. 00
  91. Battle of Alexander
      (Detail)   23 x 31-1/2 ESH   15. 00
  92. Landscape   8 x 6   AR   4. 00
  93. Landscape with
      Village   11 x 7   AR   4. 00
  94. Nativity 1523   17-1/2 x
                    14-1/2   AR   9. 50
  95. Susanna in the Bath c.18 x 23   HNA   5. 95
  96. Virgin and Child in
      Glory   26 x 17   NYGS 22. 00
D'ALTRI, ARNOLD (French, Contemporary)
  97. Idole   c. 17-1/2 x 22 AS   4. 00
AMADIO, GIOVANNI ANTONIO
  98. Gondolas (2)   15 x 40   DAC ea. 10. 00
                  8-1/2 x 23   DAC ea. 2. 50
  99. River Bridge   15 x 40   DAC   10. 00
                  8-1/2 x 23   DAC   2. 50
  100. Rome Eternal   15 x 40   DAC   10. 00
                  8-1/2 x 23   DAC   2. 50
  101. Street Cafés   15 x 40   DAC   10. 00
                  8-1/2 x 23   DAC   2. 50
AMBRASETH, F.
  102. Vers le Pacifique
      (Fair Weather Ahead) 25 x 34   CAC   12. 50
AMBROGI, MICHELOZZO See MELOZZO DA FORLI
AMECHASTEGUI
  103. Red Fox   18 x 25   AA   12. 00
AMICK, ROBERT WESLEY (American, 1879-
  104. Bounding Main   22-1/2 x 30 NYGS   10. 00
  105. Craftsman   28 x 40   CFA   15. 00
  106. Indian Scout   23-1/2x35-1/2 NYGS   16. 00
  107. Indian Weavers   22 x 28   CFA   7. 50
  108. Man O'War   20 x 26   NYGS   10. 00
                  11 x 14   NYGS   3. 00
  109. Overland Mail   26 x 40   NYGS   16. 00
  110. Promised Land   27 x 36   NYGS   16. 00

111.	Pueblo Indian	22 x 28	CFA	7.50
112.	Where the Sun Goes	18 x 30	CFA	7.50
		14 x 30	CFA	5.00
113.	Whirlaway	20 x 26	NYGS	10.00
		11 x 14	NYGS	3.00
AMIET, CUNO (Swiss, 1868-				
114.	Breton Woman	14-1/2 x 17	CAC	10.00
115.	Gladiolas	29 x 29	CFA	15.00
116.	Haymaking	21 x 31	CAC	10.00
117.	Mountain Lake	24 x 27	CAC	12.00
118.	Roses	13 x 11	CAC	5.00
119.	Zinnias	16 x 20	CFA	6.00
AMIOT, JEAN				
120.	Fishing Boats	13 x 35	CFA	15.00
121.	Home Port	24 x 48	DAC	10.00
		24 x 30	PENN	1.95
122.	Still Life with Guitar	24 x 48	DAC	10.00
AMIRY, TEYMOUR				
123.	Fantasy	18 x 22-1/2	ESH	12.00
124.	Interlude	19 x 22-1/2	ESH	12.00
ANDERSON, HARRY (American, Contemporary)				
125.	Master of Life, Health and Happiness	15-1/2 x 22	IA	5.00
126.	What Happened to Your Hand?	22 x 16	IA	5.00
		16 x 12	IA	2.50
		8-1/2 x 6-1/2	IA	1.00
ANDERSON, HEATH (American, Contemporary)				
127.	Chinese Poppies	22 x 28	IA	6.00
ANDERSON, ROLF				
128.	Beagle	15 x 12	CFA	5.00
129.	Blond Cocker Spaniel	15 x 12	CFA	5.00
130.	Setter	15 x 12	CFA	5.00
131.	Wire-Haired Terrier	15 x 12	CFA	5.00
ANDRADE, MAGDA Venezualan (Res. France) Contemporary				
132.	Blue Harmony	24 x 18-1/2	RL	10.00
ANDRE, ALBERT (French, 1869-1954)				
133.	Bakery	13 x 16	CAC	10.00
134.	Bookstalls	13 x 16	CAC	10.00
135.	Dieppe, 1894	18 x 22	NYGS	16.00
136.	Flower Vendor	13 x 16	CAC	10.00
137.	Hair Dresser	13 x 16	CAC	10.00
138.	News Vendor	13 x 16	CAC	10.00
139.	Stables	17 x 13	CAC	10.00
140.	Theatre	16 x 20	CAC	15.00
ANDRE-PETIT, H. (French, Contemporary)				
141.	Winter's Mirror	22 x 30	RL	12.50
ANDREA DAL CASTAGNO (Italian, 1410-1457)				
142.	Assumption of the Virgin c.	8 x 10	NYGS	.50
143.	David and Goliath c.	8 x 10	NYGS	.50

144.	Last Supper	8-1/2 x 19	AS	7. 50
145.	Portrait of Boccaccio	15 x 11	IA	3. 00
146.	Portrait of Dante	15 x 11	IA	3. 00
147.	Portrait of Pippo			
	Spano	15 x 9-1/2	AS	3. 25

ANDREA DI CIONE See ORCAGNE
ANDREA DA FIRENZE (Italian Ac. 1350)

148.	Dancing Girls	7-1/2x15-1/2	AS	3. 25

ANDREA DEL SARTO (ANDREA D'ANGELO) (Italian, 1486-1531)

149.	Birth of the Virgin	13 x 11	IA	3. 00
150.	Head of a Child			
	(Dr.)	14-1/2x10-1/2	NYGS	3. 00
151.	Last Supper (S. Salvi)	10 x 18	IA	10. 00
		9 x 15	IA	3. 00
152.	St. Philip the Apostle--			
	Detail of No. 151	15 x 11	IA	3. 00
153.	Head of St. Philip--			
	Detail of No. 151	15 x 11	IA	3. 00
154.	Jesus and St. John--			
	Detail of No. 151	11 x 15	IA	3. 00
155.	Madonna and Child and			
	St. John	15 x 10	IA	3. 00
		14-1/2 x 11	AS	3. 25
156.	Madonna del Sacco	10 x 15	IA	3. 00
157.	Madonna of the			
	Harpies	13 x 11	IA	3. 00
	c.	9 x 7	AP	. 50
158.	Madonna and Child--			
	Detail of No. 157.	15 x 11	AS	3. 25
159.	The Redeemer	15 x 9	IA	3. 00
160.	St. James with Two			
	Boys	15 x 8	AS	3. 25
161.	St. John	15 x 11	AS	3. 25
162.	St. John the Baptist	15 x 10	IA	3. 00
163.	Two Angels	15 x 8	IA	3. 00

ANDREOTTI, E.

164.	The Concert	19 x 28	AA	9. 00

ANDREWS, GEORGE HENRY (English, 1816-1898)

165.	At Versailles	25 x 30	AA	10. 00

ANDREWS, WALTER (American Contemporary)

166.	Blue Gulf Stream	24 x 36	NYGS	12. 00
	Detail of No. 166	16 x 30	NYGS	7. 50
167.	Breaking Surf	24 x 36	NYGS	12. 00
	Detail of No. 167	16 x 30	NYGS	7. 50
168.	Canvas - Backs at			
	Dusk	24 x 36	NYGS	12. 00
169.	Dawn over the			
	Marshes	24 x 30	NYGS	10. 00
170.	Flight at Morn	24 x 30	NYGS	10. 00
171.	Incoming Combers	23 x 36	NYGS	12. 00
	Detail of No. 171	16 x 30	NYGS	7. 50

ANGELICO, FRA. GIOVANNI DA FIESOLE (IL BEATO)

172.	Adoration of the Magi	16"Circle	PENN		1. 50
173.	Adoration of the Magi (San Marco)	11 x 11	IA		3. 00
174.	Adoration of the Magi (Cortona)	8 x 15	IA		3. 00
175.	Adoration of the Magi (With Lippi	18 x 23	HNA		5. 95
176.	Angel Adoring	11 x 7	ESH		1. 00
177.	Angel Musicians (2)	13 x 5	IA	ea.	3. 00
178.	Angel Musicians (12)	15 x 5-1/2	AS	ea.	3. 25
179.	Annunciation (San Marco)				
	Horizontal with double	16 x 22-1/2	AS		7. 50
	arch top	15-1/2x20-1/2	ESH		6. 00
		14 x 19	IA		7. 50
		13 x 17	IA		3. 00
		11-1/2 x 15	AS		3. 25
		8-1/2 x 11	IA		1. 75
		c. 8 x 10	AP		. 50
	Angel--Detail of No. 179	15 x 11	IA		3. 00
	Virgin--Detail of No. 179	15 x 11	IA		3. 00
180.	Annunciation (San Marco) - Vertical	11 x 10	IA		3. 00
181.	Annunciation (San Marco) - Vertical with arch top	13-1/2x11-1/2	AS		3. 25
		13 x 11	IA		3. 00
	Angel - Detail of No. 181	15 x 11	IA		3. 00
182.	Annunciation (Cortona)	11-1/2x13-1/2	AS		3. 25
		11 x 13	IA		3. 00
	Angel Announcing -- Detail of No. 182	15 x 11	AS		3. 25
	Virgin Annunciate-- Detail of No. 182	15 x 11	AS		3. 25
183.	Annunciation (San Marco) --Cloister Background	12-1/2x11-1/2	AS		3. 25
		11 x 10	IA		3. 00
184.	Annunciation and Adoration of the Magi	15 x 10	AS		3. 25
		15 x 9	IA		3. 00
185.	Apparition à Marie Madeleine	12 x 9	NYGS		5. 00
186.	Beheading of the Saints Cosmas and Damian	11 x 14	IA		3. 00
187.	Christ and Two Saints	11 x 15	AS		3. 25
188.	Christ as Pilgrim	11 x 15	IA		3. 00
189.	Christ Rising from the Tomb	11 x 15	IA		3. 00
190.	Communion of the Apostles	11 x 14	IA		3. 00

	Christy--Detail of			
	No. 190	15 x 11	IA	3.00
191.	Coronation of the Virgin			
	(San Marco)- Round arch	13 x 12	IA	3.00
	Christ and the Virgin			
	--Detail of No. 191	11 x 15	IA	3.00
192.	Coronation of the			
	Virgin	13 x 11-1/2	AS	3.25
193.	Coronation of the			
	Virgin (San Marco)-			
	Gothic-arched top	16 x 12	IA	3.00
194.	Coronation of the Virgin			
	(Uffizi)	15 x 11	IA	3.00
	Angels Playing (2)--			
	Details of No. 194	15 x 11	IA ea.	3.00
195.	Crucifix (Vienna)	11-1/2x7-1/2	AR	3.00
196.	Crucifix and St.			
	Dominic	15 x 11	IA	3.00
	Head of Christ--			
	Detail of No. 196	15 x 11	IA	3.00
	St. Dominic at Foot			
	of the Cross--Detail			
	of No. 196	15 x 11	IA	3.00
	Head of St. Dominic			
	--Detail of No. 196	15 x 11	IA	3.00
197.	Crucifixion (San Marco)	9 x 15	IA	3.00
	The Maries-- Detail			
	of No. 197	15 x 12	IA	3.00
	St. Dominic--Detail			
	of No. 197	15 x 11	IA	3.00
	St. Francis--Detail			
	of No. 197	15 x 11	IA	3.00
	St. Jerome--Detail			
	of No. 197	15 x 11	IA	3.00
	Head of St. Marc--			
	Detail of No. 197	15 x 11	IA	3.00
198.	Crucifixion and St.			
	Dominic	27-1/2x21-1/2	AS	7.50
		15 x 10-1/2	AS	3.25
199.	Crucifixion (Three			
	Crosses)	13-1/2x11-1/2	AS	3.25
	Figures at Foot of			
	Cross--Detail of			
	No. 199	11 x 15-1/2	AS	3.25
200.	Crucifixion of the Saints			
	Cosmas and Damian	11 x 14	IA	3.00
201.	Deposition from the			
	Cross (San Marco)--			
	Vertical	12 x 11	IA	3.00
202.	Deposition from the			
	Cross (San Marco)--			
	Horizontal	11 x 12	AS	3.25
		10 x 15	IA	3.00

203.	Descent from the Cross	11 x 12	IA	3.00
	Detail of Descent from the Cross	31-1/2 x 23	ESH	15.00
204.	Dormition of the Virgin	6 x 15	IA	3.00
205.	Entombment	13 x 11	IA	3.00
206.	Entry into Jerusalem	12 x 11	IA	3.00
207.	Flight into Egypt	19 x 19	IA	7.50
		11-1/2x12-1/2	AS	3.25
		11 x 11	IA	3.00
		8 x 9	IA	1.75
208.	Healing of Palladia	11 x 13	IA	3.00
209.	Last Judgment	8 x 15	AS	3.25
		8 x 12	IA	3.00
	Angels Dancing-- Detail of No. 209	15 x 11	IA	3.00
	Angels Dancing-- Detail of No. 209	11 x 15	IA	3.00
	The Damned-- Detail of No. 209	10 x 15	IA	3.00
	The Virgin-- Detail of No. 209	15 x 11	IA	3.00
		10 x 8	IA	1.50
210.	Lysias Delivered from the Devils	11 x 13	IA	3.00
211.	Madonna and Child with Angels (Vatican)	9 x 7	IA	1.50
212.	Madonna della Stella	16 x 11	IA	3.00
		15-1/2x8-1/2	AS	3.25
	Madonna and Child-- Detail of No. 212	15 x 11	IA	3.00
213.	Madonna of Humility (U. S. Nat'l Gallery)	25 x 18-1/2	NYGS	15.00
214.	Madonna of the Linaiuoli	15-1/2 x 10	AS	3.25
		15 x 8	IA	3.00
215.	Madonna of Peace c.	10 x 8	AP	.50
216.	Marriage of the Virgin	6 x 15	IA	3.00
217.	Martyrdom of the Saints Cosmas and Damian into the Fire	11 x 14	IA	3.00
218.	Massacre of the Innocents	11 x 11	IA	3.00
219.	Nativity of Christ	13 x 11	IA	3.00
220.	Noli Me Tangere	13-1/2x11-1/2	AS	3.25
		13 x 11	IA	3.00
221.	Pieta (Munich)	11 x 14	IA	3.00
222.	Presentation in the Temple	15 x 11	IA	3.00
223.	Resurrection of Christ	13 x 11	IA	3.00

	Angel--Detail of			
	No. 223	15 x 11	IA	3.00
224.	Road to Calvary	12 x 11	IA	3.00
225.	St. Dominic--Detail			
	of Christ Mocked	15-1/2 x 12	IA	3.50
		15 x 11	IA	3.00
226.	St. Giordano D'Alamala	15 x 11-1/2	AS	3.25
227.	St. Laurence Distributing			
	the Treasures of the			
	Church	15 x 11	IA	3.00
228.	St. Laurence Receiving			
	from Sixtus II the Treasures			
	of the Church	15 x 11	IA	3.00
229.	St. Peter Martyr	10 x 13	IA	3.00
230.	St. Raymond of			
	Cataluna	15 x 11 Oval	IA	3.00
231.	St. Thomas of			
	Aquinas	11 x 15	IA	3.00
232.	Sts. Cosmas and Damian			
	before Lysias	11 x 15	IA	3.00
233.	Transfiguration	13 x 11	IA	3.00
234.	Virgin and Child	12-1/2 x 10	ESH	2.00
235.	Virgin and Child with			
	Angels (Perugia)	15 x 10	IA	3.00
236.	Virgin and Saints	10 x 10	IA	3.00
	Four Saints (2)			
	Details of No. 236	15 x 11	IA	ea. 3.00
237.	Virgin Enthroned	14 x 12	CFA	2.50
	c.	12-1/2x9-1/2	AP	1.25
	c.	10 x 8	AP	1.00
238.	Zacharias Writing the			
	Name of John	11 x 10	IA	3.00

ANGELO, C. S.

239.	Azalea	16 x 11	CFA	12.00

ANKER, ALBERT (Swiss, 1831-1910)

240.	First Smile	17 - 12-1/2	IA	4.50
		7-1/2 x 5-1/2	IA	.30
241.	Girl Peeling Potatoes	16 x 12	CAC	4.00
242.	Grandmother	17 x 12	CAC	4.00
243.	Her Little Friend	17 x 12	CAC	4.00
244.	Home Lesson	21 x 17	CAC	7.50
		16 x 12	CAC	4.00
245.	Knitting Lesson	22 x 24	CFA	10.00
		18 x 20	CAC	7.50
246.	Parish Clerk	22-1/2 x 17	IA	7.50
247.	Pestalozzi and the			
	Children	23 x 35	CFA	12.00
		12 x 16	CAC	4.00
248.	Poultry Yard			
	(Chicken Yard)	22 x 17	CFA	7.50
		16 x 12	CAC	4.00
249.	School Boy	16 x 12	IA	4.00
		7-1/2 x 5-1/2	IA	.30

Annigoni, Pietro   19

250.	School Girl	24 x 19	CFA	10. 00
		16 x 12	IA	4. 00
		7-1/2 x 5-1/2	IA	. 30
251.	Signing the Register	21 x 35	CAC	12. 50
		11 x 18	CAC	4. 00
252	Slumberland	17 x 22	CAC	4. 00
253.	The Song	22 x 24	CAC	10. 00
		18 x 20	CAC	7. 50
254.	Strawberry Girl	16 x 12	CAC	4. 00
255.	Sunday School Walk	21 x 35	IA	12. 00
		11 x 18	IA	4. 50
256.	Tales of a Grand-father	12 x 18	CAC	4. 00
257.	Young Girl	15 x 12	CFA	4. 00
258.	Young Girl Knitting	16 x 12	CAC	4. 00
259.	The Winder	16 x 12	CAC	4. 00

ANNIGONI   PIETRO (Italian, 1910-

260.	Self-Portrait	13-1/2x10-1/2	IA	3. 00

ANSUINO DA FORLI (Italian, Ac. 1438-1448)

261.	Portrait of a Nobleman	15 x 10-1/2	AS	3. 25

ANTES, HORST (German, Contemporary)

262.	Interior IV (The Geometrician)	25-1/2 x 23	NYGS	15. 00

ANTONELLO DA MESSINA (Italian, 1430-1479)

263.	The Annunciate	15 x 11	IA	3. 00
264.	The Poet	13 x 10	IA	3. 00
265.	Portrait of a Man	12 x 9	IA	3. 00
266.	St. Jerome in his Study	18 x 14	CFA	4. 00
267.	Young Man	7 x 6	NYGS	. 50

ANTONIAZZO ROMANO(Aquilio, Marcantonio) (Italian, 1430-1509)

268.	Madonna and Child	15 x 10	IA	3. 00
269.	Virgin and Child	15 x 10-1/2	AS	3. 25

ANTUM, AERT VAN (Belgian, 1580-1620)

270.	Dutch and English War-ships in Battle against the Armada	15-1/2x31-1/2	ESH	15. 00
		8 x 10-1/2	ESH	1. 00

APOLINAR

271.	Mexican Panels I and II	21 x 8 ea.	CFA	ea. 5. 00

APPEL, KAREL (Dutch, Contemporary)

272.	Bete du Soleil (Sun Animal)	21 x 25-1/2	NYGS	12. 00
273.	Child with Hoop	25 x 19	NYGS	10. 00
274.	Composition in Red	19 x 25	NYGS	10. 00
275.	Cry for Freedom	10 x 8	AP	1. 50
276.	Dancing in Space	19 x 25	NYGS	10. 00
277.	Two Heads	19 x 25	NYGS	10. 00

APPLEYARD, J.

278.	Sunny Pastures	9 x 12	ESH	2. 00

AQUILIO, MARCANTONIO See ANTONIAZZO ROMANO

ARALDI, ALESSANDRO (Italian, 1460-1528)
279.   Portrait of Barbara
       Pallavicino   15 x 11   IA   3.00
ARCO
280.   White Sails   31-1/2 x 16   AS   15.00
ARDON, MORDECAI (Israeli, 1896-
281.   Story of a Candle   20 x 25-1/2   NYGS   12.00
ARELLANO, JUAN DE (Spanish, 1614-1676)
282.   Hydrangeas and
       Tulips   36 x 16   NYGS   15.00
283.   Roses with Blue Iris 36 x 16   NYGS   15.00
ARENAL, Luis (Mexican, 1909-
284.   The Wall   14-1/2x19-1/2 AP   5.00
                       c.   7 x 9   AP   .60
ARENTZ, JOSEPH (American, Contemporary)
285.   Coast of Maine   26 x 39   AA   12.00
                             22 x 32   AA   10.00
286.   Land's End   24 x 36   AA   12.00
287.   North Atlantic   27 x 39   AA   15.00
288.   Sand Dunes   22 x 32   AA   10.00
289.   South Atlantic   24 x 36   AA   12.00
ARENYS, RICARDO (Spanish, Contemporary)
290.   At the Start   24 x 30   NYGS   15.00
291.   Autumn Morn   23 x 46   NYGS   20.00
292.   Horses Against a
       Blue Background   31-1/2x23-1/2 NYGS   18.00
293.   Horses in the Foot-
       hills   23 x 30   NYGS   15.00
294.   In the Pasture   16 x 40   NYGS   18.00
295.   On the Range   16 x 40   NYGS   18.00
296.   Snow on the Range   25 x 30   NYGS   15.00
297.   Thoroughbreds   21 x 30   NYGS   15.00
298.   White Horses   31-1/2 x 23   NYGS   18.00
                             14 x 10   NYGS   3.00
299.   White Thoroughbreds   31-1/2 x 23   NYGS   18.00
                             14 x 10   NYGS   3.00
ARETINO See PARRI DI SPINELLI ARETINO
ARIKHA, AVIGDOR (Israeli, Contemporary)
300.   Latent Antagonism,
       1957   21 x 28   NYGS   16.00
ARKLE, WILLIAM (English, Contemporary)
301.   Turning Point   18 x 36   RL   12.50
ARLEDGE, SARA KATHRYN (American, Contemporary)
302.   Zebras   c.   7 x 9   AP   .50
ARMOUR, HAZEL (KENNEDY) (Scotch, Contemporary)
303.   Calf   12 x 9   ESH   2.00
304.   White Kitten   12 x 9   ESH   2.00
ARNEGGER, ALWIN (Austrian, 1883-1916)
305.   Riviera Splendor   24 x 36   IA   12.00
ARP, JEAN (HANS) (German, 1888-1965)
306.   Design, Study in
       Relief   10-1/2 x 10   NYGS   12.00

ARSENIO (FRA) See MASCAGNI

ARTZ, DAVID ADOLF (Dutch, 1837-1890)

307.	Sewing School	c. 8 x 10	AP	.50

ASHLEY, JAMES F.

308.	Storm Clears	24 x 36	CFA	15.00
		16 x 24	CFA	6.00
309.	Sunderland Hills	24 x 36	CFA	15.00
		16 x 24	CFA	6.00

ASSYRIA

Ashurnasirpal II
(2) (Sculpture

	Reliefs)	15 x 38	NYGS	ea. 15.00
310.	King in Chariot Hunting Lions			
311.	Assyrian Chariots Over-			
	throwing Enemy Chariots			
312.	War Chariot	23 x 31-1/2	ESH	15.00

ATHERTON, JOHN (American, 1900-1952)

313.	Harvest Bounty	21 x 14	AK	3.00

ATWOOD, JON

314.	Seafoam	24 x 36	DAC	7.50
		24 x 30	PENN	1.95

AUBERT, LOUIS (French, 1720-1780)

315.	Peep Show	11 x 8	AR	3.50
316.	Pupils in Studio	13 x 9-1/2	AR	3.50

AUDUBON, JOHN JAMES (American, 1785-1851)

317.	Blue Grosbeak	16 x 13	NYGS		3.00
318.	Blue Jay	16 x 13	NYGS		3.00
319.	Carolina Parrot	30 x 21-1/2	NYGS		12.00
320.	Carolina Turtle-Dove	21 x 17	NYGS		6.00
321.	Common Crossbill	21 x 17	NYGS		6.00
322.	Five Pairs of Wood-				
	peckers	9 x 7	CFA		1.00
323.	Flamingo	9 x 7	CFA		1.00
324.	Florida Jay	c. 23 x 18	HNA		5.95
325.	Pileated Woodpecker	30 x 19-1/2	NYGS		12.00
		c. 23 x 18	HNA		5.95
326.	Portfolio (4)	11-1/2 x 15	PENN	set	2.98
327.	Field Bunting			or	1.00 ea.
328.	Florida Jay				
329.	Prothonatary Swamp Warbler				
330.	Summer Redbird				
331.	Portfolio (4)	10 x 15	PENN	set	2.98
				or	1.00 ea.
332.	Blue-Winged Teal				
333.	Canvas-Backed Duck				
334.	Mallard Duck				
335.	Ruffed Grouse				
336.	Portfolio (30)	17 x 14	CFA	set	30.00
337.	Portrait of a Girl,				
	c. 1830	23-1/2x17-1/2	NYGS		12.00
338.	Roseate Spoonbill	7 x 9	CFA		1.00
339.	Ruby-Throated Humming-				
	bird	21 x 17	NYGS		6.00

340.	Scarlet Ibis	7 x 9	CFA	1.00
341.	Snowy Heron c.	10 x 8	NYGS	.50
342.	Summer or Wood Duck, 1825	30 x 19-1/2	NYGS	12.00
343.	Wild Turkey	22 x 15-1/2	PENN	1.50
		13-1/2 x 9	NYGS	3.00
		9 x 7	CFA	1.00
344.	Wood Ibis	9 x 7	CFA	1.00
345.	Yellow-Breasted Chat	21 x 17	NYGS	6.00

AUJAME, JEAN (French, 1905-

346.	Hetres en Normandie	16-1/2 x 22	NYGS	18.00

AUSTRALIA

347.	Aboriginal Paintings (5)	11 x 15	NYGS	ea.	2.00
348.	Fish in X-Ray Art				
349.	Mimi Spirit Woman and a Cat Fish				
350.	Spirit Man, Wili-Wilia, and the Mythical Kangaroo Man				
351.	Spirit Men, Bradbatti and Kumail-Kumail				
352.	Wet Season Seascape				
353.	United Nations World Art Series (32)	11 x 14 or 14 x 11	NYGS	ea.	2.00

AUSTRIA

354.	United Nations World Art Series (32)	11 x 14 or 14 x 11	NYGS	ea.	2.00

AUSTRIAN, BEN (American, 1906-

355.	Pipe and Letter Rack	16 x 12	CFA	5.00

AVERCAMP, HENDRICK (Dutch, 1585-1634)

356.	Ice Landscape	16 x 27-1/2	AP	15.00
357.	Winter Scene c.	20 x 24	PENN	1.50

AVERY, MILTON (American, Contemporary)

358.	Spring Orchard	23 x 30	NYGS	18.00
359.	Young Mother	24 x 18	AR	10.00

AVIGNON, SCHOOL OF (French, 15th Century) See also FROMENT

360.	Pieta of Villeneuve-les-Avignon (Attributed to Froment)	29 x 39	IA	24.00
		29 x 29-1/2	NYGS	22.00
		16-1/2x22-1/2	ESH	10.00
		11 x 15	AJ	2.50

AYLWARD, WILLIAM JAMES (American, 1875-

361.	Clipper Ship "Flying Cloud"	24 x 32	NYGS	12.00
362.	Landing of Columbus	28 x 40	CFA	15.00
363.	Landing of the Pilgrims	28 x 40	CFA	15.00
364.	U.S.S. Constitution	24 x 32	NYGS	12.00

AYME, FRANCIS (American, 19th Century)

365.	Florence en Rose	22-1/2 x 18	NYGS	16.00

AYNSCOMB-HARRIS, M. J.

366.	Boats	28 x 36	AS	20.00

367.	Bridge	24 x 36	AS		15. 00
368.	Notre Dame	22 x 40	AS		20. 00

AZTEC
369.	Four Fortunes of the Maize (3 panels)	7 x 21 (1) 6 x 11-1/2 (2)	AR set of 3		12. 00
370.	The Maize God	39 x 33	CFA		15. 00
371.	Mayan Goddess	39 x 33	CFA		15. 00

B

BABOULENE, EUGENE (French, 20th Century)
372.	Boats in Provence	17 x 22	ESH		10. 00
373.	Fishing Boats	8 x 10-1/2	ESH		1. 00
374.	Port of St. Mandrier	12 x 37	ESH		18. 00

BABYLONIA
375.	Bull	12 x 16	AR		5. 00
376.	Dragon	12 x 16	AR		5. 00

BACCICCIO, IL See GAULLI
BACCIO See BARTOLOMMEO, (FRA)
BACH, FLORENCE JULIA (American, 1887-
377.	Camelias	22 x 16	CFA		7. 50
378.	Fragrant Flowers	24 x 30	CAC		7. 50
379.	Gardenias	20 x 16	IA		3. 50
380.	Gems of the Garden	20 x 16	IA		3. 50
381.	Roses	20 x 16	IA		3. 50
382.	White Mallows	16 x 20	CAC		7. 50

BACHMANN, JOHANN (HANS) (Swiss, 1852-1917)
383.	Autumn in Bavaria	12 x 16	ESH	Pr.	4. 00
384.	Bavarian Landscape in Autumn	19-1/2x11-1/2	IA		4. 00
385.	Bavarian Moorlands	20 x 27-1/2	ESH	Pr.	8. 00
386.	Beech Forest	12 x 16	ESH	Pr.	3. 00
387.	Berchtesgaden Landscape	20 x 27-1/2	ESH	Pr.	8. 00
		16 x 20	ESH	Pr.	5. 00
388.	Brook in the Woods	23-1/2x39-1/2	ESH	Pr.	9. 00
		20 x 28	ESH	Pr.	7. 00
389.	Brook in the Mountains	23-1/2x31-1/2	ESH	Pr.	10. 00
		16 x 20	ESH	Pr.	5. 00
390.	Chalet in Tyrol	20 x 12	ESH	Pr.	4. 00
391.	Church in the Mountains	20 x 27-1/2	ESH	Pr.	8. 00
392.	Cottage in the Mountains	20 x 28	ESH	Pr.	7. 00
393.	Cottage in the Zillertal	16 x 31-1/2	ESH	Pr.	8. 00
394.	Dunes	21 x 31	CFA		7. 50
395.	Farm in the Mountains	16 x 20	ESH	Pr.	5. 00
396.	Harvest-Time	23-1/2x39-1/2	ESH	Pr.	9. 00
397.	Heath in Bloom	20 x 12	ESH	Pr.	4. 00

398.	In the Bavarian Moorland	23-1/2x31-1/2	ESH	Pr.	10.00
		16 x 20	ESH	Pr.	5.00
399.	In the Black Forest	23-1/2x39-1/2	ESH	Pr.	9.00
		20 x 28	ESH	Pr.	7.00
400.	In the Mountains	20 x 28	ESH	Pr.	7.00
401.	In the Promontory	16 x 31-1/2	ESH	Pr.	7.00
402.	In the Tyrol Mountains	20 x 27-1/2	ESH	Pr.	8.00
		16 x 20	ESH	Pr.	5.00
403.	Konigsee	20 x 28	ESH	Pr.	7.00
404.	Lake in Bavaria	20 x 27-1/2	ESH	Pr.	8.00
	Detail of No. 404	20 x 12	ESH	Pr.	4.00
405.	Landscape in Bavaria	20 x 27-1/2	ESH	Pr.	8.00
		12 x 16	ESH	Pr.	3.00
406.	Landscape in North Bavaria	20 x 27-1/2	ESH	Pr.	8.00
407.	Marshy Country	16 x 31-1/2	ESH	Pr.	8.00
408.	Misurinasee	23-1/2x39-1/2	ESH	Pr.	9.00
409.	Mountain-Forest	20 x 28	ESH	Pr.	7.00
410.	Mountain Lake in Switzerland	20 x 27-1/2	ESH	Pr.	8.00
		16 x 20	ESH	Pr.	5.00
411.	Peace of the Forest	20 x 28	ESH	Pr.	7.00
412.	Pragser Wildsee	23-1/2x39-1/2	ESH	Pr.	9.00
413.	Ramsau near Berchtesgaden	16 x 31-1/2	ESH	Pr.	8.00
414.	Springtime in Bavaria	23-1/2x31-1/2	ESH	Pr.	10.00
415.	Sunny Day near Oberstdorf	20 x 27-1/2	ESH	Pr.	8.00
416.	Sunny Landscape	20 x 27-1/1	ESH	Pr.	8.00
		16 x 20	ESH	Pr.	5.00
417.	Way in the Heathyland	20 x 27-1/2	ESH	Pr.	8.00
418.	Way in the Park	20 x 27-1/2	ESH	Pr.	8.00
		16 x 20	ESH	Pr.	5.00
419.	Wettersteingebirge	16 x 31-1/2	ESH	Pr.	7.00

BACON, PEGGY (American, Contemporary)

420.	Nobody's Pet	18 x 15	CAC		3.00
421.	Nosegay	15 x 20	NYGS		7.50

BADMIN, STANLEY R. (English, 1906-

422.	St. James Park	12-1/2 x 23	ESH		10.00

BAILEY, WILFRED

423.	Grey Lags (Taking Off)	18 x 24	AA		7.50
424.	Mallards (Landing)	18 x 24	AA		7.50

BAILLE, HERVÉ (French, 1896-

425.	Booksellers at Notre Dame	9 x 14	NYGS		3.00
426.	Place de la Concorde	9 x 14	NYGS		3.00

BAKHUYZEN, LUDOLF (Dutch, 1631-1708)

427.	Storm at Sea	11 x 13-1/2	AS		3.25

BALDASSARE, ESTENSE (Italian, 1437-1504)

428.	Family Portrait	29 x 24	NYGS		26.00

BALDOVINETTI, ALESSO (Italian, 1425-1499)
429. Virgin and Child
      (Parigi)   15-1/2x10-1/2 AS   3.25
430. Virgin Adoring the
      Child   15 x 10   IA   3.00
               c.   10 x 8   ESH   1.00
BALDUCCI, MATTEO (Italian, 1509-1541)
431. Deposition from the
      Cross   8 x 15   IA   3.00
BALDUNG (GRIEN), HANS (German, 1484-1545)
432. Head of Saturnis   13 x 10   AR   3.00
433. Holy Family   18-1/2x14-1/2   NYGS   15.00
BALESTRIERI, LIONELLO (Italian, 1874-
434. Beethoven's Sonata   19 x 44   CAC   15.00
                             12 x 26   CAC   7.50
BALLA, GIACOMO (Italian, 1874-1958)
435. Dog on Leash   23 x 28   NYGS   16.00
BAPTISTE, JOHN GASPARS (Belgian, 1620-1691)
436. Antique Flowers(2)   19 x 14   CFA   ea. 18.00
437. Blue Ribbon   18 x 14   CFA   5.00
438. Young Girl Holding
      Kitten   12 x 9   CFA   3.00
BARABINO, NICOLO (Italian, 1832-1891)
439. Madonna of the Olives 23 x 12   AS   7.50
                             15 x 9   AS   3.25
         Detail of No. 439   15-1/2x11-1/2   AS   3.25
         Detail of No. 439   20-1/2x28-1/2   AS   7.50
BARBARELLI, GIORGIO See GIORGIONE
BARBER, CHARLES E. (English-American, 1840-1917)
440. Duck Pond   22 x 26   AA   10.00
BARBIERI, GIOVANNI FRANCESCO See GUERCINO
BARD, JAMES (American, 1815-1897)
441. The Alida   18 x 32   NYGS   15.00
BARDONE, GUY (Italian, Contemporary)
442. Paysage   22-1/2x17-1/2   NYGS   18.00
443. Lee Sapins   21-1/2 x 16   NYGS   18.00
BARKER, KIT (English, 1916-
444. Marsh Grasses   27 x 36   RL   20.00
BARLE, MAURICE
445. Calvi   16 x 20   AS   2.00
446. Camargue Gypsies   20 x 30   AS   12.00
447. Les Martigues   16 x 20   AS   2.00
448. Monaco   16 x 20   AS   2.00
449. Villefranche   16 x 20   AS   2.00
BARNARD
450. Como   8 x 10   CFA   6.00
BARNES, RENEE (American, 1886-
451. Bunny Taxi   16 x 20   CFA   2.50
452. Humpty Dumpty   16 x 20   CFA   2.50
453. Nancy Lee's Playmates 16 x 20   CFA   2.50
454. Three Happy Pigs   16 x 20   CFA   2.50

BAROCCI, FEDERICO FIORI (IL BAROCCIO) (Italian, 1526-1612)
455.   Frederick of Urbino
       as a Child   15 x 10   IA   3. 00
456.   Madonna of the
       Cherries   8 x 15   IA   3. 00
457.   Nativity   14 x 11   IA   3. 00
458.   Rose   22 x 18   CFA   12. 00
459.   St. Francis   15 x 11   AS   3. 25
460.   Study of a Child (Dr.) 15 x 10-1/2   NYGS   3. 00
BARRABAND, JACQUES (French, 1767-1809)
461.   Le Grand Paradis   14 x 9   CFA   7. 50
462.   Le Paradis Emeraude   14 x 9   CFA   7. 50
463.   Le Paradis Rouge   14 x 9   CFA   7. 50
464.   Le Petit Paradis   14 x 9   CFA   7. 50
BARRATT, REGINALD (English, 1861-1917)
465.   Doorway of S. Marco   16 x 10-1/2   ESH   2. 00
466.   Horses of S. Marco   21 x 14   ESH   2. 00
BARRAUD, FRANCOIS (Swiss, 1899-1934)
467.   Ch. Davis on "The
       Traverser"   18 x 21   AA   15. 00
468.   Harbour of Barcelone   20 x 24   CAC   12. 00
469.   Will Long on "Bertha"   18 x 21   AA   15. 00
BARRIVIERA, LINO BIANCHI (Italian, 19th Century)
470.   The Christ Head   20 x 16   PENN   1. 50
BARTEL, BRONISLAW (Polish, 1887-
471.   Autumn Peeping Thru   16 x 12   CFA   1. 50
472.   Summer Flowers   16 x 12   CFA   1. 50
473.   Sunshine and Shadow   16 x 12   CFA   1. 50
474.   Sweet Summertime   16 x 12   CFA   1. 50
BARTH, PAUL BASILIUS (Swiss, 1881-1955)
475.   Legionnaires   29 x 21   CFA   12. 00
BARTLETT, WILLIAM HENRY (American, 1809-1894)
476.   View from Hyde Park   20-1/2 x 28   AA   10. 00
477.   View of Mount Vernon   15-1/2 x 21   NYGS   10. 00
478.   Washington's Tomb,
       Mount Vernon   15-1/2 x 21   NYGS   10. 00
BARTNING, LUDWIG (German, 1876-1956)
479.   Summer Beauties   20 x 24   NYGS   7. 50
BARTOLI, J.
480.   Madonna Orans   14 x 9   ESH   6. 00
BARTOLO DI FREDI (Italian, 1353-1410)
481.   Virgin and Child
       (Cusona-Siena)   15 x 11   AS   3. 25
BARTOLOMMEO (FRA BARTOLOMMEO DI PAGHOLO, KNOWN AS
BACCIO DELLA PORTA) (Italian, 1475-1517)
482.   Angel   12 x 8   AR   3. 00
483.   Angel Musician (Detail
       from "Virgin Enthroned") 11 x 15   IA   3. 00
484.   Deposition from the
       Cross   11 x 14   IA   3. 00
485.   Holy Family   12 x 11   IA   3. 00
                    c.   9 x 7   AP   . 50

486.	St. Catherine (Detail from "God in Glory")	15 x 11	IA		3.00
487.	St. Dominic	15 x 11	AS		3.25
488.	Savonarola, Portrait of	15 x 10	IA		3.00

BARTOLOMMEO DI FROSINO See FROSINO
BARTOLOMMEO VENETO See VENETO
BARTON, P.

489.	Circus Procession	10 x 30	AS		7.50
490.	Seaside Express	10 x 30	AS		7.50

BARTSCH, REINHOLD (German, 1925-

491.	In Egypt	23-1/2x39-1/2	ESH	Cv.	18.00
492.	Sorrento (Near)	24 x 32	CFA		12.00
493.	Spanish Harbour	23-1/2x39-1/2	ESH	Cv.	18.00

BASAITI, MARCO (Italian, d. 1521)

494.	Christ and His Disciples	10 x 8	CFA		3.50
495.	Christ Taking Leave of His Disciples	10 x 7-1/2	AR		3.50

BASCHENIS, Evaristo (Italian, 1617-1677)

496.	Still Life with Musical Instruments	23-1/2 x 31	CFA		15.00
		11 x 15	IA		3.00
497.	Unknown Beauty	27 x 35	CAC		12.00

BASSANO, FRANCESCO (Italian, 1549-1592)

498.	Rest During the Flight	23 x 31	CAC		12.00

BASSFORD, WALLACE (American, 1900-

499.	Bride	9 x 12	CAC		1.50
		6 x 7	CAC		1.00
500.	Bridegroom	9 x 12	CAC		1.50
		6 x 7	CAC		1.00
501.	Mardi Gras	12 x 9	CAC		1.50
		7 x 6	CAC		1.00
502.	Masquerade	12 x 9	CAC		1.50
		7 x 6	CAC		1.00

BASTIEN-LEPAGE, JULES (French, 1848-1884)

503.	Joan of Arc c.	8 x 10	AP		.50

BATEMAN, JAMES (English, 1893-

504.	Ploughing the Downs	16 x 22	ESH		15.00
505.	Ranger's Farm, Richmond Park	15-1/2 x 26	ESH		12.00

BATONI, POMPEO (Italian, 1708-1787)

506.	Holy Heart	15 x 12 Oval	IA		3.00
507.	Holy Heart of Christ	15 x 11-1/2	AS		3.25
508.	Madonna and Child	15 x 11	IA		3.00
509.	Nativity	15 x 11	IA		3.00
510.	Virgin and Child	15 x 11	AS		3.25

BAUGIN, LUBIN (French, 1610-1663)

511.	Still Life with Chess Board c.	9-1/2 x 12-1/2	AP		1.25
		6 x 8	CFA		1.00

BAUMAN, LEILA T.

512.	U. S. Mail Boat	20 x 26	NYGS		15.00

BAUMEISTER, WILLI (German, 1889-1955)
513.   Aidoneum and Perse-
       phone   c.   8 x 10   AP   .75
514.   Allegro, 1951   c.   8 x 10   AP   .75
515.   Bewegte Halde   c.   8 x 10   AP   .75
516.   Brown Composition c.   8 x 10   AP   .75
517.   Floating World on
       Blue   23 x 29   NYGS   16.00
518.   Kegelspiel   c.   8 x 10   AP   .75
519.   Kessaua/Double Ring 22-1/2x27-1/2 NYGS   20.00
520.   Masks, 1936   c.   8 x 10   AP   .75
521.   Tennis Player   c.   8 x 10   AP   .75
BAWCOMBE
522.   Street Scenes (8)   16 x 12   AK   ea. 2.50
       Continental
       Favorites (3)   11 x 8-1/2   AK   ea. 1.25
       English Views (3)
       Parisian Views (2)
BAZAS, ERIC
523.   Composition Red and
       Grey   30 x 21   RL   10.00
BAZILLE, FREDERIC (French, 1841-1870)
524.   Pink Dress   22-1/2x16-1/2 ESH   10.00
BAZIOTES, WILLIAM (American, 1912-1963)
525.   Dragon, 1950   28 x 23   NYGS   15.00
526.   Jungle   c.   8 x 10   NYGS   .50
BAZZI, GIOVANNI ANTONIO DE See SODOMA, IL
BEAL, GIFFORD (American, 1879-
527.   Circus Ponies   12 x 15   CAC   10.00
528.   The Fisher   22 x 30   CFA   12.00
BEAUGUREAU, F.
529.   Chestnut Vendor   19 x 26   RL   12.50
BEAUMONT, WILLIAM DE (American, 1890-
530.   The Fiacre   8 x 10-1/2   ESH   1.00
BEAUNEVEU, ANDRÉ (French, Ac. 1360-1403)
531.   King Richard II   24 x 12   ESH   7.50
BEAUSSIER (French, Contemporary)
532.   St. Tropez   16 x 22   NYGS   7.50
BECKER, FREDERICK (American, 1888-
533.   Still Life with
       Flowers   23 x 17   CAC   10.00
BECKER, PAULA MODERSOHN See MODERSOHN-BECKER
BECKERATH, WILLY VON (German, 1868-1938)
534.   Brahms at the Piano 18 x 22   IA   3.00
                             9 x 11   IA   1.00
BECKMANN, MAX (German, 1884-1950)
535.   Auto Portrait   c.   16 x 12   AP   2.00
536.   Cabaret Girls   29-1/2x21-1/2 NYGS   20.00
537.   Chiemsee   23 x 34   NYGS   30.00
538.   Dutch Landscape   27 x 22   CFA   12.00
539.   Lillies   29 x 16   CFA   15.00

540.	Odysseus	c. 8 x 10	AP	. 75
541.	Pic d'Aigle	26-1/2x34-1/2	NYGS	30. 00
542.	Promenade at Nice	26 x 29	CFA	20. 00
543.	Rainbow, 1942	19-1/2x31-1/2	NYGS	18. 00
544.	Seascape (The Shore)	27-1/2 x 37	NYGS	30. 00
545.	Self-Portrait	24 x 18	PENN	1. 50
546.	Still Life with Candle	19 x 14	CFA	15. 00
547.	Still Life, Lillies	30 x 17	CAC	18. 00
548.	Still Life, Yellow Orchids	28 x 22	NYGS	20. 00
549.	Summer Day by the Sea	23 x 34	NYGS	24. 00
550.	Tulips	29 x 14-1/2	NYGS	22. 00
551.	West Park, 1950	35 x 16	CFA	18. 00
552.	Winding Path in the Black Forest	33-1/2x19-1/2	NYGS	26. 00
553.	Yellow Roses	35 x 21	NYGS	22. 00

BEDA, FRANCESCO (Italian, 1840-1900)

554.	Chess Game	24 x 36	IA	10. 00

BEECHER, WILLIAM WARD

555.	Mandolin	24 x 18	AA	7. 50
556.	Three B's	24 x 18	AA	10. 00
557.	Violin	24 x 18	AA	7. 50

BEECROFT, HERBERT (English, 1865-1942)

558.	The Lord Turned and Looked Upon Peter	22 x 17	IA	5. 00
		13 x 10	IA	1. 75
559.	Open Unto Me	22 x 17	RL	7. 50
		13 x 10	RL	2. 75

BEHAM (or BOHM), BARTHEL (German, 1502-1540)

560.	Jacobea of Baden	17 x 12	AR	5. 00

BELL, BARBARA

561.	Nursery Land	18 x 22-1/2	ESH	3. 50

BELLECHOSE, HENRI (Belgian, Ac. 1415-1440)

562.	Last Communion	17 x 22-1/2	ESH	10. 00

BELLINI, GENTILE (Italian, 1429-1507)

563.	Procession of the Cross	8 x 17	IA	3. 00
564.	Rescue of the Relics of the Cross in the Canal	11 x 15	IA	3. 00

BELLINI, GIOVANNI (Italian, c. 1430-1516)

565.	Cristo in Pieta (Milan)	15 x 11	IA	3. 00
566.	The Dead Christ	15-1/2x19-1/2	ESH	10. 00
567.	Entombment of Christ	9 x 15	IA	3. 00
568.	Infant Bacchus	16 x 12	ESH	6. 00
569.	Madonna and Child in a Landscape	24 x 18-1/2	NYGS	12. 00
570.	Madonna of the Alberetti	14 x 11	AS	3. 25
571.	Madonna delle Grazie	13 x 10	IA	3. 00

572.	Madonna of the Meadows	21-1/2 x 34	NYGS	18. 00
573.	Madonna of the Trees	13 x 10	IA	3. 00
574.	Pieta (Venice)	11 x 15	IA	3. 00
575.	Pieta (Rome)	15 x 11-1/2	AS	3. 25
576.	Pieta (Milan)	11 x 14	IA	3. 00
577.	Portrait of Condottiere	20 x 14	CFA	7. 50
578.	Portrait of the Doge Leonardo Loredano	24 x 18	PENN	1. 50
		17 x 12-1/2	NYGS	5. 00
	c.	10 x 8	NYGS	. 50
	c.	9 x 7	AP	. 50
579.	St. Francis in Ecstacy	25 x 28	NYGS	16. 00
	c.	8 x 10	NYGS	. 50
580.	St. Jerome c.	9 x 7	AP	. 50
581.	Souls in Purgatory	9 x 15	IA	3. 00
582.	Transfiguration	11 x 14	IA	3. 00
583.	Virgin and Child (Venice)	15-1/2 x 9-1/2	AS	3. 25
584.	Virgin and Child with Saints	10 x 14-1/2	AS	3. 25
585.	Virgin and Child with St. George and St. Paul	11 x 15	AS	3. 25
586.	Virgin, Child, Magdalene and St. Catherine	8 x 15	AS	3. 25
587.	Virgin of the Red Cherubs	13 x 10	IA	3. 00
588.	Virgin with Sleeping Child	15 x 8	AS	3. 25

BELLINI, JACOPO (Italian, 1400-1470)

589.	Feast of the Gods c.	8 x 10	NYGS	. 50
590.	Madonna and Child (Venice)	15-1/2 x 11	AS	3. 25
		14 x 10	IA	3. 00
591.	Madonna and Child (Uffizi)	15 x 10	IA	3. 00
592.	Portrait of a Doge c.	10 x 8	NYGS	. 50
593.	Portrait of the Doge Foscari	15 x 11	AS	3. 25
594.	Portrait of a Youth c.	10 x 8	NYGS	. 50

BELLOTTO, BERNARDO (Called Canaletto) See CANALETTO
BELLOWS, GEORGE WESLEY (American, 1882-1925)

595.	Ann in a Purple Wrap	25 x 20	PENN	1. 50
596.	Both Members of this Club	17 x 24	NYGS	10. 00
	c.	8 x 10	NYGS	. 50
597.	The Dempsey-Firpo Fight, 1924	15 x 21	NYGS	7. 50
598.	Gramercy Park, 1920	18 x 24	NYGS	10. 00

599.	Lady Jean, 1924		19 x 9	NYGS	6.00
		c.	9 x 7	AP	.50
600.	The Lone Tenement		18 x 23	HNA	5.95
601.	Men on the Dock	c.	7 x 9	AP	.50
602.	Sand Cart		21 x 31	CAC	12.00
			12-1/2 x 19	NYGS	7.50
		c.	7 x 9	AP	.50
		c.	20 x 24	PENN	1.50
604.	Summer City	c.	8 x 10	NYGS	.50
605.	White Horse	c.	8 x 10	NYGS	.50

BELTRAFFIO, GIOVANNI ANTONIO (Italian, 1467-1516)

606.	Madonna and Child	14 x 11	IA	3.00
607.	Narcissus	6 x 9	IA	1.50
608.	Portrait of a Youth	12 x 9	CFA	2.00

BEMBO, BENEDETTO (Italian, Ac. 1465)

609.	Archangel Raphael with the Child Tobias	15-1/2 x 6-1/2	AS	3.25

BENALI, E; (German, 1914-

610.	Venice	23 x 31	CFA	18.00
		24 x 28	IA	12.00

BENCI, ANTONIO See POLLAIUOLO, ANTONIO
BENCI, PIERO See POLLAIUOLO, PIERO
BENEZIT, EMANUEL (French, 1887-

611.	Flowering Acaceas	20 x 25	NYGS	7.50

BENNER, GERRIT (Dutch, 1897-

612.	Chrysanthemum	24 x 19	CAC	7.50
613.	Zinnias	28 x 22	CAC	10.00

BENNETT, FRANK MOSS (English, 1874-

614.	Hunt Breakfast	22 x 32	CFA		10.00
615.	Hunts and Coaches (6)	7 x 9	CAC	set	3.00
616.	Landlord's Story	28 x 36	RL		15.00
617.	Meet at the Lodge	22 x 32	CFA		12.00
618.	Squire's Story	26 x 36	CFA		15.00

BENOIS, NADIA (Russian, Contemporary)

619.	Michaelmas Daisies	23 x 19	ESH	15.00

BENOLDI

620.	Still Life (4)	7 x 14 (2)	AK	ea.	1.50
		14 x 7 (2)		ea.	1.50

BENSA, ERNESTO (Italian, Ac. 1897)

621.	Staircase at the Bargello	24 x 15	CAC	10.00

BENSON, FRANK WESTON (American, 1862-1951)

622.	My Daughters	15 x 21	CAC	7.50

BENTON, THOMAS HART (American, 1889-

623.	Boom Town c.	8 x 10	NYGS	.50
624.	Cotton Pickers, Georgia	16 x 20	NYGS	9.00
625.	July Hay, 1943 c.	8 x 10	NYGS	.50
626.	The Ketuckian	28 x 22	NYGS	12.00
627.	Louisiana Rice Fields	11 x 19	NYGS	6.00
	c.	7 x 9	AP	.50

628.	Music Lesson	17-1/2x21-1/2	NYGS	10.00
629.	Spring Tryout	18 x 24	NYGS	10.00
630.	Threshing Wheat	22 x 36	NYGS	16.00

BENVENUTO DI GIOVANNI DEL GUASTA See GUASTA
BERCKHEYDEN HIOB AUT BRECKBERG See BRECKBURG, HIOB
BERENTZ, CHRISTIAN (1658-1722)

631.	Little House of the Dawn	14 x 11	AS	3.25
632.	Preparation for the Festival	14 x 11	AS	3.25

BERGER, PIERRE (French, Contemporary)

633.	Paris Scenes (10) (W. C.)	16 x 12	AR	ea.	6.00
634.	Canal Saint-Martin				
635.	La Madeleine				
636.	Notre Dame				
637.	Le Palais Royal				
638.	Place de la Concorde				
639.	Place Denfert-Rochereau				
640.	Place Furstenberg				
641.	Place du Tertre				
642.	La Porte-Saint-Denis				

BERGHEM, CLAES (Dutch, 1620-1683)

643.	The Ford	11 x 17-1/2	AR	4.00

BERKS, ROBERT

644.	John F. Kennedy (Sculpture)	25 x 19	AA	5.00

BERLINGHIERI, BONAVENTURA (Italian, 1210-1274)

645.	St. Francis and Scenes from his Life	15 x 8	IA	3.00
	St. Francis -- Detail of No. 645	15 x 11	IA	3.00

BERMAN, EUGENE (American, 1899-

646.	Giselle First Act Curtain	13 x 20	AR	12.00
647.	Hat Seller	25 x 19	CFA	12.00
648.	View in Perspective of a Perfect Sunset c.	18 x 23	HNA	5.95

BERNARDINO DI BETTO See PINTURICCHIO
BERNARDO, CAVALLINO See CAVALLINO
BERNATH, SANDOR (Hungarian (Res. U.S.), 1892-

649.	Schooner "Newport"	17 x 21	CAC	5.00

BERNDT, C.

650.	Sunflower	29 x 28	CFA	15.00
651.	Sunflowers	18 x 17	CFA	5.00

BERNINGHAUS, OSCAR E. (American, 1874-1952)

652.	Wild Horses	18 x 24	NYGS	10.00

BERNINI, GIOVANNI LORENZO (Italian, 1598-1680)

653.	Self-Portrait	15 x 11-1/2	AS	3.25

BERTELSMANN, WALTER (German, 1877-

654.	Low Tide	20 x 29	CFA	10.00

BERTEN

655.	Magnolia	19 x 23	CAC	7.50

BERTI, RENE (Italian, Contemporary)
656.   Steeplechasing   16 x 22   CFA   7. 50
BERTUCCI, GIOVANNI BATTISTA See UTILI
BESLER, BESIL (German, 1561-1629)
657.   Bluebell and
       Convolvulus   22-1/2 x 18   ESH   10. 00
658.   Multi-Flowered Red Lily
       and Common Contaury 22-1/2 x 18   ESH   10. 00
659.   Peruvian Scilla and
       Orchids   22-1/2 x 18   ESH   10. 00
660.   Thistle and Camomile 22-1/2 x 18   ESH   10. 00
661.   Tulips (2)   21 x 18   AL   ea. 12. 00
BESSE, RAYMOND (French, 1871-
662.   Fishing Articles   16 x 22   CAC   10. 00
BESSIL, J. R. (French, Contemporary)
663.   Voiles   27 x 32   RL   15. 00
BETZ, ANDREAS
664.   Allasio   12 x 16   ESH   4. 00
665.   Coast in Italy   12 x 16   ESH   4. 00
666.   Fall at Lake Seeham 19 x 24   CFA   10. 00
667.   Houses in Spain   20 x 23-1/2   ESH   7. 00
668.   Southern Landscape 23-1/2x39-1/2   ESH   9. 00
                          20 x 28   ESH   7. 00
                          16 x 31-1/2   ESH   7. 00
BEUCKELAER, JOACHIM (Flemish, 1535-1574)
669.   Fruit Seller   10 x 15   IA   3. 00
670.   Poultry Market   11 x 15   IA   3. 00
BEZOMBES, ROGER (French, Contemporary)
671.   Bouquet de la Jeune
       Fille   18-1/2x14-1/2   NYGS   18. 00
672.   High Summer   19 x 24   CAC   10. 00
673.   Le Melon d'Eau   18 x 13   NYGS   18. 00
BIANCHI, FRANCESCO See FERRARI
BIANCHI, LINO See BARRIVIERA
BIANCHI, PETER
674.   The Christ Head   20 x 16   DAC   5. 00
                          12 x 9   DAC   1. 50
                          10 x 8   DAC   1. 00
                          8 x 6   DAC   . 75
BICCI, LORENZO DI, THE YOUNGER (Italian, 1373-1452)
675.   Saints Cosmas and
       Damian   10 x 4   IA   1. 50
BIDDLE, GEORGE (American, 1885-
676.   Tenement   c. 7 x 9   AP   . 50
BIERSTADT, ALBERT (American, 1830-1902)
677.   Marina Grande   24 x 42   AK   12. 00
                          12 x 21   AK   3. 00
678.   Multnomah Falls   24 x 36   AA   15. 00
679.   Oregon Trail   25 x 45   AA   15. 00
680.   Rocky Mountains   26 x 39-1/2   PENN   2. 98
                          21-1/2 x 36   PENN   2. 98

681. Sierra Nevada
      Morning   25 x 39   AA   15. 00
BIGI, FRANCESCO DI CROSTOFANO See FRANCIABIGIO, IL
BIGORDI, BENEDETTO DOMINICO See GHIRLANDAIO, DOMENICO
BILLE, JACQUES (French, 1890-
682. Anemonies   20 x 16   CAC   4. 00
683. Larkspur   20 x 16   CAC   4. 00
684. Still Life with
      Pitcher   18 x 24   CAC   7. 50
685. Still Life with
      Plate   18 x 24   CAC   7. 50
BILLINGS, HENRY (American, Contemporary)
686. Arrest No. 2   c. 7 x 9   AP   . 50
BINGHAM, GEORGE CALEB (American, 1811-1879)
687. Boone with
      Pioneers   c. 7 x 9   AP   . 50
688. County Election   18 x 24   AA   12. 00
689. Fishing on the
      Mississippi   18 x 22-1/2   PENN   1. 50
690. Fur Traders Descend-
      ing the Missouri c. 20 x 24   PENN   1. 50
                         18 x 22   NYGS   12. 00
691. Raftsmen Playing
      Cards   22-1/2 x 30   NYGS   16. 00
                         5-1/2 x 7-1/2 NYGS   . 50
692. Shooting for the Beef 14 x 21   NYGS   7. 50
693. Stump Speaking   18 x 24   AA   12. 00
694. Verdict of the
      People   c.   7 x 9   AP   . 25
BINNING, BERTRAM CHARLES (Canadian, Contemporary)
695. Convoy at Rendezvous 16 x 29   CFA   15. 00
BION, CYRIL W. (English, Contemporary)
696. Evening Glow in
      Ireland   14 x 18   CFA   7. 50
697. Hills of Donegal   16 x 20   CFA   7. 50
698. Northeast Ireland 16 x 20   CFA   7. 50
699. Sunrise in Ireland 14 x 18   CFA   7. 50
BIRCH, S. J. LAMORNA (English, 1876-
700. Cornwallis Pageantry 19 x 23   RL   7. 50
701. Glorious Devon   18-1/2 x 25   RL   7. 50
702. Old Quarry   20 x 30   RL   7. 50
703. Old Stone Bridge   18 x 22   ESH   12. 00
704. Promise of Rain   16 x 22   ESH   12. 00
705. St. Ives at Low Tide 18 x 23   RL   7. 50
706. The Tay in June   18 x 23   RL   7. 50
BIRKMANN, JOHANN (Austrian, 1876-
707. Brook in the
      Mountains   16 x 20   ESH   Pr. 5. 00
708. Sailing Boats at a
      Mountain Lake   23-1/2x31-1/2 ESH   Pr. 10. 00
BIRLEY, (SIR) OSWALD (English, Contemporary)
709. Portrait of Sir Winston
      Churchill (In House of

	Commons)	20-1/2x16-1/2	ESH		10.00

BIRNEY, WILLIAM VERPLANCK (American, 1858-1909)

| 710. | Sleight of Hand | 22 x 32 | AA | | 10.00 |

BIRREN, JOSEPH P. (American, 1865-1933)

| 711. | Jonathan | 16 x 16 | CAC | | 6.00 |

BISHOP, RICHARD F. (American, 1887-

| 712. | From a Blind | 18 x 24 | AA | | 15.00 |

BISSIER, JULIUS HEINRICH (German, 1893-

713.	May 4th and 5th,				
	1961	17 x 21	NYGS		18.00
714.	Nihil Perdidi, 1961	17 x 19	NYGS		18.00

BISSIERE, ROGER (French, 1888-

715.	Painting c.	7 x 9	AP		1.00
716.	Painting (1951)	8 x 10-1/2	ESH		1.00
717.	Red, Black and				
	Orange	30-1/2 x 9	ESH		15.00
718.	Southern Cross	29-1/2 x 11	ESH		15.00

BITTNER, JOSEF

| 719. | June Flowers | 22 x 16 | NYGS | | 10.00 |

BLACKY

720.	Portraits of Children				
	(4)	16 x 12	ESH	ea.	3.00
721.	Charly				
722.	Petra				
723.	Stephan				
724.	Sylvia				

BLADEL, F.

725.	Ausfahrendes Fischer-				
	boot	20 x 12	ESH		3.00
726.	Fisher-Boats in the				
	Morning	20 x 28	ESH		7.00

BLAIR, ROBERT N. (American, Contemporary)

| 727. | Horses in the Rain | 13-1/2 x 19 | NYGS | | 7.50 |

BLAIR, STREETER (American, 1888-

| 728. | Maryland and | | | | |
| | Pennsylvania | 25 x 36 | NYGS | | 18.00 |

BLAKE, LEO B. (American, Contemporary)

729.	Berkshire Snows	20 x 24	AA		7.50
730.	The Fives Court	18 x 23-1/2	AA		18.00
731.	Mid-Winter	16 x 20	AA		5.00
732.	Old Covered Bridge	16 x 20	AA		5.00
733.	Winter in New England	20 x 24	AA		7.50

BLAKE, WILLIAM (English, 1757-1827)

734.	Beatrice Addressing				
	Dante c.	20 x 24	PENN		1.50
735.	Pilgrimage to				
	Canterbury	13 x 40	NYGS		18.00
		10 x 31	CAC		10.00
736.	Wise and Foolish				
	Virgins c.	7 x 9	AP		.25

BLANCH, ARNOLD (American, 1896-

| 737. | Floral Magic | 16-1/2 x 11 | NYGS | | 7.50 |

738.	New England	13 x 20	CAC		5. 00
739.	Outdoor Circus	12 x 20	CAC		5. 00

BLANCHARD, ANTOINE (French, Contemporary)

740.	Paris (6)	12 x 18	DAC	ea.	3. 50
741.	Cafe de la Paix	8 x 12	DAC	ea.	1. 25
742.	Champs Elysées				
743.	La Madeleine				
744.	Moulin Rouge				
745.	Notre Dame				
746.	Place de la Concorde				

BLANCHARD, CAROL (American, Contemporary)

747.	Angel	12 x 10	AA		4. 00
748.	Autumn	23 x 12	AA		10. 00
749.	Chimney Sweep	16 x 13	AA		7. 50
750.	Chris	12 x 10	AA		4. 00
751.	Grape Arbor	20 x 16	AA		10. 00
752.	Hawking (2\	16 x 12	AA	ea.	7. 50
	Departure				
	Rendezvous				
753.	Little Match Girl	16 x 13	AA		7. 50
754.	Rose Arbor	20 x 16	AA		10. 00
755.	Spring	23 x 12	AA		10. 00
756.	Summer	23 x 12	AA		10. 00
757.	Winter	23 x 12	AA		10. 00

BLANCHARD, JULES (French, 1832-1916)

758.	Copper Glow	16 x 20	RL	7. 50
759.	Oranges and Crystal	16 x 20	RL	7. 50
760.	Summer Spice	16 x 20	RL	7. 50

BLANCHET, ALEXANDRE (Swiss, 1882-

761.	Grape Harvest	24 x 24	CFA	12. 00

BLASHFIELD, EDWIN H. (American, 1848-

762.	Westward	c.	7 x 9	AP	. 50

BLECHEN, KARL EDOUARD (German, 1798-1840)

763.	Capri	28 x 40	NYGS	20. 00

BLENNER, CARL JOHN (American, 1864-

764.	The Artist's Window	25 x 30	AA	7. 50
765.	Autumn Flowers	22 x 28	CFA	7. 50
766.	Bowl of Phlox	25 x 30	AA	7. 50
767.	From My Garden	30 x 25	AA	7. 50
768.	Geraniums	20 x 24	AA	5. 00
769.	Gloucester Bouquet	30 x 25	AA	7. 50
770.	Harbor View--Phlox	28 x 22	AA	7. 50
771.	Mixed Glads	20 x 24	AA	5. 00
772.	Peonies	28 x 22	AA	7. 50
773.	Pink Gladioli	24 x 20	AA	5. 00
774.	Studio View-Phlox	20 x 24	AA	5. 00
775.	Summer Glory	20 x 16	IA	3. 50

BLES, HERRI Met DE (CIVETTA) (Flemish, 16th Century)

776.	Interrupted Music			
	Lesson	18 x 24	PENN	1. 50

BLINKS, THOMAS (English, 1860-1912)

777.	Drop!	20 x 30	AA	20. 00

(H. C. Eng.)

778.	The Rose	20 x 30	AA	20.00
				(H. C. Eng.)
779.	Shamrock	20 x 30	AA	20.00
				(H. C. Eng.)
780.	Steady!	19 x 30	AA	20.00
				(H. C. Eng.)
781.	Thistle	21-1/2 x 30	AA	20.00
				(H. C. Eng.)
782.	Twelfth of August	21-1/2 x 30	AA	20.00
				(H. C. Eng.)
783.	Unity	20 x 30	AA	20.00
				(H. C. Eng.)

BLOEMEN
| 784. | Paesaggio con Lago | 25-1/2 x 35 | CFA | 15.00 |
| 785. | Paesaggio con Cascata | 26 x 36 | CFA | 15.00 |

BLOMMERS, BERNARDUS J. (Dutch, 1845-1914)
| 786. | In the Country | c. | 7 x 9 | AP | .50 |
| 787. | Preparing for Church | c. | 7 x 9 | AP | .60 |

BLONDIN, FERNAND (Swiss, Contemporary)
788.	Porte St. Denis	8 x 12	CFA	5.00
789.	Rue Chevalier le Barre	12 x 8	CFA	5.00
790.	Rue Norvins	12 x 8	CFA	5.00

BLOOM, HYMAN (American, Contemporary)
| 791. | Anatomist, 1953 | c. | 8 x 10 | NYGS | .50 |

BLOOMSTER
| 792. | Fair Weather | 25 x 30 | CAC | 7.50 |

BLUME, PETER (American Contemporary)
793.	The Boat, 1929	16-1/2 x 20	NYGS	10.00
794.	Eternal City	c.	8 x 10	NYGS	.50
795.	Parade	c.	7 x 9	AP	.25

BOCCACCINO, BOCCACCIO, THE ELDER (Italian, 1460-1529)
| 796. | The Gypsye | 10 x 7 | IA | 1.50 |

BOCCARDI, GIOVANNI (BOCCARDINO THE ELDER) (Italian, 1460-1529)
| 797. | The Trinity | 15 x 11 | IA | 3.00 |

BOCCATI, GIOVANNI (Italian, 1420-1480)
798.	Virgin Enthroned with			
	Angel Musicians	15 x 11	IA	3.00
799.	Virgin Enthroned with			
	Angels	11 x 15	IA	3.00

BOCCIONI, UMBERTO (Italian, 1882-1916)
800.	The City Rises	20 x 30	NYGS	16.00
		c.	8 x 10	MMA	.35
801.	Dynamism of a			
	Cyclist	c.	20 x 24	PENN	1.50
802.	States of Mind:			
	The Farewells	c.	18 x 23	HNA	5.95

BOCK, LUDWIG (German, 1886-
| 803. | Still Life with Fruits | 15 x 19 | ESH | 6.00 |

BOCKER
| 804. | Stilles Moor | 26 x 34 | CFA | 18.00 |

BOCKERER, ALFRED
| 805. | Sunflowers and Poppies | 31 x 12 | CFA | 12.00 |

BODEN, LEONARD
806. H. H. The Late Pope
         Pius XII   25 x 17   AS   30. 00
         Head--Detail of
            No. 806   16 x 12   AS   22. 50
807. H. M. Elizabeth II   25 x 20   AS   30. 00
808. H. R. M. Prince Philip 25 x 20   AS   30. 00
BODENHAUSEN, MATHILDE FREIIN VON (German, 1870-
809. Madonna   23 x 18   CAC   7. 50
BODNER
810. Riding Shotgun   24 x 48   DAC   10. 00
BOEHMER, HEINRICH
811. Sylvan Solitude   22 x 30-1/2   IA   10. 00
BOGDANOVE, ABRAHAM J. , Russian (Res. U. S.) 1887-
812. Monhegan Harbor   26 x 36   CFA   15. 00
BOHROD, AARON (American, 1907-
813. America--Its History
         (Map)   22 x 32-1/2   NYGS   6. 00
814. Landscape Near
         Chicago   15 x 20   CAC   7. 50
815. St. James Park   17 x 22   CAC   7. 50
816. Waiting for 3:30   c.   8 x 10   NYGS   . 50
BOHMER, GUNTER (German, 1911-
817. Merry-Go-Round   12 x 15   CAC   10. 00
BOILANGES
818. Fery Coiffure   c.   24 x 20   PENN   1. 50
BOILLY, LOUIS LEOPOLD (French, 1761-1845)
819. Arrival of the Mail
         Coach   8 x 14   IA   3. 00
820. La Comparaison   14 x 11   CAC   12. 00
821. La Comparaison
         Petits Pieds   14 x 11   CAC   12. 00
822. Defending the Rose   18-1/2x14-1/2   CFA   20. 00
823. Politics   12 x 17   CFA   12. 00
824. Portrait of a Boy   7 x 5   IA   1. 50
825. Prelude de Nina   18-1/2x14-1/2   CFA   20. 00
                              14 x 11   CAC   12. 00
826. The Storm   11 x 13   IA   3. 00
827. La Vue Difficile   14 x 11   CAC   12. 00
BOL, FERDINAND (Dutch, 1616-1680)
828. Jacob's Dream   10 x 8   AR   4. 00
BOLSTAD, E. MELVIN (American, 1901-
         Scenes of Country Life:20 x 25 (2)   NYGS   ea. 10. 00
829.   Holiday Parade
830.   Sunday Visitors
831. Monday in the
         Country   16 x 20 (2)   NYGS   ea.   7. 50
832. Sunday in the Country
833. School's Afire   11 x 14 (2)   NYGS   ea.   3. 00
834. Sunday Fire Drill
835. Arrival at the Inn   8 x 10 (8)   NYGS   ea.   1. 50

836.   Country Lawn Party
837.   County Fair
838.   False Alarm
839.   Nine O'Clock Express
840.   School's Out
841.   Shopping on Main Street
842.   Three-Alarmer
843.   The Express   6 x 8 (8)   NYGS   ea. 1. 00
844.   Horse Trolley
845.   Morning Drive
846.   New-Fangled Engine
847.   Queen of Rails
848.   Rapid Transit
849.   Ride on Wagon
850.   Sunday Ride
BOLTRAFFIO See BELTRAFFIO
BOMBOIS, CAMILLE (French, 1883-
851.   Before Entering the
       Circus Ring   c.   8 x 10   NYGS   . 50
852.   Neighbor's Garden   24 x 18   NYGS   10. 00
853.   View of Clerval c.   18 x 23   HNA   5. 95
BONAMICI, LOUIS
854.   Eventide   22 x 28   CAC   10. 00
855.   Fishermen of
       Martinque   20 x 26   CAC   10. 00
BONESS
856.   Boats in the Twilight 14 x 27-1/2   ESH   Pr. 8. 00
857.   Calming Boats   27-1/2 x 14   ESH   Pr. 8. 00
858.   Coloured Sails   14 x 27-1/2   ESH   Pr. 8. 00
859.   Dawn Upon the
       Harbour   16 x 31-1/2   ESH   Pr. 8. 00
       Floral Subjects (3)   8 x 16   ESH   3. 00
                                                   ea. Pr.
860.   Magnolias
861.   Orchids
862.   Poinsettia
863.   Harbour-Street   27-1/2 x 14   ESH   Pr. 8. 00
864.   Red Fishing Boats   16 x 31-1/2   ESH   Pr. 8. 00
                              8 x 16   ESH   Pr. 3. 00
865.   Return by Night   16 x 31-1/2   ESH   Pr. 8. 00
                              8 x 16   ESH   Pr. 3. 00
866.   Spanish Coast   14 x 27-1/2   ESH   Pr. 8. 00
BONESTELL, CHESLEY
867.   The Sea and Me   24 x 48   DAC   10. 00
[868. No Entry]
[869. No Entry]
BONFIGLI, BENEDETTO (Italian, 1420-1496)
870.   Archangel Gabriel   11 x 12   IA   3. 00
871.   Virgin Annunciate   11 x 12   IA   3. 00
BONFORT, VERNET (French Contemporary)
872.   Flame Lilies   30 x 24   RL   17. 50

873. Pink Coffee Pot   18 x 36   RL   22. 50
BONHEUR, ROSA (French, 1822-1899)
874. Buffalo Bill   20 x 16   AA   8. 00
875. Horse Fair   17 x 36   NYGS   18. 00
                              5 x 11   NYGS   1. 00
                  c.   7 x 9   AP   . 50
876. Ploughing   c.   7 x 9   AP   . 60
BONINGTON, RICHARD PARKES (English, 1801-1828)
877. Coast of Picardy   14 x 20   ESH   12. 00
                  c.   7 x 9   AP   . 50
BONNARD, PIERRE (French, 1867-1947)
878. Almond Tree in Bloom 23 x 16   CFA   15. 00
879. Buste de Jeune Femme 10 x 8   NYGS   5. 00
880. Cannes Harbour   21-1/2x18-1/2 ESH   10. 00
881. Le Cannet   20 x 14   NYGS   7. 50
882. Chequered Table
      Cover   13 x 23-1/2 NYGS   10. 00
883. Dining Room at
      Cannet   c.   20 x 24   PENN   1. 50
884. The Farm   17-1/2x22-1/2 ESH   10. 00
885. Farm with a Red
      Roof   c.   20 x 24   PENN   1. 50
886. Fleurs Rouges   23 x 20   ESH   10. 00
887. Flowers   22 x 16   ESH   10. 00
                  c.   10 x 8   ESH   1. 00
888. Harbour of St. Tropez 16 x 20   AP   5. 00
889. The Letter   c.   23 x 18   HNA   5. 95
890. Nude at the Fire-
      place   c.   20 x 24   PENN   1. 50
                  c.   18 x 23   HNA   5. 95
891. Old Vase   22 x 18   AJ   7. 50
892. Place Clichy   c.   20 x 24   PENN   1. 50
893. Le Pont de Grenelle   18 x 22-1/2 ESH   10. 00
894. Provencal Jug   22 x 18   NYGS   7. 50
895. Rose Road   c.   20 x 24   PENN   1. 50
896. Village Fountain   18 x 22   NYGS   10. 00
897. Yellow and Red
      Still Life   c.   20 x 24   PENN   1. 50
898. Boats   20 x 28   ESH   7. 00
899. Regatta I and II   12 x 23-1/2 ESH   ea. 4. 00
BOOBIS, BRADFORD (American Contemporary)
900. Bull Fighters (2)   30 x 12   DAC   ea. 5. 00
901. English Guards (2)   30 x 12   DAC   ea. 5. 00
902. Giving Thanks   18 x 24   DAC   7. 50
                             12 x 16   DAC   3. 50
903. Masquerade Children
      (4)   12 x 9   DAC   ea. 2. 50
904. Silent Prayer   18 x 24   DAC   7. 50
                             12 x 16   DAC   3. 50
BOOTH, NINA MASON (American, 1884-
905. White Begonias   13 x 14   IA   3. 00
906. Yellow Tulips   13 x 14   IA   3. 00

BORCH, GERARD TER See TERBORCH, GERARD
BORDENAVE-AUROUS, YVONNE (French Contemporary)

907.	Long Summer Days	23-1/2 x 36	RL		12. 50	
908.	Quiet Mooring	24 x 30	RL		10. 00	

BORDI, MARIO (Italian, 1896-

909.	Freedom of the Plains	20 x 30	IA		10. 00	
910.	Rebel Herd	20 x 30	IA		10. 00	
911.	Stampede	10 x 15	AS		6. 00	
912.	Storm	20 x 24	AS		12. 00	
913.	Storm Clouds	20 x 30	AS		10. 00	

BORDONE, PARIS PASCHALINUS (Italian, 1500-1570/71)

914.	Venetian Lovers	12 x 11	IA		3. 00	

BOREIN, EDWARD (American, 1872-

915.	Steer Roping	12 x 18	AA		3. 00	

BORHORD

916.	Waiting for the 3:30 c.	8 x 10	NYGS		. 50	

BORTHWICK, ALFRED EDWARD (Scotch, 1871-

917.	The Presence	26 x 39-1/2	IA		15. 00	
		15 x 23-1/2	IA		7. 50	
		6-1/2 x 10	IA		10. 00	
					(H. C. Gr.)	

BOS, HENK (Dutch Contemporary)

918.	Antique Fruits (4)	10 x 14	DAC	set	14. 00	
919.	Breakfast Time	12 x 18	PENN		1. 50	
920.	Coffee Urn, Bread and Eggs c.	20 x 24	PENN		1. 50	
921.	Garden Bouquet	14 x 16	PENN		1. 50	
922.	Green Grapes and Strawberries	12 x 18	PENN		1. 50	
923.	Green Grapes and Zinnias c.	20 x 24	PENN		1. 50	
924.	Harvest	14 x 16	PENN		1. 50	
925.	Magnolias	40 x 30	DAC		22. 50	
		24 x 18	DAC		12. 50	
926.	Metal Pitcher, Bread and Eggs c.	20 x 24	PENN		1. 50	
927.	Metal Pitcher, Onions and Carrots c.	20 x 24	PENN		1. 50	
928.	Pitcher and Apples	16 x 14	PENN		1. 50	
929.	Pitcher and Basket of Apples c.	24 x 20	PENN		1. 50	
930.	Purple Grapes and Tomatoes	12 x 18	PENN		1. 50	
931.	Roses and Basket of Eggs c.	24 x 20	PENN		1. 50	
932.	Still Life (4)	20 x 16	DAC	ea.	5. 00	
		12 x 10	DAC	ea.	1. 50	
	Still Life (14)	13-1/2x15-1/2	DAC	ea.	5. 00	
		7 x 8	DAC	ea.	. 75	
	Still Life (4)	16 x 18	DAC	ea.	5. 00	
	Still Life (8)	8 x 8	DAC	ea.	1. 00	

933.	Still Life with Bread			
	and Pears	14 x 16	PENN	1. 50
934.	Still Life with Kettle	14 x 16	PENN	1. 50
935.	Still Life with Pitcher	14 x 16	PENN	1. 50
936.	Still Life with Plums	14 x 16	PENN	1. 50
937.	Still Life with Pottery			
	Jug	14 x 16	PENN	1. 50
938.	Still Life with Storm			
	Lantern	16 x 14	PENN	1. 50
939.	Still Life with			
	Strawberries	14 x 16	PENN	1. 50
940.	Still Life with Sun-			
	flowers	16 x 14	PENN	1. 50
941.	Still Life with			
	Tangerines	16 x 14	PENN	1. 50
942.	Still Life with Tankard	14 x 16	PENN	1. 50
943.	Tankard and Peaches	16 x 14	PENN	1. 50
944.	Wooden Basket and			
	Pitcher c.	20 x 24	PENN	1. 50
945.	Zinnias	14 x 16	PENN	1. 50

BOSCH, HIERONYMUS VAN AEKEN (Flemish,   1460-1516)

946.	Adoration of the Kings	23 x 17-1/2	AP	5. 00
947.	The Conjuror			
	(Trickster)	18 x 22	ESH	10. 00
948.	Garden of Delights	23-1/2 x 42		
	(Triptych)	(3 on 1 sheet)	NYGS	18. 00
949.	St. John at Patmos	23-1/2 x 18	NYGS	22. 00

BOSS, EDOURD (Swiss, 1873-

950.	Belpermoos	22 x 31	CAC	12. 00

BOSSCHAERTS, THOMAS WILLEBORT (Flemish, 1614-1654)

951.	Flowerpiece	12 x 8-1/2	ESH	2. 00

BOSTICK, WILLIAM A. (American Contemporary)

952.	View of Toledo, 1963	23-1/2 x 20	NYGS	12. 00

BOTKE, JESSIE ARMS (American, 1883-

953.	Cranes	25 x 30	CFA	12. 00
		17 x 20	CFA	5. 00
954.	Enchanted Pool	24 x 19	CAC	7. 50
		14 x 11	CAC	3. 00
955.	Flamingoes	25 x 30	CFA	12. 00
		17 x 20	CFA	5. 00
956.	Leadbeaters Cockatoos	18 x 22	CFA	7. 50
957.	Molucca Cockatoos	18 x 22	CFA	7. 50
958.	Nature's Dreamland	24 x 19	CAC	7. 50
959.	Royal Cockatoos	25 x 30	CFA	12. 00
		17 x 20	CFA	5. 00
960.	Tropical Beauty	25 x 30	CFA	12. 00
		17 x 20	CFA	5. 00
961.	Tropical Pool	27 x 36	NYGS	15. 00

BOTICELLI, SANDRO (ALESSANDRO DI MARIANO DEL FILIPEPI)
(Italian, 1444-1510)

962.	Adoration of the Magi,			
	1481-82	19 x 28	NYGS	16. 00

		16 x 24	PENN	1.50
		10 x 13	IA	3.00
963.	Self-Portrait-			
	Detail of No. 962	15 x 9	IA	3.00
964.	Angels - Detail of a			
	Coronation of the Virgin	11 x 15	IA	3.00
965.	Annunciation (Uffizi)	14 x 11	IA	3.00
966.	Annunciation (Florence)	10-1/2 x 11	AS	3.25
967.	Birth of Venus	16-1/2 x 26	PENN	1.50
		13 x 21	CAC	4.00
		9-1/2 x 15	AS	3.25
	c.	8 x 10	AP	.50
968.	Venus - Detail of			
	No. 967	15 x 9	IA	3.00
969.	Head of Venus -			
	Detail of No. 967	11-1/2x15-1/2	AS	3.25
970.	The Winds - Detail			
	of No. 967	11 x 15	AS	3.25
971.	Calumny of Apelles	10 x 15	IA	3.00
	Detail of No. 971	15 x 11	IA	3.00
972.	Gift Bearers	9 x 12	CFA	2.50
973.	Judith	12 x 8	IA	3.00
974.	Madonna and Child			
	(Poldi-Pezzoli, Milan)	22 x 15-1/2	AS	7.50
		18 x 12 1/2	IA	7.50
		15 x 10	IA	3.00
		13 x 9	IA	3.50
		10 x 7	IA	1.75
975.	Madonna and Child			
	with Angels	30-1/2x20-1/2	NYGS	18.00
	(Nat. Gall. - U. S.)			
976.	Madonna and Child with			
	Angels (Uffizi)	15 x 11	IA	3.00
977.	Madonna and Child with			
	Angels (Borghese)	11-1/2 Diam.	AS	3.25
		11" Diam.	IA	3.00
978.	Madonna and Child with			
	St. John (Louvre)	28 x 20	ESH	15.00
		18 x 13	ESH	7.50
		14 x 10	IA	3.00
979.	Madonna and Child with			
	St. John	16 x 11	ESH	10.00
		10-1/2 x 8	ESH	1.00
980.	Madonna and Child with			
	St. John (Pitti)	15 x 11	IA	3.00
981.	Madonna of the Lilies	22" Diam.	NYGS	12.00
		6 x 6	NYGS	.50
982.	Madonna of the			
	Magnificat	23" Diam.	AS	7.50
		19" Diam.	AS	7.50
		12" Diam.	IA	3.00
		11" Diam.	AS	3.25

983.	Angels--Detail of No. 982.	16 x 10	IA	3. 00
984.	Head of Virgin-- Detail of No. 982.	15 x 11	IA	3. 00
985.	Madonna of the Pomegranate	11" Diam.	IA	3. 00
986.	Angel--Detail of No. 985.	15 x 11	IA	3. 00
987.	Head of Virgin-- Detail of No. 985.	15 x 11	IA	3. 00
988.	Madonna of the Rose Hedge	12" Diam.	IA	3. 00
989.	Madonna of the Roses	11-1/2 Diam.	AS	3. 25
990.	Madonna of the Sea	15 x 11	IA	3. 00
991.	Madonna of the Seraphim	16 x 9	IA	3. 00
992.	Madonna with the Canopy	11" Diam.	IA	3. 00
993.	Man with a Medal	15 x 11	IA	3. 00
994.	Minerva--Head Detail from Minerva and the Centaur	15 x 11	AS	3. 25
995.	Nativity	26 x 18	ESH	20. 00
	c.	10 x 8	AP	. 50
996.	Nuptial Allegory c.	8 x 10	ESH	1. 00
997.	Pallas and the Centaur	16 x 12	IA	3. 00
998.	Portrait of a Woman	15 x 10	IA	3. 00
999.	Portrait of a Young Man	20 x 14	NYGS	12. 00
1000.	Portrait of a Youth	15-1/2 x 12	NYGS	7. 50
		8 x 6	NYGS	. 50
1001.	La Primavera (Springtime)	13-1/2 x 21	CAC	4. 00
		10 x 15	IA	3. 00
		7-1/2 x 15	AS	3. 25
1002.	Chloris--Detail of No. 1001	15 x 11	IA	3. 00
1003.	Flora--Detail of No. 1001	15 x 11	IA	3. 00
	Head of Flora-- Detail of No. 1001	15 x 11	IA	3. 00
1004.	The Graces--Detail of No. 1001	15 x 11	IA	3. 00
	One of the Graces-- Detail of No. 1001	15 x 11	IA	3. 00
1005.	Venus--Detail of No. 1001	15 x 11	IA	3. 00
1006.	Salome with the Baptist's Head	7 x 10	IA	1. 50

BOTTICELLI, SCHOOL OF

1007.	Death of Lucretia	5 x 15	AS	3. 25

BOTTICINI, FRANCESCO (Italian, 1446-1497)

1008.	Angel Announcing	15 x 11	AS	3. 25
1009.	St. Michael	15 x 7	AS	3. 25
1010.	Virgin Adoring the Child (Venice)	15-1/2x10-1/2	AS	3. 25
1011.	Virgin Adoring the Child, and Angels	11" Diam.	IA	3. 00
1012.	Virgin Annunciate	15 x 11	AS	3. 25

BOTTON, RAYMOND DE (French Contemporary)

1013.	Painting No. 1, Greek Island	24 x 40	NYGS	18. 00

BOUCHER, FRANCOIS (French, 1703-1770)

1014.	Autumn	16 x 21	NYGS	10. 00
		13 x 16	CFA	12. 00
		11 x 14	NYGS	4. 00
		10 x 12	CFA	12. 00
1015.	The Breakfast	13 x 10-1/2	IA	3. 00
1016.	Charms of the Country Life	10 x 15	IA	3. 00
1017.	Dancing Dog	10-1/2 x 8 Oval	ESH	1. 00
1018.	Diana's Rest	9 x 12	CFA	2. 50
1019.	Dispatch of the Messenger c.	8 x 10	AP	. 50
1020.	Dormeuse (Sleeper)	11 x 8-1/2	CFA	15. 00
1021.	Espieglerie (Frolic)	11 x 8-1/2	CFA	15. 00
1022.	Girl with Jug	10 x 9	CFA	5. 00
1023.	Infant Savious and the Little St. John	13 x 11-1/2 Oval	AS	3. 25
		13 x 11 Oval	IA	3. 00
1024.	Madame Bergeret	30 x 22	NYGS	16. 00
1025.	Les Marchands des Modes	12 x 16	CAC	3. 00
1026.	La Marquise de Pompadour	16 x 12	CAC	3. 00
1027.	La Musique	20-1/2 x 30	NYGS	15. 00
1028.	Musette	11 x 14	IA	3. 00
		10 x 13-1/2	IA	3. 00
		8-1/2 x 11	IA	1. 75
1029.	The Nest	10 x 15	IA	3. 00
	c.	8 x 10	ESH	1. 00
1030.	Nu De Dos	8-1/2 x 13	NYGS	4. 00
1031.	Nude	13 x 8	CFA	3. 50
1032.	Odalisque	10 x 11	CFA	2. 50
1033.	Renault and Armida	11 x 14	IA	3. 00
1034.	Repose of Diana after the Bath	11 x 14	IA	3. 00
1035.	Reposing Girl with Putto	10 x 12-1/2	AR	3. 50
1036.	Scene with Donkey and Goat c.	8 x 10	NYGS	. 50
1037.	Sleeping Shepherdess, 1750 (Bergere Endormie)	28 x 25	NYGS	16. 00

1038.	Sleeping Shepherdess			
	(Bergere Endormie)	11 x 14	IA	3. 00
		10 x 12	IA	10. 00
				(H. C. Gr.)
		8-1/2 x 11	IA	1. 75
1039.	Spring	16 x 21	NYGS	10. 00
		12 x 16	CFA	12. 00
		11 x 14	NYGS	4. 00
		10 x 12	CFA	12. 00
1040.	Summer	16 x 21	NYGS	10. 00
		11 x 14	NYGS	4. 00
		10 x 12	CFA	12. 00
1041.	La Toilette c.	20 x 24	PENN	1. 50
1042.	Water Mill	24 x 31-1/2	ESH	15. 00
		8 x 10-1/2	ESH	1. 00
1043.	Winter	16 x 21	NYGS	10. 00
		11 x 14	NYGS	4. 00
		10 x 12	CFA	12. 00

BOUDIN, EUGENE LOUIS (French, 1825-1898)

1044.	Beach at Tourgeville	18-1/2 x 27	NYGS	15. 00
1045.	Beach àt Trouville c.	18 x 23	HNA	5. 95
	c.	9-1/2 x 12-1/2	AP	1. 25
	c.	8 x 10	AP	1. 00
1046.	Beach at Viller-			
	ville	18 x 30	NYGS	16. 00
	c.	18 x 23	HNA	5. 95
1047.	Canal à Bruxelles	18-1/2x26-1/2	NYGS	15. 00
1048.	Crinolines at Trou-			
	ville	8 x 17	ESH	8. 00
1049.	Empress Eugenie			
	at Trouville	13 x 22	NYGS	7. 50
1050.	Entrance to the			
	Harbor	21 x 29	NYGS	16. 00
1051.	Fair in Brittany c.	20 x 24	PENN	1. 50
1052.	Fishing Fleet c.	8 x 10	ESH	1. 00
1053.	Harbour at Trouville	9 x 12	ESH	2. 00
1054.	Jetty at Deauville c.	18 x 23	HNA	5. 95
1055.	Return of the Terre-			
	Neuvier c.	18 x 23	HNA	5. 95
1056.	Sur La Plage	6-1/2 x 11-1/2	NYGS	7. 50
1057.	Trouville	5 x 10	CFA	1. 00
1058.	View of Trouville c.	8 x 10	ESH	1. 00

BOUGHTON, GEORGE H. (American, 1833-1905)

1059.	Pilgrims Going to			
	Church	17-1/2 x 32	NYGS	12. 00
		11-1/2 x 21	AP	3. 00
	c.	8 x 10	AP	. 50

BOUROULT, ROBERT (French Contemporary)

1060.	Village in Winter	24 x 40	RL	20. 00

BOUTS, DIRK (DIERICK DE LOUVAIN) (Dutch [Res. Belgium] 1420-
1475)
   1061.   Adoration of Three Kings --

		Triptych (Called "The			
		Pearl of Brabant")	18 x 36	IA	24. 00
1062.		St. Christopher (Right			
		Panel of No. 1061)	23-1/2 x 10	IA	12. 00

BOVE, ARMANDO MIRAVALLS (Spanish Contemporary)

1063.	Bountiful Harvest	13 x 39-1/2	NYGS	16. 00
		7-1/2 x 24	NYGS	7. 50
1064.	Dahlias with Fruit	31-1/2 x 9-1/2	NYGS	12. 00
1065.	Flamenco	16-1/2 x 30	NYGS	10. 00
1066.	Fruit and Peonies	31-1/2 x 9-1/2	NYGS	12. 00
1067.	Grapes: The			
	Blessed Land	31-1/2 x 9-1/2	NYGS	12. 00
1068.	Mirror Lake	22-1/2 x 36	NYGS	16. 00
1069.	Oranges: Land of			
	Plenty	31-1/2 x 9-1/2	NYGS	12. 00
1070.	Peonies	13 x 39	NYGS	15. 00
1071.	Roses	13 x 39	NYGS	15. 00
1072.	Spring Blooms	20 x 6-1/2	NYGS	3. 00
1073.	Still Life--Souvenirs	17 x 39-1/1	NYGS	16. 00
1074.	Street Dancing,			
	Seville	16-1/2 x 30	NYGS	10. 00
1075.	Summer Blooms	20 x 6-1/2	NYGS	3. 00

BOWERS, H. N.

1076.	Meditation	20 x 16	CFA	10. 00
1077.	Newsboy	20 x 16	CFA	10. 00

BOX, E.

1078.	Lady of the Manor	20 x 23-1/2	NYGS	12. 00

BRACKMAN, ROBERT (American, 1896-

1079.	Study--Morning			
	Interlude	20 x 15	NYGS	9. 00

BRADBURY, BENNETT (American Contemporary)

1080.	Ebb Tide	24 x 36	DAC	7. 50
		18 x 26	PENN	1. 50
		12 x 18	DAC	2. 50
1081.	Rolling Surf	24 x 48	DAC	10. 00
		24 x 30	PENN	1. 95
		15 x 30	DAC	2. 00
1082.	Shelter Bay	24 x 36	DAC	7. 50
		18 x 26	DAC	6. 00
		12 x 18	DAC	2. 50
1083.	Sunny Cove	18 x 26	PENN	1. 50

BRADSHAW, PERCY V. (English

1084.	On Lake Maggiore	9 x 10	CAC	2. 00
1085.	Street in Cassis	9 x 10	CAC	2. 00
1086.	Welsh Estuary	9 x 10	CAC	2. 00
1087.	Welsh Farm	9 x 10	CAC	2. 00

BRAGA, V.

1088.	Necklace	24 x 30	AA	7. 50

BRAMANTINO, IL See SUARDI, BARTOLOMMEO

BRANDEIS, ANTONIETTA (1849-1890)

1089.	The Ponte Vecchio	9 x 15	AS	3. 25

BRANDON, EDOUARD (French, 1831-1897)

1090.	Heder	14 x 18	NYGS	7. 50

BRANDSTATTER, P.
1091.	Madonna	23-1/2 x 20	AS		14. 00
1092.	Madonna	20 x 10	AS		7. 50
1093.	Madonna (2)	22 x 12	AS	ea.	10. 00

BRANGWYN, FRANK (English, 1867-
1094.	The Pilots c.	8 x 10	NYGS		. 50

BRAQUE, GEORGES (French, 1882-1963)
1095.	Anemones	14 x 28	CAC		16. 00
1096.	Ballet (Male No. 1)	20 x 16	CFA		7. 50
1097.	Ballet (Female No. 2)	20 x 16	CFA		7. 50
1098.	Le Billard	17 x 24	PENN		1. 50
1099.	Black Fish c.	12 x 16	AP		2. 00
1100.	Boats on Shore	17 x 23	ESH		10. 00
1101.	Bords de Mer	10 x 25	NYGS		22. 00
1102.	La Carafe c.	8 x 10	ESH		1. 00
1103.	Chrysanthemums	22 x 15	CAC		10. 00
1104.	L'Estaque c.	8 x 10	ESH		1. 00
1105.	Le Grand Gueridon	30 x 12	ESH		15. 00
1106.	Green Table Cloth	14 x 20	NYGS		7. 50
1107.	Guitar c.	18 x 23	HNA		5. 95
1108.	Harbour Scene, Antwerp	19-1/2 x 24	NYGS		12. 00
1109.	Interior	16-1/2x22-1/2	ESH		10. 00
1110.	Jug and Ivy	16 x 21	ESH		10. 00
1111.	Kitchen Table c.	8 x 10	AP		. 50
1112.	Lemon and Peaches	9 x 28	CAC		12. 00
1113.	Lemons	20 x 26	CAC		10. 00
1114.	Lemons, Peaches and Compotier	9 x 28	AA		12. 00
1115.	La Mandoline	20 x 27	CAC		15. 00
1116.	Marble Table	24 x 14-1/2	PENN		1. 50
1117.	Marine	19 x 28	CFA		15. 00
1118.	Musician c.	8 x 10	AP		. 50
1119.	Nature Morte	14-1/2 x 21	NYGS		7. 50
1120.	Nature Morte	17 x 21	NYGS		15. 00
1121.	Nature Morte	11-1/2 x 15	NYGS		15. 00
1122.	Les Peches	19 x 25	NYGS		18. 00
1123.	Pedestal Table (High, Round)	30 x 12	CAC		15. 00
1124.	Peonies, 1926	20 x 24	NYGS		12. 00
1125.	Pink Table	24 x 30	PENN		1. 95
1126.	Pitcher and Basket of Fruit	12 x 30	AR		10. 00
1127.	Red Tablecloth	18 x 22-1/2	ESH		10. 00
	c.	8 x 10	ESH		1. 00
1128.	Red Violin	17 x 22	CAC		12. 00
1129.	Round Table	24-1/2 x 19	NYGS		12. 00
1130.	Seascape	19 x 30	CFA		15. 00
1131.	Ship in the Harbor of Le Havre c.	18 x 23	HNA		5. 95

1132.	Still Life		14 x 17	AR	7.50
1133.	Still Life, 1926		18 x 22-1/2	ESH	10.00
		c.	8 x 10	ESH	1.00
1134.	Still Life, 1934		16 x 19	AR	7.50
1135.	Still Life in Black		11 x 19	CFA	5.00
1136.	Still Life: Le Jour		22 x 27-1/2	NYGS	16.00
		c.	20 x 24	PENN	1.50
1137.	Still Life, Lemons		16 x 22	AR	7.50
1138.	Still Life, Mandolin				
		c.	8 x 10	AP	.50
1139.	Still Life on a Table		30 x 12	CFA	15.00
1140.	Still Life, Pipe		11 x 14	AR	5.00
1141.	Still Life, Playing Cards		19-1/2x25-1/2	AP	6.00
1142.	Still Life, the Table, 1928		17 x 28	NYGS	16.00
1143.	Still Life, Table		14-1/2 x 24	PENN	1.50
		c.	8 x 10	AP	.25
1144.	Still Life with Banana		10-1/2 x 18	NYGS	18.00
1145.	Still Life with Bread and Jug		19 x 23	NYGS	12.00
1146.	Still Life with Fish		15 x 18	PENN	1.50
1147.	Still Life with Fruit and Glass		15 x 18	CAC	10.00
1148.	Still Life with Glass and Lemon		9 x 12	CAC	5.00
1149.	Still Life with Grapes, 1927		21 x 28-1/2	NYGS	16.00
1150.	Still Life with Lemons		12 x 32-1/2	IA	15.00
			9-1/2 x 30	ESH	15.00
1151.	Still Life with Mandolin		21 x 29	CFA	15.00
			18 x 24	PENN	1.50
		c.	18 x 23	HNA	5.95
		c.	8 x 10	AP	.50
1152.	Still Life with Playing Cards		19-1/2x25-1/2	NYGS	6.00
1153.	Still Life with Red Apple		17 x 26	CFA	12.00
1154.	Stranded Boat	c.	8 x 10	ESH	1.00
1155.	Studio		22 x 21	AA	12.00
1156.	Sugar Bowl with Fruit		9 x 30	AR	10.00
1157.	Tea Table		15 x 28	CFA	15.00
1158.	Terrace		17-1/2 x 22	ESH	10.00
1159.	Violin and Pipe with the Word "Polka"		17 x 36	NYGS	16.00
1160.	White Cloth		18 x 25	CAC	15.00
1161.	Wine Glass		18 x 28	CAC	15.00
1162.	Woman with Mandolin		24 x 18	PENN	1.50
			19 x 14	MMA	4.00

		c.	10 x 8	MMA	. 35

BRASS, ITALICO (Italian, 1870-1943)
1163. Harlequin Sonata   22 x 28   CAC   10.00
BRATBY, JOHN (English, Contemporary)
1164. Just Before They Took
       the Lighters Away   18 x 24   ESH   15.00
1165. View from the Studio
       Window   25-1/2 x 20   NYGS   18.00
BRAUER, E.
1166. Between the Birds   12 x 17   CFA   12.00
1167. The Search--Probing
       for Oil   15 x 24   CFA   15.00
BRAYER, YVES (French Contemporary)
1168. Chevaux en
       Camargue   c.   20 x 24   PENN   1.50
                           18 x 24   NYGS   22.00
1169. La Maison Blanche   17 x 23   PENN   1.50
1170. Paysage des Baux   19 x 25   NYGS   22.00
1171. La Rue St. Vincent
       sous la Neige   16 x 22   CFA   10.00
1172. Village Andalou
       (Los Palacios) c.   17-1/2 x 22   AS   4.00
BREANSKI, ALFRED DE (English, 1877-1957)
1173. Cottage Flowers   16 x 10   CAC   2.00
1174. Country Garden   16 x 10   CAC   2.00
1175. Forest Blossoms   16 x 10   CAC   2.00
1176. Highland Loch   24 x 32   CFA   10.00
BRECKBERG, HIOB (Dutch, 1628-1698)
1177. Self-Portrait   15 x 13   IA   3.00
BREMEN, MEYER VON See MEYER, JOHANN
BRESSLER, EMILE (Swiss
1178. Flowers on a Grey
       Background   20 x 15   CAC   7.50
1179. Landscape near
       Geneva   20 x 25   CFA   10.00
BRETON, JULES (French, 1827-1906)
1180. Quiet Estuary   18 x 24   CAC   10.00
1181. Shepherd's Star   26 x 20   CAC   7.50
                           20 x 16   CAC   5.00
1182. Song of the Lark   26 x 20   NYGS   12.00
                           20 x 16   AP   3.00
                           14-1/2 x 11   NYGS   3.00
                           12 x 9   CAC   2.00
                           10 x 8   NYGS   1.00
                      c.   9 x 7   AP   .50
BRETT, MOLLY
1183. All Aboard the
       Airliner   17-1/2 x 21   ESH   3.50
1184. All the Fun of the
       Fair   17-1/2 x 21   ESH   3.50
1185. Evensong   21 x 17-1/2   ESH   3.50
1186. Going to School   17-1/2 x 21   ESH   3.50

1187.	Goodnight Time	17-1/2 x 21	ESH	3.50
1188.	Kitten's Camp	9 x 13	ESH	2.00
1189.	Over the Heather	17-1/2 x 21	ESH	3.50
1190.	Playtime	17-1/2 x 21	ESH	3.50
1191.	Springtime on the Farm	17-1/2 x 21	ESH	3.50
1192.	Summer Sports	17-1/2 x 21	ESH	3.50
1193.	Teddy Bear Beach	17-1/2 x 21	ESH	3.50
1194.	Teddy Bear Camp	17-1/2 x 21	ESH	3.50
1195.	Toyland Holiday	17-1/2 x 21	ESH	3.50
1196.	Winter Games	17-1/2 x 21	ESH	3.50
1197.	Woodland Garage	8 x 13	ESH	2.00
1198.	Woodland Gardeners	17-1/2 x 21	ESH	3.50
1199.	Woodland Traffic	17-1/2 x 21	ESH	3.50

BREU, JOERG (Austrian, 1480-1537)
1200. Portrait of a Young
      Woman (Dr.)   18 x 14   PENN   1.00
BREWER
1201. Rheims Cathedral   19 x 13   CAC   3.50
                          15 x 10   CAC   2.50
BRIDGE, ELIZABETH
1202. Caballeros   16 x 30   AS   12.00
1203. Fleurs   16 x 30   AS   12.00
BRIERLY
1204. Yacht America   19 x 26   CAC   12.00
BRIGHTWELL, WALTER (American Contemporary)
1205. Daily Ride   24 x 48   DAC   10.00
1206. Day in June   24 x 48   DAC   10.00
                          12 x 30   DAC   5.00
1207. Goin' Fishin'   24 x 48   DAC   10.00
                          12 x 30   DAC   5.00
1208. Sea Harvest   24 x 48   DAC   10.00
1209. Village Smithy   24 x 48   DAC   10.00
                          12 x 30   DAC   5.00
BRIL (OR BRILL), PAOLO (OR PAUL) (Dutch, 1554-1626)
1210. Hunting Scene (2)   11 x 15   AS   ea. 3.25
1211. Landscape   10 x 15   IA   3.00
1212. Landscape   9 x 12   DAC   2.00
1213. Landscape with Procris'
      Death   11 x 15   IA   3.00
1214. Paesaggio con Cefalo
      E Procris   16 x 22-1/2   CFA   12.00
BRISCOE, ARTHUR JOHN TREVOR (English [Res. U. S.] 1873-
1215. On a Wind   14-1/2 x 23   ESH   10.00
BROCKEDON, W.
1216. Venice   8 x 10   CFA   1.00
BROMBERG, MANUEL A. (American
1217. Dr. Albert Einstein 20 x 16   CAC   5.00
BRONZINO, ALESSANDRO ALLORI DEL (Italian, 1503-1572)
1218. Christ Dead   13 x 9   AS   3.25
1219. Cleopatra   15-1/2 x 11   AS   3.25
1220. Portrait of Bianca
      Capello   15 x 10   IA   3.00

1221.	Portrait of Don Garcia de Medici, Son of Cosimo I			
		15 x 11	IA	3. 00
		14-1/2x11-1/2	AS	3. 25
1222.	Portrait of Eleanor of Toledo with Her Son,			
	John	25-1/2x20-1/2	PENN	1. 50
		14 x 11	IA	3. 00
1223.	Portrait of Eleanora of			
	Toledo	23 x 16-1/2	NYGS	24. 00
1224.	Portrait of Lucrezia			
	Panciatichi	23 x 19	AA	10. 00
		13 x 10	IA	3. 00
1225.	Portrait of a Man c.	10 x 8	NYGS	. 50
1226.	Portrait of Maria de Medici, Daughter of			
	Cosimo I	15 x 11	IA	3. 00
		14-1/2 x 11	AS	3. 25
1227.	Portrait of Stefano			
	Colonna	15 x 11	IA	3. 00
1228.	Portrait of an Unknown			
	Woman	13 x 9	AS	3. 25
1229.	Portrait of a Young			
	Man	38 x 29-1/2	NYGS	20. 00
		14 x 11	NYGS	4. 00
		10 x 8	NYGS	. 50
1230.	Venus and Cupid	12 x 9	ESH	2. 00
1231.	Young Woman and her			
	Little Boy	28 x 21	NYGS	15. 00

BROOK, ALEXANDER (American Contemporary)

1232.	Sentinels	12-1/2 x 19	NYGS		7. 50

BROOKSHAW

1233.	Melons (4)	11-1/2 x 9	IA	ea.	3. 00
1234.	Still Life (6)	16 x 12	IA	ea.	6. 00
1235.	Cherries (2)				
1236.	Peaches (2)				
1237.	Pears (2)				

BROSS

1238.	Wachtung Scene	20 x 24	CAC	15. 00

BROUWER, ADRIAEN (Flemish, 1605-1638)

1239.	The Smoker	14 x 12	AJ		2. 50
		14 x 11	IA		3. 00

BROWN

1240.	Fraince's Tavern	14 x 30	AA		12. 00
1241.	Statesmen (6)	13 x 10	AA	ea.	4. 00
1242.	Calhoun, John C.				
1243.	Clay, Henry				
1244.	Clinton, Dewitt				
1245.	Jackson, Andrew				
1246.	Marshall, John				
1247.	Webster, Daniel				

BROWN

1248.	Harbinger of Spring	15 x 18	CAC	3. 00

BROWN, ELMORE J. (American Contemporary)
1249.	Horses (4)	12 x 18	DAC	ea.	2. 50
		8 x 10	DAC	ea.	1. 25
	Horses (6)	12 x 16	DAC	ea.	2. 50
		8 x 10	DAC	ea.	1. 00

BROWN, HARLEY
1250.	Hawaiian Girl	24 x 18	AS		15. 00

BROWN, JOHN GEORGE (American, 1831-1913)
1251.	Country Gallants	26 x 40	AK		12. 00
		13 x 20	AK		3. 00

BROWNSCOMBE, JENNIE A. (American, 1850-
1252.	New Scholar	16 x 21-1/2	AA		6. 00

BRUCHHAUSER
1253.	Dancer	30 x 22	CFA		15. 00

BRUEGHEL, A.
1254.	Flowerpiece	26 x 19	NYGS		20. 00

BRUEGHEL, JAN, THE ELDER (CALLED "DE VELOURS" OR "VELVET") (Flemish, 1631-1690)
1255.	Adoration of the Kings	12-1/2x18-1/2	NYGS		12. 00
1256.	Bouquet of Flowers	22-1/2x16-1/2	ESH		10. 00
	c.	10 x 8	ESH		1. 00
1257.	Bouquet of Flowers with a Snail	22-1/2x16-1/2	ESH		10. 00
	c.	10 x 8	ESH		1. 00
1258.	Flower Piece	27-1/2 x 21	PENN		1. 50
1259.	Flowers in a Blue Vase c.	23 x 18	HNA		5. 95
		20 x 16	AR		10. 00
1260.	Flowers in a Brown Vase c.	23 x 18	HNA		5. 95
		20 x 16	AR		10. 00
1261.	Flowers in a Delft Vase	17 x 13-1/2	CFA		12. 00
1262.	Flowers in a Vase c.	24 x 20	PENN		1. 50
1263.	Still Life of Flowers	33 x 26	NYGS		18. 00
1264.	Village at the River	18 x 33	CFA		15. 00

BRUEGHEL, JAN, THE YOUNGER (Flemish, 1601-1678)
1265.	Coronation of the Virgin	32 x 23	CFA		24. 00
1266.	Landscape with Tavern	18 x 23	NYGS		20. 00
1267.	May Day Frolic	16 x 22	NYGS		10. 00
1268.	Winter Landscape	16 x 23-1/2	PENN		1. 50

BRUEGHEL, PIETER, THE ELDER (Flemish, 1525-1569)
1269.	Autumn	22 x 30	AR		12. 00
		21-1/2x29-1/2	NYGS		15. 00
		15 x 21	AR		10. 00
1270.	The Blind Leading the Blind	10 x 17	IA		3. 00

		9 x 12	CAC	2. 50
1271.	Carneval	23 x 32	CFA	18. 00
1272.	Carnival and Penitence	15 x 21	NYGS	10. 00
1273.	The Census (Numbering at Bethlehem) c.	20 x 24	PENN	1. 50
1274.	Children's Games (Children at Play)	23-1/2 x 32	IA	18. 00
1275.	Conversion of Paul	22 x 32	CFA	15. 00
1276.	Corn Harvest	8-1/2 x 12	ESH	2. 00
1277.	Harvesters	31-1/2x45-1/2	NYGS	24. 00
		21-1/2x29-1/2	NYGS	18. 00
	c.	20 x 24	PENN	1. 50
		16 x 22	AP	5. 00
		11 x 14	NYGS	4. 00
	c.	8 x 10	NYGS	. 50
1278.	Harvesters' Meal c.	20 x 24	PENN	1. 50
1279.	Hay Harvest	22 x 30	AR	12. 00
		16 x 22	AR	6. 00
1280.	Haymaking	24 x 30	PENN	1. 95
		21-1/2x29-1/2	NYGS	18. 00
1281.	Landscape	13-1/2 x 25	PENN	1. 50
1282.	Landscape with Country Dance	15 x 11	IA	3. 00
1283.	Landscape with Fall of Icarus	21-1/2x33-1/2	NYGS	16. 00
		18 x 28	DAC	7. 50
		18 x 24	PENN	1. 50
		16 x 25	AR	6. 00
		11 x 14	NYGS	4. 00
1284.	Landscape with Ice Skaters	15 x 22	AR	12. 00
1285.	Landscape with Martyrdom of St. Catherine of Alexandria	13-1/2 x 25	PENN	1. 50
1286.	Massacre des Innocents c.	17-1/2 x 22	AS	4. 00
1287.	The Misanthrope	9" Diam.	IA	3. 00
1288.	Netherlands Proverbs	23 x 32	AR	20. 00
	c.	8 x 10	NYGS	. 50
1289.	Old Shepherd	14 x 9	NYGS	3. 00
1290.	Peasant Wedding	31-1/2 x 45	AJ	20. 00
1291.	Peasants' Dance (Country Dance)	31-1/2 x 45	IA	20. 00
		20-1/2 x 30	IA	15. 00
		15 x 22	IA	10. 00
		11 x 14	NYGS	4. 00
1292.	Procession to Calvary	20 x 28	NYGS	12. 00
1293.	Skaters	16 x 22-1/2	NYGS	7. 50
1294.	Summer-Harvesters	22 x 30	AR	12. 00
		21-1/2x29-1/2	NYGS	18. 00

1295.	Tower of Babel	24 x 32	CFA	18.00
		16 x 21	NYGS	10.00
1296.	Village Wedding	11 x 14	NYGS	4.00
1297.	Wedding Dance	31-1/2 x 45	AJ	20.00
		24 x 32	NYGS	18.00
		20-1/2 x 30	IA	15.00
	c.	20 x 24	PENN	1.50
		17 x 21-1/2	NYGS	10.00
		10-1/2 x 14	NYGS	4.00
		10 x 15	CFA	1.50
	c.	7 x 9	NYGS	1.00
1298.	Merrymakers (4)			
	Details of No. 1297	8-1/2 x 6-1/2	NYGS	set 5.00
				each 1.50
1299.	Wedding Feast	31-1/2 x 45	IA	20.00
		20-1/2 x 30	IA	15.00
		16 x 23	AR	6.00
		15 x 21	IA	10.00
		11 x 14	IA	3.00
1300.	Winter: Hunters			
	in the Snow	31 x 44	NYGS	24.00
		22 x 30	IA	12.00
		21 x 29-1/2	NYGS	18.00
		18 x 23	HNA	5.95
		15 x 21	AR	10.00
		11 x 14	IA	3.00

BRUEGHEL, SCHOOL OF

1301.	Sermon of St. John	19 x 27-1/2	NYGS	12.00

BRUESTLE

1302.	Blueberry Hill	24 x 30	CAC	7.50
1303.	Blue Horizon	24 x 30	CAC	7.50
		15 x 18	CAC	3.00

BRUGGHEN See TERBRUGGHEN
BRUN See LEBRUN
BRUSH

1304.	In the Garden	28 x 12	CAC	8.00

BRUSSEL, PAUL-THEODOR VAN (Dutch, 1754-1795)

1305.	Flowerpiece	26 x 19	ESH	15.00
		13 x 10	ESH	2.00

BRUSSET

1306.	Jardin des			
	Tuileries	5 x 15	CFA	3.00
1307.	Pont Alexandre III	10 x 30-1/2	NYGS	18.00
		5 x 15	CFA	3.00

BUCHHOLZ, ROBERT

1308.	Autumn	21 x 29	CFA	10.00

BUCHOZ, PIERRE

1309.	Bouquet, Frederick V	17 x 12	CAC	10.00
1310.	Bouquet, Louis XV	17 x 12	CFA	7.50

BUCHSER, FRANK (Swiss, 1828-1890)

1311.	Plantation in			
	Virginia	12 x 17	CAC	4.00

BUCKETT, GEORGE (English [Res. U. S.] Contemporary)

1312.	Animal Whimsies (12)	14 x 11	DAC	ea.	1. 75
		10 x 8	DAC	ea.	1. 00
	Animal Whimsies (2)	11 x 14	DAC	ea.	1. 75
		8 x 10	DAC	ea.	1. 00

BUCKLE, CLAUDE (English Contemporary)

1313.	The Angler	20 x 26	ESH	8. 00
1314.	Irises	17 x 21-1/2	AS	12. 00
1315.	Neeraj the Field Worker	12-1/2x17-1/2	AS	10. 00

BUENO, PASCUAL (Spanish Contemporary)

1316.	Ibiza	26 x 36	NYGS	16. 00

BUFFET, BERNARD (French Contemporary)

1317.	Angelica and Delphiniums		21-1/2x31-1/2	ESH	15. 00
1318.	Ave Maria		18 x 31-1/2	IA	15. 00
1319.	Banks of the Marne	c.	9-1/2 x 12-1/2	AP	1. 25
		c.	8 x 10	AP	1. 00
			5 x 9	CFA	1. 00
1320.	Banks of the Seine		5 x 9	CAC	1. 00
1321.	Before Dinner		25-1/2x19-1/2	NYGS	12. 00
1322.	Birds		17-1/2x31-1/2	ESH	15. 00
1323.	Black Fishes		4 x 9	CFA	1. 00
1324.	Bouquet		22 x 18	ESH	10. 00
1325.	Breakfast		25-1/2x19-1/2	NYGS	12. 00
1326.	Brooklyn Bridge		16 x 39	NYGS	18. 00
1327.	Bullfighter		26 x 19	NYGS	15. 00
1328.	Butterfly	c.	8 x 10	ESH	1. 00
1329.	Butterflies		17-1/2x31-1/2	ESH	15. 00
1330.	Le Canal		22 x 36	CFA	18. 00
1331.	Le Canal St. Martin		17-1/2 x 30	ESH	15. 00
			14 x 22-1/2	PENN	1. 50
			13 x 22	CFA	10. 00
1332.	Canal at Meuse		18 x 24	PENN	1. 50
1333.	The Cock		16 x 11	IA	8. 00
1334.	Dallas	c.	9-1/2 x 12-1/2	AP	1. 25
		c.	8 x 10	AP	1. 00
			6 x 8	CFA	1. 00
1335.	Fishermen's Harbor		26-1/2 x 36	NYGS	18. 00
			19 x 26	CAC	20. 00
1336.	La Gare (The Station)	c.	9-1/2 x 12-1/2	AP	1. 25
		c.	8 x 10	AP	1. 00
			5 x 9	CFA	1. 00
1337.	Harbor		19-1/2 x 26	IA	20. 00
1338.	Harbor in Brittany		19 x 25	NYGS	12. 00
1339.	Head of a Clown		22 x 18	ESH	10. 00
1340.	Isola San Giorgio		22-1/2 x 30-1/2	ESH	15. 00

1341.	Lapin et Casserole Rouge (Rabbit and Red Casserole)	c.	9-1/2 x 12-1/2	AP	1. 25
		c.	8 x 10	AP	1. 00
			7 x 7	CFA	1. 00
1342.	London, Tower Bridge, 1960		19 x 30	NYGS	18. 00
1343.	Man Resting	c.	9-1/2 x 12-1/2	AP	1. 25
		c.	7 x 9	AP	1. 00
			6 x 8	CFA	1. 00
1344.	Matador		31 x 9-1/2	NYGS	12. 00
1345.	New York		17-1/2x36-1/2	NYGS	26. 00
1346.	New York Skyline		16 x 33	AP	15. 00
			14 x 30	ESH	15. 00
1347.	Orchid Still Life		19 x 25	CAC	12. 00
1348.	Paris: Arc de Triomphe	c.	24 x 20	PENN	1. 50
1349.	Paris: La Cite		19 x 27	NYGS	26. 00
1350.	Paris: Moulin de la Galette		36-1/2 x 18	ESH	18. 00
1351.	Paris: Place de la Concorde		18-1/2 x 30	ESH	15. 00
1352.	Paris: Sacre Coeur de Montmartre		16 x 21	PENN	1. 50
1353.	Paris: The Seine and Eiffel Tower	c.	20 x 24	PENN	1. 50
1354.	Piazetta San Marco		22-1/2 x 30	ESH	15. 00
1355.	Poppies		31 x 20	ESH	15. 00
			10-1/2 x 8	ESH	1. 00
1356.	Port of Beaulieu	c.	8 x 10	ESH	1. 00
1357.	Port Breton	c.	9-1/2 x 12-1/2	AP	1. 25
		c.	8 x 10	AP	1. 00
			5 x 9	CFA	1. 00
1358.	Port of La Rochelle		23-1/2 x 37	ESH	18. 00
		c.	9-1/2 x 12-1/2	AP	1. 25
		c.	8 x 10	AP	1. 00
			5 x 9	CFA	1. 00
1359.	Poster: Cannes		35 x 22-1/2	PENN	1. 00
1360.	Poster: Matador		35 x 22-1/2	PENN	1. 00
1361.	Quay D'Anjou	c.	20 x 24	PENN	1. 50
1362.	Ras Casse	c.	9-1/2 x 12-1/2	AP	1. 25
		c.	8 x 10	AP	1. 00
1363.	Red Flowers		20 x 24-1/2	AP	10. 00
		c.	8 x 10	AP	1. 00
1364.	Les Roses		18-1/2 x 23	NYGS	22. 00
1365.	Sailboat		20 x 26	AP	10. 00
		c.	8 x 10	AP	1. 00
1366.	Somme River Lock, 1962		25-1/2 x 34	NYGS	18. 00
1367.	Still Life		25 x 18	CAC	20. 00
1368.	Still Life: The Lobster		20-1/2x27-1/2	NYGS	15. 00

1369.	Still Life: Melons			
	and Pears	c.	24 x 30	PENN	1. 95
			12 x 16	DAC	2. 50
1370.	Still Life with White			
	Plate	25-1/2 x 19	IA	20. 00
1371.	Suburban Street	11 x 14	IA	8. 00
1372.	Sunflowers	24 x 18	CFA	15. 00
1373.	Toreador, 1958	31 x 9-1/2	NYGS	12. 00
1374.	Torero	31 x 21	NYGS	16. 00
1375.	Venice	21 x 27	NYGS	26. 00
1376.	White Houses in			
	Brittany	19 x 25	NYGS	12. 00
1377.	Yacht, 1963	31-1/2 x 24	NYGS	18. 00

BUFFET, MAURICE

1378.	Sluice Gate	24 x 30	RL	12. 50

BUFFMIRE, FRANK E.

1379.	Deer Hunting	16-1/2 x 24	IA	7. 50
1380.	Quail Shooting	16-1/2 x 24	IA	7. 50

BUGIARDINI, GIULIANO (Italian, 1475-1554)

1381.	Portrait entitled "The			
	Nun by Leonardo"	15 x 11	IA	3. 00
1382.	Portrait of a Lady	15 x 11	AS	3. 25
1383.	Portrait of			
	Michelangelo	14 x 11	IA	3. 00

BULGARIA

1384.	Unesco World Art			
	Series (32)	11 x 14 or		
		14 x 11	NYGS	ea.	2. 00

BULGER

1385.	Ships (4)	15 x 6	DAC	ea.	1. 50

BUNDY, EDGAR (English, 1860-1922)

1386.	Falling Leaves	28 x 40	CAC	15. 00
1387.	Woodlands	22 x 28	CAC	10. 00

BUONARROTI, MICHELANGELO See MICHELANGELO
BURCHFIELD, CHARLES (American, 1893-1967)

1388.	April Mood	c.	8 x 10	NYGS	. 50
1389.	Ice Glare		18-1/2 x 15	NYGS	7. 50
1390.	November Evening		24 x 15	PENN	1. 50
		c.	10 x 8	NYGS	. 50
1391.	Orion in Winter		20 x 23	UNICEF	10. 00
1392.	Promenade		17-1/2x23-1/2	NYGS	12. 00
			5-1/2 x 7-1/2	NYGS	. 50
1393.	Sun and Rocks		21 x 30	NYGS	16. 00
1394.	Sunflowers and			
	Red Barn		16 x 20	CAC	10. 00

BURGER, JOSEF

1395.	Mountains near			
	Garmisch	24 x 27	ESH	10. 00

BURGKMAIR, HANS (German, 1473-1531)

1396.	Emperor Maximilian			
	On Horse	17 x 11	AR	5. 00

BURI, MAX (Swiss, 1868-1925)
1397.	Accordian Player	20 x 21	CFA	10. 00
		11 x 12	CFA	4. 00
1398.	In an Alpine Inn	12 x 16	CAC	4. 00
1399.	Politicians	20 x 25	CAC	10. 00

BURKEL, HEINRICH (German, 1802-1869)
| 1400. | Garmisch Valley | 21 x 31-1/2 | NYGS | 15. 00 |

BURKHARD
| 1401. | Strandweg | 12 x 16 | CAC | 2. 00 |

BURLAMACCHI, ADOLFO FORTI
| 1402. | St. Theresa of Jesus | 14 x 8 | IA | 3. 00 |

BURLEIGH, C. H. H.
| 1403. | Ludlow | 18-1/2 x 22 | RL | 5. 00 |

BURLIN, PAUL (American Contemporary)
| 1404. | Street Scene | 20 x 15 | CAC | 5. 00 |

BURNAND
| 1405. | Peter and John | 11 x 18 | CAC | 3. 00 |

BURNE-JONES, (SIR) EDWARD (English, 1833-1898)
| 1406. | King Cophetos c. | 8 x 10 | AP | . 60 |

BURRAUD
| 1407. | Pytchley Hunt | 17 x 28 | CAC | 25. 00 |

BURRI, ALBERTO (Italian Contemporary)
| 1408. | Sacco E. Rosso S. P. 2, 1958 | 24 x 30 | NYGS | 15. 00 |

BURTON, W. F.
| 1409. | Evening Gold | 20 x 30 | AS | 12. 00 |

BUTINONE, BERNARDINO (Italian
| 1410. | Christ Disputing with the Doctors | 9-1/2 x 8 | NYGS | 12. 00 |

BUTTERSACK
| 1411. | In the Gloaming | 23 x 30 | CAC | 10. 00 |
| 1412. | Last Ray of the Sun | 12 x 21 | CAC | 5. 00 |

BUTTERWORTH, N.
1413.	Brown Beauties	9 x 12	ESH	2. 00
1414.	High Glee	9 x 12	ESH	2. 00
1415.	Ponies of the Mist	9 x 12	ESH	2. 00
1416.	Spirit of Freedom	14-1/2x22-1/2	ESH	6. 00

BUXTON, R. H. (English, 1871-
| 1417. | Check in the Valley | 16 x 25 | CAC | 7. 50 |
| 1418. | Over Hill and Dale | 16 x 25 | CAC | 7. 50 |

BYATT, EDWIN (English, 1888-1948)
| 1419. | Polegate Mill | 17-1/2 x 21 | ESH | 10. 00 |

BYRUM, RUTHVEN H. (American, 1896-
1420.	Grandview	25 x 31	CAC	7. 50
1421.	Heart of Smokies	25 x 30	CAC	10. 00
1422.	Indiana	25 x 30	AA	10. 00
1423.	Newfound Gap	25 x 31	NYGS	12. 00
1424.	Peaceful Valley	28 x 33-1/2	NYGS	12. 00
1425.	Smokey Mountain Road	25 x 30	CAC	10. 00
1426.	Song of Blossoms	25 x 30	CAC	10. 00
1427.	Sycamore Bend	25 x 30	CAC	10. 00

1428.	Tennessee	25 x 30	AA	10.00

BYZANTINE ART

1429.	Apsis with Trans- figuration (Mosaic)	14 x 10	IA	3.00
1430.	The Crucifix Who Spoke to St. Francis (Assisi)	15 x 11	IA	3.00
		10 x 8	IA	1.50
1431.	Crucifixion (Fresco)	14 x 10	IA	3.00
1432.	Emperor Constantinus IV Bestowing Privileges to the Church (Ravenna Mosaic)	14 x 10	IA	3.00
1433.	Emperor Justinianus and his Court (Ravenna Mosaic)	11 x 15	IA	3.00
1434.	Empress Theodora and her Court (Ravenna Mosaic)	11 x 15	IA	3.00
1435.	Enthroned Madonna and Child	28 x 17	NYGS	16.00
1436.	Evangeliary, Cover (2)	13 x 11	IA ea.	3.00
1437.	Evangeliary, Orna- ment Siena)	5 x 9	IA	1.50
1438.	The Holy Face (Lucca)	16 x 12	IA	3.00
1439.	Luke the Evangelist (Minature)	10 x 7	IA	1.50
1440.	Madonna of Mount Fileremo	16 x 12	IA	3.00
1441.	Mark the Evange- list (Minature)	10 x 8	IA	1.50
1442.	Saints (Codex of Indicopleustes)	12 x 12	IA	3.00
1443.	Saints Jude and Paul	10 x 7	IA	1.50
1444.	Scenes from the Life of Christ and of the Virgin	10 x 7	IA	1.50
1445.	Scenes from the Life of the Virgin	10 x 7	IA	1.50

C

CACHARD, REGIS DE (French Contemporary)

1446.	Le Bateau Rouge	30 x 40	DAC	22.50
		18 x 24	DAC	12.50
1447.	Les Chardons	30 x 40	DAC	22.50
		18 x 24	DAC	12.50
1448.	Les Fleurs, Nature Morte	40 x 30	DAC	22.50
		24 x 18	DAC	12.50

1449.	Montmartre	40 x 30	DAC	22. 50
		24 x 18	DAC	12. 50
1450.	Nature Morte sur			
	Tower Bridge	40 x 30	DAC	22. 50
		24 x 18	DAC	12. 50
1451.	Vue de la Place			
	San Marc	40 x 30	DAC	22. 50
		24 x 18	DAC	12. 50
1452.	Vue de la Salute			
	from La Piazetta	30 x 40	DAC	22. 50
		18 x 24	DAC	12. 50

CADY, WALTER HARRISON (American, 1877-)
1453.	In Old Kentucky	15 x 18	CAC	4. 00

CAGNACCI, GUIDO See CANLASSI, GUIDO
CAHOON, RALPH
1454.	The Race	22 x 32	AA	12. 00
1455.	Sailor's Wedding			
	Dance	22 x 32	AA	12. 00

CAILLEBOTTE, GUSTAVE (French, 1848-1894)
1456.	Sailing Boats			
	Argenteuil c.	10 x 8	ESH	1. 00

CALDER, ALEXANDER STERLING (American, 1898-)
1457.	Poster: Mobiles de			
	Calder (Galerie			
	Maeght)	27-1/2x20-1/2	PENN	1. 00

CALIARI, PAOLO See VERONESE, PAOLO
CALLOT, HENRI EUGENE (French, 1875-)
1458.	Harbor of Joinville	18 x 18	CAC	7. 50
1459.	Tuna Fleet	20 x 24	CAC	6. 00

CALOGERO (Italian [Res. France] Contemporary)
1460.	Dolls (4) c.	16 x 12	PENN	ea.	1. 00
	Doll at Carnival				
	Doll with Birdcage				
	Doll with Clown				
	Doll with Fishbowl				

CALVERT
1461.	Meet of the Vine			
	Hounds	17 x 28	CAC	25. 00
1462.	Wynnstay Hunt	23 x 24	CAC	28. 00
1463.	Fruit Panels (4)	30 x 10	AK	ea.	5. 00
		15 x 5	AK	ea.	1. 25

CAMERON, (SIR) DAVID Y. (Scotch, 1865-1945)
1464.	Heart of Perthshire	20 x 17-1/2	RL	10. 00

CAMPANIAN ART See ROMAN, CAMPANIAN AND POMPEIAN
MOSAICS AND FRESCOES
CAMPBELL
1465.	Blueroom Prints	21 x 18	CAC	10. 00

CAMPIGLI, MASSIMO (Italian, 1895-)
1466.	Drawing School c.	8 x 10	NYGS	. 50
1467.	Holiday, 1956	19 x 24	NYGS	12. 00

CAMPION
1468.	Sunny Day	19 x 24	CAC	7. 50

CAMPRIANI, ALCESTE (1818-1882)
1469. Landscape   9 x 15   AS   3. 25
CANALETTO (CANALE, ANTONIO, CALLED CANALETTO)
(Italian, 1697-1768) AND/OR
BELLOTTO, BERNARDO, CALLED CANALETTO (Italian, 1720-1780)
1470. Bacinio di San Marco
       from S. Giorgio
       Maggiore   17-1/2 x 26   ESH   12. 00
                         13 x 19   ESH   7. 50
1471. Bridge over the
       Brenta   19 x 28   NYGS   12. 00
1472. Bucentaur at the
       Piazetta   17 x 26   NYGS   15. 00
1473. Campidoglio   23 x 19   AS   7. 50
1474. Canal at Venice   12 x 20   PENN   1. 50
1475. Castle at Nymphen-
       burg, 1761   10-1/2 x 36   NYGS   18. 00
1476. Chiesa della Salute 18 x 13   CAC   6. 00
1477. City of London   15-1/2 x 27   ESH   10. 00
1478. City of London from
       Somerset House   17 x 30   NYGS   12. 00
1479. Colosseum   23 x 19   AS   7. 50
1480. Colosseum   11 x 15   AS   3. 25
1481. Doge Embarking on
       the Bucintoro   14-1/2x20-1/2   ESH   6. 00
1482. Doge's Palace,
       Venice   22 x 36   NYGS   26. 00
1483. Ducal Palace,
       Venice   9-1/2 x 15   AS   3. 25
1484. Eton College   16 x 28-1/2   NYGS   12. 00
1485. Fantastic Land-
       scape   17 x 20   IA   10. 00
                         11 x 13   IA   3. 00
1486. The Gazzada   10 x 15   IA   3. 00
1487. Grand Canal   23-1/2 x 32   CFA   15. 00
1488. Greenwich Hospital 17 x 27   NYGS   18. 00
1489. Imperial Castle   18 x 31   CFA   12. 00
1490. Imperial Castle,
       Schoenbrunn   18 x 32   NYGS   12. 00
1491. Imperial Chalet   17 x 31-1/2   NYGS   12. 00
1492. Landscape with
       Lagoon   17 x 20   IA   10. 00
                         11 x 13   IA   3. 00
1493. London from Rich-
       mond House   18-1/2 x 21   ESH   15. 00
1494. Murano near Venice 11 x 16   AR   5. 00
1495. Nymphenburg Castle 19 x 32   CFA   15. 00
1496. Palace of the Doge 12 x 20   DAC   5. 00
1497. Piazza San Marco
       (St. Mark's Square) 23 x 31   CFA   15. 00
                         16-1/2x24-1/2   PENN   1. 50
                         9 x 11   CFA   1. 50

1498.	Piazzetta	26 x 35	NYGS		22. 00
1499.	Place at Venice	9 x 12	DAC		2. 00
1500.	Portello and the				
	Brenta Canal at				
	Padua, c. 1735-1740	23 x 40	NYGS		20. 00
1501.	Portico with Lantern	19 x 23	NYGS		12. 00
1502.	Quay of the Piazzetta,				
	c. 1740 c.	27 x 36	NYGS		18. 00
		20 x 24	PENN		1. 50
		10 x 14	NYGS		4. 00
1503.	Reception at the Pal-				
	ace of the Doge	14-1/2x20-1/2	ESH		6. 00
1504.	Regatta on the Grand				
	Canal	17 x 26	NYGS		15. 00
		10 x 14	NYGS		4. 00
1505.	The Rialto	23 x 31	CFA		15. 00
		9-1/2 x 15	AS		3. 25
1506.	Rialto Bridge,				
	Venice	11 x 15	AS		3. 25
1507.	Rio Dei Mendicanti,				
	Venice	10 x 15	AS		3. 25
1508.	River Adige in				
	Verona	19 x 39	CFA		20. 00
1509.	Roman Ruins (2)	19 x 23	AS	ea.	7. 50
1510.	Romantic Landscape	17 x 20	IA		10. 00
		11 x 13	IA		3. 00
1511.	Ruins of a Courtyard				
	(Dr.)	11 x 8	NYGS		2. 00
1512.	St. Mark's Square,				
	Venice	11 x 15	AS		3. 25
1513.	Santa Maria Della				
	Salute	25 x 30	CFA		18. 00
1514.	Schlosshof, 1760	17 x 31-1/2	AJ		12. 00
1515.	Schlosshof in March-				
	field	17 x 31-1/2	AJ		12. 00
1516.	Schoenbrunn, 1759	18 x 31-1/2	AJ		12. 00
1517.	Square of St. Mark				
	c. 1740	27 x 36	NYGS		18. 00
		10 x 14	NYGS		4. 00
1518.	Stone Mason's Yard	10 x 13	CFA		1. 50
1519.	The Terrace,				
	c. 1745	19 x 23	NYGS		12. 00
1520.	The Thames on Lord				
	Mayor's Day	14 x 29	ESH		10. 00
1521.	Upper Grand Canal	8 x 14	CFA		1. 50
1522.	Venice	25 x 35	CFA		18. 00
		13-1/2 x 23	PENN		1. 50
1523.	Venice: Canal				
	Grande	23 x 29	CFA		18. 00
1524.	Venice: Piazza				
	San Marco	25-1/2x36-1/2	NYGS		20. 00
1525.	Venice: San Marco				
	Harbor c.	18 x 23	HNA		5. 95

1526.	Vienna Seen from			
	the Belvedere	12-1/2 x 30	AJ	7. 50
1527.	View of Dresden	21-1/2 x 37	NYGS	22. 00
1528.	View of the Ducal			
	Palace and the			
	Piazzetta	9 x 15	IA	3. 00
1529.	View of the			
	Gazzada	10 x 15	IA	3. 00
		9 x 12	ESH	2. 00
1530.	View of Grand Canal			
	in Venice	9 x 15	IA	3. 00
1531.	View of London	12 x 20	DAC	5. 00
1532.	View of London with			
	the Thames	14 x 29	ESH	10. 00
		8 x 15-1/2	ESH	3. 00
1533.	View of Munich c.	18 x23	HNA	5. 95
1534.	View of Murano			
	Canal	11 x 16	CFA	5. 00
1535.	View of Pirna	18 x 30	CFA	15. 00
1536.	View of Pirna with			
	the Fortress of			
	Sonnenschein	19 x 31	NYGS	15. 00
1537.	View of Rome	11 x 15	AS	3. 25
1538.	View of the Thames	10 x 13-1/2	ESH	3. 00
1539.	View of Vienna from			
	the Belvedere	12-1/2 x 20	NYGS	7. 50
1540.	Westminster from			
	Somerset House	17 x 30	NYGS	12. 00
1541.	Whitehall from Rich-			
	mond House	18-1/2 x 21	ESH	15. 00

CANDELL, VICTOR

1542.	Night	16 x 21	CAC	16. 00

CANEDO, ALEXANDER (Mexican [Res. U. S.] Contemporary)

1543.	Figure Study No. 1	17 x 21	IA	5. 00
1544.	Figure Study No. 2	17 x 21	IA	5. 00

CANEVARI, GIOVANNI BATTISTA (Italian, 1789-1876)

1545.	James Stuart, Son			
	of Charles I	15 x 10	IA	3. 00

CANJURA, NOE (Salvadorian Contemporary)

1546.	Maternity	23 x 11	CFA		12. 00
1547.	Sunflower	29-1/2 x 22	ESH	Cv.	15. 00

CANLASSI (OR CAGNACCI), GUIDO (Italian, 1600-1681)

1548.	Cleopatra	27-1/2 x 24	AJ	12. 00
1549.	Sybil	14 x 11-1/2	AS	3. 25
		13 x 11	IA	3. 00

CANNERT

1550.	Jonquils	20 x 16	CAC	11. 00

CATARINI, SIMONE See PESARO, SIMONE DA

CANZIANI, ESTELLA (English, 1887-   )

1551.	Piper of Dreams	16 x 12	ESH	3. 00
1552.	St. Francis	12 x 9	ESH	3. 00

CAPELLE, JAN VAN DE (Dutch, 1624-1679)

1553.	The Calm	18 x 18	ESH	12. 00

CAPULETTI, J. (Spanish, Contemporary)

1554.	Art Student	18 x 14	CAC	5.00
1555.	Artist's Palette	22 x 18-1/2	RL	10.00
1556.	New Horizons	27 x 20	CAC	12.00
1557.	Romeo and Juliet	18 x 21-1/2	RL	10.00

CARAUD, JOSEPH

1558.	Story Hour	30 x 24	IA	10.00

CARAVAGGIO, MICHELANGELO MERISI DA (Italian, 1565-1609)

1559.	Amor Sleeping	10 x 15	IA	3.00
1560.	Bacchus	20 x 17-1/2	PENN	1.50
		13 x 11	IA	3.00
1561.	Bacco Giovane	21-1/2 x 18	CFA	12.00
1562.	Basket of Fruit	11 x 14	IA	3.00
1563.	Beheading of the Baptist	10 x 15	IA	3.00
	Two Figures-- Detail of No. 1563	11 x 15	IA	3.00
	Detail of No. 1563	11 x 15	IA	3.00
1564.	Boy Bitten by a Lizard	14 x 11	IA	3.00
1565.	Boy with a Basket of Fruit	12 x 11	IA	3.00
1566.	Calling of St. Matthew	12 x 11	IA	3.00
1567.	David Showing Goliath's Head	14 x 11	IA	3.00
1568.	Deposition	15 x 10	IA	3.00
1569.	Fall of St. Paul	15 x 11	IA	3.00
1570.	Fruits and Flowers	11 x 15	AS	3.25
1571.	Giovane con Canestro di Frutta	19 x 18	CFA	12.00
1572.	Martyrdom of St. Matthew	12 x 12	IA	3.00
1573.	Mary Magdalen	9 x 8	CFA	1.00
1574.	Narciso al Fonte	22 x 18-1/2	CFA	15.00
1575.	Narcissus	13 x 11	IA	3.00
1576.	The Pilgrims Madonna	15 x 11	IA	3.00
1577.	Rest on the Flight into Egypt	10 x 8-1/2	ESH	1.00
1578.	Rest During the Flight into Egypt	11 x 14	IA	3.00
1579.	St. John in the Desert	13 x 11	IA	3.00
1580.	St. Matthew and the Angel	15 x 9	IA	3.00
1581.	Still Life c.	18 x 23	HNA	5.95
1582.	Still Life, Fruit c.	18 x 23	HNA	5.95
1583.	Victorious Cupid	15 x 11	IA	3.00

CARDELLA, TONY (French, 1898-)
1584.	Calvi Corse	12 x 16	CAC		2. 00
1585.	Cassis	12 x 16	CAC		2. 00
1586.	Hillside Homes	26 x 21	NYGS		12. 00
1587.	Mountain Village	26 x 21	NYGS		12. 00
1588.	Sanary sur Mer	12 x 16	CAC		2. 00
1589.	Saint Tropez	12 x 16	CAC		2. 00

CARINA
1590.	Ballet Elegante	14 x 11	AK	ea.	1. 50
	(4)	10 x 8	AK	ea.	1. 00
		8 x 6	AK	ea.	. 60

CARLI, RAFFAELE (Italian 15th Century)
| 1591. | Head of the Virgin | 15 x 11 | AS | | 3. 25 |

CARLSON, HARRY (American, 1895-)
| 1592. | Spring Time | 20 x 24 | CAC | | 15. 00 |

CARMONTELLE
| 1593. | Family Mozart | 12 x 8 | CAC | | 10. 00 |
| 1594. | La Sonata | 12 x 8 | CAC | | 10. 00 |

CARNEVALE DA URBINO, (FRA) CORRADINI BARTOLOMEO
(Italian, d. 1478)
| 1595. | Birth of the Virgin | | | | |
| | c. | 7 x 9 | AP | | . 25 |

CAROLSFELD, JULIUS SCHNORR VON (German, 1794-1872)
| 1596. | Madonna | 21-1/2 x 18 | ESH | | 7. 50 |

CARON
| 1597. | Emperor Augustus | | | | |
| | c. | 24 x 20 | PENN | | 1. 50 |

CARPACCIO, VITTORE (Italian, 1486-1525)
1598.	Angel Musician	15 x 11	IA		3. 00
1599.	Annunciation	12 x 11	AS		3. 25
1600.	Courtesans	15 x 10	IA		3. 00
1601.	Marriage of St.				
	Ursula	11 x 15	AS		3. 25
1602.	Meditation of the				
	Passion c.	7 x 9	AP		. 25
1603.	Miracle of the				
	Cross	10 x 11	IA		3. 00
1604.	Presentation in the				
	Temple	15 x 11	IA		3. 00
1605.	St. George and the				
	Dragon	6 x 15	IA		3. 00
1606.	St. Ursula's Dream	11-1/2x11-1/2	AS		3. 25
		11 x 11	IA		3. 00
	c.	8 x 10	NYGS		. 50

CARPENTER, MARGARET (MRS. WM. G.) (English, 1793-1872)
1607.	Bretagne	12 x 16	CAC		2. 00
1608.	Douarnenez	12 x 16	CAC		2. 00
1609.	Sisters	28 x 28	AA		10. 00

CARPIONI, GIULIO (Italian, 1611-1674)
| 1610. | Portrait | 14 x 11 | IA | | 3. 00 |

CARRA, CARLO (Italian, 1881-)
| 1611. | Still Life, 1957 | 23-1/2 x 20 | NYGS | | 12. 00 |

```
CARRACCI, ANNIBALE (Italian, 1560-1609)
  1612.  Beans-Eater        11 x 13        IA          3. 00
CARRENO DE MIRANDA, JUAN (Spanish, 1614-1695)
  1613.  Harlequin    c.    9 x 7          AP           . 25
CARRIER, JULES
  1614.  Apple Blossoms     25 x 30        CFA         10. 00
                            16 x 20        CFA          5. 00
  1615.  White and Gold
         Peonies            25 x 30        CFA         10. 00
CARRIERA, ROSALBA (Italian, 1675-1758)
  1616.  Flora              15 x 10        AS           3. 25
  1617.  Portrait of a Boy  13 x 11        AS           3. 25
  1618.  Portrait of a
         Princess of Este   15-1/2 x 11    AS           3. 25
                            14 x 11        IA           3. 00
  1619.  Self-Portrait      14 x 11        IA           3. 00
CARRUCCI, JACOPO See PONTORMO, IL
CARSON, FRANK (American, 1881-  )
  1620.  Summer Holiday     19 x 23        CAC          7. 50
CARTARINI, SIMONE See PESARO
CARTER: American
  1621.  Bronze Skyline     24 x 48        DAC         10. 00
  1622.  Grecian Columns in
         Blue               24 x 60        DAC         15. 00
                            24 x 48        DAC         10. 00
  1623.  Grecian Columns in
         Bronze             24 x 60        DAC         15. 00
                            24 x 48        DAC         10. 00
CARY, WILLIAM D. (American, 1840-1922)
  1624.  Antique Still Life
         (2)                16 x 12        AA     ea.   8. 00
         (2)                16 x 20        AA     ea.  15. 00
  1625.  Cats (2)           12 x 10        AA     ea.   5. 00
  1626.  Courtship          16 x 30        AA          15. 00
  1627.  General Robert E.
         Lee                24 x 14        AA          15. 00
  1628.  General Stonewall
         Jackson            24 x 14        AA          15. 00
  1629.  Marriage           16 x 30        AA          15. 00
  1630.  Primitive Portraits
         (2) Boy - Girl     22-1/2x17-1/2  AA     ea.  12. 00
         (2) Annie - Lionel 16 x 12        AA     ea.   8. 00
CARZOU, JEAN (French Contemporary)
  1631.  Fishing Boats      19 x 24        NYGS        12. 00
  1632.  Honfleur, 1959     19 x 24        NYGS        12. 00
  1633.  Venise             19-1/2x25-1/2  NYGS        26. 00
CASCELLA, MICHELE (Italian, 1882-  )
  1634.  Autumn in Paris    28 x 36        IA          15. 00
  1635.  Grand View of
         Portofino          26 x 48        IA          15. 00
  1636.  Green Lantern,
         Carmel-by-the-Sea  24 x 36        IA          12. 00
```

1637.	Market in Portofino	28 x 36	IA	15. 00
1638.	Ocean Avenue,			
	Carmel	24 x 36	IA	12. 00
1639.	Saint-Germain-			
	Des-Pres	10-1/2 x 15	NYGS	5. 00
1640.	Skiing in Cortina			
	D'Ampezzo	27 x 36	IA	15. 00
1641.	Spring in the Abruzzi			
	Hills	26 x 48	IA	15. 00
1642.	Sunday in Paris	26 x 48	IA	15. 00
1643.	Winter Sport--			
	Cortina D'Ampezzo	27 x 36	IA	15. 00
		16 x 20	IA	5. 00

CASELLI, SILVANO (Contemporary)

1644.	Daisy	15 x 11	IA	3. 00
1645.	Desirée	15 x 11	IA	3. 00
1646.	Flowers	22 x 16	IA	10. 00
1647.	Flowers	22 x 17	IA	10. 00
1648.	S. S. Giovanni			
	XXIII, 1960	19 x 15	IA	10. 00
1649.	Gloria and her			
	She-Cat	14 x 10	IA	3. 00
1650.	Mimosas	22 x 16	IA	10. 00
1651.	Portofino	21 x 16	IA	10. 00
1652.	Portofino	16 x 21	IA	10. 00

CASSANDRA

1653.	Classic Beauties				
	(Portraits of Women)				
	(4)	14 x 11	AK	ea.	1. 50
		14 x 8	AK	ea.	1. 25
		8 x 6	AK	ea.	. 40

CASSATT, MARY (American [Res. France] 1845-1926)

1654.	The Bath	c.	21 x 26	HNA	5. 95
		c.	18 x 24	PENN	1. 50
1655.	Boating Party	c.	18 x 23	HNA	5. 95
1656.	In the Garden		24 x 19-1/2	PENN	1. 50
1657.	Little Sisters		18 x 22	NYGS	12. 00
1658.	The Loge		28 x 22	NYGS	16. 00
1659.	La Sortie du Bain		8 x 10	CAC	1. 50
1660.	Study for Banjo				
	Lesson		16-1/2x16-1/2	PENN	1. 50
1661.	Woman and Child				
	Driving	c.	18 x 23	HNA	5. 95
1662.	Woman with Dog		30 x 20	AK	7. 50
		c.	24 x 20	PENN	1. 50
1663.	Young Mother				
	Sewing		24 x 18	PENN	1. 50
			16 x 12	PENN	1. 00

CASSINI (Italian, 1895-)

1664.	Cameos (Black)				
	(6)	14 x 9	CFA	ea.	10. 00

CASSIOLI, AMOS (Italian, 1832-1891)

1665.	Battle of Legnano	13 x 22	IA	7. 50

CASTAGNO, ANDREA DAL (Italian, 1410. 1457)

1666.	Assumption of the Virgin	c.	8 x 10	NYGS	.50
1667.	David and Goliath	c.	8 x 10	NYGS	.50
1668.	Last Supper (Florence)		8-1/2 x 19	AS	7.50
1669.	Portrait of Boccaccio		15 x 11	IA	3.00
1670.	Portrait of Pippo Spano		15 x 9-1/2	AS	3.25

CASTAGNOLA, GABRIELE (Italian, 1828-1883)

1671.	Filippo Lippi and the Nun, Buti	15 x 11	IA	3.00

CASTEL, M.

1672.	Trawlers	30 x 24	RL	15.00

CASTELLO, VALERIO (Italian, 1625-1659)

1673.	Virgin of the Veil	11 x 15	IA	3.00

CASTELLS See FERRANDIZ-CASTELLS, JUAN

CASTIGLIONE, (FRA) GIUSEPPE (Italian [Res. China] 1698-1768)

1674.	The Kirghizes Presenting Horses to the Emperor Chien Lung	12-1/2 x 40	RL	15.00

CATALONIAN ART

1675.	Nativity (Altar at Avia) (2)	c.	8 x 10	ESH	ea. 1.00
1676.	St. Martin		22-1/2 x 16	ESH	10.00
1677.	Virgin and Child		31-1/2x10-1/2	ESH	15.00

CATENA, VINCENZIO DI BIAGIO (Italian, 1470-1531)

1678.	Judith	14 x 11	IA	3.00
1679.	St. Christina	12 x 14	ESH	6.00

CATHELIN, BERNARD (French Contemporary)

1680.	Anemones on Blue	21 x 15	PENN	1.50
1681.	Autumn, 1963	28 x 18	NYGS	15.00
1682.	Spring, 1963	28 x 18	NYGS	15.00
1683.	Summer, 1963	28 x 18	NYGS	15.00
1684.	Le Vase Blanc, 1962	28 x 21	NYGS	15.00
1685.	Winter, 1963	28 x 21	NYGS	15.00
1686.	Winter Landscape near Dammartin	34 x 22-1/2	NYGS	18.00
1687.	Yellow Dahlias	28 x 19-1/2	NYGS	15.00

CATLIN, GEORGE (American)

1688.	Indian Chiefs (8)	13 x 10	PENN	set	3.98
1689.	North American Indians (6)]	11 x 16	PENN	set	3.98 or
				ea.	1.00

1690.	Ball Play Dance
1691.	Buffalo Hunt
1692.	Catching the Wild Horse
1693.	Game of the Arrow
1694.	Indian Buffalo Hunt
1695.	Snowshoe Dance

CAVEL, JACOB (Flemish, d. 1401)
1696. Composition   31-1/2 x 27   NYGS   20. 00
CAVALLINO, BERNARDO (Italian, 1622-1654)
1697. Head of a Saint   14 x 11   IA   3. 00
1698. Hi. Maria   23-1/2 x 12   ESH   4. 00
1699. Jesus Christus   23-1/2 x 12   ESH   4. 00
1700. Madonna   23-1/2 x 16   ESH   6. 00
1701. St. George   14 x 11   IA   3. 00
CAVAZZOLA, IL See MORANDO, PAOLO
CAVE PAINTING See PREHISTORIC ART
CAWTHORN
1702. Still Life Studies
       (4)   14 x 18   AK   ea. 2. 50
       (6)   7-1/2x9-1/2   AK   set 1. 00
CECCONE, ALBERTO
1703. Tuscan Landscape   11 x 13-1/2   AS   3. 25
CELESTINI, CELESTINO
1704. Still Life   15 x 18   AS   7. 50
CERCONE, ETTORE (Italian, 1850-1901)
1705. View of Torre
       Annunziata   9 x 15   IA   3. 00
CERNY, CHARLES
1706. Marine Still Life
       (4)   15 x 6-1/2   DAC   ea. 1. 50
1707. Music Lover's
       Corner   16 x 20   CAC   9. 00
1708. Poissons, 1637   13 x 16   CAC   4. 00
1709. Poissons, 1638   13 x 16   CAC   4. 00
1710. Quiet Haven   18 x 21   CAC   10. 00
1711. Rhythm and Melody   16-1/2 x 20   AP   8. 00
1712. Ship Models (6) c.   8 x 10   DAC   ea. 1. 00
1713. Submarine Garden   13 x 16   CAC   4. 00
1714. Wide World   16 x 20   CAC   9. 00
1715. World of Silence   13 x 16   CAC   4. 00
CERQUOZZI, MICHELANGELO (CALLED "DELLA BATTAGLIE" OR
'DELLE BAMBOCCIATE) (Italian, 1602-1660)
1716. Bunches of Grape   15 x 11   IA   3. 00
CERRITO
1717. La Reine de la
       Danse   12 x 16   CAC   3. 00
CESARE DA SESTO (Italian, 1477-1523)
1718. Study, St. Jerome   12-1/2x9-1/2   AR   4. 00
CEYLON
1719. UNESCO World Art
       Series (32)   11 x 14   NYGS   ea. 2. 00
                        or 14 x 11
CEZANNE, PAUL (French, 1839-1906)
1720. L'Alee à Chantilly   26 x 21   NYGS   18. 00
1721. Apple Basket   c.   10 x 8   CAC   1. 50
1722. Apples and Prim-
       roses   25 x 32   AA   15. 00
1723. Baigneuses
       (Bathers)   11 x 20   CAC   5. 00

			11 x 14	IA	3. 00
		c.	8 x 10	AP	. 50
			6 x 9	NYGS	7. 50
1724.	Le Barrage Francois				
	Zola		20-1/2 x 28	NYGS	15. 00
1725.	Bather	c.	10 x 8	MMA	. 35
1726.	Bathers in Front of				
	a Tent		23 x 29-1/2	NYGS	22. 00
1727.	Blue Vase	c.	26 x 21	HNA	5, 95
			24 x 20	PENN	1. 50
			24 x 18	DAC	7. 50
			23-1/2 x 19	NYGS	22. 00
			22-1/2 x 18	ESH	10. 00
			20 x 15-1/2	NYGS	5. 00
			8 x 7	CFA	1. 00
1728.	Boy with a Red				
	Vest		32 x 26	CAC	18. 00
			31 x 25	NYGS	28. 00
		c.	22 x 17-1/2	AS	4. 00
		c.	12-1/2x9-1/2	AP	1. 25
1729.	The Bridge	c.	20 x 24	PENN	1. 50
1730.	Bridge of Maincy		17 x 21	CFA	10. 00
		c.	8 x 10	ESH	1. 00
1731.	By the Riverside		26 x 31	CFA	20. 00
			18 x 22	CFA	12. 00
1732.	Card Players	c.	20 x 24	PENN	1. 50
	(Two Figures)		17-1/2x21-1/2	ESH	10. 00
			15 x 17	CAC	5. 00
			11 x 13	IA	3. 00
		c.	8 x 10	ESH	1. 00
1733.	Chateau de Medan		22 x 27	NYGS	15. 00
1734.	Chestnut Trees at				
	Jas de Bouffan		24 x 30-1/2	NYGS	18. 00
		c.	8 x 10	AP	. 50
1735.	Clos de Mathurins,				
	Pontoise	c.	8 x 10	ESH	1. 00
1736.	Country Landscape		23 x 32	CFA	18. 00
1737.	Dans la Valee de				
	l'Oise (In the Valley				
	of the Oise)		24 x 30	AA	15. 00
			18 x 22	IA	6. 00
1738.	Dr. Gachet's House				
	at Auvers	c.	10 x8	ESH	1. 00
1739.	Environs du Jas de				
	Bouffan		16 x 22-1/2	ESH	10. 00
1740.	L'Estaque		25 x 35	CAC	20. 00
			17 x 22	CAC	10. 00
			15-1/2x19-1/2	AP	5. 00
			11 x 14	IA	3. 00
			7 x 8	CFA	1. 00
1741.	L'Estaque	c.	16 x 12	PENN	1. 00
1742.	L'Estaque - House				
	on the Bay		11 x 18	NYGS	12. 00

		c.	8 x 10	ESH	1.00
1743.	Farm of Jas de Bouffan		20 x 25	PENN	1.50
1744.	The Farmer	c.	10 x 8	ESH	1.00
1745.	Faubourg au Printemps		18-1/2 x 22	NYGS	10.00
1746.	Flowers	c.	10 x 8	ESH	1.00
1747.	Flowers and Fruit		22 x 16	CAC	10.00
1748.	Flowers in a Small Vase		16 x 10	CFA	10.00
1749.	Fruit and Jug		19 x 24	PENN	1.50
1750.	Gardanne		16 x 19	AP	5.00
1751.	The Gardener	c.	10 x 8	ESH	1.00
1752.	Les Grandes Baigneuses	c.	8 x 10	ESH	1.00
1753.	Great Pine		11 x 12	IA	3.00
1754.	Gulf of Marseilles Seen from L'Estaque (Metropolitan, N. Y.)		25-1/2x35-1/2	NYGS	20.00
		c.	20 x 24	PENN	1.50
1755.	House at Aix-en-Provence	c.	20 x 24	PENN	1.50
1756.	House of Pere Lacroix		24 x 19-1/2	NYGS	10.00
1757.	House on the Hill (In Bellevue)		24 x 31	NYGS	20.00
			23 x 29-1/2	NYGS	26.00
1758.	In the Woods	c.	8 x 10	NYGS	.50
1759.	Jas de Bouffan		10 x 12-1/2	NYGS	15.00
1760.	Judgment of Paris		19-1/2 x 24	NYGS	18.00
1761.	King's Retreat		25 x 31	CFA	18.00
1762.	Kitchen Table		12 x 14	ESH	8.00
1763.	Lac D'Annecy		20-1/2 x 26	NYGS	12.00
		c.	8 x 10	NYGS	.50
1764.	Landscape		26 x 33	CFA	18.00
1765.	Landscape at Aix		12 x 15	AR	3.00
1766.	Landscape, Aix-en-Provence		23 x 19	CFA	16.00
1767.	Landscape, Ile de France	c.	8 x 10	ESH	1.00
1768.	Landscape in Provence	c.	18 x 23	HNA	5.95
1769.	Landscape, L'Estaque		19-1/2 x 24	AA	7.50
1770.	Landscape, Mte. Ste-Victoire		25 x 30	CAC	20.00
			18 x 22-1/2	ESH	10.00
		c.	8 x 10	ESH	1.00
1771.	Landscape with Brook		17 x 23	PENN	1.50
1772.	Landscape with Old House		26 x 31	CAC	18.00
1773.	Landscape with a Viaduct, La Montagne				

	Sainte-Victoire	25-1/2 x 32	NYGS	18. 00
		18 x 22	NYGS	9. 00
		6 x 7-1/2	NYGS	. 50
1774.	Lane of Chestnut			
	Trees	18 x 12-1/2	NYGS	16. 00
1775.	Lane Through a			
	Village	16 x 19	CAC	5. 00
1776.	Madame Cezanne	23 x 17	PENN	1. 50
	c.	10 x 8	NYGS	. 50
1777.	Madame Cezanne in			
	the Green House c.	8 x 10	AP	. 50
1778.	Madame Cezanne in			
	Red	15 x 11	IA	3. 00
1779.	La Maison du Pendu			
	(House of the Hanged			
	Man)	20-1/2x24-1/2	NYGS	12. 00
		12 x 16	AA	3. 00
		11 x 13-1/2	AS	3. 25
1780.	Mardi Gras	24 x 19	NYGS	10. 00
		20 x 16	PENN	1. 50
	c.	10 x 8	ESH	1. 00
1781.	La Mer a			
	L'Estaque	19 x 24	CAC	7. 50
1782.	Le Midi de France	24 x 30	PENN	1. 95
1783.	Milk Jug, Apples and			
	Lemon	8 x 10	ESH	1. 00
1784.	Mill at Pontoise			
	(Landscape with Mill)	26-1/2x33-1/2	IA	18. 00
		17-1/2x22-1/2	ESH	10. 00
		12 x 15	AP	5. 00
	c.	8 x 10	ESH	1. 00
1785.	La Montagne Ste-			
	Victoire (Hermitage)	19 x 23-1/2	NYGS	7. 50
		18 x 22-1/2	ESH	10. 00
1786.	La Montagne Ste-			
	Victoire (W. C.)	14 x 19	NYGS	16. 00
1787.	La Montagne Ste-			
	Victoire (W. C. -			
	Courtauld)	12-1/2 x 19	NYGS	12. 00
1788.	La Montagne Ste-			
	Victoire with Tall			
	Pine (Courtauld	20-1/2 x 28	NYGS	15. 00
1789.	La Montagne Ste-			
	Victoire with Two			
	Pines (Phillips)	23 x 28-1/2	NYGS	15. 00
	c.	18 x 23	HNA	5. 95
		17-1/2x22-1/2	ESH	10. 00
1790.	Mont Ste Victoire	14 x 21-1/2	NYGS	18. 00
1791.	Mount Ste. -Victoire,			
	c. 1890 (W. C. -			
	Tate)	14-1/2x21-1/2	NYGS	18. 00
1792.	Mount Ste. -Victoire			
	(Metropolitan, N. Y.)	9-1/2x12-1/2	AP	1. 25

1793.	Mount Ste-Victoire			
	(Zurich) c.	9-1/2x12-1/2	AP	1. 25
1794.	Mount Ste-Victoire	14-1/2 x 20	ESH	6. 00
1795.	Mount Ste-Victoire	16 x 20	PENN	1. 50
1796.	Nature Morte	14 x 20	CAC	5. 00
1797.	Onions and Bottle	18 x 22-1/2	ESH	10. 00
1798.	The Park	17 x 21	NYGS	20. 00
1799.	Paysage, La Montagne			
	Ste-Victoire (W. C.)	12-1/2 x 19	NYGS	20. 00
1800.	Peasant in a Blue			
	Blouse	22 x 18	ESH	10. 00
	c.	10 x 8	ESH	1. 00
1801.	La Pendule Noire			
	(Black Clock) c.	17-1/2 x 22	AS	4. 00
1802.	Le Pigeonnier de			
	Bellevue (Bird Tower			
	at Bellevue)	20 x 28	AP	15. 00
		14 x 19	CAC	5. 00
1803.	Pines and Rocks	23 x 18-1/2	MMA	5. 50
1804.	Pomegranates and			
	Pears c.	20 x 24	PENN	1. 50
1805.	Pommes et Oranges			
	(Apples and O			
	Oranges) c.	20 x 24	PENN	1. 50
	c.	8 x 10	ESH	1. 00
1806.	Poplars	24 x 30	CAC	15. 00
		20 x 30	ESH	15. 00
	c.	8 x 10	ESH	1. 00
1807.	Portrait of Ambrose			
	Vollard	13 x 11	IA	3. 00
1808.	Poster: Hommage a			
	Cezanne	28-1/2 x 20	PENN	1. 00
1809.	Pot de Fleurs c.	20 x 24	PENN	1. 50
1810.	Pot of Flowers with			
	Pears	17-1/2 x 21	NYGS	12. 00
1811.	Quarry of Bibemus	25-1/2 x 21	NYGS	26. 00
	c.	10 x 8	AP	. 75
1812.	Railway Cut	19 x 32	NYGS	20. 00
		13 x 21-1/2	NYGS	6. 00
1813.	Red Rock	28 x 20-1/2	NYGS	10. 00
1814.	Road and the Pond	16 x 20	NYGS	6. 00
1815.	Rocky Landscape	25 x 31-1/2	NYGS	26. 00
1816.	Roofs in Springtime			
	in Suburb	24 x 30	PENN	1. 95
		12 x 16	DAC	2. 50
1817.	La Route Tournante			
	(Winding Lane)	21-1/2 x 26	NYGS	15. 00
1818.	St. Faubourg in			
	Springtime	18-1/2 x 22	AJ	10. 00
1819.	The Seine	22 x 27	CFA	15. 00
1820.	Seine Quays c.	8 x 10	ESH	1. 00
1821.	Self-Portrait c.	24 x 20	PENN	1. 50

			24 x 18	DAC	7.50
			16 x 13	CAC	5.00
			16 x 12	DAC	2.50
		c.	10 x 8	ESH	1.00
1822.	Still Life		24 x 30	NYGS	18.00
1823.	Still Life		17-1/2x22-1/2	ESH	10.00
1824.	Still Life No. 1651		14 x 20	CAC	5.00
1825.	Still Life No. 17971		18 x 22	CAC	10.00
1826.	Still Life, Flowers		17 x 22	CAC	10.00
1827.	Still Life, Fruit c.		8 x 10	NYGS	.50
1828.	Still Life in the				
	Basket		18 x 24	PENN	1.50
1829.	Still Life with				
	Apples		19 x 25	AR	12.00
		c.	8 x 10	NYGS	.50
1830.	Still Life with a				
	Basket of Apples	c.	21 x 26	HNA	5.95
		c.	9-1/2x12-1/2	AP	1.25
		c.	8 x 10	AP	1.00
			7 x 8	CFA	1.00
1831.	Still Life with Chair,				
	Bottle and Apples		18 x 23-1/2	NYGS	20.00
1832.	Still Life with Ginger				
	Jar		18 x 22-1/2	NYGS	15.00
1833.	Still Life with				
	Jug	c.	8 x 10	ESH	1.00
1834.	Still Life with				
	Onions	c.	9-1/2x12-1/2	AP	1.25
		c.	8 x 10	AP	1.00
			7 x 8	CFA	1.00
1835.	Still Life with				
	Statue	c.	8 x 10	AP	.50
1836.	Stockade	c.	8 x 10	NYGS	.50
1837.	Tree before the				
	House		22 x 18	ESH	10.00
		c.	10 x 8	ESH	1.00
1838.	Trees and Houses		8 x 11	CFA	1.00
1839.	Uncle Dominic		20 x 16-1/2	NYGS	10.00
		c.	10 x 8	NYGS	.50
1840.	Vase of Flowers				
	(Nat. Gall. --U. S.)		28 x 23	NYGS	16.00
			20 x 16	NYGS	10.00
1841.	Vase of Flowers				
	(Durand-Ruel)		20-1/2x16-1/2	NYGS	10.00
1842.	Vase of Flowers				
	(Louvre)		20 x 15-1/2	NYGS	5.00
1843.	Vase of Tulips				
	(Art. Inst., Chicago)		22 x 16	NYGS	10.00
		c.	16 x 12	AP	2.00
1844.	Viaduct	c.	10 x 8	ESH	1.00
1845.	View of the Arc				
	Valley		22 x 18	CFA	12.00

1846.	Village Panorama	24-1/2x30-1/2	NYGS		18.00
1847.	Village Street	23 x 28-1/2	NYGS		26.00

CHABANIAN, ARSENE (Turkish Ac. 1896-1910)

1848.	Blue Horizon	22 x 30	CAC		10.00
1849.	Moonlight on the				
	Riviera	22 x 23	CAC		10.00

CHABAS, PAUL (French, 1869-1937)

1850.	September Morn	21 x 28	NYGS		12.00
		11 x 14-1/2	NYGS		3.00

CHABOR (Russian, Ac. 1928-29)

1851.	Beauty of the				
	Flowers (2)	12 x 42	CFA	ea.	18.00

CHAFFOIS, LUCIEN (French, 1925-)

1852.	Les Roses et la Mer	21 x 25	NYGS		12.00

CHAGALL, MARC (French, 1887-)

1853.	L'Acrobate	25-1/2 x 16	PENN		1.50
1854.	Les Amoureux au				
	Coq	18 x 15	NYGS		22.00
1855.	Artist and his				
	Model	28 x 20-1/2	AP		12.00
	c.	24 x 20	PENN		1.50
1856.	Artist's Model	27 x 20	CFA		15.00
1857.	Bouquet	14 x 11	NYGS		18.00
1858.	Chambon sur Lac	23-1/2x17-1/2	PENN		1.50
1859.	Circus Rider c.	20 x 24	PENN		1.50
1860.	Le Cirque, 1931	24 x 19	NYGS		12.00
1861.	Le Cirque	14 x 29	CAC		12.00
		11 x 20	CAC		5.00
1862.	Le Cirque Bleu c.	10 x 8	ESH		1.00
1863.	Clown on a White				
	Horse c.	24 x 20	PENN		1.50
1864.	The Cock	22-1/2 x 16	ESH		10.00
	c.	10 x 8	ESH		1.00
1865.	Les Deux Bouquets	28 x 21	NYGS		16.00
1866.	Evening Enchant-				
	ment	23-1/2x19-1/2	NYGS		12.00
1867.	Flowers and Lovers				
	c.	24 x 20	PENN		1.50
		24 x 18	DAC		7.50
1868.	Flying Horse c.	18 x 23	HNA		5.95
1869.	Gladioli	22-1/2 x 17	ESH		10.00
1870.	The Grand Circus	17 x 30	ESH		15.00
1871.	Green Violinist	26 x 14	CAC		15.00
1872.	I and the Village,				
	1911	28 x 22	MMA		12.00
		24 x 19	PENN		1.50
		7-1/2 x 6	NYGS		.50
1873.	Lovers above the				
	Town	16 x 23	CFA		7.50
1874.	Lovers in the Tree				
	Tops	22-1/2 x 14	ESH		10.00
1875.	Morning Mystery	23-1/2x19-1/2	NYGS		12.00

1876.	Newlyweds of the Eiffel Tower	18 x 24	PENN	1. 50
		14 x 18	CAC	5. 00
1877.	Plumes en Fleurs (Feathers in Bloom)	24 x 18	PENN	1. 50
		22 x 16	ESH	10. 00
	c.	10 x 8	ESH	1. 00
1878.	Poet Reclining	24 x 24	ESH	15. 00
1879.	Poster: Stained Glass Exhibition	32-1/2 x 21	PENN	1. 00
1880.	Poster: Venice	28-1/2 x 20	PENN	1. 00
1881.	Rabbi of Vitebsk	24 x 18-1/2	NYGS	12. 00
		24 x 18	PENN	1. 50
		14 x 11	CAC	3. 00
1882.	Rabbi with Book	24 x 18	PENN	1. 50
		14 x 11	CAC	3. 00
1883.	Rabbi with Torah	23-1/2 x 18	NYGS	12. 00
		14 x 10-1/2	NYGS	3. 00
1884.	Red House	23 x 20	CFA	12. 00
1885.	La Somnambule	25 x 20	CFA	15. 00
1886.	Synagogue in Jerusalem	19 x 24	NYGS	10. 00
1887.	Village Scene c.	8 x 10	ESH	1. 00
1888.	Violinist	23-1/2 x 20	NYGS	10. 00
		9 x 7-1/2	AP	1. 50
1889.	Woman, Flowers and Bird	10 x 7-1/2	AP	1. 50
1890.	Wounded Bird c.	8 x 10	NYGS	. 50

CHALON, LOUIS (French, 1866-)

1891.	Pas de Quatre	17 x 14	AA	5. 00

CHAMPION, THEO (German, 1887-1952)

1892.	Sunny Day	24 x 20	ESH	7. 50

CHANDOR, DOUGLAS (American, Contemporary)

1893.	H. M. Queen Elizabeth II	16 x 11-1/2	RL	5. 00

CHANDOS

1894.	San Pietro	16 x 20	AS	2. 00
1895.	Sant Antioco	16 x 20	AS	2. 00

CHANG SHU-CHI (Chinese, 1900-)

1896.	Autumn Beach	13-1/2x8-1/2	IA	2. 00
1897.	Autumn River	13 x 10	IA	2. 50
1898.	Azaleas	13-1/2x8-1/2	IA	2. 00
1899.	Begonias	13-1/2x8-1/2	IA	2. 00
1900.	Messengers of Peace	19-1/2x9-1/2	AP	1. 25
1901.	Sunset	13 x 10	IA	2. 50
1902.	Tree Peonies	9-1/2 x 14	IA	2. 50
1903.	Vanity	12-1/2x9-1/2	IA	2. 50
1904.	Visit to the Temple	13 x 10	IA	2. 50
1905.	Water Lilies	9-1/2 x 14	IA	2. 50

CHANG TA T'SIEN (Chinese)

1906.	Conversation	7 x 9-1/2	CFA	2. 00

1907.	Waterfall		7 x 9-1/2	CFA	2.00
CHAOU MENG FOU (Chinese)					
1908.	River Landscape with				
	Horses		8-1/2x12-1/2	NYGS	3.00
CHAPALLAZ					
1909.	Cabanes pres				
	Iserables		16 x 20	CAC	4.00
1910.	Champery et les				
	Dents du Midi		16 x 20	CAC	4.00
CHAPIN, JAMES (American, 1887-)					
1911.	Boy with a Book		21 x 18	NYGS	9.00
1912.	Boy with a Globe		21-1/2 x 26	NYGS	12.00
1913.	Motherhood		21-1/2x17-1/2	NYGS	12.00
1914.	Picture Book		27 x 18	NYGS	12.00
			16-1/2 x 11	NYGS	4.00
CHAPPEL, L. (American Contemporary)					
1915.	La Tango		22 x 28	CFA	7.50
CHAPUT, ROGER					
1916.	Arlequin Flutiste		24 x 16	DAC	7.50
1917.	Jeunes Femmes		24 x 30	DAC	7.50
1918.	Melancholie		24 x 16	DAC	7.50
CHARDIN, JEAN BAPTISTE SIMEON (French, 1699-1779)					
1919.	Attentive Nurse	c.	18 x 23	HNA	5.95
		c.	8 x 10	CFA	2.00
1920.	Attributes of the				
	Arts		25 x 32	NYGS	18.00
1921.	The Benedicite		14 x 11	IA	3.00
1922.	The Blessing (Grace				
	before the Meal)		24 x 18	PENN	1.50
			20 x 16	PENN	1.50
			20 x 15-1/2	NYGS	10.00
			18 x 14	CFA	5.00
			10 x 8	NYGS	1.00
			7 x 6	CFA	1.00
1923.	Bowl of Plums		16 x 20-1/2	NYGS	10.00
1924.	Boy with a				
	Teetotum	c.	9-1/2x12-1/2	AP	1.25
		c.	8 x 10	AP	1.00
			6 x 7	CFA	1.00
1925.	Child with a Top		11 x 12	IA	3.00
			10 x 11	CFA	2.50
1926.	The Designer		26 x 20	CAC	12.00
1927.	Errand Woman		13 x 11	IA	3.00
1928.	Girl with Battle-				
	dore	c.	10 x 8	ESH	1.00
1929.	Girl with Feather-				
	ball		26 x 20-1/2	NYGS	16.00
1930.	House of Cards	c.	23 x 18	HNA	5.95
		c.	10 x 8	ESH	1.00
1931.	The Kitchen Maid	c.	23 x 18	HNA	5.95
			18 x 14-1/2	NYGS	10.00
			10 x 8	CFA	2.00

1932.	Kitchen Still			
	Life	c.	8 x 10	NYGS	1.00
1933.	Laborious Mother	13 x 11	IA	3.00
1934.	Music	18-1/2 x 30	ESH	12.00
1935.	Sealing the Letter	10 x 9	CFA	.50
1936.	Soap Bubbles	21 x 17	NYGS	10.00
		11 x 9	CFA	2.00
1937.	Still Life with Flask			
	(Glass Bottle)	22 x 17-1/2	NYGS	22.00
1938.	Still Life	c.	18 x 23	HNA	5.95
1939.	Still Life with Tank-			
	ard (Pewter Pitcher)	22 x 17-1/2	NYGS	22.00
1940.	Young Governess	18 x 23	AA	7.50
		7 x 9	CFA	2.00
1941.	Youth with the			
	Violin	11 x 12	IA	3.00

CHARPENTIER, FELIX M. (French, 1844-1916)

1942.	Mlle. Du Val			
	D'Ognes	c.	8 x 10	NYGS	.50

CHASE, WILLIAM M. (American, 1849-1916)

1943.	Chrysanthemums	22 x 36	NYGS	18.00
1944.	Self-Portrait	c.	10 x 8	AP	.50

CHATER, C.

1945.	Muscovy Ducks	16 x 20	ESH	7.50
1946.	Squirrel and Butter-			
	fly Fish	14 x 18	ESH	6.00
1947.	Veiled Goldfish	14 x 18	ESH	6.00

CHAULEUR, JANE (French Contemporary)

1948.	Playmates	16 x 20	CAC	6.00
9149.	Port of Croisic	16 x 22	CFA	10.00
		8 x 10	CFA	1.00

CHAUVEAU, FRANCOIS (French, 1613-1676)

1950.	Carousel Horses			
	(A-B-C-D) (4)	16 x 11	CFA	ea. 12.00

CHAVANNES See PUVIS DE CHAVANNES

CHE T'AO (Chinese, 1630-1707)

1951.	Pavillon sous les			
	Arbers	30-1/2x14-1/2	NYGS	32.00

CHEN-CHI (Chinese Contemporary)

1952.	Artist's Home Town	14 x 18	AJ	6.00
1953.	Bamboo	33 x 12	CAC	10.00
1954.	Chrysanthemums	33 x 12	CAC	10.00
1955.	Morning Traders on			
	the Huai River	14 x 18	AJ	6.00

CHEN YANG (Chinese)

1956.	Portrait of a Lady	28 x 13	CFA	15.00

CHENG-WU-FEI (Chinese Contemporary)

1957.	Bird on Apple			
	Blossom	22 x 14-1/2	ESH	7.50
1958.	Bird on Bough with			
	Red Berries	22 x 14-1/2	ESH	7.50
1959.	Camel and Bird	22 x 17	ESH	15.00

1960.	Camellias	16 x 20	RL		6. 00
1961.	Dove with Magnolias	23-1/2 x 13	ESH		10. 00
1962.	Hibiscus	24 x 12-1/2	RL		6. 00
1963.	Peonies	24 x 12-1/2	RL		6. 00
1964.	Squirrel	23. 1/2 x 13	ESH		10. 00

CHEREPOV, GEORGE

1965.	Landscapes (4)	24 x 48	AK	ea.	6. 00
1966.	Horseshoe Path	12 x 24	AK	ea.	2. 50
1967.	Last Snow				
1968.	Memory Lane				
1969.	Sleepy Lagoon				

CHEYSSIAL, G. R. (French Contemporary)

1970.	Folie	26 x 19	RL	15. 00

CHI-PAI-SHIH

1971.	Gourds	29 x 9	CFA	7. 50
1972.	Grapes	29 x 9	CFA	7. 50

CHIENG-YING CHANG (Chinese)

1973.	Parrot and Magnolia	33-1/2 x 13	ESH	12. 00
1974.	Pink Roses and Blue Budgerigars	22 x 14-1/2	ESH	7. 50
1975.	Red Roses and Bird	22 x 14-1/2	ESH	7. 50
1976.	Roses and Bird	33-1/2 x 13	ESH	12. 00
1977.	Two Birds and Apples	23-1/2x12-1/2	ESH	10. 00
1978.	Two Budgerigars	23-1/2x13-1/2	ESH	10. 00

CHIN, K.

1979.	Suburbs of Paris	24 x 48	AK	12. 00
		12 x 24	AK	3. 00
1980.	Sunrise over Montmartre	24 x 48	AK	12. 00
		12 x 24	AK	3. 00

CHIRICO, GIORGIO DE (Italian, 1888-)

1981.	Combat	c.	20 x 24	PENN	1. 50
1982.	Disquieting Muses	c.	10-1/2 x 15	IA	3. 00
1983.	Gladiators, 1918		9 x 15	IA	3. 00
1984.	Horses	c.	10 x 8	NYGS	. 50
1985.	Italian Square		11 x 15	IA	3. 00
1986.	Italian Square, 1930		11 x 14	IA	3. 00
1987.	Juan-les Pins, 1930		28 x 21	NYGS	12. 00
1988.	Man with Two Horses on a Shore		13 x 16	IA	3. 00
1989.	Self-Portrait with Palette		17 x 13	IA	3. 00

CHIU-YING (Chinese, 16th Century)

1990.	Emperor Kwang-Wu Crossing Ford	42 x 16	NYGS	22. 00

CHOULTZE, IWAN F. (Russian [Res. U. S.] 1877-)

1991.	Blanket of Snow	24 x 32	CFA	10. 00

CHRISTUS, PETRUS (Flemish, c. 1410-1472)

1992.	Legend of St. Eligius and Godeberta	29 x 25	NYGS	18. 00

CHU, CHARLES
1993.	Apple Blossoms			
	(Two Birds)	22 x 14	AA	5. 00
1994.	Apple Blossoms			
	(One Bird)	22 x 14	AA	5. 00
1995.	Bamboo Panel			
	(Green Bird)	35 x 15	AA	7. 50
1996.	Bamboo Panel			
	(Yellow Bird)	35 x 15	AA	7. 50
1997.	Big Bamboo	24 x 30-1/2	AA	12. 00
1998.	Blue Bird	22 x 14	AA	5. 00
1999.	Blue Birds	22 x 14	AA	5. 00
2000.	Duck Panel			
	(3 Ducks)	35 x 15	AA	7. 50
2001.	Duck Panel			
	(Large Duck)	35 x 15	AA	7. 50
2002.	Pine Tree (Left)	15 x 35	AA	7. 50
2003.	Pine Tree (Right)	15 x 35	AA	7. 50
2004.	Pine Panel (Yellow			
	Birds)	35 x 15	AA	7. 50
2005.	Pine Panel (Grey			
	Bird)	35 x 15	AA	7. 50
2006.	Willows (Two			
	Swallows)	22 x 14	AA	5. 00
2007.	Willows (One			
	Swallow)	22 x 14	AA	5. 00

CHU-LUN-HAN (Chinese)
2008.	By a Waterfall	28 x 12	NYGS	48. 00
2009.	View of a Waterfall	12-1/2 x 28	NYGS	48. 00

CHU TA (Chinese 1626-1705)
2010.	Lotus	32 x 14	NYGS	15. 00

CHUANG YI
2011.	Fish	15 x 30	NYGS	10. 00

CHUGTAI, M. ABDUR RAHMAN (Pakistani)
2012.	Come Fill the Cup	30 x 24	NYGS	18. 00
2013.	For a Song	30 x 24	NYGS	18. 00

CHURCH, FREDERICK EDWIN (American, 1826-1900)
2014.	Cotopaxi, Ecuador			
	c.	8 x 10	AP	. 50
2015.	Sunset	23-1/2 x 36	NYGS	16. 00

CHURCHILL, (SIR) WINSTON (English, 1874-1965)
2016.	Cap D'Ali	20 x 24	ESH	12. 00
2017.	Manton from			
	LaPausa	17-1/2 x 27	ESH	12. 00

CIARDI, GUGLIELMO (Italian, 1842-1917)
2018.	Seascape at San			
	Giorgio	11 x 15	IA	3. 00

CIGNANI, CARLO (Italian, 1628-1719)
2019.	Madonna and Child			
	(of the Rosary)	15 x 11	IA	3. 00
2020.	Virgin and Child			
	(Florence)	15 x 11	AS	3. 25

CIGNAROLI, VITTORIO AMEDEO (Italian, 1747-1793)
2021.	Landscape	17 x 20	IA		10.00
		11 x 13	IA		3.00
2022.	Landscape with a				
	Bridge	17 x 20	IA		10.00
		11 x 13	IA		3.00

CIKOVSKY, NICOLAI (American, 1894-)
2023.	From My Window	26 x 34	CAC		12.00
2024.	Outdoor Still Life				
	c.	18 x 23	HNA		5.95
2025.	Springtime in				
	Virginia	16 x 21	NYGS		9.00

CIMA DA CONEGLIANO (Italian, 1460-1517)
2026.	Head of a Girl	9 x 7	IA		1.50

CIMABUE (GIOVANNI GUALYIERI) (Italian, 1240-1302)
2027.	Crucifix (Detail)	15 x 11	IA		3.00
2028.	Crucifix	12-1/2 x 11	AS		3.25
2029.	Head of Christ--				
	Detail of No. 2028	15-1/2x11-1/2	AS		3.25
2030.	Madonna, Angels and				
	St. Francis	11 x 11	IA		3.00
2031.	St. Francis--Detail				
	of No. 2030	15 x 10	IA		3.00

CIRINO, ANTONIO (Italian [Res. U.S.] 1889-)
2032.	Autumn Landscapes				
	(4)	10 x 12	AK	ea.	1.50
		7 x 9	AK	ea.	1.00
2033.	Home Town	25 x 30	AA		7.50
		16 x 20	AA		3.50
2034.	Shady Village	25 x 30	AA		7.50
		16 x 20	AA		3.50

CISERI, ANTONIO (Italian, 1821-1891)
2035.	The Conception	15-1/2 x 9	AS		3.25
2036.	The Deposition	10 x 15	AS		3.25
2037.	Ecce Homo	11 x 15	IA		3.00
2038.	The Holy Heart of				
	Christ	27 x 14	AS		7.50
		15 x 8	AS		3.25
	Detail of No. 2038	11-1/2x15-1/2	AS		3.25
2039.	Transport to the				
	Sepulcher	10 x 15	IA		3.00
2040.	Virgin of Lourdes	15-1/2 x 9	AS		3.25

CIUCURENCU, ALEXANDRU (Rumanian, 1903-)
2041.	Cyclamen	19 x 23-1/2	NYGS		12.00

CIZEK SCHOOL, VIENNA
2042.	Child with a Banner				
	c.	8 x 10	AP		.25
2043.	Christ with Children	14-1/2 x 22	AP		3.00
2044.	Girl with Bouquet				
	c.	8 x 10	AP		.25
2045.	Harvesters c.	8 x 10	AP		.25
2046.	Knights and Castle				
	c.	8 x 10	AP		.25

2047. Zuckermann: Spring 19 x 18   AP   1.50
CLAESZ, PIETER (Dutch, 1600-1661)
2048. Still Life with
       Musical Instruments 18 x 31-1/2   ESH   15.00
              c.   9-1/2x12-1/2   AP   1.25
                   6 x 11   CFA   1.00
CLAGHORN, JOSEPH C. (American Contemporary)
2049. At the Old Indian
       Queen   16 x 25   AA   5.00
2050. Chance Passenger   21-1/2 x 35   AA   9.00
2051. Home for the
       Holidays   16 x 25   AA   5.00
2052. Independence Hall
       (Philadelphia)   20 x 30   AA   15.00
2053. Old Bruton Church
       (Williamsburg, Va.) 20 x 30   AA   15.00
CLAPERA, PEDRO (Spanish Contemporary)
2054. Black Bull   19 x 24   NYGS   10.00
2055. Buffalo   19 x 24   NYGS   10.00
2056. Young Mother   30 x 12-1/2   AS   7.50
2057. Young Ones   30 x 12-1/2   AS   7.50
CLARK, COSMO (English 1897-)
2058. Lavender Harvest,
       Provence   22 x 30   RL   10.00
CLARK, THOMAS B. (Scotch, 1820-1876)
2059. West Highland Lands-
       cape   17 x 24   ESH   10.00
CLAUDIO DI LORENA See GELLEE, CLAUDE
CLAUSADE, P. DE (French, Contemporary)
2060. Clearing Skies   15 x 18   RL   6.00
2061. Passing Showers   15 x 18   RL   6.00
2062. Serenity   19 x 38   CFA   15.00
2063. Summer Clouds   18 x 31-1/2   RL   12.00
CLAUSEN, GUNTHER (German, 1885-)
2064. Tithe Barn   22 x 18-1/2   ESH   15.00
CLAVE, ANTONI (Spanish, Contemporary)
2065. Etagère   28 x 22-1/2   NYGS   15.00
2066. King Bacchus   26 x 19   NYGS   15.00
2067. Musician   19-1/2 x 26   NYGS   15.00
2068. Still Life, 1955   17-1/2x23-1/2 NYGS   12.00
2069. Two Fish   17 x 22-1/2   ESH   10.00
2070. Twilight   22-1/2x31-1/2 NYGS   16.00
2071. Warrior on a Red
       Background   22-1/2x17-1/2 ESH   10.00
CLAVER, FERNAND (French Contemporary)
2072. Place du Tertre   18 x 22   RL   6.00
2073. Les Tuileries   18 x 22   RL   6.00
CLAYTON, H. (English, Contemporary)
2074. Sporting Jug   22 x26   RL   15.00
2075. White Fluted Vase   22 x 26   RL   15.00
CLAYTON, W. J. M. (English Contemporary)
2076. Peacemaker   18 x 14   RL   6.00

2077.	Queen of Hearts			
	Flintlock	18 x 14	RL	6. 00
2078.	Reward Notice	18 x 14	RL	6. 00
2079.	U. S. Marshall's			
	Revolver	18 x 14	RL	6. 00
CLEMENTE, R. (Spanish Contemporary)				
2080.	Firedance	20 x 25	RL	7. 50
2081.	Guitarrista	20 x 25	RL	7. 50
2082.	Novillados	22 x 28	RL	12. 50
2083.	Red Skirt	20 x 24-1/2	RL	7. 50
CLEMENTZ, H. (German, 1852-1930)				
2084.	Christ Among the			
	Rich	15 x 19	CAC	5. 00
2085.	Christ and the			
	Doctors	24-1/2 x 36	IA	12. 00
2086.	Christ Blessing the			
	Children	28-1/2x38-1/2	IA	12. 00
		19-1/2x27-1/2	IA	6. 00
2087.	Christ in the			
	Temple	20 x 30	IA	5. 00
CLEVE, JOOS VAN (Flemish, 1518-1554)				
2088.	Joris W. Vezelier	24 x 17	NYGS	12. 00
2089.	Margarethe Boghe,			
	Wife of Joris			
	W. Vezelier	23-1/2 x 17	NYGS	12. 00
2090.	Mater Dolorosa	14 x 9	IA	3. 00
2091.	Rest During the			
	Flight into Egypt	12 x 14	IA	3. 00
CLOUET, FRANCOIS (French 1505/10-1572)				
2092.	Elizabeth of			
	Austria	14-1/2x10-1/2	AP	5. 00
2093.	Portrait of a Court			
	Lady	15-1/2 x 11	NYGS	5. 00
CLOUET, JEAN (French, 1485-1541)				
2094.	Diane de Poitiers	16-1/2x14-1/2	PENN	1. 50
2095.	Francis I	14 x 11	IA	3. 00
2096.	Henry II	12 x 9	AP	5. 00
2097.	Marie Touchet	9 x 7	NYGS	4. 00
COBB, DAVID				
2098.	Swans of Marazion	20 x 25	AS	12. 00
COBELLE, CHARLES (American Contemporary)				
2099.	Italian Fantasy	16 x 42	CAC	15. 00
2100.	Parisian Fantasy	16 x 42	CAC	15. 00
2101.	Riviera Fantasy	16 x 42	CAC	15. 00
2102.	Venetian Fantasy	16 x 42	CAC	15. 00
COCHRAN, ALLEN DEAN (American, 1888-)				
2103.	Anemones and			
	Tulips	20 x 16	CAC	3. 50
2104.	Grandeur of Summer	24 x 30	CAC	7. 50
2105.	Orchids	24 x 30	CAC	7. 50
2106.	Pansies	24 x 30	CAC	7. 50
2107.	Springtime	20 x 16	CAC	3. 50

COGGESHALL, CLAVERT (American Contemporary)

2108.	Landscape	15 x 20	NYGS	7. 50
COHELEACH, GUY (American Contemporary)				
2109.	Heading South	24 x 48	DAC	10. 00
		24 x 30	PENN	1. 95
2110.	Homecoming	24 x 60	DAC	15. 00
		24 x 48	DAC	10. 00
		24 x 30	PENN	1. 95
2111.	Secluded Rest	24 x 48	DAC	10. 00
COHRAN				
2112.	Stormy Waters c.	20 x 24	PENN	1. 50
COLANTONIO				
2113.	St. Jerome	11 x13	IA	3. 00
COLE, JOHN V. (English Contemporary)				
2114.	Spring Flowers	23 x 19	ESH	10. 00
COLEMAN, RALPH P. (American, 1892-)				
2115.	Emigrant Train c.	8 x 10	AP	. 25
2116.	The Saviour	20 x 16	IA	1. 50
		14 x 11	IA	1. 00
COLLETTI, JOSEPH (Italian [Res. U. S.] 1898-)				
2117.	Landscape, Rome	16 x 22	PENN	1. 50
2118.	Landscape, Venice	16 x 22	PENN	1. 50
COLLOMB, MME. LOUISE A. (French, 1857-)				
2119.	Cerisier en Fleurs	23-1/2 x 19	NYGS	18. 00
COLSON				
2120.	Lady Asleep	22-1/2 x 18	ESH	10. 00
		10 x 8-1/2	ESH	1. 00
COMIOTTO				
2121.	Carnations	20 x 16	CAC	4. 00
COMPTON, E. T. (Edward Theodore) (English, 1849-1921)				
2122.	Alpine Stream	23 x 31	CFA	15. 00
2123.	Konigsee	24 x 34	CFA	12. 00
CONINXLOO, EGIDE VAN (Flemish, 1544-1607)				
2124.	Osea and the Prostitute	10 x 15	IA	3. 00
CONSTABLE, JOHN (English, 1776-1837)				
2125.	Boat Building at Flatford	12-1/2 x 15	ESH	3. 00
2126.	Bridge over the Stour	17 x 26	ESH	15. 00
2127.	Cornfield	23-1/2 x 20	ESH	18. 00
	c.	23 x 18	HNA	5. 95
		21 x 17	IA	4. 00
		14 x 12	ESH	3. 00
	c.	10 x 8	AP	. 50
2128.	Cottage in a Cornfield	12 x 15	ESH	3. 00
2129.	Dedham Lock and Mill	22 x 31	NYGS	12. 00
		20 x 28	IA	7. 50
		17-1/2 x 25	ESH	15. 00

2130.	Dedham Mill	11 x 16	ESH	3.00
2131.	Flatford Mill	19 x 24	ESH	10.00
		12 x 15	ESH	3.00
		10-1/2 x 13	ESH	2.00
		7 x 9	CAC	1.00
2132.	Glebe Farm c.	8 x 10	AP	.50
2133.	Hampstead Heath	21 x 27	NYGS	15.00
		20 x 25-1/2	ESH	10.00
2134.	Hay wain, 1821	27 x 39	NYGS	18.00
		18 x 26	NYGS	10.00
	c.	20 x 24	PENN	1.50
		18 x 25-1/2	IA	7.50
		12-1/2 x 18	IA	5.00
		11 x 16	ESH	3.00
		9-1/2 x 13	ESH	2.00
2135.	Leaping Horse	20 x 26	ESH	15.00
2136.	Malvern Hall	21 x 31	AA	12.00
2137.	Old Mill	20 x 24	DAC	7.50
2138.	Salisbury Cathedral			
	c.	20 x 24	PENN	1.50
		19-1/2x25-1/2	ESH	10.00
		12 x 15-1/2	ESH	3.00
		11 x 14	IA	3.00
2139.	Salisbury Cathedral from the Bishop's Garden	15-1/2 x 20	NYGS	7.50
2140.	Stoke by Nayland	10 x 13	ESH	2.00
2141.	Valley Farm	13 x 11	ESH	2.00
	c.	10 x 8	AP	.60
2142.	View at Hampstead Heath	11 x 13	NYGS	4.00
2143.	View of Salisbury Cathedral c.	18 x 23	HNA	5.95
2144.	View on the Stour at Dedham	21 x 30	NYGS	15.00
2145.	The White Horse	25 x 36	NYGS	18.00
		18 x 26	NYGS	10.00
		5-1/2x7-1/2	NYGS	.50
2146.	Willy Lott's Cottage	11 x 16	ESH	3.00
2147.	Wivenhoe Park, Essex	19-1/2 x 36	NYGS	16.00
		18 x 24	DAC	7.50
		11 x 21	ESH	7.50
		12 x 16	DAC	2.50

CONTI, BERNARDINO DEI (Italian, 1496-1522)

2148.	The Chinese	15 x 11	AS	3.25
2149.	Portrait of Francesco Sforza as a Child	15 x 10	IA	3.00

COOK

2150.	Dog Portraits (6) c. Boston Bull Boxer	16 x 12	PENN	ea. 1.00

```
                    Cocker Spaniel
                    Collie
                    Doberman Pinscher
                    Scottish Terrier
COOK, JOHN A. (American, 1870-   )
    2151.  Setting Sail        18 x 26       PENN          1. 50
COOK, ROBERT (English Contemporary)
    2152.  Harbour Scene       19-1/2 x 27   ESH          10. 00
COOLIDGE, C. M.
    2153.  Poker Dogs (8)      9-1/2 x 14    AK      ea.   3. 00
COOPER, (SIR) GERALD
    2154.  Flowerpiece         23 x 19       ESH          15. 00
                               12-1/2x10-1/2 ESH           2. 00
    2155.  Summer Glory        22-1/2 x 27   ESH          15. 00
    2156.  Summer Splendour    22 x 28       ESH          15. 00
COOPER, W. HEATON (English Contemporary)
    2157.  Derwent Water       20 x 30       AS           12. 00
    2158.  Grasmere            18 x 26       ESH           7. 50
    2159.  Rydal Water         18 x 26       ESH           7. 50
    2160.  Ullswater           20 x 30       AS           12. 00
COPLEY, JOHN SINGLETON (English [Res. U. S. ] 1737-1815)
    2161.  Elizabeth, the Artist's
           Daughter            24 x 13       NYGS         10. 00
    2162.  Mrs. John Bacon     21-1/2 x 18   NYGS         12. 00
    2163.  Paul Revere,
           Portrait            26 x 21       NYGS         15. 00
COPPING, HAROLD (English, 1863-1932)
    2164.  The Hope of the
           World               27-1/2 x 20   IA            5. 00
                               11 x 8        IA            1. 00
COPPO DI MARCOVALDO (Italian, 14th Century)
    2165.  Crucifix            13 x 11       AS            3. 25
CORBERY
    2166.  Bouquet de Pavots   21 x 16       NYGS         18. 00
CORBIERE, ROGER DE LA (Austrian, 1893-   )
    2167.  Calm Waters         18 x 21-1/2   RL            6. 00
    2168.  Full Tide           24 x 36       RL           12. 50
    2169.  Moonlit Sea         20 x 30       RL            7. 50
    2170.  Rolling Sea         18 x 21-1/2   RL            6. 00
CORBIZZI, FILIPPO (Italian, 1494-1515)
    2171.  Nativity            15 x 11       IA            3. 00
    2172.  St. Catherine       15 x 10       IA            3. 00
CORDOBA
    2173.  Country Scenes (8)  6 x 8         CAC     ea.   2. 00
    2174.  After Lunch
    2175.  Country Home
    2176.  Farm
    2177.  Hill Town
    2178.  Late Supper
    2179.  Shore Dinner
    2180.  Tropical Breakfast
    2181.  Village
```

CORINTH, LOVIS (German, 1858-1925)
2182.	Blue Lake	22 x 30	CFA	18. 00
2183.	Bouquet	21-1/2x27-1/2	NYGS	20. 00
2184.	Carnations	15 x 18	NYGS	18. 00
2185.	Crucifixion c.	10 x 8	AP	. 60
2186.	Easter on Lake Walchen	22 x 29-1/2	NYGS	20. 00
2187.	Lake Walch, 1920	23 x 31-1/2	NYGS	20. 00
2188.	Road by the Sea	23 x 31	CAC	15. 00
2189.	Tree at Walchen Lake c.	23 x 18	HNA	5. 95
2190.	Tree on the Shore at Lake Walchen	20 x 16	AP	5. 00
2191.	Tyrolese Landscape	22 x 29	CAC	15. 00
2192.	View of the Valley of the Inn	21-1/2 x 29	NYGS	20. 00
2193.	Walchensee	27-1/2 x 35	IA	18. 00
		17-1/2 x 22	IA	12. 00
2194.	Walchenseeland- schaft c.	17-1/2 x 22	AS	4. 00

CORNEILLE (CORNELIS VAN BEVERLOO) (Dutch Contemporary)
| 2195. | Blue Summer, Closed Blinds, 1964 | 21 x 29 | NYGS | 16. 00 |

CORNELIO
| 2196. | Madonna | 23-1/2 x 20 | AS | 12. 00 |

CORNELL, HENRY (English Contemporary)
| 2197. | Happy Valley | 15 x 18 | ESH | 4. 00 |

COROT, JEAN BAPTISTE CAMILLE (French, 1796-1875)
2198.	Arleux du Nord, the Stream by the Road	19 x 23	NYGS	18. 00
2199.	The Artist's Studio	17 x 21	CAC	10. 00
	c.	18 x 23	HNA	5. 95
2200.	La Bacchanale	28 x 22-1/2	PENN	1. 50
2201.	Belfry at Douai	20 x 16	ESH	6. 00
	c.	10 x 8	ESH	1. 00
2202.	Boatman of Morte- fontaine	23 x 35	CFA	15. 00
2203.	Bridge at Nantes	18 x 24	DAC	7. 50
	c.	8 x 10	ESH	1. 00
2204.	Bridge of Narni	25-1/2 x 36	NYGS	18. 00
		16 x 24	NYGS	10. 00
		16 x 23	CFA	12. 00
2205.	Chateau-Thierry	15 x 22	CFA	7. 50
2206.	Collegiate Church at Nantes	20 x 12	NYGS	7. 50
2207.	Colosseum	11 x 15	AS	3. 25
		19 x 14	IA	3. 00
2208.	Cottage in the Wood	18 x 24	DAC	7. 50
		12 x 16	DAC	2. 50
2209.	Dance of the Nymphs	20 x 26	CAC	7. 50

		16 x 20	CAC	5. 00
		9 x 12	CAC	2. 00
	c.	8 x 10	AP	. 50
2210.	Dawn in the Glade	18 x 22	CAC	7. 50
2211.	Dock at Paques c.	8 x 10	CFA	. 50
2212.	Le Fagot Attendu	18 x 24	NYGS	18. 00
2213.	Farm at Recouvri-			
	eres c.	18 x 23	HNA	5. 95
2214.	Florence seen from			
	the Boboli Gardens	10 x 15	IA	3. 00
2215.	Forest of Coubron	29-1/2 x 24	NYGS	18. 00
2216.	The Forum Seen			
	from the Palatinos	8 x 15	IA	3. 00
2217.	Girl Meditating	17-1/2x14-1/2	NYGS	20. 00
2218.	Girl Reading by the			
	Waterside c.	19 x 23	HNA	5. 95
2219.	Girl with Red			
	Bow c.	10 x 8	ESH	1. 00
2220.	Gitana Playing the			
	Mandolin	15 x 11	IA	3. 00
2221.	The Gypsy	14-1/2 x 11	AS	3. 25
2222.	Gypsy Girl at the			
	Fountain	20 x 15	NYGS	9. 00
		10 x 7-1/2	NYGS	1. 00
2223.	Gypsy with Mando-			
	lin	27 x 19	CFA	7. 50
2224.	Houses at Honfleur	17-1/2 x 25	NYGS	12. 00
	c.	8 x 10	AP	. 50
2225.	Le Lac de Terni	24 x 36	NYGS	18. 00
		11 x 16	NYGS	4. 00
2226.	The Lake	13 x 19	CFA	10. 00
2227.	Landscape	11 x 17	AR	4. 00
2228.	Landscape near			
	Geneva	12-1/2 x 18	NYGS	7. 50
2229.	Mlle. Octavie			
	Sennegon	12 x 10	IA	3. 00
2230.	Mill at St. Nicolas-			
	les-Arras	18 x 22-1/2	ESH	10. 00
		8 x 10-1/2	ESH	1. 00
2231.	Monk with Cello c.	8 x 10	AP	. 60
2232.	Morning	11 x 12	IA	3. 00
2233.	Morning: Dance of			
	the Nymphs	17 x 22	IA	10. 00
		11 x 14	IA	3. 00
2234.	Mother and Child			
	on the Beach	14-1/2 x 18	NYGS	7. 50
2235.	Olevano Romano	8 x 13	IA	3. 00
2236.	On the Way to			
	Sevres	13 x 18	CFA	5. 00
2237.	Paysage	8 x 10	NYGS	4. 00
2238.	Pond at Ville			
	D'Avray	13 x 27	CFA	10. 00
		8 x 10-1/2	ESH	1. 00

2239.	Pont au Change,			
	Paris	18 x 26	PENN	1. 50
		12 x 16	DAC	2. 50
2240.	Le Quai des Paquis,			
	Geneva	12-1/2 x 18	NYGS	7. 50
	c.	8 x 10	ESH	1. 00
2241.	The Reader	17 x 13	CFA	10. 00
2242.	Reading Girl	16 x 12	CAC	7. 50
2243.	Remembrance of			
	Terracina	25-1/2x31-1/2	NYGS	18. 00
		11 x 13	NYGS	4. 00
2244.	Residence and			
	Factory of M. Henry	18 x 23	HNA	5. 95
2245.	The Road to Sevres	8 x 10-1/2	ESH	1. 00
2246.	Road to Sin-le			
	Noble	16-1/2x22-1/2	ESH	10. 00
		8 x 10	ESH	1. 00
2247.	Site d'Italie, 1839	21 x 32	NYGS	16. 00
2248.	Souvenir of Italy c.	8 x 10	NYGS	. 50
2249.	Souvenir de			
	Mortefontaine	16-1/2x22-1/2	ESH	10. 00
		16 x 22	CFA	12. 00
2250.	Spring	20 x 26	CAC	10. 00
		16 x 20	CAC	5. 00
		9 x 12	CAC	2. 00
	c.	8 x 10	AP	. 50
2251.	The Studio	18 x 18-1/2	ESH	10. 00
2252.	Twilight on the			
	Lake	16 x 18	CFA	12. 00
2253.	View of Florence	11 x 15	AS	3. 25
		9 x 12	DAC	2. 00
2254.	View near Volterra	22 x 30	NYGS	16. 00
2255.	Ville D'Avray	19 x 25	NYGS	12. 00
	c.	18 x 23	HNA	5. 95
		8 x 11	CFA	2. 00
2256.	Villeneuve-les-			
	Avignon c.	8 x 10	ESH	1. 00
2257.	Wagon in the Dunes	19-1/2x25-1/2	NYGS	22. 00
2258.	Woman Reading	10 x 8	CFA	1. 00
2259.	Woman Reading on a			
	Wooded Bank	21 x 17	CFA	10. 00
		12-1/2x9-1/2	AP	1. 25
2260.	Woman with a			
	Pearl c.	24 x 20	PENN	1. 50
2261.	Wood-Gatherers	17 x 21	CAC	7. 50
2262.	La Zingara	12 x 8	CFA	. 50

CORREGGIO, ANTONIO ALLEGRI DA (Italian, 1494-1534)

2263.	Antiope's Sleep	13 x 8	CFA	2. 50
2264.	Danae	16 x 11	CFA	7. 50
2265.	Danae with Cupids	11 x 14	IA	3. 00
2266.	Deposition from the			
	Cross	11 x 13	IA	3. 00

2267.	Education of Cupid	25-1/2 x 15	ESH	10.00
2268.	Holy Night	12 x 16	AP	3.00
	c.	8 x 10	AP	.50
2269.	Jupiter and Antiope c.	8 x 10	NYGS	.50
2270.	Madonna and Child (Uffizi)	8 x 6	IA	1.50
2271.	Madonna and Child (Corsini)	14 x 11	IA	3.00
2272.	Madonna della Scala	15 x 10	IA	3.00
2273.	Maria Adoring the Child	27-1/2 x 20	AS	17.50
2274.	Marriage of St. Catherine	11 x 11	IA	3.00
	c.	8 x 10	NYGS	.50
2275.	Martyrdom of Saints	11 x 13	IA	3.00
2276.	Study of an Apostle	15-1/2x9-1/2	AR	4.00
2277.	Virgin Adoring	13 x 11	IA	3.00
2278.	Virgin Adoring the Child (Florence)	13 x 11	AS	3.25
	Virgin--Detail of No. 2278	15 x 11	AS	3.25
2279.	Virgin of the Bowl	15 x 10	IA	3.00
2280.	Virgin of St. Jerome	15 x 10	IA	3.00

CORRENS, ERICH (German, 1822-1877)

2281.	Southern Belle	28 x 22	NYGS	12.00
		20 x 16	IA	3.50
	Three-Quarter Detail of No. 2281	11 x 8-1/2	NYGS	1.50
	Half-Length Detail of No. 2281	11 x 8-1/2	NYGS	1.50

COSGRAVE, JOHN O'HARA, JR. (American Contemporary)

2282.	Brig "Prince de Neufchatel" c.	12 x 16	PENN	1.00
2283.	Clipper Ship "Challenge" c.	12 x 16	PENN	1.00
2284.	Clipper Ship "Flying Cloud" c.	12 x 16	PENN	1.00
2285.	Clipper Ship "Sea Serpent" c.	12 x 16	PENN	1.00
2286.	Clipper Ship "Sovereign of the Seas" c.	12 x 16	PENN	1.00
2287.	Ship Sloop "Wasp" c.	12 x 16	PENN	1.00
2288.	Square Topsail Schooner c.	12 x 16	PENN	1.00
2289.	Topsail Schooner "Rattlesnake" c.	12 x 16	PENN	1.00

COSIMO, PIERO DI See PIERO DI COSIMO

COSSA, FRANCESCO DEL (Italian, 1439-1478)
2290. Allegory of
       Autumn   c.   8 x 10   NYGS   . 50
COSTA, LORENZO (Italian, 1460-1535)
2291. Maria   24 x 24-1/2   NYGS   24. 00
COSTIGAN, JOHN EDWARD (American, 1888-)
2292. Fishermen Three   16 x 20   CAC   7. 50
COTAN JUAN SANCHEZ See SANCHEZ Y COTAN, JUAN
COTMAN, JOHN SELL (English, 1782-1842)
2293. Greta Bridge   9 x 13   ESH   2. 00
                      c.   8 x 10   AP   . 25
COTTAVOZ, ANDRE
2294. Boats in Cannes
       Harbour   16 x 22   ESH   10. 00
COTTI, EDUARDO (Italian, 1871-)
2295. Young People (12) 15 x 6   DAC   ea. 1. 50
COULON, GEORGE (French Contemporary)
2296. Still Life with
       Bread   24 x 48   DAC   10. 00
2297. Still Life with
       Grapes   24 x 48   DAC   10. 00
                          15 x 30   DAC   2. 00
COULSON, G. D. (English Contemporary)
2298. Black Label
       Bentley   20 x 30   RL   10. 00
2299. Bristol Bulldog   22 x 28   RL   10. 00
2300. Great Western
       Express   20 x 30   RL   10. 00
2301. Iron Lady   19 x 26   RL   7. 50
COUNIS, SALOMON GUILLAUME (French [Res. Italy] 1785-1859)
2302. Paolina Buonaparte
       (La Bella Greca)   23 x 18   AA   10. 00
                          11 x 8-1/2   IA   1. 75
               Oval   10 x 8-1/2   AS   3. 25
                           8 x 7   IA   1. 50
2303. Portrait of an Un-
       known Woman
               Oval   10 x 8-1/2   AS   3. 25
COUNTER
2304. Siamese Kittens
       (2)   c.   20 x 24   PENN   ea. 1. 50
COURBET, GUSTAVE (French, 1819-1877)
2305. Amazon   c.   8 x 10   NYGS   . 50
2306. Beach at Etretat   24 x 36   NYGS   18. 00
2307. Chateau de Chillon 21 x 25   NYGS   15. 00
                          11 x 13-1/2   NYGS   4. 00
2308. Cliff of Etretat
       after Storm   c.   20 x 24   PENN   1. 50
2309. Death Halloo c.   8 x 10   AP   . 60
2310. Deer in the
       Forest   c.   18 x 23   HNA   5. 95
2311. Les Demoiselles de
       Village   21 x 25   NYGS   18. 00

2312.	Dreaming Gypsy		11 x 13-1/2	NYGS	4. 00
2313.	L'Eternité		22 x 27	NYGS	18. 00
2314.	Fishing Boats on the				
	Beach at Deauville		17 x 22-1/2	ESH	10. 00
		c.	8 x 10	ESH	1. 00
2315.	Horse in the				
	Woods	c.	8 x 10	AP	. 60
2316.	Jura Landscape		19 x 25	NYGS	22. 00
2317.	Ladies by the				
	Seine	c.	9-1/2x12-1/2	AP	1. 25
			7 x 8	CFA	1. 00
2318.	Ladies by the Water-				
	side		8 x 11	CFA	2. 50
2319.	Landscape at				
	Etretat	c.	18 x 23	HNA	5. 95
2320.	Mill on the River				
	Loue	c.	8 x 10	ESH	1. 00
2321.	The Proudhon				
	Family		22-1/2 x 17	ESH	10. 00
2322.	Sleep	c.	8 x 10	ESH	1. 00
2323.	Still Life with				
	Apples		19 x 23-1/2	NYGS	22. 00
2324.	Stone-Breakers		12 x 19-1/2	AP	5. 00
		c.	8 x 10	AP	. 50
2325.	Trellis		24 x 30	NYGS	18. 00

COURTEAU

2326.	Notre Dame	24 x 48	IA	10. 00

COURTIN, L.

2327.	Early Morning -			
	Tréboul	21 x 26	RL	10. 00

COUSE, EANGER (American, 1866-1936)

2328.	Corn Ceremony		20 x 26	CAC	6. 00
			15 x 17	CAC	3. 00
2329.	Indian Harvest	c.	8 x 10	AP	. 50
2330.	Indian Love Affair		20 x 26	CAC	7. 50
2331.	Primitive Sculptor				
		c.	8 x 10	AP	. 50
2332.	Treasure Jar		20 x 26	CAC	6. 00
			15 x 17	CAC	3. 00

COVARRUBIAS, MIQUEL (Mexican, 1902-1957)

2333.	America	25 x 36	CAC	10. 00
2334.	Diego Rivera,			
	Caricature	15-1/2 x 11	NYGS	4. 00
2335.	Flower Fiesta	28 x 22-1/2	NYGS	16. 00

COX, JOHN ROGERS (American Contemporary)

2336.	Gray and Gold	15 x 21	IA	7. 50

COYPEL, CHARLES ANTOINE (French, 1694-1752)

2337.	Democritus	13 x 11	IA	3. 00

COZENS, JOHN ROBERT (English, 1752-1799)

2338.	Lake and Town of			
	Nemi	14-1/2x20-1/2	NYGS	20. 00

CRAIG, JAMES HUMBERT (Irish, 1878-1944)
2339. Connemara (Twelve
       Pins)   16 x 20   CFA   7. 50
2340. Donegal   16 x 20   CFA   7. 50
2341. Donegal Sunlit
       Valley   15 x 20   CFA   7. 50
2342. Joyce's Country   15 x 20   CFA   7. 50
CRANACH, LUKAS (THE ELDER) (German, 1472-1553)
2343. Bethrothal of St.
       Catherine   22-1/2 x 16 NYGS   10. 00
2344. Hirschjagd   22 x 33   CFA   25. 00
2345. Luther's Daughter 12-1/2x9-1/2 AP   1. 25
2346. Madonna and Child 29-1/2x20-1/2 AS   6. 00
                          21 x 14-1/2 AS   10. 00
2347. Madonna of the
       Arbor   27-1/2 x 20 AJ   15. 00
2348. Martin Luther   8 x 6   IA   1. 50
2349. Portrait of a Woman
       (Attributed)   14-1/2 x 9-1/2 AS   3. 25
2350. Rest on the Flight
       into Egypt   22 x 16   NYGS   18. 00
2351. Self-Portrait   11 x 10   IA   3. 00
2352. Stag Hunt   22-1/2 x 32 NYGS   18. 00
                  c.   20 x 24   PENN   1. 50
GRANACH, LUKAS (THE YOUNGER) (German, 1515-1586)
2353. Portrail of a Lady 28 x 22   CAC   15. 00
                          20 x 15   AJ   7. 50
2354. Portrail of a Man 20 x 15   AJ   7. 50
CRANDALL
2355. Coast Cottage   20 x 24   CAC   10. 00
CRANE, BRUCE
2356. Winter Idyl   15 x 14   CAC   3. 00
CRAWFORD, ROBERT CREE (Scotch, 1842-1924)
2357. Overseas Highway
                  c.   8 x 10   AP   . 25
CREDI, LORENZO DI See LORENZO DI CREDI
CREPET, ANGIOLO MARIO (Italian, 1885-)
2358. Laguna   16 x 21   AS   12. 00
2359. The Mask   14 x 11   IA   3. 00
2360. The Violin   14 x 11   IA   3. 00
CRESPI, GIOVANNI MARIA (LO SPAGNUOLO) (Italian, 1665-1747)
2361. Confirmation   15 x 11   IA   3. 00
2362. Familiar Scene   15 x 11   IA   3. 00
2363. Miracle of St.
       Francis   Oval   15 x 9   IA   3. 00
CRETI, DONATI (Italian, 1671-1749)
2364. The Astronomers
       (Dr.)   7-1/2 x 10   NYGS   2. 00
CRIBB, PRESTON (English, 1876-)
2365. Ocean Racing   16 x 20   ESH   6. 00
CRISTOFANO DELL'ALTISSIMO (d. 1515)
2366. Portrait of N.
       Macchiavelli   15-1/2x11-1/2 AS   3. 25

CRIVELLI, CARLO (Italian, 1430/35-1495)
2367.	Annunciation	22-1/2 x 16	NYGS	12.00
2368.	Madonna and Child			
	c.	10 x 8	AP	.50
2369.	Madonna Enthroned	15 x 5	IA	3.00
2370.	Virgin and Child (Rome)	15-1/2 x 7	AS	3.25
2371.	Virgin and Child (Ancona)	15 x 11	AS	3.25
2372.	Virgin and Child (Venice)	15 x 10-1/2	AS	3.25
2373.	Virgin Enthroned with Child	15 x 7	IA	3.00

CROCKER, DICK
2374.	Archway	11 x 14	DAC	3.00
2375.	Center of Town	11 x 14	DAC	3.00
2376.	On the Way to Market	11 x 14	DAC	3.00
2377.	Taxco Silver Shop	11 x 14	DAC	3.00

CROPSEY, JASPER F. (American, 1823-1900)
2378.	Adirondack Mountain Stream	26 x 48	AA	15.00
2379.	Autumn Landscape	16 x 26	AA	6.00
2380.	Autumn on Hudson River	22 x 40	NYGS	18.00
2381.	Bareford Mountains	24 x 42	AK	12.00
		12 x 21	AK	3.00
2382.	Bend in the River	20 x 32	AA	10.00
2383.	Distant Foothills	12 x 20	AA	4.00
2384.	Greenwood Lake	24 x 40	AA	12.00
2385.	Hudson River Valley	26 x 48	AA	15.00
2386.	In the Catskills	26 x 48	AA	15.00
2387.	In the Valley	16 x 26	AA	6.00
2388.	Jersey Meadowland	21 x 40	AA	12.00
2389.	Lake George	24 x 40	AA	12.00
2390.	Late September	20 x 41	AA	12.00
2391.	Mountain Glimpse	25 x 38	AA	12.00
2392.	Mountain Lakes	24 x 36	NYGS	15.00
2393.	Old Red Mill	26 x 48	AA	15.00
		12 x 20	AA	4.00
2394.	River Isle	12 x 20	AA	4.00
2395.	Seclusion	12 x 20	AA	4.00
2396.	Serenity	13 x 20	AA	4.00
2397.	Starrucca Viaduct	24 x 40	AK	12.00
		12 x 20	AK	3.00
2398.	Sunset Sailing	12 x 20	AA	4.00
2399.	Susquehanna River	26 x 48	AA	15.00
		12 x 20	AA	4.00
2400.	Upper Hudson	16 x 30	AA	8.00
2401.	Village of Saugerties	16 x 30	AA	8.00
2402.	Woodland Stream	24 x 36	NYGS	15.00

2403.	Wyoming Valley	28 x 48	AA		15. 00
CROSS					
2404.	Cypresses At				
	Cagnes	24 x 30	CAC		15. 00
CROWE, B.					
2405.	Fantasia	18 x 22	AS		12. 00
2406.	Harmony	18 x 22	AS		12. 00

CUGI (Spanish [Res. U. S.] Contemporary)

2407.	Show Business				
	(4)	30 x 12	DAC	ea.	5. 00
		15 x 6	DAC	ea.	1. 50

CUNDALL, Charles (English, 1890-)

2408.	Morning in Paris	16 x 24	ESH		10. 00
2409.	Oast Cottage	20 x 24	CFA		10. 00
2410.	Regatta	15-1/2 x 26	ESH		10. 00
2411.	River Pageant	16 x 30	RL		10. 00

CUNEO, TERRENCE T. (American Contemporary)

2412.	Gradient	24 x 36	RL		15. 00

CURR, TOM (Scotch, Contemporary)

2413.	Follow Me	27-1/2 x 20	IA		5. 00
		11 x 8	IA		1. 00
2414.	The Healer	19 x 26	CAC		5. 00

CURRAN, CHARLES C. (American, 1861-1942)

2415.	Children Catching				
	Minnows	12 x 21	CAC		7. 50
2416.	Dewdrops and				
	Roses	14 x 11	CAC		3. 00

CURRIER AND IVES
CURRIER, NATHANIEL (American, 1813-1888)
IVES, JAMES MERRITT (American, 1824-1895)

2417.	Across the				
	Continent	17-1/2 x 27	NYGS		12. 00
2418.	American Express				
	Train c.	12 x 16	PENN		1. 00
2419.	American Scene,				
	Morning	16 x 24	CAC		10. 00
2420.	American Seasons				
	(4) c.	12 x 16	PENN	ea.	1. 00
2421.	Cares of a Family	18-1/2 x 24	AA		15. 00
2422.	Grist Mill	24 x 32	CAC		10. 00
2423.	Portfolio (12)	9-1/2 x 14-1/2	NYGS	set	15. 00
2424.	American Hunting Scenes			ea.	1. 50
2425.	American National Game				
	of Baseball				
2426.	Central Park, Winter				
2427.	Clipper Ship "Dreadnaught"				
2428.	Great Ocean Yacht Race				
2429.	Lightning Express Trains				
2430.	Midnight Race on the				
	Mississippi				
2431.	Peytona and Fashion				
2432.	The Road - Winter				

2433.	Rocky Mountains				
2434.	Trotting Cracks at the Forge				
2435.	Woodcock Shooting				
2436.	The Prize Boy	27 x 19-1/2	AA		16. 00
2437.	The Road - Summer				
	c.	12 x 16	PENN		1. 00
2438.	The Rocky Mountains	17-1/2x25-1/2	NYGS		12. 00
		9-1/2x14-1/2	NYGS		1. 50
2439.	Seasons (4)	9 x 12	DAC	ea.	1. 00
2440.	Ship "Great Republic" c.	12 x 16	PENN		1. 00
2441.	Ship "Nightingale" c.	12 x 16	PENN		1. 00
2442.	Steamboat "Mayflower" c.	12 x 16	PENN		1. 00
2443.	Transportation (4)	19 x 14	PENN	set	2. 98
2444.	American Express Train				
2445.	Clipper Ship "Great Republic"				
2446.	High Pressure Steamboat "Mayflower"				
2447.	The Road - Summer				
2448.	Trotting Cracks at the Forge	16 x 24-1/2	PENN		1. 50
2449.	Winter Scene, Evening	16 x 24	CAC		7. 50
2450.	Wooding Up on the Mississippi c.	12 x 16	PENN		1. 00

CURRY, JOHN STEUART (American, 1897-1946)

2451.	Elephants at the Circus c.	8 x 10	AP		. 50
2452.	Flying Codonas	18 x 15	NYGS		7. 50
2453.	Line Storm, 1935	15-1/2 x 24	NYGS		10. 00
	c.	8 x 10	AP		. 50
2454.	Spring Bouquet	16 x 21	CAC		7. 50
2455.	Wisconsin Landscape	18 x 35	CFA		15. 00
		12 x 24	PENN		1. 50

CURTIS, A.

2456.	Blacksmith Shop	24 x 36	DAC		7. 50
2457.	Mill Pond	24 x 36	DAC		7. 50

CURTIS, LELAND (American, 1897-)

2458.	Crest of the Sierras	22 x 28	CFA		7. 50
2459.	Sentinels of the West	28 x 40	CAC		15. 00

CUSA, N. W.

2460.	Carolina Wood Ducks	11 x 18	ESH		6. 00
2461.	Teal and Lilies	12 x 18	ESH		6. 00

CUVILLIES, FRANCOIS DE

2462.	Flute Player	26 x 19	AA		12. 00

2463.	Hunter	26 x 19	AA		12. 00

CUYP, AELBERT (Dutch, 1620-1691)

2464.	Horsemen and Herds-				
	men with Cattle	25 x 36	NYGS		20. 00
		9 x 13	CFA		2. 00
2465.	The Maas at				
	Dordrecht	21 x 31	CAC		16. 00
		9 x 13	CFA		2. 00
2466.	View of a Town	7 x 12	AR		3. 00

CUZ, NAN (Guatamelan Contemporary)

2467.	Madonna in Red	23-1/2 x 20	ESH	Cv.	18. 00

CYDNEY (American Contemporary)

2468.	Ballet Dancers				
	(4)	14 x 11	AK	set	3. 00
	Ballet Dancers				
	(6)	8 x 6	AK	set	1. 00
2469.	Between the Acts	20 x 16	NYGS		7. 50
		14 x 11	NYGS		3. 00
		8 x 6	NYGS		1. 00
2470.	Clowns (4)	14 x 11	NYGS	ea.	3. 00
		8 x 6	NYGS	ea.	1. 00
2471.	Curtain Call	20 x 16	NYGS		7. 50
		14 x 11	NYGS		3. 00
		8 x 6	NYGS		1. 00
2472.	Future Ballerina	16 x 20	NYGS		7. 50
		11 x 14	NYGS		3. 00
2473.	Her First Bouquet	17 x 10	NYGS		4. 00
		10 x 6	NYGS		1. 25
2474.	Little Ballerina	14 x 11	NYGS		3. 00
		8 x 6	NYGS		1. 00
2475.	Little Starlet	8 x 6	NYGS		1. 00
2476.	Paradise Island				
	I and II	40 x 15	NYGS	ea.	12. 00
		24 x 9	NYGS	ea.	5. 00
2477.	Stage Visitor	17 x 10	NYGS		4. 00
		10 x 6	NYGS		1. 25
2478.	Starlet on Stage	17 x 10	NYGS		4. 00
		10 x 6	NYGS		1. 25
2479.	Stealing the Show	14 x 11	NYGS		3. 00
		8 x 6	NYGS		1. 00
2480.	Whispering	14 x 11	NYGS		3. 00
		8 x 6	NYGS		1. 00
2481.	Young Star	17 x 10	NYGS		4. 00
		10 x 6	NYGS		1. 25

CYPRUS

2482.	UNESCO World Art				
	Series (32)	11 x 14			
	or	14 x 11	NYGS	ea.	2. 00

CZECHOSLOVAKIA

2483.	UNESCO World Art				
	Series (32)	11 x 14			
	or	14 x 11	NYGS	ea.	2. 00

D

DA COSTA, MILTON (Brazilian Contemporary)
2484.	Against a Blue Background	21 x 29-1/2	NYGS	15.00

DADDI, BERNARDO (Italian, c. 1280-1348)
2485.	Annunciation	17-1/2 x 28	NYGS	16.00
2486.	Crucifixion (School of Daddi)	14 x 9	IA	3.00
2487.	Nativity of the Virgin	15 x 11	IA	3.00
2488.	St. Catherine	7 x 9	NYGS	.50
2489.	The Virgin (Uffizi)	16 x 9	IA	3.00
2490.	The Virgin (Rome)	15 x 11	• IA	3.00
2491.	The Virgin of Succour	15 x 9	IA	3.00

DAEL, JAN FRANS VAN (Flemish, 1764-1840)
2492.	Roses, Tulips and Poppies	10-1/2 x 8	ESH	1.00

DAFFINGER, MORITZ MICHAEL (Austrian, 1790-1849)
2493.	Age of Innocence	11 x 9	NYGS	1.50
2494.	Basket with Fruit	24 x 28	IA	12.00
2495.	The Duke of Reichstadt, Son of Napoleon	9 x 7	AJ	1.00
2496.	Flower Paintings (23)	14 x 10	CFA ea.	2.50

        Alpine Rose
        Bluebells
        Bluebells (Glockenblume)
        Daphne Flower
        Devil's Eye
        Dwarf Alpine Roses
        Dwarf Box-Tree
        Field Flowers
        Forest Cyclamen
        Forget-Me-Nots
        Hedge-Rose
        Lady's Slipper
        Little Love Flowers
        Lung Weed
        Marsh Marigolds
        Meadow Anemones
        Ox Eye
        Primroses
        Purple Gentian
        Red Lilies
        Rose of France
        Snow Roses
        Sweet Peas

2497.	Madame Daffinger	11 x 9	NYGS	1.50
2498.	Princess Metternich	11 x 9	NYGS	1.50

DA FORLI, ANSUINO See ANSUINO DA FORLI
DA FORLI, MELOZZO See MELOZZO DA FORLI
DALBONO, EDOARDO (Italian, 1841-1915)
2499. From Frisio to Santa
       Lucia   10 x 15   IA   3.00
2500. Pini   9-1/2 x 12   CFA   5.00
DALBY, DAVID (OF YORK) (English, b. 1790-)
2501. Melton Hunt   24 x 37   AA   15.00
DALI, SALVADOR (Spanish Contemporary)
2502. Bacchanale   c.   9-1/2x12-1/2   AP   1.25
                     c.   8 x 10   AP   1.00
2503. Bacchanalia   12 x 16   PENN   1.00
2504. Basket of Bread   12-1/2x12-1/2 NYGS   7.50
2505. Christ of St. John
       of the Cross   36 x 20-1/2   NYGS   25.00
                          28 x 16   NYGS   12.00
                          14 x 8   NYGS   3.00
2506. Christ of St. John
       of the Cross (Dr.) 21 x 28   NYGS   12.00
                          11-1/2 x 14   NYGS   3.00
2507. Columbus Discovers
       America   28 x 21   NYGS   15.00
2508. Composition, 1942 22 x 25-1/2   NYGS   12.00
2509. Crucifixion   28 x 18   NYGS   12.00
                          26 x 16-1/2   PENN   1.50
                          14 x 9   NYGS   3.00
2510. Inventions of
       Monsters   c.   8 x 10   AP   .75
2511. Landscape of Port
       Lligat   23 x 31   NYGS   16.00
2512. Madonna of Port
       Lligat   28 x 21   NYGS   12.00
                          14 x 10-1/2   NYGS   3.00
2513. Metamorphosis of
       Narcissus   8x 12   AP   3.50
2514. Nature Morte
       Vivante   21-1/2 x 28   NYGS   15.00
2515. Persistence of
       Memory   c.   8 x 10   AP   .50
2516. Sacrament of the Last
       Supper   28 x 44   NYGS   24.00
                          19 x 30   NYGS   12.00
                          9 x 14   NYGS   3.00
                          8 x 12   IA   .50
DALLAS-SIMPSON, A. (English Contemporary)
2517. Cherry Hat   20 x 16-1/2   RL   5.00
2518. Daisy Chain   24 x 20   RL   10.00
2519. Potter's Son   20 x 16-1/2   RL   5.00
2520. Romany Boy   20 x 16-1/2   RL   5.00
2521. Scarlet Ribbons   20 x 16-1/2   RL   5.00
2522. Sea Urchin   20 x 16-1/2   RL   5.00
2523. Waif   20 x 16-1/2   RL   5.00

DALLIN, CYRUS EDWIN (American, 1861-1944)
2524. Appeal to the Great
       Spirit   17 x 14   CAC   5. 00
                         12 x 9   CAC   2. 00
DANCHIN, LEON (French Contemporary)
2525. Black Cockers   15 x 18   IA   12. 00
2526. Ducks at Dawn   18 x 19-1/2 IA   12. 00
2527. Ducks in Flight   18 x 28   IA   15. 00
2528. Ducks in the Marsh 23 x 14   IA   12. 00
2529. Gordon Setter   16 x 20   IA   12. 00
2530. Irish Setters   16 x 19   IA   12. 00
2531. Irish Setter with
       Teal   19 x 26   IA   15. 00
2532. Sketches of
       Setters   14-1/2 x 10 IA   10. 00
2533. Three Setters   11 x 16   IA   7. 50
2534. Winter Teals   16 x 22   IA   15. 00
DANHAUSER, JOSEF (Austrian, 1805-1845)
2535. Reading the Will   21 x 26   IA   12. 00
DANIELS, JOHN (Norwegian-American, 1875-)
2536. The Rockies   24 x 30   PENN   1. 95
2537. Yosemite Falls   24 x 30   PENN   1. 95
DANNOT
2538. Danzig   24 x 31-1/2 NYGS   15. 00
DANTE, JESUS
2539. Cristo-Misericordia 28 x 18   IA   10. 00
                         14 x 9   IA   2. 50
DARANIYAGALA, JUSTIN (Ceylonese, 1903-)
2540. The Fish   26 x 18-1/2 NYGS   12. 00
DARCHE, THERESE (French, 20th Century)
2541. Paris Street Scenes
       (6)   11 x 14   IA   ea. 2. 50
2542. Boulevard des Capucines
2543. Boulevard de la Madeleine
2544. Cafe de la Pais, Opera
2545. Champs Elysees
2546. Place du Chatelet
2547. Place du Tertre
       Paris Street Scenes
       (4)   16 x 20   IA   ea. 4. 00
2548. Notre Dame, Vue des
       Quais
2549. Place du Chatelet
2550. Rue de Rivoli
2551. Square St. Julien le Pauvre
       Paris Street Scenes
       (4)   20 x16   IA   ea. 4. 00
2552. Marche St. Medard
2553. Place du Tertre
2554. Quai aux Fleurs
2555. Rue du Haut Pave

DARCY
2556. Puppies and Kittens
      (4)   12 x 6   AK   ea. 1. 25

DARRO

No.	Title	Size			
2557.	Behold	10 x 8	DAC		. 60
2558.	Good Shepherd	10 x 8	DAC		. 60
2559.	Mother and Child	10 x 8	DAC		. 60

DA SESTO, CESARE See CESARE DA SESTO
DAUBIGNY, CHARLES FRANCOIS (French, 1817-1878)

No.	Title	Size			
2560.	Banks of the Oise	8 x 14	CFA		2. 50
2561.	Boats on the Oise	13 x 22	IA		10. 00
		8 x 15	IA		3. 00
2562.	Lock at Optevoz	8 x 12	ESH		2. 00

DAUMIER, HONORE (French, 1808-1879)

No.	Title	Size			
2563.	L'Amateur	13 x 10	NYGS		4. 00
2564.	The Barrel Organ c.	12-1/2x9-1/2	AP		1. 25
		8 x 6	CFA		1. 00
2565.	The Burden c.	12-1/2 x 9-1/2	AP		1. 25
		8 x 6	CFA		1. 00
2566.	The Collector	16 x 13	CFA		10. 00
2567.	Court Scene Interior	20 x 24	NYGS		12. 00
2568.	Crispin and Scapin	21-1/2 x 30	NYGS		26. 00
	c.	20 x 24	PENN		1. 50
2569.	Don Quixote	20 x 14	ESH		10. 00
2570.	The Drama	27 x 25	NYGS		26. 00
2571.	Engravings Lover				
	c.	12-1/2x9-1/2	AP		1. 25
		8 x 6	CFA		1. 00
2572.	Jeannette	11 x 8-1/2	AR		3. 00
2573.	Jugglers at Rest	20 x 25	NYGS		12. 00
2574.	Legal Sketches (6) - (B. & W.)	9 x 8	NYGS	set	5. 00 or
2575.	Plead Not Guilty			ea.	1. 00
2576.	A Respected Citizen				
2577.	So Goes his Story				
2578.	Such a Devoted Husband				
2579.	A Sure Case				
2580.	This Saintly Woman				
2581.	Legal Studies (16) (B. & W.)	size not listed	AA	set	18. 00
	Legal Studies (16) (H. C.)	size not listed	AA	set	36. 00
2582.	The Laundress c.	7 x 9	AP		. 50
2583.	Medical Studies (18) (H. C.)	size not listed	AA	set	40. 00
2584.	Notre Dame de Paris	22 x 16	PENN		1. 50
2585.	On the Barricades	22 x 17-1/2	AR		7. 50
2586.	Passers-By in Front of Print Shop	13 x 9-1/2	NYGS		6. 00
2587.	Print Collector	16 x 13	AR		10. 00
	c.	9 x 7	AP		1. 00

2588.	La Soupe	7 x 10-1/2	NYGS		4.00
2589.	Third Class				
	Carriage	18 x 24	PENN		1.50
		16 x 22	NYGS		10.00
		5-1/2 x 7-1/2	NYGS		.50
2590.	Three Lawyers	15-1/2 x 12	NYGS		7.50
2591.	Uprising	22 x 28-1/2	NYGS		16.00

DAVEY

2592.	Birds and Cats,				
	Stylized (2)	12 x 24	AK	ea.	3.00
		7 x 14	AK	ea.	1.50
	(2)	24 x 12	AK	ea.	3.00
		14 x 7	AK	ea.	1.50
2593.	Still Life (2)	10 x 20	AK	ea.	2.50
		6 x 12	AK	ea.	1.25
	(2)	20 x 10	AK	ea.	2.50
		12 x 6	AK	ea.	1.25

DAVID, GERARD JANSZ (Flemish, 1460-1523)

2594.	Adoration of the				
	Kings	22-1/2x22-1/2	NYGS		18.00
2595.	Arrest of the Judge				
	Sisamne	13 x 11	IA		3.00
2596.	Madonna with the				
	Soup	13 x 11	IA		3.00
2597.	Rest on the Flight				
	into Egypt	18 x 18	NYGS		10.00
	c.	8 x 10	NYGS		.50
2598.	Transfiguration	15 x 11	IA		3.00

DAVID, JACQUES-LOUIS (French, 1748-1825)

2599.	Bonaparte	10 x 8	CFA	1.00
2600.	Napoleon in his			
	Study	28 x 17	NYGS	12.00
		14 x 8-1/2	NYGS	4.00
2601.	Oath of the Horatii	16 x 21	PENN	1.50
2602.	Portrait of M.			
	Seriziat	14 x 11	IA	3.00
2603.	Portrait of Madame			
	Seriziat and her Son	14 x 11	IA	3.00

DAVIES, ARTHUR BOWEN (American, 1862-1928)

2604.	Italian Landscape, the			
	Apennines, 1925	28 x 43	NYGS	20.00

DAVIES, KEN

2605.	Blackboard	20 x 26	CFA	10.00
2606.	Blotter	16 x 24	CFA	10.00
2607.	Bookcase	19 x 39	CFA	15.00
2608.	End of Day	15 x 21	CFA	7.50
2609.	George Washington	11 x 8	CFA	3.00
2610.	Marine Collection	26 x 35	CFA	15.00
2611.	Old Red Mill	15 x 21	CFA	7.50
2612.	Red Accent	12 x 10	CFA	3.00
2613.	Yellow Accent	12 x 10	CFA	3.00

DA VINCI See LEONARDO DA VINCI

DAVIS, GLADYS ROCKMORE (American, 1901-)
2614. Deborah and
      Nietzsche   16 x 22   CAC   6.00
                         5-1/2 x 7   NYGS   .50
2615. Music Lesson c.   20 x24   PENN   1.50
                         16-1/2 x 22   NYGS   9.00
2616. Noel with Violin
                    c.   7 x 9   AP   .50
DAVIS, H. W. B.
2617. Mother and Son   15-1/2 x 21   ESH   4.00
                    c.   7 x 9   AP   .50
DAVIS, LOTTIE AND MOSHE
2618. Land of Our Fathers
      (Map)   22 x 32-1/2   NYGS   6.00
DAVIS, LOUIS (English Contemporary)
2619. Guardian Angel   28 x 16   ESH   10.00
DAVIS, STUART (American, 1894-1964)
2620. For Internal Use
      Only   c. 7 x 9   AP   .50
2621. Percolator, 1927   30 x 24   NYGS   18.00
2622. Pheasants   24 x 24   CFA   10.00
2623. Summer Landscape   18-1/2x26-1/2 MMA   5.00
2624. Visa   c. 8 x 10   MMA   .35
DAVIS, WILLIAM M. (American, 1836-1927)
2625. Cider Making   24 x 40   CFA   12.00
                         12 x 20   AK   3.00
DAWSON, MONTAGUE (English Contemporary)
2626. Action between Java
      and Constitution   20 x 30   RL   15.00
2627. Ariel and Taeping 29 x 36   RL   20.00
                         24 x 30   RL   15.00
2628. Days of Adventure 20 x 30   RL   10.00
2629. Eight Bells   20 x 30   RL   10.00
2530. Golden West   16-1/2 x 33   RL   10.00
2631. Horn Abeam   20 x 30   RL   15.00
2632. Neck and Neck   17 x 25   RL   7.50
2633. Ocean Racers   25 x 19   RL   7.50
2634. Racing Home the
      Cutty Sark   17 x 26   RL   10.00
2635. Racing Wings   20 x 30   RL   10.00
2636. Royal Racer   25 x 19   RL   7.50
2637. Summer Breezes--
      Off the Needles   17 x 30   RL   10.00
2638. Thermopylae Leaving
      Foochow   20 x 30   RL   10.00
2639. Winning Tack   17 x 25   RL   10.00
DAWSON, MURIEL
2640. All on a Summer's
      Day   20-1/2 x 18   ESH   3.50
2641. Blue Butterfly   21 x 17   ESH   3.50
2642. Children's Illustrations
      (12)   21 x 17-1/2   ESH   ea. 3.50

2643. Crossing the Stream
2644. Fairy Boat
2645. Feeding the Chickens
2646. Feeding the Lamb
2647. First Aconite
2648. Fun with the Chicks
2649. Gathering Apples
2650. On the Cliff Top
2651. Picking Mushrooms
2652. Roe-Deer in Summer
2653. Seat of Wisdom
2654. Tinker Tailor

	Children's Illustrations				
	(8)	17-1/2 x 21	ESH	ea.	3.50
2655.	Holy Night				
2656.	Mallard Family				
2657.	Many Friends				
2658.	Nativity				
2659.	New Yacht				
2660.	Rabbits				
2661.	Three Scotties				
2662.	Young Dignity				
	Children's Illustrations				
	(2)	17-1/2 x 22	ESH	ea.	3.50
2663.	Feeding the Calf				
2664.	Feeding the Donkeys				
	Children's Illustrations				
	(3)	15 x 12	ESH	ea.	2.50
2665.	Finding the Leveret				
2666.	Rainbow				
2667.	Upland Breezes				
	Children's Illustrations				
	(4)	12 x 15	ESH	ea.	2.50
2668.	Expectations				
2669.	Happy Childhood				
2670.	Helping Hand				
2671.	Mother Love				
2672.	Christ Child and Roe Deer	15 x 12	ESH		3.00
2673.	Fun on the Gate	19 x 21	ESH		3.50
2674.	Seat of Wisdom	21 x 16	AP		3.50
2675.	Spring of Joy	15 x 12	ESH		3.00

DEARMAN

| 2676. | Seasons (4) | 10 x 12 | AA | ea. | 5.00 |

DEBORAH

2677.	Babies, Blue Ribbon				
	(4)	11 x 14	AK	ea.	1.25
		8 x 10	AK	ea.	.75
		5 x 7	AK	ea.	.30

DE BUCOURT, R. L.

2678.	Les Bouquets	12 x 10	CFA	7. 50
2679.	Les Compliments	12 x 10	CFA	7. 50

DE CACHARD, See CACHARD, REGIS DE

DE CAILLARD

2680.	Arlequin au Violon c.	22 x 17-1/2	AS	4. 00

DE CHIRICO See CHIRICO, GIORGIO DE

DE CLAUSADE See CLAUSADE, P. DE

DE GALLARD

2681.	Bouquet d'Anemones	22 x 15	NYGS	22. 00
2682.	Le Pont Louis Philippe	27 x 19	NYGS	26. 00
2683.	Le Pont Neuf	19 x 26	NYGS	26. 00

DEGAS, EDGAR HILAIRE GERMAIN (French, 1834-1917)

2684.	L'Absinthe	c.	24 x 20	PENN	1. 50
2685.	Absinth Drinkers	c.	8 x 10	NYGS	. 50
2686.	L'Actrice dans sa Loge		30 x 26-1/2	NYGS	18. 00
2687.	After the Bath	c.	24 x 20	PENN	1. 50
		c.	12-1/2 x 9-1/2	AP	1. 25
		c.	9 x 7	AP	1. 00
2688.	Arabesque		22-1/2x12-1/2	ESH	10. 00
		c.	10 x 8	ESH	1. 00
2689.	At the Racecourse	c.	21 x 26	HNA	5. 95
2690.	At the Racetrack	c.	12 x 16	PENN	1. 00
2691.	Ballerina		15 x 12	AA	6. 00
2692.	Ballet Class		27-1/2x26	NYGS	18. 00
		c.	23 x 18	HNA	5. 95
			16 x 12	AA	3. 00
2693.	Ballet Dancer	c.	12-1/2x9-1/2	AP	1. 25
		c.	9 x 7	AP	1. 00
2694.	Ballet Dancer: Fourth Position		19 x 24	NYGS	18. 00
2695.	Ballet Encore		16 x 20	PENN	1. 50
2696.	Ballet Girl		15 x 12	AA	6. 00
2697.	Ballet Girls	c.	24 x 20	PENN	1. 50
2698.	Ballet Girls on Stage		22 x 15-1/2	NYGS	10. 00
2699.	Ballet Scene	c.	7 x 9	AP	. 75
2700.	Ballet School	c.	20 x24	PENN	1. 50
2701.	Ballet Troupe	c.	20 x 24	PENN	1. 50
2702.	Before the Ballet (Detail)		11 x 14	NYGS	3. 00
2703.	Before the Race		13 x 31	ESH	15. 00
2704.	Behind the Curtain		22-1/2x16-1/2	NYGS	10. 00
2705.	The Cabaret	c.	24 x 20	PENN	1. 50
			14 x 10-1/2	NYGS	5. 00
2706.	Cafe Concert	c.	26 x 21	HNA	5. 95
		c.	10 x 8	ESH	1. 00

2707.	Carriage at the Races	13-1/2 x 21	ESH	7.50
2708.	Classe de Danse	27 x 24	NYGS	12.00
2709.	Curtain Call c.	8 x 10	ESH	1.00
2710.	Dance Green Room			
	c.	18 x 23	HNA	5.95
2711.	Dance Lesson	13 x 10	IA	3.00
2712.	The Dances c.	24 x 20	PENN	1.50
		15 x 10	CFA	5.00
		15 x 11	AP	1.00
2713.	Dancer: Study No. One (Dr.)	16 x 10	NYGS	3.00
2714.	Dancer: Study No. Two (Dr.)	16 x 10	NYGS	3.00
2715.	Dancer Adjusting Costume	8 x 5	CFA	1.00
2716.	Dancer at the Practice Bar	31 x 19	CAC	15.00
		8 x 5	CFA	1.00
2717.	Dancer in Her Dressing Room	31 x 13	ESH	15.00
2718.	Dancer Leaning Forward	8 x 5	CFA	1.00
2719.	Dancer on Stage	22-1/2x15-1/2	ESH	10.00
		19 x 14	AP	5.00
	c.	10 x 8	ESH	1.00
2720.	Dancer Scratching Her Back c.	12-1/2x9-1/2	AP	1.25
	c.	9 x 7	AP	1.00
2721.	Dancer Tying Her Slipper	22-1/2 x 17	ESH	10.00
		11 x 10	NYGS	8.00
	c.	10 x 8	ESH	1.00
2722.	Dancer with Arms Akimbo c.	20 x 24	PENN	1.50
2723.	Dancer with Arms Behind Head	7 x 6	CFA	1.00
2724.	Dancer with Bouquet	16 x 20	PENN	1.50
		16 x 12	AA	3.00
2725.	Dancer with Fan			
	c.	24 x 20	PENN	1.50
		15 x 10	CFA	5.00
2726.	Dancer with Hand on Back	8 x 5	CFA	1.00
2727.	Dancer with Hands Behind Back	12-1/2x9-1/2	AP	1.25
	c.	9 x 7	AP	1.00
2728.	Dancers c.	23 x 18	HNA	5.95
		13-1/2x13-1/2	AR	3.00
2729.	Dancers Adjusting Their Slippers	10-1/2 x 30	ESH	15.00
		9 x 27	PENN	1.50
	c.	8 x 10	ESH	1.00

2730.	Dancers at the				
	Bar	c.	9-1/2x12-1/2	AP	1. 25
		c.	8 x 10	AP	1. 00
2731.	Dancers at the				
	Practice Bar		31 x 23	NYGS	18. 00
2732.	Dancers in Blue		22-1/2 x 21	ESH	10. 00
			17-1/2x17-1/2	AP	10. 00
		c.	10 x 8	ESH	1. 00
2733.	Dancers in Green				
		c.	10 x 8	ESH	1. 00
2734.	Dancers in Pink				
		c.	24 x 20	PENN	1. 50
2735.	Dancers in the				
	Wings		17 x 13	NYGS	5. 00
2736.	Dancers on a Red				
	Bench		19 x 21-1/2	PENN	1. 50
2737.	Dancers Preparing				
	for the Ballet		28 x 23	NYGS	16. 00
2738.	Dancing Class	c.	26 x 21	HNA	5. 95
		c.	24 x 20	PENN	1. 50
		c.	10 x 8	ESH	1. 00
2739.	Dancing Lesson		20 x 15	NYGS	5. 00
2740.	Dancing Recital		15 x 20	NYGS	7. 50
2741.	Dancing Studio		13 x 19	CFA	5. 00
2742.	La Danseuse	c.	9 x 7	AP	. 50
2743.	Danseuse au Bouquet	16 x 20	NYGS	9. 00
			6 x 7	NYGS	. 50
2744.	Danseuse Chausson	10 x 11	NYGS	7. 50
2745.	Danseuse de Bout		8 x 5	CFA	1. 00
2746.	Danseuse de Dot		16 x 10-1/2	NYGS	7. 50
2747.	Danseuse de Profil		15 x 19	NYGS	7. 50
2748.	Danseuse-Etoile	c.	22 x 17-1/2	AS	4. 00
2749.	Danseuse Rejustant		7 x 6	CFA	1. 00
2750.	Danseuses		9 x 12	NYGS	7. 50
2751.	Danseuses Roses				
		c.	23 x 18	HNA	5. 95
2752.	Danseuses Salutant	16 x 10-1/2	NYGS	7. 50
2753.	Danseuses sur un				
	Banquette		20 x 29	AR	12. 00
2754.	Ecole de Danse				
	(Dancing School)		15 x 20	NYGS	9. 00
			11 x 14	NYGS	3. 00
		c.	8 x 10	NYGS	. 50
	Detail of				
	No. 2754	c.	10 x 8	ESH	1. 00
2755.	L'Entree des				
	Masques		19 x 25-1/2	AA	12. 00
2756.	Femme a l'Ombrelle	11 x 8	NYGS	7. 50
2757.	Four Dancers		19-1/2x23-1/2	PENN	1. 50
		c.	18 x 23	HNA	5. 95
			11 x 14	NYGS	3. 00
2758.	Le Foyer de Danse a				

	Opera (Dance Foyer				
	at the Opera)	c.	20 x 24	PENN	1.50
		c.	18 x 23	HNA	5.95
			12-1/2 x 18	NYGS	6.00
		c.	8 x 10	ESH	1.00
2759.	Front of the				
	Tribune	c.	9-1/2x12-1/2	AP	1.25
			6 x 8	CFA	1.00
2760.	Girl at Ironing				
	Board	c.	24 x 20	PENN	1.50
2761.	Girl Looking Through				
	Opera Glasses		9 x 5	CFA	1.00
2762.	Half-Length Studies				
		c.	7 x 9	AP	.50
2763.	Head of a Woman		12-1/2 x 10	NYGS	12.00
2764.	Ironers		20 x 22	CFA	7.50
			10 x 11	CFA	2.50
2765.	Jeune Femme en				
	Costume de Ville		10 x 8	NYGS	7.50
2766.	Jockeys		17 x 21-1/2	NYGS	22.00
2767.	Jockeys		16 x 19	NYGS	18.00
2768.	Jockeys in the Rain		18-1/2 x 25	NYGS	15.00
2769.	Landscape		6 x 12	AR	5.00
2770.	Laundress	c.	24 x 20	PENN	1.50
2771.	Little Harlequin				
		c.	10 x 8	ESH	1.00
2772.	Mademoiselle				
	Valpincon		19 x 28	NYGS	15.00
2773.	Millinery Shop		14 x 15-1/2	AJ	6.00
2774.	Morning Bath		27 x 18	NYGS	10.00
2775.	Nude Combing Her				
	Hair	c.	8 x 10	NYGS	.50
2776.	Petit Rat		10 x 7-1/2	NYGS	7.50
2777.	Pink and Green		23-1/2x21-1/2	NYGS	15.00
2778.	Portrait of Estelle		18 x 24	PENN	1.50
2779.	Portrait of Rene de				
	Gas, 1855 (Dr.)		13 x 10-1/2	NYGS	3.00
2780.	Portrait of a Young				
	Woman		11 x 9	CFA	1.00
2781.	Race Horses		19 x 22	PENN	1.50
2782.	Racehorses at Long-				
	champs	c.	18 x 23	HNA	5.95
			16 x 19	CFA	10.00
		c.	9-1/2x12-1/2	AP	1.25
			6 x 8	CFA	1.00
2783.	Red Ballet Skirts		14 x 18	NYGS	12.00
2784.	La Repasseuse				
	(Ironer)		26 x 21	NYGS	15.00
2785.	La Repetition	c.	9 x 7	AP	.50
2786.	Seashore with Dunes		5-1/2 x 12	AJ	2.50
2787.	Seated Dancer		18 x 24	NYGS	12.00
		c.	8 x 10	ESH	1.00

2788.	The Shoe String c.	9 x 7	AP	.50
2789.	Singer with Glove c.	8 x 10	NYGS	.50
2790.	Three Dancers	25 x 19	CAC	10.00
2791.	Le Tub	6 x 9	CFA	1.00
2792.	Two Dancers on Stage	24 x 19	PENN	1.50
		24 x 18	NYGS	7.50
2793.	Two Dancers with Fan c.	24 x 20	PENN	1.50
2794.	Violinist Seated	15 x 11-1/2	NYGS	12.00
2795.	Washer Woman Carrying Washing	6 x 8	CFA	1.00
2796.	Woman Combing Her Hair c.	24 x 20	PENN	1.50
2797.	Woman in her Bath c.	9-1/2x12-1/2	AP	1.25
	c.	8 x 10	AP	1.00
2798.	Woman Washing in Her Bath	6 x 9	CFA	1.00
2799.	Woman with Chrysanthemums	28 x 35-1/2	NYGS	20.00
	c.	20 x 24	PENN	1.50
		17 x 21-1/2	NYGS	10.00
		7 x 9	AP	.50
2800.	Yellow Harlequin	23 x 12	CAC	15.00

DE GRAZIA, TED

2801.	Alone	18 x 10	AA		5.00
2802.	Boy with Rooster	13 x 10	AA		2.00
2803.	Girl with Piggy Bank	13 x 10	AA		2.00
2804.	Lost Apache	18 x 10	AA		5.00
2805.	Mariachi in Blue	24 x 8	AA		5.00
2806.	Mariachi in Red	24 x 8	AA		5.00
2807.	Navajo Campfire	23-1/2 x 48	AA		15.00
2808.	Navajo Fair	15 x 32	AA		12.00
2809.	Navajo Family	15 x 32	AA		12.00
2810.	Navajo Mother	24 x 24	AA		12.00
2811.	Navajo Wagon	15 x 32	AA		12.00
2812.	Los Ninos	24 x 36	AA		12.00
2813.	Off to Market	16 x 8	AA		4.00
2814.	Portraits (6)	12 x 9	AA	ea.	2.00
2815.	Angel Music				
2816.	Balloon				
2817.	Flower Boy				
2818.	Flower Girl				
2819.	Piccolo Pete				
2820.	Son Flowers				
2821.	Saguaro Harvest	16 x 9	AA		4.00
2822.	Waiting	16 x 8	AA		4.00
2823.	Water Maidens	16 x 9	AA		4.00

DE HEEM See HEEM

DEHN, ADOLPH ARTHUR (American, 1895-)

2824.	Caribbean Fantasy	17 x 11	NYGS	7.50
2825.	Fine Day in Missouri			
	c.	7 x 9	AP	.25
2826.	Love, Labor and			
	Leisure	22 x 33	IA	12.00
2827.	Minnesota Farm	13-1/2 x 20	NYGS	7.50
2828.	Minnesota in August	12-1/2x18-1/2	NYGS	7.50
2829.	Threshing in			
	Minnesota c.	8 x 10	NYGS	.50

DE HOOCH See HOOCH, PIETER DE

DEISTER, M. O.

2830.	Madonna	23-1/2x16-1/2	AS	14.00

DEJONGH See JONGH, TINUS DE

DEKAY, JOHN (American Contemporry)

2831.	Enchanted Forest	22 x 24	DAC	7.50
2832.	Solitude	22 x 24	DAC	7.50
2833.	Summer Reflections	36 x 24	DAC	15.00

DEKER, JEAN

2834.	Fruits (2)	11 x 14-1/2	AS	ea.	3.25

DEKONING

2835.	Gitte	20 x 12	ESH	Pr.	5.00
2836.	Portraits of Children				
	(4)	12 x 9-1/2	ESH	ea.	2.00
				Cv.	and Pr.
2837.	Susi	20 x 12	ESH	Pr.	5.00

DELACROIX, EUGENE (French, 1798-1863)

2838.	Basket of Flowers	15 x 20	CFA	7.50
2839.	Dante and Virgil			
	in Hell c.	8 x 10	NYGS	.50
2840.	Entry of the Crusaders			
	into Constantinople	18 x 24	PENN	1.50
2841.	Etude de Cavalier	26 x 20	CAC	12.00
2842.	Flower Piece	23 x 29	AR	15.00
2843.	Hamlet	11 x 8	AR	4.00
2844.	Head of a Lion	7 x 7-1/2	AR	5.00
2845.	Horse Frightened by			
	a Storm c.	20 x 24	PENN	1.50
2846.	The Horseman c.	9 x 7	AP	.50
2847.	Liberty Leading the			
	People c.	8 x 10	NYGS	.50
2848.	Lionne	7 x 7	NYGS	4.00
2849.	Odalisque	9 x 12	CFA	2.50
2850.	Ovid Among the			
	Scythians	17-1/2 x 26	NYGS	12.00
2851.	Wild Boar Hunt	21 x 27-1/2	NYGS	18.00

DE LA TOUR, MAURICE See LATOUR, MAURICE QUENTIN DE

DELAUNEY, ROBERT (French, 1885-1941)

2852.	Eiffel Tower	31 x 21	ESH	15.00
2853.	The Window c.	23 x 18	HNA	5.95

DEL COSSO

2854.	Allegory of Autumn			
	c.	7 x 9	AP	.50

DELDEVEZ
2855.   Spanish Afternoon   18 x 24   CAC   15. 00
DELLA PORTA See BARTOLOMMEO (FRA)
DELLA ROBBIA, ANDREA See ROBBIA, ANDREA DELLA
DELLA ROBBIA, LUCA See ROBBIA, LUCA DELLA
DE LONGPRE, PAUL See LONGPRE, PAUL DE
DEMAN, ALBERT (French Contemporary)
2856.   The Stream of Life   17 x 26   RL   10. 00
DE MARCO, LUIS C. (Argentinian Contemporary)
2857.   Floral Arrangement
                        c.   24 x 20   PENN   1. 50
2858.   Flowers (4)   24 x 20   DAC   ea. 7. 50
                             14 x 11   DAC   ea. 2. 50
2859.   White and Brown
        Mums   18 x 24   PENN   1. 50
2860.   Yellow Mums   18 x 24   PENN   1. 50
DEMUTH, CHARLES (American, 1883-1935)
2861.   Calla Lilies   13 x 19   CAC   5. 00
2862.   End Parade Coates-
        ville   c.   8 x 10   NYGS   . 50
2863.   Flower Study No. 1   18 x 12   NYGS   6. 00
2864.   Flower Study No. 4   18 x 12   NYGS   6. 00
2865.   I Saw the Figure 5
        in Gold   c.   20 x 24   PENN   1. 50
                        c.   7 x 9   AP   . 25
2866.   Lancaster   c.   18 x 23   HNA   5. 95
DENGEL, DIANNE (American Contemporary)
2867.   Country Bumpkins
        (4)   6 x 15   DAC   ea. 1. 50
DENIS, MAURICE (French, 1870-)
2868.   Sketches of Birds   11 x 15   ESH   8. 00
DE PISIS, FILIPO See PISIS, FILIPO DE
DE POSTELS, ROBERT See POSTELS, ROBERT DE
DE POTVIN
2869.   Porte de la
        Tournelle   24 x 48   IA   10. 00
DE PREDIS, AMBROGIO See PREDIS, AMBROGIO DE
DEPRESLE, F. FRANK (French Contemporary)
2870.   Paris Scenes (4)   40 x 10   DAC   ea. 5. 00
2871.   Bookstalls   20 x 5   DAC   ea. 1. 75
2872.   Moulin de la Galette
2873.   Notre Dame
2874.   Sacre Coeur
        Paris Scenes (2)   10 x 40   DAC   ea. 5. 00
2875.   Isle de la Cité   5 x 20   DAC   ea. 1. 75
2876.   The Seine
DERAIN, ANDRE (French, 1880-1954)
2877.   Auf der Themse c.   17-1/2 x 22 AS   4. 00
2878.   Ballet   18 x 23   CAC   15. 00
2879.   Barges on the
        Thames   18 x 23   CAC   15. 00
2880.   Barques a Grave-
        lines   c.   17-1/2 x 22 AS   4. 00

2881.	Blackfriars	19-1/2 x 24	NYGS	15. 00
2882.	Boats in Harbour			
	c.	8 x 10	ESH	1. 00
2883.	Fishing Harbour			
	c.	18 x 23	HNA	5. 95
2884.	Flowers in a Vase,			
	1932	22-1/2x28-1/2	NYGS	12. 00
2885.	Gravelines	16 x 31	NYGS	15. 00
2886.	Great Pine	23 x 28	NYGS	20. 00
2887.	Guitar Player c.	9 x 7	AP	. 50
2888.	Harbour	16 x 20	CFA	7. 50
2889.	Harlequin	23-1/2 x 20	PENN	1. 50
	c.	23 x 18	HNA	5. 95
2890.	Hyde Park	14 x 21	CFA	7. 50
2891.	Landscape	23 x 30	ESH	15. 00
2892.	Landscape, the Blue			
	Oak	23-1/2 x 30	NYGS	26. 00
		16 x 20	NYGS	5. 00
2893.	London c.	9-1/2 x 12-1/2	AP	1. 25
		6 x 8	CFA	1. 00
2894.	London Bridge,			
	1906	17 x 26	MMA	5. 00
2895.	Madonna and Child	18-1/2 x 14	NYGS	14. 00
2896.	Nude	18 x 14	CFA	5. 00
2897.	Old Bridge	25 x 31	NYGS	18. 00
2898.	Pool of London	15 x 23	NYGS	12. 00
2899.	Port of Collioure	15-1/2 x 20	AP	7. 50
2900.	Portrait of a Negro	28 x 22	NYGS	12. 00
2901.	Portrait: Venetian			
	Woman	12 x 9	NYGS	14. 00
2902.	Red Landscape	23 x 30-1/2	ESH	15. 00
	c.	8 x 10	ESH	1. 00
2903.	Sailing Boats at			
	Collioure c.	7 x 9	AP	. 75
2904.	Southern Landscape			
	c.	8 x 10	ESH	1. 00
2905.	The Thames	18 x 22	ESH	10. 00
2906.	The Tree c.	8 x 10	ESH	1. 00

DE RIBERA See RIBERA, JOSE DE
DE SALVO See SALVO, COSMO DE
DESCHAMPS, GABRIEL (French Contemporary)

2907.	Dejeuner Provencal	22 x 28	RL	12. 50
2908.	Little Boats,			
	St. Jean	23 x 28	RL	12. 50
2909.	Port de Cannes	28 x 22-1/2	RL	12. 50
2910.	Summer in Venice	30 x 22	RL	12. 50

DESIDERIO DA SETTIGNANO (Italian, 1428-1464)

2911.	St. John	15 x 11	IA	3. 00

DESMOULINS

2912.	Fruits and Flowers	24 x 30	DAC	7. 50

DESNOYER, FRANCOIS (French Contemporary)

2913.	Bridge at Albi c.	8 x 10	ESH	1. 00

2914.	Devil's Bridge	c.	8 x 10	ESH	1.00
2915.	Fishermen's Festival				
	at Sete		17-1/2 x 22	ESH	10.00
2916.	Harbour at Sete				
		c.	8 x 10	ESH	1.00
2917.	Harbour of Algier		24 x 30	CAC	15.00
2918.	Poppies and Corn-				
	flowers		22 x 18	CAC	10.00
2919.	Port of Algiers		24 x 30	ESH	15.00
2920.	Venice		13-1/2 x 23	ESH	10.00
2921.	Wild Flowers		22-1/2x18-1/2	ESH	10.00

DESOTO, MINNIE B. HALL (MRS. E.) (American, 1864-)

2922.	Christ the King		20 x 16	IA	5.00

DE SPHAER

2923.	Codice--Hunting				
	Scene		9 x 15-1/2	AS	3.25

DESPORTES, ALEXANDRE F. (French, 1661-1743)

2924.	King Charles				
	Spaniel		10-1/2 x 8	ESH	1.00
2925.	Pointer and Pheas-				
	ant		8 x 10-1/2	ESH	1.00

DESSAU

2926.	Jesus, the Children				
	are Calling		25-1/2 x 19	IA	5.00
			11 x 8	IA	1.00

DE STAEL, NICHOLAS (Russian, 1914-1952)

2927.	Les Bouteilles				
	(Bottles)	c.	12-1/2 x 9-1/2	AP	1.25
		c.	10 x 8	ESH	1.00
		c.	9 x 7	AP	1.00
2928.	Coin de Studio (Corner				
	of the Studio)	c.	12-1/2 x 9-1/2	AP	1.25
			12 x 7	CFA	1.00
		c.	9 x 7	AP	1.00
2929.	Coucher de Soleil				
	(Sunset)		19-1/2 x 27	ESH	15.00
2930.	Figure on Horse-				
	back		24-1/2 x 34	ESH	18.00
2931.	Footballers		22 x 18	ESH	10.00
2932.	Honfleur, 1952		23 x 31-1/2	NYGS	22.00
2933.	Jazz Players		22-1/2 x 16	ESH	10.00
		c.	10 x 8	ESH	1.00
2933a.	Landscape		23-1/2x31-1/2	NYGS	22.00
2934.	Landscape on the				
	Mediterranean		13 x 18	NYGS	16.00
2935.	Persimmons and a				
	Glass		22 x 27	NYGS	18.00
2936.	Sailboats at Antibes		33 x 24	NYGS	30.00
2937.	Ships	c.	18 x 23	HNA	5.95
2938.	Steamboats		22-1/2 x 18	ESH	10.00

DETLEFSON, PAUL

2939.	Autumn Interlude		24 x 48	DAC	10.00

2940.	Big Moment	24 x 48	AK	10.00
		26 x 40	AK	8.00
		18 x 24	AK	5.00
		11 x 15-1/2	AK	3.00
		5 x 8	AK	1.25
2941.	Good Old Days	26 x 40	AK	8.00
		18 x 24	AK	5.00
		11 x 15-1/2	AK	3.00
		5 x 8	AK	1.25
2942.	Happy Days	24 x 36	DAC	7.50
		12 x 18	DAC	2.50
2943.	Horse and Buggy Days	24 x 48	AK	10.00
		26 x 40	AK	8.00
		18 x 24	AK	5.00
		11 x 15-1/2	AK	3.00
		5 x 8	AK	1.25
2944.	Memories	24 x 40	DAC	8.50
		12 x 18	DAC	2.50
2945.	Old Mill Stream	24 x 40	DAC	8.50
		12 x 18	DAC	2.50
2946.	Red Caboose	24 x 30	DAC	7.50
2947.	School's Out	24 x 40	DAC	8.50
		12 x 18	DAC	2.50
2948.	Smithy	24 x 60	DAC	15.00
		24 x 48	DAC	10.00
		15 x 30	DAC	2.00
		12 x 18	DAC	2.50
2949.	Sturdy Landmark	24 x 48	AK	10.00
		26 x 40	AK	8.00
		18 x 24	AK	5.00
		11 x 15-1/2	AK	3.00
		5 x 8	AK	1.25
2950.	Spring Morn	24 x 48	DAC	10.00
		12 x 18	DAC	2.50

DEVE, EUGENE (French, 1826-1887)

2951.	Dead Calm	23-1/2 x 16	ESH	10.00
	c.	10 x 8	ESH	1.00

DEVIS, ARTHUR WILLIAM (English, 1763-1822)

2952.	Master Simpson (Friends)	31 x 25	IA	12.00
		24 x 19	IA	10.00
		18 x 14-1/2	IA	5.00
		14 x 11	IA	3.00
	Detail of No. 2952	11-1/2 x 9	IA	1.50
	c.	10 x 8	NYGS	1.00

DE ZURBURAN See ZURBURAN
DIAZ, R.

2953.	Clown au Chapeau	21 x 15	IA	6.00
2954.	Clown aux Cheveux Rouges	18-1/2 x 15	IA	6.00

2955.	Clown avec Margue-			
	rite	23-1/2 x 12	IA	6.00

DIAZ DE LA PENA, NARCISSE VIRGILE (French, 1809-1876)

2956.	Fontainebleau Woods	9 x 15	IA	3.00
2957.	Three Little Girls	24 x 16	CFA	12.00

DICKINSON, PRESTON (American, 1891-1930)

2958.	Still Life, 1928	14-1/2x20-1/2	NYGS	10.00

DIDOT

2959.	Amaryllis	31-1/2 x 14	NYGS	12.00
2960.	Iris	31 x 12	NYGS	12.00
2961.	Red Jug	13 x 31	CFA	12.00
2962.	Still Life with			
	Melon	12 x 31	NYGS	12.00
2963.	Sunflowers	31 x 12	NYGS	12.00
2964.	Yellow Lily	32 x 12-1/2	NYGS	12.00

DILL, OTTO (German, 1884-)

2965.	Summer Day in			
	Rome	21-1/2x26-1/2	ESH	10.00

DISNEY, WALT (American, 1900-1967)

2966.	Bambi Meets His			
	Forest Friends	20 x 24	NYGS	6.00
		15 x 18	NYGS	3.00
		10 x 12	NYGS	1.00
2967.	Forest Secrets	20 x 24	NYGS	6.00
		15 x 18	NYGS	3.00
		10 x 12	NYGS	1.00
2968.	Good Friends All	20 x 24	NYGS	6.00
		15 x 18	NYGS	3.00
		10 x 12	NYGS	1.00
2969.	Snow White's Last			
	Call for Dinner	20 x 24	NYGS	6.00
		15 x 18	NYGS	3.00
		10 x 12	NYGS	1.00

DIX, OTTO (German, 1891-)

2970.	Bernina	23 x 26	CAC	10.00
2971.	Mountain and			
	Stream	23 x 26	CFA	10.00
2972.	Sunrise in Hegau	24-1/2 x 28	ESH	12.00

DOBROWSKY

2973.	Blue Larkspur	20 x 12	AJ	5.00
2974.	Head of a Young			
	Girl	20 x 16	AJ	5.00

DODD, ROBERT (English, 1748-1816)

2975.	Cotton Pickers c.	7 x 9	AP	.50

DOLCI, CARLO (Italian, 1616-1686)

2976.	Ecce Homo	10 x 7	IA	1.50
2977.	The Eternal Father	10 x 14	IA	3.00
2978.	Madonna and Child	15 x 12	IA	3.00
2979.	Madonna and Child			
	c.	10 x 8	NYGS	.50
2980.	Madonna Del Dito	15 x 12	IA	3.00
		10 x 7	IA	1.50

2981.	Madonna of the Finger	13-1/2 x 11	AS	3. 25
2982.	Madonna of the Veil	14 x 11	IA	3. 00
2983.	Magdalene	15 x 11	IA	3. 00
		14-1/2 x 11	AS	3. 25
2984.	Portrait of Arnolfo de'Bardi	14 x 11	IA	3. 00
2985.	The Redeemer Oval	13-1/2 x 11	AS	3. 25
2986.	St. Agnes	13 x 11	IA	3. 00
2987.	St. Apollonia	13 x 11	IA	3. 00
2988.	St. Rosa	13 x 9	IA	3. 00
2989.	Virgin Adoring the Child	23 x 18-1/2	AS	7. 50
		14 x 11	AS	3. 25
2990.	Virgin and Child	14 x 11	IA	3. 00
2991.	Virgin and Child (Rome)	15 x 11	AS	3. 25

DOMENICHINO, IL (Italian, 1581-1641)

2992.	Chase of Diana	11 x 15	IA	3. 00
2993.	Cumaean Sibyl	15 x 11	IA	3. 00
2994.	Landscape with Figures	c. 20 x 24	PENN	1. 50
		18 x 22	DAC	7. 50
2995.	Landscape with Venus, Amor and Satyrs Oval	10 x 13	IA	3. 00

DOMENICO DI BARTOLO (Italian, 1400-1449)

2996.	Madonna and Child	15 x 8	IA	3. 00

DOMENICO DI MICHELINO See MICHELINO, DOMENICO DI
DOMENICO VENEZIANO See VENEZIANO, DOMENICO DI
DOMINIQUE

2997.	Balinesin	23-1/2 x 16	ESH	6. 00
2998.	Claudia	23-1/2 x 16	ESH	6. 00
2999.	Dieter	23-1/2 x 16	ESH	6. 00

DONATELLO (DONATO DI NICOLO DI BETTO DE'BARDI)
(Italian, 1382-1466)

3000.	Nicolo da Uzzano (Sculpture)	15 x 11	IA	3. 00
3001.	St. George (Sculpture)	15 x 11	IA	3. 00

DONGEN, CORNELIS (OR KEES) VAN (Dutch, 1877-   )

3002.	Bar du Soleil à Deauville	18-1/2 x 22	ESH	10. 00
		c. 8 x 10	ESH	1. 00
3003.	Beach at Deauville	18 x 22	CAC	10. 00
3004.	Bois de Boulogne	24-1/2 x 30	ESH	15. 00
		19 x 23	CAC	15. 00
		12 x 16	PENN	1. 00
		c. 9-1/2x12-1/2	AP	1. 25
		c. 7 x 9	AP	1. 00
3005.	Flower Basket	23 x 18	NYGS	10. 00

3006.	Park at Boulogne		6 x 8	CFA		1. 00
3007.	Tulips		19 x 36	NYGS		16. 00
			12-1/2x23-1/2	NYGS		9. 00
3008.	Versailles	c.	9-1/2x12-1/2	AP		1. 25
		c.	7 x 9	AP		1. 00
3009.	Woman at a					
	Balustrade		18 x 20	PENN		1. 50

DORING, ANTON (Swiss, 1692-)

3010.	Garden Glory	20 x 15-1/2	NYGS	7. 50
		14 x 11	NYGS	4. 00

DOSSI, DOSSO (GIOVANNI LUTERI) (Italian, 1479-1542)

3011.	Circe and her Lovers			
	in a Landscape	23 x 31-1/2	NYGS	18. 00
3012.	Jesus Christus	23-1/2 x 16	ESH	6. 00
3013.	Nymph Pursued			
	by a Satyr	10-1/2 x 15	AS	3. 25

DOU, GERARD (Dutch, 1613-1675)

3014.	Hydropic Woman	14 x 11	IA	3. 00
3015.	School Master	14 x 11	IA	3. 00

DOUGHTY

3016.	Catskill Landscape			
		c. 20 x 24	PENN	1. 50

DOUTRELEAU, P. (French Contemporary)

3017.	Reflet Blanc	24 x 37	RL	17. 50

DOVASTON

3018.	And so the Story			
	Goes	20 x 30	CAC	7. 50
3019.	Auld Lang Syne	22 x 30	CAC	7. 50

DOVE, ARTHUR C. (American, 1880-1946)

3020.	Abstract, Flour Mill,			
	1938.	26 x 16	NYGS	12. 00
3021.	Mars, Orange and			
	Green, 1935	13 x 20	NYGS	7. 50
3022.	Moon, 1935	c. 8 x 10	NYGS	. 50

DRAWBELL, M.

3023.	Leek Heads	28 x 20	AS	12. 00

DROEGE, O. (American Contemporary)

3024.	Farm House	17 x 12	CFA	25. 00

DROLLING, MICHAEL MARTIN (French, 1786-1851)

3025.	Interior of a			
	Kitchen	11 x 14	IA	3. 00

DROUAIS, FRANCOIS-HUBERT (French, 1727-1775)

3026.	Duc d'Orleans	32 x 12-1/2	AL	12. 00
3027.	Duke of Berry and the			
	Count of Provence as			
	Boys	11 x 15	IA	3. 00
3028.	Group Portrait	30 x 25	AA	12. 00
3029.	Mlle. de Charlois	32 x 12-1/2	AL	12. 00

DRUMMOND (American Contemporary)

3030.	Bayou Scene (4)	24 x 10	DAC	ea.	3. 50
		12 x 5	DAC	ea.	1. 00
3031.	Bourbon Street	15 x 40	DAC		10. 00

3032.	Capital, Williams-				
	burg	15 x 40	DAC		10. 00
3033.	Governor's Palace,				
	Williamsburg	15 x 40	DAC		10. 00
3034.	New Orleans (6)	24 x 10	DAC	ea.	3. 50
		12 x 5	DAC	ea.	1. 00
3035.	Williamsburg,				
	Virginia (4)	30 x 12	DAC	ea.	5. 00
		15 x 6	DAC	ea.	1. 50

DUCCIO DI BUONINSEGNA (Italian, 1255-1319)

3036.	Calling of the Apostles,			
	Peter and Andrew	16 x 17	NYGS	10. 00
3037.	Madonna dei Francescani			
	(The Virgin Adored)	9 x 7	IA	1. 50
3038.	The Maries at the			
	Tomb of Christ	11 x 12	IA	3. 00
	c.	8 x 10	NYGS	. 50
3039.	St. Catherine	16 x 10	IA	3. 00
3040.	The Virgin	15 x 11	IA	3. 00
3041.	Virgin and Child	15-1/2x10-1/2	AS	3. 25

DUCHAMP, MARCEL (DUCHAMP-VILLON) (French, 1888-1965)

3042.	Nude Descending a			
	Staircase c.	24 x 20	PENN	1. 50
3043.	Nude Descending a			
	Staircase No. 2,			
	1912	30 x 18	NYGS	18. 00

DUDLEY

3044.	Duneland	c.	7 x 9	AP	. 50

DUFNER

3045.	Golden Days	c.	7 x 9	AP	. 50

DUFRESNE, CHARLES (French, 1876-1938)

3046.	Still Life	24-1/2 x 30	NYGS	16. 00

DUFY, JEAN (French, 1888-1964)

3047.	Bois de Boulogne	18 x 23-1/2	CFA	12. 00
3048.	Circus Band	23-1/2 x 18	NYGS	10. 00
		14 x 11	NYGS	3. 00
3049.	Le Fiacre	18-1/2 x 24	NYGS	12. 00
3050.	Guitar Clown	23-1/2 x 18	NYGS	10. 00
		14 x 11	NYGS	3. 00
3051.	Mediterranean Scene			
	c.	18 x 24	PENN	1. 50
3052.	Le Moulin Rouge à			
	Montmartre	16 x 21	AS	10. 00
3053.	Paris: Ile de la			
	Cité	23-1/2 x 18	NYGS	15. 00
3054.	Paris: La Seine	23-1/2 x 18	NYGS	15. 00
3055.	Regatta	11-1/2 x27-1/2	PENN	1. 50
3056.	Springtime in Paris	19 x 36	NYGS	18. 00
3057.	Phaeton - Detail of			
	No. 3056	14 x 18	NYGS	4. 00
3058.	Three-Quarter Coach -			
	Detail of No. 3056	14 x 18	NYGS	4. 00

3059.	Sunday Afternoon		19 x 24	NYGS	10. 00
3060.	View of Paris		17 x 23	CFA	15. 00

DUFY, RAOUL (French, 1877-1953)

3061.	Anemones		22-1/2x16-1/2	ESH	10. 00
			18 x 13	CFA	7. 50
			17 x 12	AP	5. 00
3062.	Ascot		11 x 30	CFA	10. 00
3063.	At the Paddock		19-1/2 x 24	AR	10. 00
3064.	At the Spa	c.	8 x 10	NYGS	. 50
3065.	Baccarat Party		16 x 20	PENN	1. 50
3066.	Beach Promenade		18 x 24	NYGS	12. 00
	Beach - Detail of No. 3066.		16 x 12	NYGS	4. 00
3067.	Before the Start				
		c.	9-1/2x12-1/2	AP	1. 25
			6 x 9	CFA	1. 00
3068.	Bird in a Cage	c.	23 x 18	HNA	5. 95
			18 x 14	AP	7. 50
		c.	9 x 7	AP	. 50
3069.	Blue Mozart	c.	9-1/2x12-1/2	AP	1. 25
			6 x 8	CFA	1. 00
3070.	Boats and Seagulls	c.	9-1/2x12-1/2	AP	1. 25
			9 x 12	CFA	1. 00
3071.	Bouquet		24 x 18-1/2	NYGS	12. 00
3072.	Bullfight		20 x 24	AR	12. 00
3073.	Bunch of Anemones		22-1/2 x16-1/2	ESH	10. 00
		c.	12-1/2x9-1/2	AP	1. 25
		c.	10 x 8	ESH	1. 00
			8 x 6	CFA	1. 00
3074.	Bunch of Flowers				
		c.	9-1/2x12-1/2	AP	1. 25
			6 x 8	CFA	1. 00
3075.	The Cage	c.	24 x 20	PENN	1. 50
			18 x 14	CFA	7. 50
3076.	Caltagirone (Sicily)	c.	8 x 10	NYGS	. 50
3077.	Cargo Noir		19 x 24	CFA	10. 00
3078.	Carnival at Nice		20 x 24	AR	12. 00
			9-1/2x12-1/2	AP	1. 25
			5 x 8	CFA	1. 00
3079.	Casino de Nice		19-1/2 x 24	NYGS	12. 00
		c.	8 x 10	NYGS	. 50
3080.	Champ de Blé		21 x 26	NYGS	15. 00
3081.	Chateau and Horses		23 x 28	NYGS	15. 00
3082.	Circus		18 x 24	CAC	10. 00
3083.	Circus Band		24 x 18	CAC	10. 00
3084.	Clematites		14 x 10	NYGS	16. 00
3085.	The Concert	c.	18 x 23	HNA	5. 95
3086.	Concerte Orange		18 x 22-1/2	ESH	10. 00
3087.	Deauville		14 x 32	CFA	15. 00
		c.	18 x 23	HNA	5. 95

3088.	Deauville, 1935	17-1/2x25-1/2	NYGS	12.00
3089.	Decor for the Ballet			
	"Palm Beach"	18 x 22-1/2	ESH	10.00
3090.	Drying the Sails	12-1/2 x 30	NYGS	12.00
3091.	Gladioli	24 x 18-1/2	NYGS	12.00
3092.	Harbor	18 x 24	AA	12.00
3093.	Haymakers	14 x 18	CFA	7.50
3094.	Haymaking	14 x 18-1/2	AP	7.50
3095.	Homage to Mozart	25-1/2 x 20	NYGS	15.00
3096.	Hommage à Bach			
	c.	12-1/2x9-1/2	AP	1.25
	c.	9 x 7	AP	1.00
		8 x 6	CFA	1.00
3097.	Honfleur Harbor	18 x 24	NYGS	12.00
3098.	The Steamer -			
	Detail of No. 3097	16 x 12	NYGS	4.00
3099.	Horas du Pin	21-1/2 x 28	NYGS	12.00
3100.	Horsemen in the			
	Forest	16 x 20	AP	7.50
3101.	Jockeys c.	20 x 24	PENN	1.50
3102.	Joinville c.	20 x 24	PENN	1.50
		11-1/2 x 29	NYGS	12.00
3103.	The Lawn c.	8 x 10	CFA	1.00
3104.	Lilies	14 x 11	CFA	5.00
3105.	Mannequins at the			
	Races c.	16 x 24	PENN	1.50
3106.	Marine	6 x 8	CFA	1.00
3107.	Marne Landscape			
	c.	8 x 10	NYGS	.50
3108.	Marseille	7 x 8	CFA	1.00
3109.	Marseille, Notre			
	Dame de la Garde			
	c.	9-1/2x12-1/2	AP	1.25
	c.	7 x 9	AP	1.00
3100.	Marseilles, the Old			
	Port	18-1/2 x 24	NYGS	12.00
3111.	Mer au Havre (The			
	Sea at Le Havre)	18 x 22	NYGS	22.00
	c.	8 x 10	ESH	1.00
3112.	The Mermaid and			
	the Sailboats c.	20 x 24	PENN	1.50
3113.	Monte Carlo	19 x 23	AR	15.00
	c.	7 x 9	AP	1.00
3114.	Mozart c.	8 x 10	NYGS	.50
3115.	The Normandy Tree			
	c.	16 x 20	PENN	1.50
3116.	Open Window in			
	Nice	25-1/2x19-1/2	NYGS	18.00
		24 x 20	CAC	7.50
3117.	The Opera c.	9-1/2x12-1/2	AP	1.25
	c.	7 x 9	AP	1.00
		6 x 8	CFA	1.00

3118.	Orchestre	9 x 12	CFA	1. 00
3119.	Pablo Casals and a			
	Pianist c.	9-1/2x12-1/2	AP	1. 25
3120.	Paddock	20 x 24	CFA	15. 00
3121.	Paddock at			
	Chantilly	13 x 18	CFA	7. 50
3122.	Paddock at			
	Deauville	12 x 30	AR	10. 00
		13 x 18	CFA	7. 50
		10-1/2 x 26	PENN	1. 50
3123.	Paddock at Long-			
	champs	7 x 9	CFA	1. 00
3124.	Piazzetta	18 x 24	AA	12. 00
3125.	La Plage c.	8 x 10	ESH	1. 00
3126.	Polo	18 x 24	NYGS	12. 00
3127.	Port of Honfleur	20 x 24	CFA	15. 00
3128.	Poster: Jetty at			
	Honfleur c.	24 x 20	PENN	1. 50
3129.	Poster: Ville de			
	Honfleur	28-1/2 x 20	PENN	1. 00
3130.	Poster: Ville de			
	Nice	28-1/2x19-1/2	PENN	1. 00
3131.	Quintette c.	9-1/2x12-1/2	AP	1. 25
	c.	8 x 10	AP	1. 00
		6 x 8	CFA	1. 00
3132.	Race at Epsom	7 x 9	CAC	4. 00
3133.	Race Track, 1928			
	c.	20 x 24	PENN	1. 50
3134.	Racecourse at			
	Deauville	17 x 22-1/2	ESH	10. 00
3135.	Races at Deauville	20 x 26	CAC	15. 00
3136.	Races at Goodwood			
	c.	18 x 23	HNA	5. 95
3137.	Reception a la			
	Prefecture	6 x 8	CFA	1. 00
3138.	Red Violin	17 x 22	CFA	12. 00
		7 x 8	CFA	1. 00
3139.	Red Violin and			
	Music Sheet c.	12-1/2x9-1/2	AP	1. 25
3140.	Regatta on Thames	20 x 24	CFA	15. 00
3141.	Regatta c.	20 x 24	PENN	1. 50
		12 x 28	AP	7. 50
	c.	7 x 9	AP	1. 00
3142.	Regatta, 1938	11-1/2 x 29	NYGS	12. 00
3143.	Regatta at Cowes			
	c.	8 x 10	NYGS	. 50
3144.	Regatta at			
	Deauville	12-1/2x30-1/2	ESH	15. 00
		12 x 30	AR	10. 00
		18-1/2 x 23	ESH	10. 00
	c.	8 x 10	NYGS	. 50
	Detail of No.			
	3144 c.	8 x 10	ESH	1. 00

3145.	Regatta at Henley	19-1/2 x 26	NYGS	12.00
3146.	Roses	17 x 22-1/2	ESH	10.00
3147.	Roses in an Interior c.	9-1/2x12-1/2	AP	1.25
	c.	8 x 10	AP	1.00
		6 x 8	CFA	1.00
3148.	Rowing at Henley	19-1/2 x 26	NYGS	12.00
3149.	Sailboats at Le Havre	14 x 17	CFA	4.00
3150.	Sailboats in Normandy	12-1/2x30-1/2	ESH	15.00
3151.	St. Jeannet c.	20 x 24	PENN	1.50
3152.	San Giorgio Maggiore c.	20 x 24	PENN	1.50
3153.	Seafront at Nice	15 x 18-1/2	NYGS	7.50
3154.	Seascape c.	9-1/2x12-1/2	AP	1.25
	c.	7 x 9	AP	1.00
3155.	Self-Portrait of the Artist with his Model	16-1/2x21-1/2	NYGS	10.00
3156.	The Square, St. Cloud	24 x 19-1/2	NYGS	10.00
3157.	Stands at St. Cloud c.	9-1/2x12-1/2	AP	1.25
3158.	Strand and Casino of Nizza	15 x 18	ESH	10.00
3159.	Syracuse	18-1/2 x 25	NYGS	15.00
3160.	Toledo	6 x 8	CFA	1.00
3161.	Track No. 1	13 x 18	AR	6.00
3162.	Track No. 2	13 x 18	AR	6.00
3163.	Tulips	19 x 25	AA	12.00
3164.	Tulips and Anemones c.	8 x 10	AP	1.00
		6 x 8	CFA	1.00
3165.	United Nations Headquarters, New York	19-1/2 x 25	UNICEF	10.00
3166.	Vase of Anemones c.	23 x 18	HNA	5.95
3167.	Le Vernissage (The Gallery)	19 x 26	CFA	15.00
3168.	La Vie en Rose c.	9-1/2x12-1/2	AP	1.25
	c.	8 x 10	AP	1.00
		6 x 8	CFA	1.00
3169.	Village Garden	19-1/2x26-1/2	NYGS	12.00
3170.	Volubilis	14 x 10-1/2	NYGS	16.00
3171.	Yacht at Le Havre	18-1/2 x 22	ESH	10.00
3172.	Yacht Basin c.	8 x 10	ESH	1.00
3173.	Yachts at Deauville	14 x 18	CFA	7.50
	c.	7 x 9	AP	1.00

DULLBERG, HEINZ (German Contemporary)

3174.	Horses on the Shore	22 x 35-1/2	ESH	Cv. 18.00

DUNBAR, P.
3175. Off San Francisco   24 x 30   NYGS   12. 00
DUNLOP, RONALD OSSERY (Irish, 1894-)
3176. Conway   19 x 22-1/2   ESH   15. 00
3177. Sailing Boats at
       Itchenor   19-1/2 x 28   NYGS   12. 00
DUPLESSIS, JOSEPH S. (French, 1725-1802)
3178. Benjamin Franklin   22 x 18   NYGS   12. 00
DUPRE, JULIEN (French, 1851-1910)
3179. Gathering the Hay   18-1/2 x 25   NYGS   10. 00
DURAN, R.
3180. Cadaques   20 x 44   RL   20. 00
DURANCAMPS, F. R. (Spanish Contemporary)
3181. Bulls of Loja   17 x 40-1/2   RL   15. 00
3182. Toros en Portale   24 x 36   RL   20. 00
DURAND, ASHER BROWN (American, 1796-1886)
3183. Catskill Mountains
       near Shandaken   16-1/2 x 24   NYGS   10. 00
3184. Day of Rest   28 x 42   AA   15. 00
3185. Monument Mountain,
       Berkshires   24 x 36   NYGS   16. 00
3186. Summer Afternoon   13 x 20   AA   4. 00
3187. Sunday Morning   24-1/2 x 36   NYGS   16. 00
                           21 x 32   IA   7. 50
                           17-1/2 x 26   NYGS   10. 00
3188. White Mountain
       Scenery   26 x 39   AA   15. 00
DURAND-CHAPRON
3189. Caravelle   NYGS   18. 00
3190. Marine   22-1/2 x 13   NYGS   15. 00
DURER, ALBRECHT (German, 1471-1528)
3191. Adoration of the
       Magi   11 x 13   IA   3. 00
3192. The All Holy   22 x 20   IA   18. 00
3193. The Apostles St. John
       and St. Peter   37 x 27   NYGS   36. 00
                           27 x 10   CFA   10. 00
3194. The Apostles St. Paul
       and St. Mark   37 x 27   NYGS   36. 00
                           27 x 10   CFA   10. 00
3195. A Bunch of Violets 5 x 4   AR   3. 00
3196. Castle Court,
       Innsbruck   14-1/2x10-1/2   AR   5. 00
3197. Celandine, Study   11-1/2 x 6   AR   4. 00
3198. Christ on the Cross 12-1/2x8-1/2   AR   3. 50
3199. Columbine, Study   14 x 11-1/2   AR   4. 00
3200. Courtyard of
       Innsbruck   14-1/2x10-1/2   AR   5. 00
3201. Covered Bridge,
       Nurnberg   6 x 13   AR   4. 00
3202. Four Apostles   c. 9 x 7   AP   1. 00
3203. Hare   c. 9 x 7   AP   . 50

3204.	Head of an Angel	10 x 8	CFA	6.00
3205.	Head of an Apostle	11-1/2x9-1/2	AR	3.00
3206.	Head of Christ	10 x 8	CFA	6.00
3207.	Impenitent Thief	12-1/2x6-1/2	AR	3.50
3208.	Iris	20-1/2 x 12	AR	7.50
3209.	Large Group of Plants	16 x 12	CFA	5.00
3210.	Lavender	10 x 8	CFA	4.00
3211.	Little House by a Pond	7 x 9	AR	4.00
3212.	Little Owl	8 x 5-1/2	AR	3.50
3213.	Madonna c.	10 x 8	NYGS	.50
3214.	Madonna of the Iris c.	10 x 8	ESH	1.00
3215.	Mounted Knight	16 x 13	AR	5.00
3216.	Nurnberg from the West	6-1/2 x 14	AR	4.00
3217.	Nurnberg Wife in Ball Dress	12 x 8	CFA	4.00
3218.	Nurnberg Wife in Church Dress	12 x 8	CFA	4.00
3219.	Nurnberg Wife in House Dress	12 x 8	CFA	4.00
3220.	Pansies	11 x 6	AR	4.00
3221.	Penitent Thief	12-1/2x6-1/2	AR	3.50
3222.	Peonies	15 x 12	AR	7.50
3223.	Portrait of the Artist at Age 13	11 x 7	AR	3.00
3224.	Portrait of the Artist as a Young Man c.	10 x 8	NYGS	.50
3225.	Portrait of the Artist's Father	20 x 16	AR	12.00
		14 x 11	IA	3.00
3226.	Portrait of the Artist's Wife, Agnes Drawn	13 x 10	AR	1.50
	as St. Anne	15-1/2x11-1/2	AR	5.00
3227.	Portrait of Emperor Maximilian I	21 x 19	NYGS	10.00
		15 x 12	CFA	5.00
3228.	Portrait of Ulrich Varnbuhler	16 x 13	CFA	5.00
3229.	Praying Hands (Hands of a Praying Apostle) Sepia	17 x 12	IA	2.50
		11-1/2 x 8	AR	3.00
	Sepia	11 x 7-1/2	IA	1.00
		10-1/2x7-1/2	IA	1.50
	c.	9 x 7	AP	.35
3230.	The Quay at Antwerp	8 x 11	AR	3.00
3231.	Reunion of the Saints	22 x 20	AR	15.00

3232.	St. Jerome	16-1/2 x 11	AR	5.00
3233.	St. John's Church in Nurnberg	11-1/2 x 17	AR	7.50
3234.	Self-Portrait c.	23 x 18	HNA	5.95
		20-1/2 x 16	PENN	1.50
		19 x 14-1/2	ESH	10.00
		14 x 11	IA	3.00
		11 x 7-1/2	IA	3.00
3235.	Small Group of Plants	5 x 6	AR	3.00
3236.	Squirrels	9 x 8-1/2	NYGS	5.00
		9 x 8	CFA	1.00
3237.	Study of a Dead Roller	11 x 8	AR	3.50
3238.	Sunset	10 x 14	AR	7.50
3239.	Three Linden Trees	14-1/2 x 9-1/2	AR	5.00
3240.	Three Riders Attacked by Death	12 x 17-1/2	AR	5.00
3241.	View of Innsbruck	5 x 7	CFA	3.00
3242.	View of Trient	9 x 14	AR	3.50
3243.	Virgin Surrounded by Animals (Vierge aux Animaus)	12-1/2x9-1/2	AR	4.00
		8 x 7-1/2	NYGS	4.00
3244.	Wing of a Roller	8 x 8	AR	3.50
		6 x 6	CFA	3.50
3245.	Woman in Dance Costume c.	10 x 8	NYGS	.50
3246.	Woman's Portrait c.	9 x 7	AP	.25
3247.	Young Field Hare, Study	10 x 9	AR	3.50
		9-1/2 x 8	NYGS	7.50

DURRIE, GEORGE HARVEY (American, 1820-1863)

3248.	A Christmas Party	25 x 36	AA	15.00
3249.	Home to Thanks-giving	14-1/2x24-1/2	NYGS	7.50

DURRIEU

3250.	Adrienne	29-1/2 x 10	ESH	6.00
3251.	Pierre	20-1/2 x 10	ESH	6.00
3252.	Youth	23-1/2 x 16	ESH	6.00

DUSART, CORNELIS (Dutch, 1660-1704)

3253.	Peasants Outside an Inn	13-1/2 x 11	NYGS	4.00

DUSSO

3254.	Flores del Destino I and II	40 x 15	AK	ea.	10.00
		20 x 7-1/2	AK	ea.	2.00
3255.	Mayan Prince	40 x 15	AK		10.00
		20 x 7-1/2	AK		2.00
3256.	Mayan Princess	40 x 15	AK		10.00
		20 x 7-1/2	AK		2.00

DUTTON, HAROLD JOHN (English Contemporary)

3257.	Cornwallis	15-1/2 x 21	AA	12.00
3258.	Cosmos	15-1/2 x 21	AA	12.00
3259.	Mirage	15-1/2 x 21	AA	12.00
3260.	Shannon	15-1/2 x 21	AA	12.00

DUVAL

3261.	Chartres	c. 10 x 8	ESH	1.00

DUVENECK, FRANK (American, 1848-1919)

3262.	Whistling Boy	c. 7 x 9	AP	.50

DYCK, (SIR) ANTHONY VAN See VAN DYCK

DYF, MARCEL (French, 1899-)

3263.	At Leisure	24 x 20	DAC		7.50
		12 x 10	DAC		2.50
3264.	Autumn's Bounty	16 x 19	IA		5.00
3265.	Claudine	24 x 20	DAC		7.50
		12 x 10	DAC		2.50
3266.	Flowers from My Garden	20 x 16	IA		5.00
3267.	Garden Flowers	24 x 20	DAC		7.50
3268.	Girl with a Bird-cage	18-1/2 x 15	IA		5.00
3269.	Girl with a Mando-lin	18-1/2 x 15	IA		5.00
3270.	Orchard	20 x 24	DAC		7.50
3271.	Peonies and Roses	24 x 20	DAC		7.50
3272.	Portrait of Claudine	24 x 20	RL		10.00
3273.	Reverie	24 x 20	RL		12.50
3274.	River Valley	20 x 24	DAC		7.50
3275.	The Sonnet	21-1/2 x 18	RL		15.00
3276.	Springtime Symphony	20 x 16	IA		5.00
3277.	Summer's Offering	16 x 19	IA		5.00
3278.	Vanity	24 x 20	DAC		7.50
		12 x 10	DAC		2.50
3279.	White Gloves	24 x 20	DAC		7.50
		12 x 10	DAC		2.50

DZIGURSKI, ALEX

3280.	After the Storm	24 x 48	AA		15.00
3281.	Golden Sunset	24 x 40	AA		12.00
3282.	Imperia, Italy	16 x 20	IA		3.00
3283.	Landscapes (4)	24 x 40	AK	ea.	6.00
3284.	Autumn Morn	18 x 30	AK	ea.	4.00
3285.	Pine Brook				
3286.	Sentinel of the West				
3287.	Western Vista				
3288.	Majestic Tetons	18 x 30	AK		4.00
3289.	Nature's Majesty	18 x 30	AK		4.00
3290.	Pacific Breakers	24 x 40	AA		12.00
3291.	Positano, Italy	16 x 20	IA		3.00
3292.	Rock-Bound Coast	24 x 48	AA		15.00
3293.	White Caps	24 x 48	AA		15.00

E

EAKINS,	THOMAS (American,	1844-1916)		
3294.	The Actress	10 x 7	NYGS	.50
3295.	The Biglen Brothers			
	Racing c.	18 x 23	HNA	5.95
3296.	Cowboy Singing	21 x 17	AA	8.00
3297.	The Fairman Rogers			
	Four-In-Hand c.	18 x 23	HNA	5.95
3298.	Home Ranch	17 x 21	AA	8.00
3299.	John Biglen in a			
	Single Scull	24 x 15-1/2	NYGS	12.00
		9 x 6	NYGS	.50
3300.	Max Schmitt in a			
	Single Scull	20-1/2 x 30	NYGS	16.00
3301.	Pushing for Rail	14 x 21-1/2	NYGS	7.50
3302.	Sailboats (Hikers)			
	Racing on the			
	Delaware	12-1/2x18-1/2	NYGS	7.50
3303.	Sailing	12-1/2x18-1/2	NYGS	7.50
3304.	Starting Out After			
	Rail c.	18 x 23	HNA	5.95
3305.	Turning Stake Boat	17 x 25	PENN	1.50
3306.	Will Schuster and			
	Black-Man Going			
	Shooting, 1876	19 x 26	NYGS	15.00
		7 x 9-1/2	NYGS	1.00
EARL,	MAUDE (English, Ac.	1884-1934)		
3307.	Golden Retriever	25 x 30	AA	10.00
EARL,	RALPH (American,	1751-1801)		
3308.	William Carpenter	23-1/2x17-1/2	NYGS	12.00
EASTMAN,	JOHN (Canadian [Res.	England] Contemporary)		
3309.	Cordon Bleu and			
	Camelia	21 x 14	ESH	6.00
3310.	Dipper	21 x 14	ESH	6.00
EBBINGHAUS,	KARL (German,	1872-1950)		
3311.	Sacred Heart of			
	Jesus	39-1/2x27-1/2	IA	10.00
		29 x 21-1/2	IA	5.00
EBERHARDT See MEYER-EBERHARDT				
EDE, BASIL				
3312.	Birds (6)	15 x 11	ESH	ea. 3.00
3313.	Blue Tit and Pussy Willow			
3314.	Cock-Chaffinch and Japanese Cherry			
3315.	Goldfinch and Apple Blossom			
3316.	Great Tit and Forsythia			
3317.	Nuthatch and Silver Birch			
3318.	Robin and Wild Cherry			
EDEN				
3319.	Children's Portraits			
	(4)	14 x 11	DAC	ea. 3.50

		10 x 8	DAC	ea.	1.50
		8 x 6	DAC	ea.	1.00
3320.	Halloween Series				
	(10)	25 x 10	DAC	ea.	5.00
		15 x 6	DAC	ea.	3.00
		10 x 4	DAC	ea.	1.50
3321.	Ragga-Moppets				
	(4)	25 x 10	DAC	ea.	5.00
		15 x 6	DAC	ea.	3.00

EDWARDS, BEVERLY

3322.	Interiors (Homespun)				
	(4)	12 x 16	AK	ea.	2.50
		8 x 10	AK	ea.	1.25

EDWARDS, CARLOTTA

3323.	Ballet Practice	12 x 15	ESH		5.00
3324.	Ballet School	18 x 22	ESH		10.00
3325.	Le Cygne				
	(Opening Movement)	24 x 20	ESH		10.00
3326.	Le Cygne				
	(Closing Movement)	24 x 20	ESH		10.00
3327.	Dance of the Snow-				
	flakes	24 x 30	ESH		12.00
3328.	M. Fonteyn as				
	Ondine	24 x 20	ESH		10.00
3329.	M. Fonteyn in Les				
	Sylphides	22-1/2 x 18	ESH		10.00
3330.	M. Fonteyn and R.				
	Nureyev	24 x 20	ESH		10.00
3331.	Giselle	24 x 36	AS		7.50
3332.	Giselle				
	(M. Fonteyne)	20 x 24	ESH		10.00
		12 x 15	ESH		5.00
3333.	Giselle, Act II	16 x 20	ESH		10.00
3334.	Markova in Mazurka	20 x 24	ESH		12.00
3335.	Markova in Les				
	Sylphides	24 x 30	ESH		12.00
3336.	Memories of				
	Strauss	24 x 30	ESH		12.00
3337.	Nocturne "Les				
	Sylphides"	16 x 20	ESH		10.00
		12-1/2 x 15	ESH		5.00
3338.	Nutcracker	18 x 22	ESH		10.00
		12-1/2 x 15	ESH		5.00
3339.	Printemps à Vienne	18-1/2 x 22	ESH		10.00
		12 x 15	ESH		5.00
3340.	Swan Lake	24 x 36	AS		7.50
3341.	Swan Lake	15 x 12	ESH		5.00
3342.	Les Sylphides	24 x 36	AS		7.50
3343.	Symphonie Fant.				
	Encoul	24 x 36	AS		7.50
3344.	Ulanova in Giselle	20 x 24	ESH		10.00
3345.	La Valse	18-1/2 x 22	ESH		10.00

		18 x 22-1/2	AS		7. 50
		12 x 15	ESH		5. 00
3346.	Vilia	24 x 36	AS		7. 50
EDWARDS, LIONEL D. R. (English, 1877-)					
3347.	Enfield Hunt	12 x 17	ESH		5. 00
3348.	Hare	14 x 20			
3349.	Otter	14 x 20	CFA		5. 00
3350.	Stag	14 x 20	CFA		5. 00
EDWARDS, MAGDALENE					
3351.	Botanical Studies (8)	12 x 9	CFA	ea.	5. 00
EDZARD, DIETZ (German, 1872-1950)					
3352.	Angelica	20 x 16	AA		7. 50
3353.	At the Lodge	27 x 22	CFA		12. 00
		16 x 12	CFA		3. 00
3354.	At the Opera	27 x 22	CFA		12. 00
		16 x 12	CFA		3. 00
3355.	La Chanteuse	16 x 12	CFA		3. 00
3356.	Christine	20 x 16	AA		7. 50
3357.	Le Debut	16 x 12	CFA		3. 00
3358.	Fleurs Venitiennes	24 x 19	ESH		10. 00
3359.	Flowers and Music (2)	17 x 9	ESH	ea.	6. 00
		7 x 3-1/2	ESH	ea.	1. 00
3360.	Flowers and Music with Piano c.	18 x 23	HNA		5. 95
3361.	Flowers and Music with Violin c.	18 x 23	HNA		5. 95
3362.	Le Grand Ballet c.	20 x 24	PENN		1. 50
3363.	Grand Bouquet de Fleurs	24 x 19	ESH		10. 00
3364.	On the Banks of the Seine	18-1/2 x 23	ESH		10. 00
3365.	Les Parisiennes	17 x 21	CAC		15. 00
3366.	Place de la Concorde	28-1/2x23-1/2	NYGS		15. 00
3367.	Regate sur la Seine c.	20 x 24	PENN		1. 50
EGG, AUGUSTUS LEOPOLD (English, 1816-1863)					
3368.	The Travelling Companions	21 x 26	NYGS		15. 00
EGYPT					
3369.	Amenhopis (Black Granite Sculpture)	15 x 11	CFA		5. 00
3370.	Egyptian Cat	11 x 14	CFA		5. 00
3371.	First Sarcophagus (Treasure of Tutank-hamen	8 x 10-1/2	ESH		1. 00
3372.	Gold Funeral Mask (Treasure of Tutank-hamen)	10-1/2 x 8	ESH		1. 00

3373.	Horus the Hawk c.	7 x 9	AP		. 25
3374.	King Kephren				
	(Fourth Dynasty)	15 x 11	CFA		5. 00
3375.	King Tutankhamen, Golden				
	Effigy (14th Century				
	BC)	21-1/2 x 19	NYGS		10. 00
3376.	Lady Tent-Shenat,				
	Painted Wooden Stele				
	c.	10 x 8	ESH		1. 00
3377.	Musicians and Dancers				
	(Mural) c.	18 x 23	HNA		5. 95
3378.	Queen Nefertiti c.	9 x 7	AP		. 50
3379.	Sacred Cat				
	(Sculpture) c.	9 x 7	AP		. 25
3380.	Tomb Decoration				
	c.	8 x 10	ESH		1. 00
3381.	UNESCO World Art				
	Series (32)	11 x 14	NYGS	ea.	2. 00
	or	14 x 11			
3382.	Woman Carrying				
	Offerings c.	9 x 7	AP		1. 00
3383.	Woman of Amarna	11 x 15	CFA		5. 00

EHEMANN, HANS (German)

3384.	Algiers	20 x 12	ESH	Pr.	4. 00
3385.	Autumn in Bavaria	23-1/2x31-1/2	ESH	Pr.	10. 00
3386.	Flower Market in				
	Italy	12 x 20	ESH	Pr.	4. 00
3387.	In the Bavarian				
	Moorland	23-1/2x31-1/2	ESH	Pr.	10. 00
3388.	Mallorca	20 x 12	ESH	Pr.	4. 00
3389.	Sailing Harbour of				
	Cannes	12 x 20	ESH	Pr.	4. 00
3390.	Springtime in				
	Bavaria	23-1/2x31-1/2	ESH	Pr.	10. 00
3391.	Street in Marra-				
	kesch	20 x 12	ESH	Pr.	4. 00
3392.	Sunflowers on Red				
	Background	27-1/2 x 20	ESH	Pr.	8. 00
3393.	Venice	20 x 12	ESH	Pr.	4. 00

EICHHORN, ALFRED (Austrian, 1909-)

3394.	The Isle	17 x 26	CFA	15. 00

EICHSTAEDT, RUDOLPH (German, 1857-1926)

3395.	Christ in Emmaus	18-1/2x26-1/2	IA	7. 50

EILSHEMIUS, LOUIS MICHEL (American, 1864-)

3396.	Afternoon Wind,			
	1899 c.	8 x 10	NYGS	. 50
3397.	Village near Delaware			
	Watergap	18 x 27	PENN	1. 50

EINBECK

3398.	Monk--Cellar Man	12 x 9-1/2	ESH	Pr.	2. 00

EISENDIECK, SUZANNE (German Contemporary)

3399.	Nicole c.	24 x 20	PENN	1. 50

3400.	Nicole et			
	Nicolette	22 x 26	DAC	7. 50
	c.	20 x 24	PENN	1. 50
3401.	Sunday at Sannois	20 x 24	CAC	12. 00
EISENMAYER, ERNEST				
3402.	Study for Sculpture	21 x 14	NYGS	10. 00
ELDER, JOHN A. (American, 1833-1895)				
3403.	General T. J.			
	Jackson	30 x 22	NYGS	12. 00
		20 x 14-1/2	NYGS	6. 00
		14 x 10	NYGS	3. 00
		8 x 6	NYGS	1. 00
3404.	General Robert E.			
	Lee	30 x 22	NYGS	12. 00
		20 x 14-1/2	NYGS	6. 00
		14 x 10	NYGS	3. 00
		8 x 6	NYGS	1. 00
ELFORD, VICTOR (English Contemporary)				
3405.	Golden Evening	24 x 36	RL	12. 50
3406.	Henley Royal			
	Regatta	18 x 27	RL	7. 50
EL GRECO See GRECO, EL				
ELIOTT				
3407.	Comic Golf (4)	12 x 9	CFA	ea. 4. 00
ELLIS, DEAN (American Contemporary)				
3408.	Evening, Spain	20 x 30	NYGS	12. 00
ELMIGER, FREDERICK				
3409.	Autos, Early (6)	9 x 11	DAC	ea. 1. 00
		6 x 8	DAC	ea. . 50
		5 x 7	DAC	ea. . 30
3410.	Guards, Americana			
	(4)	15 x 6	DAC	ea. 1. 50
3411.	Regalia, Period			
	(8)	14 x 5	DAC	ea. 1. 00
3412.	Soldiers, Continental			
	(4)	14 x 5	DAC	ea. 1. 00
		9 x 4	DAC	ea. . 35
3413.	Treasure Maps (4)	11 x 14	DAC	ea. 2. 50
ELSOCHT, ROBERT				
3414.	Boulevard	28 x 36	IA	12. 00
ELWELL, FREDERICK WILLIAM (English, 1870-)				
3415.	Snapdragons	18 x 22	ESH	7. 50
EMERY, LESLIE (American Contemporary)				
3416.	Child Song	28-1/2 x 14	IA	7. 50
3417.	Children of Erin			
	(Donegal)	28-1/2 x 19	IA	10. 00
3418.	Golf Clowns (8)	12-1/2 x 10	IA	ea. 2. 00
3419.	Immaculate Heart of			
	Mary	23 x 16	IA	4. 00
		19 x 13	IA	3. 00
		12-1/2 x 9	IA	1. 00
3420.	The Phoenix	21-1/2 x 16	IA	7. 50

3421.	Tender Burden		24-1/2 x 18	IA		6.00
3422.	This is My Love		19 x 24	IA		7.50

ENDE, HANS (German, 1864-1918)

| 3423. | Twilight | | 18 x 24 | CFA | | 7.50 |

ENGEL, NISSAN (Israeli Contemporary)

3424.	Abi		16 x 12	NYGS		6.00
3425.	Anima		16 x 12	NYGS		6.00
3426.	Don Quixote		28 x 21	NYGS		15.00
3427.	El Picador		21 x 30	NYGS		16.00
3428.	Karajan		19 x 12	NYGS		6.00

ENGELHARDT, EDNA

| 3429. | Autumn Tranquility | | 24 x 48 | DAC | | 10.00 |

ENNESS, A. W.

| 3430. | Dahlias | | 13 x 11 | ESH | | 2.00 |

ENRICO, ALDO

3431.	La Gitana (4)		24 x 20	DAC	ea.	7.50
			12 x 10	DAC	ea.	2.00
3432.	Paris Twilight		24 x 48	DAC		10.00

ENSOR, JAMES (Belgian, 1860-1949)

3433.	Blue Flask	c.	18 x 23	HNA		5.95
3434.	Carnival		20-1/2 x 28	NYGS		12.00
			7 x 9	NYGS		.50
3435.	Masks	c.	16 x 12	AP		3.00
3436.	Tribulations of					
	St. Anthony	c.	8 x 10	MMA		.35

ENSTROM, IRENE (American Contemporary)

3437.	Grace		16 x 21	IA		3.00
			10 x 13-1/2	IA		2.00

EPSTEIN, (SIR) JACOB (American [Res. England] 1880-)

| 3438. | Poppies | | 17 x 22-1/2 | ESH | | 10.00 |

ERBSLOH, ADOLF (German, 1881-1947)

| 3439. | In the Alps | | 12 x 16 | ESH | | 4.00 |

ERNI, HANS (Swiss Contemporary)

| 3440. | Two Horses | c. | 18 x 23 | HNA | | 5.95 |

ERNST, MAX (German Contemporary)

3441.	Flying Geese	c.	20 x 24	PENN		1.50
3442.	Petrified City		19 x 23	NYGS		18.00

ESCHBACH, PAUL (French, 1881-)

3443.	Off Concarneau		20 x 24	CAC		6.00
3444.	Winter Sunshine		23 x 28	CAC		12.00

ESPOSITO, GAETANO (Italian, 1858-1911)

| 3445. | Sea View of Naples | | 9-1/2 x 15 | AS | | 3.25 |

ESTEVE, MAURICE (French Contemporary)

| 3446. | Composition, 1956 | | 18-1/2x22-1/2 | ESH | | 10.00 |

ETHIOPIA

3447.	UNESCO World Art					
	Series (32)		11 x 14 or			
			14 x 11	NYGS	ea.	2.00

ETNIER

| 3448. | Adolescence | c. | 7 x 9 | AP | | .25 |

ETRUSCAN ART

3449.	Amphora with Black					
	Figures		15 x 11	NYGS		4.00

3450.	Black, Figured				
	Amphora	15 x 11	NYGS		4. 00
3451.	Cithera Player (2)	15 x 11	IA	ea.	3. 00
3452.	Conversation Piece				
	(Fresco)	16 x 22	AR		12. 00
3453.	Dance Scene	11 x 15	IA		3. 00
3454.	Dancer (2)	15 x 11	IA	ea.	3. 00
3455.	Dancers	11 x 15	IA		3. 00
3456.	Family Scene	11 x 15	IA		3. 00
	Detail of No.				
	3456	15 x 11	IA		3. 00
3457.	Fight Between Greeks				
	and Amazons	10 x 15	IA		3. 00
3458.	Flute Player c.	23 x 18	HNA		5. 95
3459.	Flute Player	15 x 11	IA		3. 00
3460.	Flute Player and				
	Dancer	11 x 15	IA		3. 00
3461.	Fresco with Horses	9 x 33	NYGS		12. 00
3462.	Funeral Chorus	6 x 15	IA		3. 00
3463.	Horseman (2)	15 x 11	IA	ea.	3. 00
3464.	Lyre Player	22-1/2 x 18	ESH		10. 00
3465.	Musicians (Tomb of the				
	Leopards, Tarquinia)	15 x 30-1/2	NYGS		12. 00
3466.	The Offering	17 x 22-1/2	ESH		10. 00
3467.	Pair of Winged				
	Horses	15 x 11	NYGS		4. 00
3468.	Pipe Player c.	10 x 8	ESH		1. 00
3469.	Poster: Dancer	29 x 23	CFA		15. 00
3470.	Red-Figured Crater	15 x 11	NYGS		4. 00
3471.	Red-Figured Vase	15 x 11	NYGS		4. 00
3472.	Young Flute Player				
	and a Man (Tarquinia)				
	c.	22 x 17-1/2	AS		4. 00

EULALIE

3473.	Dog's World (4)	12 x 9	DAC	ea.	1. 50

EURICH, RICHARD (English Contemporary)

3474.	Mary Eliza	14-1/2 x 22	ESH		6. 00
3475.	Remembrance	18 x 20	ESH		10. 00

EUSTACHIO, (FRA) Italian, 1473-1555)

3476.	King David Adoring				
	(Minature)	9 x 8	IA		1. 50

EVANS, G. M.

3477.	Didst Thou Play?	8 x 15	ESH		5. 00

EVERETT, ETHEL (English Contemporary)

3478.	Little Lamb	9-1/2 x 7	ESH		2. 00

EVERGOOD, PHILIP (American, 1901-1963)

3479.	Child and Sparrow				
	(B & W)	21 x 15	AP		6. 00
3480.	Lily and the Sparrows				
	c.	23 x 18	HNA		5. 95
3481.	New Lazarus, 1949				
	c.	8 x 10	NYGS		. 50

3482. Sunny Side of the
       Street   c.   20 x 24   PENN   1. 50

                              F

FABRIANO, GENTILE See GENTILE DA FABRIANO
FAED, JOHN (Scotch, 1819-1902)
  3483. Washington on the Field
         of Trenton   26 x 20   CAC   10. 00
                           20 x 16   CAC   5. 00
FAISTAUER, ANTON (Austrian, 1887-1930)
  3484. Bunch of Flowers   21-1/2x15-1/2 AJ   5. 00
FALENS, KAREL VAN (Flemish, 1683-1733)
  3485. Alte de Chasseurs 14 x 18   CFA   12. 00
  3486. Le Chasseur Fortune 16 x 22   CFA   20. 00
  3487. Rendezvous de
         Chasse   16 x 22   CFA   20. 00
FALICK, MURRAY
  3488. Pistols, Early American
         (6)   5 x 8   IA   ea. 1. 50
FALK, HANS (Swiss Contemporary)
  3489. Three Seasons   20 x 48   CFA   30. 00
FALTER
  3490. Boyhood Days c.   20 x 24   PENN   1. 50
  3491. Horse and Buggy
         Days   c.   20 x 24   PENN   1. 50
  3492. Summer Days   c.   20 x 24   PENN   1. 50
FANTIN-LATOUR, HENRI (IGNACE HENRI JEAN THEODORE)
(FRENCH, 1836-1904)
  3493. Bouquet de Julienne
         et Fruits   19 x 18   IA   6. 00
  3494. Chrysanthemums c. 22 x 17-1/2 AS   4. 00
  3495. Chrysanthemums c. 18 x 23   HNA   5. 95
  3496. Flowers and Fruit 28 x 24   CFA   15. 00
                           23 x 18   PENN   1. 50
  3497. Portrait of Sonia c. 23 x 18   HNA   5. 95
  3498. Roses and Blue Jug 11 x 13   IA   3. 00
  3499. Still Life   c.   8 x 10   CFA   2. 00
  3500. Still Life, 1866   22 x 27   NYGS   16. 00
  3501. Still Life--Corner
         of a Table   16 x 20   CFA   7. 50
FATTORI, GIOVANNI (Italian, 1825-1908)
  3502. Repose   9 x 19   IA   3. 00
  3503. Staffato   11 x 15   AS   3. 25
  3504. The Terrace of
         Palmieri   5-1/2x15-1/2 AS   3. 25
FAUSETT, DEAN (WILLIAM DEAN) (American Contemporary)
  3505. Ancient Maple   25 x 30   AA   12. 00
  3506. Autumn in Vermont 16 x 20   AA   3. 50
  3507. Big Elms   16 x 20   NYGS   7. 50
                          11 x 14   NYGS   3. 00

3508.	Colorado Ranch	24 x 39	CFA		15. 00
		16 x 24	CFA		6. 00
3509.	Derby View,				
	Vermont	21-1/2 x 36	AA		3. 50
3510.	Freshly Fallen				
	Snow	24 x 30	PENN		1. 95
		12 x 16	PENN		1. 00
3511.	Gold of Autumn	24 x 30	PENN		1. 95
3512.	Haying Time	16 x 20	NYGS		7. 50
		11 x 14	NYGS		3. 00
3513.	Height of Summer	24 x 30	PENN		1. 95
		12 x 16	PENN		1. 00
3514.	Midsummer	24 x 36	AA		12. 00
3515.	Ripening Grain	24 x 30	PENN		1. 95
		12 x 16	PENN		1. 00
3516.	River Village	23-1/2 x 36	IA		12. 00
3517.	Road to the Hills	25 x 30	AA		12. 00
3518.	Vermont Pastorale	16 x 20	AA		3. 50
FAUST,	HEINRICH (German,	1843-1891)			
3519.	Ballet on Blue	16 x 31-1/2	ESH	Pr.	8. 00
3520.	Bunch of Apple-				
	Blossoms	20 x 27-1/2	ESH	Pr.	8. 00
3521.	Bunch of Autumn				
	Flowers	23-1/2 x 20	ESH	Pr.	8. 00
		16 x 12	ESH	Pr.	3. 00
3522.	Donkey	16 x 10	ESH	Pr.	4. 00
3523.	Foal	16 x 10	ESH	Pr.	4. 00
3524.	Greek Fishing-				
	Boats	20 x 27-1/2	ESH	Pr.	8. 00
3525.	Horses on Red				
	Background	16 x 31-1/2	ESH	Pr.	8. 00
3526.	Hunting on Horse-				
	back	16 x 31-1/2	ESH	Pr.	8. 00
3527.	Lute-Player	20 x 16	ESH	Pr.	8. 00
3528.	Mare with Foal	23-1/2 x 20	ESH	Pr.	10. 00
3529.	Monk Drinking Beer	12 x 9	ESH	Pr.	2. 00
3530.	Puszta Horses	14 x 27-1/2	ESH	Pr.	8. 00
3531.	Quiet Harbour	14 x 27-1/2	ESH	Pr.	8. 00
3532.	Rest on the Lake	18 x 23-1/2	ESH	Pr.	8. 00
3533.	Sunday Horseman	20 x 12	ESH	Pr.	4. 00
3534.	Sunny Forest	23-1/2 x 20	ESH	Pr.	8. 00
3535.	Taste of Beer	20 x 23-1/2	ESH	Pr.	10. 00
3536.	Three Horses on				
	Yellow Background	8 x 16	ESH	Pr.	3. 00
3537.	Trotting Horses	16 x 31-1/2	ESH	Pr.	8. 00
3538.	Village in Twilight	20 x 27-1/2	ESH	Pr.	8. 00
3539.	Wolfs in Hunting	16 x 31-1/2	ESH	Pr.	8. 00
FAWSETT,	GEORGE (American,	1877-)			
3540.	Ducks (6)	12 x 16	CFA	ea.	6. 00
FEI See	CHENG-WU-FEI				
FEIBUSCH,	HANS (German,	1898-)			
3541.	Mandrill and				
	Mangabeys	19 x 30	CFA		5. 00

FEININGER, LYONEL (American, 1871-1956)

3542.	Ascending Balloon			
	c.	15 x 11	AP	1.00
	c.	10 x 8	AP	1.00
3543.	Barefoot Church in			
	Halle	24-1/2 x 31	NYGS	20.00
3544.	Before the Rain	17 x 31	CFA	18.00
3545.	Big Cutters	15 x 28	ESH	12.00
3546.	Bird Cloud	17 x 28	NYGS	16.00
3547.	Blue Coast	16 x 30	NYGS	15.00
3548.	Blue Marine	18 x 32	NYGS	15.00
3549.	Blue Sails	18 x 25	NYGS	16.00
3550.	Blue Skyscrapers			
	c.	15 x 11	AP	1.00
	c.	10 x 8	AP	1.00
3551.	Cathedral in Halle	20-1/2x16-1/2	PENN	1.50
		20 x 16	AP	10.00
		13-1/2 x 12	AP	1.00
	c.	10 x 8	AP	1.00
3552.	The Church	23-1/2 x 19	PENN	1.50
3553.	The Church	16 x 25-1/2	PENN	1.50
		14 x 18	NYGS	15.00
3554.	Church at Gelmeroda			
	c.	24 x 20	PENN	1.50
3555.	Church in Erfurt	31 x 24-1/2	IA	18.00
3556.	Church of the			
	Minorites	19-1/2x16-1/2	IA	4.00
3557.	Church of Nieder-			
	grunstadt	18 x 24	PENN	1.50
3558.	Fisher off the			
	Coast	18 x 35	IA	10.00
3559.	Fishing Fleet	13-1/2 x 22	AA	10.00
3560.	Gelmeroda, 1926	27-1/2 x 22	NYGS	18.00
3561.	Gelmeroda VIII c.	8 x 10	NYGS	.50
3562.	Gelmeroda XII c.	23 x 18	HNA	5.95
3563.	Gothic Gables	15 x 24	NYGS	12.00
3564.	Market Church in			
	Halle	30 x 24	IA	18.00
		27-1/2 x 22	NYGS	20.00
		21 x 17	NYGS	6.00
3565.	Mouth of River			
	Rega	19 x 29	ESH	12.00
3566.	Mouth of River			
	Rega III	18-1/2x30-1/2	IA	12.00
3567.	Nermsdorf I	20 x 26-1/2	NYGS	22.00
3568.	Ober-Reissen	17 x 22-1/2	ESH	12.00
3569.	Orange Sails	16-1/2 x 28	IA	15.00
3570.	Peaceful Navigation			
	c.	20 x 24	PENN	1.50
3571.	Pink Cloud II	17 x 30	NYGS	20.00
3572.	Pyramid of Sails	18 x 29	NYGS	20.00
3573.	Sand Dunes and			
	Crescent Moon	16-1/2 x 28	NYGS	15.00

3574.	Sight of a Village	21 x 23-1/2	PENN		1. 50
3575.	Silver Constellation	20 x 16	AP		7. 50
3576.	The Sloop	13-1/2 x 22	AA		10. 00
3577.	Steamer "Odin II",				
	1927	21-1/2 x 32	MMA		12. 00
	c.	8 x 10	MMA		. 35
3578.	Still Life with Jugs,				
	1916	25 x 31	NYGS		18. 00
3579.	Sturmische Einfart				
	(Stormy Arrival	10 x 16	IA		8. 00
3580.	Topsail Schooner	20 x 26	AR		12. 00
3581.	Two Yachts	9-1/2 x 14	IA		8. 00
3582.	Village Street	22-1/2 x 28	NYGS		15. 00
3583.	Western Sea	23 x 29	NYGS		15. 00

FEINRICH

3584.	Girl with Sheep	12 x 9-1/2	ESH	Pr.	2. 00
3585.	Two Dancing Girls	12 x 9-1/2	ESH	Pr.	2. 00

FERGOLA, SALVATORE (Italian, 1799-1877)

3586.	Naples from Poggio-				
	reale	9 x 15	IA		3. 00

FERRANDIZ CASTELLS, JUAN (Spanish, Contemporary)

3587.	Adoration	22-1/2 x 17	NYGS	7. 50
		14 x 10	NYGS	3. 00
3588.	Holy Night	22-1/2 x 17	NYGS	7. 50
		14 x 10	NYGS	3. 00
3589.	Smiling Infancy	12 x 8	ESH	2. 50
3590.	Sweet Babe	12 x 8	ESH	2. 50

FERRARI, FRANCESCO BIANCHI (Italian, 1460-1510)

3591.	Christ in the Gethsemane			
	Garden (Detail)	14 x 11	IA	3. 00

FERRARI, GAUDENZIO (Italian, 1487-1546)

3592.	Adoration of the Magi	9 x 22	AR	4. 00

FERRUZZI, ROBERTO (Italian, 1854-1934)

3593.	Madonnina (Madonna			
	of the Street)	20 x 26	AS	7. 50
		15 x 20	IA	7. 50
		11 x 15	IA	3. 00
		11 x 14-1/2	AS	3. 25
3594.	Madonnina--Detail			
	of No. 3593	26 x 20	IA	10. 00
		23-1/2x18-1/2	IA	7. 50
		21 x 16	NYGS	5. 00
		16 x 12	AS	3. 25
		15x 11	IA	3. 00
		11 x 8-1/2	IA	1. 75
		10 x 8	NYGS	1. 00
		9-1/2 x 7	AS	3. 25

FESSLER, ALBERT

3595.	On the Costa			
	Brava	23 x 31	CFA	15. 00

FETI, DOMENICO (Italian, 1589-1624)

3596.	Prodigal Son	15 x 11	IA	3. 00

3597.	The Veil of			
	Veronica	24 x 20	NYGS	12.00

FEUCHTMAYER, JOSEPH

3598.	Honey Taster	16 x 9	CFA	5.00

FEUERBORN, JOSEPH (American Contemporary)

3599.	Cablecar to China-			
	town	40 x 20	IA	15.00
3600.	Cable Car Turn-			
	about	24 x 18	IA	10.00
3601.	Fisherman's Cove	20 x 40	IA	15.00
3602.	Golden Candles	40 x 20	IA	15.00
3603.	Hong Kong	20 x 40	IA	15.00
3604.	Matador I	36 x 12	IA	12.00
3605.	Matador II	36 x 12	IA	12.00
3606.	Opening Night	20 x 40	IA	15.00
3607.	Rickshaw Traffic,			
	Hong Kong	12 x 36	IA	10.00
3608.	Still Life	20 x 40	IA	15.00
3609.	Still Life with			
	Pineapple	36 x 20	IA	15.00

FIENE, ERNEST (American Contemporary)

3610.	Clown in Front of			
	a Mirror	20 x 16-1/2	PENN	1.50
3611.	New England Farm	16 x 21	NYGS	9.00

FIESOLE, GIOVANNI DA See ANGELICO, FRA

FILDES, SAMUEL LUKE (English, 1844-1927)

3612.	The Doctor	17-1/2 x 26	NYGS	10.00
		12 x 17	CAC	7.50
3613.	H. M. Queen			
	Elizabeth II	20 x 15	CAC	7.50

FILIPEPI, ALESSANDRO See BOTTICHELLI

FINI, LEONOR (Italian [Res. France] Contemporary)

3614.	Livia	31 x 10	NYGS	12.00
3615.	Losange	28 x 18	NYGS	15.00
3616.	Melita	31 x 10	NYGS	12.00
3617.	Two Sisters	25 x 20	CFA	15.00

FINTZ

3618.	Houses	40 x 8	DAC	5.00

FIORENTINO See ROSSO, FIORENTINO

FIORENZO DI LORENZO (Italian, 1440-1525)

3619.	Crucifixion and			
	Saints	15 x 10	IA	3.00
3620.	Miracoli di S.			
	Bernardino	15 x 11	IA	3.00
3621.	Miracoli di S.			
	Bernardino (7)	15 x 10	IA	ea. 3.00

FIORI, FEDERICO See BAROCCIO, IL

FIORI, MARIO DEL (Italian, 1603-1673)

3622.	Fruits and Flowers	4-1/2 x 15	AS	3.25

FIRLE, WALTHER (German, 1859-1935)

3623.	The Fairy Tale	18 x 24	NYGS	7.50
		11 x 14	NYGS	3.00

3624.	Sunday Devotion	22 x 31	CAC		12. 00

FISHER

3625.	Glass Bowl	20 x 16	CAC		3. 50
3626.	Springtime Symphony	20 x 16	CAC		3. 50

FLANDRIN, JULES (French, 1871-1947)

3627.	Christ Mourning				
	the City (H. C.)	20 x 16	IA		6. 00
	(B. &W.)	20 x 16	IA		4. 00
	(B. &W.)	15 x 12	IA		3. 00
3628.	Pearl Diver	17 x 21	CAC		10. 00

FLEGEL, GEORG (German, 1563-1638)

3629.	Blue Titmouse	6 x 8	NYGS		9. 00
3630.	Branch of Oranges	9 x 7	NYGS		9. 00
3631.	Centaurs and				
	Strawberries c.	10 x 8	ESH		1. 00
3632.	Crown Imperial	12 x 7-1/2	NYGS		9. 00
3633.	Garden Still Life	6 x 8-1/2	NYGS		9. 00
3634.	Ice Bird and Sea-				
	shells	5 x 7-1/2	NYGS		9. 00
3635.	Iris, Convolvulus				
	and Cherries c.	10 x 8	ESH		1. 00
3636.	Iris and Insects c.	10 x 8	ESH		1. 00
3637.	Iris, Liserons and				
	Cherries c.	8 x 10	ESH		1. 00
3638.	Still Life with				
	Parakeet	6 x 7-1/2	NYGS		9. 00

FLINT, (SIR) WILLIAM RUSSELL (English, 1880-)

3639.	Flowers and				
	Lacquer	14-1/2 x 18	ESH		15. 00
3640.	Golden Sands,				
	Bamburgh	16-1/2 x 22	NYGS		10. 00
3641.	Houses of Parlia-				
	ment	20-1/2x28-1/2	ESH		3. 00
3642.	Magna Carta	20-1/2 x 29	ESH		3. 00
3643.	Provencal Caprice	9-1/2x12-1/2	ESH		7. 50
3644.	Unwelcome Intruders	9 x 12-1/2	ESH		7. 50
3645.	Wet Sands,				
	Bamburgh	16-1/2 x 22	NYGS		10. 00

FLORENCE, SCHOOL OF (Italian 14th Century)

3646.	Chest of Nuptials	4-1/2x15-1/2	AS		3. 25
	Details (2)	8 x 15-1/2	AS	ea.	3. 25
	Details (2)	15 x 11	AS	ea.	3. 25
3647.	Feast of St. John	6 x 15-1/2	AS		3. 25
3648.	Virgin and Child	15-1/2x9-1/2	AS		3. 25

FOLLAND, R.

3649.	City Island	16-1/2 x 44	RL		15. 00
3650.	London Morning	18 x 48	RL		15. 00
3651.	Quiet Estuary	16-1/2 x 44	RL		15. 00
3652.	River Banks	16-1/2 x 44	RL		15. 00

FONTANAROSA, L.

3653.	Santa Maria from				
	San Giorgio	20 x 30	RL		15. 00

FONTANESI, ANTONIO (Italian, 1818-1882)
3654.	Alla Fonte	18 x 26	CFA		15. 00
3655.	Landscape (2)	11 x 14-1/2	AS	ea.	3. 25
3656.	Santa Trinita Bridge				
	at Florence	10 x 15	IA		3. 00

FONTANGES, J.
| 3657. | Antoinette | 8-1/2 x 7 | ESH | 1. 00 |
| 3658. | Yvette | 8-1/2 x 7 | ESH | 1. 00 |

FORABOSCO, GIROLAMO (Italian, Ac. 1631-1660)
| 3659. | Venetian Courtesan | | | | |
| | (3) | 14 x 11 | AS | ea. | 3. 25 |

FORAIN, JEAN LOUIS (French, 1852-1931)
| 3660. | Court Room: | | | | |
| | Interior | 20 x 24 | NYGS | 12. 00 |

FORD, LAUREN
3661.	Choir Practice	16 x 21	NYGS	7. 50
3662.	Guardian Angel	26 x 19-1/2	IA	7. 50
		12 x 9	IA	1. 00

FOREIN
| 3663. | Steer Roping | 12 x 18 | CAC | 3. 00 |

FORESTIER, MARINUS (English, Contemporary)
| 3664. | Golden Hour | 12 x 17 | ESH | 2. 00 |
| 3665. | Sundown | 15 x 13 | ESH | 2. 00 |

FORLI, ANSUINO DA See ANSUINO DA FORLI
FORLI, MELOZZO DA See MELOZZO DA FORLI
FORSYTH
| 3666. | Old Market Woman | | | | |
| | c. | 7 x 9 | AP | . 50 |

FORTI BURLAMACCHI See BURLAMACCHI, ADOLFO FORTI
FORTUNY Y CARBO, MARIANO (Spanish, Ac. 1838-1847)
| 3667. | In the Library | 14 x 20 | CFA | 15. 00 |

FOSTER, DERYCK (English Contemporary)
3668.	Big Class	20 x 30	AS	12. 00
3669.	Fire Flies	18-1/2x14-1/2	ESH	3. 00
3670.	Harbor Entrance,			
	Yarmouth, I. O. W.	18 x 36	AS	12. 00
3671.	Last Barge Race	20 x 30	AS	15. 00
3672.	Rounding the Buoy	20 x 27	ESH	8. 00
3673.	Royal Dragon	20 x 30	IA	10. 00
3674.	Wind Force Five	24 x 36	AS	15. 00

FOUJITA, TSUGOHARU (Japanese [Res. France] 1886-)
3675.	Cafe	c.	24 x 20	PENN	1. 50
3676.	Girl with Cat	c.	24 x 20	PENN	1. 50
3677.	Holiday		16 x 36	CFA	18. 00
3678.	In the Kitchen	c.	24 x 20	PENN	1. 50
3679.	Little Cavalier		25-1/2x18-1/2	PENN	1. 50
3680.	Quai aux Fleurs				
		c.	20 x 24	PENN	1. 50

FOUQUES, R. H. (German [Res. France]
| 3681. | Cape Finisterre | 19-1/2 x 25 | RL | 7. 50 |

FOUQUET, JEAN (French, c. 1420-1481)
| 3682. | Angel Announcing to | | | | |
| | the Virgin Her Death | 7 x 5 | IA | 1. 50 |

3683.	Annunciation	7 x 5	IA		1.50
3684.	Birth of the Baptist	7 x 5	IA		1.50
3685.	Chancellor of France	12 x 9	CFA		2.50
3686.	Death of the Virgin	7 x 5	IA		1.50
3687.	Etienne Chevalier Adoring the Madonna	7 x 5	IA		1.50
3688.	Guillaume Juvenal des Ursins	14 x 11	IA		3.00
3689.	Madonna and Child with Angels	7 x 5	IA		1.50
3690.	Marriage of the Virgin	7 x 5	IA		1.50
3691.	Portrait of Charles VII	16 x 13	PENN		1.00
3692.	Sainte Marguerite c.	8 x 10	ESH		1.00
3693.	Virgin and Child c.	10 x 8	NYGS		.50

FOURNET, L.

3694.	Finisterre	22 x 28	RL		7.50

FOWLER

3695.	Modern Still Life (4)	12 x 18	AK	ea.	2.50
		6 x 9	AK	ea.	1.00

FRA ANGELICO See ANGELICO, FRA
FRA BARTOLOMMEO See BARTOLOMMEO, FRA
FRAGONARD, JEAN-HONORE (French, 1732-1806)

3696.	Arbor with Two Children	10 x 13-1/2	NYGS		3.00
3697.	La Baiser à la Derobe	9 x 12	IA		10.00 (H. C. Gr.)
3698.	Le Billet Doux c.	10 x 8	ESH		1.00
3699.	Blind Man's Buff c.	20 x 24	PENN		1.50
3700.	Dame Langoreuse	12 x 9	IA		10.00 (H. C. Gr.)
3701.	Education is Everything c.	18 x 23	HNA		5.95
3702.	L'Etude c.	8 x 10	NYGS		.50
3703.	Farmer's Family	15 x 18-1/2	ESH		10.00
3704.	First Step	9 x 10	CAC		7.50
3705.	A Game of Horse and Rider c.	24 x 20	PENN		1.50
		24 x 18	NYGS		10.00
		16 x 12	DAC		2.50
		14 x 11	NYGS		4.00
		12 x 9	CFA		2.00
3706.	A Game of Hot Cockles	24 x 19	NYGS		10.00
		14 x 11	NYGS		4.00
		12 x 9	CFA		2.00

3707.	Gatherer of Grapes	31-1/2x24-1/2	ESH	15. 00
3708.	Girl at Her Studies			
	c.	10 x 8	ESH	1. 00
3709.	Girl Reading	22-1/2 x 18	ESH	10. 00
3710.	Girl with a Marmot	10 x 8-1/2	AR	4. 00
3711.	Good Mother Oval	12 x 10	NYGS	1. 50
3712.	Infant Cheri	9 x 10	CAC	7. 50
3713.	Inspiration	14 x 11	IA	3. 00
3714.	Lady Carving Her			
	Name c.	8 x 10	CAC	1. 00
3715.	The Letter	23 x 18	ESH	10. 00
		21 x 17	CAC	10. 00
	c.	10 x 8	ESH	1. 00
3716.	The Letter (Dr.)			
	c.	9 x 7	AP	. 25
3717.	The Love Letter	30 x 24	NYGS	18. 00
	c.	10 x 8	NYGS	. 50
3718.	Love Unto Death	18 x 12	AR	4. 00
		17 x 12	CFA	4. 00
3719.	Music Lesson	11 x 12	IA	3. 00
	c.	8 x 10	ESH	1. 00
	c.	7 x 9	AP	. 60
3720.	Oath of Love Oval	12 x 10	NYGS	1. 50
3721.	Park at Villa			
	D'Este	18 x 13	AR	4. 00
3722.	Park Landscape	11 x 14-1/2	AR	4. 00
3723.	Portrait of Constance			
	Lowendahl, Countess of			
	Turpin de Crisse			
	Oval	13 x 11	IA	3. 00
3724.	Reverence	8 x 10-1/2	NYGS	4. 00
3725.	Shepherdess	31-1/2x24-1/2	ESH	15. 00
3726.	Stolen Kiss	15 x 18-1/2	ESH	12. 00
3727.	Storming the Citadel			
	c.	8 x 10	NYGS	. 50
3728.	The Study	14 x 11	IA	3. 00
3729.	The Swing			
	(L'Escarpolette)	19 x 14-1/2	NYGS	7. 50
	c.	9 x 7	AP	. 50
	Detail of			
	No. 3729 c.	8 x 10	ESH	1. 00
3730.	A Young Girl			
	Reading	26 x 20	NYGS	15. 00
	c.	24 x 20	PENN	1. 50
		22-1/2 x 18	ESH	10. 00
		16 x 12	PENN	1. 00
		14 x 11	NYGS	3. 00
		11 x 9	CFA	2. 00
	c.	10 x 8	ESH	1. 00

FRANCA, OZZ (Brazilian [Res. U. S.] Contemporary)

3731.	City Bridge at			
	Eventide	15 x 40	DAC	10. 00
		8-1/2 x 22	DAC	2. 00

3732.	City Harbor	40 x 15	DAC	10. 00
		22 x 8-1/2	DAC	2. 50
3733.	Harbour Night			
	Scene	15 x 40	DAC	10. 00
		8-1/2 x 22	DAC	2. 50
3734.	Reflected Skyline	15 x 40	DAC	10. 00
		8-1/2 x 22	DAC	2. 50
3735.	Sailboat Topmasts	40 x 15	DAC	10. 00
		22 x 8-1/2	DAC	2. 50
3736.	Skyline Horizon	15 x 40	DAC	10. 00
		8-1/2 x 22	DAC	2. 50

FRANCESCA See PIERO DELLA FRANCESCA
FRANCESCHINI, BALDASSARE See VOLTERRANO, IL
FRANCESCHINI, MARC ANTONIO (Italian, 1648-1729)

3737.	Cupid	15 x 11	IA	3. 00
3738.	Cupid Sleeping	15 x 10-1/2	AS	3. 25
3739.	Piovano Arlotto's			
	Joke	10-1/2 x 14-1/2 AS		3. 25

FRANCIA, IL (RAIBOLINI, FRANCESCO) (Italian, 1450-1508)

3740.	Entombment	9 x 12	ESH	2. 00
3741.	Madonna and Child			
	with infant St. John	22 x 17	AA	7. 50
3742.	Madonna and Child with			
	St. Francis and			
	St. Jerome	24 x 18	AA	7. 50
3743.	Madonna, Child and			
	St. Francis c.	10 x 8	NYGS	. 50
3744.	Portrait of Evan-			
	gelista Scappi	13 x 11	IA	3. 00
3745.	St. George and the			
	Dragon c.	9 x 7	AP	. 50
3746.	St. Stephen	15 x 10-1/2	AS	3. 25

FRANCIABIGIO, IL (BIGI, FRANCESCO DI CRISTOFANO)
(Italian, 1482-1525)

| 3747. | Venus | 15 x 6 | IA | 3. 00 |

FRANCIS, DOROTHY

3748.	Eagle Heart	24 x 18	AA	10. 00
		12 x 9	AA	2. 00
3749.	Little Bluebird	24 x 18	AA	10. 00
		12 x 9	AA	2. 00

FRANCK, FREDERICK (Dutch [Res. U. S.] Contemporary)

3750.	Downtown Rhythms,			
	New York	14 x 20	NYGS	9. 00
3751.	From Manhattan			
	Bridge	14-1/2 x 20	NYGS	9. 00
3752.	Manhattan Nocturne	15-1/2 x 21	NYGS	10. 00

FRANKE

| 3753. | Ripe Sheaves | 21 x 35-1/2 | NYGS | 12. 00 |

FRANKL, FRANZ

3754.	Meadow Stream	25 x 33	CFA	12. 00
3755.	Pine Cove	25 x 33	CFA	15. 00
3756.	Winding Brook	26 x 33	CFA	12. 00

FRAZIER, KENNETH (American, 1867-1949)
| 3757. | End of the Trail | 13 x 16 | CAC | | 4. 00 |
| | | 9 x 12 | CAC | | 2. 00 |

FREDERICK, ROBERT
| 3758. | Ballet Dancers (4) | 20 x 16 | AK | ea. | 4. 00 |
| | | 12 x 9 | AK | ea. | 1. 50 |

FREEMAN, JANE (English, 1883-)
3759.	Chums	24 x 19-1/2	IA	10. 00
		14 x 11	IA	2. 00
	c.	10 x 8	IA	1. 00
3760.	Peasant Man at			
	Prayer	17 x 12	CAC	1. 50

FREITAG, CLEMENS
3761.	Birch-Grove	20 x 28	ESH	7. 00
3762.	Quiet Waters	24 x 32	IA	12. 00
3763.	Spring in the			
	Promontory	23-1/2x39-1/2	ESH	9. 00
		20 x 28	ESH	7. 00
3764.	When the Leaves			
	Begin to Fall	24 x 32	IA	12. 00

FREUND, ROBERT (German Contemporary)
3765.	Composition I	16 x 39-1/2	ESH	Cv. 15. 00
3766.	Herd of Mares	12-1/2x39-1/2	ESH	Cv. 15. 00
3767.	Matador	24-1/2x31-1/2	ESH	Cv. 15. 00

FRIEDRICH, CASPAR DAVID (German, 1774-1840)
3768.	Cross in the			
	Mountains	20 x 20	ESH	7. 00
3769.	The Lonely Tree			
	c.	18 x 23	HNA	5. 95
3770.	Summer Landscape	23 x 35	CFA	18. 00
3771.	Woman at the Window			
		17-1/2 x 13	NYGS	16. 00

FRIESZ, EMILE OTHON (French, 1879-1949)
3772.	Garden at Brun c.	20 x 24	PENN	1. 50
3773.	Port de Dieppe	23-1/2 x 20	PENN	1. 50
3774.	Port of Toulon	18 x 23	PENN	1. 50
3775.	Still Life with			
	Brigantine	20-1/2x25-1/2	NYGS	12. 00

FROLICHER, OTTO (Swiss, 1840-1890)
| 3776. | Park Landscape | 18-1/2x24-1/2 | ESH | 7. 50 |

FROMENT, NICOLAS (French, Ac. 1450-1490)
(See also SCHOOL OF AVIGNON)
3777.	Pieta d'Avignon			
	(Attributed)	16-1/2x22⁴⁴/2	ESH	10. 00
		11-1/2 x 15	AS	3. 25

FROMHOLD, MARTIN
| 3778. | Summer Bouquet | 22 x 16 | NYGS | 10. 00 |

FROMMHOLD, ERNST (German, 1879-1955)
3779.	Clearance in a			
	Wood	23-1/2x31-1/2	IA	12. 00
3780.	Down to the Valley	18 x 23-1/2	IA	6. 00
3781.	Spring	18 x 23	CFA	6. 00

3782.	Springtime	18 x 23-1/2	IA		6.00
3783.	Sunny Forest Road	18 x 23-1/2	IA		6.00
3784.	Wagon Trail	18 x 24	CAC		7.50
3785.	Woodland Stream	24 x 32	CAC		10.00

FROOT
3786.	When Evening Comes	24 x 30	CAC		10.00

FROSINO, BARTOLOMMEO DI (Italian, 1366-1440)
3787.	St. Aegidius	12 x 11	IA		3.00

FROST
3788.	Golf (12)	13 x 10	AA	ea.	6.00

FUGEL, GEBHARD (German, 1863-)
3789.	Last Supper	23 x 39-1/2	IA		10.00
		17 x 30	IA		5.00
		9-1/2 x 17	IA		2.00

FUHRIC, JOSEF VON (Austrian, 1800-1876)
3790.	St. Mary Walking over Hills	15 x 22	AJ		7.50
3791.	Virgin and Child	11 x 7	AJ		2.50

FUJIKAWA, GYO (American Contemporary)
3792.	Love in May	16 x 12	NYGS		5.00
		8 x 6	NYGS		1.50
3793.	Monkey Business	16 x 12	NYGS		5.00
		8 x 6	NYGS		1.50

FUJITA See FOUJITA
FUNK
3794.	Green Meadows	22 x 28	CAC		6.00

FUNKE-PARYS, H. W. (German, 1905-1964)
3795.	Dancers	28 x 20	ESH	Cv.	12.00

FURBER
3796.	Bouquet (12) (Months of the Year)				
	c.	16 x 12	PENN	ea.	1.00

FUSARO
3797.	Little Boats at Meze	18 x 22-1/2	ESH		10.00

FYT, JAN (Belgian, 1611-1661)
3798.	Chickens Frightened by Hawk	11-1/2 x 15	AS		3.25

G

GABRIEL
3799.	In July	31-1/2 x 20	ESH		15.00
		10-1/2 x 8	ESH		1.00

GADDI, TADDEO (ANGELO DI TADDEO) (Italian, 1300-1366)
3800.	Coronation of the Virgin	15 x 10	IA		3.00
		12 x 6	CFA		1.50
3801.	Virgin and Child (Borgo San Lorenzo, Florence)	15 x 9	AS		3.25

GAINSBOROUGH (SIR) Thomas (English, 1727-1788)

3802.	Mr. and Mrs. Andrews	18 x 31-1/2	NYGS	15. 00
3803.	The Artist's Daughter	17 x 13-1/2	PENN	1. 50
3804.	Mrs. Billington	12 x 9	ESH	2. 00
3805.	Blue Boy	31 x 22-1/2	NYGS	12. 00
		26 x 20	PENN	1. 50
		24 x 17	NYGS	10. 00
		24 x 16	CFA	10. 00
		20-1/2 x 14	AP	5. 00
		18 x 13	NYGS	5. 00
		14 x 10	NYGS	3. 00
		12 x 8-1/2	NYGS	1. 50
	c.	10 x 8	NYGS	. 50
	c.	9 x 7	AP	. 50
3806.	Count Rumford	28 x 23	NYGS	12. 00
3807.	Duchess of Devonshire	28 x 21	CAC	30. 00 Gr.
3808.	Hon. Mrs. Graham	28 x 22	CAC	30. 00 Gr.
		28 x 22	CAC	12. 00
		20 x 16	CAC	7. 50
	c.	10 x 8	NYGS	. 50
3809.	Landscape with Peasants and Horses	22-1/2 x 25	NYGS	12. 00
3810.	Miss Linley and her Brother	24 x 18	PENN	1. 50
3811.	Margaret	20 x 16	AA	6. 00
	c.	10 x 8	NYGS	. 50
3812.	Morning Walk	28 x 21	NYGS	15. 00
3813.	The Painter's Daughters	23 x 21-1/2	NYGS	18. 00
3814.	Parish Clerk	12 x 9	ESH	2. 00
3815.	Mrs. Siddons	17 x 13	CAC	5. 00
	c.	9 x 7	AP	. 50
3816.	View near King's Bromley-on-Trent	25-1/2 x 36	NYGS	18. 00
3817.	View of Dedham c.	18 x 23	HNA	5. 95

GAIR, FRANCIS

3818.	Looking Toward Chanctonbury Ring	18 x 25	CAC	7. 50
3819.	Italian Landscape	18 x 25	CAC	7. 50

GALL, DELLA

3820.	Chatou	18 x 22	CAC	7. 50
3821.	Jeune Femme	18 x 14	CAC	5. 00
3822.	Jeune Femme a la Toilette	18 x 14	CAC	5. 00
3823.	Jeune Femme and Bouquet	18 x 14	CAC	5. 00
3824.	River Seine	18 x 22	CAC	10. 00

GALLAIS
3825.	New York City Scenes					
	(4)	c.	20 x 24	PENN	ea.	1.50
3826.	Brooklyn Bridge					
3827.	Central Park					
3828.	Public Library					
3829.	Washington Square					
	New York City Scenes					
	(4)	c.	12 x 16	PENN	ea.	1.00
3830.	Art Show in Washington Square					
3831.	Lower Manhattan					
3832.	Public Library at Fifth Avenue					
3833.	Skating in Central Park					

GALLEN-KALLELA, AKSELI (Finnish, 1865-1931)
3834.	Boy with Crow	24 x 20	NYGS	10.00

GALLON, ROBERT
3835.	Afternoon	18 x 12	AA	4.00
3836.	Morning	18 x 12	AA	4.00

GAMBLE
3837.	Blossom Time	16 x 20	CAC	6.00
3838.	California Poppies	20 x 30	CAC	10.00

GAND, GIUSTO See GIUSTO DI GAND

GANSO, EMIL (American, 1895-)
3839.	Winter Morning	14-1/2 x 22	PENN	1.50

GANTNER
3840.	Le Port de			
	Strasbourg	22 x 18	NYGS	26.00

GANZIANI
3841.	Piper of Dreams	11 x 16	CAC	3.00

GARCIA
3842.	At Anchor	24 x 36	DAC	7.50
3843.	Regatta	24 x 48	DAC	10.00
3844.	Still Life	24 x 36	DAC	7.50
		24 x 30	PENN	1.95
3845.	Tall Masts	36 x 24	DAC	7.50

GARMAN, T.
3846.	Autumn Woods	19 x 22	ESH	15.00

GARNERAY, LEBRETON
3847.	Cities of U. S.,				
	Views (5)	10 x 15	CFA	ea.	12.00
3848.	Baltimore				
3849.	Boston				
3850.	New Orleans				
3851.	New York				
3852.	Philadelphia				

GAROFALO See TISI

GARRIDO, LEANDRO ROMAN (French, 1868-1909)
3853.	Minuet	24 x 32	CFA	10.00

GASSER, HENRY M.
3854.	Gondola	16 x 22-1/2	PENN		1.50
3855.	Harbor Scenes (4)	10 x 13	PENN	set	1.00
3856.	Home Port	c.	20 x 24	PENN	1.50
3857.	Inland Cove	19-1/2 x 24	PENN		1.50

3858.	Lover's Tree		16 x 22-1/2	PENN		1.50
3859.	Peaceful Harbor					
		c.	20 x 24	PENN		1.50
3860.	Solitude		19-1/2 x 24	PENN		1.50
3861.	Summer Inlet		24 x 30	CAC		15.00
3862.	Surf, Sand and					
	Rocks		19-1/2 x 24	PENN		1.50
3863.	Tranquility		19-1/2 x 24	PENN		1.50
3864.	Winter Harbor		18-1/2 x 24	PENN		1.50

GASTEIGER (German, 1871-)

3865.	Camellias in Bloom	30 x 24	CAC		7.50
3866.	Poinsettias	20 x 18	CAC		7.50

GASTON

3867.	Bridge in New York	14 x 27-1/2	ESH	Pr.	8.00
3868.	Costa del Sol	16 x 31-1/2	ESH	Pr.	8.00
3869.	Mountains in Austria	16 x 31-1/2	ESH	Pr.	8.00
3870.	Promontory	20 x 27-1/2	ESH	Pr.	8.00

GAUERMANN, FRIEDRICH (Austrian, 1807-1862)

3871.	Lake Altauseer		12 x 17-1/2	NYGS	14.00
3872.	Landscape near				
	Miesenbach		12 x 17-1/2	NYGS	14.00

GAUGUIN, PAUL (French, 1848-1903)

3873.	Alone	c.	9-1/2x12-1/2	AP	1.25
		c.	7 x 9	AP	1.00
3874.	Les Alyscamps,				
	Arles		29 x 22	NYGS	15.00
			22 x 18	AJ	15.00
		c.	10 x 8	ESH	1.00
3875.	Arearea		27 x 33-1/2	NYGS	20.00
			17 x 22	PENN	1.50
3876.	La Barriere	c.	22 x 17-1/2	AS	4.00
3877.	Bathers		23 x 29	CFA	18.00
3878.	Beach at Tahiti		23 x 18	CFA	12.00
3879.	Big Tree		16 x 20-1/2	CFA	7.50
3880.	Bonjour, Monsieur				
	Gauguin	c.	24 x 20	DAC	7.50
			23 x 18	HNA	5.95
			16 x 12	DAC	2.50
3881.	Breton Landscape		23 x 34	CFA	15.00
		c.	20 x 24	PENN	1.50
			18 x 24	DAC	7.50
			12 x 16	DAC	2.50
3882.	Breton Peasants	c.	10 x 8	ESH	1.00
3883.	Breton Village Under				
	Snow		16 x 22	ESH	10.00
3884.	Bretonne		13 x 9	NYGS	7.50
3885.	The Call (Appeal)		23 x 15	ESH	10.00
		c.	10 x 8	ESH	1.00
3886.	Cavalier		14 x 9	NYGS	7.50
3887.	Contes Barbares				
	(Barbaric Tales)		22 x 17-1/2	AS	4.00
			19 x 13	NYGS	15.00

3888.	Days of God	c.	8 x 10	CAC	1. 50
3889.	Dreamer		16 x 12	PENN	1. 00
3890.	Entrance to a Village		19-1/2 x 23	PENN	1. 50
3891.	Farm at Pouldu	c.	8 x 10	ESH	1. 00
3892.	Farmyard Scene	c.	7 x 9	AP	. 50
3893.	Fatata Te Miti		22-1/2x30-1/2	NYGS	16. 00
		c.	20 x 24	PENN	1. 50
			11 x 14	NYGS	3. 00
3894.	Fatata te Moua (Near the Mountain)		17 x 23-1/2	NYGS	7. 50
3895.	Femmes Maoris		16-1/2 x 21	NYGS	18. 00
3896.	Femmes de Tahiti		18 x 14	PENN	1. 50
3897.	Flowers and Bowl of Fruit		16-1/2 x 24	PENN	1. 50
3898.	Flowers in a Vase		10-1/2 x 8	ESH	1. 00
3899.	From Tahiti		31-1/2x24-1/2	NYGS	20. 00
3900.	Girl from Brittany in Prayer		25 x 18	NYGS	15. 00
3901.	Girl with a Fan		30 x 23-1/2	NYGS	28. 00
		c.	9 x 7	AP	1. 00
3902.	Girls with Red Flowers		7 x 6	CFA	1. 00
3903.	Haystacks		23-1/2 x 18	PENN	1. 50
3904.	I Await the Letter		20 x 26	NYGS	15. 00
3905.	I Raro Te Oviri		22-1/2x30-1/2	NYGS	16. 00
			11 x 14	NYGS	3. 00
3906.	Ia Orana Maria (Hail Mary)		30 x 23	NYGS	18. 00
		c.	24 x 20	PENN	1. 50
3907.	Landscape at Arles		24 x 18	DAC	7. 50
			16 x 12	DAC	2. 50
3908.	Landscape near Arles	c.	8 x 10	ESH	1. 00
3909.	Landscape near Pont-Aven		25 x 31-1/2	NYGS	16. 00
3910.	Landscape, Tahiti	c.	8 x 10	NYGS	. 50
3911.	Lane near Arles	c.	8 x 10	ESH	1. 00
3912.	Little Breton Girls		24 x 18	DAC	7. 50
			16 x 12	DAC	2. 50
3913.	Man with an Axe	c.	10 x 8	ESH	1. 00
3914.	Marie Henry	c.	8 x 10	CAC	1. 50
3915.	La Martinique		19-1/2 x 15	AP	5. 00
3916.	Maternity		22-1/2 x 14	ESH	10. 00
		c.	10 x 8	ESH	1. 00
3917.	Mill in Brittany		18 x 22-1/2	ESH	10. 00
		c.	8 x 10	ESH	1. 00
3918.	Nafea (When Do You Marry)		28 x 21	CFA	18. 00

		c.	24 x 20	PENN	1. 50
		c.	23 x 18	HNA	5. 95
			22-1/2 x 17	ESH	10. 00
			18 x 14	CAC	5. 00
		c.	10 x 8	ESH	1. 00
3919.	Nature Morte		14 x 18	CAC	5. 00
3920.	Nave Nave Mahana				
	(Enchanting Sun)		22 x 30	ESH	15. 00
			19 x 26	CFA	15. 00
		c.	8 x 10	ESH	1. 00
3921.	Never More		12-1/2 x 24	PENN	1. 50
3922.	The Offering c.		8 x 10	ESH	1. 00
3923.	On Horseback at the				
	Seashore		19-1/2x24-1/2	AP	10. 00
3924.	Out of Tahiti		31 x 25	CFA	18. 00
3925.	Pape Moe	c.	22 x 17-1/2	AS	4. 00
3926.	Poor Fisher	c.	24 x 20	PENN	1. 50
			13 x 11	IA	3. 00
3927.	Portrait of a Young				
	Lady	c.	8 x 10	NYGS	. 50
3928.	Red Dog	c.	8 x 10	ESH	1. 00
3929.	Reverie	c.	12-1/2x9-1/2	AP	1. 25
		c.	9 x 7	AP	1. 00
3930.	Reverie, Girl in a				
	Red Dress	c.	10 x 8	NYGS	. 50
3931.	Rider on the Coast		14 x 17	CAC	2. 00
3932.	Riders on the Beach		25 x 29	NYGS	20. 00
			15 x 18-1/2	PENN	1. 50
3933.	Riders on the Coast		33 x 30	CAC	12. 00
			29 x 23	CFA	12. 00
3934.	Schuffenecker				
	Family	c.	8 x 10	NYGS	. 50
3935.	Still Life		14 x 17	CAC	5. 00
3936.	Still Life, Flowers		25 x 30	NYGS	20. 00
			7 x 6	CFA	1. 00
3937.	Still Life (Japanese				
	Print)	c.	8 x 10	MMA	. 35
3938.	Still Life with Apples		25-1/2x29-1/2	NYGS	16. 00
3939.	Still Life with Fruit,				
	Basket, Knife		24-1/2x28-1/2	NYGS	28. 00
3940.	Still Life with				
	Mandolin		23 x 19	AJ	12. 00
3941.	Ta Matete (The				
	Market)		26 x 33-1/2	NYGS	20. 00
			24 x 30	ESH	15. 00
			18 x 24	PENN	1. 50
		c.	18 x 23	HNA	5. 95
			14-1/2x18-1/2	IA	5. 00
		c.	8 x 10	ESH	1. 00
3942.	Tahitian Girl				
	Crouching	c.	12-1/2x9-1/2	AP	1. 25
			8 x 7	CFA	1. 00

3943.	Tahitian Landscape,			
	1892	21 x 26-1/2	NYGS	12. 00
		17 x 23	CFA	10. 00
	c.	8 x 10	NYGS	. 50
3944.	Tahitian Mountains,			
	1891-93	26 x 36	NYGS	18. 00
		22-1/2 x 31	NYGS	12. 00
		14-1/2 x 20	NYGS	5. 00
		6 x 7-1/2	NYGS	. 50
3945.	Tahitian Village	33 x 26	CAC	10. 00
3946.	Tahitian Women	14 x 18	CFA	4. 00
3947.	Te Raau Rahi	23-1/2x29-1/2	NYGS	16. 00
3948.	Te Rerioa			
	(Daydreaming)	22 x 30	NYGS	15. 00
		18 x 24	PENN	1. 50
3949.	Three Puppies	23 x 16	NYGS	10. 00
	c.	10 x 8	MMA	. 35
3950.	Two Figures on a			
	Tahitian Beach	16 x 12	PENN	1. 00
		9 x 6	CFA	1. 00
3951.	Two Girls Nude	15-1/2 x 18	AP	5. 00
3952.	Two Tahitian Women			
	with Mangoes	30 x 23	CAC	15. 00
		23 x 18	NYGS	12. 00
		14 x 11	NYGS	3. 00
	c.	9 x 7	AP	. 75
3953.	Vairumati	18 x 23	CAC	15. 00
3954.	Walk near the Sea			
	c.	7 x 9	AP	. 50
3955.	We Greet Thee c.	7 x 9	AP	. 50
3956.	Where Do We Come			
	From	17 x 45	PENN	2. 98
3957.	White Horse	30-1/2 x 20	ESH	15. 00
		22 x 14	NYGS	9. 00
	c.	10 x 8	ESH	1. 00
3958.	Why Are You Angry	17-1/2x24-1/2	AA	7. 50
3959.	Woman on a White			
	Horse c.	24 x 20	PENN	1. 50
3960.	Woman with			
	Flowers	23 x 18	CAC	7. 50
3961.	Woman with			
	Gardenia c.	12-1/2x9-1/2	AP	1. 25
		9 x 5	CFA	1. 00
3962.	Woman with Mango	20 x 12	PENN	1. 50
3963.	Women Bathing	23 x 29-1/2	NYGS	20. 00
3964.	Women on the			
	Beach	6 x 8	CFA	1. 00
3965.	Women with Mangoes	30-1/2x23-1/2	NYGS	15. 00
	c.	10 x 8	ESH	1. 00
3966.	The Yellow Christ	26 x 21	NYGS	15. 00

GAULLI, GIOVANNI BATTISTA (IL BACCICCIO) (Italian, 1639-1709)

3967.	Tobias and the			
	Archangel	5 x 15	IA	3. 00

		Detail of No.			
		3967	11 x 15	IA	3. 00
GAWRILOW					
3968.	Warm Evening	c.	7 x 9	AP	. 60
GAZZERA, ROMANO (Italian Contemporary)					
3969.	Amaryllys		14 x 11	IA	3. 00
3970.	Dahlias on the				
	Shore		14 x 11	IA	3. 00
3971.	Great Dahlias		11 x 14	IA	3. 00
3972.	Island of Geraniums		14 x 11	IA	3. 00
3973.	Oriental Garden		14 x 11	IA	3. 00
3974.	Oriental Pansy		14 x 11	IA	3. 00
3975.	Red Berries		23 x 18-1/2	AS	7. 50
3976.	Red Canas		11 x 14	IA	3. 00
3977.	Red Flowered Tree		14 x 11	IA	3. 00
3978.	Sunflowers		14 x 11	IA	3. 00
3979.	Wild Carnations		14 x 11	IA	3. 00
3980.	The Zinnia and the				
	Butterfly		17 x 23	AS	7. 50
GEBERT, M.					
3981.	Fishing-Boats with				
	Cottage		20 x 27-1/2	ESH	Pr. 8. 00
GELLÉE, CLAUDE (CLAUDE OF LORRAINE) (French, 1600-1682)					
3982.	Classical Landscape		20 x 26	NYGS	18. 00
3983.	Country Feast	c.	8 x 10	CFA	5. 00
3984.	David at Cave				
	Adullum	c.	8 x 10	NYGS	. 50
3985.	Herdsman Driving				
	Cattle	c.	20 x 24	PENN	1. 50
3986.	Landing at Latium		7 x 10	CFA	5. 00
3987.	Landscape		11 x 15	IA	3. 00
3988.	Landscape with Herd		11 x 7	CFA	4. 00
GENERALIC, IVAN (Croatian Contemporary)					
3989.	Autumn in the				
	Village		18-1/2 x 21	ESH	10. 00
3990.	Harvest	c.	20 x 24	DAC	7. 50
3991.	Rest at Noontime				
		c.	20 x 24	DAC	7. 50
GENOUD					
3992.	Lipari Island		12 x 16	CAC	10. 00
GENT, VAN					
3993.	Adoration of the				
	Magi	c.	7 x 9	AP	. 25
3994.	Magnolia		24 x 31	CAC	10. 00
GENTH					
3995.	Spanish Dancers		20 x 30	CAC	10. 00
GENTILE DA FABRIANO (GENTILE DI NICOLO DI GIOVANNI MASSI)					
(Italian, 1360-1427)					
3996.	Adoration of the				
	Magi		11-1/2 x 15	AS	3. 25
		c.	7 x 9	AP	. 60
	Detail of No.				
	3996		11 x 15	IA	3. 00

3997.	Coronation of the			
	Virgin	32 x 23	IA	24.00
3998.	Flight into Egypt	9 x 15	AS	3.25
		5 x 16	IA	3.00
3999.	Madonna and Child	15 x 11	IA	3.00
4000.	Virgin and Child	11 x 10-1/2	AS	3.25

GENTILESCHI, ORAZIO LOMI DE (Italian, 1562-1647)

4001.	Annunciation	15 x 10	IA	3.00
4002.	The Lute Player	26 x 23	NYGS	16.00

GENTILINI, FRANCO (Italian Contemporary)

4003.	Portraits (8)	14 x 11	DAC	ea. 3.50
	Portraits (2)	24 x 20	DAC	ea. 7.50

GEORGHIOU, GEORGE POL (Greek, 1901-   )

4004.	Fumagusta Harbour	19 x 24	NYGS	12.00

GERARD, FRANCOIS (French, 1770-1837)

4005.	Eros and Psyche	13 x 9	CFA	2.50
4006.	Napoleon	12 x 9	IA	3.00

GERICAULT, JEAN-LOUIS ANDRÉ THEODORE (French, 1791-1824)

4007.	The Coal Wagon	16-1/2 x 26	NYGS	12.00
4008.	English Boy	18 x 13-1/2	NYGS	7.50
4009.	Epsom Derby	19 x 24	CFA	12.00
	c.	9-1/2x12-1/2	AP	1.25
		8 x 11	CFA	1.00
4010.	Head of a Horse	10-1/2 x 8	ESH	1.00
4011.	Horse Race c.	8 x 10	ESH	1.00
4012.	Horses at Market	9 x 12	AR	5.00
4013.	Polish Trumpeter	15-1/2x12	NYGS	12.00
4014.	Trumpeter of the			
	Hussars c.	10 x 8	AJ	2.50

GEROME, LEON (French, 1824-1904)

4015.	La Madeleine a			
	Paris	20 x 24	CAC	15.00
4016.	La Place de la			
	Concorde a Paris	20 x 24	CAC	15.00

GERRY, SAMUEL LANCASTER (American, 1813-1891)

4017.	New England Home-			
	stead c.	18 x 23	HNA	5.95

GERWIN, FRANZ (German Contemporary)

4018.	Coke Furnace	27 x 35	CFA	15.00
4019.	Pulse of Industry	26 x 36	NYGS	18.00

GESSNER, RICHARD (German, 1894-   )

4020.	Steel Works	21 x 41	ESH	15.00

GHERARDO DEL FORA (Italian, 1444-1529)

4021.	Choral Page	15 x 10	IA	3.00
4022.	Missal Page with			
	Annunciation	14 x 10	IA	3.00

GHIBERTI, LORENZO (Italian, 1378-1455)

4023.	Marten Stalking Bird	16 x 11	CFA	5.00

GHILCHIK, D.

4024.	Rain on the Way	20 x 30	AS	7.50

GHIRLANDAIO, DOMENICO (BIGORDI, BENEDETTO DOMENICO)
(Italian, 1449-1494)

4025.	Adoration of the Shepherds	11 x 11	IA	3.00
4026.	Angel Appearing to Zacharias	10 x 14-1/2	AR	4.00
4027.	Annunciation	11 x 15	IA	3.00
4028.	Banquet of Jesus	9 x 15-1/2	AS	3.25
4029.	Birth of the Baptist	10 x 15	IA	3.00
4030.	Birth of the Virgin	9 x 15	IA	3.00
4031.	Five Women - Detail of No. 4030	11 x 15	IA	3.00
4032.	Birth of the Virgin	15-1/2x11-1/2	AS	3.25
4033.	Head of Ludovica Tornabuoni - Detail of No. 4032	15-1/2x11-1/2	AS	3.25
4034.	Francesco Sassetta and Son Teodoro	23 x 16	NYGS	10.00
4035.	Head of the Virgin	15 x 11	AS	3.25
4036.	Last Supper	9 x 14	IA	3.00
4037.	St. James - Detail of No. 4036	15 x 11	IA	3.00
4038.	St. Thomas - Detail of No. 4036	15 x 11	IA	3.00
4039.	Madonna, Angels and Saints	11 x 14	IA	3.00
4040.	Maid with a Tray of Fruit	15-1/2 x 17	AS	3.25
4041.	Old Man with a Child c.	24 x 20	PENN	1.50
		15 x 11	IA	3.00
4042.	Piero Di Lorenzo De'Medici (Miniature)	13 x 8	IA	3.00
4043.	Portrait of a Young Lady	15-1/2x11-1/2	AS	3.25
4044.	Vision of Santa Fina	14-1/2x18-1/2	ESH	12.00
4045.	Visitation of the Virgin	9 x 15	IA	3.00
4046.	Giovanna Tornabuoni - Detail of No. 4045	15 x 11	IA	3.00
	Three Women - Detail of No. 4045	15-1/2x11-1/2	AS	3.25
	Four Women - Detail of No. 4045	15-1/2x11-1/2	AS	3.25
	Head of Giovanna Tornabuoni - Detail of No. 4045	15-1/2x11-1/2	AS	3.25

GHIRLANDAIO, RIDOLFO (Italian, 1483-1561)

4047.	Portrait of a Man (The Goldsmith)	15 x 11	IA	3.00
4048.	Portrait of a Woman	14-1/2 x 11	AS	3.25

GIACOMETTI, ALBERTO (Swiss Contemporary)

4049.	Head of the Artist's			
	Mother	17 x 12	NYGS	18. 00

GIAMBELLINO, IL See BELLINI, GIOVANNI
GIAMBONO, MICHELE (Italian, Ac. 1420-1462)

4050.	Virgin and Child	15 x 11	AS	3. 25

GIANUZZI, GIULIO See ROMANO, GIULIO
GIAQUINTO, CORRADO (Italian, 1699-1755)

4051.	Assumption of the			
	Virgin	15 x 9	IA	3. 00

GIBB, WILLIAM

4052.	Musical Instruments			
	(12)	9 x 13	NYGS	set 20. 00 or
				ea. 2. 00

    Bagpipes, Continental
    Bagpipe, Northumbrian and Lowlands
    Clavichord
    Drums of India
    Guitar
    Hellier Stradivarius
    Mandoline and Quinterna
    Organ, Chamber
    Spinnet, Double
    Spinnet, Upright
    State Trumpet and Kettledrum
    Viola da Gamba

GIG

4053.	Pity Kitty (4)	22 x 15	DAC	ea. 7. 50
		12 x 8	DAC	ea. 2. 50
4054.	Pity Puppy (4)	12 x 8	DAC	ea. 2. 50

GIGANTI, G.

4055.	Marini di Posillipo	16-1/2 x 11	CFA	10. 00
4056.	Marini of Sorrento	16-1/2 x 11	CFA	10. 00

GILBERT, JANE (American Contemporary)

4057.	Girl with Cat	14 x 10-1/2	AR	6. 00
4058.	Girl with Flowers	20 x 16	AR	10. 00

GILDER

4059.	Breton Coast	13 x 35	CFA	15. 00

GILLES, WERNER (German, 1894-)

4060.	Fishing	15 x 22	ESH	7. 50

GILLET, EDWARD FRANK (English, 1874-1927)

4061.	"Forrard"	10 x 14	ESH	3. 00
4062.	"Hoic! Cover Hoic!"	10 x 14	ESH	3. 00
4063.	"Whoo-oop"	10 x 14	ESH	3. 00

GILLIES, MARGARET (English, 1803-1887)

4064.	Landscape	13 x 18	NYGS	16. 00
4065.	Landscape with Trees	13 x 18	NYGS	16. 00

GILROY, JOHN (English Contemporary)

4066.	Ayame (Iris)	24 x 19-1/2	ESH	10. 00
4067.	Bara (Rose)	24 x 19	ESH	10. 00
4068.	Flamenco	19-1/2 x 26	ESH	7. 50
4069.	High Tee	9-1/2 x 21	ESH	3. 00
4070.	It's a Miss	9-1/2 x 21	ESH	3. 00

4071.	Kiku			
	(Chrysanthemum)	24 x 19	ESH	10. 00
4072.	Maya	19 x 14	ESH	6. 00
4073.	Mother Love	15 x 20	ESH	5. 00
4074.	Parquita	23-1/2x19-1/2	ESH	10. 00
GINGER,	PHYLLIS			
4075.	Town Center	19 x 30	CFA	5. 00
GINNER	(English Contemporary)			
4076.	Salisbury Cathedral			
	c.	7 x 9	AP	. 50
GIORDANO,	F.			
4077.	Fisherman of			
	Capri	19-1/2x23-1/2	AS	12. 00
GIORGIONE	(BARBARELLI,	GIORGIO) (Italian,	1478-1510)	
4078.	Adoration of the			
	Shepherds	24 x 30	NYGS	18. 00
		19-1/2 x 24	PENN	1. 50
		6 x 7-1/2	NYGS	. 50
4079.	Boy with an			
	Arrow	13 x 11	IA	3. 00
4080.	The Bravo	13 x 11	IA	3. 00
4081.	Christ Supporting			
	the Cross	16 x 8	IA	3. 00
4082.	The Concert	11 x 14	IA	3. 00
	Head - Detail of			
	No. 4082	15 x 11	IA	3. 00
4083.	Concert Champetre			
	(Pastoral Symphony)	24 x 30	NYGS	26. 00
		11 x 13	IA	3. 00
4084.	Double Portrait	13 x 11	IA	3. 00
4085.	Evander and Aeneas	24 x 28	ESH	12. 00
4086.	Judith	15-1/2 x 12	ESH	12. 00
4087.	Landscape with			
	Figures	10 x 14	IA	3. 00
4088.	Laura	14 x 11	IA	3. 00
4089.	The Mocked Christ	11 x 14	IA	3. 00
4090.	An Old Woman	13 x 11	IA	3. 00
4091.	Solomon's Judgment	14 x 11	IA	3. 00
4092.	The Storm	17 x 15	IA	3. 00
4093.	The Tempest c.	10 x 8	NYGS	. 50
4094.	Three Philosophers			
	c.	18 x 23	HNA	5. 95
		11 x 13	IA	3. 00
4095.	Trial by Fire	11 x 14	IA	3. 00
GIOTTINO	(MASO DI BANCO) (Italian Ac.	1336-1350)		
4096.	Deposition from the			
	Cross	15-1/2 x 11	AS	3. 25
		14 x 12	IA	3. 00
GIOTTO	DI BONDONE (Italian,	1266-1336)		
4097.	Apparition of St. Francis			
	to Fra Agostino	11-1/2 x15-1/2	AS	3. 25
		11 x 15	IA	3. 00

4098.	Ascension of Christ	11 x 12	IA		3.00
4099.	Ascension of St. John, the Evangelist	11 x 15	IA		3.00
	St. John - Detail of No. 4099	15 x 11	IA		3.00
	Details of No. 4099 (2)	15 x 11	AS	ea.	3.25
4100.	Banquet of Herod - Details (2)	15 x 11	AS	ea.	3.25
4101.	Baptism of Christ	11 x 12	IA		3.00
4102.	Brother Leo Sees the Heavenly Throne	9 x 8	IA		1.50
4103.	Canonisation of St. Francis	9 x 8	IA		1.50
4104.	The Capture of Christ	29-1/2 x 30	NYGS		30.00
4105.	Christ on the Mount of Olives	45 x 20	CAC		6.00
		30 x 16	CAC		1.50
4106.	The Clarisses Mourning St. Francis	9 x 8	IA		1.50
4107.	Crucifix	14 x 13	IA		3.00
		9 x 8	IA		1.50
4108.	Crucifixion	11 x 12	IA		3.00
4109.	Dante, Portrait c.	9 x 7	AP		.25
4110.	Death of the Knight of Celano	12 x 11	IA		3.00
		8 x 8	IA		1.50
4111.	Death and Obseques of St. Francis (Assisi)	9 x 8	IA		1.50
4112.	Death of St. Francis (S. Croce)	11-1/2x15-1/2	AS		3.25
		11 x 15	IA		3.00
	Detail of No. 4112	14-1/2 x 11	AS		3.25
	Detail of No. 4112	11 x 15	IA		3.00
4113.	Deposition	20 x 19	IA		7.50
		12 x 11	IA		3.00
4114.	Entry into Jerusalem	12 x 13	IA		3.00
4115.	Flight into Egypt	19 x 19	IA		7.50
		11 x 11	IA		3.00
	c.	7 x 9	AP		.50
4116.	Holy Family	30 x 16	CAC		1.50
4117.	Honorius III Approving the Franciscan Order	11 x 15	IA		3.00
4118.	Innocent III Approves the Order	14 x 11	IA		3.00
		9 x 8	IA		1.50
4119.	Innocent III Dreams of St. Francis	9 x 8	IA		1.50

4120.	Joachim and the				
	Shepherds	c.	18 x 23	HNA	5. 95
4121.	Judas Kiss		11 x 11	IA	3. 00
	Detail of No.				
	4121		15 x 11	IA	3. 00
4122.	A Knight Verifies				
	the Stigmata		9 x 8	IA	1. 50
4123.	Maria and the				
	Angels		29-1/2x26-1/2	NYGS	30. 00
4124.	Angel - Detail of				
	"Madonna and Angels"				
			15 x 11	IA	3. 00
4125.	Marriage of the				
	Virgin		11 x 12	IA	3. 00
4126.	Meeting at the				
	Golden Gate		11 x 12	IA	3. 00
	Joachim and Anne-				
	Detail of No.				
	4126		15 x 11	IA	3. 00
4127.	Miracle of the				
	Source		15 x 11	IA	3. 00
			10 x 8	IA	1. 50
4128.	Nativity		11 x 14	IA	3. 00
4129.	Noli Me Tangere		28 x 30-1/2	NYGS	30. 00
			11 x 12	IA	3. 00
	Magdalene and Jesus -				
	Detail of No.				
	4129		15 x 11	IA	3. 00
4130.	Presentation of the				
	Virgin		11 x 12	IA	3. 00
	Detail of No.				
	4130		15 x 11	IA	3. 00
4131.	Resurrection of				
	Lazarus		11 x 12	IA	3. 00
	Detail of No.				
	4131		15 x 11	IA	3. 00
4132.	St. Clara		15 x 11	IA	3. 00
4133.	St. Francis and the				
	Birds (Gold Back-				
	ground)		21 x 18-1/2	ESH	10. 00
4134.	St. Francis and the				
	Sultan		9 x 8	IA	1. 50
4135.	St. Francis Appearing				
	to Gregory IX		9 x 8	IA	1. 50
4136.	St. Francis Appears in				
	Chapter of Arles		10 x 15	IA	3. 00
4137.	St. Francis Being				
	Honored by a Man		9 x 8	IA	1. 50
4138.	St. Francis Celebrates				
	the Crib at Greccio		12 x 11	IA	3. 00
			8 x 8	IA	1. 50
4139.	St. Francis Dreaming				
	a Palace		8 x 8	IA	1. 50

4140.	St. Francis Drives Out the Devils from Arezzo	9 x 8	IA	1.50
4141.	St. Francis Giving his Cloak	23-1/2x20-1/2	AA	12.00
4142.	St. Francis Healing a Devotee	8 x 8	IA	1.50
4143.	St. Francis Hearing the Voice of the Crucifix	9 x 8	IA	1.50
4144.	St. Francis in the Chariot of Fire	14 x 11	IA	3.00
		9 x 8	IA	1.50
4145.	St. Francis in the Presence of the Sultan	15 x 10	IA	3.00
4146.	St. Francis Liberates a Man from Prison	8 x 8	IA	1.50
4147.	St. Francis Preaching Before Honorius III	14 x 11	IA	3.00
		8 x 8	IA	1.50
4148.	St. Francis Preaching to the Birds (Assisi)	14-1/2 x 11	AS	3.25
		10 x 7	IA	1.75
4149.	St. Francis Receiving the Stigmata (Assisi)	8 x 8	IA	1.50
4150.	St. Francis Receiving the Stigmata (S. Croce)	13 x 11	IA	3.00
4151.	St. Francis Resuscitates a Woman	8 x 8	IA	1.50
4152.	St. Francis Speaking to the Birds	20 x 18	ESH	10.00
		15 x 11	IA	3.00
		10 x 8	IA	1.50
4153.	St. Francis Transported into Ecstasy	9 x 8	IA	1.50
4154.	St. Francis Waives his Inheritance	10 x 15	IA	3.00
4155.	Virgin and Child (Florence)	15 x 11	AS	3.25
4156.	Vision of a Brother and of the Bishop	9 x 8	IA	1.50

GIOTTO, SCHOOL OF

4157.	Crucifixion and Saints	15 x 8	IA	3.00
4158.	Dante, Portrait	15 x 11	IA	3.00

GIOVANNI DA COMO See GIOVANNI DA MILANO
GIOVANNI DA FIESOLE See ANGELICO, FRA
GIOVANNI DA MILANO (Italian, Ac. 1349-1369)

4159.	Madonna and Child	15 x 9	IA	3.00
4160.	Presentation in the Temple -	15 x 10	IA	3.00
4160-a	Details of No. 4160	10 x 15	IA	3.00

GIOVANNI DEL BIONDO (Italian, Ac. 1377-1392)
4161.   Madonna and Saints   15 x 8   IA   3. 00
GIOVANNI DI PAOLO (Italian c. 1403-1482)
4162.   Flight into Egypt
                          c.   18 x 23   HNA   5. 95
                               11 x 12   AS   3. 25
4163.   Foreboding of Mary   28 x 39-1/2   ESH   10. 00
                               21-1/2 x 29   ESH   7. 00
4164.   Holy Mary   28 x 39-1/2   ESH   10. 00
4165.   Madonna Immaculata   28 x 39-1/2   ESH   10. 00
                               21-1/2 x 29   ESH   7. 00
4166.   Madonna in the
        Moonlight   21-1/2 x 29   ESH   7. 00
4167.   Mater Dulce   28 x 39-1/2   ESH   10. 00
                               21-1/2 x 29   ESH   7. 00
4168.   Our Lord on Mount
        of Olives   21-1/2 x 29   ESH   7. 00
4169.   Paradise   7-1/2x15-1/2   AS   3. 25
4170.   St. Jerome and the
        Lion   15 x 11   IA   3. 00
4171.   Virgin of Humility   15 x 11-1/2   AS   3. 25
                               15 x 11   IA   3. 00
GIOVANNI PISANO See PISANO, GIOVANNO
GIRALT LERIN, JUAN (Spanish Contemporary)
4172.   Backstage   22-1/2 x 30   NYGS   12. 00
4173.   Danza Gitana,
        Granada   20 x 40   NYGS   15. 00
4174.   Gypsy Dance, 1962   24 x 19-1/2   NYGS   7. 50
4175.   Spanish Dance   24 x 19-1/2   NYGS   7. 50
GIRARD, M.
4176.   Metropolitan Bridge 24 x 48   DAC   10. 00
                               15 x 40   DAC   10. 00
                               15 x 30   DAC   2. 00
4177.   Siamese Cats (4)   20 x 12   DAC   ea.   3. 00
                               10 x 6   DAC   ea.   1. 00
GIRTIN
4178.   Rainbow over the
        Exe   11-1/2x19-1/2   NYGS   18. 00
GISSING, ROLAND (Canadian Contemporary)
4179.   Bow River Valley
        (Banff, Alta. , Can.) 20 x 25   IA   7. 50
4180.   Foothills of the
        Rockies   20 x 25   IA   7. 50
GIUNTA PISANO (Italian, 1202-1258)
4181.   Curcifix   14-1/2x11-1/2   AS   3. 25
GIUSTO DI GAND (Flemish, c. 1440-1475)
4182.   Communion of the
        Apostles   11 x 12   IA   3. 00
GLACKENS, WILLIAM J. (American, 1870-1938)
4183.   Beach at Annisquam   16-1/2 x 20   NYGS   10. 00
4184.   Chez Mouquin   c.   20 x 24   PENN   1. 50
4185.   Dream Ride   15 x 17   NYGS   7. 50

4186.	Hammerstein's Roof Garden	c.	24 x 20	PENN	1.50
4187.	Luxembourg Gardens	c.	20 x 24	PENN	1.50
4188.	Soda Fountain	c.	8 x 10	NYGS	.50

GLANNON, EDWARD JOHN (American Contemporary)

4189.	Corner of the Pasture	12 x 18	CAC	3.00

GLASSI, H.

4190.	In the Sunny South	20 x 28	ESH	7.00

GLENDENING, ALFRED A. (English, Ac. 1861-1903)

4191.	Harvest Time	24 x 48	AK	12.00
		12 x 24	AK	3.00

GLICKLICH

4192.	Spring Song	17 x 13	CAC	3.50
		12 x 9	CAC	2.00

GLINTZ

4193.	Autumn Flowers	18 x 24	CAC	7.50
4194.	Bell Flowers	21 x 28	CAC	9.00
4195.	Sailing Harbour	21 x 28	CAC	9.00

GLITSCH

4196.	Camp Flowers	18 x 13	CAC	2.00
4197.	Freisia	17 x 13	CFA	5.00
4198.	Mimosa	17 x 13	CFA	5.00

GÖB, EWALD

4199.	Late Summer Day in the Promontory	23-1/2x39-1/2	ESH	9.00
		20 x 28	ESH	7.00
4200.	On the Heath	23-1/2x39-1/2	ESH	9.00
		20 x 28	ESH	7.00

GODRON, J. B.

4201.	Madonna	21 x 20	ESH	12.00
		13 x 12	ESH	6.00

GOES, HUGO VAN DER (Flemish, 1440-1482)

4202.	Adoration	24-1/2 x 37	NYGS	20.00
4203.	Holy Family	7 x 8	NYGS	.50
4204.	Portinari Triptych	11 x 26	IA	10.00
		7 x 17	AS	3.25
4205.	Floral Still Life. - Detail of No. 4204	15 x 11	IA	3.00
4206.	St. Margaret - Detail of No. 4204	15 x 11	IA	3.00

GOGH, VINCENT VAN See VAN GOGH, VINCENT

GOLDING, CECIL (American Contemporary)

4207.	Adonis	39 x 12	CAC	15.00
4208.	Autumn Leaves	30 x 25	CAC	7.50
4209.	Ballet Figures (2) Delight Exaltation	16 x 12	NYGS	ea. 3.00
	Ballet Figures (7) Delight Enchantment Exaltation	7-1/2 x 6	NYGS	ea. 1.00

Gaiety
Grace
Joy
Rapture

4210.	Birds (10)	24-1/2x19-1/2	NYGS	ea.	10. 00
	American Robin	16 x 12	NYGS	ea.	5. 00
	Baltimore Oriole				
	Blossom-Headed Parakeet				
	Blue Jay				
	Brown Thrasher				
	Cardinal				
	Red-Capped Fruit Dove				
	Red-Shafted Flicker				
	Rose-Breasted Grosbeak				
	Yellow-Billed-Cuckoo				
4211.	Blue and White	28 x 34	CAC		10. 00
4212.	Christ Preaching on the				
	Sea (After Hofmann)	22-1/2 x 36	IA		15. 00
4213.	Dixie Memories	28 x 34	CAC		10. 00
		20 x 24	CAC		5. 00
4214.	Flowering Dogwood	25 x 31	CAC		7. 50
		17 x 21	CAC		3. 00
4215.	Gleam O'Gold	28 x 34	CAC		10. 00
		20 x 24	CAC		7. 50
4216.	Jenny Lind	28 x 22	NYGS		12. 00
		11 x 8-1/2	NYGS		1. 50
4217.	Keep 'Em Flying	20 x 16	CAC		2. 50
		14 x 11	CAC		1. 00
4218.	Niche, Fruit and				
	Flowers	33-1/2 x 10	NYGS		10. 00
4219.	Portico, Fruit and				
	Flowers	33-1/2 x 10	NYGS		10. 00
4220.	Temple Dancer	24 x 20	CAC		7. 50
4221.	Tulips	17 x 21	CAC		3. 00
4222.	Venus	39 x 12	CAC		15. 00

GOLINKIN, JOSEPH WEBSTER (American, 1896-)

4223.	Endeavor II and				
	Ranger	23 x 17	CAC		15. 00
4224.	Hambletonian	17 x 23	CAC		15. 00

GÖLLNER, KURT (German, 1880-)

| 4225. | Chalet in the | | | | |
| | Mountains | 20 x 27-1/2 | ESH | Pr. | 8. 00 |

GONNER, P. (German)

4226.	Song Birds (6)	12 x 9	DAC	ea.	. 30
	Bluebird	8 x 6	DAC	ea.	. 20
	Cardinal				
	Goldfinch (2)				
	Robin				
	Rusty Blackbird				

GONZALES, XAVIER (American, 1898-)

| 4227. | Hong Kong | 21 x 32 | NYGS | | 15. 00 |
| 4228. | Personnage | 15 x 11 | NYGS | | 12. 00 |

GOODMAN, ELSA
 4229. Christ in Gethsemane
     (After Hofmann) 40 x 30   IA   12. 00
GOODWIN, ROBIN
 4230. Homing on a Fresh
     Westerly   20 x 30   AS   15. 00
 4231. Yealm River, Newton
     Ferrers   16 x 26   AS   12. 00
GORDON
 4232. Dancer (2)   23-1/2 x 16 ESH ea. 6. 00
GORKY, ARSHILE (American, 1904-1948)
 4233. Agony   c. 8 x 10   MMA   . 35
 4234. The Betrothal c. 9 x 7   AP   . 50
 4235. Liveris Cock's Comb,
     1944   c. 8 x 10   NYGS   . 50
 4236. Water of the Flowery
     Mill   28 x 24   NYGS   16. 00
GORTER, ARNOLD MARC (Dutch, 1866-)
 4237. December   27 x 21   CAC   10. 00
 4238. Spring   19 x 31   CAC   10. 00
GOSSART, JAN See MABUSE
GOTTLIEB, ADOLPH (American, 1903-)
 4239. Thrust, 1959   28 x 23   NYGS   16. 00
GOUGH, (MISS) (English, [Res. India] Ac. 1840-43)
 4240. Barbados Pride 21 x 30   RL   6. 00
 4241. Citrus Maxima 21 x 30   RL   6. 00
 4242. Dillenia and
     Hibiscus   21 x 30   RL   6. 00
 4243. Hibiscus and
     Stribilanthes   21 x 30   RL   6. 00
 4244. Lotus Flowers 21 x 30   RL   6. 00
 4245. Tobacco Plant 21 x 30   RL   6. 00
GOULD, JOHN (English, 1804-1881)
 4246. Birds (16)   12 x 9   CAC ea. 1. 00
             8 x 6   CFA ea. 1. 00
GOYA Y LUCIENTES, FRANCISCO DE (Spanish, 1746-1828)
 4247. Be Careful with That
     Step (B & W)   12 x 8   NYGS   2. 00
 4248. Blindman's Buff 15 x 20   CAC   4. 00
           11 x 13-1/2 AS   3. 25
 4249. Bullfight   19 x 24   NYGS   10. 00
          15-1/2 x 24 PENN   1. 50
 4250. Don Manuel Osorio
     de Zuniga   30 x 23   NYGS   16. 00
           24 x 18   PENN   1. 50
           23 x 17-1/2 AP   5. 00
          19-1/2 x 15 NYGS   9. 00
           14 x 11   NYGS   4. 00
          12-1/2 x 9 NYGS   1. 00
        c. 9 x 7   AP   . 50
 4251. Dona Arias de
     Enriques   15 x 11   AS   3. 25

4252.	Dona Isabel Cobos				
	de Porcel	26 x 17	NYGS	12. 00	
	c.	23 x 18	HNA	5. 95	
		18-1/2x12-1/2	PENN	1. 00	
4253.	Gossiping Women	16 x 40	NYGS	18. 00	
4254.	Group of Children				
	c.	8 x 10	NYGS	. 50	
4255.	Lady Reading a				
	Letter	22-1/2x15-1/2	ESH	10. 00	
4256.	Maja Dressed	11 x 21-1/2	PENN	1. 50	
		7-1/2x14-1/2	AS	3. 25	
4257.	Maja Nude	16 x 32	NYGS	12. 00	
	c.	8 x 10	ESH	1. 00	
		7-1/2x14-1/2	AS	3. 25	
4258.	Picnic c.	10 x 8	ESH	1. 00	
4259.	Portrait of the				
	Artist	17 x 13	CAC	7. 50	
4260.	Portrait of Countess				
	Casa-Flores	15 x 10	IA	3. 00	
4261.	Portrait of El Conde				
	de Teba c.	10 x 8	NYGS	. 50	
4262.	Portrait of				
	Ferdinand VII	13 x 10	IA	3. 00	
4263.	Queen Maria				
	Louise	35 x 25	NYGS	32. 00	
4264.	El Quitasol	11 x 15	AS	3. 25	
4265.	Senora Sabasa				
	Garcia	23-1/2x19-1/2	PENN	1. 50	
	c.	23 x 18	HNA	5. 95	
	c.	22 x 17-1/2	AS	4. 00	
		20 x 16	NYGS	9. 00	
4266.	Spring	20 x 13	CFA	7. 50	
4267.	Victor Guye c.	23 x 18	HNA	5. 95	
4268.	Vintage	21 x 15	CAC	4. 00	
4269.	Water Carrier	22 x 16	NYGS	10. 00	
GOYEN,	JAN VAN (Dutch, 1596-1656)				
4270.	Landscape, Dordrecht				
		9-1/2 x 16	AR	4. 00	
4271.	Riverside Village	8 x 10-1/2	ESH	1. 00	
4272.	Village Landscape	19-1/2x31-1/2	ESH	15. 00	
GOZZOLI,	BENOZZO (Italian, 1420-1497)				
4273.	Angel (Head)	15 x 11	IA	3. 00	
4274.	Angel Adoring (2)	15 x 11	IA	ea. 3. 00	
4275.	Angel Gardener	15-1/2 x 11	AS	3. 25	
4276.	Angels Adoring (2)	11 x 15	IA	ea. 3. 00	
4277.	Journey of the Magi:				
4278.	Emperor Paleologue				
	Section	11 x 14-1/2	AS	3. 25	
		15 x 11	IA	3. 00	
4279.	Emperor Paleologue -				
	Detail of No.				
	4277	20 x 26-1/2	AS	7. 50	

		11 x 15	IA		3.00
		10-1/2 x 15	AS		3.25
4280.	Lorenzo De Medici				
	Section	11 x 14	AS		3.25
		15 x 11	IA		3.00
4281.	Lorenzo De Medici -				
	Detail of No.				
	4277	20 x 26-1/2	AS		7.50
		11 x 15	IA		3.00
		10-1/2 x 15	AS		3.25
4282.	Lorenzo De Medici				
	(Head) - Detail of				
	No. 4277	15-1/2x11-1/2	AS		3.25
	Piero De Medici -				
	Details (2) of No.				
	4277	11 x 15	IA	ea.	3.00
4283.	Giuliano De Medici				
	Section	11 x 15	AS		3.25
4284.	Giuliano De Medici -				
	Detail of No.				
	4277	11 x 15	IA		3.00
4285.	Marriage of St.				
	Catherine	7 x 11	IA		3.00
4286.	Miracle of St.				
	Dominic	9 x 13	IA		3.00
4287.	St. Augustine Brought				
	to School	11 x 13	IA		3.00
4288.	St. Augustine Leaving				
	Rome for Milan	11 x 12	IA		3.00
4289.	St. Augustine Teaching				
	Philosophy	11 x 13	IA		3.00
4290.	St. Sebastian	15 x 11	IA		3.00
4291.	Tower of Babel				
	(2 Details)	11 x 15	IA	ea.	3.00
4292.	Tower of Babel				
	(2 Details)	15 x 11	IA	ea.	3.00

GRABAR

4293.	Russian Winter c.	7 x 9	AP	.50

GRABWINKLER, PAUL (Austrian, 1880-)

4294.	Fall of the Year	12 x 16	IA	2.50

GRADL, HERMANN (German, 1883-)

4295.	River View	22-1/2 x 28	ESH	10.00

GRAF, URS (Swiss, 1487-1529)

4296.	Blue Room	17-1/2x13-1/2	NYGS	9.00
4297.	Home Sweet Home	17-1/2x13-1/2	NYGS	9.00
4298.	Place of Execution	9 x 9-1/2	AR	3.00

GRAHAM, ROBERT MAC D. (American Contemporary)

4299.	Still Life (6)	8 x 10	NYGS	ea.	1.50
				set	7.50

GRAILLY, VICTOR DE (French [Res. U. S.] Ac. 1840-1870)

4300.	View of Mount			
	Vernon	15-1/2 x 21	NYGS	10.00

4301.	Washington's Tomb,			
	Mount Vernon	15-1/2 x 21	NYGS	10.00

GRANDMA MOSES See MOSES
GRANT, CHARLES

4302.	An English Lady in Calcutta, 1848	24 x 17	AA	10.00
4303.	An Englishman in Calcutta, 1848	24 x 17	AA	10.00

GRANT, (SIR) FRANCIS (Scotch, 1803-1878)

4304.	Breakfast Scene at Melton, 1834	20-1/2 x 28	NYGS	15.00
4305.	Quorn Hounds	20 x 27	CAC	25.00
4306.	Sir Richard Sutton	17 x 28	CAC	25.00
4307.	Sir Richard Sutton and the Quorn Hounds	20 x 34	CAC	36.00

GRANT, GORDON (American, 1875-1962)

4308.	Harbor Traffic	17 x 21-1/2	NYGS	7.50
4309.	In with the Tide	25 x 30	CAC	7.50
4310.	Last Rays c.	7 x 9	AP	.50
4311.	Wind and Tide	16-1/2x21-1/2	NYGS	7.50
4312.	Winter Landscape	20 x 25	CAC	7.50

GRAU-SALA, EMILIO (Spanish Contemporary)

4313.	Vaudeville Artist No. 1	18 x 15	CAC	10.00

GRAULÉ

4314.	Blossom Valley	24 x 48	DAC	10.00
		12 x 24	DAC	3.50
4315.	Country Autumn	24 x 48	DAC	10.00
		12 x 24	DAC	3.50

GRAVES, MORRIS (American Contemporary)

4316.	Bird Searching	30 x 15	NYGS	15.00
4317.	Birds on the Beach			
	c.	11 x 15	AP	1.00
	c.	7 x 9	AP	1.00
4318.	Duck Resting	19 x 30	CFA	7.50
4319.	Duckling	13 x 17	CFA	5.00
4320.	Little Known Bird of the Inner Eye c.	8 x 10	NYGS	.50
4321.	Maribou	17 x 25	CFA	5.00
4322.	Woodpeckers	30-1/2 x 21	NYGS	15.00

GRAY, MARIE CHILTON (American, 1888-)

4323.	Delphinium and White Peonies	25 x 30	CAC	7.50

GRAY, RALPH W. (American, 1880-)

4324.	Home Camp in March	14 x 18	AJ	6.00

GRECO, EL (DOMENICO THEOTOCOPULI) (Spanish, 1541-1614)

4325.	Annunciation	25 x 17	NYGS	15.00
4326.	Apostles Peter and Paul	26 x 22	NYGS	12.00
4327.	Christ Blessing c.	23 x 18	HNA	5.95

4328.	Christ Driving the Traders from the Temple	20 x 24	NYGS	18. 00
4329.	Christ Healing the Blind Man	28 x 34-1/2	IA	15. 00
4330.	Christ in the Garden of Gethsemane c.	7 x 9	AP	. 50
4331.	Head of Christ c.	24 x 20	PENN	1. 50
4332.	The Holy Family c.	7 x 9	AP	. 50
4333.	Laocoon c.	23 x 18	HNA	5. 95
4334.	Mary Magdalen	21-1/2x16-1/2	NYGS	12. 00
4335.	Mater Dolorosa	26 x 20	IA	18. 00
		20-1/2x14-1/2	ESH	10. 00
	c.	10 x 8	ESH	1. 00
4336.	St. Jerome	28-1/2x24-1/2	NYGS	18. 00
4337.	St. John the Baptist c.	9 x 7	AP	. 50
4338.	St. Martin and the Beggar	24 x 13	PENN	1. 50
		24 x 12-1/2	NYGS	12. 00
		10 x 5	NYGS	. 50
4339.	View of Toledo	28 x 25	NYGS	18. 00
		24 x 21-1/2	NYGS	12. 00
		24 x 18	PENN	1. 50
		18 x 16	AP	5. 00
		14 x 12-1/2	NYGS	4. 00
	c.	9 x 7	AP	. 50
		8 x 7	NYGS	. 50
4340.	The Virgin with St. Ines and St. Thecla	28 x 15-1/2	PENN	1. 50
		24 x 12-1/2	NYGS	12. 00

GREECE

4341.	Antiquities (3)	9 x 24 (1)	AR	set 12. 00
		8-1/2 x 12 (2)	AR	of 3
4342.	Apollo's Oxen Stolen by Hermes (Detail of Vase)	10-1/2 x 13	ESH	8. 00
4343.	Chariot (Detail of Vase)	10 x 17	ESH	8. 00
4344.	Discobolus (Sculpture) c.	9 x 7	AP	. 25
4345.	Exaltation of the Flower (Bas Relief)	18-1/2 x 21	ESH	10. 00
4346.	Ganymede Pursued by Zeus (Detail of Vase)	15-1/2 x 12	ESH	8. 00
4347.	Greek Scrolls (Black) (4)	7 x 10	CFA	ea. 4. 00
4348.	Maenads, Attic Vase (Detail)	18 x 22-1/2	ESH	10. 00

4349.	Parthenon Frieze (Elgin Marbles):			
4350.	Horsemen in the Panathenaic Procession	21 x 35-1/2	NYGS	16. 00
4351.	Horsemen Preparing for the Panathenaic Procession	21-1/2x35-1/2	NYGS	16. 00
4352.	Quadriga - Vix Vase	23 x 30	ESH	15. 00
	c.	8 x 10	ESH	1. 00
4353.	Stag (Detail of Vase)	11 x 17	ESH	8. 00
4354.	UNESCO World Art Series (32)	11 x 14		
	or	14 x 11	NYGS ea.	2. 00
4355.	Victory of Samothrace (Sculpture)	9x 7	AP	. 25

GREEN, M. GHIGLION (French Contemporary)

4356.	L'Eglise St. Pierre	20-1/2 x 25	RL	10. 00
4357.	Haymakers	19-1/2 x 24	RL	10. 00

GREENE, ELMER

4358.	Gardenia	20 x 16	IA	3. 50
4359.	Satin Gown	22 x 26	CAC	7. 50
4360.	Still Life (8)	24 x 30	CAC ea.	7. 50
4361.	Antique Plate			
4362.	Blue Bowl			
4363.	Brass Vase			
4364.	Garden's Gift			
4365.	Garnet Vase			
4366.	Harmony			
4367.	Magnolia			
4368.	Symphony of Flowers			
	Still Life (2)	24 x 36	CAC ea.	10. 00
4369.	Basket of Sunshine			
4370.	Medley of Spring			
	Still Life (2)	22 x 33	CAC ea.	7. 50
4371.	Chinese Basket			
4372.	Orchid and White			

GREENWOOD, MARION (American Contemporary)

4373.	Haitian Dancers	12 x 18	NYGS	7. 50

GREER, A. D.

4374.	Blue and White	25 x 30	AA	7. 50
4375.	Glade Water	25 x 30	CAC	7. 50
4376.	May Blossoms	25 x 30	IA	7. 50

GREIG, D.

4377.	Fine Sailing Day	15 x 12	ESH	6. 00
4378.	Preparing to Sail	12 x 15	ESH	6. 00
4379.	Sparkling Water	15 x 12-1/2	ESH	6. 00
4380.	Summer Sunshine	12 x 15	ESH	6. 00
4381.	West Country Harbour	12 x 15	ESH	6. 00
4382.	Yachting Panorama	10 x 15	ESH	6. 00

GRELLETTE
4383.	Sacred Heart of Jesus		20 x 16	CAC	6.00
			12 x 9	CAC	2.00
4384.	Sacred Heart of Mary		20 x 16	CAC	6.00
			12 x 9	CAC	2.00

GREUZE, JEAN-BAPTISTE (French, 1725-1805)
4385.	Broken Jug	c.	24 x 20	PENN	1.50
		Oval	13 x 11	IA	3.00
			12 x 9	CFA	2.50
4386.	Broken Pitcher		18 x 14	CAC	7.50
		c.	10 x 8	NYGS	.50
4387.	Dairymaid	Oval	13 x 11	IA	3.00
4388.	Dead Bird		14 x 11	IA	3.00
4389.	L'Enfant a l'Ecuelle		14 x 8	NYGS	4.00
4390.	Girl with a Puppy	c.	10 x 8	ESH	1.00
4391.	Girl with a Rose	c.	10 x 8	ESH	1.00
4392.	Head of a Girl		16 x 14	CAC	5.00
4393.	Little Girl with a Dog		14 x 11	IA	3.00
4394.	Mild Maid		18 x 14	CAC	7.50
			12 x 9	CFA	2.50
			11 x 9	CAC	5.00
		c.	10 x 8	NYGS	.50
4395.	Recreation		20 x 16	CFA	8.00
4396.	Sophie Arnold		18 x 15	ESH	10.00
4397.	Study of a Woman		17 x 13	CAC	5.00
4398.	Wool Winder		20 x 16-1/2	NYGS	10.00
4399.	Young Boy	c.	10 x 8	ESH	1.00
4400.	Young Girl with a Bird		16 x 13	CAC	5.00

GRIFFITH, E. N.
4401.	Bachelor's Friends	24 x 31	CFA	15.00
		6 x 7	CFA	1.00

GRIFFIN, K. A.
4402.	Becalmed Feluccas	20 x 30	AS	15.00
4403.	Bowsprit	16 x 36	AS	12.00
4404.	Calm	22 x 30	AS	15.00
4405.	Homecoming	20 x 30	AS	15.00

GRIGORESCU, NICOLAE (Rumanian, 1858-1907)
4406.	The Gypsy	27-1/2x14-1/2	NYGS	12.00

GRIMM, H. (German)
4407.	Indian Chief Monument Valley	16 x 12	ESH	Pr.	3.00
4408.	Mexican Fishers	16 x 23-1/2	ESH	Pr.	8.00
4409.	Princess White Stripe	16 x 12	ESH	Pr.	3.00
4410.	Two Girls on Yellow	22-1/2 x14	CFA		10.00

GRIMM, PAUL (American, 1875-)

4411.	Bouquet with				
	Gladiolus	19-1/2x27-1/2	ESH	Pr.	8. 00
4412.	Desert Beauty	16 x 20	ESH	Pr.	5. 00
4413.	Desert Domain	25 x 31	NYGS		12. 00
		16-1/2 x 21	NYGS		7. 50
		9 x 11	NYGS		1. 50
4414.	Grandmother and				
	Child	27-1/2 x 20	ESH	Pr.	8. 00
4415.	Joshua	16 x 20	ESH	Pr.	5. 00
4416.	Jucca, California	16 x 20	ESH	Pr.	5. 00
4417.	Mexico	16 x 20	ESH	Pr.	5. 00
4418.	Old Mission	12 x 16	ESH	Pr.	3. 00
4419.	Old Weaver	16 x 20	ESH	Pr.	5. 00
4420.	Pleasant Retreat	25 x 31	NYGS		12. 00
		16-1/2 x 21	NYGS		7. 50
		9 x 11	NYGS		1. 50
4421.	View into Mountains	23-1/2 x 20	ESH	Pr.	8. 00

GRIMOU, ALEXIS (French, 1678-1733)

4422.	Girl Pilgrim	14 x 10	IA		3. 00
4423.	Young Pilgrim (2)	14-1/2 x 11	AS	ea.	3. 25
4424.	Youthful Pilgrim	14 x 10	IA		3. 00

GRIS, JUAN (Spanish, 1887-1927)

4425.	Black Palette	c.	18 x 23	HNA	5. 95
4426.	Breakfast	c.	8 x 10	MMA	. 35
4427.	Checkerboard		16 x 20	CFA	7. 50
			11 x 14	AR	5. 00
4428.	Le Compotier		24-1/2 x 20	NYGS	12. 00
4429.	Guitar and Flowers				
		c.	8 x 10	MMA	. 35
4430.	Guitarist		23 x 15	AR	7. 50
4431.	Harlequin		20 x 13	AR	7. 50
4432.	Maker of Preserves		24 x 20	CAC	12. 00
4433.	Nature Morte		10 x 14	NYGS	15. 00
4434.	Poster: L'Atelier				
	of Juan Gris		27-1/2x20-1/2	PENN	1. 00
4435.	Le Sac de Café				
		c.	17-1/2 x 22	AS	4. 00
4436.	Still Life		22-1/2x18-1/2	ESH	10. 00
4437.	Still Life, 1915		15-1/2x19-1/2	NYGS	6. 00
4438.	Still Life / Album		22 x 28	NYGS	20. 00
4439.	Still Life Before Open				
	Window, Place Ravignon				
		c.	20 x 24	PENN	1. 50
4440.	Still Life with Open				
	Book		16 x 20	NYGS	10. 00
4441.	Violin et Verres (Violin				
	and Glasses)		19-1/2 x 24	AA	15. 00

GRISOT, P.

4442.	After Rehearsal	24 x 19-1/2	RL		10. 00
4443.	Portraits of Girls				
	(4)	12 x 9	DAC	ea.	2. 00

GROFE, MARY
| 4444. | Roses and Larkspur | 14 x 15 | CFA | 1.50 |
| 4445. | Zinnias and Lark-spur | 14 x 15 | CFA | 1.50 |

GROMAIRE, MARCEL (French, 1892-)
| 4446. | Brooklyn Bridge | 18-1/2x22-1/2 | IA | 10.00 |

GROPPER, WILLIAM (American, 1897-)
4447.	America--Its Folklore (Map)	22 x 32-1/2	NYGS	6.00
4448.	Cossacks	14 x 18	CAC	10.00
4449.	Diogenes	18 x 12	CAC	10.00
4450.	On Stage	18 x 14	CAC	10.00
4451.	Races	18 x 14	CAC	10.00
4452.	Senate	15 x 20	NYGS	9.00
4453.	Senator	14 x 18	NYGS	7.50
4454.	The West	16 x 20	CAC	10.00
4455.	Woodcutter	18 x 14	CAC	10.00

GROSE, DAVID
4456.	Balloon with Horse-man	18 x 24	AA	12.00
4457.	Blackberry Patch	10 x 30	AA	12.00
4458.	Caleb	13 x 10	AA	6.00
4459.	Cape Cod, Mass. (4)	15 x 10-1/2	AA	ea. 5.00
4460.	Faneuil Hall, Boston			
4461.	House of Seven Gables			
4462.	State House, Boston			
4463.	Wight Grist Mill			
	Cape Cod, Mass. (4)	10 x 8	AA	ea. 2.50
4464.	Light House			
4465.	Old House			
4466.	Old Mill			
4467.	Windmill			
4468.	Cape Harbour	8 x 10	AA	2.50
4469.	Clipper Nightingale	13-1/2 x 20	AA	10.00
4470.	Elm Street Trolley	11 x 16	AA	6.00
4471.	Fuller Family	12 x 16	AA	8.00
4472.	Ghosted Autos	18 x 24	AA	12.00
4473.	Ghosted Trolleys	18 x 24	AA	12.00
4474.	Landscape	14 x 22-1/2	PENN	1.50
4475.	Locust Trees	10 x 30	AA	12.00
4476.	Main Street Trolley	11 x 16	AA	6.00
4477.	New England Barn	28 x 13	AA	12.00
4478.	New England Church	28 x 13	AA	12.00
4479.	New England Scenes (6)	29 x 10	AA	ea. 12.00
4480.	Ancient Cape-Codder			
4481.	Cape Cod Meeting House			
4482.	Christopher Wren Church			
4483.	Old Mill			
4484.	Old North Church			
4485.	Old South Meeting House			

4486.	Old Manse	10-1/2 x 15	AA	5.00
4487.	Sea Gulls	8 x 10	AA	2.50
4488.	U. S. S. Constitution			
		13-1/2 x 20	AA	10.00
4489.	Verity	13 x 10	AA	6.00
4490.	Wayside Inn	10-1/2 x 15	AA	5.00
4491.	Winged Balloon	18 x 24	AA	12.00

GROSS

4492.	Landscape	14 x 22-1/2	PENN	1.50

GROSSI, O. (American Contemporary)

4493.	Still Life, Golden			
	(2)	18 x 26	AK	ea. 6.00

GROSZ, GEORGE (German-American, 1893-1959)

4494.	Central Park	17-1/2x13-1/2	NYGS	7.50
4495.	Funeral of the Poet			
	Panizza	c. 12 x 16	AP	2.00
4496.	Man of Opinion	c. 8 x 10	NYGS	.50
4497.	Manhattan	22 x 16	AP	15.00
		c. 9 x 7	AP	.25
4498.	Manhattan Harbor	22 x 16-1/2	NYGS	10.00
4499.	Piece of My World			
		c. 8 x 10	NYGS	.50

GROTH

4500.	Bullfight	16 x 22	CAC	24.00

GRUND, NORBERT (Austrian, 1717-1767)

4501.	Walk in the Park	24 x 18	DAC	7.50
		16 x 12	DAC	2.50

GRÜNEWALD (OR GRUENEWALD), MATTHIAS (German, c. 1470-1531)

4502.	Angel Concert with			
	Madonna and Child	20 x 22	CAC	12.00
4503.	Angel Musician	23 x 18	ESH	10.00
4504.	Ascension	30 x 19	CAC	18.00
4505.	Christ on the Cross	20 x 22	CAC	12.00
4506.	Concert of the			
	Angels	13 x 21	ESH	5.00
4507.	Crucifixion	37 x 28	NYGS	36.00
		24 x 18	NYGS	15.00
		19 x 16-1/2	AP	5.00
4508.	Madonna			
	(Isenheimer Altar)	30 x 23-1/2	NYGS	26.00
4509.	Moonlight	23 x 29	CAC	10.00
4510.	Portrait of a Saint			
	in Prayer	14 x 11-1/2	AR	4.00
4511.	Stuppach Madonna	33-1/2 x 28	NYGS	10.00
4512.	Virgin and St. John	31 x 25	ESH	15.00

GUARDI, FRANCESCO DE' (Italian, 1712-1793)

4513.	Arco E. Marina			
	(Arch and Seaway)	12 x 21	CFA	12.00
4514.	Brenta Canal	12 x 21	CFA	12.00
4515.	Bridge at Venice	12 x 20	DAC	5.00
4516.	Colonnades	30 x 23	CFA	15.00

4517.	Departure of the Bocentauro	20 x 30	ESH	15. 00
4518.	La Dogana, Venice	22 x 28	NYGS	15. 00
4519.	La Dogana and Santa Maria Della Salute	13 x 21-1/2	NYGS	12. 00
4520.	Doge's Palace, Venice	22 x 28	NYGS	15. 00
		17 x 23	AR	15. 00
4521.	Ducal Palace, Venice c.	18 x 23	HNA	5. 95
4522.	Fantastic Landscape	15-1/2 x 40	NYGS	18. 00
4523.	Flowers	21 x 31	NYGS	16. 00
4524.	Grand Canal	22 x 40	CFA	25. 00
4525.	Grand Canal Rialto Bridge	12 x 18	CFA	7. 50
4526.	Grand Canal, San Geremia	22 x 37	NYGS	22. 00
4527.	Isle of St. Giorgio Maggiore	11 x 15	AS	3. 25
4528.	Ladies and Patricians	8 x 15	AS	3. 25
4529.	Lagoon of Venice	9 x 12	ESH	5. 00
4530.	Little Square of St. Marcus	9 x 15	AS	3. 25
4531.	Monastery of St. Zacary	8 x 15	AS	3. 25
4532.	Old Fishery	9 x 15	AS	3. 25
4533.	Peristylium of a Villa	8 x 6	IA	1. 50
4534.	La Place Saint-Marc	9-1/2x13-1/2	NYGS	4. 00
4535.	Rio dei Mendicanti at Venice	8 x 6	IA	1. 50
4536.	Ruins on the Seashore	14 x 10	CFA	1. 50
4537.	San Giorgio Maggiore	16 x 30	NYGS	12. 00
4538.	Santa Maria Della Salute	21 x 28	NYGS	15. 00
		19 x 26	ESH	15. 00
		13 x 21	NYGS	10. 00
4539.	Seascape with Archway	9 x 15	IA	3. 00
4540.	Seaport with Classic Ruins	8 x 12	CFA	2. 00
4541.	Scene in Venice	23 x 34	CFA	20. 00
4542.	Sultan's Favorite	18 x 25	NYGS	12. 00
4543.	Summer Day in the Palace Garden	18 x 25	NYGS	12. 00
4544.	Venice: San Giorgio Maggiore	16 x 30	NYGS	12. 00
4545.	Venise	10 x 15	NYGS	4. 00

4546.	View of the Canale di Brenta	9 x 15	IA		3.00
4547.	View of the Laguna at Venice	10 x 15	IA		3.00
4548.	View on the Cannareggio	16 x 25	NYGS		12.00

GUASTA, BENVENUTO DI GIOVANNI DEL (Italian, 1436-1518)

4549.	Angels (Detail from "The Virgin and Saints)	15 x 11	IA		3.00
4550.	Hercules at the Crossroads	11" Diam.	AS		3.25

GUBA, RUDOLF (German, Ac. 1940-)

4551.	Idle Hours	24 x 28	CFA		10.00
4552.	Lighter in the Morning	23-1/2x35-1/2	ESH		18.00
4553.	Sailing Boats	23-1/2x31-/2	ESH	Pr.	10.00
		16 x 20	ESH	Pr.	5.00

GUBLER, MAX

4554.	Old Man and the Sea	39 x 27	CFA		30.00

GUDIOL, MONTSERRAT (Spanish Contemporary)

4555.	Motherhood	26 x 19	NYGS		12.00

GUERCINO, IL (BARBIERI, GIOVANNI FRANCESCO) (Italian, 1591-1666)

4556.	Di Porti Estiui	14 x 19	CFA		10.00
4557.	Ecce Homo	14-1/2x11-1/2	AS		3.25
		14 x 11	IA		3.00
4558.	Susanna and the Elders (Dr.)	11-1/2x10-1/2	NYGS		3.00

GUERIN, FRANCOIS (French, 1735-1791)

4559.	The Artist's Daughter	18 x 14-1/2	NYGS		10.00
4560.	Lady Reading with Child	10 x 12	AR		4.00
4561.	Lady Writing with Child	10 x 12	AR		4.00
4562.	Lady's Phaeton c.	8 x 10	ESH		1.00

GUERMACHEFF, MICHEL

4563.	Lengthening Shadows	19 x 22-1/2	CAC		5.00
4564.	Sunset Glory	19 x 22-1/2	CAC		5.00

GUIDI, TOMMASO See MASACCIO

GUIDI, VIRGILIO

4565.	Portrait of the Artist's Daughter	14-1/2x11-1/2	AS		3.25

GUIDO DA SIENA (Italian, 14th Century)

4566.	Madonna and Child	15 x 10	IA		3.00
4567.	Virgin Enthroned	15-1/2 x 10	AS		3.25

GUIDONE (GUIDO DI GRAZIANO) (Italian, 1278-1302)

4568.	Frate Guido di S. Galgano	14 x 9	IA		3.00

GUIGOU, PAUL CAMILLE (French, 1834-1871)

4569.	Provencal Landscape	c. 8 x 10	ESH		1.00

GUILLAUMIN, ARMAND (French, 1841-1927)
4570.	Pointe de la Beau-			
	mette, Agay c.	18 x 23	HNA	5. 95
4571.	Riviera (Agay)	22 x 27	NYGS	12. 00
4572.	Die Roten Felsen			
	von Agay c.	17-1/2 x 22	AS	4. 00

GUION, MOLLY (American Contemporary)
4573.	Jade and China	24 x 20	NYGS	10. 00
4574.	Rose Goddess	24 x 20	NYGS	10. 00

GUYS, CONSTANTIN (French, 1805-1892)
4575.	La Caleche	7 x 10	NYGS	4. 00
4576.	Dancer	12 x 9	AR	5. 00
4577.	English Family			
	Outing	10 x 8	ESH	1. 00
4578.	Horse and Carriage	8 x 10	ESH	1. 00
4579.	Hyde Park	8 x 10	ESH	1. 00
4580.	Ladies at the Theatre	7 x 10	CFA	5. 00
4581.	Lady in Blue and			
	Green	12 x 8-1/2	AR	5. 00
4582.	Riders in the Bois			
	de Boulogne	10 x 8	ESH	1. 00
4583.	Two Ladies in a			
	Theatre Box	7 x 10	AR	5. 00

GWATHMEY, ROBERT (American Contemporary)
4584.	Soft Crabbing c.	18 x 23	HNA	5. 95

H

HACKER, A. (English, 1858-1919)
4585.	Christ on the Mount			
	of Olives	20 x 40	AS	12. 00
		14 x 31	AS	7. 50

HACKER, PHILIPPE
4586.	Lake of Albano	9 x 12	DAC	2. 00

HACKERT, JACOB PHILIPP (German, 1737-1807)
HAGEDORN, KARL (German [Res. England] 1889-)
4588.	Rough Waters	17 x 24	CFA	6. 00

HAGER, WILHELM (German Contemporary)
4589.	Garden Poppies	22 x 31-1/2	ESH	Cv. 15. 00
4590.	Midday in the			
	Harbour	22 x 31-1/2	ESH	Cv. 15. 00

HAHN, WILLIAM (American, 1840-1890)
4591.	Autumn	14 x 39-1/2	ESH	8. 00
4592.	Autumn	16 x 31-1/2	ESH	7. 00
4593.	Steep Coast	14 x 39-1/2	ESH	8. 00
4594.	Surf	16 x 31-1/2	ESH	7. 00
4595.	Up in Central Park	20 x 40	AA	15. 00

HAHN VIDAL, MARGARITA See VIDAL
HAIDER, KARL (German, 1846-1912)
4596.	Foothills of the			
	Alps	18 x 21-1/2	NYGS	16. 00

HAKENBECK

4597.	Peter at the Zoo	20 x 14	AP	5.00

HALEWIJN, WILLIAM

4598.	Boy of Haifa	27 x 21-1/2	IA	10.00
4599.	Leila: Girl of Jerusalem	27 x 17-1/2	IA	10.00
4600.	Palestine: Refugee-Mother	27 x 20	IA	10.00

HALL, HAINES (American, Ac. 1959-)

4601.	Gardenias	17 x 18	IA	3.00
		9 x 10	IA	1.00
4602.	Magnolia Blossoms	17 x 18	IA	3.00
		9 x 10	IA	1.00

HALLIDAY, EDWARD (English, 1902-)

4603.	Prince Philip, Duke of Edinburgh	20 x15	CAC	7.50

HALS, DIRCK (Dutch, 1591-1656)

4604.	The Solo	15 x 11-1/2	AJ	5.00

HALS, FRANS (Flemish, 1580-1666)

4605.	Bohemian Girl	24 x 20	PENN	1.50
4606.	La Bohemienne	22-1/2x20-1/2	NYGS	22.00
4607.	Boy with a Lute	24 x 19	PENN	1.50
4608.	Claes Duyst van Voorhout c.	8 x 10	NYGS	.50
4609.	Family Group	15 x 25	ESH	12.00
4610.	Fenyntje van Steenkiste	14 x 10	IA	3.00
4611.	Fisher Maiden c.	23 x 18	HNA	5.95
4612.	The Gypsy	15 x 14	CFA	5.00
		12 x 11	IA	3.00
4613.	Happy Reveller	23-1/2 x 19	PENN	1.50
4614.	Hille Bobbe	19 x 16	CAC	4.00
		7 x 6	NYGS	.50
4615.	The Jester	26 x 22-1/2	NYGS	18.00
		26 x 22	AP	15.00
		22 x 16	CAC	18.00
	c.	9 x 7	AP	.50
4616.	Laughing Cavalier	19 x 15	ESH	15.00
		16-1/2 x 13	NYGS	6.00
		12 x 9	CAC	2.00
	c.	9 x 7	AP	.50
4617.	Portrait of Jasper Schade von Westrum	24 x 18	PENN	1.50
4618.	Portrait of an Officer c.	23 x 18	HNA	5.95
		11 x 9	CFA	2.00
4619.	Portrait of a Woman c.	10 x 8	NYGS	.50
4620.	Rummelpot Player	24 x 18	CFA	15.00
4621.	Singing Boy	7 x 6	NYGS	.50
4622.	Singing Boys c.	23 x 18	HNA	5.95
	c.	9 x 7	AP	.60

4623.	W. Van Heythuysen	25 x 16-1/2	ESH		12. 00

HAMBOURG, ANDRÉ (French Contemporary)

4624.	Venise: Vue de Torcello	17-1/2 x 25	NYGS		22. 00

HAMEN Y LEON, JUAN VAN DER (Spanish, 1596-1632)

4625.	Still Life (Attributed)	24 x 32	NYGS		15. 00
4626.	Still Life: Flowers and Fruit (Attributed)	23 x 30	NYGS		16. 00
		10 x 14	NYGS		4. 00
	Detail of No. 4626	17 x 27	NYGS		12. 00

HAMILTON, FRANK M.

4627.	New Orleans Panels (4)	36 x 15	AK	ea.	7. 50
		19 x 8	AK	ea.	2. 50
		10 x 4	AK	ea.	1. 00

HAMILTON, LETITIA M. (Irish Contemporary)

4628.	Gateway to Wales	16 x 20-1/2	ESH		12. 00
4629.	Poplars, Jura Valley	17-1/2 x 21	ESH		12. 00

HAMILTON, WILLIAM (English, 1751-1801)

4630.	Times of Day (4)	12 x 10	CFA	set	25. 00

HAN JO-CHO (Chinese, 1050-1125)

4631.	Sparrows in Rice Field	10" - Ovoid	NYGS		10. 00

HAN-KAN (Chinese 8th Century)

4632.	Tarters Bringing a Tribute of Horses (Attributed)	12 x 40	NYGS		18. 00

HANFT, WILLY (German, 1888-)

4633.	Beechen Alley	23-1/2x31-1/2	IA		10. 00
4634.	Birches	22-1/2 x 30	IA		10. 00
4635.	Garda Lake	24 x 32	CFA		12. 00
4636.	Spring	18 x 23-1/2	IA		6. 00
4637.	Sunny Way	24 x 32	CAC		10. 00
4638.	Sylvan Silence	24 x 32	IA		10. 00

HANKE

4639.	Ducks	31-1/2 x 16	ESH		7. 00
4640.	Swans	31-1/2 x 16	ESH		7. 00

HANKEY, WILLIAM LEE (English, 1869-)

4641.	Anchors Aweigh	20 x 24	CAC		6. 00
4642.	Arrival in Port	20 x 24	CAC		6. 00
4643.	Awaiting the Tide	26 x 31	CAC		10. 00
4644.	Breton Harbour	18 x 22	CAC		7. 50
4645.	Coombe Village, Oxfordshire	20 x 24	CAC		6. 00
4646.	Departing Fishermen	20 x 24	CAC		6. 00
4647.	Drifting	22 x 28	CAC		10. 00
4648.	Fish Quay, St. Ives	18 x 22	CAC		7. 50
4649.	Fisherman's Cove	26 x 31	NYGS		12. 00
4650.	Gay Normandy	20 x 24	CAC		6. 00
4651.	Mentone	18 x 22	CAC		5. 00
4652.	Mussel Boats, Honfleur	18 x 22	CAC		7. 50

4653.	Peaceful Waters	18-1/2 x 22	ESH		12. 00
4654.	Quaint Brittany	20 x 24	CAC		6. 00
4655.	St. Tropez Harbor	20 x 24	CAC		6. 00
4656.	Summer in Devonshire	25 x 31	NYGS		12. 00
4657.	Village Pond, Oxfordshire	20 x 24	CAC		6. 00

HANN, GEORGE

4658.	La Cote D'Azur	18-1/2 x 22	ESH		6. 00
4659.	Mediterrancan Street	18-1/2 x 22	ESH		6. 00

HANSEN

4600.	Questionable Companions	c. 20 x 24	PENN		1. 50

HAPP, HANS (German, 1889-)

4661.	Candlelight	27 x 23	ESH		12. 00
4662.	Old Well	27-1/2 x 23	ESH		12. 00

HARBART, GERTRUDE (American Contemporary)

4663.	Nickel Plate Road	17 x 39-1/2	NYGS		16. 00

HARDER, ALEXANDER (German, 1901-)

4664.	Coast of Lebanon	23 x 31	NYGS		22. 00
4665.	Old Fisherman	19 x 15	CAC		3. 50

HARDY, HEYWOOD (English, 1843-1932)

4666.	Breaking Cover	22 x 30	CAC		25. 00
4667.	Lost Scent	22 x 30	CAC		25. 00
4668.	Sporting Scene	17 x 25	CAC		5. 00

HARLOW, HARRY M. (American, 1882-)

4669.	Mrs. Waddell and Children	25 x 32	CAC		10. 00

HARNDEN

4670.	Still Life (2)	14 x 36	AK	ea.	10. 00
		10 x 26	AK	ea.	5. 00
		7 x 18	AK	ea.	3. 00
		4 x 10	AK	ea.	1. 00
	Still Life (2)	10 x 26	AK	ea.	5. 00
		7 x 18	AK	ea.	3. 00
		4 x 10	AK	ea.	1. 00

HARNETT, R. F.

4671.	Cats, Dogs and Horses (6)	24 x 12	AK	ea.	3. 00
		12 x 6	AK	ea.	1. 25
4672.	Favorite Birds (4)	36 x 12	AK	ea.	5. 00
4673.	Fruits Aglow (4)	11 x 14	AK	ea.	1. 50
4674.	Italy Romantic (4)	12 x 18	AK	ea.	2. 50
4675.	Lady Fair (Portraits of Women) (4)	20 x 16	AK	ea.	5. 00
		14 x 11	AK	ea.	2. 50
		10 x 8	AK	ea.	1. 25
4676.	Wild Flower Panels (4)	24 x 8	AK	ea.	2. 50
		14 x 6	AK	ea.	1. 00

4677.	Wild Flowers					
	(4)		12 x 9	AK	ea.	1.00

HARNETT, WILLIAM M. (American, 1848-1892)

4678.	Antique Violin		25 x 16	CFA	7.50
4679.	Banker's Table	c.	18 x 23	HNA	5.95
4680.	Bard of Avon		24 x 18	AA	10.00
4681.	Cremona Violin	c.	23 x 18	HNA	5.95
4682.	Emblems of Peace		21 x 26	CFA	12.00
			6 x 7	CFA	1.00
4683.	Evening's Comfort		9 x 12	CFA	3.00
4684.	Faithful Colt		22 x 18	PENN	1.50
4685.	Just Dessert		21 x 25	CFA	15.00
		c.	20 x 24	PENN	1.50
		c.	18 x 23	HNA	5.95
			16 x 20	AP	6.00
			6 x 7	CFA	1.00
4686.	Literature		14 x 19	CFA	5.00
			6 x 7	CFA	1.00
4687.	Music and Literature				
			23-1/2x31-1/2	NYGS	18.00
			16 x 21	PENN	1.50
			11 x 14	NYGS	3.00
4688.	My Gems	c.	18 x 23	HNA	5.95
4689.	Old Cremona		21 x 16	PENN	1.50
4690.	Old Models		30 x 16	CFA	15.00
4691.	Old Refrain		22-1/2x15-1/2	NYGS	7.50
4692.	Smoking		14 x 19	CFA	5.00
			6 x 7	CFA	1.00
4693.	Still Life with Copper Tankard, Jugs and Fruit	c.	18 x 23	HNA	5.95
4694.	Still Life with Pewter Tankard, Wine Bottle and Cooler	c.	18 x 23	HNA	5.95

HARRISON, JOHN CYRIL (English Contemporary)

4695.	Alpine Stream	24 x 31	CAC	15.00
4696.	Mallard Rising	13-1/2 x 19	ESH	5.00
4697.	Passing Mallards	18 x 24	CFA	7.50
4698.	Widgeon on Tideway	18 x 24	CFA	7.50

HART, ERNEST (American Contemporary)

4699.	Cocker Spaniels	16 x 22	NYGS	7.50
4700.	English Setters	16 x 22	NYGS	7.50
4701.	Irish Setters	16 x 22	NYGS	7.50
4702.	Pointers	16 x 22	NYGS	7.50

HART, GEORGE OVERBURY "POP" (American, 1868-1933)

4703.	Bahamas	12 x 19	NYGS	7.50

HARTLEY, MARSDEN (American, 1878-1943)

4704.	Fish House, New England	15 x 20	NYGS	9.00
4705.	Fox Island, Maine	20 x 25	PENN	1.50
4706.	Portrait of a German Officer	c.	10 x 8	NYGS	.50

4707.	Wild Roses, 1942	22 x 28	NYGS		16.00

HARTMANN, NORBERT (German Contemporary)

4708.	Palamos	20 x 27-1/2	ESH		12.00

HARTNETT

4709. Floral Subjects

	(2)	24 x 48	AK	ea.	8.00
		15 x 30	AK	ea.	7.50
		7 x 15	AK	ea.	2.00

Floral Subjects

	(2)	30 x 15	AK	ea.	7.50
		15 x 7	AK	ea.	2.00

HARTUNG, HANS (German Contemporary)

4710. Painting T 1962

	L 7	8-1/2 x 37	ESH		18.00

HARVEY, GEORGE (1801-1878)

4711.	Casenovia, N. Y.	26 x 48	AA		15.00

HARVEY, HAROLD (English, 1874-1942)

4712.	Blue Door, Newlyn	22 x 18	CAC		5.00

HASCH, KARL (Austrian, 1835-1897)

4713.	Landscape in Fall	24 x 48	AK		12.00
		12 x 24	AK		3.00

HASEGAWA

4714.	Ming Horse	30 x 40	CAC		45.00

HASLEHURST, ERNEST WILLIAM (English, 1866-)

4715.	By the Stream	10 x 15	ESH		2.00
4716.	Mill Stream	10 x 15	ESH		2.00

HASSAM, CHILDE (American, 1859-1935)

4717.	Bailey's Beach, 1901				
		22 x 24	NYGS		10.00
4718.	Church at Old Lyme	27 x 24	IA		12.00
	c.	9 x 7	AP		.50
4719.	Golden Afternoon, Oregon, 1908	29-1/2 x 39	NYGS		20.00
4720.	Winter Nightfall in the City, 1889	14-1/2 x 19	NYGS		7.50

HASSELL, CLEMENTS (English, Ac. 1950)

4721.	Blue Window in Cassis	24 x 20	CAC		10.00

HAUGHTON, W.

4722.	Irish Peat Bog, County Mayo	16 x 20	AS		6.00
4723.	St. Ives	16 x 20	AS		6.00

HAUSEN, PETER

4724.	Larkspur and Marguerites	31 x 12	CFA		12.00

HAVELL, ROBERT, JR. (American, 1793-1878)

4725.	The Blenheim Leaving Start Hotel	10 x 16	CAC		12.00
4726.	Land of Promise	26 x 36	AA		15.00
4727.	Partridge Shooting	11 x 15	CAC		24.00
4728.	Pheasant Shooting	11 x 15	CAC		24.00
4729.	Shootings (4)	8 x 12	CAC	set	24.00

4730.	Snipe Shooting	11 x 15	CAC	24.00
4731.	View of Ossining, 1856	28 x 37-1/2	NYGS	18.00
4732.	Wild Duck Shooting	11 x 15	CAC	24.00

HAWLEY, PETE

4733.	Copy Kittens (4)	10 x 8	DAC	ea.	1.00

HAWTHORNE, CHARLES WEBSTER (American, 1872-1930)

4734.	Trousseau	22 x 22	CAC	7.50

HAYMSON, JOHN (American Contemporary)

4735.	Arlington, Va., Robert E. Lee, Home	20 x 16	AA	7.50
4736.	Autos, Old	12 x 30	AA	10.00
4737.	Balloon No. 1	30 x 12	AA	10.00
4738.	Balloon No. 2	30 x 12	AA	10.00
4739.	Banjo	30 x 12	AA	10.00
4740.	Blast Furnace	30 x 12	AA	10.00
4741.	Blue Vase	30 x 12	AA	10.00
4742.	Boston, Mass.: Old North Church	30 x 12	AA	10.00
		20 x 16	AA	7.50
4743.	Old South Meeting House	30 x 12	AA	10.00
		20 x 16	AA	7.50
	Charleston, S. C.:			
4744.	Dock Street Theatre	16 x 12	AA	5.00
4745.	Garden Gate	16 x 12	AA	5.00
4746.	Meeting Street	16 x 12	AA	5.00
4747.	St. Philip's Church	16 x 12	AA	5.00
4748.	Charlottesville, Va., Thomas Jefferson's Home, Monticello	18 x 24	AA	12.00
	Chicago, Ill.:			
4749.	Aerial View	24 x 18	AA	10.00
4750.	Boulevard Bridge	20 x 16	AA	7.50
		12 x 9	AA	2.00
4751.	Michigan Boulevard	20 x 16	AA	7.50
		12 x 9	AA	2.00
4752.	Skyline	20 x 40	AA	20.00
4753.	Under the Clock	20 x 16	AA	7.50
4754.	Water Tower	24 x 18	AA	10.00
4755.	Corn	12 x 30	AA	10.00
4756.	Driftwood	12 x 30	AA	10.00
4757.	Fire Engines, Old	12 x 30	AA	10.00
4758.	Floral Subjects (5)	30 x 12	AA	ea. 10.00
4759.	Blue Vase			
4760.	Bowl			
4761.	Green Vase			
4762.	Vase			
4763.	White Vase			
	Floral Subjects (2)	27 x 20	AA	ea. 12.00
4764.	Fall in Manhattan			
4765.	Spring in Manhattan			

	Floral Subjects (2)	24 x 16-1/2	AA	ea.	12.00
4766.	Bouquet and Vieux Carré				
4767.	Bouquet and Governor's Palace				
4768.	Florence, Italy:				
	Piazza	12 x 16	AA		5.00
4769.	French Chateaux				
	(4)	12 x 9	AA	ea.	2.00
4770.	Chamford				
4771.	Destendre				
4772.	Sainte Mesme				
4773.	Villandry				
4774.	Fruit Subjects (4)	30 x 12	AA	ea.	10.00
4775.	Blackberries				
4776.	Cherries				
4777.	Grapes				
4778.	Strawberries				
	Fruit Subjects (4)	20 x 30	AA	ea.	15.00
4779.	Apple Bough				
4780.	Grape Cluster				
4781.	Mexican Fruit:	Grapes			
4782.	Mexican Fruit:	Pineapple			
4783.	Giant Metropolis	24 x 54	AA		30.00
4784.	Grain Elevator	20 x 16	AA		7.50
	Greece:				
4785.	Mykonos	16 x 29-1/2	AA		15.00
4786.	Poros Harbor, 1967	31 x 36	NYGS		18.00
	Jamaica, B.W.I.:				
4787.	Kingston	16 x 12	AA		5.00
4788.	Street Scene	16 x 12	AA		5.00
4789.	Locomotives, Old	12 x 30	AA		10.00
	London, England (4)	16 x 12	AA	ea.	5.00
4790.	Changing the Guard				
4791.	Mansion House				
4792.	Old Curiosity Shop				
4793.	Tower Bridge				
	London, England (2)	12 x 30	AA	ea.	10.00
4794.	Changing the Guard at Buckingham Palace				
4795.	London Bridge				
4796.	London, England: Houses				
	of Parliament	20 x 40	AA		20.00
4797.	Los Angeles, Cal.:				
	Civic Center	16 x 20	AA		7.50
4798.	Mandolin	30 x 12	AA		10.00
	Mexico (6)	12 x 16	AA	ea.	5.00
4799.	Flower Seller				
4800.	Fountain				
4801.	Market at Patzinaro				
4802.	Mexican Family				
4803.	Taxco				
4804.	Taxco Cathedral				

4805.	Mexico, Cuernavaca Market	12 x 30	AA	10.00

4805. Mexico, Cuernavaca
Market   12 x 30   AA   10.00
Nassau, Bahamas
(2)   12 x 16   AA   5.00
4806. Gregory's Arch
4807. Waterfront
4808. New England Harbors
(6)   12 x 16   AA   ea. 5.00
4809.   Boothbay (2)
4810.   Gloucester (2)
4811.   Rockport (2)
New Orleans, La.
(2)   20 x 16   AA   ea. 7.50
4812.   Lace Balconies
4813.   Old Residence
New Orleans, La.
(2)   30 x 12   AA   ea. 10.00
4814.   Prete House
4815.   Vieux Carré
New York, N. Y.
(10)   30 x 12   AA   ea. 10.00
4816.   Brooklyn Bridge Arch
4817.   Central Park
4818.   Central Park Skating
4819.   Central Park, Winter Night
4820.   Grand Central Terminal
4821.   Pan-Am Building
4822.   Rockefeller Center
4823.   Statue of Liberty
4824.   Stock Exchange
4825.   United Nations Secretariat
New York, N. Y. (6) 12 x 30   AA   ea. 10.00
4826.   Downtown Skyline
4827.   George Washington Bridge
4828.   New York from Brooklyn
4829.   Public Library
4830.   Skyline, Lower New York from Brooklyn
4831.   United Nations Skyline
New York, N. Y. (5) 16 x 20   AA   ea. 7.50
4832.   Central Park Lake
4833.   Fulton Market
4834.   Hudson River Skyline
4835.   Philharmonic Hall, Lincoln Center
4836.   The Plaza
New York, N. Y. (12)20 x 16   AA   ea. 7.50
4837.   Lever House
4838.   Little Church Around the Corner
4839.   Lower Park Avenue
4840.   Metropolitan Museum
4841.   Rockefeller Center
4842.   St. Patrick's Cathedral No. 1
4843.   St. Patrick's Cathedral No. 2

4844.	Skyline			
4845.	Stock Exchange			
4846.	U. S. Treasury Building			
4847.	Vanderbilt Avenue			
4848.	Washington Square			
	New York, N. Y. (2) 15 x 18-1/2	NYGS	ea.	6.00
4849.	Public Library			
4850.	Rockefeller Plaza			
	New York, N. Y. (2) 18-1/2 x 15	NYGS	ea.	6.00
4851.	Fifth Avenue			
4852.	Grand Central Terminal			
	New York, N. Y.:			
4853.	Brooklyn Bridge			
	Harbor	20 x 40	AA	20.00
4854.	Central Park Sky-			
	line	20 x 26	AA	12.00
4855.	East River Harbor	20 x 40	AA	20.00
4856.	Empire State Build-			
	ing	24 x 18	AA	12.00
4857.	George Washington			
	Bridge, Night	21 x 29	AA	12.00
4858.	Lower New York			
	Bay	16-1/2 x 25	AA	15.00
4859.	Mid-Town Water-			
	front	16-1/2 x 25	AA	15.00
4860.	New York City No. 1			
	(Sheet of 8)	9 x 12 ea.	AA	10.00 sheet
4861.	New York City No. 2			
	(Sheet of 7)	9 x 12 ea.	AA	9.00 sheet
4862.	Queensborough Bridge,			
	Night	18 x 21	AA	10.00
4863.	Tugs at Work	24 x 34	AA	20.00
4864.	United Nations			
	Panorama	20 x 40	AA	20.00
4865.	Washington Square			
	Park	16 x 12	AA	5.00
	Paris, France:			
4866.	Arc de Triomphe	20 x 16	AA	7.50
4867.	Boulevard des			
	Italiens	16 x 12	AA	5.00
4868.	Les Bouquinistes	30 x 12	AA	10.00
4869.	Eiffel Tower	32 x 11	AA	12.00
4870.	Kiosk and Café	16 x 12	AA	5.00
4871.	Left Bank	30 x 12	AA	10.00
4872.	Louvre	15 x 30	AA	15.00
4873.	La Madeleine	30 x 12	AA	10.00
		32 x 11	AA	12.00
4874.	Moulin Rouge	16 x 12	AA	5.00
4875.	Opera House	25 x 38	AA	18.00
4876.	Palais Justice	25 x 38	AA	18.00
		15 x 30	AA	15.00

4877.	Place de la Concorde	25 x 38	AA		18. 00
4878.	Pont des Arts	11 x 32	AA		12. 00
4879.	Pont Neuf	11 x 32	AA		12. 00
4880.	Rue de Rivoli	16 x 12	AA		5. 00
4881.	Saint Germain	30 x 12	AA		10. 00
	Philadelphia, Pa.:				
4882.	Betsy Ross House	16 x 12	AA		5. 00
4883.	Cradle of Liberty	20 x 16	AA		7. 50
4884.	Elfreth's Alley	16 x 12	AA		5. 00
4885.	Independence Hall	18 x 24	AA		12. 00
4886.	Rittenhouse Square	20 x 16	AA		7. 50
		16 x 12	AA		5. 00
4887.	Portraits (2)	26 x 20	AA	ea.	20. 00
4888.	Portraits, Mexican Children (4)	26 x 17	AA	ea.	15. 00
4889.	Quebec, Canada, Chateau-Frontenac	16 x 12	AA		5. 00
4890.	Rome, Italy: (2) Theatre de Marcal;	33 x 17	AA	ea.	15. 00
4891.	Column Pedestal of a Temple Rome, Italy (2)	12 x 16	AA	ea.	5. 00
4892.	Pantheon				
4893.	St. Peter's				
	St. Augustine, Fla.: (2)	12 x 16	AA	ea.	5. 00
4894.	Oldest House in U. S.				
4895.	Oldest Schoolhouse in U. S.				
	San Francisco, Cal. (2)	20 x 16	AA	ea.	7. 50
4896.	Cable Cars				
4897.	Fishermen's Wharf				
4898.	San Francisco, Cal. Skyline	20 x 40	AA		20. 00
	Schools, Colleges, Universities (9)	16 x 12	AA	ea.	5. 00
4899.	Annapolis, Md.				
4900.	The Citadel				
4901.	Columbia				
4902.	Cornell				
4903.	Harvard, the Yard				
4904.	Princeton, Nassau Hall				
4905.	West Point				
4906.	William and Mary				
4907.	Yale				
4908.	Ships, Old	12 x 30	AA		10. 00
	Spain:				
4909.	Cordova	30 x 12	AA		10. 00
4910.	Santiago	30 x 12	AA		10. 00
4911.	Verona	20 x 30	AA		18. 00
4912.	Steamboats	12 x 30	AA		10. 00

4913.	Still Life with				
	Moulin	34 x 28	AA		15. 00
4914.	Still Life with Bottle				
	and Fruit	31 x 36	NYGS		18. 00
4915.	Texas, The Alamo	16 x 12	AA		5. 00
	Texas (2)	20 x 16	AA	ea.	7. 50
4916.	Cat Cracker				
4917.	Oil Fields				
4918.	Texas, Oil Refinery	30 x 12	AA		10. 00
4919.	Three Owls	13 x 30	AA		12. 00
4920.	Trotters	12 x 30	AA		10. 00
4921.	Valley Forge, Pa.	16 x 12	AA		5. 00
	Venice, Italy:				
4922.	Canal	16 x 12	AA		5. 00
4923.	Doge's Palace	20 x 40	AA		20. 00
4924.	Gondolas	12 x 16	AA		5. 00
4925.	St. Marks	16 x 12	AA		5. 00
	Washington, D. C.:				
4926.	The Capitol	20 x 16	AA		7. 50
4927.	The Capitol at				
	Night	20 x 16	AA		7. 50
4928.	Jefferson Memorial	30 x 12	AA		10. 00
4929.	Lincoln Memorial	12 x 30	AA		10. 00
4930.	Mount Vernon, Va.,				
	Washington's Home	16 x 20	AA		7. 50
4931.	National Gallery of				
	Art	16 x 20	AA		7. 50
4932.	U. S. Supreme Court				
	Building	30 x 12	AA		10. 00
		20 x 16	AA		7. 50
4933.	Washington Monu-				
	ment	30 x 12	AA		10. 00
4934.	Washington News	12 x 16	AA		5. 00
4935.	The White House	12 x 30	AA		10. 00
	Williamsburg, Va.:				
4936.	Brick House Tavern	30 x 12	AA		10. 00
4937.	Bruton Parish	30 x 12	AA		10. 00
4938.	Colonial Court				
	House	20 x 16	AA		7. 50
4939.	Governor's Palace	30 x 12	AA		10. 00
		29-1/2x24-1/2	AA		12. 00
		20 x 16	AA		7. 50
4940.	Palace Gardens	29-1/2x24-1/2	AA		12. 00
4941.	View of Williams-				
	burg	20 x 40	AA		20. 00
4942.	Williamsburg, Va.				
	(8)	12 x 9	AA	ea.	2. 00

HAYS, WILLIAM JACOB (American, 1872-1934)

| 4943. | Westchester Hills | 27 x 36 | NYGS | 16. 00 |

HAYWARD, PETER

| 4944. | Aristocrats | 25 x 30 | CAC | 7. 50 |
| 4945. | Brookside Mill | 24 x 48 | DAC | 10. 00 |

4946.	Indian Summer	24 x 48	DAC	10.00
4947.	Quiet City	24 x 40	DAC	8.50
4948.	Windswept Palms	24 x 40	DAC	8.50

HEALY, GEORGE P. A. (American, 1813-1894)

| 4949. | Abraham Lincoln, 1857 | 27-1/2 x 20 | NYGS | 12.00 |

HEBLING, T.

| 4950. | Mozart | 28 x 22 | CFA | 12.00 |

HECHT, ZOLTAN (American, 1890-)

| 4951. | Skaters | 16 x 20 | CAC | 10.00 |

HECKE, JAN VAN DEN (Belgian, 1620-1684)

| 4592. | Flowerpiece | 19 x 25 | ESH | 15.00 |
| | | 10 x 13 | ESH | 2.00 |

HECKEL, ERICH (German, 1883-)

4953.	Dangaster Landscape	18 x 19-1/2	NYGS	6.00
4954.	Mountain Village	29 x 26	NYGS	18.00
4955.	White House in Dangast	c. 18 x 23	HNA	5.95

HEDA, WILLIAM CLAESZ (Dutch, 1594-1682)

4956.	Dessert	17 x 14	CFA	8.00
4957.	Still Life	18 x 24	PENN	1.50
4958.	Still Life	c. 18 x 23	HNA	5.95

HEEM, JAN DAVIDSZ. DE (Dutch, 1606-1684)

| 4959. | Still Life with Ham, Lobster and Fruit, 1656 | c. 22 x 31 | NYGS | 15.00 |
| 4960. | Vase of Flowers | c. 23 x 18 | HNA | 5.95 |

HEEMSKERCK, EGBERT VAN (Dutch, 1610-1680)

| 4961. | House Wife | 14 x 11 | IA | 3.00 |
| 4962. | Young Girl | 21 x 16 | NYGS | 20.00 |

HEFFNER, J.

| 4963. | Spring Landscape | 26 x 33 | CFA | 15.00 |
| 4964. | Springtime | 24 x 33 | CFA | 15.00 |

HEGETSCHWEILER, MAX (Swiss, 1902-)

| 4965. | Studio | 12 x 14 | CAC | 10.00 |

HEGNER

| 4966. | Street at Nessebar | 15 x 20 | AP | 5.00 |

HEIDINGSFELD, FRITZ (German, 1907-)

4967.	Coast of East Lake	21 x 27-1/2	ESH	10.00
4968.	East Lake	21 x 28	ESH	10.00
4969.	Ibiza	12 x 16	ESH	4.00

HEIMBACH, WOLFGANG (German, 1610-1678)

| 4970. | Kitchen | 11 x 15 | IA | 3.00 |

HEINBACH, JOHANN (German, 1694-1764)

4971.	Heathy Land	20 x 27-1/2	ESH	Pr.	8.00
4972.	Landscape in Upper-Bavaria	20 x 27-1/2	ESH	Pr.	8.00
4973.	Mountains in Switzerland	20 x 27-1/2	ESH	Pr.	8.00
4974.	Mountains near Salzborg	20 x 27-1/2	ESH	Pr.	8.00

HELCK, PETER (American Contemporary)
4975.	Autos (4)	12 x 18	DAC	ea.	2. 50
4976.	Barney Oldfield	8 x 12	DAC	ea.	1. 00
	Benz, 1910				
4977.	Dario Festa				
	Peugeot, 1915				
4978.	Felice Nazzard Fiat,				
	1907				
4979.	George Robertson				
	Locomobile, 1908				

HELPS, R.
| 4980. | Ice-Cream Man | 8-1/2 x 13 | ESH | | 2. 00 |
| 4981. | Seaside Fun | 8-1/2 x 13 | ESH | | 2. 00 |

HELSTROM, BESSIE (American Contemporary)
| 4982. | White Hydrangeas | 25 x 30 | CFA | | 10. 00 |

HEMPFING, WILHELM (German, 1886-1951)
| 4983. | Dreamer's Cove | 22 x 30-1/2 | IA | | 10. 00 |

HEMSLEY, WILLIAM (English Contemporary)
| 4984. | What's O'Clock | 12-1/2 x 15 | ESH | | 5. 00 |

HENCKE, ALBERT (American, 1865-1936)
4985.	Nursery Stories (4)	20 x 16	CFA	ea.	2. 50
4986.	Dick Whittington				
4987.	Goosey Gander				
4988.	Jack and the Beanstalk				
4989.	Little Red Riding Hood				
	Nursery Stories (2)	16 x 20	CFA	ea.	2. 50
4990.	Girl and Swing				
4991.	See Saw				
4992.	Mary and her Little				
	Lamb	22 x 28	CFA		2. 50
4993.	Noah's Ark	28 x 40	CFA		15. 00

HENDERSON, CHARLES COOPER (English, 1803-1877)
4994.	Calais Express	15 x 25	AA		7. 50
		9 x 14	AA		2. 00
4995.	Going Easy	13 x 24	CAC		10. 00
4996.	Got Hold	13 x 24	CAC		10. 00
4997.	Leeds to London	24 x 36	AA		15. 00
4998.	London Royal Mail	15 x 25	AA		7. 50
		9 x 14	AA		2. 00

HENKEL
| 4999. | The Cuartette | 16 x 20 | AP | | 10. 00 |

HENNER, JEAN-JACQUES (French, 1829-1905)
5000.	Alsation Girl,				
	1873	11 x 7	NYGS		6. 00
5001.	Fabiola	19 x 14-1/2	IA		7. 50
		15 x 11	AS		3. 25
		14 x 11	IA		3. 00
		10 x 8	IA		1. 75
5002.	Reader	11 x 14	IA		3. 00

HENRI, ROBERT (American, 1865-1929)
5003.	Herself, 1913	20-1/2 x 17	NYGS		9. 00
5004.	Himself, 1913	20-1/2 x 17	NYGS		9. 00
		8-1/2 x 6-1/2	NYGS		. 50

HENRIOT, J. DURAND (French Contemporary)
5005.   Beach at Noon   22 x 30   RL   15. 00
HENRY, EDWARD LAMSON (American, 1841-1919)
5006.   Childhood of Rapid
        Transit   15 x 32-1/2   NYGS   36. 00
5007.   Country Breakfast   18 x 26   DAC   7. 50
5008.   Days Before Rapid
        Transit   13 x 34   NYGS   36. 00
5009.   Days of Yore   22 x 32   CFA   12. 00
5010.   First Railway Train   24 x 48   AA   15. 00
5011.   Home Again   24 x 40   CFA   12. 00
                              12 x 20   AK   3. 00
5012.   The 9:45 Accommodation,
        Stratford, Conn.   15 x 30   AA   12. 00
5013.   Off the Main Road   18 x 26   DAC   7. 50
5014.   Old Dutch Church   18 x 34   NYGS   36. 00
5015.   The Planet   15 x 32   NYGS   36. 00
5016.   St. John's Church   21-1/2x17-1/2 NYGS   30. 00
5017.   Sunday Morning   21-1/2 x 40   AA   15. 00
5018.   Wedding in the
        Thirties   16 x 25   PENN   1. 50
HENRY, JAMES LEWIS (English, 1855-1919)
5019.   According to Law   14 x 18   CFA   15. 00
HENRY, MICHEL (French, 1928-)
5020.   Andalusian Land-
        scape   24 x 32-1/2   RL   20. 00
5021.   Bronze and Grey   30 x 15   RL   15. 00
5022.   Les Cardons   24-1/2 x 30   RL   20. 00
5023.   Compotier D'Oranges 24 x 24   RL   10. 00
HENRY, PAUL EDMUND (Irish, Ac. 1874-1904)
5024.   Stormy Day in
        Connemara   18 x 22   NYGS   .   7. 50
HEPPLE, NORMAN (English Contemporary)
5025.   Her Mother's Hat   31 x 24   RL   15. 00
HERMES, GERTRUDE (English Contemporary)
5026.   Donkey Ride   16 x 12   CFA   5. 00
HERRING, JOHN FREDERICK (English, 1795-1865)
5027.   Breaking Cover   17-1/2x30-1/2 NYGS   12. 00
                              13 x 20-1/2   NYGS   6. 00
                              6-1/2 x 11   NYGS   1. 00
5028.   Call of the Hunt   24 x 36   RL   15. 00
5029.   End of Hunt   17-1/2x30-1/2 NYGS   12. 00
                              13 x 20-1/2   NYGS   6. 00
                              6-1/2 x 11   NYGS   1. 00
5030.   Fox Hunting Scenes
        (4)   9 x 16   IA   ea. 2. 50
5031.   Breaking Cover
5032.   The Death
5033.   Full Cry
5034.   The Meet
5035.   Full Cry   17-1/2x30-1/2 NYGS   12. 00
                              13 x 20-1/2   NYGS   6. 00
                              6-1/2 x 11   NYGS   1. 00

5036.	The Meet	17-1/2x30-1/2	NYGS		12. 00
		13 x 20-1/2	NYGS		6. 00
		6-1/2 x 11	NYGS		1. 00
5037.	Views of Florence	13 x 17	CFA		12. 00
HERRING-HARRIS					
5038.	Full Cry (4)	20 x 32	AA	ea.	25. 00
HERTENSTEIN					
5039.	Hans Holbein, the				
	Younger c.	9 x 7	AP		. 25
HERVÉ, JULES R. (French, 1887-)					
5040.	Alsatian Landscape				
	(Thann)	25 x 32	NYGS		12. 00
5041.	Bois de Boulogne	22-1/2 x 28	RL		12. 50
5042.	Evening--Place du				
	Chatelet	24 x 30	RL		12. 50
5043.	Feeding the Pigeons	29 x 22	RL		12. 50
5044.	Mountain Idyll	25 x 32	NYGS		12. 00
HESS, JULIUS (German, 1878-)					
5045.	Landscape with Pines	23 x 30	ESH		10. 00
5046.	Paris--Montmartre	14 x 39-1/2	ESH		8. 00
5047.	Still Life	14 x 39-1/2	ESH		8. 00
HESS, PETER HEINRICH LAMBERT VON (German, 1792-1871)					
5048.	Am Chiemsee	29 x 25	CFA		15. 00
5049.	Lake Chiemsee	19-1/2 x 17	NYGS		6. 00
HESSELIUS, JOHN (American, 1728-1778)					
5050.	Charles Calvert,				
	1761	24 x 19	NYGS		12. 00
HEWES, MADELINE (American Contemporary)					
5051.	The Blessing Strive	24 x 30	CFA		15. 00
HEYDEN, JAN VAN DER (Dutch, 1630-1712)					
5052.	Square in Utrecht	17-1/2x23-1/2	NYGS		10. 00
HIBBARD, ALDRO THOMPSON (American, 1886-)					
5053.	Little Town of				
	Weston	24 x 32	IA		10. 00
HICKS, EDWARD (American, 1780-1849)					
5054.	Cornell Farm c.	18 x 23	HNA		5. 95
5055.	Falls of Niagara	27 x 32	NYGS		18. 00
5056.	Peacable Kingdom	18 x 24-1/2	PENN		1. 50
	c.	18 x 23	HNA		5. 95
		17-1/2 x 23	NYGS		10. 00
		5-1/2 x 7-1/2	NYGS		. 50
5057.	Residence of David				
	Twing	16 x 19	IA		7. 50
HIDALGO, ALEJANDRO RANGEL (Mexican Contemporary)					
5058.	Consuelo	20 x 15	NYGS		7. 50
		7-1/2 x 6	NYGS		1. 50
5059.	Future Scientist	20 x 16-1/2	NYGS		7. 50
		7-1/2 x 6	NYGS		1. 50
5060.	Going to Market	16 x 12	NYGS		5. 00
		8 x 6	NYGS		1. 50
5061.	Indita	20 x 15	NYGS		7. 50
		7-1/2 x 6	NYGS		1. 50

5062.	Indito	20 x 15	NYGS		7. 50
		7-1/2 x 6	NYGS		1. 50
5063.	José	20 x 15	NYGS		7. 50
		7-1/2 x 6	NYGS		1. 50
5064.	Little Bird Vendor	16 x 12	NYGS		5. 00
		8 x 6	NYGS		1. 50
5065.	Little Caballero	20 x 15	NYGS		7. 50
		7-1/2 x 6	NYGS		1. 50
5066.	Little Flower Vendor	15-1/2x12-1/2	NYGS		5. 00
		8 x 6	NYGS		1. 50
5067.	Little Fruit Vendor	15-1/2x12-1/2	NYGS		5. 00
		8 x 6	NYGS		1. 50
5068.	Little Senorita	20 x 15	NYGS		7. 50
		7-1/2 x 6	NYGS		1. 50
5069.	Love Letter	20 x 16-1/2	NYGS		7. 50
		7-1/2 x 6	NYGS		1. 50
5070.	La Madona de				
	Guadalupe	20 x 27-1/2	NYGS		10. 00
		11 x 15	NYGS		4. 00
		8 x 11	NYGS		2. 00

HIEBLE, W.

5071.	Chinese Road	24-1/2 x 20	ESH	Pr.	6. 00
5072.	Egyptian Priestess	20 x 21	ESH	Pr.	8. 00
5073.	Regatta	9 x 33-1/2	ESH		12. 00
5074.	Still Life	9 x 33-1/2	ESH		12. 00

HIERER, A.

5075.	Fishing Boats	23-1/2x39-1/2	ESH		9. 00
		20 x 28	ESH		7. 00
		16 x 31-1/2	ESH		7. 00
5076.	Furioso	20 x 23-1/2	ESH		7. 00
5077.	Nocturno	23-1/2 x 20	ESH		7. 00

HIEU, T.

5078.	Horses	7 x 9-1/2	CFA		2. 00
5079.	Horses in Woodland	7 x 9-1/2	CFA		2. 00

HIGGINS, WILLIAM VICTOR (American, 1884-)

5080.	Fiesta Day	30 x 32	IA		18. 00

HIGHMORE

5081.	General Wolfe	19 x 15	ESH		7. 00

HILAIR, JEAN BAPTISTE (French, 1753-1822)

5082.	Music Lesson	14 x 11-1/2	AS		3. 25
5083.	Music Lesson Oval	12 x 11	IA		3. 00
5084.	The Reading	14 x 11-1/2	AS		3. 25
5085.	The Reading Oval	12 x 11	IA		3. 00

HILAIRE, C. (French Contemporary)

5086.	Les Acides	20 x 26	RL		20. 00
5087.	Paddock c.	20x 24	PENN		1. 50
5088.	Regatta c.	20 x 24	PENN		1. 50
5089.	Tropicana	24 x 30	RL		17. 50

HILDER, EDITH (English Contemporary)

5090.	Summer Glory	20 x 24-1/2	ESH		10. 00
5091.	Wildflowers with Lands-				
	capes (4)	17 x 17	ESH	ea.	3. 00
	(With Rowland Hilder)				

HILDER, ROWLAND (English Contemporary)

5092.	Anne Hathaway's Cottage	11 x 15	ESH	4. 00
5093.	Autumn	15 x 22	ESH	5. 00
5094.	Birdham Pool	13 x 18	ESH	5. 00
5095.	Blossom Time in England	9 x 13	ESH	2. 00
5096.	Bridge Over the Medway	8-1/2 x 13	ESH	2. 00
5097.	Christmas at the Mill	9 x 13	ESH	2. 00
5098.	A Corner of Britain	9 x 12	ESH	2. 00
5099.	Crockham Hill	19 x 26	ESH	10. 00
5100.	Eynsford	20 x 27	ESH	10. 00
5101.	Farm Pond	19 x 26-1/2	ESH	10. 00
5102.	Farm Road	16 x 20	ESH	6. 00
5103.	A Fresh Breeze	20-1/2x28-1/2	ESH	12. 00
5104.	Home Farm	11 x 18	ESH	2. 00
5105.	In the Days of Sail	20-1/2 x 29	ESH	12. 00
5106.	Kentish Lane	12 x 18	ESH	5. 00
5107.	Minsmere	20-1/2x28-1/2	ESH	12. 00
5108.	Morning Sunshine	19 x 26	ESH	10. 00
5109.	Near Shoreham, Kent	8-1/2 x 13	ESH	2. 00
5110.	Passing Shower	12-1/2 x 18	ESH	3. 00
5111.	Plough Teams	12 x 18	ESH	3. 00
5112.	Sea Breeze at Whitstable	9 x 13	ESH	2. 00
5113.	September Day in the Highlands	9 x 13	ESH	2. 00
5114.	Skiddaw	8-1/2 x 13	ESH	2. 00
5115.	Spring	15 x 22	ESH	5. 00
5116.	Springhead Cottage	12 x 18	ESH	3. 00
5117.	Tintern Abbey, Monmouthshire	8-1/2 x 13	ESH	2. 00
5118.	The Weald	15 x 22	ESH	5. 00
5119.	Westerham Mill	10 x 14	ESH	2. 00
5120.	Willie Lott's Cottage	8-1/2 x 13	ESH	2. 00
5121.	Windsor from the River	8-1/2 x 13	ESH	2. 00
5122.	Wroxham Bridge, Norfolk	12 x 19-1/2	ESH	5. 00

HILL, J. S.

5123.	Bevy of Quails	18-1/2 x 24	AA	15. 00

HILLIARD

5124.	Queen Elizabeth I c.	24 x 20	PENN	1. 50

HILLIER, TRISTRAM (English Contemporary)

5125.	Blue Cart	18 x 24	ESH	15. 00
5126.	Country Lane	20 x 24	RL	10. 00
5127.	Flooded Meadow	18 x 24	RL	10. 00

5128.	January Landscape	20 x 24	ESH	15. 00
5129.	Salamanca	18 x 28	RL	15. 00

HILTON, ROGER (English Contemporary)

5130.	March 1960 (Grey and White with Ochre)	18-1/2 x 28	NYGS	15. 00

HINDU ART

5131.	Four Birds	c.	10 x 8	ESH	1. 00
5132.	Horse and Groom (Kotah School)	c.	8 x 10	ESH	1. 00
5133.	Kangra--Krishna and Radha	c.	8 x 10	ESH	1. 00
5134.	Mara	c.	10 x 8	ESH	1. 00
5135.	Princess and her Attendant	c.	8 x 10	ESH	1. 00
5136.	Temple Rubbings: Dancer (2)	c.	24 x 20	PENN ea.	1. 50
5137.	Two Cranes	c.	8 x 10	ESH	1. 00

HIRSCH, JOSEPH (American Contemporary)

5138.	Circus	c.	18 x 23	HNA	5. 95
5139.	Philosopher		24-1/2x18-1/2	NYGS	12. 00

HIS, RENÉ (French, 1881-)

5140.	Red Boat	18 x 23	RL	7. 50

HITCHCOCK, GEORGE (American, 1850-1913)

5141.	Flight into Egypt	24 x 36	NYGS	15. 00
		16 x 24	NYGS	7. 50

HITCHCOCK, HAROLD

5142.	Serenity	25 x 18	AS	17. 50
5143.	Woodland Pool	15 x 22	AS	12. 00

HITCHENS, SYDNEY IVON (English, 1893-)

5144.	Boat on the Pond	13-1/2 x 41	NYGS	18. 00
5145.	Boathouse, Early Morning	16 x 27	ESH	15. 00
5146.	Edge of the Wood	13-1/2 x 36	NYGS	15. 00
5147.	Flower Composition	17-1/2 x 26	NYGS	12. 00

HOANG-TICH-CHU (Chinese Contemporary)

5148.	Planting Rice	15 x 19-1/2	AP	5. 00

HOBBEMA, MEINDERT (Dutch, 1638-1709)

5149.	Avenue, Middleharnis, Holland	26 x 35	NYGS	20. 00
		19 x 26	NYGS	15. 00
		16 x 21-1/2	ESH	6. 00
		13-1/2 x 26	NYGS	5. 00
		10 x 13	ESH	2. 00
5150.	Avenue of Trees	c.	7 x 9	AP	. 50
5151.	Entrance to a Village	18 x 24	PENN	1. 50
5152.	Landscape with Falconer	28 x 37-1/2	NYGS	28. 00
5153.	Landscape, Wooded Road	29 x 36	NYGS	20. 00
5154.	The Mills	21 x 31-1/2	ESH	15. 00
		8 x 10-1/2	ESH	1. 00

5155.	River Landscape		26 x 34	NYGS	16. 00
5156.	Ruins of Brederode				
	Castle	c.	20 x 24	PENN	1. 50
5157.	Sunlit Landscape		11 x 14	IA	3. 00
5158.	View on a High				
	Road		26 x 36	NYGS	20. 00
5159.	Village Avenue		18 x 26	DAC	7. 50
			12 x 16	DAC	2. 50
5160.	Village near a Pool				
		c.	18 x 23	HNA	5. 95
5161.	Village with				
	Watermill		25 x 35	CFA	18. 00
5162.	Watermill with a				
	Red Roof	c.	20 x 24	PENN	1. 50
			18 x 24	DAC	7. 50
			12 x 16	DAC	2. 50

HODGKINS, FRANCES (New Zealand, 1869-1947)

5163.	Wings on Water	19 x 27-1/2	NYGS	12. 00

HODLER, FERDINAND (Swiss, 1853-1918)

5164.	Breithorn	c.	18 x 23	HNA	5. 95
5165.	Meditation		22-1/2 x 16	NYGS	12. 00
5166.	Woodland		19 x 26	NYGS	12. 00

HOECKER

5167.	Girl with a Cat	c.	7 x 9	AP	. 50

HOFFNAGEL, JORIS (OR GEORG) (Flemish, 1542-1600)

5168.	Jousting Horses	18-1/2x21-1/2	ESH	10. 00

HOFER, KARL (German, 1878-1955)

5169.	Farewell in a				
	Dream		27 x 30	NYGS	20. 00
5170.	Girls Throwing				
	Flowers		28 x 22	CAC	12. 00
5171.	Italian Landscape		24 x 29	NYGS	18. 00
5172.	Italian Landscape,				
	Agnuzzo		25 x 36	NYGS	18. 00
5173.	Landscape at				
	Muzzano		15-1/2x20-1/2	AP	5. 00
5174.	Musicians		30 x 25	NYGS	26. 00
5175.	Still Life with				
	Fruit		16 x 24	NYGS	12. 00
5176.	Still Life with				
	Grapefruit		18 x 23	NYGS	12. 00
5177.	Still Life with				
	Lemons		18-1/2 x 22	NYGS	22. 00
5178.	Three Masks		19-1/2 x 16	IA	6. 00
		c.	9 x 7	AP	. 75

HOFLER, MAX (English, d. 1962)

5179.	Capital City at				
	Night		17-1/2 x 26	ESH	7. 50
5180.	Lights of West-				
	minster		17-1/2 x 26	ESH	7. 50
5181.	London from Primrose				
	Hill		19 x 24	ESH	7. 50

5182.	Old Mill	10 x 12	ESH	2. 00
5183.	Oxfordshire Farm	18-1/2 x 22	ESH	10. 00
5184.	Peaceful Waters	10 x 12	ESH	2. 00
5185.	Sunlit Cove	10 x 12	ESH	2. 00

HOFMANN, HANS (American, 1881-1966)

5186.	Veluti in Speculum	28 x 24	NYGS	16. 00

HOFMANN, HEINRICH (German, 1824-1911)

5187.	Christ and the Rich				
	Young Ruler	27 x 36	IA		15. 00
		19 x 24	IA		5. 00
		8 x 9-1/2	IA	Gr.	10. 00
5188.	Christ at Thirty-				
	Three	20 x 16	IA		4. 00
		12 x 9	IA		1. 00
		9-1/2x7-1/2	NYGS		1. 00
5189.	Christ at Twelve	20 x 16	NYGS		7. 50
		9-1/2x7-1/2	NYGS		1. 00
5190.	Christ in the Garden				
	of Gethsemane	30 x 22	NYGS		12. 00
		24 x 17-1/2	NYGS		9. 00
		20 x 14-1/2	IA		4. 00
		10 x 7	NYGS		1. 00
5191.	Christ in the				
	Temple	27 x 36	IA		15. 00
		18 x 24	NYGS		9. 00
		7 x 9-1/2	NYGS		1. 00
5192.	Christ Preaching				
	by the Sea	22-1/2x35-1/2	NYGS		15. 00
5193.	Christus	10 x 8	IA	Gr.	10. 00

HOFMANN, KARL (Austrian, 1852-1926)

5194.	In the Forest	23-1/2x31-1/2	ESH	Pr.	10. 00

HOGARTH, WILLIAM (English, 1697-1764)

5195.	Graham Children	22-1/2 x 25	NYGS	12. 00
5196.	Marriage a la Mode:			
	Signing of the			
	Marriage Contract	21-1/2 x 28	NYGS	15. 00
5197.	The Marriage			
	Contract	21-1/2 x 28	NYGS	15. 00
5198.	Rake's Progress			
	c.	8 x 10	NYGS	. 50
5199.	The Shrimp Girl			
	c.	24 x 20	PENN	1. 50
	c.	9 x 7	AP	. 50

HOITSU, SAKAI See SAKAI HOITSU

HOKUSAI (Japanese, 1760-1849)

5200.	The Wave	c.	7 x 9	AP	. 50

HOLBEIN, HANS, THE YOUNGER (German, 1497-1543)

5201.	Anne of Cleves,			
	Queen of England	14 x 10	IA	3. 00
5202.	B. von Hartenstein			
	c.	9 x 7	AP	. 25
5203.	Duchess of Milan	9 x 4	CFA	. 80

5204.	Earl de la Warr		24 x 14	ESH	10.00
5205.	Edward VI as a Child				
	(Prince of Wales)		22 x 17	NYGS	10.00
			8 x 6	NYGS	.50
5206.	Erasmus	c.	24 x 20	PENN	1.50
		c.	10 x 8	NYGS	.50
5207.	Jane Seymour		24 x 17	NYGS	10.00
5208.	Lady Lee	c.	9 x 7	AP	.25
5209.	Merchant George				
	Gisze		34-1/2x30-1/2	IA	20.00
			33 x 26	NYGS	22.00
			25-1/2x22-1/2	IA	15.00
		c.	9 x 7	AP	.60
			7 x 6	NYGS	.50
5210.	Portrait of an				
	Elderly Man		7 x 5	NYGS	.50
5211.	Portrait of Erasmus		14 x 11	IA	3.00
5212.	Portrait of Henry				
	VIII		13 x 11	IA	3.00
5213.	Portrait of a Lady		20 x 15	CFA	7.50
5214.	Portrait of a Man		18 x 13-1/2	AJ	7.50
5215.	Portrait of Richard				
	Southwell		14 x 11	IA	3.00
5216.	Self-Portrait		9 x 7	IA	3.00
5217.	Sir Thomas More		29 x 23	NYGS	18.00
			8 x 6	NYGS	.50

HOLE, WILLIAM (English, Ac. 1600-1630)

5218.	Christ Weeping over				
	Jerusalem	10 x 15	IA	Gr.	15.00
		7 x 10	IA	Gr.	10.00

HOLESCH

5219.	Chargers	20 x 26	PENN	1.50
5220.	Courtship	24 x 20	PENN	1.50
5221.	Quartet	26 x 19	PENN	1.50
5222.	Rehearsal	26 x 19	PENN	1.50

HOLLAND

5223.	Federal Hall	17-1/2 x 22	PENN	1.50

HOLMES, CALVIN JOSEPH (American Contemporary)

5224.	In Wordworth's			
	Country	20 x 29	ESH	5.00

HOLST, JOHANNES

5225.	Schooner	22 x 31	IA	15.00

HOLUSA

5226.	Country Girl	c.	24 x 20	PENN	1.50
5227.	Harbor Reflections				
		c.	20 x 24	PENN	1.50

HOMER, WINSLOW (American, 1836-1910)

5228.	Boys in a Pasture				
		c.	18 x 23	HNA	5.95
			15 x 22	PENN	1.50
5229.	Breezing Up		19-1/2 x 31	NYGS	15.00
			18 x 24	PENN	1.50
		c.	18 x 23	HNA	5.95

		15 x 24	NYGS	10. 00
5230.	Bridle Path, White			
	Mountains c.	20 x 24	PENN	1. 50
	c.	18 x 23	HNA	5. 95
5231.	Coming Storm	13 x 19	CAC	5. 00
5232.	Country School	22 x 40	CFA	12. 00
	c.	18 x 23	HNA	5. 95
		11 x 20	AK	3. 00
5233.	Country Store	11-1/2 x 18	NYGS	7. 50
5234.	Croquet Scene c.	20 x 24	PENN	1. 50
		18 x 24	DAC	7. 50
		15 x 25	NYGS	12. 00
		12 x 16	DAC	2. 50
5235.	Eight Bells	18 x 21-1/2	PENN	1. 50
5236.	Flower Garden and			
	Bungalow, Bermuda	12 x 18	AJ	6. 00
5237.	Fog Warning	16-1/2 x 26	PENN	1. 50
		13 x 21	AP	3. 00
	c.	7 x 9	AP	. 50
5238.	Girl Picking Apple			
	Blossoms c.	20 x 24	PENN	1. 50
5239.	Gloucester Farm			
	c.	18 x 23	HNA	5. 95
5240.	Gulf Stream	18-1/2 x 30	AA	10. 00
	c.	18 x 23	HNA	5. 95
		11 x 20	NYGS	7. 50
	c.	8 x 10	NYGS	. 50
5241.	Herring Net	18-1/2 x 30	NYGS	12. 00
	c.	20 x 24	PENN	1. 50
		18 x 26	DAC	7. 50
5242.	Homosassa River	18 x 12-1/2	NYGS	7. 50
5243.	Hudson River			
	Logging	13 x 19	NYGS	7. 50
5244.	The Hunter c.	23 x 18	HNA	5. 95
5245.	Moonlight at Woods			
	Island Light c.	7 x 9	AP	. 50
5246.	Negro Cabins and			
	Palms c.	7 x 9	AP	. 50
5247.	North Woods Club,			
	Adirondacks	12-1/2 x 18	AJ	6. 00
5248.	Northeaster	25-1/2x37-1/2	NYGS	20. 00
	c.	18 x 23	HNA	5. 95
		7 x 11	NYGS	1. 00
	c.	7 x 9	AP	. 50
5249.	Palm Tree, Nassau	19-1/2x13-1/2	NYGS	7. 50
		18 x 12	AJ	6. 00
		9 x 6	NYGS	. 50
5250.	Portage	14 x 21	NYGS	7. 50
5251.	Rapids, Hudson			
	River	15 x 21-1/2	NYGS	7. 50
5252.	Shell Heap	18 x 12-1/2	NYGS	7. 50
5253.	Skating at the			
	Central Park	12-1/2 x 19	NYGS	7. 50

5254.	Sloop, Bermuda	13-1/2x19-1/2	NYGS		7.50
		12-1/2 x 18	AJ		6.00
5255.	Snap the Whip	24 x 38	AA		15.00
	c.	20 x 24	PENN		1.50
	c.	18 x 23	HNA		5.95
5256.	Sponge Fishing,				
	Bahamas	14 x 18-1/2	NYGS		7.50
5257.	Stowing the Sail,				
	Bahamas	14 x 22	AP		7.50
5258.	Sunlight on the				
	Coast	25 x 40	AK		12.00
		12 x 20	AK		3.00
5259.	Sunset, Saco Bay				
	c.	20 x 24	PENN		1.50
5260.	Turkey Buzzard	12-1/2 x 18	NYGS		6.00
5261.	Waterfall in the				
	Adirondacks	13-1/2x19-1/2	NYGS		7.50
5262.	Weaning the Calf	19 x 30	NYGS		12.00
5263.	Weatherbeaten c.	18 x 23	HNA		5.95
		16 x 27-1/2	PENN		1.50
5264.	Woodman and Fallen				
	Tree c.	18 x 23	HNA		5.95
HONDA					
5265.	Oriental Birds and				
	Flowers (4)	24 x 8	AK	ea.	2.50
		12 x 4	AK	ea.	1.00
HONDEKOETER, MELCHIOR (Dutch, 1636-1695)					
5266.	Chickens	11-1/2 x 15	AS		3.25
HONTHORST, GERARD VAN (Dutch, 1590-1656)					
5267.	Adoration of the				
	Infant Jesus	11 x 15	IA		3.00
5268.	A Supper	10 x 15	IA		3.00
HOOCH, PIETER DE (Dutch, 1629-1683)					
5269.	Boy with Pome-				
	granates	22 x 17-1/2	ESH		12.00
5270.	Card Players	30 x 25-1/2	IA		18.00
		19-1/2x16-1/2	ESH		6.00
5271.	Cellar Room	20 x 19	PENN		1.50
5272.	Courtyard of a				
	Dutch House	17-1/2 x 14	ESH		12.00
5273.	Courtyard with				
	Arbour	22 x 18-1/2	ESH		15.00
5274.	Dutch Courtyard				
	c.	24 x 20	PENN		1.50
		19-1/2 x 17	NYGS		10.00
		10 x 9	CFA		2.00
		7-1/2x6-1/2	NYGS		.50
5275.	Dutch Courtyard with				
	Pump c.	7 x 9	AP		.50
5276.	Dutch Interior	29 x 25	NYGS		20.00
5277.	Interior	14 x 11	IA		3.00
5278.	Interior of a Dutch				
	House c.	10 x 8	NYGS		.50

5279.	Interior with			
	Soldiers	17-1/2 x 15	ESH	7. 50
5280.	Maternal Duty	11 x 12	IA	3. 00
5281.	The Mother	17 x 18-1/2	NYGS	15. 00
5282.	Pantry	20 x 19	AP	5. 00
5283.	The Players	11-1/2x14-1/2	AS	3. 25
5284.	The Sentinel	13-1/2 x 11	AS	3. 25
5285.	Storage Room c.	7 x 9	AP	. 50
5286.	The Wardrobe	10 x 11	IA	3. 00
5287.	Woman at the			
	Window	20 x 20	NYGS	10. 00
5288.	Woman Drinking with			
	Two Men c.	20 x 24	PENN	1. 50
5289.	Woman Peeling			
	Apples	22 x 17-1/2	ESH	15. 00
5290.	Woman Weighing			
	Gold c.	18 x 23	HNA	5. 95

HOOWIJ, JAN (Dutch [Res. U. S.] Contemporary)

5291.	Balinese Girl c.	24 x 20	PENN	1. 50
		24 x 18	DAC	7. 50
5292.	Ponte Vecchio	15 x 30	DAC	2. 00

HOPF, H.

5293.	Almond Blossoms	23-1/2x31-1/2	ESH	Pr. 10. 00
5294.	Lake in Bavaria	12 x 16	ESH	Pr. 3. 00
5295.	Landscape in Upper-			
	Bavaria	12 x 16	ESH	Pr. 3. 00
5296.	Landscape near			
	Munich	12 x 16	ESH	Pr. 3. 00
5297.	San Vigilio, Lake of			
	Garda	20 x 27-1/2	ESH	Pr. 8. 00
5298.	Sunflowers	23-1/2x31-1/2	ESH	Pr. 10. 00
5299.	View from the			
	Forest	20 x 27-1/2	ESH	Pr. 8. 00

HOPKING, NOEL HUBERT (English Contemporary)

| 5300. | Two Fawns | 12 x 9 | ESH | 2. 00 |
| 5301. | Two Squirrels | 12 x 7 | ESH | 2. 00 |

HOPKINS, LYMAN

5302.	Anchors	10 x 24	AA	7. 50
5303.	At the Dock	22 x 5-1/2	AA	4. 00
5304.	Ebb Tide	10 x 24	AA	7. 50
5305.	Fishing Boats	5-1/2 x 22	AA	4. 00
5306.	Lobster Buoy	10 x 24	AA	7. 50
5307.	Low Tide	10 x 24	AA	7. 50
5308.	Rocky Coast	10 x 24	AA	7. 50
5309.	Sea Gulls	5-1/2 x 22	AA	4. 00
5310.	Sea Gulls	22 x 5-1/2	AA	4. 00
5311.	Traulers	10 x 24	AA	7. 50

HOPPER, EDWARD (American, 1882-1967)

5312.	Captain Strout's			
	House	13 x 19	CFA	5. 00
5313.	Circus Wagon	13 x 19	CFA	5. 00
5314.	Early Sunday Morn-			
	ing	23 x 40	CFA	15. 00

5315.	Ground Swell		15 x 21	NYGS	7. 50
5316.	House by the Rail- road	c.	8 x 10	MMA	. 35
5317.	House on Pamet River		15 x 19	NYGS	7. 50
			13 x 16	PENN	1. 00
5318.	Lighthouse at Two Lights	c.	20 x 24	PENN	1. 50
		c.	18 x 23	HNA	5. 95
			12 x 16	PENN	1. 00
		c.	7 x 9	AP	. 50
5319.	Marshall's House		13 x 19	CFA	5. 00
5320.	Night Hawks	c.	8 x 10	NYGS	. 50
5321.	Rockland Harbor, Maine		13 x 19	CFA	5. 00
5322.	Rooms by the Sea, 1951		22 x 30	NYGS	16. 00
5323.	Seven A. M.		18 x 24	PENN	1. 50

HOPPMAN, HEIN

5324.	Fishing Boats on Shore	18 x 24	ESH	10. 00

HOPPNER, JOHN (English, 1758-1810)

5325.	Miss Euston	18 x 14	CFA	5. 00
5326.	Jessamy Bride	11 x 9	ESH	2. 00
5327.	Little Bo Peep (Miss Harriet Ann Seale)	31 x 25	NYGS	16. 00
		24 x 19-1/2	NYGS	10. 00

HORTER, EARL (American, 1881-)

5328.	Gloucester Docks	14 x 19	NYGS	7. 50

HOSCH, G.

5329.	Lake in the Mountains	23-1/2x31-1/2	ESH	Pr. 10. 00

HOUEI TSONG (EMPEROR) (Chinese [Sung Dynasty--South] 1082-1184)

5330.	La Perruche aux Cinq Couleurs (The Five-Colored Parrot)			
	Part I: Peinture	20-1/2x27-1/2	NYGS	58. 00
	Part II: Calligraphie	20-1/2 x 27	NYGS	58. 00

HOUSTON, ROBERT (Scotch, 1891-)

5331.	Firth of Clyde	18 x 24	CFA	10. 00
5332.	Isle of Arran	18 x 24	CFA	10. 00
5333.	Isle of Bute	18-1/2 x 24	ESH	15. 00
5334.	Sannox Bridge	18 x 21	ESH	7. 50

HOUTMAN, M.

5335.	Basket of Fruit	13 x 15	CFA	7. 50
5336.	Bowl of Fruit	13 x 15	CFA	7. 50

HOVENDEN, THOMAS (Irish-American, 1840-1895)

5337.	Breaking Home Ties	16 x 22	AA	7. 50

HOWARD, RICHARD
5338.	Soldiers, Revolutionary (3)	21 x 17	AA		9.00 Sheet
5339.	Still Life, Stylized (2)	16 x 12	AA	ea.	8.00
5340.	Antique Pineapple				
5341.	Antique Watermelon				
5342.	Victorian Portraits (2)	12 x 10	AA	ea.	5.00
	Victorian Portraits (4)	10 x 8	AA	ea.	4.00

HOWLAND, ALFRED C. (American, 1838-1909)
5343.	Buffalo Hunt	17-1/2x23-1/2	PENN		1.50
5344.	Fourth of July Parade	24 x 40	NYGS		15.00

HSIANG-SHENG-MO
5345.	Autumn Wind	28 x 12	NYGS		48.00

HUBER, WOLF (German, 1480-1549)
5346.	Adoration of the Kings	28 x 18	NYGS		22.00
5347.	Annunciation to Joachim	28 x 18	NYGS		22.00
5348.	Flight into Egypt	22 x 22	NYGS		22.00
5349.	Head of a Girl	9 x 7	AR		3.00
5350.	Joachim and Anna	28 x 18	NYGS		22.00
5351.	Landscape	13 x 18	AR		7.50

HUBERGER, TUGOMIR (Hungarian Contemporary)
5352.	Adriatic Harbor	15 x 35-1/2	CFA		15.00
5353.	City at Night	32 x 31	CFA		18.00
5354.	Deep Sea	19 x 38	ESH	Cv.	18.00
5355.	Jesus Christus	23-1/2x22	ESH	Cv.	15.00
5356.	Mediterranée	21-1/2x39-1/2	ESH	Cv.	18.00
5357.	New York - Manhattan	19 x 39-1/2	ESH	Cv.	18.00
5358.	Royal Panther	16 x 38	ESH	Cv.	15.00
5359.	Still Life	13 x 39-1/2	ESH	Cv.	15.00
5360.	Still Life with Fruits	22 x 27	CFA		15.00

HUERTES, SEGUNDO (Argentinian Contemporary)
5361.	Spring in the Mountains	24 x 48	NYGS		16.00

HUET, JEAN BAPTISTE (French, 1745-1811)
5362.	Milkmaid	10 x 8	ESH		1.00
5363.	Times of Day (4)	8 x 11	CFA	ea.	6.00
5364.	L'Apres Midi				
5365.	Le Matin				
5366.	Le Midi				
5367.	Summer - Le Soir				

HUGGINS
5368.	South Sea Whale Fishery	17 x 22-1/2	AA		15.00

HUGO, JEAN (French, 1894-   )

5369.	Paris Street	15 x 18	CAC	10.00
		7 x 9	CAC	4.00
5370.	Place du Tertre	15 x 18	CAC	10.00
		7 x 9	CAC	4.00
5371.	Seascape	15 x 18	CAC	10.00
		7 x 9	CAC	4.00
5372.	Winter Sports	15 x 18	CAC	10.00
		7 x 9	CAC	4.00

HULDAH (HULDAH CHERRY JAFFE) (American Contemporary)

5373.	Avant le Rideau	25 x 20	NYGS	12.00
		14 x 11	NYGS	3.00
		7-1/2x6-1/2	NYGS	1.00
5374.	Big Brother	20 x 16	NYGS	7.50
		14 x 11	NYGS	3.00
		7-1/2 x 6	NYGS	1.00
5375.	Cafe - Promenade	20 x 25	NYGS	12.00
		11 x 14	NYGS	3.00
	Detail of			
	No. 5375	25 x 20	NYGS	12.00
		14 x 11	NYGS	3.00
		7-1/2 x 6	NYGS	1.00
5376.	Curtain Time	15 x 30	NYGS	12.00
		7 x 14	NYGS	3.00
5377.	Les Deux Camarades	25 x 20	NYGS	12.00
		20 x 16	NYGS	7.50
		14 x 11	NYGS	3.00
		7-1/2 x 6	NYGS	1.00
	Detail of			
	No. 5377	14 x 11	NYGS	3.00
5378.	Flower Market	20 x 25	NYGS	12.00
		11 x 14	NYGS	3.00
	Detail of			
	No. 5378	25 x 20	NYGS	12.00
		14 x 11	NYGS	3.00
		7-1/2 x 6	NYGS	1.00
5379.	His Rose	20 x 16	NYGS	7.50
		14 x 11	NYGS	3.00
		7-1/2 x 6	NYGS	1.00
5380.	Ice Cream Vendor	25 x 20	NYGS	12.00
		20 x 16	NYGS	7.50
		14 x 11	NYGS	3.00
		7-1/2 x 6	NYGS	1.00
5381.	In Central Park	25 x 20	NYGS	12.00
		20 x 16	NYGS	7.50
		14 x 11	NYGS	3.00
		7-1/2 x 6	NYGS	1.00
5382.	La Jeune Ballerina	25 x 20	NYGS	12.00
		14 x 11	NYGS	3.00
		7-1/2 x 6	NYGS	1.00
5383.	Little Sister	20 x 16	NYGS	7.50
		14 x 11	NYGS	3.00
		7-1/2 x 6	NYGS	1.00

5384.	May Bud	20 x 16	NYGS		7. 50
		14 x 11	NYGS		3. 00
		7-1/2 x 6	NYGS		1. 00
5385.	Maytime	15 x 30	NYGS		12. 00
		7x 14	NYGS		3. 00
5386.	Mois de Mai	31-1/2 x 10	NYGS		12. 00
		20 x 6	NYGS		4. 00
5387.	Portrait Heads				
	(4)	7-1/2 x 6	NYGS	ea.	1. 00
5388.	Annette				
5389.	Marianne				
5390.	Suzanne				
5391.	Yvonne				
5392.	Premiere au				
	Rendezvous	25 x 20	NYGS		12. 00
		20 x 16	NYGS		7. 50
		14 x 11	NYGS		3. 00
		7-1/2 x 6	NYGS		1. 00
	Detail of				
	No. 5392	14 x 11	NYGS		3. 00
5393.	Printemps	31-1/2 x 10	NYGS		12. 00
		20 x 6	NYGS		4. 00
5394.	Sailboat Pond	25 x 20	NYGS		12. 00
		20 x 16	NYGS		7. 50
		14 x 11	NYGS		3. 00
		7-1/2 x 6	NYGS		1. 00
5395.	La Sylphide	23-1/2 x 29	NYGS		12. 00
5396.	Tavern on the Green	25 x 20	NYGS		12. 00
		20 x 16	NYGS		7. 50
		14 x 11	NYGS		3. 00
		7-1/2 x 6	NYGS		1. 00
5397.	White Roses	25 x 30	NYGS		12. 00

HULK
5398.	English Country-				
	side	26 x 48	AA		15. 00

HUMPHRIS, D. (English, d. 1965)
| 5399. | Motley | 25 x 20 | RL | | 10. 00 |

HUNDEBERG
5400.	Active White and				
	Red	25 x 30	CFA		18. 00

HUNDERTWASSER, FRIEDRICH (Austrian Contemporary)
5401.	The Large Way	29 x 29	CFA		20. 00
5402.	Martha	22 x 35	NYGS		20. 00
5403.	The Singing Bird	25-1/2 x 18	AJ		15. 00
5404.	Town on the Silver				
	River	19 x 22	NYGS		16. 00
5405.	Yellow Ships	28 x 18	NYGS		15. 00

HUNT, CECIL ARTHUR (English, 1873-)
5407.	Ben Nevis	14-1/2 x 19	ESH		10. 00
5408.	Snowdon	17 x 21	ESH		12. 00

HUNT, PETER
| 5409. | Four Seasons (4) | 20 x 16 | AA | ea. | 6. 00 |

HUNT, V.
5410. Harvest Time   24 x 40   DAC   8.50
HUNT, WILLIAM HOLMAN (English, 1827-1910)
5411. The Hireling
      Shepherd   18 x 26   NYGS   15.00
5412. Light of the World   28 x 14   IA   6.00
                             24 x 12   IA   4.50
                             19 x 10   IA   2.50
                             12 x 6   IA   .50
             c.   9 x 7   IA   .50
HUNT, WILLIAM MORRIS (American, 1824-1879)
5413. Hurdy-Gurdy Boy   26 x 20   CFA   7.50
                          16 x 12   AK   2.50
HUNTER, ROBERT DOUGLAS (American Contemporary)
5414. Arrangement with
      Lemons and Limes   24 x 40   DAC   8.50
5415. Still Life (4)   12 x 30   DAC   ea.   5.00
                          6 x 15   DAC   ea.   1.50
5416. Still Life Arrange-
      ment with Oranges   24 x 48   DAC   10.00
HUNTINGTON, DANIEL P. (American, 1816-1906)
5417. Abraham Lincoln   24 x 18   DAC   7.50
                          16 x 12   DAC   2.50
HURD, PETER (American Contemporary)
5418. Bonfire   c.   18 x 24   PENN   1.50
5419. Dry River   c.   24 x 18   PENN   1.50
5420. The Gate and
      Beyond   c.   18 x 23   HNA   5.95
5421. Rainy Season   c.   18 x 24   PENN   1.50
5422. Rancheria   12-1/2 x 22 PENN   1.50
                             12 x 22   NYGS   7.50
5423. Rio Hondo   22 x 29   NYGS   12.00
5424. Valley Farm   c.   24 x 18   PENN   1.50
HUTTER, WOLFGANG (Austrian Contemporary)
5425. Lovers   18-1/2 x 26 NYGS   12.00
HUTTON, CLARKE (English, 1898-)
5426. Harlequinade   19 x 30   CFA   5.00
HUYGENS
5427. Profusion of Beauty   20 x 16   PENN   1.50
HUYSUM, JAN VAN (Dutch, 1628-1749)
5428. Basket with Flowers 15-1/2 x 13   NYGS   16.00
5429. Flowers in a Vase   24 x 20   NYGS   15.00
5430. Fruit and Flowers   11 x 9   ESH   2.00
5431. Fruits and Flowers 15-1/2 x 13   NYGS   16.00
5432. Garden Gaiety   20 x 16   NYGS   7.50
5433. Gardener's Gift   20 x 16   NYGS   7.50
HYAMS, MARTHA (American Contemporary)
5434. Bird Lovers   12 x 21   NYGS   6.00
5435. Story Teller   12 x 21   NYGS   6.00

IBARRARAN, JOSE
 5436. Sacred Heart of
        Jesus   22-1/2 x 16   IA   3. 00
                           12-1/2 x 9   IA   . 60
IBARZ ROCA, MIGUEL (Spanish Contemporary)
 5437. Blue Vase   28 x 22   NYGS   15. 00
 5438. Costa Catalina,
        St. Pol, 1962   17 x 39   NYGS   18. 00
 5439. Little Harbor
        (Ibiza)   20-1/2 x 39   NYGS   18. 00
 5440. Spring Song   23-1/2 x 30   NYGS   15. 00
IGOR
 5441. Portraits (4)   24 x 20   DAC   ea. 7. 50
                           12 x 10   DAC   ea. 2. 00
IMMEL, PAUL J.
 5442. Flower Paintings
        (8)   16 x 16   AA   ea. 2. 50
                Anemones
                Cosmos
                Dahlias
                Dainty Bess Rose
                Daisies
                Moss Rose
                Phlox
                Wall Flowers
        Flower Paintings
        (8)   12 x 16   AA   ea. 1. 50
                Calendula (2)
                Cosmos
                Daffodils
                Dahlias
                Gladioli
                Petunia
                Study in Purple
        Flower Paintings (4) 16 x 20   AA   ea. 3. 00
                Daffodils
                Helenium and Coreopsis
                Marguerites
                Single Camelias
 5443. Gettysburg Address 20 x 16   AA   5. 00
                           11-1/2 x 9   AA   1. 50
INDIA, FRANCESCO See TORBIDO, IL
INDIA (Country)
 5444. UNESCO World Art
        Series (32)   11 x 14
                     or   14 x 11   NYGS   ea. 2. 00
INDUNO, GEROLAMO (Italian, 1827-1890)
 5445. Antiquary   15 x 11   IA   3. 00

INGRES, JEAN AUGUSTE DOMINIQUE (French, 1780-1867)

5446.	Baigneuse	c.	12-1/2x9-1/2	AP	1.25
			11 x 7	CFA	1.00
5447.	La Comtesse				
	D'Haussonville		30 x 21-1/2	NYGS	16.00
5448.	Gounod, Charles De				
	(DR.)		12 x 9	NYGS	3.00
5449.	Gounod, Mme. Charles				
	De (DR.)		12 x 9	NYGS	3.00
5450.	La Grande Odilisque		6 x 11	CFA	1.00
5451.	Mme. Riviere	c.	10 x 8	NYGS	.50
5452.	Mlle. Riviere	c.	23 x 18	HNA	5.95
5453.	Mme. de Sennones				
		c.	24 x 20	PENN	1.50
5454.	Petite Baigneuse				
		c.	10 x 8	ESH	1.00
5455.	Portrait of Mlle.				
	Rinieri	c.	12-1/2x9-1/2	AP	1.25
5456.	Raoul Rochette		12 x 9	AR	3.00
5457.	Reclining Odalisque		16 x 30	ESH	15.00
5458.	The Source (Spring)		15 x 7	IA	3.00
		c.	12-1/2x9-1/2	AP	1.25
			11 x 5	CFA	1.00
5459.	The Turkish Bath				
		c.	9-1/2x12-1/2	AP	1.25
			8 x 8	CFA	1.00
5460.	Turkish Women		9"-Diam.	NYGS	.50

INGWERSEN, JAMES

5461.	Portraits (2)	20 x 16	IA	ea.	3.00
5462.	Gary				
5463.	Gretchen				
5464.	Karen	26 x 20	IA		6.00

INNESS, GEORGE (American, 1825-1894)

5465.	After a Summer				
	Shower	c.	7 x 9	AP	.50
5466.	Autumn Oaks		20 x 30	NYGS	12.00
			6 x 9-1/2	NYGS	.50
5467.	Catskill Mountains		18 x 26	DAC	7.50
		c.	20 x 24	PENN	1.50
5468.	Coming Storm		18 x 27	PENN	1.50
5469.	Hillside in Etretat				
		c.	20 x 24	PENN	1.50
5470.	June		18 x 27	PENN	1.50
5471.	Lackawanna Valley		24 x 36	NYGS	16.00
		c.	18 x 23	HNA	5.95
5472.	Passing Shower		12 x 19	NYGS	6.00
5473.	Peace and Plenty		31 x 45	AJ	20.00
			20-1/2 x 30	NYGS	12.00
			16-1/2 x 24	PENN	1.50
			7 x 10-1/2	NYGS	.50

IRAN

5474.	UNESCO World Art		
	Series (32)	11 x 14	

| | or | 14 x 11 | NYGS | ea. | 2. 00 |

IRANIAN ART (Fifth Century B. C.)

5475.	Archer of the Royal Guard (Facing Right)	30 x 11	ESH	15. 00
5476.	Archer of the Royal Guard (Facing Left)	30 x 11	ESH	15. 00
5477.	Khusran Discovers Chirin	c. 10 x 8	ESH	1. 00
5478.	Lion	20 x 36-1/2	ESH	18. 00
5479.	Picnic in a Garden	c. 10 x 8	ESH	1. 00

ISABEY, LOUIS GABRIEL EUGENE (French, 1803-1886)

| 5480. | Hungarian Count | 11 x 9 | NYGS | 1. 50 |

ISRAEL

| 5481. | UNESCO World Art Series (32) | 11 x 14 | | | |
| | | or 14 x 11 | NYGS | ea. | 2. 00 |

ISRAELS, IZACK (Dutch, 1865-)

| 5482. | Girl Riding a Donkey | 14 x 19-1/2 | NYGS | 5. 00 |

ITAYA, FOUSSA (Japanese Contemporary)

5483.	Hideaways	24 x 26	RL	10. 00
5484.	Intruder	18 x 23	RL	7. 50
5485.	Playtime	18 x 23	RL	10. 00

IVERD, EUGENE (American, 1893-)

5486.	Admiration	21 x 14	CFA	2. 50
5487.	Happy Days	22 x 28	CFA	10. 00
5488.	Looking Forward	22 x 28	CFA	7. 50
5489.	Old and New	22 x 28	CFA	7. 50

J

JACOB, ALEXANDRE (French, 1876-)

5490.	L'Hiver	14 x 17-1/2	RL	5. 00
5491.	Le Printemps	14 x 17-1/2	RL	5. 00
5492.	Spring in Normandy	18 x 13	RL	5. 00
5493.	Winter in the Marshes	18 x 22	RL	7. 50
5494.	Winter Sun	23-1/2 x 30	RL	10. 00

JACOBSEN, AUGUST (Norwegian, 1868-)

5495.	Shady Nook	22 x 30-1/2	IA	10. 00
		17 x 23-1/2	IA	6. 00
		12 x 16	IA	2. 50

JACOPO DA BOLOGNA (Italian, Ac. 1490-1530)

| 5496. | Pieta | 15 x 11-1/2 | AS | 3. 25 |

JACOPO DEL SELLAIO (Italian, 1442-1493)

| 5497. | Banquet of the Queen Vasti | 11 x 15 | IA | 3. 00 |

JACQUE, CHARLES EMILE (French, 1813-1894)

| 5498. | Sheepfold | c. 7 x 9 | AP | . 60 |

JACUS, JEAN (French Contemporary)

5499.	Ships of Thought	20 x 24	RL	7. 50
5500.	Timeless City	19 x 25	RL	7. 50

JAFFE, ARTHUR (American Contemporary)

5501.	Anemone	10 x 14	AJ	3. 00
5502.	Autumn's Paint Box	15 x 10-1/2	IA	3. 00
5503.	Between Seasons	10 x 14	AJ	3. 00
5504.	Cosmos (W. C.)	8-1/2 x 12	AJ	1. 50
5505.	Crimson Ramblers	10 x 14	AJ	3. 00
5506.	Dachstein (W. C.)	13 x 19-1/2	AJ	4. 00
5507.	Early Morning Mist	26 x 18	CFA	10. 00
5508.	Fall on the Ranch	10 x 14	AJ	3. 00
5509.	Garden Wall with Grinnel Glacier	12 x 8-1/2	AJ	1. 50
5510.	Greeting the Sunrise	22 x 28	AJ	10. 00
5511.	Grundlsee (W. C.)	13 x 19-1/2	AJ	4. 00
5512.	Ichabod Verdure	24 x 18	CFA	10. 00
5513.	Indian Lookout	10 x 14	AJ	3. 00
5514.	June Bouquet	10 x 14	AJ	3. 00
5515.	Maple Family	10 x 14	AJ	3. 00
5516.	Montana Mountains	8-1/2 x 12	AJ	1. 50
5517.	Rain Forest	26 x 18	CFA	10. 00
5518.	St. John's Garden	8-1/2 x 12	AJ	1. 50
5519.	Spring in the Air	15 x 10-1/2	IA	3. 00
5520.	Spring in the Hills	15 x 10-1/2	IA	3. 00
5521.	Sugar Maples	15 x 10-1/2	IA	3. 00
5522.	Yuletime in the Valley	10 x 14	AJ	3. 00

JAMBOR, LOUIS (Hungarian, 1884-)

5523.	Jesus of Nazareth	21 x 16	IA	1. 50
		12 x 9	IA	. 75
5524.	The Lord's Supper	24-1/2 x 18	IA	5. 00
		17 x 12-1/2	IA	2. 00

JAKUCHI ITO (Japanese, 1713-1800)

5525.	Cog's	30 x 18	CFA	40. 00

JAMES, DAVID (English, Ac. 1881-)

5526.	Atlantic Roll	18 x 36	ESH	12. 00
5527.	Flowing Tide	20 x 40	AS	20. 00

JAMES, M. C.

5528.	Spring Flowers	25 x 19	ESH	10. 00
5529.	Summer Flowers	25 x 19	ESH	10. 00

JAMES, WILLIAM (English, Ac. 1761-1771)

5530.	Entrance to the Grand Canal from the Piazzetta	22 x 40	RL	20. 00
5531.	Venice	24-1/2 x 40	AS	20. 00

JAMIESON, MITCHELL (American Contemporary)

5532.	Convoy Entering Mers-El-Kebir	12 x 18	NYGS	4. 00
5533.	Gray Morning	12 x 18	NYGS	4. 00

JANCH, MICHAEL

5534.	Garden Flowers	20 x 15-1/2	NYGS	7. 50
		14 x 11	NYGS	4. 00

JANK, ANGELO (German, 1868-1935)
5535.	Full Cry	24 x 33	NYGS	18. 00

JANSEM, JEAN
5536.	Nature Morte	19 x 26	NYGS	26. 00
5537.	Still Life	24 x 31	IA	18. 00

JAPAN
5538.	UNESCO World Art Series (32)	11 x 14		
	or	14 x 11	NYGS	ea. 2. 00

JAQUES, PIERRE (Swiss Contemporary)
5539.	Blooming Orchard	21 x 28-1/2	NYGS	10. 00
5540.	Blue-Winged Teal	16 x 28	ESH	7. 50
5541.	Enchanted Road	21 x 26	NYGS	10. 00
5542.	Rolling Wheatfields	16 x 39	NYGS	15. 00
5543.	Shovelers on the Mud	22 x 28	ESH	7. 50
5544.	Swiss Village	15 x 39	NYGS	15. 00
5545.	Teal and Willows	22 x 28	ESH	7. 50
5546.	Yacht Basin, Geneva	21 x 26-1/2	NYGS	12. 00

JARVIS, W. FREDERICK (American Contemporary)
5547.	New York Yacht Club Trophy Race, Cowes Regatta	13 x 30	ESH	10. 00

JAWLENSKY, ANDREJ ALEXEJEWITSCH (Russian, 1902-)
5548.	Child with Doll c.	15 x 11	AP	1. 00
	c.	9 x 7	AP	1. 00
5549.	Girl with Peonies	28 x 21	NYGS	18. 00
5550.	Haus in Baumen	21 x 20	CFA	12. 00
5551.	Head with Open Eyes c.	15 x 11	AP	1. 00
	c.	9 x 7	AP	1. 00
5552.	Lady with a Fan	21 x 15	NYGS	6. 00
5553.	Licht und Schatten, 1958 c.	17-1/2 x 22	AS	4. 00
5554.	Meditation I, II, III (Air-Blue, Fire-Orange, Water-Green)	7 x 5 ea.	NYGS	16. 00 sheet
5555.	Mediterranean at Marseilles	17 x 25	NYGS	24. 00
5556.	Moon Light c.	7 x 9	AP	. 75
5557.	Rose in Blue Vase	23 x 10	CFA	12. 00
5558.	Still Life	19 x 21	AP	10. 00
5559.	Still Life with Flowers and Cock	21 x 19	ESH	10. 00
5560.	Street in Murnau	19-1/2 x 21	NYGS	15. 00
5561.	Stummer Schmerz c.	22 x 17-1/2	AS	4. 00
5562.	Variation	20-1/2 x 15	NYGS	20. 00

JEN JEN FA (Chinese 13th Century)
5563.	Chevaux au Paturage	19-1/2 x 30	NYGS	46. 00

JENKINS, PAUL (American Contemporary)
5564. Phenomena: Sun Over
       the Hourglass, 1966 21 x 40   NYGS   20. 00
JENNINGS, WALTER ROBIN (English Contemporary)
5565. Country Companions 20 x 24   AS   7. 50
5566. Edge of the Village   9 x 12   ESH   3. 00
JEUDWINE, ESME
5567. Flowers for You   13-1/2 x 10   ESH   2. 50
5568. A Little One   13-1/2 x 10   ESH   2. 50
5569. Noah's Ark   18-1/2x13-1/2 ESH   2. 50
5570. Picnic   18-1/2x13-1/2 ESH   2. 50
JIDEL
5571. Parisian Water-
       colors   13 x 19   CFA   25. 00
JOHN, C. R. D'OYLY (English Contemporary)
5572. Behind the Piazza
       San Marco   21 x 15   RL   7. 50
5573. Café Bar   17 x 21-1/2   RL   6. 00
5574. Old Archway   17 x 25   RL   7. 50
5575. Old Bridge, Venice 17 x 24-1/2   RL   7. 50
5576. San Giorgio from the
       Riva Schiavoni   21 x 15   RL   7. 50
JOHNSON, AVERY F. (American Contemporary)
5577. Bahama Chores   16 x 22   CFA   10. 00
5578. Bahama Morning   16 x 22   CFA   10. 00
JOHNSON, CECILE (American Contemporary)
5579. Harbor Towns (4)   12 x 30   DAC   ea.   5. 00
5580.   Cape Cod Harbor
5581.   Chatham
5582.   Sag Harbor
5583.   Well Fleet
JOHNSON, EASTMAN (American, 1824-1906)
5584. The Boy Lincoln
                      c.   7 x 9   AP   . 50
5585. Child with Rabbit   26 x 20   AK   7. 50
                           16 x 12   AK   2. 50
5586. Old Stage Coach   22 x 40   CFA   12. 00
                           11 x 20   AK   3. 00
5587. Savoyard Boy   26 x 22   AK   7. 50
                           16 x 13   AK   2. 50
5588. Scissors Grinder   26 x 20   CFA   7. 50
                           16 x 12   AK   2. 50
JOHNSON, M.
5589. Jane Lumb   24 x 18   RL   10. 00
5590. Sibylla   24 x 18   RL   10. 00
JOHNSTONE, JANET (English Contemporary)
5591. Wild Ponies at the
       Ford   28 x 14   ESH   6. 00
5592. Wild Ponies in an
       Autumn Frost   28 x 14   ESH   6. 00
JONES, ALFRED GARTH (English, 1872-1930)
5593. Holiday in France   16-1/2 x 20   ESH   12. 00

JONES, BARBARA (English Contemporary)
5594.   Fair Ground   19 x 30   CFA   5. 00
JONES, D.
5595.   March of the Kings   28 x 36   RL   15. 00
JONES, JOE (American, 1909-1963)
5596.   Chapel in the Park   24 x 20   NYGS   20. 00
5597.   Quiet Cove   11-1/2 x 18   NYGS   7. 50
5598.   Rockport   24 x 36   NYGS   15. 00
5599.   Setting Sail   17-1/2 x 36   NYGS   15. 00
            Detail of
            No. 5599   11-1/2 x 18   NYGS   7. 50
JONGKIND, JOHAN B. (Dutch, 1819-1891)
5600.   Harbor at Honfleur   7 x 9   NYGS   . 50
5601.   Leaving Honfleur   20 x 28   ESH   15. 00
5602.   River Meuse, 1866   14 x 20   NYGS   7. 50
5603.   View of Grenoble,
            1877   9 x 14-1/2   NYGS   3. 00
JORDAENS, JACOB (Flemish, 1593-1678)
5604.   Adam and Eve   c.   8 x 10   NYGS   . 50
5605.   Pan and Syrinx   14 x 11   IA   3. 00
5606.   Satyr and Peasant   13 x 11   IA   3. 00
JORDI See MERCADÉ
JOSY (Ps. for SUSSMAYR, JOSEPH)
JULES, MERVYN (American Contemporary)
5607.   Circus   c.   7 x 9   AP   . 50
5608.   Cobblers   14-1/2x18-1/2 NYGS   7. 50
5609.   Hot Jazz   14 x 17   AR   10. 00
5610.   Little Hippo   c.   7 x 9   AP   . 25
JUNGHANNS, JULIUS PAUL (Austrian c. 1876-1958)
5611.   Coming Home   19 x 32-1/2   ESH   15. 00
5612.   The Hunt   20 x 27   ESH   10. 00
..5613.   Mother and Son   23-1/2 x 21   ESH   12. 00
JÜRK (JURK-LAUTEN), HANS (German Contemporary)
5614.   Amaryllis   23-1/2 x 12   ESH   4. 00
5615.   Boats (2)   23-1/2 x 12   ESH   ea. 4. 00
5616.   Garden-Poppies   31-1/2 x 16   ESH   7. 00
5617.   Magnolias   23-1/2 x 12   ESH   4. 00
5618.   Still Life (2)   23-1/2 x 12   ESH   ea. 4. 00
            Still Life (2)   16 x 31-1/2   ESH   ea. 7. 00
5619.   Sun Flowers   31-1/2 x 16   ESH   7. 00

K

KACZ See KOMAROMI-KACZ
KAGIE, JAN
5620.   Pines on the Dunes   19-1/2 x 30   RL   7. 50
KAHILL, JOSEPH B. (American, 1882-)
5621.   Collector   20 x 24   NYGS   9. 00
                                          11 x 14   NYGS   3. 00
KALCKREUTH, PATRICK VON (German, 1898-
5622.   Fishing Boats   18 x 25   CFA   7. 50

5623.	High Sea	26 x 39	IA	15. 00
5624.	High Sea No. 2	13 x 19	CFA	5. 00
5625.	Isle of Helgoland	17 x 24	CFA	6. 00
5626.	Sailing Home	23 x 17	CFA	7. 50
5627.	Waves	18 x 23	CFA	7. 50

KALF, WILLEM (Dutch, 1622-1693)

5628.	Still Life	26 x 21-1/2	NYGS	12. 00

KAN, M. J. E. G. VAN (Dutch, 1886-1930)

5629.	Flower Paintings			
	(6)	20 x 8	ESH	ea. 4. 00
	Blue Lilies			
	Corn-Cobs			
	Orchid			
	Poinsettia			
	Poppy			
	Sunflowers			

KANDINSKY, WASSILY (Russian, 1866-1944)

5630.	L'Arc Noir, 1912			
	c.	20 x 24	PENN	1. 50
5631.	Arrow Composition	16 x 22-1/2	ESH	10. 00
5632.	Calm	20-1/2 x 31	NYGS	15. 00
5633.	Capricious Line	26 x 14	AA	15. 00
5634.	Le Cercle Rouge			
	c.	17-1/2 x 22	AS	4. 00
5635.	Composition c.	20 x 24	PENN	1. 50
5636.	Composition No. 711	16-1/2 x 23	AP	10. 00
5637.	Composition, 1914	24 x 18	AR	12. 00
5638.	Composition, 1934	17-1/2 x 23	NYGS	10. 00
5639.	Dream Improvisation	27-1/2x27-1/2	NYGS	20. 00
5640.	Heavenly Bodies	21-1/2 x 16	PENN	1. 50
5641.	Heavy Red c.	18 x 23	HNA	5. 95
5642.	Improvisation No. 10	8 x 10	ESH	1. 00
	c.	7 x 9	AP	. 75
5643.	Improvisation XIX	27 x 31-1/2	IA	18. 00
5644.	Improvisation No. 30	28 x 28	CFA	15. 00
5645.	Improvisation			
	No. 35	18 x 24	PENN	1. 50
5646.	Intersecting Lines	24 x 35	CFA	18. 00
5647.	Lyrisches	17 x 23-1/2	PENN	1. 50
5648.	Mountain Landscape /			
	Church	13 x 18	NYGS	6. 00
5649.	Paysage	13 x 16	NYGS	16. 00
5650.	Perpetual Line	24-1/2x35-1/2	NYGS	20. 00
5651.	Points in a Bow			
	c.	23 x 18	HNA	5. 95
5652.	Poster (With Klee):			
	Aquerelles, 1930			
	c.	30 x 20	PENN	1. 00
5653.	Poster: Epoque du			
	Bauhaus	29 x 22-1/2	PENN	1. 00
5654.	Poster (With Klee)			
	Galerie Berggruen	30 x 20	PENN	1. 00

5655.	Poster: Oeuvres				
	Inconnu		28 x 21	PENN	1. 00
5656.	Romantic Landscape		28 x 32	NYGS	20. 00
5657.	Schweres Rot	c.	22 x 17-1/2	AS	4. 00
5658.	Street at Murnau		13 x 17-1/2	NYGS	15. 00
5659.	Suprematist				
	Composition		23 x 19	NYGS	12. 00
5660.	Symmetrical Accord		24-1/2x31-1/2	NYGS	20. 00
5661.	Whirling	c.	11 x 15	AP	1. 00
		c.	7 x 9	AP	1. 00

KANE, JOHN (American, 1860-1934)

5662.	From my Studio				
	Window	c.	8 x 10	NYGS	. 50
5663.	The Schooner				
	Montanna		20-1/2 x 26	AA	12. 00
			10 x 13	AA	2. 00

KANELBA, RAYMOND (Polish, [Res. France] 1900-1961)

5664.	Little Musician	14 x 11-1/2	NYGS	7. 50

KANO TANNYU (Japanese, 1602-1674)

5665.	Summer Palace	20-1/2 x 28	NYGS	24. 00

KARFOIL, BERNARD (American, 1866-1952)

5666.	The Laurent Pony				
	Cart		16 x 20	NYGS	9. 00
		c.	7 x 9	AP	. 50

KASSEL, F.

5667.	Boy and his Dog	24 x 20	DAC	7. 50
		12 x 10	DAC	1. 50
5668.	Daily Task	24 x 20	DAC	7. 50
		12 x 10	DAC	1. 50
5669.	Girl with Basket	24 x 20	DAC	7. 50
		12 x 10	DAC	1. 50
5670.	Grandmother's			
	Pride	24 x 20	DAC	7. 50
		12 x 10	DAC	1. 50
5671.	Little Helper	24 x 20	DAC	7. 50
		12 x 10	DAC	1. 50
5672.	Mother Love	24 x 20	DAC	7. 50
		12 x 10	DAC	1. 50
5673.	Spinning Wheel	24 x 20	DAC	7. 50
		12 x 10	DAC	1. 50
5674.	Three Generations	24 x 20	DAC	7. 50
		12 x 10	DAC	1. 50

KATZ, MANÉ See MANÉ-KATZ

KAULBACH, WILHELM VON (German, 1805-1874)

5675.	Artist's Daughter	21 x 14	CAC	5. 00
		7 x 6	CAC	1. 00
5676.	Gretel	12 x 9	NYGS	1. 50
		7-1/2 x 6	NYGS	1. 00
5677.	Hansel	12 x 9	NYGS	1. 50
		7-1/2 x 6	NYGS	1. 00

KAUTZKY, THEODORE (TED) (American, 1896-1953)

5678.	Cape Ann Harbor	25 x 30	CFA	10. 00

		13 x 18	PENN		1.50
5679.	Church Street	25 x 30	CFA		10.00
5680.	Connecticut Hills	20 x 24	CAC		6.00
5681.	Country Holiday	20 x 24	CAC		6.00
5682.	Fisherman's Harbor	20 x 24	CAC		6.00
5683.	Hilltop Haven	22 x 28	CFA		7.50
5684.	Normandy Road	22 x 28	CFA		7.50
5685.	October Sunshine	20 x 24	CAC		6.00
5686.	Peaceful Cove	22 x 28	CFA		7.50
5687.	Peaceful Valley c.	20 x 24	PENN		1.50
5688.	Quiet Inlet	13 x 18	PENN		1.50
5689.	Schooner in Harbor	20 x 24	CAC		6.00
5690.	Sunny Brittany	22 x 28	CFA		7.50
5691.	Village Street	25 x 30	CFA		10.00
5692.	Winter in New England	20 x 24	CAC		6.00

KAYMAR

5693.	Nature Studies (6) Fall (2) Grape Leaves Queen Anne's Lace Summer (2)	28 x 13-1/2	AA	ea.	7.50

KEANE, MARGARET (American Contemporary)

5694.	Black Dress	20 x 10	JM		10.00
5695.	Circe (jg)	23 x 35	JM		15.00
5696.	Coffee Break	24 x 27	JM		15.00
5697.	Escape	35 x 20	JM		20.00
5698.	In Between	28 x 19	JM		15.00
5699.	Mother and Child	30 x 18	JM		15.00
5700.	On the Beach	34 x 22	JM		15.00
5701.	On the Threshold	34 x 21	JM		15.00
	Paintings of Young People (12)	12 x 9	JM	ea.	3.00
5702.	Awakening				
5703.	Bull Fight Day				
5704.	Destiny				
5705.	Edge of Summer				
5706.	Emerging				
5707.	Farmer's Daughter				
5708.	Freshmen				
5709.	Many Views				
5710.	Reflection				
5711.	Reply				
5712.	Storm				
5713.	Transition				
5714.	Secret	30 x 14	JM		10.00
5715.	Three Harlequins	29 x 23	JM		15.00
5716.	Youth	24 x 12	JM		10.00

KEANE, WALTER (American Contemporary)

5717.	Alone	29 x 37	JM		25.00
5718.	Backstage	31 x 19	JM		15.00
5719.	Beachhead	12 x 24	JM		15.00

5720.	Dragon on Parade	9 x 12	JM		2. 00
5721.	Girl of China	29 x 14	JM		20. 00
5722.	Grant Avenue,				
	San Francisco	28 x 18	JM		15. 00
5723.	Lookout	40 x 18	JM		15. 00
5724.	No Dogs Allowed	24 x 12	JM		15. 00
	Paintings of Young				
	People (12)	12 x 9	JM	ea.	3. 00
5725.	At the Fair				
5726.	Ballerina				
5727.	Blond Boy				
5728.	Boy and his Dog				
5729.	First Grail				
5730.	Girl and her Cat				
5731.	Gypsies				
5732.	Little Ones				
5733.	Lost				
5734.	Rejected				
5735.	Waiting for Grandmother				
5736.	Watching				
5737.	Peace on Earth	33 x 28	JM		25. 00
5738.	Runaway	40 x 14	JM		25. 00
5739.	Steep Climb	40 x 20	JM		20. 00
5740.	Stray	24 x 12	JM		15. 00
5741.	Waif	30 x 14	JM		20. 00

KEANE, WILLIAM

5742.	Old Banjo	25 x 16	CFA		7. 50

KEEN, LILA MOORE

5743.	Camelias (4)	20 x 16	AA	ea.	3. 50
	Chandieri Elegans				
	Dr. W. G. Lee				
	Latifolia				
	Rev. John Bennett				
	Camelias (2)	16 x 12	AA	ea.	2. 50
	Alba Fimbriata (White)				
	Japonica Triphosa (White)				

KEISEKI

5744.	Summer	24 x 10	CAC	12. 00

KEITH, WILLIAM (American, 1839-1911)

5745.	Cypress Point	17 x 40	NYGS	15. 00
		11 x 26	NYGS	7. 50

KELLY, FELIX (New Zealander Contemporary)

5746.	Drifter and Paddle			
	Steamer	19 x 30	CFA	5. 00

KELLY, (SIR) GERALD (English, 1879-)

5747.	Albert Memorial	12-1/2 x 20	NYGS	7. 50
5748.	The Discovery-			
	Embankment	12-1/2 x 20	NYGS	7. 50
5749.	Peaches	20 x 22-1/2	AS	12. 00
5750.	Pont St. Marie	16 x 20	AS	7. 50
5751.	St. Clement Danes			
	and Lawcourts	12-1/2 x 20	NYGS	7. 50

5752.	St. Paul's Cathedral	12-1/2 x 20	NYGS		7.50
5753.	The Yellow Tamein	24 x 19	RL		15.00

KELLY, J. REDDING (American Contemporary)

5754.	Abraham Lincoln	18 x 15	NYGS		5.00
		9 x 7-1/2	NYGS		1.50

KELSEY, RICHMOND I. (American Contemporary)

5755.	Morro Bay	12 x 18	DAC		2.50
		8 x 12	DAC		1.25
5756.	Noyo Estuary	12 x 18	DAC		2.50
		8 x 12	DAC		1.25
5757.	Noyo River	12 x 18	DAC		2.50
		8 x 12	DAC		1.25
5758.	Port Noyo	12 x 18	DAC		2.50
		8 x 12	DAC		1.25

KEMENY, LYDIA (English Contemporary)

5759.	Red Chair	32 x 20	NYGS		16.00

KEMP-WELCH, LUCY (English, 1868-)

5760.	Behind the Plow	16 x 20	CAC		5.00

KENNEDY, CECIL (English, 1905-)

5761.	Delphiniums and				
	Lilies	10 x 8	CFA		1.00
5762.	Peonies	30 x 22-1/2	ESH		15.00

KENT, LESLIE (English, Ac. 1940-)

5763.	October Morning	18 x 22	ESH		10.00

KENT, ROCKWELL (American, 1882-)

5764.	Adirondacks	12 x 17	PENN		1.00
5765.	Mount Equinox,				
	Winter	20 x 26	CAC		10.00
5766.	Polar Expedition				
	c.	8 x 10	NYGS		.50
5767.	Winter, A View of				
	Monhegan, Maine	28 x 35	NYGS		18.00
		16-1/2 x 22	NYGS		10.00

KENTLEY

5768.	Autos, Antique (4)	9-1/2 x 18	AK	ea.	2.00
5769.	Dogs, Playful (4)	10 x 20	AK	ea.	2.00

KERR, VERNON

5770.	Four Seasons of the				
	Sea (4)	12 x 24	IA	ea.	5.00
5771.	Autumn Glow				
5772.	Spring Tide				
5773.	Summer Surf				
5774.	Winter Sea				
5775.	Glowing Surf	24 x 48	IA		15.00
5776.	Incoming Tide	20 x 40	IA		12.00
5777.	Laguna Surf	24 x 48	IA		15.00
5778.	Moon Light	20 x 40	IA		12.00
5779.	Peace and Solitude	24 x 48	IA		15.00
5780.	Sea Rhythm	24 x 48	IA		15.00

KESSEL, VAN

5781.	Gold Goblet and				
	Flowers	16 x 22-1/2	ESH		10.00

5782.	Insects	c.	8 x 10	ESH	1. 00

KEYSER, THOMAS DE (Dutch, 1596-1667)

| 5783. | Portrait of an Old |||||
| | Woman || 15 x 11 | IA | 3. 00 |

K'IEOU YING (Chinese)

| 5784. | Scene on the Yangtse |||||
| | River || 15 x 31 | ESH | 15. 00 |

KING, HENRIETTA (American)

| 5785. | Ten P. M. || 18 x 22 | CAC | 5. 00 |

KING, PAUL (American, 1867-1947)

5786.	Dream	24 x 20	AA	7. 50
5787.	Magnolias	28 x 31	CAC	10. 00
5788.	Mystery of the East	24 x 20	NYGS	10. 00
5789.	Peace	24 x 20	AA	7. 50

KIRCHNER, ERNST LUDWIG (German, 1880-1938)

5790.	Berlin Street Scene				
		c.	20 x 24	PENN	1. 50
5791.	Davos in the Snow				
		c.	18 x 23	HNA	5. 95
5792.	Dresden-Friedrich,				
	1909		17 x 21	NYGS	6. 00
5793.	Klostersu Mountain		25 x 25	CFA	18. 00
5794.	Mountain Landscape		18 x 30	AJ	15. 00
5795.	Rhine Bridge	c.	12 x 16	AP	2. 00
5796.	Self-Portrait with				
	Model	c.	12 x 13-1/2	AP	1. 00
		c.	7 x 9	AP	1. 00
5797.	Two Peasants	c.	24 x 20	PENN	1. 50

KISLING, MOISE (OR MAURICE) (Polish, 1891-)

| 5798. | Woman with a |||||
| | Shawl | c. | 24 x 20 | PENN | 1. 50 |

KISSELOWA, JELENA A. (Russian, 1878-)

| 5799. | Russian Peasant |||||
| | Woman | c. | 7 x 9 | AP | . 50 |

KLEE, PAUL (Swiss, 1879-1940)

5800.	Actor's Mask		16 x 14-1/2	AR	12. 00
5801.	Aquarium Green-				
	Red	c.	11 x 15	AP	1. 00
		c.	7 x 9	AP	1. 00
5802.	Arab Song		26 x 18	NYGS	12. 00
5803.	Around the Fish		18 x 25	MMA	6. 00
5804.	Ballet Scene		11-1/2 x 15	NYGS	15. 00
5805.	Banner at the				
	Pavilion		16 x 24	CFA	10. 00
5806.	La Belle Jardiniere				
		c.	24 x 20	PENN	1. 50
5807.	Bird Garden		18 x 26-1/2	AA	15. 00
5808.	Blossoms in the				
	Twilight		13 x 31	CFA	12. 00
5809.	Blue Head		19-1/2 x 13	AR	10. 00
5810.	Blue Night		19 x 29-1/2	ESH	15. 00
5811.	Boats and Cliffs		13 x 20	CAC	5. 00

5812.	Branches in the Autumn	c.	12 x 16	AP	2. 00
5813.	Buffoonery	c.	11 x 15	AP	1. 00
		c.	7 x 9	AP	1. 00
5814.	By the Troutstream		12 x 9	NYGS	10. 00
5815.	Caprice in February		20 x 15	CFA	7. 50
5816.	Castle and Sun	c.	23 x 18	HNA	5. 95
5817.	Chapel, 1917		12-1/2 x 7	NYGS	10. 00
5818.	Columns and Crosses		16 x 22	CFA	12. 00
5819.	Composition, 1914	c.	7 x 9	AP	. 50
5820.	Dancer		21 x 21	NYGS	16. 00
5821.	Drummer	c.	7 x 9	AP	. 75
5822.	Ecstasy	c.	7 x 9	AP	. 75
5823.	Embrace		18 x 14	AR	5. 00
			10 x 8	AR	2. 00
5824.	Equals Infinity	c.	8 x 10	MMA	. 35
5825.	Fire at Full Moon	c.	18 x 23	HNA	5. 95
5826.	Fish Magic		23-1/2 x 30	NYGS	18. 00
		c.	18 x 23	HNA	5. 95
		c.	8 x 10	ESH	1. 00
		c.	7 x 9	AP	. 75
5827.	Flower Girl		16 x 19	AR	10. 00
5828.	Fruit D'Azur	c.	7 x 9	AP	. 75
5829.	Garden Under Water	c.	23 x 18	HNA	5. 95
5830.	Le Gilet Rouge (Red Waistcoat)		22-1/2x14-1/2	ESH	10. 00
		c.	9 x 7	AP	. 75
5831.	Girl with Flag	c.	20 x 24	PENN	1. 50
5832.	Head of a Man	c.	24 x 20	PENN	1. 50
5833.	The Holy One	c.	15 x 11	AP	1. 00
		c.	9 x 7	AP	1. 00
5834.	Indian Story		16 x 20	PENN	1. 50
5835.	Jardin Erotique		16 x 15	NYGS	18. 00
5836.	Landscape in Motion		16 x 25	NYGS	20. 00
5837.	Landscape of the Past		9 x 10	NYGS	12. 00
5838.	Landscape, Yellow Birds		19 x 24	CFA	12. 00
		c.	7 x 9	AP	. 75
5839.	Legend of the Nile		27 x 24	NYGS	20. 00
5840.	Lying Down		16-1/2 x 27	NYGS	16. 00
5841.	Man on a Tight Rope		12 x 7-1/2	NYGS	3. 00
5842.	Mask, 1939		21 x 22	AR	10. 00
			16 x 17	AR	7. 50
5843.	Nestling Birds		17 x 23	AR	12. 00
5844.	Once from the Gray of Night Emerged	c.	7 x 9	AP	. 75

5845.	Oriental Castle		10 x 12	NYGS	10.00
5846.	Picture Album		24 x 22-1/2	NYGS	15.00
5847.	Picture Sheet	c.	7 x 9	AP	.75
5848.	Pink-Yellow, Windows				
	and Roofs		12 x 9-1/2	NYGS	12.00
5849.	Poster: Berggruen				
	et Cie		30 x 20	PENN	1.00
5850.	Poster (With Kandinsky):				
	Galerie Berggruen		30 x 20	PENN	1.00
5851.	Poster: Twelve				
	Aquarelles		35 x 19	PENN	1.00
5852.	Red Waistcoat		22-1/2 x 15	ESH	10.00
5853.	Refuge	c.	11 x 15	AP	1.00
		c.	7 x 9	AP	1.00
5854.	Revolution of the				
	Viaduct	c.	12 x 13-1/2	AP	1.00
		c.	7 x 9	AP	1.00
5855.	Rich Harbour		13-1/2x29-1/2	NYGS	12.00
5856.	River Regulizing				
	Territory		14 x 21	IA	12.00
5857.	Senecio, 1922		16 x 14-1/2	AR	12.00
5858.	Sinbad the Sailor		16 x 23	PENN	1.50
5859.	Small Rhythmic				
	Landscape		11 x 9	NYGS	12.00
5860.	Sparce Foliage		11 x 16	ESH	8.00
5861.	Still Life, 1940		22-1/2 x 18	AP	10.00
5862.	They're Biting		12 x 9	AR	3.00
5863.	Tomcat, 1930		10 x 13	NYGS	10.00
5864.	Traveling Circus		25 x 19-1/2	NYGS	16.00
5865.	Tree House	c.	11 x 15	AP	1.00
		c.	7 x 9	AP	1.00
5866.	Twittering Machine				
		c.	8 x 10	MMA	.35
5867.	Understanding One		21 x 15	AR	12.00
			10 x 7	AR	2.00
5868.	Vigilant Angel		18 x 14	AR	5.00
			10 x 8	AR	2.00
5869.	Warning of the				
	Ships	c.	7 x 9	AP	.75
5870.	Woman in Costume				
		c.	9 x 7	AP	.75

KLEIN, H.

5871.	Boats at Night	16 x 31-1/2	ESH	7.00

KLEPICH, FRED

5872.	Sunday Walk	16 x 20	IA	5.00

KLINE, FRANZ (American, 1910-1962)

5873.	Black, White and			
	Gray, 1959		NYGS	18.00

KLITZ

5874.	Horseguards at			
	Wellington Arch	15 x 30	ESH	8.00
5875.	Piccadilly Circus	15 x 30	ESH	8.00

5876.	Westminster Bridge and the Houses of Parliament	15 x 30	ESH		8. 00

KLUGE, CONSTANTIN (Latvian, 1912-)

5877.	Elysee Club	22 x 22	RL		15. 00
5878.	Lady of the Sampans	25 x 20	RL		12. 50
5879.	La Madeleine	20 x 24	CAC		10. 00

KNATHS, KARL (American, 1891-)

5880.	Cin-Zin	20 x 24	NYGS		12. 00

KNELL, KARL (Swiss, 1880-1954)

5881.	Cyclops	19 x 26	CFA		25. 00
		15-1/2 x 21	AA		15. 00
5882.	Geyser	19 x 26	AA		15. 00
5883.	War Ships (4)	6 x 10	CFA	ea.	6. 00
5884.	Man of War Cutter				
5885.	Gun Battleship				
5886.	Gun Frigate				
5887.	Sloop of War				

KNELL, WILLIAM ADOLPHUS (English, d. 1875)

5888.	The Fleet, 1800	24 x 36	RL		15. 00

KNIGHT, CHARLES K. (English, 1901-)

5889.	Ditchling Beacon	18 x 23	ESH		15. 00

KNIGHT, (DAME) LAURA (English, 1877-)

5890.	Ballet	18 x 21	ESH		15. 00
5891.	Carnival	20 x 26	CFA		12. 00
5892.	Flight	24 x 20	ESH		12. 00
5893.	Month of May	20 x 16	CAC		6. 00
5894.	Normandy	22 x 28	CAC		10. 00
5895.	Rural Courtship	30 x 24	AA		12. 00

KNOX, W.

5896.	The James Baines	30 x 40	RL		20. 00

KO SHANG LAN (Chinese)

5897.	Two Horses	30 x 15-1/2	NYGS		12. 00

KOBATA

5898.	Mother and Child	28 x 18	AK		7. 50
		18 x 12	AK		3. 00

KOBEL, ALFRED (Swiss Contemporary)

5899.	Comtesse D'Orsay	11 x 9	NYGS		1. 50

KOBELL

5900.	Landscape near Munich	16 x 21	NYGS		16. 00
5901.	View on the Lake	15 x 13	NYGS		12. 00

KOHLER, FRITZ (German, 1887-)

5902.	River Landscape	23 x 29	ESH		12. 00

KOHLSTÄDT, FRITZ (German Contemporary)

5903.	Lofoten	20 x 36	ESH	Cv.	15. 00
5904.	Red Reef	15-1/2x31-1/2	ESH	Cv.	15. 00
5905.	Yellow Cloud	25-1/2x31-1/2	ESH	Cv.	15. 00

KOKOSCHKA, OSKAR (Austrian, 1886-)

5906.	Amsterdam	23 x 33	NYGS		20. 00
	c.	17-1/2 x 22	AS		4. 00
5907.	Augustus Bridge, Dresden	21 x 31	AR		15. 00

5908.	Boat in Dogana, Venice	25 x 31-1/2	NYGS	20. 00
5909.	Castles in Amsterdam	24 x 33	CAC	15. 00
5910.	Charles Bridge, Prague	24 x 30	DAC	7. 50
		12 x 16	DAC	2. 50
5911.	Clown and Dog	22 x 15	CFA	10. 00
5912.	Coliseum, Rome	24 x 33	CFA	20. 00
5913.	Courmayeur	24-1/2 x 36	NYGS	20. 00
5914.	Delphi	24 x 35	CFA	18. 00
5915.	Dresden Neustadt (from Studio Window) c.	20 x 24	PENN	1. 50
5916.	Hamburg Harbor, 1961	25 x 33-1/2	NYGS	22. 00
5917.	Karlsbrücke in Prague	19-1/2x27-1/2	NYGS	12. 00
	c.	18 x 23	HNA	5. 95
5918.	London, Tower Bridge	23-1/2 x 29	NYGS	20. 00
5919.	Lyon	27 x 36	NYGS	20. 00
5920.	Matterhorn	27 x 36	NYGS	20. 00
5921.	Polperro, Cornwall	16 x 23	AP	7. 50
5922.	Roses at Villeneuve	16-1/2 x 21	NYGS	12. 00
5923.	Self-Portrait, 1913	23 x 14	NYGS	10. 00
5924.	Tempest c.	7 x 9	AP	. 50
5925.	Terrace Gardens at Richmond	25 x 36	NYGS	20. 00
5926.	Thames Landscape c.	12 x 16	AP	2. 00
5927.	Venice, Bacino di San Marco	18-1/2 x 25	ESH	15. 00
5928.	Venice, St. Maria della Salute	25-1/2 x 35	NYGS	20. 00
5929.	View of Dresden	16 x 23	NYGS	10. 00
5930.	View in the Rhone Valley c.	18 x 23	HNA	5. 95
5931.	View of the Thames	17-1/2 x 25	ESH	15. 00

KOLBE, GEORG (German, 1877-1947)

5932.	Hands	9 x 11	CFA	3. 50

KOLLWITZ, KATHE (German, 1867-1945)

5933.	Devotion (DR. -B&W)	14 x 11	AR	2. 00
5934.	The Family (Dr. -B&W)	14 x 11	AR	2. 00
5935.	Mother and Child (Dr. -B&W)	24-1/2 x 19 sheet	IA	6. 00
5936.	Mother and Children (Dr. -B&W)	14 x 11	AR	2. 00
5937.	Self-Portrait with Karl (Dr. -B&W)	14 x 11	AR	2. 00

5938.	Slumber (Dr. -B&W)	24-1/2 x 19 sheet	IA		6. 00

KOLMAN, REID
5939.	Duck Decoys (4) Mallard Drake Mallard Hen Pintail Drake Pintail Hen	10 x 13	AA	ea.	5. 00

KOMAROMI-KACZ, ENDRÉ (Hungarian, 1880-1948)
5940.	Christ and the Little Children	28 x 39	IA		15. 00
		17 x 24	IA		7. 50
		10 x 14	IA		3. 00
5941.	Madame Butterfly	18 x 30	CFA		10. 00

KONDIG
5942.	Geranium and Begonia	19 x 15	CAC		5. 00

KONINCK, DAVID (Dutch, 1636-1687)
5943.	The Dog	11 x 15-1/2	AS		3. 25
5944.	Rabbits	11 x 15-1/2	AS		3. 25

KONRAD, IGNACE
5945.	Breaking Cover	9 x 16	CAC		2. 50
5946.	Concours Hippique	21 x 29	CAC		9. 00
5947.	The Death	9 x 16	CAC		2. 50
5948.	Full Cry	9 x 16	CAC		2. 50
5949.	Joy of the Gallop	13-1/2 x 19	IA		5. 00
5950.	Mare and Foal in the Paddock	13 x 19	CAC		5. 00
5951.	The Meet	9 x 16	CAC		2. 50
5952.	The Meeting	21 x 29	IA		10. 00
5953.	Out to Grass	13 x 19	CAC		5. 00
5954.	Steeplechase	21 x 29	IA		10. 00
5955.	Thoroughbreds at Large	13-1/2 x 19	IA		5. 00

KOONING, WILLIAM DE (Dutch [Res. U. S.] Contemporary)
5956.	Woman I	c.	8 x 10	MMA		. 35

KOPMAN, BENJAMIN (Russian [Res. U. S.] 1887-)
5957.	Artist at the Easel	c.	23 x 18	HNA		5. 95

KORTHALS, JAN (OR JOHANNES) (Dutch Contemporary)
5958.	Ceylon	18 x 14	DAC		2. 50
5959.	Colombo (4)	18 x 14	DAC	ea.	2. 50
5960.	Italian Cities (6)	16 x 12	DAC	ea.	1. 75
5961.	Kandy	18 x 14	DAC		2. 50
5962.	London Views (6)	16 x 12	DAC	ea.	1. 75

KOSA, EMIL JEAN (French [Res. U. S.] 1903-)
5963.	Junction at Acton	14 x 19	CFA		5. 00
5964.	Meeting Place	24 x 36	CFA		15. 00
		16 x 24	CFA		6. 00

KOSHANG LAN (Chinese 19th Century)
5965.	Two Horses (With Wang Kwan)	30 x 15-1/2	NYGS		12. 00

KOZLOW, RICHARD (American Contemporary)
  5966.   Formentor   21-1/2 x 24   IA   12. 00
  5967.   Luquillo   19 x 17   IA   12. 00
  5968.   Mirador   20 x 24   IA   12. 00
KRAUS, AUGUST (German, 1868-1934)
  5969.   Summer Day   22 x 31   CFA   12. 00
KRAUS, FRIEDRICH (German, Ac. 1852-1880)
  5970.   Mother Love   26 x 20   AK   7. 50
KREIBACH
  5971.   Albert Schweitzer
                          c.   9 x 7   AP   1. 00
KREUL, JOHANN
  5972.   Beautiful Girl of
          Nuremberg   16 x 12   ESH   Pr. 3. 00
KRIESCH, LAURA (Hungarian, 1879-)
  5973.   Confectioner in
          Cairo   10 x 14   CFA   7. 50
  5974.   Fruit Market   10 x 14   CFA   7. 50
  5975.   In the Hammam   10 x 14   CFA   7. 50
  5976.   Return from the
          Oasis   10 x 14   CFA   7. 50
KRINGS, HUGO (German, 1878-)
  5977.   Reading Man   21 x 17   CFA   6. 00
  5978.   Smoker   19 x 16   CFA   10. 00
  5979.   Spinner   19 x 16   CFA   6. 00
  5980.   Young Mother   19 x 16   CFA   10. 00
KROGER, FLORENCE (American Contemporary)
  5981.   Babies (4)   12 x 10   DAC   ea. 1. 50
  5982.   The Boy Jesus   24 x 20   NYGS   7. 50
                               20 x 16   PENN   1. 50
                               18 x 15   NYGS   4. 00
                               10 x 8   NYGS   1. 00
  5983.   Boy Praying   c.   10 x 8   DAC   1. 00
  5984.   Girl Praying   c.   10 x 8   DAC   1. 00
  5985.   Kittens (4)   12 x 9   DAC   ea. 1. 50
          Religious Paintings
          (4)   20 x 16   DAC   ea. 3. 75
  5986.   Christ at Twelve
  5987.   The Lord's Image
  5988.   Madonna and Child
  5989.   Mary
KROLL, LEON (American, 1884-)
  5990.   Nina   15 x 19   CAC   10. 00
  5991.   Willows   14 x 20   NYGS   7. 50
KRONBERG, LOUIS (American, 1870-   )
  5992.   Dancer in Pink   24 x 17   CFA   7. 50
                               19 x 14   CFA   3. 00
  5993.   Dancer in White   24 x 17   CFA   7. 50
                               19 x 14   CFA   3. 00
KRÜGER, ERNA (German, 1883-)
  5994.   Almond Blossoms   31-1/2 x 28   ESH   18. 00
  5995.   Brook in the Woods   20 x 28   ESH   7. 00

5996.	Flowers in Autumn	23-1/2x31-1/2	ESH	9.00
5997.	Garden-Poppies	20 x 28	ESH	7.00
5998.	Height of Summer	20 x 28	ESH	7.00
5999.	Lilacs	20 x 28	ESH	7.00
6000.	On the Havelsee	23 x 31-1/2	ESH	15.00
6001.	Peonies with Lark-spur	20 x 28	ESH	7.00
6002.	Roses	20 x 28	ESH	7.00
6003.	Spreewald in Autumn	20 x 28	ESH	7.00
6004.	Spreewald in Spring	20 x 24	ESH	7.00
6005.	Spring Sunshine	24 x 32	IA	10.00
6006.	Summer Landscape	24 x 32	IA	7.50
		17-1/2x23-1/2	IA	5.00
6007.	Summer's Glory	24 x 32	IA	10.00
6008.	Sunflowers	20 x 28	ESH	7.00
6009.	When the Leaves Begin to Fall	24 x 32	IA	7.50
		17-1/2x23-1/2	IA	5.00

KRUMMACHER, KARL (German, 1867-1955)

6010.	Cornfield	18 x 26	CFA	7.50
6011.	Spring Blossoms	19 x 27	CFA	7.50

KUHN, WALT (American, 1880-1949)

6012.	Blue Clown	24 x 20	NYGS	12.00
6013.	Clown with Black Wig	24 x 18	PENN	1.50
6014.	Dressing Room	24 x 18	PENN	1.50
6015.	Ducks	25 x 18	PENN	1.50

KULISIEWICZ, TADEUSZ (Polish, 1899-)

6016.	Portrait, 1954 (Dr.)	14 x 12	NYGS	6.00

KUNDIG, R.

6017.	Landscape with Lake	24 x 29	CFA	12.00

KUNIYOSHI, YASUO (American, 1893. 1953)

6018.	Fish Kite	c.	8 x 10	NYGS	.50
6019.	I'm Tired		19 x 14-1/2	NYGS	7.50
			16 x 12	PENN	1.00
6020.	Japanese Toy Tiger and Odd Objects		13-1/2x19-1/2	NYGS	7.50
		c.	7 x 9	AP	.25

KUNTZ, ROGER (American Contemporary)

6021.	Apartment Houses	16 x 12	CAC	12.00
6022.	Arcade	12 x 16	CAC	12.00
6023.	Backstage	16 x 12	CFA	12.00
6024.	Bar Lesperance	16 x 12	CAC	12.00
6025.	Intermission	16 x 12	CFA	12.00
6026.	Latin Quarter Hotel	16 x 12	CAC	12.00
6027.	New Orleans Square	12 x 16	CAC	12.00
6028.	Old New Orleans	12 x 16	CAC	12.00
6029.	The Seine	12 x 16	CFA	12.00
6030.	Sidewalk Cafe	12 x 16	CAC	12.00

KUPETSKY

6031.	Flute Player	20 x 16	CAC	10.00

KURZ, LOUIS (OR EMIL) (Austrian [Res. U. S.] 1833-1921) and
ALLISON, ALEXANDER
  6032. Civil War Battles
         (36)   15 x 21   CAC   ea. 2. 00
            Assault of Fort Sanders
            Battle of Antietam
            Battle of Atlanta
            Battle of Bull Run
            Battle of Cedar Creek
            Battle of Champion Hill
            Battle of Chancellorsville
            Battle of Chattanooga
            Battle of Chickamauga
            Battle of Cold Harbor
            Battle of Corinth
            Battle of Five Forks
            Battle of Fort Donelson
            Battle of Franklin
            Battle of Fredericksburg
            Battle of Gettysburg
            Battle of Kennesaw Mountain
            Battle of Lookout Mountain
            Battle of Missionary Ridge
            Battle of the Monitor and the Merrimac
            Battle of Nashville
            Battle of Olustee
            Battle of Opequon
            Battle of Pea Ridge
            Battle of Resaca
            Battle of Shiloh
            Battle of Spotsylvania
            Battle of Stone River
            Battle of the Wilderness
            Battle of Williamsburg
            Battle of Wilson's Creek
            Capture of Fort Fisher
            Fall of Petersburg
            Fort Pillow Massacre
            Siege of Vicksburg
            Storming of Fort Wagner
KUTTER, JOSEPH (Luxemburgian, 1894-1941)
  6033. Calvi on Corsica   25-1/2x31-1/2 NYGS   18. 00
  6034. Clown   23 x 19-1/2   NYGS   18. 00
  6035. Clown with
        Accordion   21 x 16-1/2   NYGS   6. 00
  6036. Flowers   22-1/2 x 17   NYGS   6. 00

L

LADELL, EDWARD (English, Ac. 1850-1886)
  6037. Still Life (2)   12 x 16   AS   ea. 6. 00

6038.	Tower of London	19 x 30	CFA		5. 00

LAESSIG
6039.	Flowers (4)	15 x 6	DAC	ea.	1. 50

LA FONTAINE, THOMAS S. (English Contemporary)
6040.	Beaufort Hunt	18 x 26	ESH		10. 00
6041.	Lindsay Arabs	17 x 25	ESH		12. 00

LA FRESNAYE, ROGER DE (French, 1885-1925)
6042.	Conquest of the Air, 1913	20 x 24	MMA		7. 50

LAKEN
6043.	Hunting Recollections (6)	10 x 13	CAC	ea.	30. 00

LA MANOLA
6044.	Adeline Plunkett	14 x 10	CAC		2. 50

LAMARQUE
6045.	Citadel	28 x 36	RL		17. 50

LA MASSON, PAUL (French)
6046.	Bicycle	10 x 8	CFA		1. 50
6047.	Carnaval	8 x 10	CFA		1. 50
6048.	Carousel	10 x 8	CFA		1. 50
6049.	County Fair	8 x 10	CFA		1. 50

LAMBERT, GEORGES (French Contemporary)
6050.	Le Bal	30 x 20	RL		12. 50

LAMBERTINI, MICHELE (Italian, 1440-1469)
6051.	Virgin and Child	15 x 10	AS		3. 25

LAMPI, JOHANN BATTISTA (Austrian-Italian, 1751-1838)
6052.	Elisabeth, Princess of Württenberg	15 x 11	IA		3. 00

LAMPITT, RONALD
6053.	Early Morning on the Weald	17 x 20	ESH		10. 00
6054.	Four Ponies in an Autumn Landscape	12 x 15	ESH		6. 00
6055.	Return to the Farm	12 x 17	ESH		6. 00
6056.	Spring Landscape	17 x 21	ESH		10. 00
6057.	Spring Sunshine	17 x 21-1/2	ESH		10. 00

LAMPRECHT, ANTON (German, 1901-)
6058.	Blue Window	23-1/2x31-1/2	ESH		15. 00
6059.	Easter-Tide	23-1/2x31-1/2	ESH	Cv.	15. 00
6060.	Fisher-Boats in the Lagoon	23-1/2x31-1/2	ESH	Cv.	15. 00
6061.	Gay Flowers	26 x 20	ESH		10. 00

LANCASTER, PERCY (English, 1878-)
6062.	White Mill	15 x 12	ESH		6. 00

LANCRET, NICOLAS (French, 1690-1743)
6063.	Autumn	16-1/2 x 22	IA		10. 00
		13 x 15	CFA		10. 00
		12 x 14	CFA		15. 00
		10 x 14	IA		3. 00
		9 x 12	IA	Gr.	10. 00
6064.	Bird Cage	17 x 18	CFA		15. 00
6065.	Cage	14 x 10	IA		3. 00

6066.	La Camargo Dansant (The Dancer Camargo)	18-1/2 x 26	NYGS		12.00
		9 x 12	IA	Gr.	10.00
		12 x 9	CFA		2.00
	c.	10 x 8	ESH		1.00
6067.	Dancing	16-1/2 x 22	IA		10.00
6068.	Golden Days	16 x 22	CFA		10.00
6069.	In the Golden Days of Old	16-1/2 x 22	IA		10.00
6070.	Innocence	22 x 22	CAC		7.50
		19 x 19	AS		7.50
		16 x16	CAC		5.00
		11 x 11	CFA		2.50
		10-1/2x10-1/2	AS		3.25
		8 x 8-1/2	IA		1.75
6071.	Menuett	9 x 12	IA	Gr.	10.00
6072.	Music Lesson	22 x 22	CAC		7.50
		19 x 19	AS		7.50
		16 x 16	CAC		5.00
		11 x 11	CFA		2.50
		10-1/2x10-1/2	AS		3.25
		8 x 8-1/2	IA		1.75
6073.	Pastorale--Dancing	16 x 22	CFA		10.00
6074.	Picnic After the Hunt	23-1/2 x 29	NYGS		16.00
6075.	Spring (Le Printemps)				
		13 x 15	CFA		10.00
		12 x 14	CFA		15.00
		10 x 14	IA		3.00
		9x 12	IA	Gr.	10.00
6076.	Summer	17 x 22-1/2	ESH		10.00
		12 x 14	CFA		15.00
		10 x 14	IA		3.00
6077.	Winter	12 x 14	CFA		15.00
		10 x 14	IA		3.00
6078.	Winter, the Skaters				
	c.	8 x 10	ESH		1.00

LAND, ERNEST ALBERT

6079.	Home Sweet Home	18 x 26	DAC		7.50

LANDORI

6080.	Interlude	31 x 21	CFA		16.00
6081.	Modern Ballet	14 x 34	CFA		15.00
6082.	Riders on the Beach	13 x 34	CFA		15.00

LANDSEER, (SIR) EDWIN HENRY (English, 1802-1873)

6083.	An Aristocrat	c.	7 x 9	AP		.50
6084.	Dignity and Impudence					
		c.	7 x 9	AP		.50
6085.	Distinguished Member of the Humane Society					
			16 x 20	CAC		5.00
			9 x 12	CAC		2.00

6086.	Monarch of the Glen	26 x 20	CAC		7. 50
6087.	Shoeing the Mare c.	7 x 9	AP		. 50

LANE, HARRY (American, 1891-)

6088.	Flower Paintings (2)	16 x 20	CFA	ea.	2. 50
	Anemones	13 x 16	CFA	ea.	1. 50
	Pansies Flower Paintings (3)	20 x 16	CFA	ea.	2. 50
	Cyclamen	16 x 13	CFA	ea.	1. 50
	Magnolias Primroses				

LANE, ROBERT BRYAN

6089.	Optimist	21 x 16	CFA		5. 00

LANG, HERMANN (German, 1856-1916)

6090.	Cross in the Mountains	20 x 25	AS		10. 00

LANGLAIS, X.

6091.	Dreaming	36 x 28-1/2	RL		12. 50

LANGLET, P.

6092.	Christ, Blessing	20 x 16	AS		6. 00

LANGSHIH-NING (Chinese)

6093.	One Hundred Horses in Pasture	13-1/2 x 22	ESH		10. 00

LA PAGLIA, ANTHONY (American)

6094.	Song Birds (3)	22-1/2x18-1/2	NYGS	ea.	7. 50
	Blue Grosbeak	16 x 12	NYGS	ea.	3. 00
	Blue Jay Cardinal				

LA PICQUE, CHARLES (French, 1898-)

6095.	Before the Start	16 x 26	PENN		1. 50

LARSEN, CHRISTIAN (Danish-Argentinian Contemporary)

6096.	Day-Dreaming	19 x 25-1/2	UNICEF		10. 00

LARSEN, C. B.

6097.	Christina	23 x 17	IA		6. 00

LARSEN, LUCAS

6098.	Seascape	10 x 15	ESH		6. 00
6099.	Surf	20 x 24	ESH		10. 00

LARSEN, OLE (Swedish Contemporary)

6100.	Teamwork	25 x 30	IA		7. 50

LASARD, LOU-ALBERT

6101.	Meo mit Pferochen	21 x 16	CFA		5. 00
6102.	Orientalische Szene	28 x 19	CFA		12. 00

LASCAUX CAVES See PREHISTORIC ART

LASINIO, GIOVANNI PAOLO (Italian, 1789/96-1855)

6103.	Planets (6)	13 x 16	CFA	ea.	10. 00

LASZLO, PHILIP ALEXIUS DE (Hungarian, 1869-1940)

6104.	Roosevelt, Theodore (Portrait)	23-1/2 x 18	NYGS		12. 00

LA TOUR, GEORGE DE (French, d. 1652)

6105.	New Born	8 x 9	CFA		1. 00

6106.	St. Madeleine	c.	12-1/2x9-1/2	AP	1.25

LA TOUR, HENRI FANTIN See FANTIN-LATOUR
LA TOUR, MAURICE QUENTIN DE (French, 1704-1788)

6107.	La Butte de				
	Montmartre	c.	10 x 8	ESH	1.00
6108.	Fortune Teller		16 x 19-1/2	AP	7.50
6109.	Nativity (Rennes)				
		c.	8 x 10	ESH	1.00
	Detail of				
	No. 6109		21 x 16	ESH	10.00
6110.	Nativity (Louvre)				
		c.	8 x 10	ESH	1.00
6111.	Prisoner		19 x 12-1/2	ESH	10.00
6112.	St. Joseph Charpen-				
	tier		25 x 18	PENN	1.50
6113.	Ste. Madeleine	c.	9 x 7	AP	1.00
			8 x 6	CFA	1.00
6114.	St. Sebastian Nursed				
	by St. Irene		15 x 20	AJ	7.50

LAUFMAN, SIDNEY (American, 1891-)

6115.	Summer Landscape	13 x 17	CAC	10.00

LAUMONIER, ELY

6116.	Les Alpilles Provence			
		24 x 48	AK	12.00
		12 x 24	AK	3.00
6117.	Environs de Nice	24 x 48	AK	12.00
		12 x 24	AK	3.00
6118.	Olive Grove	22 x 28	RL	10.00

LAURENCIN, MARIE (French, 1885-1956)

6119.	Arabesque	21 x 18	CAC	15.00
6120.	Dancers	18 x 22-1/2	ESH	10.00
6121.	Les Deux Amies	22 x 18-1/2	NYGS	10.00
		14 x 11-1/2	NYGS	3.00
6122.	Four Girls	14 x 20	CAC	15.00
6123.	Girl in Red	17 x 14	CFA	5.00
6124.	Girl with Lillies	12 x 18	CAC	15.00
6125.	Girl with Rose	17 x 21	CAC	15.00
6126.	Helene	21 x 18	CAC	15.00
6127.	In the Park	26-1/2 x 19	NYGS	12.00
	c.	23 x 18	HNA	5.95
		20 x 14	NYGS	7.50
		8-1/2 x 6	NYGS	.50
6128.	Jeanette	16 x 13	CAC	6.00
6129.	La Jeune Mere	22 x 18-1/2	NYGS	10.00
6130.	Portrait of Mlle.			
	Chanel	c.	24 x 20	PENN	1.50
6131.	La Princesse de			
	Cleves	16 x 19-1/2	NYGS	7.50
6132.	Rosette Girl with			
	Fan	19 x 14	CAC	12.00
6133.	Self-Portrait	16 x 13	CAC	6.00

6134.	Sisters		24 x 30	DAC	7. 50
		c.	20 x 24	PENN	1. 50
6135.	Tanzerinnen	c.	17-1/2 x 22	AS	4. 00
6136.	Yvette, Girl with				
	Mandolin		19 x 14	CAC	12. 00
			16 x 13	CAC	6. 00

LAURENS, HENRI (French, 1885-1954)

6137.	Head	11-1/2 x 9	NYGS	15. 00

LAURENT

6138.	Endymion and Diane	15 x 11	AS	3. 25

LAURJAN

6139.	Red Sideboard	17 x 22	CAC	10. 00

LAURRAIN, CLAUDE See GELLÉE, CLAUDE

LAUTERBURG

6140.	Geraniums	30 x 25	CAC	15. 00

LAUTH, ROBERT (German, 1896-)

6141.	Spanish Coast	20 x 23-1/2	ESH	7. 00
		10 x 12	ESH	3. 00
6142.	Spanish Harbour	20 x 23-1/2	ESH	7. 00
		10 x 12	ESH	3. 00

LAUTREC See TOULOUSE-LAUTREC

LAVARENNE, P.

6143.	Song of Dawn	28 x 36-1/2	RL	15. 00

LAVAUX, GREGOIRE (French)

6144.	Autumn Morning	24 x 30	CAC	10. 00

LAVREINCE, NICHOLAS (French-Swedish, 1737-1807)

6145.	Le Concert Agree-			
	able	11 x 14	CFA	12. 00
6146.	La Partie de			
	Musique	11 x 14	CFA	12. 00
6147.	Promenade	6-1/2x4-1/2	AR	3. 00

LAVRILLIER, G. (French Contemporary)

6148.	Red and White Roses	22-1/2 x 18	RL	6. 00

LAWRENCE, EDITH M. (English, Ac. 1884-1886)

6149.	Roses (4) (H. C.)	12 x 9	CFA	ea.	3. 00
6150.	Roses - Black back-				
	ground (8)	12 x 9	CFA	ea.	5. 00

LAWRENCE, (SIR) THOMAS (English, 1769-1830)

6151.	Calmady Children		28" Diam.	NYGS	15. 00
			20" Diam.	NYGS	12. 00
			9" Diam.	NYGS	1. 50
		c.	7 x 9	AP	. 50
6152.	Fluyder Children		28 x 17	NYGS	15. 00
		c.	9 x 7	AP	. 50
6153.	The Hon. Caroline				
	Upton	c.	24 x 20	PENN	1. 50
6154.	The Hon. Mrs.				
	Ashley		10 x 8	CFA	6. 00
6155.	Lady Templeton and				
	her Son		31 x 21-1/2	NYGS	16. 00
6156.	Master Lambton		28 x 22	NYGS	12. 00
			14 x 11	NYGS	4. 00

			10 x 8	CFA	6.00
		c.	9 x 7	AP	.50
	Detail of No. 6156		14 x 11	IA	3.00
6157.	Miss Baring	c.	10 x 8	NYGS	.50
6158.	Miss Croker		20 x 16	AA	5.00
			18 x 14	CFA	5.00
6159.	Miss Murray		28 x 21-1/2	IA	12.00
			14 x 11	NYGS	4.00
			10 x 8	CFA	6.00
	Detail of No. 6159		14 x 11	IA	3.00
6160.	Miss West		27 x 22	CAC	10.00
			7-1/2 x 6	NYGS	.50
6161.	Pinkie		31 x 22	NYGS	12.00
			26 x 20	PENN	1.50
			24 x 17	NYGS	10.00
			24 x 16	CFA	10.00
			20 x 16	AA	5.00
			18 x 14	CFA	5.00
			18 x 13	NYGS	5.00
			14 x 10	NYGS	3.00
			12 x 8	NYGS	1.50
		c.	9 x 7	AP	.50
6162.	Portrait of Lord				
	Seaham as a Boy		20 x 16	IA	6.00
			14 x 11	IA	2.50

LAYCOX, JACK

6163.	Buena Vista	18 x 24	DAC	12.50

LAYTON, MARGARET

6164.	Antique Shop	10 x 30	CAC	10.00
6165.	Blinky	12 x 9	AA	5.00
6166.	Engine 32	20 x 10	AA	7.50
6167.	Hook and Ladder	20 x 10	AA	7.50
6168.	Maison Dubois	23 x 10	CAC	7.50
6169.	Mal's Restaurant	25 x 12	CAC	10.00
6170.	March Gallery	30 x 10	CAC	10.00
6171.	Perfume Shop	10 x 30	CAC	10.00
6172.	Twelfth Step Cafe	30 x 10	CAC	10.00
6173.	Village Cafe	23 x 10	CAC	7.50
6174.	Wade Gallery	25 x 12	CAC	10.00
6175.	Winky	12 x 9	AA	5.00

LEADER, BENJAMIN WILLIAM (B. W.) English, 1831-1923)

6176.	By Mead and Stream	17 x 28-1/2	NYGS	24.00
6177.	Gleam before the Storm	18 x 27-1/2	NYGS	24.00
6178.	Golden Hours	24 x 40	AS	20.00
6179.	Way to the Village Church	18 x 27	NYGS	24.00

LE BA DANG (Vietnamese [Res. France] Contemporary)

6180.	Les Branches Mortes	25 x 30	RL	15.00
6181.	Emperor's Festival	30 x 23	RL	17.50

6182.	Fishing Nets	25 x 30	RL		15. 00
6183.	Forest	28 x 36	RL		20. 00
6184.	Horsemen	24 x 30	RL		17. 50
6185.	Oriental Sunset				
	(3 panels)	30 x 13 ea.	RL	set	30. 00
6186.	Sampans	24 x 30	RL		17. 50
6187.	Three Boats	24 x 31	RL		15. 00

LEBOURG, ALBERT (French, 1849-1928)

6188.	Paris, Le Pont Neuf	13-1/2x22-1/2	ESH		10. 00

LE BRETON, CONSTANT (French, 1895-)

6189.	Baltimore, View	12 x 16	CFA		12. 00
6190.	Boston, View I and				
	II (2)	12 x 16	CFA	ea.	12. 00
6191.	Ducal Palace	20 x 24	CFA		12. 00
6192.	Grand Canal	20 x 24	CFA		12. 00
6193.	Landscape with				
	Boats	19 x 23	CFA		10. 00
6194.	Los Angeles, View	12 x 16	CFA		12. 00
6195.	New Orleans, View	12 x 16	CFA		12. 00
6196.	New York-Brooklyn,				
	View	12 x 16	CFA		12. 00
6197.	San Francisco,				
	View	12 x 16	CFA		12. 00

LE BRUN, LOUISE ELISABETH VIGÉE (French, 1755-1842)

6198.	Artist and Daughter				
	c.	9 x 7	AP		. 50
6199.	The Dauphin				
	and his Sister	10-1/2 x 8	ESH		1. 00
6200.	Madame Elisabeth				
	Le Brun	11 x 9	CFA		6. 00
6201.	Madame Le Brun				
	and her Daughter	17 x 13	NYGS		5. 00
6202.	Marie Antoinette,				
	Queen of France	8 x 10-1/2	ESH		1. 00
6203.	Mrs. Molé-Raymond	14 x 10	IA		3. 00
6204.	Portrait of Madame				
	Le Brun	11 x 8	CFA		1. 00
6205.	Self-Portrait	14 x 11	AS		3. 25
		13 x 11	IA		3. 00
	Head--Detail of				
	No. 6205	15 x 11	IA		3. 00
6206.	Self-Portrait with				
	Daughter (2)	14 x 11	IA	ea.	3. 00

LEBRUN, RICO (American, 1900-1964)

6207.	Anna	20 x 10	NYGS		7. 50
6208.	Figure in Rain c.	10 x 8	NYGS		. 50

LE CERVIN

6209.	Matterhorn	27 x 35	CAC		12. 50

LE CLEAR, THOMAS (American, 1818-1882)

6210.	Buffalo Newsboy	26 x 21	AK		7. 50
		16 x 13	AK		2. 50

LE COMTE, PAUL EMILE (French, 1877-1950)

6211.	Old House c.	18 x 23	PENN		1. 50

LEE
| 6212. | Go-Go (4) | | 15 x 6 | DAC | ea. | 1. 50 |

LEE, DORIS E. (American Contemporary)
6213.	Apple Pickers		10 x 16	NYGS	5. 00
6214.	Arbor Day	c.	8 x 10	NYGS	1. 50
6215.	Corn Pickers		10 x 16	NYGS	5. 00
6216.	Thanksgiving, 1935	9 x 13	NYGS	3. 00
		8 x 11	NYGS	1. 50
6217.	Tropical Bird	12 x 18	NYGS	7. 50
6218.	Winter in the Catskills	14 x 20	NYGS	7. 50

LEE-HANKEY See HANKEY, WILLIAM LEE
LEEMPUTTER
| 6219. | Homeward Bound | 20 x 26 | CAC | 7. 50 |

LEGA, SILVESTRO (Italian, 1826-1895)
| 6220. | Lady of the Garden | 11 x 15 | IA | 3. 00 |

LEGARES, JOSE OLIVET (Spanish Contemporary)
| 6221. | In the Foothills | 25 x 35 | NYGS | 16. 00 |

LEGER, FERNAND (French, 1881-)
6222.	Abstraction		25 x 20	CAC	15. 00
6223.	Big Julie	c.	8 x 10	MMA	. 35
6224.	Blue Basket		24-1/2 x 19	NYGS	12. 00
6225.	Composition, 1920	11 x 8	AP	2. 00
6226.	King of Hearts	19 x 30	CFA	7. 50
6227.	Leisure--Homage to Louis David	c.	20 x 24	PENN	1. 50
6228.	Poster: Musee des Arts Decoratifs	30 x 20	PENN	1. 00
6229.	Sitting Woman	c.	9 x 7	AP	. 75
6230.	Still Life	c.	18 x 23	HNA	5. 95
6231.	Still Life with Fruit	c.	20 x 24	PENN	1. 50
6232.	Three Women	19 x 25	MMA	7. 50
6233.	Women and Child	15-1/2x22-1/2	ESH	10. 00
6234.	Yellow Flowers in a Blue Vase	25 x 20	NYGS	12. 00

LEHUCHER
| 6235. | Anemones | 21 x 27 | CAC | 7. 50 |
| 6236. | Spring Flowers | 21 x 27 | CAC | 7. 50 |

LEIBL, WILHELM (German, 1844-1900)
| 6237. | Old Woman in Church | 21 x 13 | CAC | 5. 00 |
| 6238. | Three Women in Church | 21 x 13 | NYGS | 6. 00 |

LEIGH, WILLIAM R. (American, 1866-1955)
6239.	Bull Diving	22 x 18	CFA	7. 50
6240.	Bull Dogging	22 x 18	CFA	7. 50
6241.	Double Crosser	22 x 18	CFA	7. 50
6242.	Greased Lightning	22 x 18	CFA	7. 50
6243.	Navajo Pony	12 x 16	AA	5. 00
6244.	White Navajo Pinto	12 x 16	AA	5. 00

LEIPOLD, KARL (German, 1864-1943)
6245.	Dutch Sailboats	21 x 29	CAC	12. 00
6246.	Old Dutch Mill	29 x 25	CAC	10. 00
6247.	Rialto Bridge	22 x 26	CAC	10. 00

LEITCH, WILLIAM LEIGHTON (Scotch, 1804-1883)
6248.	Amalfi	8 x 10	CFA	6. 00
6249.	Balsano	8 x 10	CFA	6. 00
6250.	Milan	8 x 10	CFA	6. 00

LEITH-ROSS, HARRY (American, 1886-)
6251.	Northern Lake	19 x 27	IA	10. 00
6252.	Old Mill	19 x 27	IA	10. 00

LELONG, PIERRE EMILE (American, 1908-)
6253.	Paris Street Scenes				
	(20)	9-1/2 x 12 (14)	IA	ea.	3. 50
	L'Arc de				
	Triomphe	12 x 9-1/2 (6)	IA	ea.	3. 50
	Les Bouquinistes				
	Les Champs-Elysees				
	La Conciergerie				
	Les Invalides				
	la Madeleine				
	Moulin Rouge				
	Notre Dame				
	Notre Dame (L'Abside)				
	Notre Dame et la Seine				
	L'Opera				
	Le Pantheon				
	Place de la Concorde				
	Place du Tertre				
	Place Vendome				
	Pont Alexandre III				
	Le Pont Marie				
	Le Pont Neuf				
	Rue Norvins				
	La Tour Eiffel				

LE MAISTRE, ALEXIS (French, 19th Century)
6254.	Fisherman's			
	Cottage	17 x 22	ESH	6. 00

LE MASSON See LA MASSON

LE NAIN, LOUIS (French, 1593-1648)
6255.	Blacksmith at his			
	Forge	20 x 17	ESH	10. 00
6256.	Card Player c.	16 x 12	PENN	1. 00
6257.	Family of Peasants			
	c.	20 x 24	PENN	1. 50
6258.	Peasants Home from			
	Haymaking	17 x 22-1/2	ESH	10. 00

LENARD, JACQUES
6259.	Flowerpiece	8 x 10	CFA	1. 00

LENBACH, FRANZ VON (German, 1836-1904)
6260.	Shepherd Boy	16 x 22	IA	7. 50
		8 x 12	ESH	2. 00

LENORE
6261.	Bouquet Ballet (4)	14 x 11	AK	ea.	1.50
		14 x 8	AK	ea.	1.25
		10 x 8	AK	ea.	1.00
		8 x 6	AK	ea.	.60

LEONARDO DA VINCI (Italian, 1452-1519)
6262.	Adoration of the				
	Magi (Florence)	11-1/2x15-1/2	AS		3.25
6263.	Annunciation c.	20 x 24	PENN		1.50
		7 x 15	AS		3.25
		6 x 14	IA		3.00
	Angel--Detail of				
	No. 6263	15 x 11	IA		3.00
6264.	Baptism of Christ				
	c.	8 x 10	NYGS		.50
6265.	Beatrici D'Este				
	(Attributed)	15 x 10	IA		3.00
6266.	La Belle Ferroniere				
	c.	8 x 10	NYGS		.50
6267.	Christ (Head)	13-1/2 x 10	ESH		10.00
6268.	Ginevra De'Benci	15 x 14	NYGS		10.00
6269.	Isabelle D'Este	17 x 12-1/2	NYGS		7.50
6270.	The Last Supper				
	(Unrestored)	16-1/2 x 32	ESH		15.00
		16 x 32	IA		15.00
		13 x 23	IA		7.50
		11 x 22	NYGS		6.00
		7 x 11	IA		1.75
	c.	7 x 9	AP		.50
6271.	The Last Supper				
	(Restored)	21 x 40	NYGS		12.00
		15-1/2 x 30	NYGS		6.00
		14 x 25	PENN		1.50
		10 x 20	NYGS		3.00
		9 x 15	IA		3.00
6272.	Leda and the Swan	14 x 11	IA		3.00
6273.	Madonna and Child				
	(Florence)	15 x 11-1/2	AS		3.25
6274.	Madonna and Child				
	(Dr.)	14-1/2x10-1/2	NYGS		3.00
6275.	Madonna, Child,				
	St. Anne and				
	St. John	22 x 16	PENN		1.50
		22 x 15	ESH		15.00
6276.	Mona Lisa				
	(La Gioconda) c.	24 x 20	PENN		1.50
	c.	23 x 18	HNA		5.95
		21 x 14-1/2	AP		5.00
		19 x 13	IA		5.00
		18-1/2 x 13	NYGS		5.00
		15 x 11	IA		3.00
	c.	10 x 8	ESH		1.00

			10 x 6-1/2	NYGS	1. 00
			9 x 7	IA	1. 75
6277.	Portrait of Unknown				
	Woman		14 x 10	IA	3. 00
6278.	The Redeemer		13-1/2x10-1/2	IA	3. 50
			14 x 11	IA	3. 00
			10 x 7-1/2	IA	1. 75
6279.	St. Anne	c.	10 x 8	NYGS	. 50
6280.	St. Anne (Head)		16 x 12	PENN	1. 00
		c.	9 x 7	AP	. 60
6281.	St. John the Baptist		13 x 10	IA	3. 00
			12 x 9	CFA	2. 50
6282.	St. Peter		6 x 4-1/2	AR	3. 00
6283.	The Saviour (Head)				
		c.	10 x 8	ESH	1. 00
6284.	Self-Portrait				
	(Presumed)		14 x 11	IA	3. 00
6285.	Virgin and Child				
	with St. Anne and				
	John the Baptist				
	(Dr.)		30 x 22	NYGS	15. 00
6286.	Virgin, Child and				
	St. Anne		14 x 11	IA	3. 00
	Detail--Head of				
	St. Anne		15 x 11	IA	3. 00
6287.	Virgin of the Rocks		28 x 18	NYGS	15. 00
			15 x 9	AS	3. 25
	Detail of No.				
	6287		22-1/2 x 19	ESH	10. 00
		c.	10 x 8	ESH	1. 00
6288.	Woman in Profile				
	(Dr.)		14-1/2 x 10	NYGS	3. 00

LE PRINCE, JEAN BAPTISTE (French, 1733-1781)

6289.	Russian Interior		7 x 6	AR	3. 50

LERIN See GIRALT LERIN
LEROLLE, HENRI (French, 1848-1929)

6290.	Arrival of the				
	Shepherds		16 x 20	NYGS	7. 50
		c.	8 x 10	IA	. 50

LESAOUT

6291.	Paris Scenes (8)				
		c.	8 x 10	DAC	ea. 1. 00

LETELLIER

6292.	L'Etang	18 x 27	NYGS	18. 00

LEUTZE, EMANUEL G. (American, 1816-1868)

6293.	Washington Crossing			
	the Delaware	18 x 30	NYGS	15. 00
		16 x 28	CAC	10. 00
		7-1/2 x 14	NYGS	3. 00

LEVER

6294.	The Mayflower Yacht				
		c.	7 x 9	AP	. 25

LEVI, JULIAN EDWIN (American, 1900-)
6295.   New England Dock   13 x 10   CAC   10. 00
LEVIER, CHARLES
6296.   Fleurs devant La
        Campagne   24 x 18   DAC   12. 50
6297.   Flowers and Fruits 15 x 30   DAC   2. 00
6298.   Flowers by an Open
        Window   c.   24 x 20   PENN   1. 50
6299.   Nappe Jaune   36 x 24   DAC   15. 00
6300.   Still Life before
        Window   24 x 48   DAC   10. 00
LEVINE, JACK (American Contemporary)
6301.   Biblical Kings and
        Rabbis (Portraits)
        (6)   10 x 8   NYGS   ea.   3. 00
                                                   or   15. 00
                                                   set
6302.   Hillel
6303.   King Asa
6304.   King David
6305.   King Saul
6306.   Maimonides
6307.   Yehudah
6308.   The Inauguration
                       c.   18 x 23   HNA   5. 95
6309.   String Quartette c. 7 x 9   AP   . 50
6310.   The Trial   c.   8 x 10   NYGS   . 50
LEVY, RUDOLF (German, 1875-1943)
6311.   Still Life with
        Green Jug   21 x 25-1/2   NYGS   20. 00
LEWIS, EDMUND DARCH (American, 1835-1910)
6312.   Landscape   23 x 36   NYGS   16. 00
LEWSEY, TOM
6313.   Shoal Water   17 x 24   ESH   10. 00
LEYSTER, JUDITH (Dutch, 1610-1660)
6314.   The Jester   22 x 19   PENN   1. 50
L'HERMITTE, LEON AUGUSTIN (French, 1844-1925)
6315.   Haymakers   c.   7 x 9   AP   . 50
6316.   Haymaking   18-1/2 x 25   NYGS   7. 50
6317.   Supper at Emmaus   23-1/2 x 34   NYGS   18. 00
        Christ (Head)--
        Detail of No.
        6317   20 x 16   NYGS   7. 50
                            10 x 8   NYGS   1. 50
LHOTE, ANDRÉ (French, 1885-)
6318.   The Model   19 x 13   CFA   5. 00
LI LING (Chinese, Ming Dynasty)
6319.   Polo Players   7 x 29   NYGS   6. 00
LI LONG MEIN (Chinese)
6320.   Horse and Groom   10 x 30   CFA   30. 00
LI TANG (Chinese, Ac. 1100-1130)
6321.   Returning from
        Festival   10 x 11   NYGS   30. 00

LIANG K'AI (Chinese, Ac. c. 1200)
6322.	Le Poete Li Tai Po	30 x 13	CFA	30. 00

LIER, ADOLF HEINRICH (German, 1826-1882)
6323.	Harvest	23 x 35	CFA	15. 00
6324.	Landscape (Starnberger Lake)	25 x 36	CFA	18. 00
6325.	Start of the Hunt	21 x 16	NYGS	6. 00
6326.	Surf	23-1/2x39-1/2	ESH	9. 00

LIER, CLAIRE
6327.	Boy with Colt	23-1/2 x 16	ESH	6. 00
6328.	Girl with Shetland Pony	23-1/2 x 16	ESH	6. 00
6329.	We Three	20 x 16	NYGS	6. 00

LIGNON, BERNARD (French Contemporary)
6330.	Cask	23 x 28	RL	12. 50
6331.	Clown	26-1/2 x 13	NYGS	22. 00
6332.	Le Vase Blanc	28-1/2x19-1/2	RL	15. 00
6333.	Water Carnival	24-1/2 x 30	RL	20. 00

LIGOZZI, JACOPO (Italian, 1543-1627)
6334.	Anacardio	15 x 10-1/2	AS	3. 25
6335.	Fig with Birds	15 x 10-1/2	AS	3. 25
6336.	Fortune	15 x 9	AS	3. 25

LIMBOURG, POL DE (French, Ac. 1402-1416)
6337.	Book of Hours of the Duc de Berry (2)	10 x 8	ESH	ea.	1. 00

LIMOUSE
6338.	Nature Morte aux Figues	c.	17-1/2 x 22	AS	4. 00

LINARD
6339.	Bouquet of Flowers		17 x 22	CAC	10. 00
6340.	Flowerpiece Toile	c.	12-1/2x9-1/2	AP	1. 25

LINDERUM, RICHARD (German, 1851-   )
6341.	Ave Maria	20 x 14	NYGS	9. 00

LINT, E. VAN
6342.	Paesaggio No. 43 and No. 45	7 x 11	CFA	ea.	5. 00

LIOTARD, JEAN ETIENNE (Swiss, 1702-1789)
6343.	The Painter's Niece, Mlle. Lavergne, 1746	20 x 16	NYGS	10. 00
6344.	Portrait of a Lady	10 x 8-1/2	AR	4. 00
6345.	The Soltaness (Lady Mary-Adelaide of France)	11 x 13-1/2	AS	3. 25
6346.	Young Girl Singing into a Mirror	24 x 20	CFA	10. 00

LIPCHITZ, JACQUES (French, 1891-   )
6347.	Sauvetage	12-1/2 x 10	NYGS	12. 00

LIPKIN, AILEEN
6348.	Peasant on a Donkey	32 x 20	IA	15. 00

6349.	Walking Nuns	33 x 20	IA	15. 00
LIPPI, FILIPPINO (Italian, 1457-1504)				
6350.	Angel Adoring	21 x 9-1/2	ESH	7. 50
6351.	Angel Announcing	11" Diam.	IA	3. 00
6352.	Apparition of the Virgin			
	to St. Bernard	12 x 11	IA	3. 00
6353.	Esther and Ahasverus	5 x 15	IA	3. 00
6354.	Madonna Adoring the			
	Child	15 x 11	IA	3. 00
6355.	Madonna and Child	30 x 21-1/2	NYGS	26. 00
6356.	Portrait of an			
	Old Man	13-1/2 x 11	AS	3. 25
		13 x 10	IA	3. 00
6357.	Portrait of a Young			
	Man	20 x 14	NYGS	12. 00
6358.	St. Peter and St. Paul			
	before the Proconsul	11 x 15	AS	3. 25
6359.	Self-Portrait	15 x 11	IA	3. 00
		15 x 8	AS	3. 25
6360.	Virgin Adoring the			
	Child	15 x 11	AS	3. 25
6361.	Virgin Adoring the			
	Child	15-1/2 x 11	AS	3. 25
6362.	Virgin Annunciate	11" Diam.	IA	3. 00
LIPPI, (FRA) FILIPPO (Italian, 1406-1469)				
6363.	Adoration of the			
	Child	15 x 9	IA	3. 00
6364.	Angel Adoring	18 x 8	CFA	3. 00
6365.	Angel Announcing	14 x 5	IA	3. 00
6366.	Madonna and Child			
	and Stories from her			
	Life	11" Diam.	IA	3. 00
	Virgin (Head)--			
	Detail of No.			
	6366	15 x 11	IA	3. 00
6367.	Virgin Adoring	15-1/2x11-1/2	AS	3. 25
6368.	Virgin Adoring	15 x 11	AS	3. 25
6369.	Virgin Adoring the			
	Child (Uffizi)	12 x 11	IA	3. 00
	Detail of No.			
	6369	17 x 13	IA	3. 00
6370.	Virgin Annunciate	14 x 5	IA	3. 00
6371.	Virgin and Child	15-1/2x10-1/2	AS	3. 25
	Virgin--Detail of			
	No. 6371	19-1/2x15-1/2	AS	7. 50
		16 x 11-1/2	AS	3. 25
		12 x 9-1/2	AS	3. 25
6372.	Virgin and Child			
	(Venice)	15 x 11	AS	3. 25
6373.	Virgin and Child			
	(Florence	15 x 11	AS	3. 25
6374.	Virgin and Child and			
	Sacred History	11-1/2" Diam.	AS	3. 25

LIPPINCOTT, EDWARD
6375. Solid Comfort   24 x 30   DAC   7. 50
LIPPO MEMMI See MEMMI, LIPPO
LIPPO VANNI See VANNI, LIPPO
LISS, GIOVANNI See LYS, JAN VAN
LITT
6376. Oriental Girls
        (Portraits) (4)   20 x 16   AK   ea. 5. 00
                           15 x 11   AK   ea. 2. 50
                           11 x 8   AK   ea. 1. 25
                            7 x 5   AK   ea.   . 75
LITTLEJOHNS, JOHN (English, 1874-)
6377. Between Showers   18 x 22   CFA   10. 00
6378. Bridge at Sedbergh 17-1/2 x 22   ESH   10. 00
6379. Old Watermill   16-1/2 x 20   ESH   12. 00
6380. Sussex Farm   18 x 21   ESH   15. 00
                           17 x 20   ESH   6. 00
LIVINGSTON, ALINE
6381. Raggedy Romeo   16 x 21   AA   4. 00
LLOVERAS, FEDERICO (Spanish Contemporary)
6382. Bay of Naples   25 x 34   NYGS   18. 00
6383. Bay of Palma de
        Mallorca   25 x 34   NYGS   18. 00
                           12 x 16   NYGS   4. 00
6384. California Desert
        near Palm Springs 13 x 39-1/2   NYGS   15. 00
6385. Castel S. Angelo,
        Rome   25 x 34   NYGS   18. 00
                           12 x 16   NYGS   4. 00
6386. Chicago Financial
        District   31-1/2x12-1/2 NYGS   12. 00
6387. Chicago Skyline   13 x 39-1/2   NYGS   18. 00
6388. Columbus Monument,
        Barcelona   31-1/2 x 12   NYGS   12. 00
6389. Florence   25 x 34   NYGS   18. 00
6390. Giralda, Sevilla   31-1/2 x 12   NYGS   12. 00
6391. Loire, Chateau
        d'Amboise   13-1/2 x 39   NYGS   18. 00
6392. London, Houses of
        Parliament   17 x 39   NYGS   18. 00
6393. Madrid, Puente de
        Segovia   17 x 39   NYGS   18. 00
6394. Mallorca Harbor   13-1/2 x 39   NYGS   18. 00
6395. Miami   13 x 39-1/2   NYGS   15. 00
6396. New Orleans   15 x 39-1/2   NYGS   18. 00
6397. New York, Lower
        Manhattan   17 x 39-1/2   NYGS   18. 00
6398. New York, Wall
        Street   31-1/2x12-1/2 NYGS   12. 00
6399. Palma de Mallorca   13-1/2 x 39   NYGS   18. 00
6400. Paris, Ile de la
        Cité   17 x 39   NYGS   18. 00

6401.	Paris, Le Pont Neuf	17 x 39	NYGS	18. 00
6402.	Paris, la Tour Eiffel	31-1/2 x 12	NYGS	12. 00
6403.	The Parthenon, Athens	25 x 34	NYGS	18. 00
		12 x 16	NYGS	4. 00
6404.	Piazza S. Pietro (St. Peter's Square, Rome)	25-1/2 x 34	NYGS	18. 00
		12 x 16	NYGS	4. 00
6405.	San Francisco-Oakland Bridge	17 x 39-1/2	NYGS	18. 00
6406.	San Marco, Venezia	31-1/2 x 12	NYGS	12. 00
6407.	Sorrento	17 x 40	NYGS	18. 00
6408.	Street in Chelsea	13-1/2x39-1/2	NYGS	18. 00
6409.	Venice	13-1/2 x 39	NYGS	18. 00
6410.	Washington, D. C.	17 x 39-1/2	NYGS	18. 00
6411.	Windsor Castle	17 x 39	NYGS	18. 00

LLOVET, RAMON (Spanish Contemporary)

6412.	Flowers and Pigeons	19-1/2 x 39	NYGS	18. 00

LOBLEY, JOHN HODGSON (English, 1878-)

6413.	Old Harry Rocks	16-1/2 x 21	ESH	12. 00
		16 x 20	ESH	6. 00

LOCHNER, STEFAN (German, 1400-1451)

6414.	Adoration	22 x 24	CFA	15. 00
		20 x 21	CFA	6. 00
6415.	Annunciation (2 Parts)	32-1/2 x 16	NYGS	20. 00
	(2 on 1 sheet)	22 x 11-1/2	NYGS	18. 00
	(2 on 1 sheet)			
6416.	Madonna in the Rose Garden	c. 23 x 18	HNA	5. 95
6417.	Madonna of the Rose Arbor	18-1/2x14-1/2	IA	12. 00
		16 x 12-1/2	IA	7. 50
	c.	9 x 7	AP	. 50

LOCKE, JUSTIN

6418.	Tata Domingo	24-1/2 x 10	IA	10. 00

LOCKWOOD, WARD (American, 1894-)

6419.	Fragments of Elegance	22-1/2 x 30	IA	15. 00
6420.	Horses in Winter	c. 7 x 9	AP	. 50
6421.	Young Sculptress	26 x 18	IA	10. 00

LODI, AGASTINO DA (Italian, Ac. 1500)

6422.	Leave-Taking of Jesus	15 x 11	AS	3. 25

LOEDERER

6423.	Brahms at Home	16 x 24	CAC	4. 00

LOESCH, ERNST (German, 1860-1946)

6424.	Lilacs	22 x 26	IA	6. 00

LOEWENGRUND
| 6425. | Rooftops | 17 x 21 | CAC | 7. 50 |

LOGAN, MAURICE (American, Ac. 1940)
| 6426. | Old Dock | 14 x 20 | IA | 7. 50 |

LONGHI, PIETRO (Italian, 1702-1785)
6427.	Apothecary	14 x 11	AS	3. 25
6428.	Dancing Master	14 x 11-1/2	AS	3. 25
		14 x 11	IA	3. 00
6429.	Dentist (Chemist's Shop)	15 x 11	IA	3. 00
6430.	Familiar Concert	11 x 14	IA	3. 00
6431.	Kiss of the Hand	24 x 19	CFA	12. 00
6432.	Longhi Painting Portrait of a Lady	14 x 11	AS	3. 25
6433.	Marriage	14 x 11	IA	3. 00
6434.	Tailor	24 x 19	CFA	12. 00
		14 x 11	IA	3. 00
6435.	Venetian Lady	9 x 8	CFA	5. 00

LONGPRE, PAUL DE (American, 1855-1911)
| 6436. | Flower Paintings (8) | 14 x 11 | NYGS | ea. 2. 50 |

Delight (Rose)
Enchanting
Fairy Lustre
Fleurs de Louis
Gentle Waking
Red Velvet
White Prince
Winsome

LONGSTAFF, W.
| 6437. | Arundel | 14 x 21 | ESH | 12. 00 |
| 6438. | Sussex Downs | 19 x 23 | ESH | 12. 00 |

LOPEZ, BEV
| 6439. | Juveniles, Blue Ribbon (4) | 12 x 9 | AK | ea. . 75 |

LOPEZ, GRACE
6440.	Kittens, Blue Ribbon (4)	10 x 12	AK	ea. . 75
6441.	Puppies, Blue Ribbon (4)	10 x 12	AK	ea. . 75
		5 x 7	AK	ea. . 30

LORENZ, CARL (Austrian, 1871-)
6442.	Coast of Jugoslavia	6-1/2 x 16	ESH	Pr. 4. 00
6443.	Mount Cervin	16 x 6-1/2	ESH	Pr. 4. 00
6444.	Pine Trees with Vesuvius	16 x 6-1/2	ESH	Pr. 4. 00
6445.	Riviera	6-1/2x15-1/2	ESH	Pr. 4. 00

LORENZETTI, AMBROGIO (Italian, Ac. 1324-1347)
| 6446. | Castle on the Sea | 9 x 13-1/2 | AS | 3. 25 |
| 6447. | Castle on the Shore | 10 x 15 | IA | 3. 00 |

6448.	Country Life	7 x 15-1/2	AS	3.25
6449.	Effect of Good Government in the Country	24 x 30	NYGS	12.00
6450.	Good Government	15 x 9	IA	3.00
	Peace--Detail of No. 6450	16 x 12	IA	3.00
6451.	Madonna and Child	15 x 9	IA	3.00
6452.	Madonna and Child and Two Saints	14 x 7	IA	3.00
6453.	Madonna and Saints	15 x 10	IA	3.00
6454.	St. Dorothea	15 x 10	IA	3.00
6455.	St. Michael (Asciano-Siena)	13-1/2 x 11	AS	3.25
6456.	Town Life	7 x 15-1/2	AS	3.25
	Detail of No. 6456	11 x 15-1/2	AS	3.25
6457.	View of a City	10 x 15	IA	3.00
		9 x 13-1/2	AS	3.25
6458.	Virgin and Child (Siena)	15-1/2 x 8	AS	3.25
6459.	Virgin and Child (Siena)	15-1/2 x 9	AS	3.25

LORENZETTI, PIETRO (Italian, c. 1280-1348)

6460.	Birth of the Virgin	16 x 10	IA	3.00
6461.	Descent from the Cross	11 x 15	IA	3.00
6462.	Madonna and Sts. John and Francis	11 x 15	IA	3.00
6463.	Virgin and Child (Arezzo)	15 x 10	AS	3.25

LORENZO DI CREDI (SCIARPELLONI, LORENZO) (Italian, 1459-1537)

6464.	Annunciation	14 x 11-1/2	AS	3.25
		13 x 11	IA	3.00
	Virgin--Detail of No. 6464	10 x 8	IA	1.50
6465.	Holy Family	11" Diam.	IA	3.00
6466.	Madonna and Child (Vatican)	15 x 11	IA	3.00
6467.	Madonna and Child with St. John (Borghese)	11" Diam.	IA	3.00
6468.	Portrait of a Young Girl c.	8 x 10	NYGS	.50
6469.	Portrait of a Youth in a Black Cap	12 x 11	IA	3.00
6470.	Portrait of a Youth in a Red Cap	14 x 10	IA	3.00
6471.	Portrait of Verrocchio	15 x 10	IA	3.00
6472.	Venus	15 x 7	AS	3.25

LORENZO MONACO (Italian, 1370-1425)
6473.	Adoration of the Magi	10 x 15	IA	3.00
6474.	Annunciation (Florence)	15 x 11	AS	3.25
6475.	Crucifixion	9 x 15	IA	3.00
6476.	Madonna and Saints	15 x 11	IA	3.00

LORENZO DI PIETRO See VECCHIETTA, IL
LORENZO DA SAN SEVERINO (Italian, 1445-1503)
6477.	Virgin and St. Anne	15 x 7	IA	3.00

LORENZO VENEZIANO (Italian, 1400-1461)
6478.	Marriage of St. Catherine	15 x 19-1/2	AS	3.25
6479.	Virgin and Child	15 x 9	AS	3.25

LORI, FLORA
6480.	Zinnias	16-1/2 x 23	AS	7.50

LORJOU, BERNARD (French, 1908-)
6481.	Composition in Blue	c. 24 x 20	PENN	1.50
		24 x 18	DAC	12.50
6482.	Composition in Orange	c. 20 x 24	PENN	1.50
		18 x 24	DAC	12.50
6483.	Flowers and Pineapple	22 x 27-1/2	NYGS	16.00
6484.	Green Dish	22-1/2 x 23	NYGS	18.00
6485.	Red Sideboard	17-1/2x22-1/2	ESH	10.00

LORRAIN, CLAUDE See GELLEE, CLAUDE
LOTIRON, ROBERT (French, 1886-)
6486.	Fishmongers	c. 8 x 10	ESH	1.00

LOTTO, LORENZO (Italian, 1480-1556)
6487.	Gentleman with Gloves	14 x 11	IA	3.00
6488.	Nativity, 1523	18 x 13-1/2	NYGS	7.50
6489.	Portrait of Bernardo de Rossi	14 x 11	IA	3.00
6490.	Portrait of a Youth	11 x 12	IA	3.00
6491.	St. Catherine of Alexandria	14 x 11	IA	3.00
6492.	Three Ages of Man	11 x 14	IA	3.00
		c. 7 x 9	AP	.60

LOTZE, KARL (German, 1892-)
6493.	Does at Night	29 x 22	ESH	15.00

LOWRIE, AGNES POTTER (English-American, 1892-)
6494.	Blue Compote	18 x 22	CFA	5.00
		6 x 8	CFA	1.00
6495.	Red Compote	18 x 22	CFA	5.00
		6 x 8	CFA	1.00
6496.	Watermelon	19 x 28	CFA	10.00

LOWRY, LAURENCE STÉPHAN (English, 1887-)
6497.	At the Seaside	20 x 24	NYGS	15.00
6498.	Canals and Factories	24 x 30	NYGS	15.00

6499.	Children's Play-			
	ground	18 x 24	NYGS	15. 00
6500.	Lancashire Village	14 x 20	NYGS	12. 00
6501.	Northern River			
	Scene	16 x 24	ESH	15. 00
6502.	Old Church and			
	Steps	24 x 20	NYGS	15. 00
6503.	On the Sands, Berwick			
	on Tweed	20 x 23-1/2	NYGS	15. 00
6504.	Outside the Mills	11 x 20	NYGS	7. 50
6505.	Village Square	18 x 24	NYGS	16. 00

LUCAS, EUGENIO (Spanish, 1824-1870)

| 6506. | Aveyron | 23 x 28 | CAC | 10. 00 |

LUCCA

6507.	Harbour by Night	16 x 31-1/2	ESH	Pr.	8. 00
		8 x 16	ESH	Pr.	3. 00
6508.	Still Life with				
	Banjo	16 x 31-1/2	ESH	Pr.	8. 00
		8 x 16	ESH	Pr.	3. 00

LUCCHA, SCHOOL OF (Italian, 14th Century)

| 6509. | Crucifix | 14-1/2x11-1/2 | AS | 3. 25 |

LUCE, MAXIMILIEN (French, 1858-1941)

| 6510. | Pastoral | 25-1/2 x 36 | NYGS | 16. 00 |

LUCIANI, SEBASTIANO See PIOMBO, SEBASTIANO DEL
LUCIONI, LUIGI (American, 1900-)

6511.	Autumn Landscape	16 x 24	PENN	1. 50
6512.	Peace in the Valley	20 x 24	NYGS	10. 00
6513.	Route Seven	16 x 21	NYGS	9. 00
6514.	Sunlit Patterns	14 x 20	NYGS	7. 50
6515.	Vermont Landscape			
	c.	20 x 24	PENN	1. 50
6516.	Vermont Pastoral	19-1/2 x 33	NYGS	12. 00
6517.	White Birches in			
	Vermont c.	20 x 24	PENN	1. 50

LUDLUM, JOHN P. American, Ac. 1952)

| 6518. | Ballerina | 22 x 18 | CAC | 6. 00 |
| 6519. | Scheherazade | 22 x 18 | CAC | 6. 00 |

LUINI, BERNARDINO (Italian, 1475-1532)

6520.	Holy Family c.	8 x 10	NYGS	. 50
6521.	Little St. John with			
	the Lamb	10 x 9	IA	1. 50
6522.	Madonna of the			
	Carnation	17 x 16	AA	7. 50
6523.	Madonna of the Rose			
	Bower	12 x 11	IA	3. 00
6524.	Portrait of a Lady	16 x 11	AR	5. 00
6525.	Silence	9 x 7	CFA	2. 50
6526.	Virgin (Head) c.	9 x 7	AP	. 50
6527.	Virgin and Child	11 x 8	IA	1. 50

LUKS, GEORGE B. (American, 1867-1933)

| 6528. | Spielers c. | 20 x 24 | PENN | 1. 50 |

LUNDBERG, GUSTAF (Swedish, 1695-1786)

| 6529. | Portrait of Boucher | 12 x 9 | CFA | 2. 50 |

LUPAS, LOUIS (American Contemporary)
6530. Johnson, Lyndon
       Baines (DR.)   16 x 13   NYGS   4. 00
6531. Johnson, Lyndon
       Baines, 1962 (DR.)   13 x 17   NYGS   4. 00
6532. Kennedy, John F.   28 x 20   NYGS   12. 00
6533. Kennedy, John F.
       (DR.)   16 x 13   NYGS   4. 00
                             13-1/2 x 10   NYGS   3. 00
6534. Musicians (8)   14 x 11   CAC   ea.   3. 00
6535.   Beethoven   10 x 8   CAC   ea.   1. 00
6536.   Brahms
6537.   Dvorak
6538.   Grieg
6539.   Puccini
6540.   Rachmaninoff
6541.   Rossini
6542.   Sibelius
LURCAT, JEAN (French, 1892-)
6543. Acapulco   c.   17-1/2 x 22   AS   4. 00
6544. Big Cloud   16 x 24   NYGS   12. 00
6545. Brazil (Detail from
       KLM Tapestry) c.   8 x 10   ESH   1. 00
6546. Coq Blanc   23 x 15   NYGS   18. 00
6547. Garden in the Night   16 x 22-1/2   ESH   10. 00
6548. Guerrier   23 x 14   NYGS   22. 00
6549. Man   31 x 14   ESH   15. 00
6550. Man and the Star   29-1/2 x 24   ESH   15. 00
6551. Papillon   16 x 22-1/2   NYGS   26. 00
6552. Papillon Bleu   28 x 21-1/2   NYGS   22. 00
6553. Ram in the Night   21-1/2x28-1/2 ESH   15. 00
LUSCHNER, H.
6554. Flamingo-Blossoms   16 x 12   ESH   Pr.   3. 00
6555. Flower Paintings (2) 31-1/2 x 9   ESH   ea.   8. 00
                                                     Pr.
       Cactus Flower
       Clivia
6555a. On Lago-Maggiore   18 x 23-1/2   ESH   Pr.   8. 00
6556. Paris   18 x 23-1/2   ESH   Pr.   8. 00
6557. Red Cactus   16 x 12   ESH   Pr.   3. 00
6558. Venice with Campanile
                             14 x 27-1/2   ESH   Pr.   8. 00
6559. Yellow Cactus   16 x 12   ESH   Pr.   3. 00
LUTHY, JOHANNES (Swiss, 1803-1863)
6560. Florals, Fragrant
       (4)   16 x 12   AK   ea.   1. 50
                             12 x 9   AK   ea.   1. 00
                             8 x 6   AK   ea.   . 40
LUTI, BENEDETTO (Italian, 1666-1724)
6561. Head of a Cherub   12 x 10   IA   3. 00
LYNCH, J. H. (English, d. 1868)
6562. Autumn Leaves   23 x 19   IA   7. 50

6563.	Tina	23 x 19	IA		6. 00

LYNE, MICHAEL (English Contemporary)

6564.	Beaufort at Worcester Lodge	15 x 21	RL		7. 50
6565.	Cotswold at Shipton Oliffe	15 x 21	RL		7. 50
6566.	Devon and Somerset Hounds	10-1/2 x 10	ESH		2. 00
6567.	Duke of Beaufort's Hunt	13 x 20	CFA		7. 50
6568.	Royal Agricultural Beagles at Jarvis Quarry	15 x 21	RL		7. 50
6569.	Whaddon Chase at Waterloo	15 x 21	RL		7. 50

LYNN

6570.	Flowers (4)	18 x 14	AK	ea.	3. 00
		12 x 10	AK	ea.	3. 00

LYS, JAN VAN (German, c. 1629)

6571.	Venus at the Mirror	14 x 11	IA		3. 00

M

MA LIN (Chinese, Sung Dynasty South)

6572.	Lake Shore in Autumn	10-1/2 x 11	NYGS	32. 50
6573.	Two Birds	9-1/2 x 9	NYGS	24. 00

MA YUAN (Chinese, 13th Century)

6574.	Canoe in Moonlight	29 x 14	CFA	36. 00
6575.	Landscape with Willows	9-1/2 x 10	NYGS	24. 00

MABUSE (GOSSART, JAN) (Flemish, 1470-1541)

6576.	Adam and Eve	10 x 8	AR	3. 00
6577.	Adoration of the Kings	22 x 20	ESH	10. 00
6578.	Triptych Malvagna	11 x 15	IA	3. 00

MAC BRYDE, J. ROBERT (Scotch Contemporary)

6579.	Still Life with Basket	17-1/2 x 21	ESH	15. 00

MAC DONALD, RICHARD (English Contemporary

6580.	The Kite	20 x 32-1/2	RL	12. 50
6581.	Still Life with Thunder	24 x 17	RL	12. 50

MAC DONALD-WRIGHT, STANTON (American, 1890-)

6582.	Synchromy in Blue-Green	c.	8 x 10	NYGS	. 50

MAC EWEN

6583.	With Grandma	c.	7 x 9	AP	. 50

MAC GREGOR, ROBERT (Scotch, 1848-1922)

6584.	American Clipper "Lightning"	22 x 32	AA	10. 00

6585.	The "Ariel"		22 x 32	AA		10. 00
6586.	Before the Wind		24 x 32	CFA		10. 00
6587.	Blue Waters	c.	20 x 24	PENN		1. 50
			16 x 24	IA		5. 00
6588.	Cutty Sark		24 x 20	AA		7. 50
			12 x 10	AA		2. 00
6589.	Flying Cloud		20 x 30	AA		8. 00
6590.	Good Going		20 x 30	AA		10. 00
6591.	Outward Bound		16 x 24	IA		5. 00
6592.	Red Jacket		24 x 20	AA		7. 50
			12 x 10	AA		2. 00
6593.	The "Torrens"		20 x 30	AA		8. 00

MACHOUREK

6594.	Flower Study on Green		24 x 20	DAC		7. 50
6595.	Flower Study on Red		24 x 20	DAC		7. 50
6596.	Matador (2)		40 x 20	DAC	ea.	15. 00
			20 x 10	DAC	ea.	3. 50
6597.	Senora		24 x 20	DAC		7. 50
6598.	Senorita		24 x 20	DAC		7. 50

MAC IVER, LAUREN (American Contemporary)

6599.	Manhattan		36 x 20	NYGS		18. 00
6600.	Oil Splatters on Leaves	c.	8 x 10	NYGS		. 50
6601.	Venice	c.	7 x 9	AP		. 50

MACKE, AUGUST (German, 1887-1914)

6602.	African Landscape		18 x 22	ESH		10. 00
6603.	Blick ins Gartenhaus		14 x 10	CFA		10. 00
6604.	Blue Girl Reading Book		23 x 17	PENN		1. 50
6605.	Children on the Water		16 x 22	ESH		10. 00
6606.	Girl with Aquarium	c.	16 x12	AP		2. 00
6607.	Girl with Blue Birds		22 x 30-1/2	NYGS		26. 00
6608.	Girl with Bowl	c.	23 x 18	HNA		5. 95
6609.	Gladiolas		30 x 24	CAC		15. 00
6610.	Indians on Horseback		15-1/2 x 21	NYGS		6. 00
6611.	Kandern		9-1/2x12-1/2	NYGS		12. 00
6612.	Lady at Hatter's Shop	c.	9 x 7	AP		. 75
6613.	Lady in Green Jacket	c.	9 x 7	AP		. 75
6614.	Landscape with Cow and Camel		18 x 21	CFA		15. 00
6615.	Millinery Shop at Promenade		20 x 29	CFA		15. 00
		c.	20 x 24	PENN		1. 50
6616.	Mother and Child		13-1/2 x 12	AP		1. 00
		c.	9 x 7	AP		1. 00

6617.	People on a Blue			
	Lake	23-1/2 x 19	IA	15. 00
6618.	Port of Duisberg	17 x 15	CAC	5. 00
6619.	Schaufenster mit			
	Gelben Baumen	19 x 13	CFA	12. 00
6620.	Walk Among			
	Flowers c.	20 x 24	PENN	1. 50
6621.	Yellow Coat	11-1/2x17-1/2	NYGS	16. 00
6622.	Zoological Gardens	19 x 31	NYGS	20. 00

MACKENZIE, HELEN (Scotch Contemporary)

| 6623. | Homeguard | 11 x 13 | ESH | 3. 00 |

MACLAGAN, PHILIP (English Contemporary)

| 6624. | Roses | 12 x 9 | ESH | 2. 00 |

MACLET, ELISEE (French, 1881-)

| 6625. | Red Mill | 20 x 28 | NYGS | 12. 00 |

MAES, NICOLAES (Dutch, 1632-1693)

6626.	Asking a Blessing	24 x 20	DAC	7. 50
6627.	Duchess of Mazarin	20 x 15	CAC	10. 00
6628.	Grace before Meat			
	c.	9 x 7	AP	. 60
6629.	Old Woman Dozing			
	over a Book c.	18 x 23	HNA	5. 95
6630.	The Prayer	23 x 19	PENN	1. 50
6631.	The Spinner c.	20 x 24	PENN	1. 50
6632.	Young Girl Peeling			
	Apples c.	8 x 10	NYGS	. 50

MAESTRO DEL CASSONE ADIMARE

6633.	Marriage of Lisa			
	Ricasoli and Boccaccio			
	Adimari	8 x 38	IA	10. 00
		6 x 15	IA	3. 00

MAESTRO DEL CASSONI JARVES (Italian, 15th Century)

| 6634. | Griselda Legend | 6 x 15 | IA | 3. 00 |

MAESTRO DELLA NATIVITA DI CASTELLO

6635.	Virgin and Child			
	(S. Giovanni			
	Valdarno)	15-1/2 x 11	AS	3. 25

MAESTRO DI SAN FRANCESCO

| 6636. | St. Anthony | 15 x 7 | IA | 3. 00 |

MAGNASCO, ALESSANDRO (Italian, 1677-1749)

| 6637. | Baptism of Christ | 24 x 30 | NYGS | 18. 00 |

MAGNUS, JOSEF (Austrian, Contemporary)

6638.	Jenny Lind	28 x 22	IA	6. 00
		20 x 16	IA	3. 50
		12 x 9	IA	1. 00

MAGRITTE, RENÉ (Belgian, 1898-)

| 6639. | Empire of Light | 19 x 24 | CFA | 7. 50 |

MAI-THU

6640.	The Class	10-1/2 x 30	ESH	15. 00
6641.	Game of Chess	8 x 34-1/2	ESH	18. 00
6642.	Larkspurs	10 x 8	ESH	1. 00
6643.	Recreation	10-1/2 x 30	ESH	15. 00

6644.	Still Life with				
	Orchids	10 x 8	ESH		1.00
6645.	Two Little Girls	8 x 10	ESH		1.00

MAI-VAN-NAM (Chinese Con temporary)

6646.	Walking to Market	12 x 19-1/2	AP		5.00

MAILE, BEN

6647.	Thenets	13 x 37	AS		12.00
6648.	West Side	20 x 34-1/2	AS		15.00

MAILLOL, ARISTIDE (French, 1861-1944)

6649.	Day and Night				
	(DR.)	25-1/2 x 19	IA		15.00
6650.	Head of a Young				
	Girl	17 x 24	NYGS		10.00
6651.	Nude	8 x 10	NYGS		12.00

MAINARDI, SEBASTIANO (Italian, 1460-1513)

6652.	Madonna, Child and				
	Angels	11" Diam.	IA		3.00
6653.	Portrait of a Girl	10 x 6	CFA		1.00
6654.	Portrait of a Man	17 x 13	NYGS		15.00

MAINO See MAYNO

MAIO, SALVATORE DE (American Contemporary)

6655.	Guys and Dolls (Children's				
	Portraits) (27)				
6656.	At the Beach, Ocean				
	Breeze (2)	36 x 13	AK	ea.	10.00
		22 x 8	AK	ea.	4.00
		15 x 5-1/2	AK	ea.	2.00
		8 x 4	AK	ea.	1.00
6657.	Ballerinas (2)	30 x 15	AK	ea.	10.00
	Ballerina with				
	Flower	15 x 7	AK	ea.	2.50
	Ballerina with				
	Shoe	8 x 4	AK	ea.	1.00
6658.	Ballet Teens (5)	36 x 13	AK	ea.	10.00
	Blue	22 x 8	AK	ea.	4.00
	Red	15 x 5-1/2	AK	ea.	2.00
	Bloomer Girl				
	Easter Bonnet				
	Blue				
	Easter Bonnet				
	Pink				
6659.	Harlequins (4)	36 x 13	AK	ea.	10.00
		30 x 15	AK	ea.	10.00
		22 x 8	AK	ea.	4.00
		15 x 7	AK	ea.	2.50
		8 x 4	AK	ea.	1.00
6660.	Flora Dora Girls (4)	24 x 18	AK	ea.	10.00
	Pink Lady	14 x 11	AK	ea.	3.50
	Serenade in	10 x 8	AK	ea.	2.00
	Blue				
	Sunbonnet Sue				
	Tangerine				

6661.	Mardi Gras (2)	30 x 15	AK	ea.	10. 00
	Boy	15 x 7	AK	ea.	2. 50
	Girl	8 x 4	AK	ea.	1. 00
6662.	Portraits, Spanish				
	(4)	30 x 15	AK	ea.	10. 00
	Countess	15 x 7	AK	ea.	2. 50
	Flamenco Dancer				
	Senorita				
	Valiant Matador				
6663.	Teen Musicale (4)	24 x 18	AK	ea.	10. 00
	Drummer	14 x 11	AK	ea.	3. 50
	Guitarist	10 x 8	AK	ea.	2. 00
	Pianist				
	Vocalist				

MAJEWICZ, GEORGE (Silesian, 1897-)

6664.	Herd of Elephants	23-1/2x31-1/2	ESH	Cv.	15. 00
6665.	Lions	23-1/2x31-1/2	ESH	Cv.	15. 00
6666.	Wild Horses	24-1/2x35-1/2	ESH	Cv.	18. 00

MAJOR, HENRY (American, 1889-)

6667.	"Gay Philosopher"				
	Series (6)	20 x 16	NYGS	ea.	6. 00
6668.	End of a Perfect	14 x 11	NYGS	ea.	2. 00
	Day	7-1/2 x 6]	NYGS	ea.	1. 00
6669.	TheGay Philosopher--				
	Why Worry?				
6670.	Philosopher's Heir				
6671.	Philosopher's Offspring				
6672.	Philosopher's Quartet				
6673.	Philosopher's Wife				

MAJOREL, F.

6674.	Jonquilies	24-1/2 x 20	AS		12. 00

MAKIELSKI, BRONISLAU (American, 1901-)

6675.	Blue Ridge Mountains				
	of Virginia	25 x 30	IA		7. 50

MALER, HANS (German, 1488-1529)

6676.	Maria of Burgundy	20 x 12	AJ		7. 50

MALEVITCH, KASIMIR (Russian, 1878-1935)

6677.	Suprematist Composition,				
	1914 (Airplane				
	Flying)	23 x 19	NYGS		12. 00

MANCINI, ANTONIO (Italian, 1852-1930)

6678.	O' Prevetariello	14 x 11	IA		3. 00

MANCINI, DOMENICO (Italian, 16th Centruy)

6679.	Italian Boy with				
	Violin c.	9 x 7	AP		. 60
6680.	Musician	13 x 11	IA		3. 00

MANDON, EDOUARD (French Contemporary)

6681.	Evening Calm	18 x 27	ESH		10. 00
6682.	Song of the Surf	17-1/2 x 31	RL		7. 50
6683.	Surf	20 x 35-1/2	ESH		15. 00
6684.	Tide at Dawn	18 x 31-1/2	RL		10. 00
6685.	Tumbling Waves	16 x 32	RL		7. 50

MANE-KATZ (Russian [Res. France] 1894-1962)
6686.   Flower Cart   20 x 16   UNICEF   10. 00
MANESSIER, ALFRED (French Contemporary)
6687.   Alleluia of the
        Fields   18-1/2x18-1/2   AP   10. 00
6688.   Crown of Thorns   23 x 19   CFA   12. 00
6689.   Evening in a Little
        Harbor   22 x 30   CFA   18. 00
6690.   Festival in Zeeland   31 x 12   NYGS   18. 00
6691.   Night   c.   18 x 23   HNA   5. 95
MANET, EDOUARD (French, 1832-1883)
6692.   Amazon   11 x 15   IA   3. 00
6693.   Balcony   9 x 6   NYGS   . 50
6694.   Ballet Espagnol   25 x 37   NYGS   18. 00
6695.   Bar at the Folies
        Bergere   21-1/2x28-1/2   NYGS   12. 00
                       c.   20 x 24   PENN   1. 50
                       c.   8 x 10   NYGS   . 50
                               6 x 8   CFA   1. 00
6696.   The Boat   15-1/2x19-1/2   AP   5. 00
6697.   Boating   c.   7 x 9   AP   . 50
6698.   Boy with Cherries   28 x 18   CAC   7. 50
                               22-1/2x18-1/2   ESH   10. 00
                       c.   10 x 8   ESH   1. 00
6699.   Boy with Sword c.   10 x 8   NYGS   . 50
6700.   The Breakfast c.   20 x 24   PENN   1. 50
                               18 x 24   DAC   7. 50
6701.   Breadfast at the
        Studio   26 x 35   CFA   18. 00
6702.   Bunch of Flowers   14 x 10   AR   5. 00
6703.   Bust of a Woman   12 x 10   CFA   2. 50
6704.   Eel and Red Mullet   10 x 12   IA   3. 00
6705.   Fifer Boy   31-1/2 x 19   NYGS   18. 00
                       c.   24 x 16   PENN   1. 50
                               23-1/2 x 14   AP   10. 00
                       c.   9 x 7   AP   . 50
6706.   Figure of a Boy
        (Leon Leenhoff)
        (DR.)   12 x 6   NYGS   3. 00
6707.   Flowers in a Crystal
        Vase   c.   10 x 8   ESH   1. 00
6708.   Flute Player   18 x 11   CFA   4. 00
6709.   Gare St. -Lazare   22-1/2x28   NYGS   16. 00
                       c.   18 x 23   HNA   5. 95
6710.   Girl at Folies
        Bergere   9 x 6   NYGS   . 50
6711.   Guitar and Sombrero   17-1/2 x 28   NYGS   15. 00
6712.   In a Boat   22 x 30   NYGS   16. 00
                               5-1/2x7-1/2   NYGS   . 50
6713.   In the Conservatory
                       c.   7 x 9   AP   . 25
6714.   In the Greenhouse
                       c.   8 x 10   NYGS   . 50

6715.	Lola de Valence		15 x 11	IA	3. 00
6716.	Lunch in the Studio		27 x 35-1/2	NYGS	22. 00
6717.	Luncheon on the				
	Grass	c.	20 x 24	PENN	1. 50
6718.	Mlle. Marguerite		22 x 18	CFA	15. 00
6719.	Music at the				
	Tuileries	c.	20 x 24	PENN	1. 50
6720.	Naked Blonde	c.	10 x 8	ESH	1. 00
6721.	Olympia		10 x 14-1/2	AJ	2. 50
		c.	9-1/2x12-1/2	AP	1. 25
		c.	7 x 9	AP	1. 00
6722.	On a Balcony		15 x 10-1/2	AJ	2. 50
		c.	10 x 8	ESH	1. 00
6723.	Les Paveurs, Rue				
	de Berne (Road-				
	menders of Rue de				
	Berne		21-1/2x26-1/2	NYGS	15. 00
			21 x 26	ESH	15. 00
6724.	Peonies	c.	24 x 20	PENN	1. 50
		c.	23 x 18	HNA	5. 95
6725.	Picnic	c.	8 x 10	NYGS	. 50
		c.	7 x 9	AP	. 60
6726.	Picnic on the				
	Grass		9 x 12	CFA	2. 50
6727.	Pink Rose and Yellow				
	Rose		12-1/2x9-1/2	NYGS	7. 50
			8 x 6	CFA	1. 00
6728.	Piper	c.	10 x 8	AP	. 50
6729.	The Plum		14 x 9	IA	3. 00
6730.	Port of Bordeaux				
		c.	8x 10	ESH	1. 00
6731.	Portrait of the				
	Barmaid		20-1/2x12-1/2	ESH	12. 00
6732.	Portrait of Berthe				
	Morisot	c.	22 x 17-1/2	AS	4. 00
6733.	Portrait of Irma				
	Brunner	c.	26 x 21	HNA	5. 95
		c.	24 x 20	PENN	1. 50
		c.	10 x 8	ESH	1. 00
6734.	Portrait of Mme.				
	Blumer	c.	10 x 8	CFA	1. 00
6735.	Reading	c.	7 x 9	NYGS	. 50
6736.	River at Argenteuil		16 x 27	ESH	15. 00
			10 x 17-1/2	ESH	5. 00
6737.	Roses in a Vase				
		c.	12-1/2x9-1/2	AP	1. 25
		c.	9 x 7	AP	1. 00
6738.	Roses and Tulips in				
	a Vase		18 x 11	CFA	5. 00
6739.	Self-Portrait	c.	10 x 8	NYGS	. 50
6740.	Servante de Bocks		24 x 19	NYGS	12. 00
		c.	9 x 7	NYGS	. 50

6741.	Study of a Woman	20 x 16	PENN	1.50
6742.	Vase of Peonies	20 x 15-1/2	PENN	1.50
	c.	10 x 8	ESH	1.00
6743.	Villa Bellevue	35 x 27	CAC	18.00
		25 x 20	CFA	12.00
	c.	22 x 17-1/2	AS	4.00
6744.	Waitress Serving			
	Beer c.	24 x 20	PENN	1.50
6745.	White Lilac	22 x 17	NYGS	22.00
6746.	Woman with Ribboned			
	Hat	23 x 19-1/2	NYGS	24.00
6747.	Woman's Portrait	21 x 17	PENN	1.50
6748.	Women Bathing	15 x 11	IA	3.00

MANGUIN, HENRI CHARLES (French, 1874-1943)

6749.	Port of St. Tropez	22-1/2 x18-1/2	ESH	10.00

MANTEGNA, ANDREA (Italian, 1431-1506)

6750.	Ascension	15 x 7	IA	3.00
6751.	Cardinal Mezzarota			
	c.	8 x 10	NYGS	.50
6752.	Christ in the Garden			
	of Olives	20 x 28	NYGS	15.00
6753.	Madonna and Child	21 x 17	ESH	10.00
		14 x 11	IA	3.00
6754.	Madonna with Sleeping			
	Child	17-1/2 x 13	NYGS	18.00
6755.	Parnassus (Parigi)	11 x 14	AS	3.25
6756.	Portrait of Elisabetta			
	Gonzaga	14 x 10	IA	3.00
6757.	St. George	15 x 7-1/2	AS	3.25
		15 x 7	IA	3.00
		10 x 5	NYGS	.50
6758.	Virgin Enthroned			
	with Saints	15 x 25	IA	10.00

MAPAI

6759.	Italian Views (7)	8 x 10	CFA	ea.	6.00

MAPPLE, ADRIAN

6760.	Silver Stream	16-1/2 x 22	ESH	7.50

MARATTA, CARLO (Italian, 1625-1713)

6761.	Holy Family	15 x 11	IA	3.00
6762.	Holy Night	31 x 24	IA	12.00
		23-1/2 x 18	IA	7.50
		21 x 16-1/2	NYGS	6.00
		21 x 16	IA	4.00
	Detail of No.			
	6762	15 x 20	IA	10.00
		11 x 15	IA	3.00
6763.	Portrait of a			
	Gentleman	13 x 11	IA	3.00
6764.	Portrait of a Man	13 x 11	IA	3.00

MARC, A. (Serbian, [Res. France] 1894-1964)

	European Landscapes			
	(W. C.) (61)	8 x 12	CAC	ea.	1.50

6765.	Albi
6766.	Bad Kreuznach
6767.	Barche Isola dei Pescatori
6768.	Basel
6769.	Bernkastel
6770.	Chillon
6771.	Clavedeleralp
6772.	Cochem
6773.	Cote D'Azur
6774.	Dents du Midi
6775.	Dinkelsbuhl
6776.	Evelone
6777.	Firenze
6778.	Firenze, Palazzo Vecchio
6779.	Firenze, Ponte Vecchio
6780.	Fluelen
6781.	Geneve
6782.	Grindelwald
6783.	Heidelberg
6784.	Innsbruck
6785.	Iserables
6786.	Isola Bella Sbocco Sul Lago
6787.	Isola dei Pescatori
6788.	Isola dei Pescatori Barche Alla Rivoca
6789.	Jungfrau
6790.	Lago di Como Nesso
6791.	Lago di Como Varenna
6792.	Ligerz Cieresse
6793.	Luzern
6794.	Mallorca
6795.	Maloja
6796.	Matterhorn
6797.	Menton
6798.	Michelstadt
6799.	Montreux
6800.	Morges
6801.	Mourillon
6802.	Murten
6803.	Mythen
6804.	Nordlingen
6805.	Paris, Les Bouquinistes
6806.	Paris, La Madeleine
6807.	Paris Montmartre
6808.	Paris, Notre Dame
6809.	Paris, Place de la Concorde
6810.	Paris, Place du Tertre
6811.	Port Mejean
6812.	Rivaplana
6813.	Roma Arco di Constantino
6814.	Roma, Piazza San Pietro
6815.	Ruthenberg
6816.	St. Gallen

6817.	St. Sophorin
6818.	San Salvatore
6819.	Solothurn
6820.	Thunersee
6821.	Toledo
6822.	Treib
6823.	Urnersee
6824.	Zermatt
6825.	Zurich

European Landscapes
(W. C.) (11)   12 x 8   CAC   ea.   1.50

6826.	Bern
6827.	Cordoba
6828.	Granada
6829.	Morcote
6830.	Piz Roseg
6831.	St. Luc
6832.	St. Moritz
6833.	St. Ursanne
6834.	Schaffhausen
6835.	Sevilla
6836.	Zuoz

European Landscapes
(W. C.) (19)   12 x 16   CAC   ea.   2.00

6837.	Bad Kreuznach
6838.	Baie de Menton
6839.	Beilstein
6840.	Erlach
6841.	Firenze, Panorama
6842.	Friebourg
6843.	Furstenau
6844.	Gandria
6845.	Gribourg
6846.	Lac Leman
6847.	Miltenberg
6848.	Oberengadin
6849.	Palma de Mallorca
6850.	Piz Bernina
6851.	Roma, Tempie e Chiesa
6852.	Rothenburg
6853.	Sarlat
6854.	Stein am Rhine
6855.	Vaumarcus

European Landscapes
(W. C.) (12)   25 x 12   CAC   ea.   2.50

6856.	Angler's Paradise
6857.	Brook
6858.	Coast of Italy
6859.	Cottage in Brittany
6860.	Dreamy Corner
6861.	Harbor in Brittany
6862.	Little Flemish Town

6863.	Old Canal Bridge				
6864.	Pine Trees				
6865.	Riviera				
6866.	Small Canal				
6867.	Terrace by the Sea				
	European Landscapes				
	(W. C.) (4)	12 x 25	CAC	ea.	2.50
6868.	Country Fair				
6869.	Fair Grounds				
6870.	Kirmes				
6871.	Roundabouts				
	European Landscapes				
	(W. C.) (9)	16 x 20	CAC	ea.	5.00
6872.	Avignon				
6873.	Eiger Monch Jungfrau von Schynige Platte				
6874.	Farm by the River				
6875.	Harbor at Rockport, Mass.				
6876.	The Lock				
6877.	Martiques				
6878.	Paris, Montmartre				
6879.	Paris, Notre Dame				
6880.	Rosegtal Piz Roseg und Sellagruppe				
	European Landscapes:				
	(2)	12 x 14	CAC	ea.	4.00
6881.	Venezia, Bacinio de San Marco				
6882.	Venezia, Canale della Giudecca				
6883.	Paris, Notre Dame	18 x 24	CAC		10.00
6884.	Schaffhausen	16 x 12	CAC		2.00
6885.	Werdenberg	20 x 30	CAC		18.00
MARC,	FRANZ (German, 1880-1916)				
6886.	Abstract Form	18 x 22	CFA		15.00
6887.	Animals at Bay c.	18 x 23	HNA		5.95
6888.	Animals' Lot c.	7 x 9	AP		.50
6889.	Blue Fox	12 x 16	ESH		4.00
6890.	Blue Horse	28 x 21	NYGS		20.00
		21-1/2 x 16	AP		6.00
	c.	9 x 7	AP		.50
6891.	Blue Horses	17 x 29	CFA		12.00
6892.	Deer in Flower Garden	21-1/2 x 30	NYGS		20.00
6893.	Deer in the Forest	21 x 32	CFA		18.00
		27 x 29-1/2	NYGS		28.00
6894.	Gazelle	15 x 18	NYGS		15.00
		15 x 17-1/2	NYGS		7.50
	c.	8 x 10	ESH		1.00
6895.	Horse and Eagle	26 x 36	IA		20.00
6896.	Landscape with Horse	22 x 29	NYGS		26.00
		16 x 22	NYGS		18.00

6897.	Large Blue Horses			
	c.	7 x 9	AP	. 50
6898.	Little Blue Horse	22 x 28	NYGS	20. 00
6899.	Monkeys	12 x 13-1/2	AP	1. 00
	c.	7 x 9	AP	1. 00
6900.	Red and Blue Horses	10 x 13	CFA	7. 50
6901.	Red Deer	22 x 31-1/2	IA	18. 00
		15 x 21	IA	10. 00
6902.	Red Horses	22 x 31-1/2	IA	18. 00
		20-1/2 x 31	NYGS	20. 00
		14 x 21	IA	5. 00
		13 x 19-1/2	NYGS	15. 00
	c.	7 x 9	AP	. 50
6903.	Sheep	16 x 23-1/2	PENN	1. 50
6904.	Stag in the Woods	21 x 31-1/2	IA	18. 00
		14 x 21	IA	10. 00
6905.	Three Deer	23-1/2x31-1/2	NYGS	20. 00
6906.	Three Horses c.	18 x 23	HNA	5. 95
		10-1/2 x 16	IA	5. 00
6907.	Tiger	30 x 27	NYGS	20. 00
		19 x 17-1/2	NYGS	6. 00
6908.	Tower of Blue Horses	29 x 19	NYGS	18. 00
		21 x 14	CFA	6. 00
6909.	Two Deer	22 x 21	CFA	18. 00
6910.	Two Sheep	19 x 29	NYGS	20. 00
6911.	Yellow Horses	20 x 31-1/2	NYGS	20. 00

MARCA-RELLI, CONRAD (American Contemporary)

6912.	Steel Grey	30 x 26	NYGS	18. 00

MARCEL, RENÉE (French, 1899-)

6913.	Boats in the Dawn	16 x 31-1/2	ESH	7. 00
6914.	Boats in Shimmering Light	20 x 39-1/2	ESH	9. 00
6915.	Harbour Symphony	20 x 39-1/2	ESH	9. 00
6916.	Porto Ferraio	20 x 39-1/2	ESH	9. 00
6917.	Sunset	16 x 31-1/2	ESH	7. 00

MARCH, L.

6918.	Trout River	27 x 20	RL	7. 50

MARCHAND, ANDRÉ (French, 1877-1951)

6919.	Basket of Tomatoes	20 x 25	CAC	15. 00

MARCOUSSIS, LOUIS C. (Polish, 1884-)

6920.	Goldfish Bowl	10 x 30-1/2	ESH	15. 00

MAREES, HORST DE (German, 1896-)

6921.	St. Martin and the Beggar	37 x 24	NYGS	30. 00

MARGARITONE D'AREZZO (Italian, 1216-1293)

6922.	Crucifix	14 x 8	IA	3. 00

MARGOTTI, FRANCESCO (Italian, c. 1868)

6923.	Jesus Sleeping	11 x 13	IA	3. 00

MARGOTTON, RENÉ (French Contemporary)

6924.	La Pecheuse	26 x 19	RL	15. 00

6925.	Vase of Canna	30 x 15	RL		15. 00

MARGULES, DE HIRSCH (American, 1899-)

6926.	Fishing Boats	16 x 22-1/2	AR		7. 50

MARIANA

6927.	Samplers (4)	9 x 7	AA	ea.	2. 50

MARIANI, LEE (American Contemporary)

6928.	Columbus Circle	16 x 24	CFA	15. 00
6929.	Golden Gate	20 x 26	CAC	15. 00
6930.	Grand Army Plaza	16 x 24	CFA	15. 00
6931.	New York Harbour	20 x 24	CAC	15. 00

MARIANO

6932.	Painted Cock	c.	9 x 7	AP	. 25

MARIESCHI, MICHELE (Italian, 1696-1743)

6933.	Landscape (2)	10 x 15-1/2	AS	3. 25
6934.	Santa Maria Della Salute	20 x 30	CFA	15. 00

MARIN, JOHN (American, 1872-1953)

6935.	Boats and Sea, Deer Island, Maine	12 x 16	CAC	1. 50
6936.	Broadway Night	12 x 16	CAC	1. 50
6937.	Cape Split, Maine	15 x 20-1/2	NYGS	7. 50
6938.	Circus Elephants	19 x 24	NYGS	15. 00
6939.	Circus Forms c.	7 x 9	AP	. 60
6940.	Circus Horses c.	20 x 24	PENN	1. 50
6941.	Deer Isle, Maine	17-1/2x20-1/2	PENN	1. 50
6942.	Deer Isle Islets, Maine, 1922	17 x 20	NYGS	10. 00
		12 x 14	NYGS	3. 00
6943.	Fishermen and Boats	18 x 23	NYGS	12. 00
6944.	From the Bridge	18 x 22	PENN	1. 50
6945.	Headed for Boston c.	7 x 9	AP	. 50
6946.	Lower Manhattan from the River	21-1/2 x 26	NYGS	15. 00
	c.	8 x 10	MMA	. 35
6947.	Maine Islands	16-1/2x19-1/2	NYGS	10. 00
		12 x 14	NYGS	3. 00
	c.	8 x 10	NYGS	. 50
6948.	Movement: Boats and Objects, Blue-Gray Sea	22 x 28	NYGS	16. 00
6949.	Movement on the Road	18 x 22	PENN	1. 50
6950.	Movement No. 2, Related to Downtown	12 x 16	CAC	1. 50
	c.	7 x 9	AP	. 60
6951.	New Mexico No. 2, Area Near Taos	12 x 16	CAC	1. 50
6952.	On Morse Mountain c.	7 x 9	AP	. 60
6953.	Peach Trees in Blossom c.	8 x 10	NYGS	2. 00

6954.	Phippsburg, Maine	12 x 16	CAC		1. 50
	c.	7 x 9	AP		. 60
6955.	Pine Tree	16 x 20	CFA		7. 50
6956.	Sketches (W. C.) (8)	8 x 10	NYGS	ea.	2. 00
6957.	Adirondacks Along Ausable River				
6958.	Equestrians				
6959.	Going Through the Thoroughfare				
6960.	Lions in the Ring				
6961.	Peach Trees in Blossom				
6962.	Ramapo River near Suffern, N. Y.				
6963.	Three-Master				
6964.	Women and Sea				
6965.	Storm over Taos				
	c.	7 x 9	AP		. 60
6966.	Street Seeing c.	7 x 9	AP		. 25
6967.	Sunset	15 x 17-1/2	NYGS		7. 50
6968.	Tunk Mountains, Autumn,				
	Maine, 1945	25 x 30	NYGS		18. 00
	c.	8 x 10	NYGS		. 50
6969.	Two-Masters Becalmed				
		12 x 16	CAC		1. 50

MARINI, MARINO (Italian, 1901-)

6970.	Cavallo	23 x 17	CFA	12. 00
6971.	Le Cheval (Horse)	24 x 17	ESH	10. 00
		18-1/2x12-1/2	NYGS	4. 00
		18 x 12	AP	3. 00
6972.	Departure	24 x 16-1/2	NYGS	12. 00
6973.	Due Cavalieri	23 x 17	CFA	12. 00
6974.	Giocollieri	23 x 17	CFA	12. 00
6975.	Horse and Acrobat	22-1/2 x 16	ESH	10. 00
6976.	Horse and Jugglers	24 x 18	PENN	1. 50
6977.	Horse on Red Ground			
		28 x 21	CFA	25. 00
6978.	Horse with Acrobats	31 x 25	NYGS	22. 00
6979.	Horseman	24 x 18	NYGS	12. 00
		18 x 12-1/2	AP	3. 00
6980.	Paard (Gray Horse)	21 x 15-1/2	NYGS	6. 00
6981.	Red Horse	30 x 22	NYGS	16. 00
6982.	Red Rider	28 x 20	CFA	15. 00
		27-1/2 x 19	IA	15. 00
6983.	Representation in			
	Blue	24 x 18	PENN	1. 50
6984.	The Rider	22-1/2 x 18	ESH	10. 00
6985.	Two Riders	29-1/2x20-1/2	NYGS	22. 00

MARIO DEI FIORI (NUZZI, MARIO) (Italian, 1603-1673)

| 6986. | Flowers and Fruit | 8 x 30 | IA | 10. 00 |
| 6987. | Fruit | 8 x 30 | IA | 10. 00 |

MARION

| 6988. | Papagena | 21 x 15 | AS | 7. 50 |
| 6989. | Papageno | 21 x 15 | AS | 7. 50 |

MARMA, R.

| 6990. | Florence, Landmarks | | | | |
| | (3) | 20 x 7 | AL | ea. | 5. 00 |

Piazza S. Spirito
La Sinagoga
Via Orivolo

| (5) | | 11 x 14 | AL | ea. | 5.00 |

Mercato dell'Pulci
Mercato di S. Pietro
Ponte Vecchio
Via Alzani
Volta dei Tintori

MARMION, SIMON (French, 1425-1489)

6991.	Christ of Sorrows				
		c.	10 x 8	ESH	1.00
6992.	Virgin of Sorrows				
		c.	10 x 8	ESH	1.00

MARQUE, A.

| 6993. | Still Life (2) | 24 x 20 | DAC | ea. | 7.50 |
| 6994. | Still Life (2) | 20 x 24 | DAC | ea. | 7.50 |

MARQUE, JAY

| 6995. | Blue Lamp | 20-1/2 x 17 | AS | 7.50 |
| 6996. | Grey Jug | 20-1/2 x 17 | AS | 7.50 |

MARQUET, ALBERT (French, 1875-1947)

6997.	Barques a La Rochelle	21-1/2 x 26	NYGS	15.00
6998.	Beach at Les Sables D'Olonne	18 x 22-1/2	ESH	10.00
6999.	Boat Scene c.	20 x 24	PENN	1.50
7000.	Bridge at St. Michel	17 x 22	CAC	10.00
7001.	Carnival on the Beach c.	7 x 9	AP	.75
7002.	Coulours of Naples	18 x 23	ESH	10.00
7003.	Ete, La Plage des Sables	19-1/2 x 24	PENN	1.50
7004.	Harbour of Naples			
		c.	8 x 10	ESH	1.00
7005.	Ile de France	21 x 26	CFA	12.00
7006.	Die Marne bei Varenne-St. Hilaire c.	17-1/2 x 22	AS	4.00
7007.	Notre Dame de Paris	18 x 22-1/2	NYGS	10.00
7008.	Paris in Autumn	23 x 18	CAC	12.00
7009.	Paris in Grey Weather	18 x 23	CAC	12.00
7010.	Paris in Winter	18 x 23	CFA	12.00
7011.	Plage de Fecamp			
		c.	20 x 24	PENN	1.50
7012.	Pont Neuf	19-1/2 x 24	NYGS	12.00
		18 x 22	CAC	7.50
7013.	Pont Neuf au Soleil	17 x 23	NYGS	22.00
7014.	Le Pont St. Michel	20 x 24	NYGS	10.00
		17 x 22	ESH	10.00
7015.	Port of Algiers	21 x 25-1/2	NYGS	12.00

7016.	Port D'Audierne	21 x 26	NYGS	15. 00
7017.	Port du Havre	15 x 18	CAC	5. 00
7018.	River Landscape			
	c.	18 x 23	HNA	5. 95
7019.	Road to LaFrette	24 x 30	ESH	15. 00
		8 x 10	ESH	1. 00
7020.	Sailboats at La			
	Rochelle	13 x 13	CFA	5. 00
7021.	St. Gervais Church,			
	Paris	19 x 23	CFA	15. 00
7022.	Seascape	19 x 25	CFA	10. 00
7023.	The Seine and Notre			
	Dame of Paris	18 x 23	HNA	5. 95
7024.	The Seine near			
	Poissy	18 x 22-1/2	ESH	10. 00
		8 x 10	ESH	1. 00
7025.	Three Boats c.	9-1/2x12-1/2	AP	1. 25

MARRUCCI CIPRIANO (Italian Contemporary)

7026.	Venetian Masquerade	18 x 27	AS	7. 50

MARSH, REGINALD (American, 1898-1954)

7027.	High Yaller	20 x 15	NYGS	9. 00

MARSHALL, G.

7028.	Spring	21 x 16	IA	3. 50

MARSHALL, J. FRITZ (English, 1859-1932)

7029.	Cocks (2)			
	(Peace and War)	21 x 15-1/2	AA	ea. 10. 00

MARSHALL, WILLIAM E. (American, 1837-1906)

7030.	Abraham Lincoln			
	(B & W)	21 x 15-1/2	NYGS	15. 00

MARSTON, FREDA (English, 1895-1949)

7031.	Glen Falloch	17-1/2 x 21	ESH	10. 00
7032.	Sussex Landscape	9 x 12	ESH	2. 00

MARSTON, ST. CLAIR (English, 1886-)

7033.	Bluebell Time	20 x 24	CFA	10. 00
7034.	Corfe Castle	16 x 24	CAC	6. 00
7035.	Delphiniums	16 x 12	CAC	1. 75

MARTELLINI, GASPARE (Italian, 1785-1857)

7036.	Head of a Girl	15 x 11	IA	3. 00
7037.	Barges on the Seine	18 x 24	CAC	7. 50

MARTIAL, LUCIEN JEAN (French, 1892-)

7038.	Honfleur	28 x 35	RL	15. 00

MARTIN

7039.	Beach in Blue Sun			
	Shades	15 x 25	CFA	15. 00

MARTIN, ANSON A.

7040.	The Bedale Hunt	21 x 31	CFA	30. 00

MARTIN, DAVID STONE (American Contemporary)

7041.	Clarinetist	14 x 11	CFA	7. 50
7042.	Doorstep	11 x 15	CFA	7. 50
7043.	Halsted Street	17 x 11	CFA	7. 50
7044.	Jazz Band	11 x 17	CFA	7. 50
7045.	Music Store	11 x 17	CFA	7. 50

7046.	Musical Interior	17 x 11	CFA	7.50
7047.	Piano Lesson	14 x 11	CFA	7.50
7048.	Rent Party	17 x 11	CFA	7.50
7049.	Rhythm Section	17 x 11	CFA	7.50
7050.	Trombonist	14 x 11	CFA	7.50

MARTIN, FLETCHER (American, 1904-)

7051.	Clown Act	11-1/2x15-1/2	NYGS	7.50
7052.	The Golden Eagle			
	c.	7 x 9	AP	.25

MARTIN, HOMER (American, 1836-1897)

7053.	Harp of the Winds	22 x 31	NYGS	12.00
		15-1/2 x 22	NYGS	7.50
	c.	8 x 10	NYGS	.50
	c.	7 x 9	AP	.50

MARTIN, MAURICE (French Contemporary)

7054.	Chartres	22 x 25	RL	10.00
7055.	View of the Seine			
	c.	20 x 24	PENN	1.50

MARTINEZ, ALFREDO RAMOS (Mexican, 1872-1946)

7056.	Flower Vendors	11 x 18	AR	3.00

MARTINI, FRANCESCO See FRANCESCO DI GIORGIO MARTINI
MARTINI, JOSEPH DE (American, 1896-)

7057.	Moonlight	11 x 20	NYGS	7.50
7058.	The Road to Calvary			
	c.	10 x 8	ESH	1.00

MARTINI, SIMONE (Italian, 1284-1344)

7059.	Annunciation			
	(Florence)	11 x 15-1/2	AS	3.25
		11 x 13	IA	3.00
	c.	8 x 10	NYGS	.50
	Angel--Detail of			
	No. 7059	15-1/2x11-1/2	AS	3.25
		15 x 11	IA	3.00
	Head of the Virgin--			
	Detail of No.			
	7059	15 x 11	AS	3.25
7060.	Annunciata	15 x 11	IA	3.00
7061.	Crucifixion and			
	Saints	16 x 8	IA	3.00
7062.	Giudoriccio of Fogliano			
		6 x 16	IA	3.00
	Detail of No.			
	7062	11 x 15	IA	3.00
7063.	Madonna	15 x 11	IA	3.00
7064.	Madonna and Child	16 x 11	IA	3.00
7065.	Madonna with Child	29-1/2 x 22	NYGS	28.00
7066.	Madonna Enthroned			
	and Saints	15 x 10	IA	3.00
7067.	La Maesta (Siena)	10-1/2 x 15	AS	3.25
7068.	St. Claire (Assisi)	15 x 11	AS	3.25
7069.	St. Francis (Assisi)	15 x 11	AS	3.25

MARUSSIG

7070.	Still Life	c.	7 x 9	AP	.50

MAS, PIERRE
7071. Golden Corn and
       Teasels   24 x 20   AS   15. 00
MAS Y FONDEVILA, ARCADIO (Spanish, 1850-)
7072. Bouquet in White
       Vase   c. 24 x 20   PENN   1. 50
MASACCIO (GUIDI, TOMMASO) (Italian, 1401-1428)
7073. Adam and Eve   15-1/2 x 7   AS   3. 25
7074. Adam and Eve Driven
      out of Paradise
      (Brancacci)   14 x 11   NYGS   2. 00
        Detail of No.
        7074   14 x 11   NYGS   2. 00
7075. Adoration of the
      Magi   c.   7 x 9   AP   . 25
7076. Crucifixion   15 x 11   IA   3. 00
                 10 x 7   NYGS   . 50
7077. Expulsion from
      Paradise   15 x 8   IA   3. 00
                 10 x 4   NYGS   . 50
7078. St. Anne, Madonna
      and Child with Angels
                15 x 9   IA   3. 00
7079. St. Peter Baptizing the
      Neophytes (Brancacci)
               11 x 14   NYGS   2. 00
        Two Heads--
        Detail of No.
        7079   14 x 11   NYGS   2. 00
        Kneeling Neophyte,
        Detail of No.
        7079   14 x 11   NYGS   2. 00
7080. St. Peter Christening
      the Idolatres   15 x 11   AS   3. 25
7081. St. Peter Curing the
      Sick by his Shadow 11 x 14   NYGS   2. 00
        Two Heads, Detail
        of No. 7081   14 x 11   NYGS   2. 00
        A Sick Man, Detail
        of No. 7081   14 x 11   NYGS   2. 00
7082. St. Peter Distributing
      the Goods of the
      Community to the Faith-
      ful and Death of Ananias
      (Brancacci)   11 x 14   NYGS   2. 00
        Group of the Faith-
        ful, Detail of
        No. 7082   14 x 11   NYGS   2. 00
        Woman and Child,
        Detail of No.
        7082   14 x 11   NYGS   2. 00
        St. Peter, St. John
        and Group of the

	Faithful, Detail of No. 7082	14 x 11	NYGS	2.00
	St. Peter Enthroned (Brancacci) Details:			
7083.	Head of St. Peter	14 x 11	NYGS	2.00
7084.	Head of a Carmelite	14 x 11	NYGS	2.00
7085.	Two Carmelites	14 x 11	NYGS	2.00
7086.	Male Figure (Head of Masaccio)	14 x 11	NYGS	2.00
7087.	St. Peter Giving Alms to the Poor	15 x 11	AS	3.25
7088.	St. Peter Healing the Sick	15 x 11	AS	3.25
7089.	St. Peter Raising the Son of Theophilus--3 Details:			
7090.	Theophilus	14 x 11	NYGS	2.00
7091.	St. Peter, St. Paul and Group of By- standers	11 x 14	NYGS	2.00
7092.	Group of Bystanders	11 x 14	NYGS	2.00
7093.	St. Peter and St. John Almsgiving	15 x 10	IA	3.00
	Woman and Child, Detail of No. 7093	15 x 9	IA	3.00
7094.	Tribute Money (Brancacci)	15 x 22	NYGS	5.00
	Central Group, Detail of No. 7094	11 x 14	NYGS	2.00
	An Apostle (Head) Detail of 7094	14 x 11	NYGS	2.00
	Jesus (Head), Detail of No. 7094	14 x 11	NYGS	2.00
	St. John (Head), Detail of No. 7094	14 x 11	NYGS	2.00
	St. Peter (Head), Detail of No. 7094	14 x 11	NYGS	2.00
7095.	St. Peter Extracting Coin from Fish's Mouth, Detail of 7094	14 x 11	NYGS	2.00
	St. Peter Handing Coin to Tax Collector Detail of No. 7094	14 x 11	NYGS	2.00
	Three Apostles (Heads), Detail of No. 7094	11 x 14	NYGS	2.00
	Two Apostles and the Tax Collector,			

	Detail of No.			
	7094	11 x 14	NYGS	2. 00
7096.	The Trinity with the Virgin and St. John the Evangelist (Santa Maria Novella), 2 Details:			
	The Donor, Detail of No. 7096	14 x 11	NYGS	2. 00
	Wife of the Donor, Detail of No. 7096	14 x 11	NYGS	2. 00

MASCAGNI, DONATI (CALLED FRA ARSENIO) (Italian, 1579-1636)

7097.	Pieta	15 x 10	IA	3. 00

MASOLINO DA PANICALE (Italian, 1383-1447)

7098.	Two Noblemen (Florence)	15-1/2 x 11	AS	3. 25

MASON, ROY M. (American, 1886-)

7099.	Falcon's Nest	21-1/2 x 30	IA	12. 00
7100.	Fisherman's Hangout	14-1/2 x 20	IA	7. 50
7101.	Gleaners	21-1/2 x 30	IA	12. 00
7102.	Montezuma Marshes	21-1/2 x 30	IA	12. 00
7103.	Open Season	21-1/2 x 30	IA	12. 00
7104.	Piney Creek	21-1/2 x 30	IA	12. 00
7105.	Pintail Point	21-1/2 x 30	IA	12. 00
7106.	The Ritz	21-1/2 x 30	IA	12. 00

MASON, FRANK W.

7107.	Heading for Home	15 x 23	CFA	7. 50
7108.	Homeward Bound	15 x 23	CFA	7. 50

MASSA, FREDERICK (American Contemporary)

7109.	Roman Vista	20 x 48	AK	10. 00
7110.	Venetian Vista	20 x 48	AK	10. 00

MASSI, GENTILE See GENTILE DA FABRIANO

MASSON, ANDRÉ (French, 1896-)

7111.	House of the Vestals	22 x 26-1/2	ESH	12. 00

MASSON, HENRI (Belgian [Res. Canada] 1907-)

7112.	Gaspé Village	23 x 31	CFA	18. 00

MASSYS, CORNELIS (Flemish, 1508-1575)

7113.	Arrival in Bethlehem	21 x 29-1/2	NYGS	16. 00
		15-1/2 x 22	NYGS	7. 50

MASSYS, JAN (Flemish, 1505-1575)

7114.	Portrait of Andrea Doria	15 x 10	IA	3. 00

MASSYS, QUENTIN See METSYS, QUENTIN

MASTER, WERDEN

7115.	Vision of St. Hubert	12-1/2x8-1/2	ESH	2. 00

MASTER OF CASTELSARDO (Sardinian, 16th Century)

7116.	Ancona di Saccardo	15 x 11	IA	3. 00

MASTER OF COLOGNE

7117.	Madonna with Sweet Pea	21 x 13-1/2	NYGS	18. 00

MASTER OF THE HALF-LENGTH
7118.	Girl Playing a Lute	10-1/2 x 8	ESH	1. 00
7119.	Musical Trio	9 x 8	AJ	2. 50
7120.	Portrait of a Lady	20 x 15-1/2	AJ	7. 50

MASTER OF THE HOLY KINDRED (German, Ac. 1485-1515)
7121.	Three Angels	8 x 10-1/2	ESH	1. 00

MASTER OF THE LIFE OF MARY
7122.	Angels Playing Music			
	c.	7 x 9	AP	1. 00
7123.	Annunciation	29 x 35	IA	20. 00
	c.	18 x 23	HNA	5. 95
		16-1/2 x 20	NYGS	6. 00

MASUDA, MAKOTO (Japanese Contemporary)
7124.	Cote D'Azur	25 x 32-1/2	RL	12. 50
7125.	Frenchman's Quay	25 x 32-1/2	RL	12. 50

MATHAUSER
7126.	Behold the Man	21 x 37	CAC	15. 00
7127.	Christ before Pilate	21-1/2 x 38	IA	12. 00
7128.	Golgatha	21 x 38	IA	12. 00

MATHIEU, PAUL (Belgian, 1872-1932)
7129.	Les Capetiens Partout	15 x 30	ESH	15. 00
7130.	Composition, 1958	21-1/2x35-1/2	NYGS	22. 00
7131.	Paris - Capitale des Arts	12 x 36	ESH	18. 00
7132.	Victory of De Nain	14-1/2 x 37	ESH	18. 00

MATISSE, HENRI (French, 1869-1954)
7133.	Amber Necklace c.	10 x 8	ESH	1. 00
7134.	Anemones	25 x 31-1/2	NYGS	20. 00
7135.	Anemones by the Window	22 x 18	CAC	10. 00
7136.	Asphodeles	30 x 23	NYGS	20. 00
	c.	10 x 8	ESH	1. 00
7137.	Blossoming Garden	19 x 24	CFA	12. 00
7138.	La Blouse Romaine	24 x 18-1/2	PENN	1. 50
7139.	Blue Nude	13 x 20	PENN	1. 50
7140.	Blue Room	21-1/2 x 18	NYGS	15. 00
7141.	Blue Window	25-1/2 x 17	MMA	10. 00
	c.	9 x 7	AP	. 60
7142.	Bouquet c.	9 x 7	AP	. 50
7143.	Carnival in Nice	15 x 23	CFA	12. 00
7144.	Coffee c.	10 x 8	NYGS	. 50
7145.	Conversation Piece	18-1/2 x 22	ESH	10. 00
7146.	The Dancer	19 x 30	CFA	7. 50
7147.	La Danse (DR.)	18 x 24	NYGS	10. 00
7148.	La Danse	18 x 12	NYGS	7. 50
7149.	Fauve Landscape			
	c.	8 x 10	ESH	1. 00
7150.	Femme au Bijou Bleu c.	9 x 7	AP	. 50
7151.	Flower Petals	11 x 47	NYGS	18. 00
7152.	Flowers and Fruits	24 x 19	CFA	15. 00
7153.	Girl Reading	20 x 24	CFA	15. 00

7154.	Girl with Anemones				
	c.	20 x 24	PENN	1. 50	
7155.	Girl with Anemones	24 x 20	CFA	15. 00	
	c.	10 x 8	ESH	1. 00	
7156.	Goldfish	17 x 14	CAC	10. 00	
7157.	Le Grand Atelier	20 x 24	NYGS	10. 00	
	c.	8 x 10	ESH	1. 00	
7158.	Grand Interieur				
	Rouge	22 x 14-1/2	NYGS	12. 00	
7159.	Green Pumpkin	32 x 26	CAC	18. 00	
7160.	The Gypsy c.	24 x 20	PENN	1. 50	
7161.	Harmony in Blue				
	c.	7 x 9	AP	. 50	
7162.	Idol	20 x 24	DAC	7. 50	
7163.	Interior at Nice c.	9-1/2x12-1/2	AP	1. 25	
		6 x 8	CFA	1. 00	
7164.	Interior with Black				
	Fern	22-1/2 x 17	ESH	10. 00	
7165.	Interior with Egg				
	Plants	18 x 24	PENN	1. 50	
7166.	Interior with Egyptian				
	Curtain	22-1/2 x 17	ESH	10. 00	
7167.	Interior with Flowers	24 x 15	PENN	1. 50	
7168.	Interior with Violin				
	c.	20 x 24	PENN	1. 50	
7169.	Large Studio c.	8 x 10	ESH	1. 00	
7170.	Marguerite Reading				
	c.	18 x 23	HNA	5. 95	
7171.	Narcissi and Fruit	24 x 19-1/2	NYGS	12. 00	
7172.	Notre Dame	17-1/2x14-1/2	AP	6. 00	
7173.	Odalisque	21 x 14	NYGS	18. 00	
7174.	Odalisque with Raised				
	Arms c.	8 x 10	NYGS	. 50	
7175.	Open Window,				
	Collioure c.	10 x 8	ESH	1. 00	
7176.	Piano Lesson c.	8 x 10	MMA	. 35	
7177.	Pineapple and				
	Anemones c.	8 x 10	MMA	. 35	
7178.	Plum Blossoms	26 x 20	DAC	7. 50	
	c.	24 x 20	PENN	1. 50	
7179.	Poster: Nice,				
	Travail et Joie	28-1/2 x 20	PENN	1. 00	
7180.	Poster: The Sculpture				
	of Matisse	28-1/2 x 20	PENN	1. 00	
7181.	Purple Robe	20 x 16	PENN	1. 50	
7182.	Red Studio c.	8 x 10	MMA	. 35	
7183.	Reverie	25 x 20	CFA	15. 00	
7184.	River Landscape	22-1/2x18-1/2	AJ	10. 00	
7185.	Sketches (8) c.	8 x 10	MMA	ea.	. 35
7186.	Still Life c.	20 x 24	PENN	1. 50	
7187.	Still Life, Apples on				
	a Pink Tablecloth	23 x 28	NYGS	16. 00	

7188.	Still Life by the Window		22 x 18-1/2	ESH	10. 00
7189.	Still Life, Flowers and Fruit		18 x 23	HNA	5. 95
7190.	Still Life, Pineapple	c.	8 x 10	NYGS	. 50
7191.	Still Life with Apples		25-1/2x29-1/2	NYGS	16. 00
7192.	Still Life with Dahlias		19 x 24	PENN	1. 50
		c.	8 x 10	ESH	1. 00
7193.	Still Life with Goldfish		24 x 15	NYGS	10. 00
7194.	Still Life with Green Carpet		17-1/2x22-1/2	ESH	10. 00
7195.	Still Life with Lemons		16 x 19	NYGS	10. 00
7196.	Still Life with Magnolia		20 x 28	CFA	15. 00
7197.	Still Life with Oysters	c.	18 x 23	HNA	5. 95
		c.	7 x 9	AP	. 50
7198.	Still Life with Peaches		18 x 23	CAC	15. 00
7199.	Still Life with Pineapple		22 x 28	AA	15. 00
7200.	Studio		16 x 20	AP	10. 00
7201.	Studio Quai St. Michel	c.	20 x 24	PENN	1. 50
7202.	Studio with La Danse	c.	8 x 10	ESH	1. 00
7203.	Tabac Royal		24 x 30	DAC	7. 50
		c.	21 x 26	HNA	5. 95
7204.	Two Young Girls	c.	24 x 20	PENN	1. 50
7205.	White Dress		15 x 19	CFA	7. 50
7206.	Woman with Aquarium	c.	8 x 10	CAC	1. 50
7207.	Woman with Blue Hat	c.	9 x 7	AP	. 50
7208.	Young Girl in White Dress		15 x 19	AP	7. 50

MATTA, ROBERTO (Chilean [Res. U. S.] Contemporary)

7209.	Who's Who	23 x 29-1/2	NYGS	15. 00

MATTEO DI GIOVANNI DI BARTOLO (Italian, 1430-1495)

7210.	Massacre of the Innocents	11 x 11	IA	3. 00
7211.	St. Barbara	15 x 11	IA	3. 00
7212.	St. Lucy (Arezzo)	15 x 11	AS	3. 25
7213.	St. Magdalene	16 x 12	IA	3. 00
7214.	Virgin and Child (Siena)	15-1/2 x 11	AS	3. 25

MATTHEW, K. (American Contemporary)
7215.	Spring Idyll	23 x 32	NYGS	10.00

MAURER, ALFRED HENRY (American, 1868-1932)
7216.	Outside the Town	18 x 23	CAC	7.50
7217.	Still Life with Doily	17-1/2 x 21	NYGS	12.00
	c.	8 x 10	NYGS	.50

MAUVE, ANTON RUDOLF (Dutch, 1838-1888)
7218.	Return to the Fold	c.	7 x 9	AP	.50
7219.	Spring		9 x 14	CAC	2.50

MAX, GABRIEL (Austrian, 1840-1915)
7220.	Christ Healing the Sick Child	13 x 8	CAC	1.50
7221.	St. Veronica's Veil	22 x 17-1/2	IA	7.50
		20 x 16	IA	5.00
		12 x 9-1/2	IA	1.50
		11 x 9	IA	1.75

MAXIMILIAN, B. P.
7222.	Christ	20 x 40	AS	12.00
7223.	Christ	20 x 27-1/2	AS	10.00

MAYNO, FARY JUAN (Spanish, 1569-1649)
7224.	Adoration of the Magi	c.	8 x 10	NYGS	.50

MAZETTI
7225.	European Landscapes (4)	12 x 16	CAC	ea.	2.00
7226.	Chillon				
7227.	Glerolles				
7228.	Matterhorn				
	Monte Rosa				
	European Landscapes (2)	8 x 12	CAC	ea.	1.50
7229.	Austria				
7230.	Zarmatt				

MAZZOLA, FRANCESCO See PARMIGIANINO
MAZZON SCHOOL, MILAN
7231.	My Cat Awakes (Granata)	c.	7 x 9	AP	.50
7232.	Pork Butcher's Wife	c.	7 x 9	AP	.50

MAZZONOVITCH
7233.	April the 20th	16 x 16	CAC	6.00

MC FEE, HENRY LEE (American, 1886-1953)
7234.	Still Life: Apples	20 x 15	NYGS	7.50

MC GILL
7235.	Blue Bonnets	22 x 28	CAC	7.50

MC GINNIS, EVELYN
7236.	Desert Landscapes (4)	18 x 36	AA	ea.	12.00
7237.	Desert Calm				
7238.	Desert Peace				
7239.	Palo Verde Tree in Desert				

7240.	Smoke Treet in Desert				
	Desert Landscapes				
	(2)	15 x 30	AA	ea.	7. 50
7241.	Heart of the Desert				
7242.	Sunlight and Shadows				
7243.	Desert Mood (2)	24 x 8	AA	ea.	3. 00
	Desert Mood (2)	8 x 24	AA	ea.	3. 00

MC GREGOR, WILLIAM (English Contemporary)

7244.	Ben Lomond from				
	Loch Ard	15 x 28	RL		6. 00
7245.	Carbis Bay	17 x 22	RL		6. 00
7246.	Loch Leven	18 x 24	RL		6. 00
7247.	Loch Long	18 x 24	RL		6. 00
7248.	Loch Sunart	24 x 48	RL		20. 00
7249.	Off the Coast of				
	Arran	15 x 28	RL		6. 00
7250.	View of St. Mawes	17 x 22	RL		6. 00

MC KENNEY AND HALL

7251.	Indian Portraits (8)	16 x 12	PENN	ea.	1. 00
7252.	Chief Naw-Kaw				
7253.	Chief of Musquakees				
7254.	Chief of the Sioux				
7255.	Chippeway Chief				
7256.	Great Walker				
7257.	Ioway Chief				
7258.	Pawnee Brave				
7259.	Sleepy Eye				

MC KNIGHT, DODGE (American, 1860-1950)

7260.	Winter Landscape	14 x 18	AJ		6. 00

MEADOWS, J. E. (English, 1828-1888)

7261.	Near Brading	24 x 40	RL		20. 00
7262.	Old Red Lion Inn	26 x 40	AA		12. 00
7263.	Valley Farm	24 x 40	AA		12. 00

MEDEIROS, M.

7264.	Ballerinas (2)	16 x 12	AK	ea.	5. 00
	Ballerina in	10 x 8	AK	ea.	2. 00
	Gold				
	Ballerina in Pink				
7265.	Florals, Majestic				
	(4)	36 x 24	AK	ea.	7. 50
	Autumn Bouquet	18 x 12	AK	ea.	3. 00
	Golden Mums				
	Orange Poppies				
	Summer Bouquet				
7266.	Guys and Dolls (6)	30 x 15	AK	ea.	10. 00
	Boobsy Girl	15 x 7	AK	ea.	2. 50
	Farmer Boy	8 x 4	AK	ea.	1. 00
	Farmer Girl				
	Jackie Boy				
	Not Guilty				
	Swing Time				
7267.	Gypsies (2)	28 x 18	AK	ea.	7. 50

	Gypsy with Basket	18 x 12	AK	ea.	3. 00
	Gypsy with Urn				
7268.	Landscapes (4)	20 x 48	AK	ea.	10. 00
7269.	Coast of Spain				
7270.	French Village				
7271.	Italian Wharf				
7272.	Spanish Bay				
7273.	Little Women (2)	36 x 24	AK	ea.	7. 50
7274.	Harmony in Yellow	18 x 12	AK	ea.	3. 00
7275.	Melody in Pink				
7276.	Madonnas (2)	28 x 18	AK	ea.	7. 50
	Asleep	18 x 12	AK	ea.	3. 00
	Awake				
7277.	Musicians (2)	36 x 13	AK	ea.	10. 00
7278.	Guitar Player	22 x 8	AK	ea.	4. 00
7279.	Trumpet Player	15 x 5-1/2	AK	ea.	2. 00
7280.	Portraits (Children)	12 x 18	AK	ea.	5. 00
7281.	Book Mates	8 x 12	AK	ea.	2. 50
7282.	By the Fireside				
7283.	Feathered Friends				
7284.	Puppy Love				

MEDICI ART TREASURES

	(12)	10 x 13	NYGS	ea. or set	1. 50 15. 00
7285.	Agate Cup				
7286.	Cosimo II De'Medici				
7287.	Cup with Hercules				
7288.	Ewer--Lapis Lazuli				
7289.	Ewer--Silver Gilt				
7290.	Flask--Gold				
7291.	Jasper Vase				
7292.	Jewel Case				
7293.	Red Jasper				
7294.	Rock Crystal				
7295.	Tiberio				
7296.	Venus and Cupid				

MEEK, THOMAS

7297.	New York Landmarks (3)	17 x 26	AL	ea.	10. 00
	Grand Central, Madison Square Park, Public Library				
7298.	Rome, Landmarks (4)	22-1/2x16-1/2	AL	ea.	10. 00
7299.	Column Marcus Aurelius				
7300.	Forum of Trajan and Church of S. Maria				
7301.	Piazza S. Pietro				
7302.	S. Maria Trastavere				

MEGARGEE, LON (American, 1886-)

7303.	Home on the Ranch	16 x 20	NYGS		6. 00

		12 x 15	NYGS		4. 00
7304.	Saturday Night on				
	the Ranch	16 x 20	NYGS		6. 00
		12 x 15	NYGS		4. 00

MEI FENG (Chinese, 16th Centruy)
7305.	Lotus Flowers	29 x 16	CFA		15. 00

MEIERSDORF
7306.	Jazz (4)	17 x 21	AA	ea.	5. 00
7307.	Big Bass Trio				
7308.	Hot Licks				
7309.	In the Groove				
7310.	Quintet				

MEISSONIER, JEAN LOUIS ERNEST (French, 1815-1891)
7311.	At the Relay	6 x 8	IA	1. 50
7312.	The Chess Game	14 x 10	CFA	15. 00
7313.	Halting at an Inn	8 x 10	CAC	1. 00
7314.	Soldiers Gambling	8 x 10	CAC	1. 00

MEISTER DES HAUSBUCHES (German, 1460-1490)
7315.	Three Hovering			
	Angels	12 x 15	NYGS	7. 50

MEISTERMANN, GEORG (German Contemporary)
7316.	Fish, Oxen and			
	Bird	24 x 29-1/2	NYGS	16. 00

MELATTI
7317.	Vase of Flowers	30 x 40	DAC	22. 50
	c.	20 x 24	PENN	1. 50
		18 x 24	DAC	12. 50

MELCHERS, GARI (American, 1860-1932)
7318.	Mother and Child	19-1/2 x 17	NYGS	9. 00
	c.	10 x 8	NYGS	. 50
7319.	Penelope	28 x 26	CAC	15. 00
7320.	Pipers of Balmoral			
	c.	7 x 9	AP	. 50

MELOZZO DA FORLI (Italian, 1438-1494)
7321.	Angel Announcing	15 x 8	IA		3. 00
7322.	Angel Musicians				
	(2)	14 x 11-1/2	AS	ea.	3. 25
7323.	Archangel Gabriel	27 x 14	CFA		12. 00
		22-1/2x11-1/2	ESH		15. 00
7324.	Sixtus IV Appoints				
	Platina his	15 x 11	IA		3. 00
	Librarian				
	Cardinale Giuliano				
	della Rovere -				
	Detail of No.				
	7324	15 x 11	IA		3. 00
	Platina - Detail				
	of No. 7324	15 x 11	IA		3. 00

MELROSE, ANDREW (American, 1836-1901)
7325.	Crossing the Stream	24 x 40	AK	12. 00
		12 x 20	AK	3. 00

MEMLING, HANS (Flemish, 1433-1494)
7326.	Crucifixion	14 x 11	IA	3. 00

7327.	Madonna and Child				
	c.	10 x 8	NYGS		.50
7328.	Madonna and Child				
	Enthroned	26-1/2 x 18	NYGS		22.00
7329.	Madonna and Child				
	with Angels	20 x 16	NYGS		10.00
	(Nat. Gall.,				
	U.S.) c.	10 x 8	NYGS		.50
7330.	Portrait of a Man	10 x 7	NYGS		.50
7331.	Portrait of Unknown				
	Man	13 x 9	IA		3.00
7332.	Portrait of Unknown				
	Man	10 x 7	IA		3.00
7333.	Portrait of a Young				
	Man	15 x 11	NYGS		7.50
7334.	Procession of the				
	Kings c.	7 x 9	AP		.60
7335.	St. Benedict	15 x 11	IA		3.00
7336.	Virgin Entrhoned and				
	Two Angels	15 x 11	IA		3.00
7337.	Virgin of the Throne				
	(Florence)	15 x 11	AS		3.25

MEMMI, LIPPO (Italian, 1317-1347)

7338.	Crucifixion and				
	Saints	16 x 8	IA		3.00
7339.	Madonna Enthroned				
	and Saints	10 x 15	IA		3.00
7340.	St. Dominic	15 x 12	IA		3.00

MENABONI, ATHOS (American Contemporary)

7341.	Birds (3)	22 x 28	ESH	ea.	7.50
	Bufflehead				
	Hooded Merganser				
	Valley Quail				
	Birds (2)	18 x 14	CAC	ea.	12.00
	Cardinal				
	Red-Winged Blackbird				

MENGS, ANTON RAPHAEL (German, 1728-1799)

7342.	Cupid	17 x 14	ESH		6.00
7343.	Portrait of the				
	Artist's Daughter	15 x 11	AS		3.25
7344.	Rest on the Flight				
	into Egypt	19 x 26	NYGS		10.00

MENZ, WILLY (German, 1890-)

7345.	Commerce	19 x 23	CFA	7.50

MENZEL, ADOLPH VON (German, 1815-1905)

7346.	Flute Concert	20 x 29	CFA	12.00
7347.	Garden of the			
	Ministry	13 x 21	AR	10.00
7348.	Round Table	24 x 20	NYGS	9.00

MERCADÉ, JORDI (KNOWN AS "JORDI") (Spanish Contemporary)

7349.	Coastal Town in Spain			
		22 x 35-1/2	NYGS	16.00

7350.	Musical Clowns	21-1/2 x 30	RL		17.50
7351.	Pueblo Costero	21-1/2 x 30	RL		17.50

MERCIER
| 7352. | Sidewalks of New York | 19 x 28-1/2 | AA | | 15.00 |

MERISI, MICHELANGELO See CARAVAGGIO
MERKER, ERICH (German, 1891-)
| 7353. | Furnace | 25 x 34 | CFA | | 15.00 |
| 7354. | Industry | 26 x 34 | CFA | | 15.00 |

MERRILL, WILLIAM
| 7355. | Moppets (4) | 30 x 12 | DAC | ea. | 5.00 |
| | | 15 x 6 | DAC | ea. | 1.50 |

MERRIOTT, JACK
| 7356. | Springtime | 20 x 24 | AS | | 7.50 |

MERTE, OSCAR (German)
| 7357. | Across the Field | 23-1/2 x 37 | NYGS | | 18.00 |

MERTON, JOHN RALPH (English Contemporary)
| 7358. | Sixteen to Eighteen | 27-1/2x27-1/2 | RL | | 25.00 |

MERYON
| 7359. | San Francisco | 7 x 37 | CAC | | 15.00 |

MESCHES, ARNOLD (American Contemporary)
| 7360. | Industrial No. 1 (Cars and Trucks) | 12 x 16 | CFA | | 12.00 |
| 7361. | Industrial No. 2 (Wire Fence) | 12 x 16 | CFA | | 12.00 |

MESSINA See ANTONELLO DA MESSINA
MESTROVIC, IVAN (Yugoslavian 1883-)
| 7362. | Immortal Indian (Sculpture) c. | 7 x 9 | AP | | .25 |

METCALF, WILLARD L. (American, 1858-1925)
7363.	Golden Carnival	28 x 31	NYGS		16.00
7364.	Icebound c.	7 x 9	AP		.50
7365.	North Country	30-1/2 x 34	NYGS		18.00
7366.	November Mosaic	28 x 31	NYGS		16.00

METELLI, ORNEURE (Italian, 1872-1938)
| 7367. | Public Gardens at Terni | 18 x 27 | CFA | | 12.00 |

METLI
| 7368. | Calla Lilies | 22 x 18 | CAC | | 12.00 |

METSU, GABRIEL (Dutch, 1629-1667)
7369.	The Hunter and the Lady	15 x 11	IA		3.00
7370.	Letter Reader	20-1/2 x 16	NYGS		10.00
7371.	Letter Writer	20-1/2 x 16	NYGS		10.00
7372.	Vegetable Market	22-1/2 x 18	ESH		10.00
7373.	Violoncello Player	22-1/2 x 17	ESH		15.00

METSYS, JAN See MASSYS, JAN
METSYS, QUENTIN (Flemish, 1466-1530)
| 7374. | Erasmus, Portrait | 15 x 11 | IA | | 3.00 |
| 7375. | The Pawn-Broker and his Wife (Le Preteur sur Gages) c. | 20 x 24 | PENN | | 1.50 |

		11 x 11	IA	3. 00
7376.	Pierre, Gilles,			
	Portrait	15 x 11	IA	3. 00
7377.	Virgin and Child	15 x 10	IA	3. 00

METZINGER, JEAN (French, 1883-1957)

7378.	The Port, 1912	28 x 34	NYGS	20. 00

MEULEN, PIETER VAN DER (Belgian, Ac. 1660)

7379.	Royal Hunt	30 x 36	NYGS	16. 00

MEUNIER, CONSTANTIN (Belgian, 1831-1905)

7380.	Courting Days	19 x 16	CAC	5. 00
7381.	Wedding Bells	19 x 16	CAC	5. 00

MEXICO

7382.	UWA Series (32)	11 x 14		
	or	14 x 11	NYGS	ea. 2. 00

MEYER, JOHANN GEORGE (VON BREMEN) (German, 1813-1886)

7383.	Holiday with Grand-			
	father	25 x 39	AA	12. 00

MEYER, MAURICE

7384.	Evening Tide	24 x 60	DAC	15. 00
		24 x 48	DAC	10. 00
		24 x 30	PENN	1. 95
		15 x 30	DAC	2. 00

MEYER-EBERHARDT, CURT (German, 1895-)

7385.	Fawn	19 x 15	NYGS	6. 00
7386.	Poodle	21-1/2x14-1/2	NYGS	6. 00
7387.	Winter Worries	18 x 17	CAC	10. 00

MICHAUD, LEONIE (French, 1873-)

7388.	Juan	24 x 18	AK	6. 00
7389.	Juanita	24 x 18	AK	6. 00

MICHELANGELO BUONARROTI (Italian, 1475-1564)

7390.	Creation of Adam			
	(Man) (Sistine)	22 x 46	CFA	18. 00
		11 x 22-1/2	AP	5. 00
		11 x 15	IA	3. 00
	Adam (Figure) -			
	Detail of No.			
	7390	11 x 15	IA	3. 00
	Adam (Head) -			
	Detail of No.			
	7390	15 x 11	IA	3. 00
	God the Father -			
	Detail of No.			
	7390	11 x 15	IA	3. 00
	God (Head) - Detail			
	of No. 7390	15 x 11	IA	3. 00
	Hands of God and			
	Adam - Detail of			
	No. 7390	11 x 15	IA	3. 00
7391.	Creation of Adam and			
	Original Sin (Sistine			
	Chapel)	11 x 15	IA	3. 00
7392.	David (Sculpture)	15-1/2 x 11	AS	3. 25

7393.	Epiphany (DR.)	21 x 15-1/2	NYGS		10.00
7394.	Holy Family	11" Diam.	IA		3.00
7395.	Madonna and Child (DR.)	21 x 15-1/2	NYGS		10.00
7396.	Nude Decorative Figures (2)	15 x 11	IA	ea.	3.00
7397.	Original Sin (Expulsion from Paradise) (Sistine Chapel)	11 x 15	IA		3.00
7398.	Adam and Eve - Detail of No. 7397	11 x 7-1/2	NYGS		4.00
	Adam (Head) - Detail of No. 7397	15 x 11	IA		3.00
	Eve (Head) - Detail of No. 7397	15 x 11	IA		3.00
7399.	Pieta (Sculpture)	28 x 22	NYGS		12.00
		14 x 11	NYGS		3.00
		12 x 9	AP		1.50
7400.	Mater Dolorosa - Detail of No. 7399	20 x 16	NYGS		7.50
7401.	Prophet Daniel (Sistine Chapel)	15 x 11	IA		3.00
	Head of Daniel - Detail of No. 7401	15 x 11	IA		3.00
7402.	Prophet Ezechial (Sistine Chapel)	15 x 11	IA		3.00
	Head of Ezechial - Detail of No. 7402	15 x 11	IA		3.00
7403.	Prophet Isaiah (Sistine Chapel)	23-1/2x17-1/2	CFA		12.00
		15 x 11	IA		3.00
		10 x 7-1/2	IA		1.75
	Head of Isaiah - Detail of No. 7403	15 x 11	IA		3.00
		14-1/2 x 11	AS		3.25
7404.	Prophet Jeremiah (Sistine Chapel)	15 x 11	IA		3.00
	Head of Jeremiah - Detail of No. 7404	15 x 11	IA		3.00
		14-1/2 x 11	AS		3.25
7405.	Prophet Joel (Sistine Chapel)	15 x 11	IA		3.00
	Head of Joel - Detail of No. 7405	15 x 11	IA		3.00
		11 x 8	IA		1.75

7406.	Prophet Jonah (Sistine Chapel)	15 x 11	IA	3.00
	Head of Jonah - Detail of No. 7406	15 x 11	IA	3.00
7407.	Prophet Zacharias	15 x 11	IA	3.00
	Head of Zacharias - Detail of No. 7407	15 x 11	IA	3.00
7408.	Sibyl: Cumean (Sistine Chapel)	15 x 11	IA	3.00
	Head of Cumean Sibyl - Detail of No. 7408	15 x 11	IA	3.00
7409.	Delphic Sybil c.	24 x 20	PENN	1.50
		23 x 17	CFA	12.00
		15 x 11	IA	3.00
	Head of Delphic Sybil - Detail of No. 7409	15 x 11	IA	3.00
		14-1/2 x 11	AS	3.25
7410.	Lybian Sibyl	15 x 11	IA	3.00
	Head of Lybian Sibyl - Detail of No. 7410	15 x 11	IA	3.00
7411.	Persian Sibyl	15 x 11	IA	3.00
	Head of Persian Sibyl - Detail of No. 7411	15 x 11	IA	3.00
7412.	Study	16 x 9	AR	4.00
7413.	Three Male Figures	11-1/2 x 8	AR	3.50

MICHELINO DI BESOZZO (DOMENICO DI) (Italian, 1417-1491)

7414.	Dante and his Book	20 x 25	ESH	12.00
7415.	Marriage of St. Catherine	15 x 11	IA	3.00

MICHETTI, FRANCESCO PAOLO (Italian, 1851-1929)

7416.	Self-Portrait	14 x 11	IA	3.00

MIERIS, FRANS VAN (ELDER) (Dutch, 1635-1681)

7417.	Chamber Music	19-1/2 x 16	AP	9.00
7418.	Charlatan	14 x 10	IA	3.00
7419.	Repast of Two Old People	13 x 11	IA	3.00

MIGLIARO, VINCENZO (Italian, 1858-1938)

7420.	Carmella	15 x 11	IA	3.00
7421.	La Luciana	14 x 10	IA	3.00

MIGNARD, PIERRE (Italian, 1612-1695)

7422.	Duchess of Maine as a Girl	15 x 11	IA	3.00
7423.	Madonna of the Grapes	24 x 18	IA	7.50
		14-1/2 x 11	AS	3.25
		10-1/2 x 9	IA	1.75

7424.	Portrait of the Countess of Grignan - Oval -	14 x 11-1/2	AS	3. 25

MIGNON, ABRAHAM (German, 1640-1679)

7425.	Fruits	11 x 15	AS	3. 25

MIJA (Japanese)

7426	Hiroshige	c.	7 x 9	AP	. 50

MILBOURNE, CHARLES

7427.	Government House	17 x 22	PENN	1. 50

MILLAIS, (SIR) JOHN EVERETT (English, 1829-1896)

7428.	Boyhood of Raleigh	15 x 17-1/2	ESH	
		8 x 9	NYGS	. 50
7429.	Cherry Ripe	15 x 10	ESH	6. 00
7430.	Souvenir of Velasquez			
		11 x 9	ESH	2. 00

MILLER, HENRY ARTHUR (Russian-American 1897-)

7431.	Abstract, 1965	c.	11 x 15	AP	1. 00
		c.	7 x 9	AP	1. 00
7432.	City in Turmoil	c.	11 x 15	AP	1. 00
		c.	7 x 9	AP	1. 00
7433.	Flying Bird	c.	11 x 15	AP	1. 00
7434.	Flying Fish	c.	7 x 9	AP	1. 00
7435.	Two Heads	c.	11 x 15	AP	1. 00
		c.	7 x 9	AP	1. 00

MILLER, MARY (American Contemporary)

7436.	Peace Rose	20 x 16	IA	4. 00
7437.	Quiet Moment	30 x 24	IA	15. 00
7438.	Rose Bouquet	20 x 16	IA	4. 00
		12 x 9	IA	1. 50
7439.	Young Mother and Child	30 x 24	IA	15. 00

MILLET, JEAN FRANCOIS (French, 1814-1875)

7440.	The Angelus	20 x 24	IA	7. 50
		17 x 20-1/2	IA	10. 00
		11 x 14	NYGS	3. 00
		11 x 13	IA	3. 00
		9 x 11-1/2	IA	1. 75
		7-1/2 x 10	IA	. 50
7441.	La Becquée	10-1/2 x 8	NYGS	4. 00
7442.	Bundlers	11 x 13	IA	3. 00
7443.	Feeding her Birds	20 x 16	AP	5. 00
		c.	9 x 7	AP	. 50
7444.	First Step	c.	7 x 9	AP	. 25
7445.	Girl Gleaner	15-1/2 x 12	AR	4. 00
7446.	Gleaner	16 x 12	CFA	4. 00
7447.	The Gleaners (Les Glaneuses)	c.	20 x 24	PENN	1. 50
		17-1/2x23-1/2	NYGS	7. 50
		16-1/2 x 22	IA	10. 00
		11 x 14	IA	3. 00
		10-1/2 x 14	NYGS	3. 00
		8-1/2 x 11	IA	1. 75

		8 x 10-1/2	NYGS		1.00
	c.	8 x 10	IA		.50
7448.	Going to Work c.	9 x 7	AP		.50
7449.	Man with a Hoe	14-1/2 x 18	IA		3.00
7450.	Retour des Champs	12 x 9	NYGS		4.00
7451.	Shepherdess with her Sheep	11 x 14	IA		3.00
7452.	The Spinner: Goat-Herdess of the Auvergne	14 x 11	IA		3.00
7453.	Young Shepherdess with Flock	17 x 21	IA		10.00

MINAMI, KUNZO (Japanese, 1883-1950)

7454.	Crane and Fancy	24 x 18	PENN		1.50
7455.	Odd Birds Bathing	24 x 18	PENN		1.50
7456.	Odd Birds in a Tree	24 x 18	PENN		1.50
7457.	Weathervane Crane	24 x 18	PENN		1.50

MINAUX, ANDRE (French Contemporary)

7458.	Fishing Boats on the Beach	18-1/2 x 22	ESH		10.00
7459.	Pastry Cook	22-1/2 x 16	ESH		10.00

MINERVA

7460.	Boudoirs, Early American (4)	10 x 13	AK	ea.	1.75
		8 x 10	AK	ea.	1.00
		5 x 7	AK	ea.	.60

MIRO, JOAN (Spanish, 1893-   )

7461.	Birds' Wings Glide over the Moon c.	10 x 8	ESH		1.00
7462.	Characters of the Night c.	7 x 9	AP		.50
7463.	Comets	10 x 31-1/2	PENN		1.50
7464.	Composition	19-1/2 x 14	ESH		10.00
7465.	Composition, 1930	18 x 24	PENN		1.50
7466.	Composition, 1933	20 x 22	AR		12.00
7467.	Composition, 1949 c.	20 x 24	PENN		1.50
7468.	Composition, 1950	13-1/2 x 18	AR		12.00
7469.	Composition, 1963	24 x 18	PENN		1.50
7470.	Dog Barking at the Moon c.	18 x 23	HNA		5.95
		16 x 20	AR		7.50
		8 x 10	AR		2.00
7471.	The Farm c.	20 x 24	PENN		1.50
7472.	Femmes, Oiseau au Claire de Lune	23 x 18-1/2	NYGS		12.00
7473.	Fighting Cock	16 x 12	AR		5.00
		10 x 8	AR		2.00
7474.	Figures Under the Moon	20 x 6	AR		5.00
7475.	Fragment c.	20 x 24	PENN		1.50

7476.	Fragment of a Triptych	26 x 20	PENN	1.50
7477.	Fresco, 1951	10 x 31	AR	12.00
7478.	Harlequin's Carnival	16 x 22-1/2	ESH	10.00
7479.	Man, Woman and Child	23 x 20	NYGS	16.00
7480.	Maternity	24 x 19	AR	10.00
7481.	Menagerie	20 x 28	CFA	15.00
7482.	Moon	12 x 16	AR	5.00
		8 x 10	AR	2.00
7483.	Mural	8 x 39	CAC	15.00
7484.	Nursery Decorations	6 x 24	AR	5.00
7485.	Painting, 1952	12 x 31-1/2	ESH	15.00
7486.	Painting, 1963 c.	8 x 10	MMA	.35
7487.	Personnages Inverses c.	20 x 24	PENN	1.50
7488.	Personnages Orageux	18 x 22-1/2	ESH	10.00
7489.	Portrait No. 1	23-1/2x18-1/2	PENN	1.50
7490.	Poster: Art, Sculptures, Graphique	28-1/2x 20	PENN	1.00
7491.	Rays of the Sun	18 x 25	CAC	7.50
7492.	Rooster	17 x 12	CAC	6.00
7493.	Le Soleil	25 x 19	CAC	12.00
7494.	Summer	16 x 12	AR	5.00
		10 x 8	AR	2.00
7495.	The Sun	8 x 10	AR	2.00
7496.	Woman and Birds in Front of the Sun	21 x 15	IA	7.50
7497.	Woman and Bird in the Night	6 x 24	AR	5.00

MITCHELL, BRUCE (American Contemporary)

7498.	Fire Island Landing	12-1/2 x 19	NYGS	6.00
7499.	My Hideaway	24 x 30	AA	10.00
7500.	Spring Breakup in the Laurentians	24 x 30	AA	10.00

MITCHELL, JAMES A. (English, 1902-)

7501.	Close Ashore	15 x 30	DAC	5.00
7502.	Land's End	24 x 48	DAC	10.00
		c. 20 x 24	PENN	1.50
		12 x 30	DAC	5.00
7503.	Off the Highlands	15 x 30	DAC	5.00
7504.	Out Islands Schooner	15 x 30	DAC	5.00
7505.	Sea Eagle	26 x 40	AA	15.00
7506.	Tropic Landfall	15 x 30	DAC	5.00

MITCHELL, J. E.

7507.	Conch Boat	18 x 12	DAC	2.50
7508.	Derelict Sloops	18 x 12	DAC	2.50
7509.	Fishing Sloops	18 x 12	DAC	2.50
7510.	High and Dry	18 x 12	DAC	2.50

MITSOKI TOSA See TOSA MITSUOKI

MIXER

7511.	Palomino	21 x 16	CFA	7. 50
7512.	Quarter Horse	21 x 16	CFA	7. 50

MODERSOHN-BECKER, PAULA (German, 1876-1907)

7513.	Bauern-Madchen mit Verschrankten Armen c.	22 x 17-1/2	AS	4. 00
7514.	Flower Still Life	23-1/2 x 17	NYGS	12. 00
7515.	Still Life c.	18 x 23	HNA	5. 95

MODIGLIANI, AMADEO (Italian, 1884-1920)

7516.	The Algerian	22 x 13	CFA	12. 00
7517.	Alice c.	24 x 20	PENN	1. 50
7518.	Boy in Blue	23 x 14	AA	10. 00
7519.	Caryatid	21 x 17	ESH	10. 00
7520.	Girl in Pink	21 x 15-1/2	AA	7. 50
	c.	10 x 8	NYGS	. 50
7521.	Girl with Black Tie	22-1/2 x 17	ESH	10. 00
	c.	10 x 8	ESH	1. 00
7522.	Girl with Braids c.	26 x 21	HNA	5. 95
7523.	Grocer's Daughter c.	12-1/2x9-1/2	AP	1. 25
		7 x 6	CFA	1. 00
7524.	Gypsy Woman with Baby	24 x 15	NYGS	10. 00
	c.	23 x 18	HNA	5. 95
		16 x 12	PENN	1. 00
7525.	Jeanne	26 x 16	CAC	12. 00
7526.	Little Milkmaid	22-1/2x14-1/2	ESH	10. 00
7527.	Little Peasant	16 x 10-1/2	AP	3. 00
7528.	Mme. Amedee with Cigarette c.	16 x 12	PENN	1. 00
7529.	Mme. Kisline c.	16 x 12	PENN	1. 00
7530.	Peasant Boy	16 x 10	AR	3. 00
7531.	Portrait	18 x 12-1/2	NYGS	7. 50
7532.	Portrait of Jeanne Hebuterne	26-1/2x17-1/2	NYGS	18. 00
7533.	Portrait of Lady Van Muyden	15-1/2 x 11	AS	3. 25
7534.	Portrait of Mme. Hayden c.	24 x 20	PENN	1. 50
7535.	Portrait of Mme. Zborowska	21 x 16	NYGS	10. 00
7536.	Portrait of a Woman	9 x 7	NYGS	. 50
7537.	Portrait of a Young Woman c.	23 x 18	HNA	5. 95
7538.	Recling Nude	21-1/2 x 32	NYGS	16. 00
		20 x 30	ESH	15. 00
		17 x 26	CAC	15. 00
		17 x 23	IA	12. 00
7539.	Seated Nude c.	24 x 20	PENN	1. 50
		22-1/2x14-1/2	ESH	10. 00

7540.	Self-Portrait	c.	10 x 8	ESH	1. 00
7541.	Two Lovers		24 x 19	PENN	1. 50
7542.	Venus	c.	7 x 9	AP	. 60
7543.	Woman with a Baby		24 x 15	PENN	1. 50
7544.	Woman with Blue Eyes		10 x 6	CFA	1. 00
7545.	Woman with Brown Hair	c.	16 x 12	PENN	1. 00
7546.	Woman with a Collar		22-1/2 x 15	ESH	10. 00
7547.	Woman with a Necklace	c.	9 x 7	AP	. 50
7548.	Woman with Red Hair		24 x 15	PENN	1. 50
		c.	16 x 12	PENN	1. 00
7549.	Woman with Ruffled Blouse	c.	24 x 20	PENN	1. 50
7550.	The Young Apprentice		11 x 7	CFA	1. 00
7551.	Young Girl with Blue Eyes	c.	12-1/2x9-1/2	AP	1. 25
7552.	Young Woman with Earrings	c.	10 x 8	ESH	1. 00

MOELLEN, VAN DER

| 7553. | Cities of Lille and Tournai | | 14 x 34-1/2 | CFA | 30. 00 |

MOELLER, LOUIS C.

| 7554. | Cronies | | 18 x 24 | AA | 8. 00 |
| 7555. | Local Adversaries | | 18 x 24 | AA | 8. 00 |

MOESLER

| 7556. | Birth of the Flag | | 30 x 40 | CFA | 15. 00 |

MOLLENHAUER, ERNST (German, 1892-)

| 7557. | Harbour at East Lake | | 23 x 27 | ESH | 10. 00 |
| 7558. | Landscape North Sea | | 27 x 22 | ESH | 12. 00 |

MOLNÉ (Spanish, 1907-)

| 7559. | Red and Gold | | 20 x 24 | RL | 10. 00 |

MONACO, LORENZO (FRA LORENZO DEGLI ANGELI) See
LORENZO MONACO
MONAHAN, HUGH C. (Irish [Res. Canada] Contemporary)

| 7560. | Greylag on the Loch | | 16 x 24 | RL | 7. 50 |
| 7561. | Mallard, Anglesay | | 16 x 24 | RL | 7. 50 |

MONDRIAN, PIET (Dutch, 1872-1944)

7562.	Blue Chrysanthemum, 1922	c.	11 x 9-1/2	NYGS	7. 50
7563.	Blue Rose,	c. 1922	11 x 8	NYGS	7. 50
7564.	Composition, 1913		15 x 19-1/2	NYGS	6. 00
7565.	Composition in Bleu		19-1/2x17-1/2	NYGS	5. 00
7566.	Horizontal Trees	c.	20 x 24	PENN	1. 50

7567.	Large Chrysanthemum,			
	c. 1908	16 x 10	NYGS	7. 50
7568.	Opposition of Lines,			
	Red and Yellow	17 x 13	NYGS	10. 00
7569.	Painting No. 1,			
	1921	19 x 12	AR	7. 50
7570.	Poster: L'Art			
	Hollandais	28-1/2 x 19	PENN	1. 00
7571.	Rose in Tumbler,			
	1922	9-1/2x7-1/2	NYGS	7. 50
7572.	Trafalgar Square	20 x 16-1/2	MMA	6. 00
MONET,	CLAUDE (French, 1840-1926)			
7573.	Amsterdam c.	17-1/2 x 22	AS	4. 00
7574.	Anemones c.	10 x 8	ESH	1. 00
7575.	Argenteuil	22 x 25-1/2	NYGS	10. 00
		18 x 21	CFA	10. 00
		8 x 10	CFA	1. 00
7576.	Banks of the Seine,			
	Vetheuil	22 x 30	NYGS	16. 00
7577.	La Barque Bleue			
	(Blue Boat)	21 x 25	NYGS	12. 00
	c.	9-1/2x12-1/2	AP	1. 25
		7 x 8	CFA	1. 00
7578.	Le Bassin			
	d'Argenteuil	22 x 29-1/2	NYGS	16. 00
		21 x 29	CFA	12. 00
	c.	20 x 24	PENN	1. 50
		18 x 26	DAC	7. 50
		16 x 22-1/2	ESH	10. 00
	c.	8 x 10	ESH	1. 00
7579.	Bateaux de Plaisance			
	(Pleasure Boats)	18 x 25	ESH	10. 00
	c.	12 x 16	PENN	1. 00
7580.	Beach at Saint-			
	Adresse	22 x 30	AA	15. 00
		15 x 20	IA	5. 00
7581.	Beach at Trouville	22 x 26	CFA	12. 00
		18 x 22	PENN	1. 50
7582.	Boat Races at			
	Argenteuil	11 x 19	CFA	5. 00
7583.	Boating on the Epte	11 x 12	IA	3. 00
7584.	Boats and Regatta			
	at Argenteuil	18 x 30	ESH	15. 00
	c.	8 x 10	ESH	1. 00
7585.	Boats at Argenteuil	24 x 31	NYGS	18. 00
	c.	20 x 24	PENN	1. 50
7586.	Boats at Etretat	21-1/2 x 27	NYGS	18. 00
7587.	Boats on Beach c.	20 x 24	PENN	1. 50
7588.	Boats on the Seine	6 x 9	NYGS	. 50
7589.	Bordighera	18-1/2x21-1/2	ESH	10. 00
	c.	8 x 10	ESH	1. 00
7590.	Les Bords de la			
	Seine	21 x 27-1/2	ESH	15. 00

7591.	Bridge at Argenteuil				
			24 x 30	CFA	15. 00
			20-1/2x28	NYGS	20. 00
		c.	18 x 23	HNA	5. 95
			16-1/2x22-1/2	ESH	10. 00
		c.	8 x 10	ESH	1. 00
7592.	Camille Monet with Son and Nurse in the Garden	c.	18 x 23	HNA	5. 95
7593.	Canal de Zandaam		12 x 21	ESH	6. 00
7594.	Cap d'Antibes		25 x 35	NYGS	20. 00
			21 x 28-1/2	AR	12. 00
7595.	Cape Martin		19-1/2x24-1/2	PENN	1. 50
7596.	Chateau-Gaillard		17 x 22-1/2	ESH	10. 00
7597.	Chrysanthemums		16 x 20	PENN	1. 50
7598.	Coast near Dieppe		15 x 20	AP	5. 00
7599.	Coast of Etretat		15 x 19	AP	5. 00
		c.	7 x 9	AP	. 60
7600.	Corn Poppies	c.	18 x 23	HNA	5. 95
		c.	9-1/2x12-1/2	AP	1. 25
7601.	Daughter Painting in a Landscape	c.	9-1/2x12-1/2	AP	1. 25
			6 x 7	CFA	1. 00
7602.	Etretat		18 x 22-1/2	ESH	10. 00
7603.	Fisherman's Cottage on Cliffs	c.	18 x 23	HNA	5. 95
7604.	Fishing on the Seine		23 x 31-1/2	IA	15. 00
7605.	Flower Beds	c.	20 x 24	PENN	1. 50
7606.	Fruit Still Life		23 x 29	CFA	18. 00
7607.	Garenne Bezons		19 x 25	ESH	10. 00
7608.	La Grenouillere		16-1/2x22-1/2	ESH	10. 00
7609.	Haystack at Sunset	c.	18 x 23	HNA	5. 95
7610.	Houses of Parliament	c.	9-1/2x12-1/2	AP	1. 25
7611.	Houses of Parliament, Sunset	c.	18 x 23	HNA	5. 95
7612.	Impression at Sunrise		18-1/2 x 24	ESH	10. 00
7613.	In the Garden	c.	10 x 8	ESH	1. 00
7614.	Jean Monet on a Mechanical Horse		19 x 23	NYGS	12. 00
		c.	8 x 10	ESH	1. 00
7615.	Landscape near Vetheuil		22 x 29-1/2	AJ	12. 00
			22 x 27	NYGS	12. 00
7616.	London Parliament		16 x 17-1/2	AP	5. 00
7617.	Madame Monet in her Garden at Giverny		22-1/2x16-1/2	IA	6. 00
7618.	Monet's House at Argenteuil		25 x 20-1/2	NYGS	18. 00

7619.	On the Seine	19 x 33	CFA	15. 00
7620.	Palazzo da Mula,			
	Venice	24-1/2 x 32	NYGS	18. 00
	c.	18 x 23	HNA	5. 95
7621.	Pond at Argenteuil	14 x 19	CFA	4. 00
7622.	Pool with Nympheas	13 x 14	CFA	5. 00
7623.	Poppies	15 x 20	AP	10. 00
7624.	Quai du Louvre,			
	Paris	22 x 31-1/2	ESH	15. 00
		8 x 10-1/2	ESH	1. 00
7625.	Red Boats	22 x 30	NYGS	16. 00
7626.	Regatta	19 x 29	NYGS	26. 00
7627.	Regatta at Argenteuil	14 x 22-1/2	ESH	10. 00
		13x 20	AP	6. 00
	c.	9-1/2x12-1/2	AP	1. 25
		5 x 9	CFA	1. 00
7628.	The River	21 x 26	NYGS	15. 00
		20 x 24	DAC	7. 50
7629.	Road in Snow at			
	Honfleur	5 x 8	CFA	1. 00
7630.	Rocks at Belle			
	Isle c.	8 x 10	NYGS	. 50
7631.	Rouen Cathedral, West			
	Facade, Sunlight	28 x 18-1/2	NYGS	12. 00
	c.	10 x 8	ESH	1. 00
7632.	Rowing Boat at			
	Giverny	8 x 10-1/2	ESH	1. 00
7633.	Sailing Boats	15-1/2 x 21	ESH	6. 00
7634.	Sailing Boats at			
	Argenteuil	17 x 22-1/2	ESH	10. 00
	c.	8 x 10	ESH	1. 00
7635.	Sea at Etretat c.	8 x 10	ESH	1. 00
7636.	Seacoast at Trouville			
	c.	20 x 24	PENN	1. 50
7637.	The Seine at			
	Argenteuil	21 x 28-1/2	NYGS	26. 00
		19 x 25	AJ	12. 00
	c.	7 x 9	NYGS	. 50
7638.	The Seine at Bougival			
		16 x 22-1/2	ESH	10. 00
	c.	8 x 10	ESH	1. 00
7639.	The Seine at Vetheuil			
		20 x 33-1/2	NYGS	20. 00
		17-1/2 x 30	RL	10. 00
7640.	Snow at Argenteuil	11 x 13	IA	3. 00
7641.	Still Life	20 x 28	NYGS	16. 00
7642.	Still Life: Apples			
	and Grapes	22 x 27	CAC	12. 00
7643.	Still Life: Fruit	23-1/2 x 29	NYGS	20. 00
7644.	Stone Pines,			
	Antibes	25 x 32	CFA	15. 00
7645.	Street in Fecamp	24 x 18	PENN	1. 50

7646.	Studio Boat		15 x 20	NYGS		6. 00
7647.	Summer (Fields in					
	Spring)		28 x 35	NYGS		20. 00
			18 x 22-1/2	NYGS		15. 00
			6 x 7	NYGS		. 50
7648.	Sunflowers		30 x 24	NYGS		18. 00
		c.	10 x 8	NYGS		. 50
7649.	Sunset at Vetheuil					
		c.	8 x 10	ESH		1. 00
7650.	Train Station St.					
	Lazare	c.	8 x 10	NYGS		. 50
7651.	Tulip Field		18 x 22-1/2	ESH		10. 00
		c.	8 x 10	ESH		1. 00
7652.	Tulip Fields at					
	Sassenheim		18 x 24	PENN		1. 50
7653.	Tulips in Holland		19 x 24	PENN		1. 50
7654.	Vase of Chrysanthemems					
		c.	23 x 18	HNA		5. 95
7655.	Vencie, San Giorgio					
	Maggiore		18 x 22-1/2	ESH		10. 00
7656.	View of Amsterdam,					
	West Church Tower		19-1/2 x 24	NYGS		12. 00
7657.	Water Lilies	c.	23 x 18	HNA		5. 95
			16-1/2 x 16	IA		6. 00
			14 x 13	CFA		5. 00
		c.	9-1/2x12-1/2	AP		1. 25
			7 x 7	CFA		1. 00
7658.	Water Lilies					
	(Orangerie) - 2 Parts					
			12-1/2 x 30 ea.	NYGS	ea.	10. 00
7659.	Weeping Willow		27 x 24	NYGS		12. 00
7660.	White and Purple					
	Water Lilies		27 x 36	NYGS		20. 00
7661.	Windmills		9 x 15-1/2	ESH		2. 00
7662.	Wisteria		24 x 32	NYGS		15. 00
7663.	Woman with a					
	Parasol		22-1/2 x 15	ESH		10. 00
7664.	Water Lilies -					
	Detail of No. 7663		13-1/2x30-1/2	ESH		15. 00
		c.	8 x 10	ESH		1. 00
7665.	Women in a Garden					
		c.	20 x 24	PENN		1. 50
7666.	Yellow Iris		37 x 18	NYGS		15. 00
7667.	Yellow Iris with					
	Pink Cloud	c.	9-1/2x12-1/2	AP		1. 25
			6 x 6	CFA		1. 00
7668.	Zaandam		17 x 26-1/2	NYGS		10. 00
MONETTI						
7669.	Alpine Slope		40 x 15	DAC		10. 00
7670.	Alpine Stream		40 x 15	DAC		10. 00
7671.	Serene Setting		24 x 48	DAC		10. 00
			15 x 30	DAC		2. 00

MONIER, MADELEINE
7672. Bouquet (2)   27-1/2 x 21   IA   ea. 10. 00
MONNOYER, JEAN-BAPTISTE (PÈRE) (French, 1634-1699)
7673. Basket of Flowers   8 x 10-1/2   ESH   1. 00
7674. Basket of Flowers
       (2)   22 x 18   CFA   ea. 12. 00
MONREALESE, IL See NOVELLI, PIETRO
MONTAGU, RODERIC
7675. Castle San Angelo   30 x 40   CAC   120. 00
7676. Piazza Palladino   30 x 40   AL   24. 00
7677. Romantic Scenes (4) 28 x 11   CAC   ea. 10. 00
7678.   Garden of Flowers
7679.   Garden of Love
7680.   Garden of Romance
7681.   Garden of Sceret Love
       Romantic Scenes (2) 18 x 28   CAC   ea. 12. 00
7682.   Della Fortuna
7683.   Isle of Istria
       Romantic Scenes (2) 20 x 16   AL   ea. 8. 00
7684.   Capricio Venezia
7685.   Marina di Giorgio, Venezia
       Romantic Scenes (4) 11 x 14   AL   ea. 5. 00
7686.   Ascola Piceno
7687.   Castel Del Monte
7688.   Tarquina
7689.   Urbino
       Romantic Scenes (3) 14 x 11   CAC   ea. 5. 00
7690.   Camp Vaccinio
7691.   Carriage of Love
7692.   The Prince
       Romantic Scenes (2) 7 x 18   AL   ea. 5. 00
7693.   Barcarolle, Venezia
7694.   Lido, Venezia
       Romantic Scenes (3) 18 x 7   CAC   ea. 5. 00
7695.   Flower Girl
7696.   Villa Della Rose
7697.   Villa Umberto
MONTEZ, PAULINO (Portuguese, 1897-)
7698. Daybreak   36 x 24   DAC   7. 50
7699. Nightfall   36 x 24   DAC   7. 50
MONTI, VINCENZO
7700. Ancona Sunset   25 x 30   CFA   15. 00
7701. Portofino   24 x 27   CFA   15. 00
MONTICELLI, ADOLPHE (French, 1824-1886)
7702. Les Martigues   9 x 14   IA   3. 00
MONTINI
7703. Monique   c. 24 x 20   PENN   1. 50
MONTJOIE, LOUIS (French, Ac. 1748-89)
7704. Street Scenes, French
       (6)   8 x 10   CFA   ea. 6. 00
           Le Carousel
           Le Lapin Agile

Moulin Rouge
Place de la Concorde
Rue de L'Abrevoir
Rue Norvins

MONTLACK

7705.	Spring Idyll	30 x 25	CAC	10.00
7706.	Stillness of Eternity	30 x 25	CAC	10.00

MONTPEZAT, HENRI D'AINECY DE (French, 1817-1859)

7707.	The Ponychaise	17 x 22-1/2	ESH	10.00
7708.	The Tilbory c.	8 x 10	ESH	1.00

MOORE, HENRY (English, 1898-)

7709.	Family Group c.	20 x 24	PENN	1.50
7710.	Group of Figures	17 x 12	CFA	6.00
7711.	Ideas for Metal Sculpture, 1937	15-1/2 x 22	NYGS	18.00
7712.	Reclining Figure in a Landscape	15 x 23	NYGS	15.00
7713.	Sculptural Objects	19 x 30	CFA	7.50
7714.	Standing Figures	18-1/2x10-1/2	NYGS	7.50
7715.	Two Women Seated	24 x 22	NYGS	12.00
		23 x 22	AR	15.00

MOORE, NELSON AUGUSTUS (American, 1824-1902)

7716.	Barefoot Prodigy c.	24 x 20	PENN	1.50
7717.	West Springfield c.	20 x 24	PENN	1.50
		18 x 26	DAC	7.50

MOPP, MAXIMILIAN (Austrian, 1885-)

7718.	Chess with Emanuel Lasker	16 x 20	AR	7.50
		8 x 10	AR	1.50
7719.	String Quartet	16 x 20	AR	7.50
		8 x 10	AR	1.50
	c.	7 x 9	AP	1.00
7720.	Symphony	21 x 31	NYGS	16.00

MOR, ANTHONIS (Dutch, 1519-1575)

7721.	Portrait of a Boy	15-1/2 x 10	NYGS	5.00

MORA

7722.	Teuzitlian Market c.	7 x 9	AP	.60

MORADO

7723.	Way to the Quarry c.	7 x 9	AP	.60

MORAN, THOMAS (American, 1837-1926)

7724.	Dream City	20 x 24	AA	10.00
7725.	Gen. Wayne at Stony Point	18 x 30	CAC	10.00
7726.	Grand Canyon	24 x 32	AA	12.00
		20 x 30	CAC	10.00

MORANDI, GIORGIO (Italian, 1890-)

7727.	Natura Morta	14-1/2 x 14	NYGS	18.00
7728.	Still Life c.	12 x 16	AP	2.00

7729.	Still Life with Jug			
	and Bottle	15 x 13	NYGS	15. 00

MORANDO, PAOLO (IL CAVAZZOLA) (Italian, 1486-1522)

7730.	Madonna and Child	7 x 6	IA	1. 50

MOREAU, JEAN MICHEL (THE YOUNGER) (French, 1741-1814)

7731.	French Park	9 x 14	AR	4. 00
		7 x 11	CAC	3. 00

MOREAU, LUC ALBERT (French, 1882-1948)

7732.	Knockout	17-1/2 x 24	PENN	1. 50

MOREDA

7733.	Madonna	19 x 14	AS	12. 00

MORELLI, DOMENICO (Italian, 1826-1901)

7734.	Mater Purissima	20 x 28	IA	10. 00
7735.	Potiphar's Wife	11 x 13	IA	3. 00

MORGANTHULER

7736.	Winter	25 x 31	CFA	15. 00

MORISOT, BERTHE (French, 1841-1895)

7737.	Bassinet	c.	12 x 16	AP	2. 00
7738.	Children of Gabriel				
	Thomas		22 x 17	CAC	10. 00
7739.	The Cradle	c.	24 x 20	PENN	1. 50
			16 x 12	AA	3. 00
		c.	10 x 8	ESH	1. 00
7740.	Eugene Manet a				
	L'Ile de Wight	c.	17-1/2 x 22	AS	4. 00
7741.	Farm in Normandy		10 x 12	IA	3. 00
7742.	Femme a L'Eventail				
		c.	22 x 17-1/2	AS	4. 00
7743.	Girl Writing a				
	Letter	c.	10 x 8	ESH	1. 00
7744.	Hortensia	c.	20 x 24	PENN	1. 50
7745.	Jour d'Eté		16 x 26	NYGS	15. 00
7746.	On the Lake	c.	9-1/2x12-1/2	AP	1. 25
7747.	On the Lake in the				
	Bois de Boulogne		18-1/2x22-1/2	ESH	10. 00
7748.	On the Terrace		20 x 16	CFA	12. 00
		c.	9-1/2x12-1/2	AP	1. 25
		c.	9 x 7	AP	1. 00
			7 x 6	CFA	1. 00
7749.	Portrait of a Young				
	Girl	c.	23 x 18	HNA	5. 95
7750.	Skating in the Bois		20 x 16	PENN	1. 50
7751.	Swans		11 x 14-1/2	ESH	8. 00
7752.	Thames Estuary				
		c.	10 x 8	ESH	1. 00
7753.	Two Children		22-1/2 x 18	ESH	10. 00
7754.	Young Girl Waiting				
		c.	10 x 8	ESH	1. 00

MORLAND, GEORGE (English, 1763-1804)

7755.	Check	c.	8x 10	ESH	1. 00
7756.	Death	c.	8 x 10	ESH	1. 00
7757.	End of the Hunt		23-1/2 x 31	NYGS	18. 00

7758.	Fox Hunting (4)	7-1/2 x 9	AA	ea.	4.00
7759.	Going into Cover				
	c.	8 x 10	ESH		1.00
7760.	Going Out c.	8 x 10	ESH		1.00
7761.	Inside of a Stable	12-1/2 x 18	NYGS		5.00
7762.	Laundrymaid	11 x 9	ESH		2.00
7763.	Shepherds Reposing	22 x 17	CAC		12.00
7764.	Weary Sportsman	22 x 17	CAC		12.00

MORO, GIUSEPPE (Italian, 1888-)

7765.	Princess Isabella				
	Maria	26 x 20	CAC		12.00

MORODER, A.

7766.	Madonna	20 x 19	AS		10.00
		10 x 9	AS		4.00

MORONE, FRANCESCO (Italian, 1473-1529)

7767.	St. John the Baptist	11 x 7-1/2	AR		3.00

MORONI, GIOVAN BATTISTA (Italian, 1525-1578)

7768.	Count P. Secco				
	Suardi	16 x 8	IA		3.00
7769.	Gentleman in Adoration				
	before the Madonna	20 x 22	NYGS		12.00
7770.	Tailor	23 x 17-1/2	NYGS		12.00

MOROT, PIERRE

7771.	Street Scenes, Paris				
	(6) Arc de Triomphe	24 x 10	AA		8.00
	Notre Dame-Book-				
	stalls	12 x 27	AA		10.00
	Petite Rue	24 x 10	AA		8.00
	Place Fursten-				
	berg	18 x 24	AA		12.00
	Place du Tertre	18 x 24	AA		12.00
	Sacre Coeur	12 x 27	AA		10.00

MORRIS, (SIR) CEDRIC (English, 1889-)

7772.	Yellow Irises	22 x 18	ESH		15.00

MORRIS, GEORGE FORD (American, 1877-1961)

7773.	Man O'War	9-1/2x12-1/2	NYGS		2.00
7774.	Man O'War - Study				
	of Head	17 x 13	NYGS		4.00
7775.	Whirlaway	9-1/2x12-1/2	NYGS		2.00
7776.	Whirlaway - Study of				
	Head	17 x 13	NYGS		4.00

MORSE, SAMUEL F. B. (American, 1791-1872)

7777.	General Lafayette	24 x 16-1/2	NYGS		12.00

MOSES, (GRANDMA), ANNA MARY ROBERTSON (American, 1860-1961)

7778.	Apple Butter Making	11 x 13	CFA		2.00
7779.	Christmas at Home	10 x 13	CFA		2.00
7780.	Country Fair c.	12 x 16	PENN		1.00
7781.	Dead Tree c.	20 x 24	PENN		1.50
		16 x 20	CFA		7.50
7782.	Grandma to Big				
	City c.	12 x 16	PENN		1.00

7783.	It's Haying Time	18 x 23	PENN	1.50
7784.	Joy Ride	18 x 24	PENN	1.50
7785.	Old Checkered House	18 x 22	CAC	10.00
7786.	Old Homestead	23 x 27	CAC	18.00
7787.	Out for the Christmas Trees	18 x 24	PENN	1.50
7788.	Portfolio (6)	12 x 16	CFA	set 15.00
7789.	Sugaring Off	18 x 24	PENN	1.50
7790.	Threshers c.	12 x 16	PENN	1.00
7791.	Winter Twilight c.	12 x 16	PENN	1.00

MOSKOWITZ, SHIRLEY (American Contemporary)

7792.	An Ode to a Summer Floral	24 x 18	PENN	1.50

MOSLEY, CHARLES (English, 1720-1770)

7793.	The Ballet	19 x 30	CFA	5.00

MOSTAERT, JAN (Flemish, c. 1475-1555)

7794.	A Fair (Detail)	22 x 31-1/2	ESH	15.00

MOTHERWELL, ROBERT (American, 1915-1966)

7795.	Cambridge Collage	28 x 19	NYGS	15.00
7796.	Poster for Exhibition: Robert Motherwell	34-1/2x22-1/2	MMA	1.95

MOULY, MARCEL (French Contemporary)

7797.	Festival of Ships	23 x 30	RL	15.00
7798.	Fisher-Boats	20 x 36	ESH	(Cv.) 15.00
7799.	Spanish Balcony	23 x 30	RL	12.50
7800.	Street in Spain	23 x 29	RL	12.50
7801.	Venice in Blue Light	22 x 30	RL	15.00
7802.	Venice Vert et Gris	23 x 29	RL	12.50

MOUNT, WILLIAM SIDNEY (American, 1807-1868)

7803.	Bargaining for a Horse	19 x 24	NYGS	12.00
7804.	Dancing on the Barn Floor	20 x 26	AK	7.50
		12 x 16	AK	2.50
7805.	Music is Contagious	20 x 26	AK	7.50
		12 x 16	AK	2.50

MOZAIEK

7806.	Three-Dimensional Teens (4)	11 x 14	DAC	ea. 1.50
7807.	Watch the Birdie (4)	12 x 9	DAC	ea. 1.50

MU CH'I (Chinese [Sung Dynasty South] c. 1230-1275)

7808.	Wild Goose Flying (Einfallende Wildganz)	28-1/2 x 11	NYGS	16.00
7809.	Wild Goose Resting (Sitzende Wildganz)	28-1/2 x 11	NYGS	16.00

MUELLER

7810.	Study in an Evening Landscape c.	12 x 16	AP	2.00

MUGHAL
7811.	Prince Riding an Elephant	c.	7 x 9	AP		.50

MÜLLER, ERICH MARTIN (German, 1888-)
7812.	Lake in Bavaria	21 x 30	ESH		10.00
7813.	Majesty of the Mountains	21 x 28-1/2	ESH		10.00

MÜLLER, KARL K. (German, 1876-1955)
7814.	Bouquet of Flowers with Larkspur	31-1/2x23-1/2	ESH	Pr.	10.00

MUNCH, ANKA (Danish, 1876-)
7815.	Portraits (6)	13 x 5	ESH	ea. Pr.	3.00
	Anette				
	Jackie				
	Madleine				
	Marika				
	Marilyn				
	Yvonne				

MUNCH, EDVARD (Norwegian, 1863-1944)
7816.	Bridge	24 x 24	NYGS		12.00
7817.	Farmyard	26 x 34	NYGS		18.00
7818.	Manor House	16 x 22	CFA		6.00
7819.	Park in Kosen	23 x 26-1/2	AR		15.00
		23 x 26	CFA		15.00

MUNCHAUSEN, AUGUST VON (American Contemporary)
7820.	American Sports (6)	12 x 16	IA	ea.	2.50
7821.	Baseball (2)				
7822.	Fencing (2)				
7823.	Football (2)				
7824.	Ballet Scenes (2)	22 x 28	NYGS	ea.	10.00
7825.	Corps du Ballet Russe	13 x 16	NYGS	ea.	3.00
7826.	Pas de Trois Ballet Scenes (2)	16 x 20	NYGS	ea.	6.00
7827.	Finale	13 x 16	NYGS	ea.	3.00
7828.	Interlude Ballet Scenes (2)	20 x 16	NYGS	ea.	6.00
7829.	Pose Classique	16 x 13	NYGS	ea.	3.00
7830.	Variation Classique Ballet Scenes (2)	20 x 16	NYGS	ea.	6.00
7831.	En Presentation				
7832.	Sur la Pointe Ballet Scenes (2)	16 x 13	NYGS	ea.	3.00
7833.	Pas de Deux- Swan Lake Variation-Swan Lake				

MUNDING, A.
7835.	Fir Forest	12 x 16	ESH	Pr.	3.00
7836.	View in the Black Forest	20 x 27-1/2	ESH	Pr.	8.00

MUNKACSY, MIHALY (Hungarian, 1844-1909)
7837.	The Saviour	32 x 23-1/2	IA		12.00

		24 x 18	NYGS	10.00
		14 x 10	NYGS	3.00

MÜNNICH, HEINZ
7838. At the Mediterranean

	(2)	19 x 12	ESH	ea.	3.00
7839.	City Vista	24 x 36	DAC		7.50
	c.	24 x 30	PENN		1.95
7840.	In the Sunny South	18 x 23-1/2	ESH		7.00
7841.	Italian Harbour	23-1/2x39-1/2	ESH		9.00
7842.	Reflected City	24 x 36	DAC		7.50
	c.	24 x 30	PENN		1.95
7843.	Southern Landscape	18 x 23-1/2	ESH		7.00

MUNNINGS, (SIR) ALFRED J. (English, 1878-1965)

7844.	After the Race	19 x 25	RL	10.00
7845.	Belvoir Hounds Exercising in the Park	20 x 24	RL	15.00
7846.	Black Knight	17 x 12	RL	6.00
7847.	Full River	18-1/2 x 24	RL	10.00
7848.	Gypsy Life	19 x 24	RL	10.00
7849.	Major T. Bouch, MFH, with the Belvoir Hounds	20 x 24	RL	15.00
7850.	November Morning in the Pytchley Country	17 x 20	RL	15.00
7851.	October Meeting	18 x 29	RL	15.00
7852.	Prince of Wales	11 x 14	ESH	2.00
7853.	Saddling Paddock, Cheltenham, March Meeting	16 x 25	RL	10.00
7854.	Studies of Pixie, an Exmoor Foal	15-1/2 x 15	RL	5.00

MUNOZ, ALBERTO (Spanish Contemporary)

7855.	Mallorca	22 x 30	NYGS	12.00

MUNTER, GABRIELE (German, 1877-)

7856.	Haywagon	15 x 18-1/2	NYGS	6.00
7857.	Mountain View	17 x 20	CFA	6.00

MURILLO, BARTOLOME ESTEBAN (Spanish, 1618-1682)

7858.	Boys Eating c.	23 x 18	HNA	5.95
7859.	Children of the Shell c.	7 x 9	AP	.50
7860.	The Divine Shepherd (Madrid)	15 x 11-1/2	AS	3.25
	The Infant Jesus - Detail of No. 7860	14 x 10	IA	3.00
		10 x 8	IA	1.50
7861.	Ecce Homo	13 x 11	IA	3.00
		10 x 7	NYGS	.50
7862.	Game of Dice	27-1/2 x 20	NYGS	18.00
7863.	Girl and her Duenna	29 x 24	NYGS	18.00
	c.	24 x 20	PENN	1.50
		10 x 9	CFA	2.00

7864.	Grape and Melon			
	Eaters	27-1/2 x 19	NYGS	18.00
7865.	Immaculate			
	Conception	35-1/2 x 24	IA	15.00
		23-1/2 x 16	IA	7.50
		20 x 10-1/2	IA	5.00
		13 x 10	IA	3.00
		11 x 8	IA	1.75
	c.	10 x 8	NYGS	.50
	c.	9 x 7	AP	.60
7866.	The Infant St. John			
	c.	23 x 18	HNA	5.95
7867.	Jesus Feeding the			
	Five Thousand	16 x 39	IA	12.00
7868.	Madonna and Child	24 x 18	DAC	7.50
		24-1/2 x 17	IA	7.50
		16 x 12	DAC	2.50
	Detail of No.			
	7868	15 x 11	IA	3.00
		10 x 7	IA	1.75
7869.	Madonna and Child			
	(Rome)	15 x 11-1/2	AS	3.25
7870.	Madonna and Child--			
	Detail (Florence)	16 x 12	AS	3.25
7871.	Madonna and Child			
	(Corsini)	15 x 11	IA	3.00
		10 x 8	NYGS	.50
7872.	Marriage of St.			
	Catherine	11 x 14	IA	3.00
7873.	Moses Striking the			
	Rock	16 x 39	IA	12.00
7874.	Pastry Eaters	27-1/2 x 23	NYGS	18.00
		22 x 18	DAC	7.50
	c.	9 x 7	AP	.60
7875.	St. Joseph and the			
	Holy Child	24 x 18	NYGS	10.00
7876.	The Santiago Madonna			
		24 x 17	AA	7.50
7877.	Street Urchin	13 x 10-1/2	AJ	2.50
7878.	Urchins	20 x 15-1/2	NYGS	7.50
7879.	Virgin and Child			
	c.	9 x 7	AP	.50
7880.	Virgin of the			
	Chaplet	15 x 10	AS	3.25
MURIS, GEORGE				
7881.	Down to the Sea	18-1/2 x 22	ESH	7.50
7882.	Flower Shop	18-1/2 x 22	ESH	7.50
7883.	Mediterranean			
	Harbour	18-1/2 x 22	ESH	7.50
7884.	Riviera	18-1/2 x 22	ESH	7.50
MURPHY, H. DUDLEY (American, 1867-1945)				
7885.	Silver Bowl	25 x 30	CFA	12.00

MURRAY, ALBERT K. (American, 1906-)
7886.   Aligning   14 x 21   NYGS   6. 00
7887.   Fisherman's Wharf
                c.   20 x 24   PENN   1. 50
7888.   Georgetown, Great
        Exuma, B. W. I.   12 x 18   NYGS   4. 00
7889.   Golden Harvest c.   20 x 24   PENN   1. 50
7890.   Lattice Bridge c. 20 x 24   PENN   1. 50
7891.   Lighthouse Cove c. 20 x 24   PENN   1. 50
MUSCHA
7892.   Gandria   20 x 27-1/2   ESH   Pr. 8. 00
MUSIC, ANTONIO ZORAN (Austrian [Res. France] 1909-)
7893.   Suite Byzantine   23-1/2x28-1/2   NYGS   15. 00
MUTI, RUTILIO
7894.   Panorama Mugello   20 x 30   AS   15. 00
MYERS, FRANK H. (American, 1899-)
7895.   Early Moonlight   24 x 30   IA   10. 00

N

NANTEUIL, ROBERT (French, 1623-1678)
7896.   Portrait of Louis
        XIV   14 x 11-1/2   AS   3. 25
NASH, JOHN H.
7897.   Cornfield   19 x 21   ESH   15. 00
7898.   Duckpond   17 x 21-1/2   ESH   15. 00
7899.   Road to the Farm   15-1/2 x 21   ESH   15. 00
7900.   Window in Bucks   21-1/2 x 18   ESH   15. 00
NASH, PAUL (English, 1889-1946)
7901.   Aylesbury Plain   19 x 24   CAC   10. 00
7902.   Pond in the Field   20 x 28   CFA   12. 00
7903.   Sussex Landscape   15 x 21   AP   5. 00
7904.   Threshing   c. 7 x 9   AP   . 50
7905.   Wood on the Downs   16-1/2 x 21   ESH   15. 00
NASMYTH, ALEXANDER (Scotch, 1758-1840)
7906.   England's Capital   9-1/2 x 13   ESH   2. 00
NATOIRE, CHARLES JOSEPH (French, 1700-1777)
7907.   Girl with Tambourine
                            11 x 8   AR   3. 50
NATTIER, JEAN MARC (French, 1685-1766)
7908.   Anne Henriette   11 x 15   IA   3. 00
                            8 x 11   IA   1. 75
7909.   Infanta Isabella of
        Parma   10-1/2 x 8   ESH   1. 00
7910.   Mme. De Caumartin
        as Hebe   28 x 22   NYGS   16. 00
7911.   Mme. Louise de
        France   22-1/2x17-1/2   ESH   10. 00
                            10-1/2 x 8   ESH   1. 00
7912.   Mme. Sophie de
        France   30 x 24   IA   12. 00

			20 x 16	IA	6.00
			14 x 11	IA	3.00
			10 x 8	NYGS	.50
7913.	Mme. Victoire de				
	France		20 x 16	IA	6.00
			14 x 11	IA	3.00
7914.	Marie Adelaide,				
	Daughter of Louis				
	XV		11 x 15	IA	3.00
			8 x 11	IA	1.75
			8 x 10	NYGS	.50
7915.	Marie Zepherine,				
	Daughter of Louis				
	XV		12 x 15	IA	3.00
			11 x 14-1/2	AS	3.25
7916.	Portrait de Jeune				
	Femme		9 x 8	CFA	6.00
7917.	Princess Mary Anne		11 x 15	CFA	3.00
7918.	Princess Mary				
	Louise		11 x 15	AS	3.25

NAUJOK, CURT (German, 1898-1927)
| 7919. | St. Cecelia | 10 x 7-1/2 | IA | Gr. 10.00 |
| | | 9 x 7 | CAC | 5.00 |

NAVIASKY, PHILIP (English, 1894-)
| 7920. | Market Day in | | | |
| | Toledo | 18 x 22 | NYGS | 7.50 |

NAY, ERNST WILHELM (German Contemporary)
7921.	Blue Umber	17 x 24	NYGS	20.00
7922.	Ecsatic Blue	31 x 22	NYGS	20.00
7923.	Green Planes	21 x 33-1/2	NYGS	20.00
7924.	Green Slices	21 x 33	CFA	18.00
7925.	Motion	33-1/2 x 25	NYGS	28.00
7926.	Red and Blue	31-1/2 x 24	NYGS	20.00
7927.	Yellow Vermilion	16-1/2x23-1/2	NYGS	20.00

NEER, AERT VAN DER (Dutch, 1604-1677)
7928.	Skating on the			
	Dike	c. 20 x 24	PENN	1.50
7929.	Winter Landscape	11 x 12	IA	3.00

NEGRETE, EZEQUIEL (Mexican Contemporary)
| 7930. | Labor in the Fields | 7 x 9 | AP | .60 |

NEGRETTI, JACOPO See PALMA IL VECCHIO

NELSON, GEORGE LAURENCE (American, 1887-)
7931.	Delft Bowl	16 x 20	CAC	35.00
7932.	Oriental Splendor	24 x 30	CAC	7.50
7933.	Purple Symphony	20 x 16	CAC	3.50

NERFIN
| 7934. | Promenade No. 1 and | | | |
| | No. 2 | 20 x 48 | AK | ea. 10.00 |

NERI DI BICCI (Italian, 1419-1491)
| 7935. | Virgin Adoring the | | | |
| | Child | 11 x 13 | IA | 3.00 |

NEROCCIO DI BARTOLOMMEO LANDI (Italian, 1447-1500)
| 7936. | Madonna and Child | 16 x 8 | IA | 3.00 |

7937.	St. Catherine of Siena	15 x 11	AS	3.25
7938.	St. Michael	15-1/2 x 5	AS	3.25
7939.	Virgin and Child	14-1/2 x 11	AS	3.25

NEUBERT

7940.	Sailing Boats at the Harbor	16 x 25	AP	5.00

NEVILLE

7941.	Long Crendon	16 x 20	CAC	4.00
7942.	Polperro	16 x 20	CAC	4.00
7943.	Wickham	12 x 16	CAC	2.00
7944.	Wiltshire Lane	12 x 16	CAC	2.00

NEVINSON, CHRISTOPHER RICHARD (Austrian [Res. England] 1889-)

7945.	After the Storm	18 x 23	ESH	10.00
7946.	Hark, Hark, the Lark	16 x 20	ESH	12.00
7947.	Spring in Suffolk	17-1/2 x 22	ESH	15.00

NEWELL, J. P. (American, Ac. 1858-1866)

7948.	Newport, Rhode Island in 1730)	14 x 22	NYGS	18.00

NEWTON, ALGERNON H. (English, 1881-)

7949.	Whispering Breeze	18-1/2 x 28	RL	10.00

NEWTON, PARKER (American, d. 1928)

7950.	Still Life with Violin	18 x 24-1/2	ESH	10.00

NGUYEN-DUC-NUNG (Chinese Contemporary)

7951.	Dawn	13 x 20	AP	5.00

NGUYEN-VAN-BINH (Chinese Contemporary)

7952.	Bamboo	12-1/2x19-1/2	AP	5.00

NICHOLS, DALE (American, 1904-)

7953.	Company for Supper	27 x 36	NYGS	15.00
		19-1/2 x 26	NYGS	10.00
		6 x 8	NYGS	.50
7954.	End of the Hunt	19-1/2 x 26	NYGS	10.00
7955.	Evening in the Country	20 x 26	NYGS	10.00
7956.	Grains of Wheat	6 x 10	NYGS	.50
7957.	Summer's Bounty	20 x 26	NYGS	10.00

NICHOLSON, BEN (English, 1894-)

7958.	Argolis 1959	24 x 45	NYGS	24.00
7959.	March 14 - 47 (Still Life on a Table)	21 x 22-1/2	NYGS	12.00

NICHOLSON, JOHN M. (English, 1901-)

7960.	In Old England	26 x 36	CFA	15.00
7961.	Pebble	9 x 7	NYGS	7.50
7962.	St. Ives Rooftops	18 x 27	NYGS	18.00

NICHOLSON, WINIFRED ROBERTS (English Contemporary)

7963.	Crete	c. 18 x 23	HNA	5.95
7964.	Flowers in a Jug	21 x 15	CFA	10.00

NICO, S.

7965.	Juveniles (4)	10 x 8	DAC	ea. 1.25

NICOL, FRANCOIS PAUL (French, 1879-)
7966.	Bambina	18 x 15	IA	6. 00
7967.	Lapland Boy	18 x 15	IA	6. 00
7968.	Mimosa	20 x 16-1/2	IA	10. 00
7969.	Serenata	18 x 15	IA	6. 00
7970.	Sorrentina	26-1/2x20-1/2	IA	15. 00

NICZKY, EDVARD (German, 1850-1919)
| 7971. | Path in Forest | 26 x 20 | AK | 7. 50 |

NIGG, JOSEPH (Austrian, 1782-1885)
7972.	Floral and Fruit	26 x 21	CAC	20. 00
7973.	Floral and Fruit (4)	25 x 20	CAC	ea. 20. 00
7974.	Floral and Fruit	24 x 19	CAC	20. 00
7975.	Flowers in a Land-scape	21 x 15-1/2	NYGS	7. 50
7976.	Flowers on a Marble Table	21 x 15-1/2	NYGS	7. 50
7977.	Grandmother's Bouquet (2)	21 x 15-1/2	AJ	ea. 7. 50

NIKKELIN, J. M. VAN (Dutch, 1690-)
| 7978. | June Blossoms | 20 x 16 | NYGS | 7. 50 |

NIKOLSKY, A. L.
| 7979. | Autumn Harmony | 22-1/2x29-1/2 | AS | 7. 50 |

NINNES, BERNARD TREVORROW (English, 1899-)
| 7980. | Summer Seas | 18 x 22 | ESH | 10. 00 |

NINO
| 7981. | La Dore | 12 x 16 | CAC | 2. 00 |
| 7982. | Lallier | 12 x 16 | CAC | 2. 00 |

NISHIMOURA, KEOU
| 7983. | Plage au Portugal | 20 x 32 | AS | 15. 00 |

NIVEN, MARGARET (English Contemporary)
7984.	Flowers (4)	22 x 18	ESH	ea. 12. 00
7985.	April Flowers			
7986.	Autumn Flowers			
7987.	Garden Flowers			
7988.	Summer Flowers			

NIVERT, GEORGETTE (French Contemporary)
7989.	Bridesmaid	24 x 20	RL	7. 50
7990.	Consolation	20 x 17	RL	6. 00
7991.	Innocence	20 x 17	RL	6. 00
7992.	Philomena	24 x 20	RL	7. 50

NOBLE, JAMES CAMPBELL (Scoth, 1846-1913)
| 7993. | Still Life, Flowers and Fruit | 16 x 30 | ESH | 15. 00 |
| 7994. | Still Life with Wine and Fruit | 16 x 30 | ESH | 18. 00 |

NOCKOLDS, ROY
| 7995. | Rolls-Royce | 16 x 19-1/2 | ESH | 6. 00 |

NOIREAUT, L.
| 7996. | Humorist | 12 x 9 | CFA | 1. 50 |
| 7997. | Old Salt | 12 x 9 | CFA | 1. 50 |

NOKINA KAIOKU (Japanese, 1798-1863)
| 7998. | Wintry Landscape | 24 x 10-1/2 | IA | 12. 00 |

NOLAN
7999.	Floating Flowers	25 x 20	NYGS		18. 00
8000.	Humming Bird and Vine	25 x 20-1/2	NYGS		18. 00

NOLDE, EMIL (German, 1867-1956)
8001.	Heavy Seas at Sunset	13-1/2 x 18	NYGS		10. 00

NOORDT, VAN
8002.	Girl with a Pigeon	12 x 9	ESH		3. 00

NORO KAISEKI (Japanese, 1747-1828)
8003.	Summer Landscape	24 x 10-1/2	IA		12. 00

NORWAY
8004.	UWA Series (32)	11 x 14 or 14 x 11	NYGS	ea.	2. 00

NOTTI, GHERARDO DELLE (Dutch, 1590-1656)
8005.	Young Man with the Bat	14 x 11	AS		3. 25

NOURSE, ELIZABETH (American, 1859-1938)
8006.	Mother and Children	20 x 13	CAC		7. 50

NOVELLI, PIETRO (IL MONREALESE) (Italian, 1603-1644)
8007.	Portrait of a Child	15 x 11	IA		3. 00

NOWAK, HEINZ (German)
8008.	Red Bridge	13 x 35-1/2	CFA		18. 00
8009.	Repose	27-1/2 x 23	CFA		15. 00

NUVOLONE, CARLO FRANCESCO (Italian, 1608-1661)
8010.	Virgin and Child	c. 7 x 9	AP		. 50

O

OBSTNER, J.
8011.	Orange Girl	20 x 16	ESH	Pr.	5. 00

OCHTERVELT, JACOBUS (Dutch, 1635-1709)
8012.	Music Lesson	25 x 20	NYGS	18. 00
8013.	Music Party	23 x 18	NYGS	16. 00
8014.	Musicians	30 x 24	CFA	18. 00
		25 x 20	NYGS	12. 00
		24 x 20	DAC	7. 50
		16 x 12	DAC	2. 50

O'CONNELL, DAVID
8015.	Christ the Comforter	23 x 18	AS	12. 00
8016.	Last Supper	18-1/2 x 24	ESH	10. 00
8017.	Our Lady of Walsingham	21 x 21	ESH	10. 00
8018.	Sacred Heart of Jesus	19-1/2 x 15	IA	8. 50
8019.	Sacred Heart of Mary	19-1/2 x 15	IA	8. 50
8020.	The Saviour	24 x 18-1/2	ESH	12. 00
8021.	Transfiguration	21 x 21	ESH	10. 00

O'CONNOR, JOHN (English Contemporary)
8022.	Lake in Autumn	19 x 26	RL	10. 00

OERDER, FRANS (Dutch, 1876-)
8023.	Blossom Time	28 x 34	NYGS	12. 00
		17 x 20-1/2	NYGS	5. 00
8024.	Magnolias	28 x 34	NYGS	12. 00
		25-1/2 x 32	NYGS	10. 00
		17 x 20-1/2	NYGS	5. 00

OGDEN
8025.	Silvery Night	24 x 29	CAC	6. 00
		16 x 20	CAC	3. 00
8026.	Winter Silence	24 x 29	CAC	6. 00
		16 x 20	CAC	3. 00

O'GORMAN
8027.	Self-Portrait	c.	9 x 7	AP	. 60

OGURI SOTAN (Japanese, 15th Century)
8028.	Spring Landscape	24 x 10-1/2	IA	12. 00

O'HIGGINS
8029.	Man of the Twentieth				
	Century	c.	9 x 7	AP	. 60

OKADA, KENZO (Japanese Contemporary)
8030.	Eventails	22 x 27-1/2	NYGS	15. 00

OKAMURA, ARTHUR (American Contemporary)
8031.	Stray Cur, Eucalyptus			
	Grove, 1961	25 x 40	NYGS	20. 00

O'KEEFFE, GEORGIA (American, 1887-)
8032.	Autumn Leaves	20 x 15-1/2	NYGS	9. 00
8033.	Black Iris c.	8 x 10	NYGS	. 50
8034.	Pelvis with Distance c.	8 x 10	MMA	. 35
8035.	Ram's Head with			
	Hollyhock and Little			
	Hills	25 x 30	NYGS	18. 00
8036.	White Canadian Barn			
	No. 2, 1932	12 x 30	NYGS	15. 00
8037.	White Flower	25 x 30	NYGS	18. 00

OLA
8038.	Swiss Guard (2)	40 x 20	DAC	ea.	15. 00
		20 x 10	DAC	ea.	3. 50

OLSSON, JULIUS (English, d. 1942)
8039.	Off the Western Land	19 x 25	CAC	5. 00

OLSZEWSKI, KARL EWALD (Austrian, 1884-)
8040.	Coming Storm	16 x 22	CFA	7. 50
8041.	Flying Swans	22 x 31	CFA	15. 00
8042.	Geese Before the			
	Storm	25 x 35-1/2	NYGS	16. 00
8043.	Sea Gulls	22 x 30	CFA	12. 00

OOMELING, F.
8044.	Wedding Feast in			
	Holland	22 x 31	CAC	7. 50

OPPER, E. (American, 1880-)
8045.	Fire Engine	23 x 30-1/2	NYGS	15. 00
		11 x 14	NYGS	3. 00
		5-1/2x7-1/2	NYGS	1. 00

ORLANDINI, ORLANDO PALADINO (Italian, 1905-)
8046.	Chrysanthemums	20 x 25	CFA		10. 00

OROVIDA (Miss Orovida Camille Pissarro) English, 1893-)
8047.	Man and Beast	22 x 19	ESH		15. 00

OROZCO, JOSE CLEMENTE (Mexican, 1883-1949)
8048.	Cabaret	c.	20 x 24	PENN		1. 50
8049.	Hispano-American					
	Mural		8 x 8	NYGS		. 50
8050.	Mexican Pueblo		20 x 24-1/2	NYGS		12. 00
8051.	Sutlers	c.	7 x 9	AP		. 60
8052.	Zapatistas		24-1/2x30	NYGS		18. 00
			6 x 7-1/2	NYGS		. 50

ORTLIP
8053.	Golden Age	c.	7 x 9	AP		. 50

OS, GEORGIUS J. VAN (Dutch, 1782-1861)
8054.	Bouquet with Crown				
	Imperials	31-1/2 x 22	ESH		15. 00
		10-1/2 x 8	ESH		1. 00
8055.	Vase of Mixed				
	Flowers	13 x 10	ESH		2. 00

OSTADE, ADRIAEN VAN (Dutch, 1610-1685)
8056.	Backgammon Players	9 x 7-1/2	AR		3. 50
8057.	Les Buveurs	8 x 9-1/2	NYGS		4. 00
8058.	Country Inn	21-1/2 x 16	NYGS		12. 00
8059.	Dutch Tavern	9 x 7-1/2	AR		3. 50

OSTHAUS, EDMUND HENRY (American, 1858-1928)
8060.	Hunting Dogs (4)	12 x 18	AK	ea.	2. 50
		6 x 9	AK	ea.	1. 00
8061.	In Action	20 x 26	IA		7. 50

OSWALD, CARLOS (Italian-Brazilian, 1882-)
8062.	Last Supper	16-1/2x28-1/2	IA		8. 00
		11-1/2 x 20	IA		4. 50
8063.	Sacred Heart of				
	Jesus	23 x 17	IA		6. 00
		18 x 13	IA		4. 50

OTTEMA
8064.	Blossom Time	24 x 30	CAC		10. 00
8065.	Summer Idyl	22 x 18	CAC		6. 00

OTTER, THOMAS P. (American, Ac. 1860)
8066.	On the Road	24 x 48	AK		12. 00
		12 x 24	AK		3. 00

OUDOT, ROLLAND (French [Res. U. S.] 1897-)
8067.	Church of Magagnose	12 x 17	CAC		6. 00
8068.	Folies Bergeres				
		c.	22 x 17-1/2	AS		4. 00
8069.	Gladiolus	23 x 17	CFA		10. 00
8070.	Harvest	21 x 29	CAC		12. 00
8071.	Route de Provence	16-1/2 x 22	NYGS		18. 00
8072.	Village near Houdan	10 x 16	CFA		5. 00

OUDRY, JEAN BAPTISTE (French, 1686-1755)
8073.	Macaw	c.	10 x 8	ESH		1. 00

OUTIN, PIERRE (French, 1840-1899)
8074.	The Toast	28 x 23	NYGS		12. 00

OWENS, CHARLES (American Contemporary)
8075.	Custom House	7 x 10	CFA	6.00
8076.	Gravesend	7 x 10	CFA	6.00
8077.	Sheerness	7 x 10	CFA	6.00

OXTOBY, DAVID (English Contemporary)
| 8078. | The Ray | 28 x 28 | RL | 10.00 |

P

PACCHIA, GIROLAMO DEL (Italian, 1477-1535)
| 8079. | Madonna and Child with St. John | 12" Diam. | IA | 3.00 |

PACH, WALTER (American, 1883-)
8080.	Musicians (B&W) (9)	12 x 9	CFA	ea. 2.50
8081.	Bach			
8082.	Beethoven			
8083.	Brahms			
8084.	Haydn			
8085.	Liszt			
8086.	Mozart			
8087.	Schubert			
8088.	Wagner			
8089.	Weber			

PACHECO, FRANCISCO (Spanish, 1571-1654)
| 8090. | Water Carriers c. | 7 x 9 | AP | .60 |

PADOVANINO, IL (ALESSANDRO VAROTARI) (Italian, 1580-1650)
| 8091. | Portrait of a Woman | 14 x 11 | IA | 3.00 |

PADUA, PAUL MATHIAS (German-Austrian, 1903-)
8092.	Before the Mirror	19 x 15	ESH	7.50
8093.	Brother and Sister	17 x 13	ESH	6.00
8094.	Flowers on White	19 x 23	CFA	12.00
8095.	Hollywood Swing	27 x 22	IA	12.00
8096.	Lady in Front of a Mirror	23 x 17	CFA	10.00
8097.	Love Letter	28 x 24	CFA	15.00
8098.	Old Farmer	10-1/2 x 8	ESH	4.00
8099.	Reading Lady	22 x 18	CFA	10.00
8100.	Sunshine Lady	22-1/2 x 17	IA	10.00

PAGHOLO, BARTOLOMMEO DI See (FRA) BARTOLOMMEO, KNOWN AS BACCIO DELLA PORTA

PAILES, ISSAAK (Russian-French, 1895-)
| 8101. | Nature Morte | 16 x 20 | PENN | 1.50 |

PAILLAVA
| 8102. | Floral Panels (4) | 42 x 10 | DAC | ea. 5.00 |
| | | 21 x 5 | DAC | ea. 1.75 |

PALIZZI, GIUSEPPE (Italian, 1812-1888)
| 8103. | Asinello | 12 x 9 | CFA | 5.00 |
| 8104. | Friars and Peasants (2) | 10 x 15 | IA | ea. 3.00 |

8105.   Vitellini Bianchi   15 x 20-1/2   CFA   12.00
PALLAS, REINHOLD (German, 1901-   )
8106.   Terrace on the
        Riviera   25-1/2x31-1/2   ESH   15.00
PALMA IL VECCHIO (PALMA, JACOPO OR GIACOMO) (Italian,
1480-1528)
8107.   Christ on the Mount
        of Olives   11 x 8   AR   3.00
8108.   Holy Conversation   9-1/2 x 15   AS   3.25
8109.   St. Barbara   15 x 7   IA   3.00
PALMEIRO, JOSE (Spanish [Res. France] Contemporary)
8110.   Little Harbour   19 x 26   RL   10.00
8111.   El Puerto del Mar   25 x 36   RL   20.00
PALMER, ROD
8112.   Bright Cloud   9 x 12   NYGS   15.00
PALMERO, A.
8113.   Horses of the Night   18 x 36   RL   12.50
PALUÉ, PIERRE (French Contemporary)
8114.   Approaching Twilight,
        Arcachon   22 x 30   NYGS   12.00
8115.   Barque Orange a la
        Teste   18 x 24   DAC   12.50
8116.   Coastline at
        Arcachon   22 x 30   NYGS   12.00
8117.   Filets a Aquillon   18 x 24   DAC   12.50
8118.   Port d'Eyrac   18 x 24   DAC   12.50
8119.   Red Boat   18 x 36   NYGS   16.00
8120.   Yellow Boat   18 x 36   NYGS   16.00
PAN, ARTHUR (Hungarian [Res. England] Contemporary)
8121.   H.M. the Queen in
        Coronation Robes   26 x 18   RL   12.50
PANET, ANDRÉ
8122.   Souvenir de Paris   16 x 36   NYGS   15.00
PANINI, GIOVANNI PAOLO (Italian, 1691-1764)
8123.   Antique Roman
        Architecture (2)   19 x 15   CFA   ea. 18.00
8124.   Interior of St.
        Peters   9 x 14   CFA   1.50
8125.   Marcus Aurelius   33-1/2x26-1/2   AL   18.00
8126.   Piazza del Quirinale 26 x 25   CFA   18.00
8127.   Piazza di S. Maria
        Maggiore   26 x 25   CFA   18.00
8128.   Roman Ruins   11 x 15   IA   3.00
8129.   Roman Ruins   14-1/2 x 11   AS   3.25
8130.   Roman Ruins (2)   15 x 11   AS   ea. 3.25
8131.   Roman Ruins (2)   27 x 19-Oval   AS   ea. 7.50
8132.   Roman Ruins (2)   27 x 20   CFA   ea. 10.00
8133.   View of the Roman
        Forum, 1747   24-1/2 x 40   NYGS   20.00
PAOLO, GIOVANNI See GIOVANNI DE PAOLO
PAPA IBRA TALL (Senegalese Contemporary)
8134.   Wonders of the
        Brush   19 x 13   UNICEF   10.00

PARADISE, PHIL (American Contemporary)
8135.	Beach at Cortez	6-1/2 x 10	AR	1.00
8136.	Fisher Folk at			
	Guayamas	6-1/2 x 10	AR	1.00
8137.	Flower Vendor	20 x 13	AR	6.00
		10 x 6-1/2	AR	1.00
8138.	Maria	20 x 12	AR	6.00
		10 x 6	AR	1.00
8139.	Marimba Players	18 x 25	AR	10.00
		18 x 24	AP	10.00
	c.	7 x 9	AP	.50
8140.	Sunday Morning	20 x 13	AR	6.00
		10 x 6-1/2	AR	1.00
8141.	Tomas	20 x 12	AR	6.00
		10 x 6	AR	1.00

PAREDES, JOSÉ M. DE (Mexican [Res. U. S.] Contemporary)
| 8142. | Royal Visitors in | | | |
| | Watteau's Studio | 20 x 30 | CFA | 30.00 |

PARIZOT, L.
8143.	Notre Dame (B & W)	8 x 12	CFA	5.00
8144.	Le Quai de Tournelle			
	(B & W)	8 x 12	CFA	5.00

PARK, JOHN ANTHONY (English, 1880-)
| 8145. | Church in the | | | |
| | Fields | 17 x 21 | CAC | 7.50 |

PARKINSON, G.
| 8146. | Fishing Port, | | | |
| | Evening | 20 x 40 | AS | 15.00 |

PARMIGIANINO, IL (MAZZOLA, FRANCESCO) (Italian, 1503-1540)
8147.	Marriage of St.			
	Catherine	9 x 15	IA	3.00
8148.	Portrait of a Woman			
	Called "The Fair"	15 x 9	IA	3.00

PARRI DI SPINELLO ARETINO (Italian, 1387-1453)
| 8149. | Virgin of the | | | |
| | Misericordia | 11 x 11 | IA | 3.00 |

PARRISH, MAXFIELD (American, 1870-1965)
8150.	Canyon	15 x 12	NYGS	2.00
8151.	Daybreak	18 x 30	NYGS	12.00
		10 x 18	CAC	6.00
		6 x 10	NYGS	1.00
8152.	Dreaming	18 x 30	CAC	12.00
		10 x 18	CAC	6.00
8153.	Evening	15 x 12	CAC	2.00
8154.	Garden of Allah	9 x 18	NYGS	6.00
8155.	Hilltop	30 x 18	CAC	12.00
		20 x 12	CAC	6.00
		10 x 6	NYGS	1.00
8156.	Lute Players	18 x 30	CAC	12.00
		10 x 18	CAC	6.00
		12 x 15	CAC	2.00
		6 x 10	CAC	1.00

8157.	Morning	15 x 12	CAC	2.00
		10 x 6	CAC	1.00
8158.	Page	12 x 10	NYGS	2.00
8159.	Prince	12 x 9	CAC	2.00
8160.	Quiet Solitude	17 x 14	AK	4.00
		12 x 9	AK	2.00
8161.	Reveries	16 x 12	CAC	2.00
8162.	Romance	14 x 23	CAC	8.00
8163.	Rubaiyat	8 x 30	CAC	9.00
8164.	Sheltering Oaks	17 x 14	AK	4.00
		12 x 9	AK	2.00
8165.	Stars	30 x 18-1/2	NYGS	12.00
		20 x 12	NYGS	6.00
8166.	Tranquility	29-1/2 x 24	NYGS	12.00
		16-1/2x13-1/2	NYGS	6.00
		11-1/2 x 9	NYGS	2.00
8167.	Twilight	22-1/2 x 18	NYGS	12.00
		17 x 14	AK	4.00
		12 x 9	AK	2.00
8168.	Under Summer Skies	17 x 14	AK	4.00
		12 x 9	AK	2.00
8169.	White Birch	11 x9	NYGS	2.00
8170.	Wild Geese	15 x 12	NYGS	2.00

PARSONS, ALFRED (English, 1847-1920)

| 8171. | Bredon-on-the-Avon | 24 x 36 | NYGS | 15.00 |
| | | 16 x 24 | NYGS | 10.00 |

PARTIKEL, ALFRED (German, 1888-1946)

| 8172. | In the Valley | 26 x 35 | CFA | 15.00 |

PASCIN, JULES (American, 1885-1930)

| 8173. | Woman in Red | 24 x 20 | PENN | 1.50 |

PASKIN, JOSHUA

| 8174. | Flower Sprays (2) | 24 x 18 | DAC | ea. 12.50 |
| | (2) | 18 x 24 | DAC | ea. 12.50 |

PASMORE, VICTOR (English, 1908-)

| 8175. | Quiet River | 15 x 20 | AP | 6.00 |

PATENIER (OR PATINIR), JOACHIM (Flemish, 1480-1524)

8176.	Flight into Egypt c.	18 x 23	HNA	5.95
8177.	Rest on the Flight into Egypt (Detail)	31-1/2x18-1/2	ESH	15.00
8178.	St. Jerome in a Rocky Landscape	14 x 13	CFA	4.00

PATER, JEAN BAPTISTE JOSEPH (French, 1695-1736)

8179.	Arlequin et Pierrot	9 x 12	IA	Gr. 10.00
8180.	Blind Man's Buff	20 x 25-1/2	NYGS	12.00
8181.	Dance	25 x 34	NYGS	18.00
8182.	La Danse	12 x 10	IA	Gr. 10.00
8183.	L'Escarpolette	12 x 10	IA	10.00
8184.	Fete Champetre	9 x 12	IA	Gr. 10.00
		9 x 11	CFA	2.00
8185.	Meeting in a Park	11 x 13	IA	3.00

8186.	Meeting Outside a			
	Park	16-1/2 x 20	IA	10.00
8187.	Toilette	13 x 11	IA	3.00

PATINIR See PATENIER
PATRICK, JOHN DOUGLAS (American, 1863-)

| 8188. | Der Clown | 23-1/2 x 16 | ESH | 6.00 |

PATRICK, JAMES MC INTOSH (Scotch, 1907-)

8189.	Autumn Idyll	27 x 36	NYGS	16.00
8190.	Autumn in Kinnordy	16 x 22	CFA	10.00
8191.	Farm in Angus	16 x 22	CFA	10.00
8192.	Late Summer in			
	Scotland	19 x 27	NYGS	12.00
8193.	Spring in Eskadale	16 x 24	NYGS	7.50
8194.	Summer in Angus	16 x 22	NYGS	7.50
8195.	Winter in Angus	16-1/2 x 22	NYGS	7.50
	c.	7 x 9	AP	.25

PAUL, RICHARD (American, 1775-1830)

| 8196. | Old Surrey | 22 x 30 | AA | 10.00 |

PAULI, FRITZ (Swiss, 1891-)

| 8197. | Barbara | 24 x 19 | CFA | 10.00 |

PEALE, JAMES (American, 1749-1831)

| 8198. | Fruit | 17 x 27 | NYGS | 12.00 |
| | | 9 x 14 | NYGS | 4.00 |

PEALE, REMBRANDT (American, 1778-1860)

8199.	Thomas Jefferson	18 x 15	NYGS	5.00
		17 x 14	IA	7.50
		9 x 7-1/2	NYGS	1.50

PEARSON, MARGUERITE S. (English, 1898-)

8200.	Allegro	25 x 30	AA	10.00
		10 x 12	AA	2.00
8201.	At the Melodeon	25 x 30	AA	10.00
		10 x 12	AA	2.00
8202.	Blue Danube	25 x 30	AA	10.00
		10 x 12	AA	2.00
8203.	Blue Kimono	25 x 30	AA	10.00
8204.	Canterbury Bells	20 x 24	AA	5.00
8205.	Hostess	28 x 23-1/2	AA	7.50
8206.	The Letter	26 x 22	AA	7.50
8207.	Moment Musicale	25 x 30	AA	10.00
		10 x 12	AA	2.00
8208.	Song	24 x 28	AA	7.50
8209.	Zinnias	20 x 24	AA	5.00

PECHAUBES, EUGENE (French, 1890-)

8210.	The Chase	15 x 30	DAC	5.00
8211.	Fox Hunt	12 x 16	DAC	2.50
8212.	Military Horsemen,			
	French (6)	9-1/2x8-1/2	IA	ea. 5.00
	First Empire:			
	Carabineer			
	Imperial Guards, Officer			
	of Artillery			
	Imperial Guards, Officer			
	of Cuirasseers			

Second Empire: Hussar
Imperial Guards, Officer
of Cuirasseers
Imperial Guards, Officer
of Fifth Hussars

8213.	Start	12 x 16	DAC	2.50

PECHSTEIN, MAX (German, 1881-1955)

8214.	Blossoming Tree by the River	19 x 23-1/2	NYGS	12.00
8215.	Boat at Sunrise c.	18 x 23	HNA	5.95
		17 x 19-1/2	NYGS	6.00
8216.	Boats on Beach	25 x 29	CFA	18.00
8217.	Fisherman	18 x 22	CFA	15.00
8218.	Lupow Estuary	14 x 23	NYGS	6.00
8219.	Rising Sun	23-1/2x29-1/2	NYGS	20.00
8220.	Stormy Ocean	23 x 27-1/2	ESH	10.00
8221.	Sun on Baltic Beach	22 x 27-1/2	NYGS	15.00
	c.	18 x 23	HNA	5.95

PEDERSEN, CARL-HENNING (Danish Contemporary)

8222.	Blue Birds, 1962	31-1/2x26-1/2	NYGS	15.00

PEDRO, LUIS MARTINEZ (Cuban Contemporary)

8223.	Espacio Azul	25 x 30	NYGS	15.00

PEEL

8224.	Cottage in Surrey	22 x 26	AA	10.00
8225.	Country Lane	22 x 26	AA	10.00

PEIFFER

8226.	Tropical Fruits	12 x 19	NYGS	18.00

PEINER, WERNER (German, 1897-)

8227.	Good Earth	21 x 35-1/2	NYGS	15.00

PELAEZ

8228.	Still Life c.	7 x 9	AP	.25

PELHAM, GENE (American Contemporary)

8229.	Colonial Americana (4)	12 x 17	AK	ea. 5.00
8230.	Bennington Station	6 x 9	AK	ea. 2.00
8231.	Cambridge Station			
8232.	Dover Valley			
8233.	Pawlet Spring Country Scenes (6)	11 x 14	NYGS	ea. 3.00
8234.	Covered Bridge	6 x 7-1/2	NYGS	ea. 1.00
8235.	Green Pastures			
8236.	Hillside Stream			
8237.	Twin Pines			
8238.	Wayside Barn			
8239.	Willow Pond			
8240.	No. 1, 1967	36 x 33	NYGS	18.00
8241.	Peaceful Waters	25 x 31	NYGS	10.00
		17 x 21	NYGS	7.50
		9 x 12	NYGS	1.50
8242.	Rolling Hills	24 x 36	NYGS	12.00

		17 x 21	NYGS		7.50
		9 x 12	NYGS		1.50
8243.	Sunny Valley	24 x 36	NYGS		12.00
		17 x 21	NYGS		7.50
8244.	Valley Stream	24 x 36	NYGS		12.00
		17 x 21	NYGS		7.50

PELLERANO, JOHN (American Contemporary)
8245. Jazz Performers
       (8)   18 x 12   IA   ea. 2.50
8246.   Baritone Sax
8247.   Drummer
8248.   Guitarist
8249.   On the Vibes
8250.   Playing the Slush Pump
8251.   Rhythm Man
8252.   Sax Man
8253.   Swing Clarinet

PEMBERTON-LONGMAN, JOANNE
8254. Sea Holly   AS   5.00
8255. Secret   24 x 20   AS   15.00
8256. The Towans   AS   5.00

PENNACCHI, PIER MARIA (Italian, 1464-1514)
8257. Annunciation   11 x 10   IA   3.00

PERCY, SIDNEY
8258. Gypsy Encampment   24-1/2 x 39   AA   12.00
8259. Lake Country   24 x 36   IA   12.00

PEREIRA, IRENE RICE (American Contemporary)
8260. Myths (4) (B & W)   12 x 16   AR   ea. 2.50
8261. Oblique Progression
                          c.   7 x 9   AP   .50
8262. Spring Twelve
       O'Clock   c.   8 x 10   NYGS   .50

PERFALL, ERICH VON (German, 1881-)
8263. Freight Ships on
       River   21 x 27-1/2   ESH   10.00
8264. March on Lower
       Rhine   21 x 28   ESH   10.00

PERI, LUCIEN (English, 1880-1949)
8265. Italian Landscape   20 x 12   ESH   Pr. 4.00
8266. Madonna della
       Serra   15 x 22   CFA   10.00
                                7 x 10   CFA   1.00
8267. San Cipriano,
       Corsica   18-1/2 x 25   RL   7.50
8268. Still Waters   18-1/2 x 25   RL   7.50

PERREAL, JEAN (MASTER OF MOULINS) (French, 1445-1534)
8269. Portrait of a Woman 15 x 11-1/2   AS   3.25

PERRONNEAU, JEAN BAPTISTE (French, 1715-1783)
8270. Girl with a Kitten   22-1/2x18-1/2   NYGS   18.00
                                12 x 9   CFA   3.00
                          c.   10 x 8   ESH   1.00

PERRY, ENOCH W. , JR. (American, 1831-1915)
8271. The Pemigewasset
      Coach   22 x 36   NYGS   16. 00
PERSIAN MURALS
      Garden Scenes (4) 11 x 14   NYGS ea. 4. 00
8272.   Girl with a Drinking Cup
8273.   Lady in a Garden
8274.   Persian Games
8275.   Summer's Day
8276.   In a Garden   16 x 25   NYGS   12. 00
8277.   Poem   18 x 18   NYGS   7. 50
8278.   Resting under a
        Tree   18 x 18   NYGS   7. 50
8279.   Time for Recreation 16 x 25   NYGS   12. 00
PERTHUIS
8280.   Still Life (6)   15 x 6   DAC   ea. 1. 50
PERUGINO (PIETRO VANNUCCI) (Italian, 1445-1523)
8281.   Archangel Michael 22 x 10   ESH   12. 00
8282.   Baldassare Monaco 8 x 7   IA   1. 50
8283.   Crucifixion   8 x 15   IA   3. 00
        The Virgin and
        St. Bernard--
        Detail of No.
        8283   15 x 11   IA   3. 00
8284.   Crucifixion, Christ
        and the Magdalene 15 x 11   IA   3. 00
8285.   Crucifixion with the
        Virgin and St. John 24 x 13   NYGS   12. 00
8286.   Francesco delle
        Opere   13 x 11   IA   3. 00
8287.   Lamentation of
        Christ   9 x 7-1/2   AR   3. 00
8288.   Madonna   10 x 7   NYGS   . 50
8289.   Madonna and Angels 12 x 11   IA   3. 00
8290.   Madonna and Child 20 x 15   CFA   7. 50
8291.   Madonna and Child
        with Two Saints   20 x 15   NYGS   7. 50
8292.   Magdalene   15-1/2 x 11 AS   3. 25
8293.   Portrait of Baldasar,
        Monk Valombrosian 11 x 10-1/2 AS   3. 25
8294.   Portrait of Don Biagio
        Milanesi   15-1/2x10-1/2 AS   3. 25
8295.   Portrait of a Young
        Man   15 x 10-1/2 AS   3. 25
8296.   St. Mary Magdalene 15 x 11   IA   3. 00
8297.   St. Michel   15 x 11   IA   3. 00
8298.   The Virgin Adoring
        the Child   23 x 19   AS   7. 50
                           16 x 12   AS   3. 25
8299.   Virgin and Child
        Enthroned and Saints
        (Rome)   13-1/2x11-1/2 AS   3. 25
                           13 x 11   IA   3. 00

```
                The Virgin - Detail
                of No. 8299      15 x 11       IA        3. 00
8300.   Virgin with Child and
                Saints (Parigi)    11" Diam.    AS        3. 25
8301.   The Virgin (Head)   15-1/2 x 11    AS        3. 25
8302.   A Youth            15 x 10       IA        3. 00
PESARO,  SIMONE DA (CARTARINI, SIMONE) (Italian, 1612-1648)
8303.   Holy Family        15 x 11       IA        3. 00
PESELLINO,  FRANCESCO (Italian, 1422-1457)
8304.   Madonna and Child
                with St. John   c.   9 x 7        AP         . 50
8305.   Miracle of St.
                Anthony            9 x 15       IA        3. 00
PETER,  WENCESLAUS (OR WENZEL) (Austrian, 1742-1829)
8306.   Hungarian Countess  11 x 9            NYGS      1. 50
PETERSON,  ROGER TORY (American, 1908- )
8307.   Baltimore Butterfly  11 x 8-1/2       NWF       1. 00
8308.   Canada Geese       11 x 8-1/2       NWF       1. 00
PETO,  JOHN FREDERICK (American, 1854-1907)
8309.   Books of Learning   9 x 12       CFA        3. 00
8310.   Evening's Comfort   9 x 12       CFA        3. 00
8311.   Letter Rack        25 x 21       CFA       15. 00
                            c.   24 x 20       PENN       1. 50
8312.   Old Companions     23 x 31       NYGS      15. 00
                            11 x 14       NYGS       3. 00
8313.   Old Cremona    c.   18 x 23       HNA        5. 95
8314.   Poor Man's Store
                            c.   18 x 23       HNA        5. 95
PETRIE,  GRAHAM (English, 1859-
8315.   The Backs, Cambridge
                            11-1/2 x 14       ESH        2. 00
8316.   Lago Maggiore      11 x 15       ESH        2. 00
8317.   Market Place, Venice
                            12 x 14       ESH        2. 00
8318.   Rio Veneziano      11 x 15       ESH        2. 00
PETTENKOFEN,  AUGUST (Austrian, 1822-1889)
8319.   Children           10-1/2 x 12    NYGS      10. 00
PETTIE,  JOHN (Scotch, 1839-1893)
8320.   The Vigil      c.   7 x 9        AP         . 50
PETTIT,  W. S.
8321.   Now that April's
                Here            20 x 24       ESH       15. 00
PHELAN
8322.   The "Charles
                Morgan"         15 x 18       AA        10. 00
8323.   The "Rattlesnake"   15 x 18       AA        10. 00
8324.   Recipes (4)        12 x 9        AA    ea.   1. 50
PHIDIAS (Greek, B. C. 490-  )
8325.   Parthenon Rider     9 x 11       CFA        3. 50
PHILIPP,  ROBERT (American, 1895-  )
8326.   Cup of Chocolate   16 x 20       AR         6. 00
8327.   Girl at the Piano   25 x 30       CFA       15. 00
```

8328.	Girl in Blue	24 x 30	DAC	7.50
8329.	Rendezvous	16-1/2 x 21	IA	3.00

PHILIPP, WERNER (English Contemporary)

8330.	Shelter Cove Ranch	16-1/2 x 21	IA	3.00

PHILIPPE, W.

8331.	La Mer	20 x 24	CFA	15.00

PHILPOT, LEONARD D. (English, 1877-)

8332.	Orchids	20 x 15	CFA	7.50

PIAZZETTA, GIOVANNI BATTISTA (Italian, 1682-1754)

8333.	Country Girl	13 x 11	IA	3.00
8334.	Fortune-Teller	15 x 11	IA	3.00
8335.	Nude in the Sun			
	(DR.)	14-1/2x10-1/2	NYGS	3.00
8336.	St. John Nepomuceno	13-1/2 x 11	AS	3.25

PICABIA, FRANCIS (Spanish, 1878-1953)

8337.	Amorous Display	26 x 19	AR	10.00

PICART LE DOUX, CHARLES ALEXANDRE (French, 1881-)

8338.	L'Oiseau Lyre	26 x 19-1/2	NYGS	18.00

PICASSO, PABLO (RUIZ) (Spanish, 1881-)

8339.	Absinthe Drinker	27-1/2x20-1/2	IA	18.00
8340.	Abstract Harlequin			
	c.	12-1/2x9-1/2	AP	1.25
	c.	9 x 7	AP	1.00
8341.	Acrobat's Family	28 x 20	NYGS	12.00
8342.	L'Acrobate a la			
	Boule	24 x 15	NYGS	10.00
	(Acrobat on a			
	Ball)	20 x 12	PENN	1.50
8343.	Aficionado	9 x 5	CFA	1.00
8344.	Antique Bust	22 x 30	CFA	15.00
		6 x 8	CFA	1.00
8345.	Arlequin, 1917 c.	24 x 20	PENN	1.50
8346.	Arlequin c.	12-1/2x9-1/2	AP	1.25
	c.	10 x 8	CFA	1.00
8347.	Arlequin au Cafe	22-1/2x16-1/2	ESH	10.00
8348.	The Artist's Son	21 x 15	CFA	10.00
8349.	Artist's Son, Age			
	Three, as Harlequin			
	c.	22 x 17-1/2	AS	4.00
		21 x 15-1/2	NYGS	7.50
		16 x 12	PENN	1.00
		15-1/2x11-1/2	NYGS	3.00
	c.	12-1/2x9-1/2	AP	1.25
8350.	Attente, 1901 c.	24 x 20	PENN	1.50
8351.	Balcony	9 x 6	NYGS	.50
8352.	Ballerina c.	12-1/2x9-1/2	AP	1.25
		8 x 6	CFA	1.00
8353.	Bandilleros (B & W)	12 x 16-1/2	AA	6.00
8354.	Bathers, 1918 c.	12 x 16	PENN	1.00
8355.	Bay at Cannes	20 x 30	ESH	15.00
8356.	Before the Thrust	16 x 22	AP	10.00
8357.	Black Bust c.	12-1/2x9-1/2	AP	1.25
	c.	9 x 7	AP	1.00

8358.	Blue Boy, 1905	24 x 13	NYGS	12. 00
8359.	Blue Boy - Detail (Drawing) of No. 8358	14 x 11	NYGS	3. 00
8360.	Blue Nude	24 x 18	PENN	1. 50
		16 x 12	PENN	1. 00
8361.	Boats on Beach	5 x 7	NYGS	. 50
8362.	Bouquet	26 x 20	AR	6. 00
		23 x 15	AP	6. 00
8363.	Boy and Horse	24 x 16	PENN	1. 50
8364.	Boy in Red Harlequin Jacket	23 x 17	CAC	15. 00
8365.	Boy Leading a Horse	28 x 16-1/2	MMA	6. 50
8366.	Boy with Collar	16 x 12	PENN	1. 00
		7 x 5	CFA	1. 00
8367.	Boy with Pipe c.	26 x 21	HNA	5. 95
8368.	Bull Ring c.	20 x 24	PENN	1. 50
8369.	Bullfight	18 x 21-1/2	ESH	10. 00
	c.	8 x 10	ESH	1. 00
		5 x 7	NYGS	. 50
8370.	Cafe at Royan	20 x 27-1/2	IA	15. 00
	c.	8 x 10	ESH	1. 00
8371.	Candle, Pitcher and Saucepan	9-1/2x12-1/2	AP	1. 25
	c.	7 x 9	AP	1. 00
8372.	Candle, Vase and Blue Casserole	6 x 8	CFA	1. 00
8373.	Casserole Emaillée	19 x 24	PENN	1. 50
		18 x 24	NYGS	10. 00
		12 x 16	PENN	1. 00
8374.	The Charge (B & W)	12 x 16-1/2	AA	6. 00
8375.	The Chemise (Woman in Chemise)	28 x 22	CFA	18. 00
		18 x 15	AR	4. 00
8376.	Chest of Drawers with Still Life c.	8 x 10	ESH	1. 00
8377.	Child with a Dove	28 x 20-1/2	NYGS	15. 00
		18 x 13	AR	3. 00
		16 x 12	PENN	1. 00
		14 x 10	NYGS	4. 00
8378.	Children Reading	19-1/2 x 15	AR	7. 50
	c.	9 x 7	AP	. 50
8379.	Citron et Orange	16 x 20	PENN	1. 50
8380.	Classical Head c.	24 x 20	PENN	1. 50
8381.	Cock	20 x 15	AP	8. 00
	c.	9 x 7	AP	. 50
8382.	Composition: Peasants c.	20 x 24	PENN	1. 50
8383.	Compote Dish and Pitcher by the Window	21 x 28-1/2	NYGS	16. 00

8384.	Compote with Fruit and Guitar		17 x 22	CFA	10.00
8385.	La Compotier		15 x 20 Oval	AR	7.50
8386.	Contemplation	c.	10 x 8	ESH	1.00
8387.	La Corrida		15 x 21	NYGS	15.00
8388.	La Corrida (B & W)		12 x 32	NYGS	15.00
8389.	The Couple		19 x 11-1/2	NYGS	22.00
			10 x 7	AR	2.00
8390.	Curtain for the Ballet "Parade"				
		c.	8 x 10	ESH	1.00
			6 x 7	NYGS	.50
8391.	Dancers	c.	12-1/2x9-1/2	AP	1.25
			7 x 6	CFA	1.00
8392.	Les Demoiselles d'Avignon (Maids from Avignon)		22 x 23	MMA	7.50
		c.	7 x 9	AP	1.00
			6 x 6	CFA	1.00
8393.	Don Quixote		26 x 20	CFA	6.00
			20 x 17	AR	5.00
8394.	Don Quixote (DR.)		16 x 13-1/2	AP	3.00
8395.	Donkey Driver	c.	9-1/2x12-1/2	AP	1.25
			9 x 12	CFA	1.00
8396.	The Dove	c.	9-1/2x12-1/2	AP	1.25
			9 x 12	CFA	1.00
8397.	The Embrace	c.	12-1/2x9-1/2	AP	1.25
8398.	The Family	c.	10 x 8	ESH	1.00
8399.	Family Dispossessed		14 x 10	CFA	5.00
8400.	Family of Acrobats with Monkey	c.	20 x 24	PENN	1.50
8401.	Family of Saltimbanques		26 x 24	AA	15.00
			24 x 18	PENN	1.50 '
		c.	9 x 7	AP	.25
8402.	Fan, Salt Box and Melon	c.	20 x 24	PENN	1.50
8403.	La Femme Assise		28 x 21-1/2	NYGS	15.00
8404.	La Femme Bleue		24 x 17-1/2	NYGS	12.00
			19 x 16	CFA	7.50
8405.	Femme en Chemise		28 x 23	NYGS	18.00
8406.	Femme et Enfant		16 x 12-1/2	NYGS	18.00
8407.	Femme Qui Pleure		23-1/2 x 19	NYGS	12.00
8408.	Fillette a la Boule		23 x 16	CAC	15.00
8409.	Fillette au Chien		27 x 18	NYGS	12.00
8410.	Fish Net	c.	12-1/2x9-1/2	AP	1.25
			8 x 6	CFA	1.00
8411.	Fisherman's Farewell				
		c.	9-1/2x12-1/2	AP	1.25
			7 x 6	CFA	1.00
8412.	Flower Seller		14 x 21	NYGS	12.00
8413.	Flowers, 1903		25 x 19	NYGS	15.00

8414.	Flowers, 1907 c.	10 x 8	ESH	1.00
8415.	Forces of Life and the Spirit Triumphing over Evil (UNESCO Mural) c.	8 x 10	ESH	1.00
8416.	Girl Before a Mirror	28 x 20	PENN	1.50
8417.	Girl in a Chair	10 x 7	AR	2.00
8418.	Girl on a Beach Ball c.	10 x 8	ESH	1.00
8419.	Girl on a Divan	8 x 10	AR	2.00
8420.	Girl on the Wall	28 x 22	CFA	15.00
8421.	Girl Reading	22-1/2 x 28	AJ	15.00
8422.	Girl with a Jug	26 x 21	NYGS	18.00
8423.	Girl with Mandolin	23-1/2 x 17	NYGS	12.00
		8 x 6	CFA	1.00
8424.	Glass, Bottle and Paper c.	9-1/2x12-1/2	AP	1.25
		6 x 8	CFA	1.00
8425.	The Gourmet	28 x 20-1/2	NYGS	15.00
		20 x 14-1/2	NYGS	7.50
	c.	9 x 7	AP	.50
8426.	Green Still Life	22 x 30	ESH	12.00
		19 x 26	MMA	7.50
8427.	Grille	9 x 6	CFA	1.00
8428.	Guernica	22 x 49	PENN	2.98
		16 x 35-1/2	NYGS	12.00
		8-1/2 x 19	NYGS	4.00
8429.	Guitar (Still Life)	20 x 22-1/2	AJ	10.00
		17 x 22	AP	10.00
8430.	Guitar and Bottle	16 x 15	CFA	7.50
8431.	Guitar and Grapes	25 x 18-1/2	AA	12.00
8432.	Hands Holding Flowers	23 x 16	CFA	6.00
8433.	Harlequin	22-1/2x17	ESH	10.00
		21 x 16	CFA	10.00
	c.	12-1/2x9-1/2	AP	1.25
	c.	9 x 7	AP	.50
		7 x 4	CFA	1.00
8434.	Harlequin, 1917	28-1/2 x 22	NYGS	16.00
8435.	Harlequin, 1923 c.	10 x 8	ESH	1.00
8436.	Harlequin and Boy	23 x 18-1/2	NYGS	15.00
8437.	Harlequin and Mirror	24 x 19	PENN	1.50
8438.	Harlequin on Horseback, 1905 c.	24 x 20	PENN	1.50
		24 x 16-1/2	NYGS	15.00
		14 x 9-1/2	NYGS	3.00
8439.	Harlequin with Mask	17-1/2x22-1/2	ESH	10.00
8440.	Harlequin's Family	7 x 5	CFA	1.00
8441.	Head of Harlequin			
	c.	24 x 20	PENN	1.50

8442.	Head of a Woman		20 x 14	NYGS	15. 00
			7 x 7	NYGS	. 50
8443.	Interior at Nice		8 x 6	CFA	1. 00
8444.	The Ironer		9 x 5	NYGS	. 50
8445.	L'Italienne (Italian Woman)		22 x 15	ESH	10. 00
			10-1/2 x 8	ESH	1. 00
8446.	The Jester		26 x 20	AR	6. 00
			23 x 16	CFA	6. 00
8447.	Jeune Homme et Cheval		19-1/2x12-1/2	NYGS	18. 00
8448.	Juan-les Pins		24 x 30	DAC	7. 50
		c.	8 x 10	ESH	1. 00
		c.	7 x 9	AP	. 50
8449.	Juggler with Still Life, 1905		29 x 20	NYGS	16. 00
8450.	Lamp and Bowl of Fruit	c.	24 x 20	PENN	1. 50
8451.	Landscape		20 x 28	NYGS	20. 00
8452.	Landscape with Dead Tree		17-1/2x22-1/2	ESH	10. 00
8453.	Lemon and Oranges		14 x 17	CFA	5. 00
8454.	Liseuse Grise		24 x 14	PENN	1. 50
		c.	16 x 12	PENN	1. 00
8455.	Little Girl with Basket		9 x 4	NYGS	. 50
8456.	Little Shepherd		21 x 15-1/2	NYGS	7. 50
			15-1/2x11-1/2	NYGS	3. 00
8457.	Lobster and Cat	c.	20 x 24	PENN	1. 50
8458.	The Lovers		27 x 20	NYGS	15. 00
			24 x 18	PENN	1. 50
		c.	23 x 18	HNA	5. 95
			20 x 15	AP	7. 50
			10 x 14-1/2	NYGS	7. 50
			16 x 12	PENN	1. 00
			14 x 11	NYGS	3. 00
8459.	Lovers in the Street	c.	12-1/2 x9-1/2	AP	1. 25
			11 x 7	CFA	1. 00
		c.	9 x 7	AP	1. 00
8460.	Ma Jolie		23-1/2 x 21	AR	12. 50
8461.	Madame Canals	c.	24 x 20	PENN	1. 50
8462.	Madame Jacqueline R.	c.	12-1/2x9-1/2	AP	1. 25
			8 x 6	CFA	1. 00
8463.	Man with Guitar		8 x 6	CFA	1. 00
8464.	Mandolin and Guitar		19-1/2 x 28	AA	15. 00
			8 x 10-1/2	ESH	1. 00
8465.	Matador	c.	30 x 24	PENN	1. 95
8466.	Maternité		18 x 12	NYGS	18. 00
8467.	Maternité, 1903		18 x 16	NYGS	10. 00

8468.	Maternity	26 x 20	AR	15. 00
		19 x 15	AR	7. 50
	c.	12-1/2x9-1/2	AP	1. 25
	c.	9 x 7	AP	1. 00
8469.	Midget Dancer c.	24 x 20	PENN	1. 50
8470.	Minotauromachy (B & W)	19-1/2 x 27	NYGS	7. 50
8471.	Modern Madonna	24 x 24	CAC	18. 00
8472.	The Mother, 1901	24 x 16-1/2	NYGS	12. 00
		21-1/2 x 15	AP	10. 00
	c.	12-1/2x9-1/2	AP	1. 25
	c.	9 x 7	AP	1. 00
8473.	Mother and Child, 1921	25 x 28	NYGS	16. 00
8474.	Mother and Child, 1922	28 x 22-1/2	NYGS	16. 00
		20 x 16	PENN	1. 50
8475.	Mother and Child (Blue)	27-1/2x21-1/2	IA	15. 00
		24 x 18-1/2	PENN	1. 50
8476.	Mother and Child with Shawl c.	24 x 20	PENN	1. 50
8477.	Motherhood (B & W)	20 x 15	AA	10. 00
8478.	The Mothers	14-1/2 x 18	ESH	10. 00
	c.	8 x 10	ESH	1. 00
8479.	Moulin de la Galette	21-1/2 x 28	NYGS	15. 00
	c.	20 x 24	PENN	1. 50
8480.	The Muse, 1935	8 x 10	AR	2. 00
8481.	Nature Morte	24 x 30	DAC	7. 50
8482.	Nature Morte au Cerises	15 x 23-1/2	PENN	1. 50
8483.	Nature Morte aux Poissons	19-1/2 x 24	NYGS	18. 00
8484.	Night Fishing at Antibes, 1939	12 x 20-1/2	MMA	3. 00
8485.	Nude, Half-Length	24 x 19	NYGS	10. 00
		14 x 11	NYGS	3. 00
8486.	Nude from the Back c.	12-1/2x9-1/2	AP	1. 25
	c.	9 x 7	AP	1. 00
8487.	Nude with a Towel	28 x 21-1/2	NYGS	15. 00
8488.	Nude Woman Lifting her Arm c.	12-1/2x9-1/2	AP	1. 25
		10 x 8	CFA	1. 00
8489.	The Old Guitarist	30 x 20	NYGS	18. 00
		14 x 11	NYGS	3. 00
8490.	The Painter at Work	28 x 21	NYGS	22. 00
		24 x 19-1/2	NYGS	24. 00
8491.	Palette and Bust	14 x 18	CFA	7. 50
8492.	Peace, 1952	18 x 36	NYGS	12. 00

8493.	Picador with Lance, (B & W)	17 x 12	AA		7. 50
8494.	Pierrot, 1918	24 x 19	PENN		1. 50
8495.	Pierrot Seated	21 x 16	NYGS		6. 00
8496.	Pierrot with Flowers	21 x 15-1/2	NYGS		7. 50
		15-1/2x11-1/2	NYGS		3. 00
8497.	Pierrot with Mask	21 x 15-1/2	NYGS		7. 50
		15-1/2x11-1/2	NYGS		3. 00
8498.	Pigeons	22 x 18	ESH		10. 00
8499.	Portrait, 1938 c.	10 x 8	ESH		1. 00
8500.	Portrait de Femme	22-1/2 x 18	PENN		1. 50
		16 x 12	PENN		1. 00
8501.	Portrait of Dora Maar	10-1/2 x 8	ESH		1. 00
8502.	Portrait of Gertrude Stein	8 x 7	NYGS		. 50
8503.	Portrait of M. G. Coquiot, 1901 c.	24 x 20	PENN		1. 50
8504.	Portrait of Jaime Sabartes c.	24 x 20	PENN		1. 50
8505.	Portrait of Madame "Z"	22-1/2 x 18	ESH		10. 00
8506.	Portrait of a Young Woman, Version XIII	22-1/2 x 18	ESH		10. 00
	c.	10 x 8	ESH		1. 00
8507.	Posters (9) c.	30 x 21-1/2	PENN	ea.	1. 00
	L'Attente				
	Le Cubisme (Galerie Bryelen)				
	Harlequin				
	Madam Canals				
	Maitres de L'Art Moderne				
	Maitres Contemporains				
	Midget Dancer				
	Mother and Child				
	Portrait (Galerie Bryelen)				
8508.	Procession	14 x 20	AA		7. 50
8509.	La Ronde	26 x 20	AR		7. 50
8510.	Rooster	19 x 15	AR		6. 00
		14 x 11	AP		5. 00
8511.	Saltimbanque	19 x 13	NYGS		18. 00
	c.	24 x 20	PENN		1. 50
8512.	Saltimbanque's Family with a Dog c.	7 x 9	AP		. 75
8513.	Seated Acrobat c.	20 x 24	PENN		1. 50
8514.	Seated Acrobat with a Child c.	10 x 8	ESH		1. 00
		9 x 6	CFA		1. 00
8515.	Seated Bather	28 x 23	NYGS		15. 00
8516.	Seated Nude	22 x 16	ESH		10. 00
		17 x 14	CFA		7. 50
		10 x 7	CFA		1. 00

8517.	Seated Pierrot	c.	12-1/2x9-1/2	AP	1.25
8518.	Seated Woman	c.	9 x 7	AP	1.00
8519.	Self-Portrait		24 x 18	PENN	1.50
8520.	Self-Portrait as Harlequin at Lapin Agile		19 x 19	ESH	10.00
		c.	8 x 10	ESH	1.00
8521.	Snowy Morning	c.	9-1/2x12-1/2	AP	1.25
8522.	Les Soupeurs		16-1/2 x 24	PENN	1.50
8523.	Southern Landscape		15 x 22-1/2	ESH	10.00
			8 x 10-1/2	ESH	1.00
8524.	Still Life		16 x 20	IA	7.50
8525.	Still Life		8 x 5	CFA	1.00
8526.	Still Life, 1901		21 x 28-1/2	NYGS	16.00
8527.	Still Life, 1903	c.	8 x 10	ESH	1.00
8528.	Still Life, 1918		18 x 24	NYGS	10.00
8529.	Still Life, Antique Bust		17-1/2 x 24	AR	12.00
8530.	Still Life in a Landscape	c.	8 x 10	ESH	1.00
8531.	Still Life on a Table	c.	9-1/2x12-1/2	AP	1.25
		c.	7 x 9	AP	1.00
8532.	Still Life with Antique Head		18 x 24	PENN	1.50
		c.	18 x 23	HNA	5.95
			15 x 20	NYGS	7.50
			12 x 16	PENN	1.00
8533.	Still Life with Black Head		5 x 7	NYGS	.50
8534.	Still Life with Casserole	c.	18 x 23	HNA	5.95
8535.	Still Life with Fish		24 x 18	DAC	7.50
			16 x 12	DAC	2.50
			10 x 8	ESH	1.00
8536.	Still Life with Guitar		18 x 22-1/2	AA	12.00
			18 x 22	ESH	10.00
			14 x 17	CFA	7.50
8537.	Still Life with Head	c.	20 x 24	PENN	1.50
8538.	Still Life with Mandolin, 1923		20-1/2 x 28	NYGS	15.00
8539.	Still Life with Mandolin, 1924		17 x 23	NYGS	10.00
8540.	Still Life with Red Shawl		8 x 7	NYGS	.50
8541.	Still Life with Wallpaper		13 x 17	NYGS	15.00
8542.	Still Life with Yellow Jug		5 x 7	NYGS	.50
8543.	The Studio		31 x 21	CFA	15.00

			22-1/2 x 18	ESH	10. 00
		c.	10 x 8	MMA	. 35
8544.	Summer Bouquet		26 x 20	AA	7. 50
8545.	Sylvette XIII	c.	20 x 24	PENN	1. 50
8546.	Tete de Jeune				
	Homme		24 x 17-1/2	NYGS	12. 00
8547.	Three Musicians,				
	1921		21 x 23	MMA	6. 00
		c.	18 x 23	HNA	5. 95
			17 x 19	PENN	1. 50
		c.	9-1/2x12-1/2	AP	1. 25
		c.	8 x 10	MMA	. 35
8548.	The Thrust				
	(B & W)		14 x 20	AA	7. 50
8549.	La Toilette		28 x 18	NYGS	15. 00
			16 x 12	PENN	1. 00
			8 x 6	CFA	1. 00
8550.	Toros and Toreros				
	(4)		14-1/2 x 20	CFA	10. 00
8551.	The Tragedy		25 x 16	PENN	1. 50
			24 x 15-1/2	NYGS	12. 00
		c.	23 x 18	HNA	5. 95
		c.	16 x 12	PENN	1. 00
8552.	Tumblers	c.	10 x 8	ESH	1. 00
8553.	Turkish Shawl		22 x 17-1/2	ESH	10. 00
8554.	Turkish Woman	c.	12 x 10	AP	1. 00
8555.	Two Brothers		8 x 6	CFA	1. 00
8556.	Two Children		18-1/2x22-1/2	AP	10. 00
8557.	Two Harlequins,				
	1905		26 x 19	NYGS	12. 00
			14 x 10	NYGS	3. 00
8558.	Two Sisters		8x 5	CFA	1. 00
8559.	Ulysses and the				
	Sirens	c.	12-1/2x9-1/2	AP	1. 25
			8 x 5	CFA	1. 00
8560.	Vase with Flowers		26 x 20	AA	7. 50
8561.	Villa au Palmier		22 x 28-1/2	NYGS	26. 00
8562.	The Violin		24 x 18	CFA	15. 00
8563.	War, 1952		18 x 36	NYGS	12. 00
8564.	White Clown		20 x 13	PENN	1. 50
8565.	Window		8 x 6	CFA	1. 00
8566.	Woman	c.	23 x 18	HNA	5. 95
8567.	Woman, a Portrait		21 x 15-1/2	PENN	1. 50
8568.	Woman Asleep		7 x 5	NYGS	. 50
8569.	Woman at her				
	Mirror		8 x 10-1/2	ESH	1. 00
8570.	Woman Before a				
	Mirror		27-1/2 x 22	NYGS	20. 00
8571.	Woman Carrying				
	Bread	c.	10 x 8	ESH	1. 00
8572.	Woman in Blue		10-1/2 x 8	ESH	1. 00
8573.	Woman in Blue				
	Stockings		9 x 7	NYGS	. 50

8574.	Woman in a Chemise			
		28 x 24	AJ	18. 00
		18 x 15	AR	4. 00
8575.	Woman in White	22 x 18	AP	3. 00
		17 x 14	CFA	7. 50
	c.	16 x 12	AP	2. 00
8576.	Woman of Majorca			
	c.	10 x 8	ESH	1. 00
8577.	Woman on a Wall	7 x 6	CFA	1. 00
8578.	Woman Sitting	28 x 21	CFA	15. 00
8579.	Woman with Blue			
	Veil c.	24 x 20	PENN	1. 50
		10 x 8	CFA	1. 00
8580.	Woman with Book	28 x 20-1/2	NYGS	15. 00
8581.	Woman with a			
	Cape c.	24 x 20	PENN	1. 50
8582.	Woman with a Fan	6 x 5	CFA	1. 00
8583.	Woman with a Fish			
	Hat, 1949	27-1/2 x 22	NYGS	15. 00
8584.	Woman with a			
	Flowered Hat	19-1/2 x 16	AR	7. 50
8585.	Woman with a Hat	19 x 16	CFA	7. 50
8586.	Woman with			
	Tambourine c.	20 x 24	PENN	1. 50
8587.	Woman's Figure	13-1/2 x 8	NYGS	2. 00
8588.	Woman's Profile on			
	Red c.	16 x 12	PENN	1. 00
8589.	Wounded Bird c.	8 x 10	NYGS	. 50
8590.	Young Girl Seated	24 x 18	PENN	1. 50
8591.	Young Girl with Arm			
	Upraised	19 x 16	CFA	7. 50

PICKEN, GEORGE ALEXANDER (American, 1898-)
8592.	Hawthorne, New York	7 x 20	NYGS	7. 50

PICKENS, ALTON (American Contemporary)
8593.	Carnival, 1949 c.	8 x 10	NYGS	. 50

PICKERSGILL, HENRY W. (English, 1782-1875)
8594.	Lady in Blue	28 x 22	CFA	10. 00

PICKETT, JOSEPH (American, 1848-1918)
8595.	Coryell's Ferry	23 x 30	CFA	12. 00
		19 x 24	PENN	1. 50
	c.	8 x 10	NYGS	. 50
8596.	Manchester Valley	22-1/2 x 30	NYGS	15. 00
	c.	8 x 10	MMA	. 35
		5 x 7	NYGS	. 50

PICOT, FRANCOIS EDOUARD (French, 1786-1868)
8597.	Eros and Psyche	10 x 12	CFA	2. 50

PIEPER, JOSEF (German, 1907-)
8598.	Children with Bird	19 x 24	CFA	15. 00
8599.	Two Figures	34 x 24	CFA	18. 00

PIERO DELLA FRANCESCA (FRA SAN SEPOLCRO) (Italian, 1416-1492)
8600.	Annunciation	15 x 9	IA	3. 00

8601.	Chosroes Defeated by				
	Heraclius	7 x 15	IA		3.00
	Details of No.				
	8601 (2)	15 x 11	IA	ea.	3.00
8602.	Death and Burial of				
	Adam	11 x 15	IA		3.00
	Adam - Detail				
	of No. 8602				
	Two Figures -				
	Detail of No.				
	8602	15 x 11	IA		3.00
8603.	Dream of Constantine				
	(Detail)	15 x 11	IA		3.00
8604.	Duchess of Urbino	15 x 11	IA		3.00
	c.	9 x 7	AP		.25
8605.	Duke of Urbino	15 x 11	IA		3.00
	c.	9 x 7	AP		.25
8606.	Empress Helen and				
	the Discovery of the				
	Cross	12 x 11	IA		3.00
8607.	Flagellation	10 x 14	IA		3.00
8608.	Madonna of the				
	Childbirth	13-1/2 x 11	IA		3.00
8609.	Madonna of				
	Senigallia	12 x 10	IA		3.00
8610.	Magdalena	15 x 10	IA		3.00
8611.	Nativity	30-1/2x29-1/2	NYGS		28.00
8612.	Our Lady of Mercy	15 x 10	IA		3.00
8613.	Portrait of a Girl				
	c.	9 x 7	AP		.60
8614.	The Queen of Sheba				
	Adoring the Cross	15 x 11	IA		3.00
8615.	Queen of Sheba -				
	Detail of No. 8614	15 x 11	IA		3.00
	c.	10 x 8	NYGS		.50
8616.	Queen of Sheba and				
	Maids c.	18 x 23	HNA		5.95
8617.	Recognition of the				
	Cross	11 x 15	IA		3.00
8618.	Resurrection	12 x 10	IA		3.00
8619.	Solomon's Reception				
	of the Queen of				
	Sheba	11 x 15	IA		3.00
8620.	Victory of Constantine				
	over Maxentius	11 x 14	IA		3.00
8621.	Virgin Enthroned				
	with Saints and Federico				
	da Montefeltro	15 x 10	IA		3.00
8622.	Virgin of Misericordia				
	(San Sepolcro, Arezzo)				
		15 x 10	AS		3.25

PIERRE, GUSTAVE (French, 1875-)
8623. Antique Bas Relief
       (3-in-1 panel)   7 x 25   CFA   15. 00
8624. The Traveler   c.   20 x 24   PENN   1. 50
PIETRO DA CORTONA (BERRETINI) (Italian, 1596-1669)
8625. Aenea and Venus   11 x 15   IA   3. 00
8626. Age of Silver   15 x 11   AS   3. 25
PIETRO DI COSIMO (PIERO DI LORENZO) (Italian, 1462-1521)
8627. Portrait of a Floren-
       tine Lady (The
       Magdalene)   14 x 11   IA   3. 00
8628. Portrait of a Gentle-
       woman   15 x 11   AS   3. 25
8629. Simonetta Vespucci
       (Cleopatra?)   14 x 10   IA   3. 00
PIETRO DI GIOVANNI D'AMBROGIO (Italian, Ac. 1428-1447)
8630. Adoration of the
       Shepherds(Detail) c. 10 x 8   ESH   1. 00
8631. Saint Bernardine of
       Siena   15 x 11-1/2   AS   3. 25
PIKE, JOHN (American Contemporary)
8632. Ahead of the Wind   18 x 26   PENN   1. 50
8633. Bearsville Store   18 x 26   PENN   1. 50
8634. Campers   18 x 26   PENN   1. 50
8635. Fritzi and Fred   18 x 26   PENN   1. 50
8636. I'll Show the Way   18 x 26   PENN   1. 50
8637. Lake Lure   20 x 26   NYGS   10. 00
8638. Perfect Morning   21 x 27   NYGS   12. 00
8639. Water in the Flat-
       lands   18 x 26   PENN   1. 50
PILKINGTON, FLORA (English Contemporary)
8640. Passing of June   14 x 10   ESH   2. 00
PINTURICCHIO (BERNARDINO DI BETTO) (Italian, 1454-1513)
8641. Assumption of the
       Virgin   15 x 11   IA   3. 00
8642. "Cavaliere di Rodi"
       Alberto Arringhieri
       (The Knight of Rhodes)
                           11 x 11   ESH   6. 00
                           10 x 12   IA   3. 00
8643. Madonna and Child
       (Rome)   13-1/2x11-1/2 AS   3. 25
8644. Madonna and Child   13 x 11   IA   3. 00
8645. Madonna and Child
       and Saints   14 x 9   IA   3. 00
8646. Madonna and Saints 14 x 10   IA   3. 00
8647. Meeting of Frederic
       III with Eleanor of
       Portugal   15 x 9   IA   3. 00
8648. Nativity   15 x 10   IA   3. 00
       Virgin--Detail
       of No. 8648   15 x 11   IA   3. 00
                           11 x 8-1/2   IA   1. 75

8649.	Virgin Adoring			
	(Fome)	15 x 11	AS	3. 25
PIOMO,	SEBASTIANO DEL (Italian, 1485-1547)			
8650.	Christopher Columbus			
	c.	10 x 8	NYGS	. 50
8651.	The Magdalene	15 x 10	IA	3. 00
8652.	Portrait (Formerly			
	called "The Fornarina")			
		14 x 11	IA	3. 00
8653.	Portrait of Young			
	Roman Lady c.	23 x 18	HNA	5. 95
PIOT,	ANTOINE (French, Ac. 1870)			
8654.	Poppy Girl	29 x 22	AA	10. 00
PIPER,	JOHN (English, 1903-)			
8655.	Cottages	16 x 20	NYGS	10. 00
8656.	Pointe du Chateau	20 x 27	ESH	10. 00
8657.	Rowlestone Tympanum			
	with Hanging Lamp	20 x 27	ESH	10. 00
8658.	St. Mary le Port	18 x 15	AP	6. 00
PIPPAL,	HANS ROBERT (Austrian, Contemporary)			
8659.	Girl with a Flower	24 x 18	IA	12. 00
8660.	Young Girl	24 x 18	IA	12. 00
PIPPIN,	HORACE (American, 1888-1946)			
8661.	Holy Mountain III	23-1/2 x 28	NYGS	15. 00
8662.	Victorian Interior,			
	1946 c.	20 x 24	PENN	1. 50
PIRANESI,	GIAN BATTISTA (Italian, 1728-1778)			
8663.	Ancient Temple			
	Ruins c.	12 x 16	PENN	1. 00
8664.	Arch of Augustus,			
	Colonnades and			
	Fountain c.	12 x 16	PENN	1. 00
8665.	The Campidoglio,			
	View	18 x 24	PENN	1. 50
8666.	Clocks (4)	14 x 11	CFA ea.	6. 00
8667.	Fantasy of a Palace			
	with a Fountain	10 x 15	NYGS	3. 00
8668.	Imperial Mausoleum			
	c.	12 x 16	PENN	1. 00
8669.	Italian Ruins			
	(B & W)	24 x 36	CFA	24. 00
8670.	Italian Views (6)			
	(B & W)	8 x 12	CFA ea.	7. 50
8671.	Italian Views (6)			
	(H. C.)	8 x 13	CFA ea.	10. 00
8672.	Piazza del Popolo,			
	View	18 x 24	PENN	1. 50
8673.	Piazza della Rotunda,			
	Fiew	18 x 24	PENN	1. 50
8674.	Sant Angelo Bridge			
	and Castle, View	18 x 24	PENN	1. 50
8675.	Santa Maria Maggiore			
	c.	12 x 16	PENN	1. 00

8676.	St. Peter's Piazza			
	and Colonnades c.	12 x 16	PENN	1.00

PISANO, ANTONIO (CALLED PISANELLO) (Italian, 1397-1455)

8677.	Etude d'Oiseaux	6 x 8	NYGS	4.00
8678.	Portrait of a			
	Woman (Verona)	15-1/2x11-1/2	AS	3.25
8679.	Princess of Este	13 x 10	IA	3.00
8680.	Vision of St. Eustace			
		21 x 25-1/2	NYGS	12.00

PISANO, GIOVANNI (Italian, c. 1245-1314)

8681.	Madonna and Child			
	(Ivory)	15 x 11	IA	3.00

PISIS, FILIPO DE (Italian, 1896-1956)

8682.	Chiesa della Salute,			
	1947	30 x 23	NYGS	16.00
8683.	Flowers, 1937	24-1/2 x 19	NYGS	12.00

PISSARRO, CAMILLE (French, 1830.1903)

8684.	Avenue de L'Opera			
	in 1900	24 x 30	ESH	15.00
8685.	Blossoming Plum			
	Tree	19 x 24	CFA	15.00
8686.	Bords de l'Eau a			
	Pontoise, 1872	22 x 36	NYGS	18.00
8687.	Blvd. Montmartre	20 x 25	AR	12.00
	c.	18 x 23	HNA	5.95
		15-1/2x18-1/2	AP	5.00
8688.	Blvd. Montmartre			
	at Night	20 x 21-1/2	NYGS	12.00
8689.	Bridge at Bruges	18 x 21-1/2	NYGS	12.00
8690.	Canal of the Loing	8 x 10	CFA	1.00
8691.	Chestnut Trees	15 x 19-1/2	AP	7.50
8692.	Church at Knoche			
	c.	8 x 10	ESH	1.00
8693.	Church and Castle			
	at Eragny c.	8 x 10	ESH	1.00
8694.	Conversation	13 x 10	IA	3.00
8695.	Entrance to a			
	Village	18 x 22-1/2	ESH	10.00
	c.	8 x 10	ESH	1.00
8696.	Flowery Plum Trees	10 x 12	IA	3.00
8697.	French Winter			
	Scene	24 x 30	DAC	7.50
8698.	Garden of the			
	Tuileries	23 x 33	CFA	18.00
8699.	L'Hermitage c.	10 x 8	ESH	1.00
8700.	In the Garden	18 x 24	PENN	1.50
8701.	Landscape	16 x 19	AP	5.00
8702.	Meadow at Mont			
	Foucauld c.	8 x 10	ESH	1.00
8703.	Morgen in Eragny	17-1/2x22	AS	4.00
8704.	Morning at the			
	Louvre	6 x 8	CFA	1.00

8705.	L'Oise near Pontoise					
			16 x 20	NYGS	10. 00
8706.	Orchard	c.	8 x 10	ESH	1. 00
8707.	Pavillion de					
	Flore	c.	8 x 10	ESH	1. 00
8708.	Place du Theatre					
	Francais	c.	9-1/2x12-1/2	AP	1. 25
			7 x 9	CFA	1. 00
8709.	Pont de Pierre,					
	Rouen		16-1/2 x 23	PENN	1. 50
8710.	Pontoise		24 x 30	PENN	1. 95
			12 x 16	DAC	2. 50
8711.	Les Quais a Rouen		20 x 23-1/2	PENN	1. 50
8712.	Red Roofs		18 x 22	ESH	10. 00
		c.	8 x 10	ESH	1. 00
			7 x 8	CFA	1. 00
8713.	River Bank		21-1/2 x 36	AA	15. 00
8714.	The Road	c.	8 x 10	NYGS	. 50
			6 x 8	CFA	1. 00
8715.	Road Along the					
	Railway		6 x 9	NYGS	. 50
8716.	Road to Ennery		18 x 22-1/2	ESH	10. 00
8717.	Road to Louveciennes					
		c.	18 x 23	HNA	5. 95
		c.	8 x 10	ESH	1. 00
8718.	Route de Versailles					
	a Louveciennes		22 x 17-1/2	AS	4. 00
8719.	The Seine at Marly		17 x 23	NYGS	15. 00
8720.	Snowy Morning	c.	7 x 9	AP	1. 00
8721.	Street in Rouen		22-1/2x17-1/2	ESH	10. 00
8722.	Towpath		24-1/2 x 30	ESH	15. 00
		c.	20 x 24	PENN	1. 50
		c.	9-1/2x12-1/2	AP	1. 25
		c.	8 x 10	ESH	1. 00
8723.	View from					
	Louceciennes		18 x 28	ESH	15. 00
8724.	View of the Seine		18 x 21-1/2	ESH	10. 00
8725.	Village Market	c.	20 x 24	PENN	1. 50
8726.	Winter Scene	c.	24 x 30	PENN	1. 95
PITLOO, ANTON VAN (Dutch, 1780-1837)						
8727.	View of Ischia		10 x 15	IA	3. 00
PITTONI, GIOVANNI BATTISTA (Italian, 1687-1767)						
8728.	Nativity		15 x 11	IA	3. 00
PIZZANELLI, LEONARDO (Italian Contemporary)						
8729.	Cinzia		13 x 11	IA	3. 00
8730.	Flowers		13 x 11	IA	3. 00
8731.	Little Gypsy		15 x 10	IA	3. 00
8732.	Reading Little Girl		17 x 14	IA	7. 50
8733.	Resting Model		13 x 11	IA	3. 00
8734.	Young Mother		13 x 11	IA	3. 00
8735.	Young Pupil		13 x 11	IA	3. 00
PLUIM, R.						
8736.	Paris Views (6)		11 x 14	DAC	ea. 1. 50

```
                  Montmartre,  Sacre  Coeur
                  Notre  Dame
                  Place  de  la  Concorde
                  Place  de  L'Opera
                  Quai  des  Grands  Augustins
                  Rue  Mouffetard
PLUVINEL
  8737.   Riding Horses (4)    12 x 16        CFA      ea.  12. 00
PODESTI,  FRANCESCO (Italian,  1800-1895)
  8738.   Giuseppi Verdi and
          the Countess Zaccaria
                            17-1/2x22-1/2    NYGS          10. 00
POITEAU
  8739.   Antique Fruit
          Prints (5)          13 x 10        NYGS     ea.   3. 00
          (6)                 10 x 7         NYGS     ea.   2. 00
POLAND
  8740.   UWA Series (32)     11 x 14        NYGS     ea.   2. 00
                       or     14 x 11
POLLAIUOLO,  ANTONIO (BENCI,  ANTONIO) (Italian,  1433-1498)
  8741.   Hercules and Antaeus 7 x 4        IA                1. 50
  8742.   Hercules and the
          Hydra                7 x 5        IA                1. 50
  8743.   Portrait of a Lady  15 x 11       IA                3. 00
  8744.   Princess of Este    13 x 10       IA                3. 00
POLLAIUOLO,  PIERO (BENCI,  PIERO) (Italian,  1443-1496)
  8745.   Coronation of the
          Virgin and Saints   14 x 10       IA                3. 00
  8746.   Portrait of Galeazzo
          Sforza (by Piero and
          Antonio Pollaiuolo) 15 x 10       AS                3. 25
POLLARD,  JAMES (English,  1797-1859)
  8747.   West Country Mails  11 x 16       CFA              12. 00
POLLOCK,  JACKSON (American,  1912-1956)
  8748.   Blue Poles     c.    8 x 10       NYGS              . 50
  8749.   Composition         24 x 19       PENN              1. 50
  8750.   Number 27,  1950    13-1/2x29-1/2 NYGS             16. 00
  8751.   Poster for Exhibition:
          Jackson Pollock     32 x 24       MMA              10. 00
  8752.   Water Beast,  1945  13-1/2x39-1/2 NYGS             18. 00
POLLONI,  SILVIO (Italian,  1888-  )
  8753.   Tropical Fish (6)    9 x 7        NYGS     set   5. 00 or
                                                    ea.   1. 00
POMPEIAN ART
  8754.   Aldobrandini Nuptials 9 x 29      IA                7. 50
  8755.   Amphora with Raven  17 x 12       CFA              10. 00
  8756.   Animals of the Nile
          (3)                  9 x 15       IA       ea.   3. 00
  8757.   Bacchante           14 x 11       IA                3. 00
  8758.   Chiron and Achilles 11 x 10       IA                3. 00
  8759.   Diana               17 x 12       CFA              10. 00
  8760.   Dionysical Frieze of
          the Villa dei Misteri
```

	(11 prints)	13 x 48	IA	ea.	3.00
8761.	Eros Punished by Venus	15 x 10	IA		3.00
8762.	Festival Dance	17 x 12	CFA		10.00
8763.	Feston with Masks (Mosaic)	6 x 16	IA		3.00
8764.	Heracles Strangling the Serpents	14 x 10	IA		3.00
8765.	Iphigenia's Sacrifice	13 x 11	IA		3.00
8766.	Leda	17 x 12	CFA		10.00
8767.	Medea before Murdering her Children	14 x 11	IA		3.00
8768.	Mosaics (4)	11 x 11	IA	ea.	3.00
	Doves around a Cup				
	Philosophers				
	Sea Animals				
	Strolling Players				
	Mosaics (2)	10 x 10	IA	ea.	3.00
	Cat and Fowls				
	Chained Dog				
	Mosaics:				
	Comic Scene	13 x 10	IA		3.00
	Parrots on a Cup	13 x 11	IA		3.00
	Skull and Symbols	12 x 10	IA		3.00
8769.	Paintings, Antique (8)	11 x 15	IA	ea.	3.00
8770.	Bacchic Festival of Cupids				
8771.	Cupids as Dyers				
8772.	Cupids as Florists				
8773.	Cupids as Locksmiths				
8774.	Cupids as Perfumers				
8775.	Cupids as Wine Merchants				
8776.	Cupids Playing with a Target				
8777.	Punishment of Circe				
	Paintings, Antique (3)	15 x 11	IA	ea.	3.00
8778.	Cupid Driving a Crab				
8779.	Cupid Driving Two Dolphins				
8780.	Daedalus Showing the Wooden Cow to Pasiphae				
8781.	Perseus and Andromeda	15 x 11	IA		3.00
8782.	Telephus Nursed by the Hind	14 x 10	IA		3.00
8783.	Theseus the Rescuer	12 x 11	IA		3.00
8784.	Venus and Mars	14 x 10	IA		3.00
8785.	Wall Decoration	15 x 12	IA		3.00
8786.	Wounded Enea	13 x 10	IA		3.00

PONTORMO (CARRUCCI, JACOPO) (Italian, 1494-1557)

8787.	Child with Dog	15 x 10-1/2	AS		3.25

8788.	Portrait of Cardinal Cervini	14 x 11-1/2	AS		3. 25
8789.	Portrait of Cosimo De'Medici, Pater Patriae	15 x 11	IA		3. 00
8790.	Portrait of Giuliano De'Medici	15 x 11	IA		3. 00
8791.	Three Graces (DR.)	14-1/2x10-1/2	NYGS		3. 00

PORDENONE, GIOVANNI (Italian, 1483-1539)

8792.	Study of a Nude	11 x 7	AR		3. 00

PORTER, SOPHIE (American)

8793.	Coffee Pot	15 x 15	NYGS		7. 50
8794.	From Garden and Orchard	28 x 14	NYGS		10. 00
8795.	Fruits and Flowers	28 x 14	NYGS		10. 00
8796.	Tea Pot	15 x 15	NYGS		7. 50

PORTINARI, CANDIDO (Brazilian, 1903-)

8797.	Coffee Bearers	23 x 28	NYGS		16. 00
	c.	7 x 9	AP		. 50

PORTUGAL   (17th Century)

8798.	Hunting Scenes (2)	11 x 15	AS		3. 25

POSSE, W.

8799.	Greek Landscape	14 x 35	CFA		15. 00

POSTELS, ROBERT N. DE (American, 1908-)

8800.	The Happy Hours	16 x 34	NYGS		10. 00
		10-1/2 x 22	NYGS		5. 00

POT, HENDRIK GERRITSZ (Dutch, 1600-1657)

8801.	The Miser	11 x 10	IA		3. 00

POTHAST, BERNARD J. C. (Dutch, 1882-)

8802.	Her First Lesson	21 x 25-1/2	NYGS		10. 00

POTRONAT, L. (French, 20th Century)

8803.	Landscapes (6)	12 x 16	DAC	ea.	2. 50
8804.	At the Wharf	8 x 10	DAC	ea.	1. 00
8805.	Going Ashore				
8806.	Marine Plaza				
8807.	Old Road				
8808.	Seaview Hill				
8809.	Winding Shore				
8810.	Saint Raphael	23 x 28	IA		12. 00

POTTER, PAULUS (Dutch, 1625-1665)

8811.	Calving Cow	10-1/2 x 9	AR		3. 00
8812.	Hawking Party	11 x 12-1/2	ESH		2. 00
8813.	White Horse	8 x 10-1/2	ESH		1. 00

POTTHAST, EDWARD HENRY (American, 1857-1927)

8814.	Children by the Sea	12 x 16	NYGS		6. 00
8815.	Holiday c.	7 x 9	AP		. 50

POUCETTE

8816.	Boats at Deauville	19-1/2 x 15	PENN		1. 50
8817.	Harlequin and Mandolin	20 x 10	PENN		1. 50
8818.	Harlequin with Guitar	20 x 10	PENN		1. 50

8819.	Imaginary Landscape			
		19-1/2 x 15	PENN	1.50
POURBUS, FRANS (Flemish, 1568-1622)				
8820.	Portrait of a Man	15 x 11	IA	3.00
8821.	A Youth	15 x 11	IA	3.00
POUSSIN, NICOLAS (French, 1594-1665)				
8822.	Annunciation	8 x 9	AR	3.00
8823.	Assumption of the Virgin	26 x 19	NYGS	12.00
8824.	Funeral of Phocion	7 x 10	NYGS	.50
8825.	Holy Family on the Steps	19 x 28	NYGS	15.00
		16-1/2 x 24	PENN	1.50
8826.	Landscape with Orpheus	9 x 15	IA	3.00
8827.	Moise Sauvé des Eaux	9 x 12-1/2	NYGS	4.00
8828.	Orpheus and Eurydice c.	10 x 8	ESH	1.00
8829.	Ponte, Molle, Rome	9 x 14	CFA	4.00
POWELL				
8830.	Over the Salt Flats	13-1/2 x 20	NYGS	7.50
PRADIER, RAOUL (French, 1929-)				
8831.	Primavera	30 x 15	RL	15.00
PREDIS, AMBROGIO DE (Italian, 1455-1522)				
8832.	Portrait of a Youth	15 x 12	IA	3.00
PREHISTORIC ART				
8833.	Altamira: Bison I and II c.	8 x 10	ESH ea.	1.00
	Lascaux:			
8834.	Bull and Horses			
	c.	8 x 10	ESH	1.00
8835.	Bulls, Horses and Stags c.	10 x 8	ESH	1.00
8836.	Le Cheval Chinois (Chinese Horse)	17-1/2x22-1/2	ESH	10.00
8837.	Chinese Horse (Second) c.	8 x 10	ESH	1.00
8838.	Drawings from Lascaux Caves c.	20 x 24	PENN	1.50
8839.	Five Horses and Cow c.	8 x 10	ESH	1.00
8840.	Great Hall of the Bulls	14-1/2x30-1/2	ESH	15.00
	c.	8 x 10	ESH	1.00
8841.	Red Bull c.	8 x 10	ESH	1.00
8842.	Swimming Stags c.	8 x 10	ESH	1.00
8843.	Two Bulls c.	8 x 10	ESH	1.00
	NIAUX:			
8844.	Bison Wounded by Arrows c.	8 x 10	ESH	1.00
8845.	Three Bisons c.	10 x 8	ESH	1.00

8846.	Wild Pony	c.	10 x 8	ESH	1.00
	Pech-Merle:				
8847.	Horses and Ritual				
	Hands	c.	8 x 10	ESH	1.00
8848.	Saharan Rock Painting:				
	Bowman of Jabbaren		16-1/2x22-1/2	ESH	10.00
8849.	Dancers	c.	10 x 8	ESH	1.00
8850.	Oxen	c.	10 x 8	ESH	1.00
	Miscellaneous:				
8851.	Falling Bison		17-1/2 x 25	AP	7.50
8852.	Grazing Reindeer		17-1/2 x 25	AP	7.50
8853.	Jumping Cow	c.	18 x 23	HNA	5.95

PRENDERGAST, MAURICE (American, 1859-1924)

8854.	Autumn Festival				
		c.	8 x 10	NYGS	.50
8855.	Boat Landing		14-1/2x24	PENN	1.50
8856.	Central Park		14 x 22	PENN	1.50
			14 x 21-1/2	NYGS	12.00
8857.	Ponte della Paglia				
		c.	18 x 23	HNA	5.95
8858.	The Swans		16-1/2 x 23	PENN	1.50

PRENTICE, L. W.

8859.	Basket of Apples	20 x 16	CFA	7.50
8860.	Pail of Apples	20 x 16	CFA	7.50

PRESSMANE, JOSEPH (Polish-French, 1904-)

8861.	Enghien in the Snow	17-1/2 x 21	ESH	10.00

PRETI, CLITOFONTE (Italian, 19th Centrury)

8862.	Maternity	15 x 10	IA	3.00

PREUSS, ROGER

8863.	Snow Geese Winging			
	South	8-1/2 x 11	NWF	1.00

PREVOST, ALEXANDRE (French, Ac. 1850-1886)

8864.	French Street Scenes				
	(2)	12 x 30	DAC	ea.	5.00

PRICE

8865.	Lyric Art (4)	9 x 28	DAC	4.00

PRIESTMAN, BERTRAM (English, 1868-)

8866.	Mill on the Marsh	16 x 20	ESH	10.00

PRIMATICCIO, FRANCESCO (Italian, 1504-1570)

8867.	Ceres on a Couch	7-1/2 x 11	AR	3.00

PRINZ, KARL LUDWIG (Austrian, 1875-)

8868.	Lilac Time	19-1/2 x 29	NYGS	10.00

PROOM, AL

8869.	Accent in White	15 x 30	AA	12.00
8870.	Basket	15 x 30	AA	12.00
8871.	Dignity	23-1/2 x 11	AA	7.50
8872.	Grace	23-1/2 x 11	AA	7.50

PROTIC, MIODRAG (Yugoslavian Contemporary)

8873.	Still Life with			
	Pitcher	21 x 25	NYGS	12.00

PRUD'HON, PIERRE PAUL (French, 1758-1823)

8874.	Head of Vengeance	19 x 15	NYGS	6.00

8875.	Imperatrice			
	Josephine		NYGS	4. 00

PURRMANN, HANS (German, 1880-)

8876.	Castagnola	26 x 29	CFA	15. 00
8877.	Fountain in Triente	23 x 28	ESH	12. 00
8878.	Landscape in			
	Ischia	23 x 28	CFA	15. 00
8879.	Porto d'Jochia	19-1/2x23-1/2	NYGS	15. 00
8880.	Road with Palm			
	Tree c.	18 x 23	HNA	5. 95
8881.	Street Scene	22 x 27-1/2	NYGS	20. 00

PUSHMAN, HOVSEP (Armenian, 1877-1966)

8882.	When Autumn is			
	Here	22-1/2x15-1/2	NYGS	10. 00

PUVIS DE CHAVANNES, PIERRE CECIL (French, 1824-1898)

8883.	Hope	11 x 12	IA	3. 00
8884.	St. Genevieve c.	9 x 7	AP	. 60
8885.	Wine Press c.	8 x 10	NYGS	. 50

PUY, JEAN (French, 1876-)

8886.	Market at Sanary	23 x 30-1/2	ESH	15. 00
8887.	Port at Douellan			
	c.	8 x 10	ESH	1. 00
8888.	Red Sails	14-1/2x22-1/2	ESH	10. 00

PYON, SANG-BYOK

8889.	Cats and Sparrows	24 x 12	ESH	10. 00

Q

QUA

8890.	Busy Harbor	16 x 30	AA	12. 00
8891.	Canton Water Front	16 x 30	AA	12. 00

QUANTE, OTTO (German, 1875-)

8892.	Good Reading	16-1/2 x 19	NYGS	6. 00
8893.	No Worries	19 x 16	NYGS	6. 00
8894.	Puppet Show	19 x 16	NYGS	6. 00
8895.	Spring Dance	16 x 19	NYGS	6. 00

QUINTAINE, ROGER (French Contemporary)

8896.	La Camargue	25 x 40	RL	15. 00
8897.	Evening in the			
	Camargue	24 x 30	RL	15. 00
8898.	Reflections in the			
	Fall	26 x 36	RL	20. 00

QUIZET, LEON ALPHONSE (French, 1885-1955)

8899.	Le Moulin de la			
	Galette et la Villa			
	Medicis	20 x 24	NYGS	12. 00

R

RAEBURN, (SIR) HENRY (Scotch, 1756-1823)
8900. Boy with a Rabbit   26 x 20   CAC   7.50
                              20 x 16   CAC   5.00
                              12 x 9   CAC   2.00
                       c.   9 x 7   AP   .50
8901. Col Charles
       Christie   28 x 23   NYGS   12.00
8902. The Drummond
       Children   11 x 7   NYGS   .50
8903. English Officer   28 x 22   CAC   10.00
8904. Miss Eleanor
       Urquhart   19-1/2 x 16   NYGS   10.00
8905. Mrs. Lauzun   c.   10 x 8   NYGS   .50
RAFFAELLINO DEL GARBO (Italian, 1466/70-1524)
8906. Studies of Hands
       for a Madonna   12-1/2x9-1/2   AR   4.00
RAFFAELLO SANZIO (KNOWN AS "RAPHAEL") (Italian, 1483-1520)
8907. Alba Madonna   24" Diam.   NYGS   16.00
                           16" Diam.   PENN   1.50
                            8" Diam.   NYGS   .50
8908. Andrea Navagero
       and Agostino
       Beazzino   10 x 15   IA   3.00
8909. Angel Playing the
       Lute   11 x 13   IA   3.00
8910. Angiolo Doni   15 x 11   IA   3.00
8911. Ansidei Madonna   20-1/2x13-1/2   ESH   12.00
8912. Bindo Altoviti   23 x 17-1/2   AA   7.50
8913. A Child (Rome)   15 x 6   AS   3.25
8914. Classic Figures
       (4)   18 x 8   CFA   ea. 4.00
8915. Coronation of the
       Virgin   15 x 9   IA   3.00
8916. Cowper Madonna   21-1/2 x 16   PENN   1.50
8917. Deposition (Rome)   12 x 11-1/2   AS   3.25
8918. La Disputa   18 x 24   IA   7.50
                            8 x 11   IA   1.75
8919. La Donna Gravida   14 x 11   IA   3.00
8920. La Donna Velata   10 x 8   NYGS   .50
8921. Entombment   11 x 12   IA   3.00
8922. La Fornarina   15 x 10-1/2   AS   3.25
8923. Four Designs   9 x 14   AR   3.00
8924. Heraclitus   9 x 7   NYGS   .50
8925. Holy Family   13 x 8   CFA   2.50
8926. Madonna and Child
       (DR.)   14-1/2x10-1/2   NYGS   5.00
8927. Madonna "La Belle
       Jardiniere"   15 x 10   IA   3.00
8928. Madonna del Cardellino
       (Goldfinch)   15 x 11   AS   3.25
                            15 x 10   IA   3.00

	Head of Madonna - Detail of No.			
	8928	16 x 12	IA	3.00
		10 x 8	IA	1.50
8929.	Madonna of Foligno	15 x 10	IA	3.00
		10-1/2x9-1/2	AS	3.25
	Angel - Detail			
	of No. 8929	15 x 11	IA	3.00
	St Jerome (Head) Detail of No.			
	8929	15 x 11	IA	3.00
8930.	Madonna del			
	Granduca	30 x 20	ESH	15.00
		24-1/2 x 18	IA	7.50
		24 x 14	NYGS	10.00
		21 x 14	AP	5.00
		16 x 11	IA	3.00
		10 x 7	IA	1.75
	c.	9 x 7	AP	.50
8931.	Madonna of the Maison			
	d'Orleans	14 x 8	IA	3.00
8932.	Madonna in the			
	Meadow	12 x 10	ESH	2.00
8933.	Madonna with the			
	Pomegranate	16 x 11	AR	5.00
8934.	Madonna della Sedia			
	(of the Chair)	29" Diam.	IA	12.00
		24" Diam.	NYGS	9.00
		20" Diam.	IA	10.00
		16" Diam.	AP	5.00
		12" Diam.	IA	3.50
		11" Diam.	IA	3.00
		9" Diam.	NYGS	1.00
		8-1/2" Diam.	IA	1.75
	(gold border)	22 x 18	NYGS	7.50
8935.	Madonna of San Sisto			
	(Sistine)	35 x 26	CAC	15.00
		27 x 23	CFA	12.00
		24 x 18	NYGS	10.00
		21 x 15-1/2	NYGS	7.50
		15 x 11	IA	3.00
		10 x 7	NYGS	1.00
8936.	Madonna Tempi	21 x 14	AP	5.00
8937.	Madonna della Tenda	28 x 20	CAC	15.00
		22 x 17	CAC	12.00
8938.	Marriage of the			
	Virgin	15 x 10	IA	3.00
	The Virgin - Detail of No.			
	8938	10 x 8	IA	1.50
8939.	La Muta	14 x 11	IA	3.00
8940.	Niccolini-Cowper			
	Madonna	24 x 16-1/2	NYGS	12.00

8941.	Pope Julius II	13 x 11	IA	3.00
8942.	Portrait of Francesco Maria della Rovere, Duke of Urbino	15 x 11	IA	3.00
		9 x 7	NYGS	.50
8943.	Portrait of Madalena Strozzi-Doni	15 x 11	IA	3.00
		10 x 8	NYGS	.50
8944.	Portrait of Perugino (Supposed)	15 x 10	IA	3.00
8945.	Portrait of Tommaso Inghirami	15 x 11	IA	3.00
8946.	Portrait of a Young Nobleman	20-1/2 x 14	NYGS	10.00
8947.	Psychée	10-1/2 x 7	NYGS	4.00
8948.	Resurrection of Christ	13 x 11	IA	3.00
8949.	St. John in the Desert	12 x 11	IA	3.00
8950.	School of Athens	18 x 24	IA	7.50
		8 x 11	IA	1.75
8951.	A Scribe	9 x 7	NYGS	.50
8952.	Self-Portrait	15 x 11	AS	3.25
		14 x 11	IA	3.00
8953.	Small Cowper Madonna	21 x 16	NYGS	10.00
	c.	10 x 8	NYGS	.50
	c.	9 x 7	AP	.50
8954.	Studies of Movements	14 x 9	AR	3.00
8955.	Three Studies of the Virgin	11 x 8	AR	3.00
8956.	Transfiguration	15 x 10	IA	3.00
8957.	Veiled Lady (La Fornarina?)	15 x 11	IA	3.00
8958.	The Virgin	10 x 8	IA	1.50
8959.	Virgin with the Blue Diadem (Virgin of the Veil)	15 x 11	IA	3.00
8960.	Virgin of Divine Love (Attrib.)	14 x 11	IA	3.00
8961.	Virgin of the Impannata	14 x 11	AS	3.25
8962.	Virgin with the Child and St. John (DR.)	14-1/2x10-1/2	NYGS	5.00
8963.	Vision of Ezechiel (Florence)	15 x 10	AS	3.25
8964.	Young Man	19 x 14	CAC	7.50

RAIBOLINI, FRANCESCO See FRANCIA, IL
RAIMONDI, ALDO (Italian, 1902-)

8965.	Floral Paintings (8)	9 x 7	NYGS	set 10.00

Alpine Star				ea.	1.50
Clivia	7 x 5		NYGS	set	6.00
Cornflower				ea.	1.00
Cyclamen					
Marguerite					
Narcissus					
Poppy					
Rose					

RAIN, CHARLES (American Contemporary)
8966.	Dark Stranger	24 x 30	CFA		15.00

RAJKO (Yugoslavian Contemporary)
8967.	Hawaii, 1963	24 x 20	NYGS		7.50
8968.	Tahiti, 1963	24 x 20	NYGS		7.50

RAKER, JAMES (American Contemporary)
8969.	Afternoon	10 x 8	AR		2.00
8970.	Becalmed	10 x 8	AR		2.00
8971.	Boy with Horse	10 x 8	AR		2.00
8972.	Redbird and Cat	10 x 8	AR		2.00

RANKEN, WILLIAM (Scotch, 1881-1941)
8973.	In Swallowfield Park	20-1/2x13-1/2	ESH		6.00

RAOUX, JEAN
8974.	Young Girl Reading a Letter	19 x 15	CFA		10.00

RAPHAEL See RAFFAELLO SANZIO

RAUSCHENBERG, ROBERT (American Contemporary)
8975.	Rebus	c. 20 x 24	PENN		1.50
8976.	Reservoir	30 x 21-1/2	NYGS		18.00

RAVENET
8977.	El Janguey	c. 7 x 9	AP		.25

RAWSON, CARL W. (American, 1884-)
8978.	Autumn Farewell	19-1/2 x 25	IA		6.00
8979.	Blue Spruce	25 x 32	IA		12.00
8980.	Lake Superior	25 x 32	IA		12.00
8981.	Landscapes (6)	12 x 15	IA	set	10.00
8982.	Autumn Reflections				
8983.	Fruitage of Autumn				
8984.	Offshore Wind				
8985.	Superior Days				
8986.	When Autumn Comes				
8987.	Where the Fisherfolk Live				
8988.	Winter	25 x 32	IA		12.00

RAY
8989.	Rope Dancer	c. 8 x 10	NYGS		.50

RAY, ROBERT
8990.	Sunflowers	26-1/2 x 38	IA		12.00

RAY, RUTH
8991.	Horses (4)	18 x 24	DAC	ea.	7.50
8992.	Copper Queen				
8993.	Golden Ruler				
8994.	Handsome Witch				
8995.	Storm Queen				

REDON, ODILON (French, 1840-1916)

8996.	Anemones	9 x 8	CFA	1. 00
8997.	Big Tree	19-1/2 x 14	NYGS	5. 00
8998.	Blue Vase on Dark			
	Background c.	10 x 8	ESH	1. 00
8999.	Bouquet of Flowers/			
	Green Vase	28 x 20-1/2	NYGS	15. 00
9000.	Cyklops c.	8 x 10	MMA	. 35
9001.	Field Flowers	16-1/2 x 21	PENN	1. 50
9002.	Flower Still Life	26 x 19	NYGS	15. 00
9003.	Flowers c.	18 x 23	HNA	5. 95
9004.	Flowers in a Blue			
	Vase	23 x 17-1/2	AR	12. 00
9005.	Flowers in a Jar	22 x 16	ESH	10. 00
9006.	Girl and Flowers	18 x 23	PENN	1. 50
9007.	Large Green Vase			
	c.	23 x 18	HNA	5. 95
		22 x 17	PENN	1. 50
9008.	Ophilie	18 x 26	PENN	1. 50
9009.	Pegasus	15-1/2 x 21	AP	4. 00
9010.	Phaeton	19 x 23-1/2	NYGS	12. 00
9011.	Red Boat	18 x 24	CFA	12. 00
9012.	Still Life	21 x 16	AA	7. 50
9013.	Turquoise Vase with			
	Flowers c.	23 x 18	HNA	5. 95
9014.	Vase de Fleurs	17 x 22	NYGS	22. 00
9015.	Vase of Flowers	26 x 19	MMA	6. 50
9016.	Vase of Flowers	25 x 19	CFA	10. 00
		19 x 16	CFA	10. 00
		8 x 6	CFA	1. 00
9017.	Vase of Flowers			
	c.	26 x 21	HNA	5. 95
		22-1/2 x 18	ESH	10. 00
		10-1/2x12-1/2	PENN	1. 50
9018.	Wildflowers	24 x 18	NYGS	12. 00

REDOUTE, PIERRE JOSEPH (French, 1759-1840)

9019.	Auriculas and				
	Camelias	22 x 17	ESH		10. 00
9020.	Bouquet (2)	12 x 9	CFA	ea.	5. 00
	Blue Bow				
	Pink Bow				
9021.	Cactus	19 x 14	CFA		5. 00
9022.	Choix de Camellias	19 x 14	CFA		7. 50
9023.	Choix de Fleurs	19 x 14	CFA		7. 50
9024.	Fruit in Goblet	22 x 17	ESH		10. 00
9025.	Mixed Bouquet	19 x 14	CFA		5. 00
9026.	Moss Rose c.	12-1/2x9-1/2	AP		1. 25
9027.	Red and Pink Roses	19 x 14	CFA		5. 00
9028.	Rosa Damascena				
	Aurora c.	12-1/2x9-1/2	AP		1. 25
	c.	9 x 7	AP		1. 00
9029.	Rosa Damascena				
	Celsiana c.	12-1/2x9-1/2	AP		1. 25

9030.	Rosa Muscosa				
	Multiplex	c.	9 x 7	AP	1. 00
9031.	Rosa Multiflora				
	Carnea	c.	12-1/2x9-1/2	AP	1. 25
		c.	9 x 7	AP	1. 00
9032.	Rose-Carnation		12-1/2x9-1/2	CFA	1. 00
9033.	Rose d'Enfante		11 x 19	CAC	3. 00
9034.	Roses de Cumber-				
	land		15 x 10	CAC	5. 00
9035.	Roses de Paris		8 x 5	CFA	3. 00
9036.	Roses (6)		15-1/2x10-1/2	CFA	8. 00
	Roses (3)		12-1/2x9-1/2	CFA	ea. 1. 00
	Pink				
	White and Pink				
	Yellow				
9037.	Rosier (3)		15 x 10	CAC	ea. 5. 00
	Rosier a Cent Feuilles				
	Rosier des Parfumeurs				
	Rosier Grandeur Royale				
9038.	Yellow and Pink				
	Roses		19 x 14	CFA	5. 00
REED					
9039.	Canterbury Pilgrims		16 x 60	CAC	10. 00
REEKIE, G.					
9040.	Blue Bowl		14 x 36	RL	10. 00
9041.	Harmony in Pewter		12 x 48	RL	20. 00
9042.	Pewter Jug		14 x 36	RL	10. 00
REGGIANINI					
9043.	Mother's Birthday		19 x 27	AA	9. 00
REGNAULT, HENRI (French, 1843-1871)					
9044.	Automdon		16 x 17	CAC	3. 50
9045.	Salome	c.	8 x 10	NYGS	. 50
REGNIER, CHARLES (German, 1811-1862)					
9046.	Mounted Knights (4)		19 x 12	CFA	ea. 10. 00
REHN, FRANK K. M. (American, 1848-1914)					
9047.	In the Glittering				
	Moonlight		24 x 36	NYGS	15. 00
REID					
9048.	Coming of the White				
	Man	c.	7 x 9	AP	. 50
REMBRANDT HARMENSZ VAN RIJN (Dutch, 1606-1669)					
9049.	Adoration des Bergers				
	(Adoration of the				
	Shepherds)		12 x 10	CFA	1. 00
			9 x 8	NYGS	4. 00
9050.	The Apostle Paul		26 x 20	IA	12. 00
9051.	Aristotle Contemplating				
	a Bust of Homer		28 x 27	CFA	15. 00
9052.	The Artist's Mother		24x18-1/2-Oval	NYGS	10. 00
9053.	The Atrist's Son,				
	Titus (Reading)		19-1/2 x 17	NYGS	10. 00

9054.	The Artist's Son,			
	Titus (undated)	25 x 21	NYGS	12.00
	(Norton-Simon			
	Coll'n.)	24 x 18	PENN	1.50
	c.	16 x 12	PENN	1.00
		14 x 12	NYGS	4.00
9055.	The Artist's Son,			
	Titus, 1655	30-1/2 x 23	NYGS	18.00
	(Metropolitan, N.Y.)	14 x 10	NYGS	4.00
9056.	Bathsheba	10 x 10	CFA	2.50
9057.	Bethsabea Bathing	11 x 11	IA	3.00
9058.	Bridal Couple	20 x 30	DAC	7.50
	c.	20 x 24	PENN	1.50
9059.	Christ	24-1/2 x 20	PENN	1.50
	c.	16 x 12	PENN	1.00
9060.	Christ (Head) c.	24 x 20	PENN	1.50
9061.	Danae	25 x 28	NYGS	16.00
9062.	Descent from the			
	Cross	28 x 22	NYGS	15.00
		28 x 21-1/2	IA	12.00
9063.	The Disciples at			
	Emmaus c.	10 x 8	ESH	1.00
9064.	The Elephant	12 x 16	CFA	5.00
9065.	Girl at Open Half-			
	Door c.	24 x 20	PENN	1.50
9066.	Girl with a Broom	26 x 22	NYGS	12.00
	c.	23 x 18	HNA	5.95
		20 x 16-1/2	PENN	1.50
		19-1/2 x 17	IA	4.00
		10 x 9	CFA	2.00
9067.	Golden Helmet	25 x 19	IA	18.00
		23 x 17	IA	4.00
		21 x 15-1/2	AP	5.00
	c.	10 x 8	ESH	1.00
9068.	Good Samaritan	11 x 13	IA	3.00
9069.	Hendrikje Stoffels	29 x 20	NYGS	26.00
		26 x 21-1/2	NYGS	12.00
	c.	23 x 18	HNA	5.95
		7 x 5	NYGS	.50
9070.	Jacob Blessing his			
	Children	27 x 32-1/2	NYGS	22.00
9071.	Jacob's Dream	27 x 33	IA	18.00
9072.	Jesus, Good			
	Samaritan	18-1/2x15-1/2	NYGS	15.00
9073.	Jewish Bride c.	7 x 9	AP	.60
9074.	Judah Asking Jacob	7 x 9-1/2	AR	3.00
9075.	Man at a Door	8 x 5	AR	3.00
9076.	The Man with the			
	Golden Helmet	26 x 20	IA	18.00
		26 x 19	NYGS	18.00
		25 x 19	IA	18.00
	c.	24 x 20	PENN	1.50

			c.	23 x 18	HNA	5. 95
				23 x 17	IA	4. 00
				19 x 14	IA	7. 50
				16 x 12	DAC	2. 50
			c.	9 x 7	AP	. 60
9077.	Masters of the Cloth					
	Guild			20 x 30	NYGS	12. 00
9078.	The Mill			25 x 30	NYGS	18. 00
9079.	Night Watch			37 x 44-1/2	IA	24. 00
				23 x 28	NYGS	12. 00
				20 x 23	DAC	7. 50
				18 x 21-1/2	PENN	1. 50
			c.	7 x 9	AP	. 50
9080.	Old Man with a Red					
	Cap			20 x 14	CFA	14. 00
				7 x 5	NYGS	. 50
9081.	Old Soldier			22-1/2 x 9	ESH	6. 00
9082.	Philosphe en Lisant			21 x 16	PENN	1. 50
9083.	The Philosopher, c.					
	1650			24 x 19	NYGS	12. 00
	(U. S. Nat. Gall'y.)			24 x 18-1/2	IA	12. 00
9084.	Philosopher (DR.)			8 x 9	AR	3. 00
9085.	Pilgrims at Emmaus			11 x 11	AS	3. 25
9086.	Polish Nobleman			11 x 8	CFA	2. 00
9087.	Polish Rider			25 x 29	NYGS	18. 00
				12 x 14	NYGS	4. 00
9088.	Portrait of the					
	Admiral's Wife			36-1/2x29-1/2	NYGS	20. 00
9089.	Portrait of a Lady					
	with an Ostrich-					
	Feather Fan	c.		23 x 18	HNA	5. 95
9090.	Portrait of an Old					
	Man (Detail, Head)			15 x 11	AS	3. 25
9091.	Portrait of a Rabbi			28 x 23	NYGS	16. 00
9092.	Portrait of Rembrandt					
	and Saskia			24 x 20	DAC	7. 50
9093.	Rembrandt's Mother			13 x 11	ESH	5. 00
9094.	Rest on the Flight					
	into Egypt			8 x 12-1/2	AR	3. 00
9095.	St. Joseph's Dream			23 x 18	NYGS	10. 00
9096.	Saskia	c.		24 x 20	PENN	1. 50
				20 x 16	CFA	12. 00
				19-1/2 x 16	IA	12. 00
9097.	Saskia at Toilet					
	Table			9-1/2x7-1/2	AR	3. 00
9098.	Self-Portrait			18-1/2 x 15	NYGS	20. 00
				11 x 8	NYGS	. 50
9099.	Self-Portrait (Metal					
	Collar)			13-1/2 x 11	AS	3. 25
				13 x 11	IA	3. 00
9100.	Self-Portrait (White					
	Cap)			21-1/2x18-1/2	PENN	1. 50

	c.	16 x 12	PENN		1.00
		10 x 8	CFA		2.00
9101.	Self-Portrait (Louvre) (Skull Cap)	13 x 11	IA		3.00
9102.	Self-Portrait (As an Officer)	15 x 10	IA		3.00
9103.	Self-Portrait	26-1/2 x 22	NYGS		18.00
	c.	10 x 8	NYGS		.50
9104.	Stormy Landscape	20 x 28	CFA		18.00
		7 x 10	AR		3.00
9105.	The Student	30 x 33-1/2	NYGS		20.00
		25-1/2 x 29	AA		10.00
		17 x 19	NYGS		6.00
9106.	Study of an Old Man				
	c.	16 x 12	PENN		1.00
		8 x 5-1/2	AR		3.00
9107.	Supper at Emmaus	17-1/2 x 17	IA		7.50
		11 x 11	IA		3.00
9108.	Syndics c.	7 x 9	AP		.50
9109.	Syndics of the Drapers Guild	7 x 10	NYGS		.50
9110.	Three Elephants	10 x 14	AR		3.00
9111.	Titus	20 x 17	CFA		10.00
9112.	Toilette of Saskia	9 x 7	CFA		3.00
9113.	Young Girl at an Open Half-Door	26 x 22	NYGS		12.00
		24 x 20	DAC		7.50
		14 x 12	NYGS		4.00
		9-1/2 x 8	NYGS		1.00
9114.	Young Girl at a Window	18-1/2 x 16	IA		7.50
9115.	Young Girl at Open Half-Window	30 x 24	CFA		15.00
9116.	Young Warrior	25 x 19	ESH		15.00

REMINGTON, FREDERIC (American, 1861-1909)

9117.	Apache	16 x 22	PENN		1.50
	c.	12 x 16	PENN		1.00
9118.	Argument with the Town Marshall	16 x 24	AA		5.00
9119.	Attack on the Supply Wagons	16 x 24	CFA		5.00
9120.	Benighted for Dry-Camp c.	7 x 9	AP		1.00
9121.	Bronco Busters (2)	15 x 11	PENN	set	1.00
9122.	Running Bucker				
9123.	Sunfisher				
9124.	Buckskins (8)	16 x 12	PENN	set	2.98
				or ea.	1.00
9125.	Arizona Cowboy				
9126.	Army Packer				
9127.	Breed				

Rendle, J. Morgan 43

9128.	Cavalry Officer			
9129.	Cheyenne Buck			
9130.	Old Raymon			
9131.	Sioux Chief			
9132.	Trapper			
9133.	Coming and Going of the Pony Express	13-1/2 x 20	AA	5.00
9134.	The Cowboy	26 x 18	AA	10.00
9135.	Dash for Timber	22 x 38-1/2	AA	15.00
9136.	Dismounted: The Fourth Troopers Moving	20 x 29	AA	12.00
		18 x 24	PENN	1.50
9137.	Emigrants	17-1/2 x 26	NYGS	10.00
9138.	Episode of a Buffalo Hunt	26 x 20	AA	12.00
9139.	Long-Horn Cattle Sign c.	7 x 9	AP	1.00
9140.	Navajo Raid c.	7 x 9	AP	1.00
9141.	Old Time Plains Fight	16 x 23-1/2	PENN	1.50
9142.	Prospecting for Cattle Range	22 x 38	AA	15.00
9143.	Scout: Friends or Enemies?	19-1/2 x 29	AA	12.00
		18 x 24	PENN	1.50
9144.	Smoke Signal	24 x 38-1/2	AA	15.00
9145.	Stampeded by Lightning	20 x 30	AA	12.00
9146.	Victory Dance	20-1/2 x 29	AA	12.00
	Western Scenes (6)	8 x 12	NYGS	set 7.50 or ea. 1.50
9147.	Aiding a Comrad			
9148.	Change of Ownership			
9149.	Emigrants			
9150.	Fight for the Waterhole			
9151.	Flight			
9152.	New Year on the Cimarron			

RENDLE, J. MORGAN (English, 1889-)

9153.	Alfristan Church	14 x 19	ESH	6.00
9154.	Boating Lake	18 x 22	ESH	10.00
9155.	Downland Farm	15 x 20-1/2	ESH	6.00
9156.	Fringe of the Downs	15 x 19	ESH	6.00
9157.	South Heighton Farm	18-1/2 x 22	ESH	7.50
9158.	Sussex Downs	13-1/2 x 17	ESH	6.00

RENI, GUIDO (Italian, 1575-1642)

9159.	Adoration of the Shepherds by Night	22 x 14	RL	7.50
9160.	Archangel Michel	15 x 11	IA	3.00
9161.	Aurora c.	7 x 9	AP	.50
		6 x 13	IA	3.00

9162.	Bacchus	14 x 11	IA	3.00
9163.	Baptism of Jesus	15 x 11	IA	3.00
9164.	Cardinal Bernardino			
	Spada	15 x 9	IA	3.00
9165.	Chaste Susan	11 x 15	AS	3.25
9166.	Christ on the Cross	15 x 11	IA	3.00
9167.	Cleopatra	15 x 11	IA	3.00
9168.	Ecce Homo	14 x 10	IA	3.00
9169.	Massacre of the			
	Innocents	15 x 9	IA	3.00
9170.	Portrait of Beatrice			
	Cenci	15-1/2 x 11	AS	3.25
		15 x 11	IA	3.00
9171.	St. John the Baptist	13 x 11	IA	3.00
9172.	St. Joseph	13 x 11	IA	3.00
9173.	Youth of the Virgin	17 x 25	ESH	15.00

RENOIR, PIERRE AUGUSTE (French, 1841-1919)

9174.	Amazon	26 x 22	NYGS	12.00
9175.	Apple Vendor c.	24 x 20	PENN	1.50
9176.	Artist Sisley and his			
	Wife	21 x 15	NYGS	20.00
9177.	At the Concert c.	24 x 20	PENN	1.50
9178.	At the Grenouillere	12 x 16	AA	3.00
9179.	At the Seashore c.	8 x 10	NYGS	.50
9180.	Au Cirque Fernando			
	(Two Little Circus			
	Girls)	28 x 21	NYGS	15.00
	c.	24 x 20	PENN	1.50
		24 x 18	DAC	7.50
		16 x 12	DAC	2.50
9181.	Bal a Bougival (Dance			
	at Bougival)	32 x 17	NYGS	18.00
	c.	26 x 21	HNA	5.95
	c.	24 x 20	PENN	1.50
9182.	Balancoire (Swing)	31 x 24-1/2	NYGS	15.00
		24 x 18	PENN	1.50
	c.	23 x 18	HNA	5.95
		22 x 17	ESH	10.00
		16 x 12	AA	3.00
	c.	12-1/2x9-1/2	AP	1.25
	c.	10 x 8	ESH	1.00
	c.	9 x 7	AP	1.00
9183.	The Bath	18-1/2x15-1/2	NYGS	15.00
9184.	Bather with Griffon	15 x 9	IA	3.00
9185.	Bathers at Guernsey	12-1/2 x 16	NYGS	10.00
9186.	Bathing Nude with			
	Long Hair	10 x 8	CFA	1.00
9187.	Bathing Woman on a			
	Rock	19-1/2x15-1/2	AP	5.00
9188.	Bergere	15 x 11	NYGS	7.50
9189.	Boating	24 x 30	DAC	7.50
	c.	20 x 24	PENN	1.50

9190.	Boating Party		16 x 22-1/2	ESH	10.00
		c.	8 x 10	ESH	1.00
	Girl with a Dog	--			
	Detail of No.				
	9190	c.	10 x 8	ESH	1.00
9191.	Boating Party at				
	Chatou	c.	18 x 23	HNA	5.95
9192.	Breakfast		31 x 25	CFA	18.00
9193.	By the Seashore				
		c.	24 x 20	PENN	1.50
			22 x 17-1/2	NYGS	10.00
		c.	9 x 7	AP	.50
9194.	The Caillebotte				
	Children	c.	12 x 16	PENN	1.00
		c.	9-1/2x12-1/2	AP	1.25
			6 x 8	CFA	1.00
9195.	Chalands sur la				
	Seine		18 x 24-1/2	PENN	1.50
9196.	Child in White		24 x 19-1/2	NYGS	12.00
		c.	16 x 12	PENN	1.00
		c.	9 x 7	AP	.50
	Detail of No.				
	9196		16 x 12-1/2	NYGS	5.00
9197.	Child and Nurse-				
	maid	c.	12 x 16	PENN	1.50
9198.	Children at the				
	Seashore		25 x 18	PENN	1.50
9199.	Claude Dessinant		12 x 9-1/2	NYGS	7.50
9200.	Cock-Pheasant in the				
	Snow	c.	9-1/2x12-1/2	AP	1.25
9201.	Confidences	c.	23 x 18	HNA	5.95
9202.	Cornfield		13 x 16	CFA	2.00
9203.	Cup of Chocolate				
		c.	10 x 8	NYGS	.50
9204.	Dancer		30-1/2x20-1/2	NYGS	16.00
9205.	Excursionist		13 x 10	IA	3.00
9206.	Farmhouse, les				
	Collettes	c.	8 x 10	ESH	1.00
9207.	Field Flowers		30 x 22-1/2	NYGS	26.00
9208.	Fille au Chapeau		13 x 9	NYGS	7.50
9209.	Fillette a la				
	Gerbe	c.	10 x 8	ESH	1.00
9210.	Fillette au Chapeau				
	Bleu	c.	22 x 17-1/2	AS	4.00
9211.	Flowers and Cat		21 x 17	PENN	1.50
9212.	Fruits of the Midi		15 x 20	CFA	7.50
		c.	7 x 9	AP	.50
9213.	Gabrielle and Coco		9 x 8	NYGS	.50
9214.	Gabrielle and Jean		25-1/2 x 21	NYGS	12.00
			10 x 8	CFA	1.00
9215.	Gabrielle and Rose		24 x 19-1/2	PENN	1.50

9216.	Gabrielle with Jean Renoir and a Little Girl		16-1/2x22-1/2	ESH	10.00
9217.	Garden at les Collettes	c.	8 x 10	ESH	1.00
9218.	Garden Walk	c.	8 x 10	ESH	1.00
9219.	Girl Adjusting Earrings		23 x 19	PENN	1.50
9220.	Girl at the Piano	c.	24 x 20	PENN	1.50
9221.	Girl Combing her Hair	c.	12-1/2x9-1/2	AP	1.25
9222.	Girl in Pink	c.	9-1/2x12-1/2	AP	1.25
		c.	6 x 8	CFA	1.00
9223.	Girl in Violet		15 x 11	CFA	5.00
9224.	Girl Lying at Water's Edge	c.	9-1/2x12-1/2	AP	1.25
			6 x 8	CFA	1.00
9225.	Girl Reading		22 x 18	NYGS	16.00
			21 x 18	CFA	12.00
			21 x 17	PENN	1.50
			20 x 16	NYGS	6.00
			9 x 7	NYGS	.50
9226.	Girl with a Basket of Fish		31 x 10	NYGS	12.00
9227.	Girl with a Basket of Oranges		31 x 10	NYGS	12.00
9228.	Girl with a Cat		26-1/2 x 20	AA	12.00
			24 x 19	NYGS	12.00
9229.	Girl with a Falcon		13 x 8	NYGS	.50
9230.	Girl with Flowing Hair		25-1/2 x 21	NYGS	26.00
9231.	Girl with a Hat		21 x 16	CFA	7.50
			20-1/2 x 16	AR	7.50
9232.	Girl with a Hoop		29-1/2x17-1/2	NYGS	16.00
9233.	Girl with a Watering Can		30 x 22	NYGS	16.00
			24 x 17-1/2	PENN	1.50
		c.	23 x 18	HNA	5.95
			22 x 16	NYGS	10.00
			14 x 11	NYGS	3.00
			12 x 9	ESH	2.00
			9 x 6	CFA	1.00
9234.	Girls in Open Air		19 x 16	NYGS	18.00
9235.	Girls Picking Flowers		16-1/2 x 21	NYGS	10.00
			16 x 20	CFA	10.00
			7 x 8	CFA	1.00
9236.	Les Grands Boulevards		16-1/2x20-1/2	IA	6.00
			8 x 9	NYGS	.50
9237.	La Grenouillere		24 x 33	CFA	15.00

9238.	Guitar Player	c.	7 x 9	AP	. 50
9239.	Her First Night		15 x 12	AR	3. 00
9240.	Idyle		24 x 18	PENN	1. 50
9241.	In the Meadow		28 x 22	AA	15. 00
			24 x 19	PENN	1. 50
9242.	In the Nursery		24 x 30	NYGS	18. 00
9243.	Ingenue		24 x 18	PENN	1. 50
9244.	Jacque Fray (Baby)				
		c.	16 x 12	PENN	1. 00
9245.	Jean Renoir Drawing		17-1/2 x 21	NYGS	15. 00
9246.	Jean Renoir Sewing		21-1/2 x 18	AA	7. 50
9247.	Jeanne Samary	c.	16 x 12	AP	2. 00
		c.	9 x 7	AP	. 50
9248.	Jeune Baigneuse		15 x 12	NYGS	3. 00
9249.	Jeune Femme en				
	Bleu		15-1/2 x 10	NYGS	15. 00
9250.	Jeunes Filles				
	Assises		25-1/2x21	NYGS	18. 00
9251.	Lady at the Piano		30 x 24	CFA	18. 00
			24 x 20	DAC	7. 50
			22 x 17-1/2	NYGS	10. 00
			14 x 11	NYGS	3. 00
		c.	9 x 7	AP	. 50
9252.	Lady Sewing		20 x 16-1/2	AJ	7. 50
			20 x 16	CFA	7. 50
			9 x 7-1/2	IA	. 50
9253.	Lady with a Muff		15 x 10-1/2	NYGS	3. 00
9254.	Lady with a				
	Parasol	c.	20 x 24	PENN	1. 50
			18-1/2 x 22	NYGS	15. 00
			18 x 22	NYGS	12. 00
9255.	Lady with Umbrella		19 x 23	CFA	15. 00
9256.	Landscape		10 x 13-1/2	AR	5. 00
9257.	Landscape at Guernsey				
			7 x 8	CFA	1. 00
9258.	Landscape near				
	Menton	c.	20 x 24	PENN	1. 50
		c.	18 x 23	HNA	5. 95
9259.	Large Vase of				
	Flowers		30 x24	IA	4. 00
			24 x 18	IA	3. 00
			22-1/2 x 17	IA	4. 00
9260.	Liseuse		17 x 14-1/2	NYGS	7. 50
		c.	10 x 8	ESH	1. 00
9261.	Liseuse Blanche	c.	24 x 20	PENN	1. 50
9262.	Little Girl with the				
	Sheaf		13-1/2 x 11	AS	3. 25
9263.	Little Gleaner		13 x 11	IA	3. 00
9264.	Little Irene		24 x 20	DAC	7. 50
9265.	Little Margot				
	Berard		16 x 12-1/2	AP	4. 00
		c.	9 x 7	AP	. 50

9266.	Little Nude in			
	Blue	20 x 16	NYGS	10. 00
		15-1/2 x 12	NYGS	3. 00
9267.	La Loge	28 x 22-1/2	NYGS	15. 00
		23-1/2 x 16	PENN	1. 50
9268.	Lovers c.	18 x 23	HNA	5. 95
9269.	Luncheon	31-1/2 x25-1/2	NYGS	20. 00
9270.	Luncheon of the			
	Boating Party	26-1/2 x 36	AA	18. 00
	(Phillips Coll'n.)	20-1/2 x 28	NYGS	12. 00
		18 x 24	PENN	1. 50
	Girl with a Dog --			
	Detail of No.			
	9270	22-1/2x18-1/2	ESH	10. 00
9271.	Mme. Charpentier and			
	her Children	24 x 30	NYGS	18. 00
	c.	8 x 10	NYGS	. 50
	Charpentier Children			
	- Detail of No.			
	9271	22 x 18	NYGS	10. 00
9272.	Mme. Henriot c.	18 x 23	HNA	5. 95
		18 x 22	NYGS	10. 00
	c.	12 x 16	PENN	1. 00
	c.	8 x 10	MMA	. 35
		7 x 8	CFA	1. 00
9273.	Mme. Renoir c.	23 x 18	HNA	5. 95
9274.	Mlle. Irene	19-1/2 x 16	IA	12. 00
		18 x 14-1/2	IA	5. 00
9275.	Mlle. Lacaux	22 x 17-1/2	NYGS	10. 00
9276.	Meadow c.	7 x 9	AP	. 50
9277.	Mixed Flowers in a			
	Vase c.	23 x 18	HNA	5. 95
9278.	Moss Roses c.	10 x 8	ESH	1. 00
9279.	Mother and Child	10 x 6	CFA	1. 00
9280.	Mother and Children	24 x 15	NYGS	12. 00
	c.	12-1/2x9-1/2	AP	1. 25
	c.	9 x 7	AP	1. 00
9281.	Moulin de la			
	Gallette	23-1/2x31-1/2	NYGS	15. 00
	c.	20 x 24	PENN	1. 50
		16-1/2x22-1/2	ESH	10. 00
		16 x 22	CFA	10. 00
		10-1/2x14-1/2	AJ	2. 50
	c.	8 x 10	ESH	1. 00
		9 x 6	CFA	1. 00
	Head of a Girl -			
	Detail of No.			
	9281 c.	10 x 8	ESH	1. 00
	Head of a Woman -			
	Detail of No.			
	9281 c.	10 x 8	ESH	1. 00

	Heads of Two Men -			
	Detail of No.			
	9281 c.	10 x 8	ESH	1.00
	Still Life, Glass-			
	ware - Detail of			
	No. 9281 c.	10 x 8	ESH	1.00
9282.	The Musical Mendes			
	Sisters	24 x 20	DAC	7.50
9283.	Near the Lake	20 x 24	NYGS	12.00
9284.	Noirmoutier	17 x 21	CAC	7.50
9285.	Nu (Nude)	11 x 10-1/2	NYGS	7.50
9286.	Nu au Soleil (Nude			
	in the Sun)	26-1/2 x 21	NYGS	12.00
	c.	12-1/2x9-1/2	AP	1.25
9287.	Nude Gabrielle	15 x 36	NYGS	18.00
9288.	Nude in a Landscape	25-1/2x20-1/2	NYGS	12.00
9289.	Nude Seated in a			
	Landscape	9 x 8	CFA	1.00
9290.	Nude Studies	12-1/2 x 16	ESH	10.00
9291.	Les Nymphs	15 x 20	PENN	1.50
9292.	Oarsmen at Chatou	29 x 35-1/2	NYGS	20.00
9293.	On the Terrace	30 x 24	IA	4.00
		27-1/2 x 22	NYGS	12.00
	c.	23 x 18	HNA	5.95
		22 x 18	IA	3.00
		20 x 16-1/2	AP	7.50
	c.	10 x 8	IA	.50
	c.	9 x 7	AP	.50
9294.	The Orange Vendor	13 x 11	AR	5.00
9295.	Paris Boulevard in			
	Spring	19-1/2 x 24	NYGS	22.00
9296.	Petite Fille	7 x 6	CFA	1.00
9297.	Petite Fille au			
	Chapeau	21 x 16	PENN	1.50
9298.	Picnic	19-1/2 x 24	PENN	1.50
9299.	Pink Roses c.	10 x 8	ESH	1.00
9300.	Place Clichy	25-1/2x21-1/2	NYGS	15.00
	c.	10 x 8	ESH	1.00
9301.	Pont de Chemin			
	de Fer c.	20 x 24	PENN	1.50
9302.	Portrait of Gabrielle	23 x 16	PENN	1.50
9303.	Portrait de Jeune			
	Fille	15 x 12	NYGS	3.00
9304.	Portrait of Lucie			
	Berard	15 x 11	NYGS	3.00
9305.	Portrait of a Model			
	c.	10 x 8	ESH	1.00
9306.	Portrait of a Young			
	Girl	25-1/2 x 21	NYGS	12.00
		20-1/2 x 16	NYGS	5.00
9307.	La Premiere			
	Sortie	25-1/2 x 20	ESH	15.00
9308.	Printemps a Chatou	22 x 27	NYGS	15.00

9309.	Reader	16 x 12	AA	3.00
9310.	Reading Girl in White	18 x 20	ESH	10.00
9311.	Reading Girl with Straw Bonnet	18-1/2 x 16	AP	5.00
9312.	Rose and Blue	23 x 15	AA	10.00
		14 x 9	NYGS	3.00
		9 x 5	CFA	1.00
9313.	Roses	25-1/2 x 21	NYGS	18.00
		25 x 20	CFA	15.00
		20-1/2 x 17	NYGS	10.00
	c.	10 x 8	ESH	1.00
9314.	Roses Mousseuses	21 x 16	PENN	1.50
9315.	Rower's Lunch	20 x 24	NYGS	12.00
9316.	St. Mark's Square	24 x 31	CFA	18.00
9317.	Sea and Cliffs c.	9-1/2x12-1/2	AP	1.25
		6 x 8	CFA	1.00
9318.	Seated Bather c.	8 x 10	MMA	.35
9319.	Seated Nude c.	12-1/2x9-1/2	AP	1.25
		8 x 6	CFA	1.00
9320.	A Scene at Moulin de la Gallette	11 x 16	ESH	8.00
9321.	The Seine at Argenteuil	18 x 21-1/2	NYGS	18.00
	c.	8 x 10	ESH	1.00
9322.	The Seine at Champrosay	21 x 25	NYGS	12.00
9323.	The Seine at Chatou			
	c.	18 x 23	HNA	5.95
9324.	Self-Portrait	11 x 8	NYGS	.50
9325.	La Serenade	13-1/2 x 10	NYGS	8.00
9326.	Sitting Nude c.	16 x 12	PENN	1.00
		9 x 7	CFA	1.00
9327.	Skiff	24 x 30	DAC	7.50
		18 x 24	NYGS	12.00
9328.	Sleeping Girl with a Cat	26-1/2 x 20	AA	12.00
9329.	Sloping Pathway in a Field c.	9-1/2x12-1/2	AP	1.25
		6 x 8	CFA	1.00
9330.	Small Painter	14 x 11	AR	5.00
9331.	Smiling Woman	14 x 11	IA	3.00
9332.	La Source	30 x 24	NYGS	18.00
9333.	Spring Flowers c.	23 x 18	HNA	5.95
9334.	Standing Bather c.	12-1/2x9-1/2	AP	1.25
9335.	Still Life with Peaches	21 x 25-1/2	MMA	4.00
9336.	Strand of Guernsey	12 x 16	AJ	10.00
	The Swing (See Balancoire)			
9337.	Therese Berard			
	c.	9 x 7	AP	.50
9338.	Thoughtful	24 x 20	DAC	7.50

9339.	Three Bathers	c.	20 x 24	PENN	1. 50
9340.	Tree Near the				
	Farm		19 x 22	ESH	10. 00
		c.	8 x 10	ESH	1. 00
9341.	Two Bathers	c.	9-1/2 x 12-1/2	AP	1. 25
9342.	Two Children in				
	White		24 x 14-1/2	PENN	1. 50
9343.	Two Girls at the				
	Piano	c.	26 x 21	HNA	5. 95
			22 x 18	NYGS	10. 00
			16 x 12	AA	3. 00
			14 x 11-1/2	NYGS	3. 00
		c.	12-1/2x9-1/2	AP	1. 25
		c.	10 x 8	ESH	1. 00
		c.	9 x 7	AP	1. 00
9344.	Two Girls in Blue				
		c.	23 x 18	HNA	5. 95
9345.	Two Girls in a				
	Meadow		21 x 17	CFA	10. 00
		c.	12-1/2x9-1/2	AP	1. 25
	Two Little Circus				
	Girls (See Au Cirque				
	Fernando)				
9346.	Two Sisters		28 x 22	NYGS	16. 00
			19 x 17	CFA	10. 00
9347.	Two Women with				
	Umbrellas		15 x 11	ESH	8. 00
9348.	Two Young Girls				
		c.	7 x 9	CFA	1. 00
9349.	Vase of Roses	c.	10 x 8	ESH	1. 00
9350.	Venice, Gondola		21 x 25	NYGS	16. 00
9351.	Venice, St. Mark's				
	Square		24-1/2 x 31	NYGS	20. 00
9352.	View of Cagnes		14 x 18	NYGS	15. 00
9353.	View of the Post				
	Office	c.	8 x 10	ESH	1. 00
9354.	White Roses	c.	8 x 10	ESH	1. 00
9355.	Woman Asleep	c.	12-1/2x9-1/2	AP	1. 25
			8 x 6	CFA	1. 00
9356.	Woman in a Veil		16 x 11	AR	7. 50
9357.	Woman Tying up her				
	Shoe		18 x 20-1/2	NYGS	15. 00
9358.	Woman with a Cat		24 x 19-1/2	PENN	1. 50
			20 x 16	CFA	10. 00
		c.	12-1/2x9-1/2	AP	1. 25
			8 x 7	CFA	1. 00
9359.	Woman with Lilacs		23 x 18	NYGS	12. 00
9360.	Women in a Field		23 x 28	ESH	15. 00
		c.	8 x 10	ESH	1. 00
9361.	Women with Hats				
		c.	8 x 10	ESH	1. 00
9362.	Young Girl		24 x 20	CFA	15. 00

9363.	Young Girl at Piano	8 x 6	CFA	1. 00
9364.	Young Girl Bathing			
	c.	9-1/2x12-1/2	AP	1. 25
	c.	7 x 9	AP	1. 00
9365.	Young Girl Combing			
	her Hair	17 x 14	CFA	7. 50
		8 x 6	CFA	1. 00
9366.	Young Girl with a			
	Blue Hat c.	12-1/2x9-1/2	AP	1. 25
9367.	Young Girl with			
	Daisies	22 x 18-1/2	ESH	10. 00
9368.	Young Girl with			
	Hat c.	24 x 20	PENN	1. 50
9369.	Young Sea-Fisher			
	c.	12-1/2x9-1/2	AP	1. 25
9370.	Young Shepherd	20 x 24-1/2	NYGS	12. 00
9371.	Yvone and Christine			
	at the Piano	24 x 30	NYGS	12. 00

RENOUF, EMILE (French, 1845-1894)

9372.	The Helping Hand	22 x 32	IA	10. 00
		11 x 14	IA	3. 00

REPIN, ILYA (Russian, 1844-1930)

9373.	Cossack Letter	23 x 38	AJ	15. 00

RETTIG, MARTIN (American Contemporary)

9374.	Roses	24 x 22	CFA	10. 00

REUTHER, WOLF (German Contemporary)

9375.	Cock	25 x 20	IA	12. 00
9376.	Duet	24 x 19-1/2	IA	15. 00
9377.	Rooster	25 x 19	CFA	15. 00
9378.	El Toro	25 x 20	IA	15. 00

REYNOLDS, (SIR) JOSHUA (English, 1723-1792)

9379.	Age of Innocence	20 x 16	CAC	6. 00
		16 x 13	NYGS	6. 00
		12 x 9	CAC	2. 00
	c.	10 x 8	ESH	1. 00
	c.	9 x 7	AP	. 50
9380.	Captain Bligh	28-1/2 x 23	AA	10. 00
9381.	Dr. Samuel Johnson			
	c.	10 x 8	NYGS	. 50
9382.	Georgiana Elliott	30 x 25	NYGS	18. 00
9383.	Heads of Angels	20 x 16	CAC	5. 00
	c.	10 x 8	ESH	1. 00
9384.	Holy Family	10-1/2 x 15	ESH	10. 00
9385.	Infant Samuel at			
	Prayer	24 x 20	NYGS	10. 00
		23 x 18-1/2	IA	7. 50
		14 x 10	NYGS	3. 00
		11 x 8	IA	1. 75
	c.	10 x 8	NYGS	1. 00
	c.	9 x 7	AP	. 50
9386.	Lady Betty Hamilton	31 x 22	NYGS	16. 00
		23-1/2 x 16	NYGS	10. 00

		18 x 13	NYGS		5.00
		14 x 10	NYGS		3.00
9387.	Lady Caroline				
	Howard	25-1/2x20-1/2	PENN		1.50
		20 x 16	CAC		7.50
	c.	16 x 12	PENN		1.00
9388.	Lady Elizabeth Delme				
	and her Children	31 x 19	NYGS		15.00
9389.	Lady in Yellow	19-1/2 x 16	NYGS		10.00
9390.	Master Hare	24 x 19-1/2	PENN		1.50
		12-1/2 x 10	IA		3.00
9391.	Miss Bowles	16-1/2x12-1/2	NYGS		5.00
	c.	9 x 7	AP		.50
9392.	Miss Crewe	19 x 15	ESH		12.00
9393.	Miss Mary Hickey	20 x 16	NYGS		10.00
9394.	Mrs. Smith and her				
	Children c.	7 x 9	AP		.50
9395.	Nellie O'Brien	17 x 13	NYGS		5.00
9396.	Portrait of a Lady	28 x 22	CAC		6.00
9397.	Simplicity	17 x 14	CAC		5.00
		17 x 13	CAC		5.00
		12 x 9	CAC		2.00
9398.	Young Shepherd	19 x 15-1/2	ESH		10.00

RIAB

9399.	Pointer Hunting-Dog	11 x 15-1/2	CFA	12.00
9400.	Setter Hunting-Dog	11 x 15-1/2	CFA	12.00

RIASNI, B.

9401.	Bouquets (6)	16 x 12	DAC	ea.	1.75
		10 x 8	DAC	ea.	.75

RIBERA, JUSEPE DE (CALLED LO SPAGNOLETTO) (Spanish, 1588-1652)

9402.	Madonna and Child	24 x 20	NYGS	10.00
9403.	St. Jerome	10 x 15	IA	3.00
9404.	St. Mary of Egypt	14 x 11	IA	3.00

RICCI, MARCO (Italian, 1676-1729)

9405.	The Falls	14-1/2 x 11	AS	3.25
9406.	Landscape	11 x 15	AS	3.25

RICCIARDI, VITTORIO

9407.	Sunlit Haven	24 x 36	NYGS	12.00

RICHARDS, FREDERICK THOMPSON (American, 1864-1921)

9408.	Golf Through the			
	Ages (6)	11 x 7	CFA	set 30.00

RICHARDSON, CHARLES (English, Ac. 1855-1901)

9409.	New Quay	17 x 39	AS	7.50
9410.	Peaceful Haven	10 x 31-1/2	AS	10.00
9411.	Quiet Harbour	10 x 31-1/2	AS	10.00

RICHARDSON, VOLNEY ALLAN (American, 1880-)

9412.	Bowl of Mums	25 x 30	AA	10.00
9413.	Crabapple and			
	Dogwood	25 x 30	AA	10.00

RICHMOND, L.

9414.	The Harbour, St.			
	Ives	18 x 22	ESH	10.00

		10 x 12	ESH		2. 00
RICHTER, GUSTAV KARL LUDWIG (German,			1823-1884)		
9415.	The Artist's Sister	27-1/2 x 22	NYGS		12. 00
		11 x 9	NYGS		1. 50
RICO, DANIEL (American Contemporary)					
9416.	City Dawn	36 x 24	DAC		7. 50
9417.	City Dusk	36 x 24	DAC		7. 50
RICO DA CANDIA, ANDREA DI (Italian, 14th Century)					
9418.	Virgin and Child	14-1/2x11-1/2	AS		3. 25
RIDINGEN					
9419.	Spanish Riding School				
	(4)	14 x 13-1/2	CFA		20. 00
RIEFEL, CARLOS VON					
9420.	Fruit (6)	16 x 20	IA	ea.	4. 50
RIERA ROJAS, R. See ROJAS					
RIETTI, ARTURO (Italian, 1863-1942)					
9421.	Toscanini	21-1/2 x 18	AA		10. 00
RIGAUD, HYACINTHE (French, 1659-1743)					
9422.	Portrait of a Child	14-1/2x11-1/2	AS		3. 25
RIGNANO					
9423.	Musicians, Old World				
	(2)	30 x 15	AK	ea.	10. 00
		15 x 7	AK	ea.	2. 50
RIGOULTS, VAN					
9424.	Flowers and Fruits	12-1/2 x 10	ESH		2. 00
RINALDI, M.					
9425.	Atlantic Sunrise	20 x 24	IA		7. 50
9426.	Breaking Surf	27-1/2 x 30	IA		12. 00
9427.	Rocky Point	20 x 24	AA		7. 50
RIOPELLE, JEAN-PAUL (Canadian Contemporary)					
9428.	Du Noir Qui se				
	Lève, 1962	24 x 19	NYGS		15. 00
RITTER, JULIAN (American Contemporary)					
9429.	American Venus	18 x 36	IA		12. 00
9430.	Bullfight	24 x 48	IA		18. 00
9431.	Clowns (10)	7 x 5-1/2	IA	ea.	. 50
9432.	Clowns (4)	18 x 14	IA	ea.	4. 00
	Adlai	10 x 8	IA	ea.	2. 00
	Gent				
	Maestro				
	Micky				
9433.	Clowns (2)	12-1/2x9-1/2	IA	ea.	1. 50
	Helter				
	Skelter				
9434.	Jane	24 x 12	IA		7. 50
		16 x 8	IA		4. 00
9435.	Leo	24 x 12	IA		7. 50
		16 x 8	IA		4. 00
9436.	Model Studies (2)	12 x 24	IA	ea.	7. 50
9437.	Ruby	20 x 24	IA		8. 00
RIVERA, DIEGO (Mexican, 1886-1958)					
9438.	Delfina Flores	26 x 20	NYGS		12. 00

9439.	Flower Seller	13-1/2 x 18	NYGS	6.00
		6 x 8	NYGS	1.00
9440.	Flower Vendor	28 x 28	NYGS	15.00
		18 x 18	NYGS	6.00
	c.	9 x 7	AP	.50
9441.	Indian Girl	16 x 12	NYGS	4.00
9442.	Man and Machinery			
	(Mural) c.	9 x 7	AP	.50
9443.	Mexican Child c.	9 x 7	AP	.50
9444.	Mother's Helper	13-1/2 x 18	NYGS	6.00
		6 x 8	NYGS	1.00
9445.	Native Girl	16 x 12	NYGS	4.00
9446.	Oaxaca	10-1/2x15-1/2	NYGS	4.00
		6 x 8	NYGS	1.00
9447.	Rug Weaver	10-1/2x15-1/2	NYGS	4.00
		6 x 8	NYGS	1.00

RIVERS, LARRY (American Contemporary)

9448.	Flowers in a Vase	30 x 26-1/2	NYGS	16.00

RJEPIN

9449.	A. Rubinstein c.	9 x 7	AP	.60

ROBBIA, ANDREA DELLA (Italian, 1435-1525)

9450.	Bambino (Bas			
	Relief) c.	7 x 9	AP	.25
9451.	Head of a Child	13 x 11	IA	3.00
9452.	Singing Boys (Bas			
	Relief) c.	7 x 9	AP	.25

ROBBIA, LUCA DELLA (Italian, 1400-1482)

9453.	Madonna of the Apple			
	(Terra-Cotta)	15 x 11	IA	3.00
9454.	Madonna with the			
	Lilies	20 x 16	NYGS	7.50

ROBERT, CHARLES (TASSY) (French, 1882-   )

9455.	Maternity	27 x 19	CFA	10.00

ROBERT, HUBERT (French, 1733-1808)

9456.	Fantastic Ruins	11 x 15	AS	3.25
9457.	The Fountains	28 x 24	NYGS	15.00
		14 x 13	NYGS	4.00
9458.	The Landing	28 x 24	NYGS	15.00
		14 x 12	NYGS	4.00
9459.	Landscape	15 x 8	IA	3.00
9460.	The Obelisk	28 x 24	NYGS	15.00
		14 x 12	NYGS	4.00
9461.	Old Bridge	27 x 36	NYGS	18.00
	c.	18 x 23	HNA	5.95
		8 x 11	CFA	2.00
9462.	Old Temple	28 x 24	NYGS	15.00
		14 x 12	NYGS	4.00
9463.	Park	23 x 11-1/2	IA	10.00
9464.	Park Landscape	14-1/2x7-1/2	IA	3.00
9465.	Paysage	14 x 10-1/2	NYGS	4.00
9466.	Roman Garden	28 x 20	NYGS	12.00
		14 x 10	NYGS	4.00

9467.	Roman Ruins	11 x 15	IA		3. 00
9468.	Ruins	23 x 11-1/2	IA		10. 00
9469.	Ruins of a Porch	14-1/2x7-1/2	IA		3. 00
9470.	Terrace	28 x 20	NYGS		12. 00
		14 x 10	NYGS		4. 00
9471.	Terrace of the Chateau				
	de Marly	24-1/2 x 36	NYGS		18. 00
		18 x 24	DAC		7. 50
9472.	Set of Four Subjects	14 x 12	NYGS	set	15. 00
	Fountains				
	Landing				
	Obelisk				
	Old Temple				

ROBERTI, DOMENICO (Italian, 1642-1707)

9473.	Spring	32 x 10	AL		15. 00
9474.	Summer	32 x 10	AL		15. 00
9475.	Tempio Borghese	32 x 12	AL		15. 00
9476.	Tempio Calonna	32 x 12	AL		15. 00
9477.	Tempio Corsini	32 x 11	AL		15. 00
9478.	Tempio Doria	32 x 11	AL		15. 00

ROBERTI, ERCOLE (Italian, 1456-1496)

9479.	Ginevra Bentivoglio	21 x 14-1/2	NYGS		10. 00
		12 x 8	CFA		2. 00
9480.	Giovanni Bentivoglio	21 x 14-1/2	NYGS		10. 00
		12 x 8	CFA		2. 00
9481.	Israelites	10 x 22	ESH		6. 00

ROBERTO

9482.	Flora Bella (4)	30 x 10	AK	ea.	4. 00
		21 x 7	AK	ea.	2. 50
		12 x 4	AK	ea.	1. 00

ROBIE (OR ROBBIE), JEAN BAPTISTE (Belgian, 1821-1910)

9483.	Cascade of Flowers	36 x 24	AA		12. 00

ROBUSTI, JACOPO See TINTORETTO
ROCA See IBARZ ROCA, MIGUEL
ROCCO

9484.	Paris Scenes (2)	24 x 48	AK	ea.	6. 00
9485.	Arc de Triumphe	12 x 24	AK	ea.	2. 50
9486.	Moulin Rouge				

ROCKWELL, NORMAN (American, 1894-)

9487.	Four Seasons (4 on one				
	sheet)	11 x 8 ea.	NYGS	sheet	5. 00

RODEWALD, CLAUDE (Alsacian [Res. U. S.] 1923-1945)

9488.	French Scenes (2)	20 x 24	AA	ea.	12. 00
9489.	Montmartre				
9490.	Rue Royale				
	French Scenes (2)	18 x 24	AA	ea.	10. 00
9491.	Monaco				
9492.	Nice				
	French Scenes (2)	16 x 20	AA	ea.	10. 00
9493.	Moulin Rouge				
9494.	Place du Tertre				
	French Scenes (2)	14 x 20	AA	ea.	10. 00

9495.	Cour de Rohan			
9496.	Petit Cafe			
ROESEN,	SEVERIN (American, 1815-1871)			
9497.	Boy with Still Life	26 x 20	AK	7. 50
		16 x 12	AK	2. 50
9498.	Still Life	20 x 26	AK	7. 50
		12 x 17	AK	2. 50
ROHLFS,	CHRISTIAN (German, 1849-1938)			
9499.	Canna Indica	20 x 15	AP	7. 50
9500.	Red Canna Lilies	21-1/2 x 29	NYGS	22. 00
9501.	Sunflowers c.	20 x 24	PENN	1. 50
ROHRICHT,	WOLF (German, 1886-1953)			
9502.	Frozen River	19 x 25	ESH	7. 50
9503.	Osteria	24 x 20	ESH	12. 00
9504.	Summer in Italy	21 x 25-1/2	ESH	10. 00
ROJAS,	R. RIERA (Spanish Contemporary)			
9505.	La Cuadrilla	23 x 24	NYGS	10. 00
9506.	El Matador	23 x 24	NYGS	10. 00
9507.	Picador Y Banderilleros			
		23 x 24	NYGS	10. 00
9508.	Picadores	23 x 24	NYGS	10. 00
ROKA,	C.			
9509.	Gypsy Girl	24 x 19-1/2	IA	12. 00
ROLING,	ALPHONS (Dutch, 1904-)			
9510.	Bouquet with			
	Anemones	20 x 17	PENN	1. 50
ROLLAND,	MARTIN			
9511.	Mood Indigo	24 x 48	DAC	10. 00
ROLOFF,	A.			
9512.	Approaching Storm	20-1/2 x 27	ESH	15. 00
9513.	Burning Prairies	16 x 22	NYGS	6. 00
9514.	Galloping Horses	21 x 33-1/2	NYGS	16. 00
9515.	Horses in a Storm	24 x 30	IA	12. 00
ROMAKO,	ANTON			
9516.	Gardener	19 x 15	ESH	6. 00
ROMAN AND CAMPAGNIAN DECORATION (See also POMPEIAN ART)				
9517.	Alexander the Great	11 x 15	IA	3. 00
9518.	Bacchante	22 x 18	ESH	10. 00
		14 x 11	IA	3. 00
9519.	Battle of Ixus	8 x 15	IA	3. 00
9520.	Cock Fight	11 x 11	IA	3. 00
9521.	Darius	11 x 15	IA	3. 00
9522.	Diana	14 x 10	IA	3. 00
9523.	Diana di Stabia c.	22 x 17-1/2	AS	4. 00
9524.	Flora	14 x 11	IA	3. 00
9525.	Hercules and the			
	Hesperides	14 x 10	IA	3. 00
9526.	Icarus' Fall	15 x 10	IA	3. 00
9527.	Idyllic Landscape	11 x 11	IA	3. 00
9528.	Iphigenia in Tauris	15 x 11	IA	3. 00
9529.	Leda	14 x 10	IA	3. 00
9530.	Orestes and Pylades	10 x15	IA	3. 00

9531.	Paquius Proculus and				
	his Wife	13 x 11	IA		3. 00
9532.	The Rider	17 x 22-1/2	ESH		10. 00
9533.	Roman Heads (2)	16 x 11	CFA	ea.	12. 00
9534.	Roman Frieze I and II				
	(B & W)	28-1/2 x 16	AA	ea.	8. 00
9535.	Roman Wall Painting-				
	Spring c.	18 x 23	HNA		5. 95
9536.	Sapho	11 x 11	IA		3. 00
9537.	Still Life with				
	Chickens	17 x 22-1/2	ESH		10. 00
9538.	Three Graces	13 x 11	IA		3. 00
9539.	Waterfowl (Mosaic)	15-1/2x31-1/2	ESH		15. 00

ROMANO, GIULIO (GIANNUZZI, GIULIO) (Italian, 1492-1546)

9540.	Apollo and the Muses	11 x 25	IA		7. 50
		7 x 15	IA		3. 00

ROMANO, UMBERTO (American, 1905-)

9541.	Lancer	20 x 25-1/2	NYGS		12. 00

ROMBOUTS, THEODOR (Flemish, 1597-1637)

9542.	Gamblers	11 x 15	IA		3. 00

ROMNEY, GEORGE (English, 1734-1802)

9543.	Elizabeth Sutherland	9 x 8	CFA		6. 00
9544.	Lady Hamilton	19 x 17	CAC		7. 50
		12 x 9	ESH		2. 00
9545.	Lady Hamilton as a				
	Bacchante	25 x 20	CAC		10. 00
		16 x 13	CAC		5. 00
9546.	Lady Lilith	18 x 15	ESH		12. 00
9547.	Little Bo Peep	20 x 15	NYGS		9. 00
9548.	Mme. de Genlis	19 x 14-1/2	ESH		12. 00
9549.	Miss Willoughby				
	c.	23 x 18	HNA		5. 95
		20 x 15-1/2	NYGS		9. 00
	c.	16 x 12	PENN		1. 00
		11 x 8-1/2	NYGS		1. 50
9550.	Mrs. Davenport	19-1/2 x 16	NYGS		10. 00
		12 x 10	NYGS		1. 00

ROSA, SALVATORE (Italian, 1615-1673)

9551.	Bridge of Tivoli	11 x 15	IA		3. 00
9552.	Dirupi in Riva				
	Almare	14-1/2 x 35	CFA		15. 00
9553.	Landscape: Peace				
	Setting Fire to the				
	Weapons	10 x 15	IA		3. 00
9554.	Sea View	14-1/2 x 23	AS		7. 50
9555.	Sea View	14-1/2 x 23	AS		7. 50
		11 x 14-1/2	AS		3. 25
9556.	Seascape	11 x 15	IA		3. 00
9557.	View of a Bay	11 x 14	IA		3. 00

ROSAI, OTTONE (Italian, 1895-1957)

9558.	The Road	15 x 11	AS		3. 25
9559.	Sea View	11 x 15	AS		3. 25

9560.	Three Houses	15 x 11	AS	3. 25
9561.	Winter	10-1/2 x15	AS	3. 25

ROSAN, LOUIS (French Contemporary)

9562.	La Rochelle	21 x 28-1/2	NYGS	12. 00
9563.	Little Harbor in			
	Brittany	21 x 28-1/2	NYGS	12. 00

ROSE, IVER (American, 1899-)

9564.	Hi Ya Folks	22 x 16	NYGS	10. 00
9565.	Show's On	22 x 16	NYGS	10. 00

ROSENSTOCK, W.

9566.	Glory of Summer	28 x 22	AA	7. 50
9567.	Summer Symphony	28 x 22	AA	7. 50

ROSENTHAL, TOBY EDWARD (American, 1848-1917)

9568.	The Cardinal's			
	Portrait	19 x 24	IA	7. 50
		9-1/2 x 12	IA	1. 50
9569.	His Madonna	24-1/2 x 19	NYGS	7. 50
		13-1/2x10-1/2	NYGS	3. 00
9570.	Seine Madonna	25 x 19	IA	7. 50
		20 x 16	IA	8. 50
		16 x 12	IA	5. 50
		12 x 9	IA	3. 50

ROSS, C. CHANDLER (American, 1888-1952)

9571.	Eastern Tranquility	20 x 24	NYGS	10. 00
9572.	Eternal East	26 x 22	NYGS	10. 00
9573.	Oriental Rider	26 x 22	NYGS	10. 00
9574.	Oriental Simplicity	20 x 24	NYGS	10. 00

ROSS, MARGARET

	Children's				
	Illustrations (4)	17-1/2 x 20	ESH	ea.	3. 00
9575.	Baby Show				
9576.	Bedtime				
9577.	Going to School				
9578.	Village Shop				
	Children's				
	Illustrations (4)	10 x 13-1/2	ESH	ea.	2. 00
9579.	Baking Day				
9580.	Fishing				
9581.	In the Fields				
9582.	Packing the Picnic				

ROSELLI, COSIMO (Italian, 1439-1507)

9583.	Madonna and Child			
	with Two Angels	16 x 10	IA	3. 00

ROSSI, CARLO

9584.	Breakers at Sunset	20 x 39	IA	12. 00

(IL) ROSSO FIORENTINO (GIOVANNI BATTISTA DI JACOPO)
(Italian, 1494-1541)

9585.	Angel Playing the			
	Lute	11 x 13-1/2	AS	3. 25
		11 x 13	IA	3. 00
9586.	Moses Defending the			
	Daughters of Jethro	15 x 11	IA	3. 00

ROTARI, PIETRO (Italian, 1707-1762)
9587.   Girl with a Flower
        in her Hair   20 x 15-1/2   NYGS   10. 00
ROTH, ETIENNE
9588.   Brother and Sister
                      c.   24 x 20   PENN   1. 50
                          12 x 10   DAC   2. 00
9589.   Fillettes (4)   10 x 8   DAC   ea. 1. 50
9590.   Friendship   c. 24 x 20   PENN   1. 50
                          12 x 10   DAC   2. 00
9591.   My Pride   24 x 20   DAC   7. 50
                          12 x 10   DAC   2. 00
9592.   Reverie   24 x 20   DAC   7. 50
                          12 x 10   DAC   2. 00
ROTHENSTEIN, (SIR) WILLIAM ("WILL") (English, 1872-)
9593.   Little Princess   22 x 19   ESH   15. 00
ROTIG, S. F.
9594.   L'Alerte   17-1/2 x 24   IA   15. 00
9595.   Ducks Landing   17-1/2 x 24   IA   15. 00
9596.   Pointers and
        Pheasants   16 x 23   IA   10. 00
9597.   Setters et Canards 16 x 23-1/2   IA   10. 00
ROUAULT, GEORGES (French, 1871-1958)
9598.   Afterglow, Galilee 19 x 25   NYGS   16. 00
9599.   L'Ange Gardien   15 x 12   NYGS   18. 00
9600.   Biblical Landscape 18-1/2 x 24-1/2 PENN   1. 50
9601.   Blue Bird   22-1/2 x 16   ESH   10. 00
9602.   Bouquet No. 1 and
        No. 2   14 x 9-1/2   NYGS   ea. 5. 00
9603.   Christ and the
        Fishermen   20-1/2 x 29   NYGS   16. 00
                      c. 18 x 23   HNA   5. 95
9604.   Christ Mocked by
        Soldiers   29-1/2 x 23   AP   7. 50
                          26 x 20   CFA   7. 50
                      c. 9 x 7   AP   . 50
9605.   Christian Intimacy 15 x 22-1/2   IA   10. 00
9606.   Christian Nocturne
                      c. 20 x 24   PENN   1. 50
9607.   Le Cirque (4)   12 x 8   AR   ea. 5. 00
9608.   Clown, 1920   23 x 16-1/2   NYGS   10. 00
9609.   Clown (Head)   25 x 18   PENN   1. 50
9610.   Le Duo   21 x 14   NYGS   22. 00
9611.   Ecce Homo   30 x 21   IA   15. 00
9612.   Fleurs Decoratifs 14 x 10   CFA   7. 50
9613.   Flight into Egypt 22 x 17   ESH   10. 00
9614.   Flowers in a Vase 22 x 18   PENN   1. 50
9615.   Harlequin and a
        Dog   23-1/2 x 15   AR   12. 00
9616.   Head of a Boy c. 24 x 20   PENN   1. 50
9617.   Heads of Two Clowns
                          24 x 18   PENN   1. 50

9618.	L'Hiver	15 x 11	NYGS	18. 00
9619.	Die Italienerin c.	22 x 17-1/2	AS	4. 00
9620.	Jeanne D'Arc	16 x 13	CAC	6. 00
9621.	Judgement of Christ	16 x 23	PENN	1. 50
9622.	Madame "X"	20 x 14	AR	7. 50
9623.	Motherhood	18-1/2x14-1/2	IA	5. 00
9624.	The Old King	25 x 17	PENN	1. 50
		23 x 16	ESH	10. 00
		22 x 16	AP	10. 00
	c.	9 x 7	AP	. 50
9625.	Parade	23-1/2 x 15	AR	12. 00
9626.	Pierrot	30 x 19-1/2	AA	15. 00
		19 x 14	CFA	7. 50
		12-1/2x8-1/2	NYGS	4. 00
		9 x 6	NYGS	. 50
9627.	Pierrot Pointing			
	c.	20 x 24	PENN	1. 50
9628.	Pierrots	21 x 16-1/2	NYGS	22. 00
9629.	Poster: Clown and			
	Girl	29-1/2 x 21	PENN	1. 00
9630.	Poster: "Passion"	28 x 19-1/2	PENN	1. 00
9631.	La Sainte Face			
	(The Holy Face)	20 x 14-1/2	NYGS	7. 50
	c.	16 x 12	PENN	1. 00
9632.	Sainte-Marthe	18 x 14-1/2	NYGS	22. 00
9633.	Sainte-Veronique	19 x 14	NYGS	22. 00
9634.	Seated Clown			
	(Wise Pierrot) c.	26 x 21	HNA	5. 95
9635.	Small Magician	24 x 19	PENN	1. 50
9636.	Sorrowing Christ			
	c.	10 x 8	ESH	1. 00
9637.	Stella Vespertina	16 x 10	NYGS	22. 00
9638.	La Sybelle	21 x 15	AR	10. 00
9639.	Wounded Clown	30-1/2x18-1/2	ESH	15. 00
	c.	9 x 7	AP	. 50
ROUAULT, I.				
9640.	Sainte Therese de			
	L'Enfante Jesus	16 x 10-1/2	NYGS	12. 00
ROUAULT, RAOUL				
9641.	Sailing Boats at			
	Anchor	16 x 24-1/2	ESH	10. 00
ROUF				
9642.	Clowns (2)	16 x 12	ESH ea.	3. 00
9643.	Horses (2)	20 x 16	ESH ea.	5. 00
9644.	Sailing Boats (2)	20 x 16	ESH ea.	3. 00
ROUSSEAU, HENRI JULIEN (LE DOUANIER) (French, 1844-1910)				
9645.	The Angler c.	8 x 10	ESH	1. 00
9646.	Bois de Vincennes	20 x 24	CFA	15. 00
9647.	Bunch of Wild			
	Flowers c.	10 x 8	ESH	1. 00
9648.	Carnival Night c.	24 x 20	PENN	1. 50
	c.	23 x 18	HNA	5. 95

9649.	The Cart of Pere					
	Juniet		23-1/2 x 32	NYGS		15.00
		c.	20 x 24	PENN		1.50
9650.	Cascade		16 x 20	NYGS		7.50
9651.	Edge of the Forest		19 x 15-1/2	AP		5.00
9652.	Equatorial Jungle		26 x 23-1/2	NYGS		16.00
9653.	Flowers		14-1/2 x 12	AR		3.00
9654.	Flowers in a Jar					
		c.	10 x 8	ESH		1.00
9655.	I, Myself	c.	16 x 12	AP		2.00
9656.	In the Forest		21-1/2x18-1/2	NYGS		12.00
9657.	In the Park		14 x 18	CFA		7.50
9658.	Jungle, Setting Sun		18 x 26	PENN		1.50
9659.	Jungle Sunset	c.	18 x 23	HNA		5.95
9660.	Landscape with Mill		14 x 25	AP		5.00
9661.	Lion in the Jungle		14 x 18	ESH		10.00
9662.	Le Moulin d'Alfort					
		c.	17-1/2 x 22	AS		4.00
9663.	On the River	c.	7 x 9	AP		.50
9664.	Self-Portrait	c.	24 x 20	PENN		1.50
		c.	23 x 18	HNA		5.95
9665.	Sleeping Gypsy		20 x 31	MMA		6.50
		c.	8 x 10	MMA		.35
9666.	Snake Charmer		10 x 11	CFA		2.50
9667.	Springtime in the					
	Valley of the Bievre		20 x 17	AA		7.50
9668.	Summer	c.	8 x 10	ESH		1.00
9669.	Tiger Hunt		16-1/2 x 20	NYGS		16.00
9670.	Toll Gate		16 x 12-1/2	NYGS		12.00
9671.	Vase of Flowers		14-1/2 x 12	AP		3.00
9672.	Virgin Forest at					
	Sunset		19-1/2x27-1/2	NYGS		15.00
9673.	Waterfall		24 x 31	NYGS		18.00

ROUSSEAU, THEODORE (French, 1812-1867)

9674.	The Oaks	9 x 14	IA	3.00
9675.	Spring	8 x 12	ESH	2.00

ROUX, ANTOINE (French, 1765-1835)

9676.	The Barque "Rosalie"				
		c.	8 x 10	ESH	1.00
9677.	The Brig "Solide"				
		c.	8 x 10	ESH	1.00

ROWLANDSON, THOMAS (English, 1756-1827)

9678.	End of the Mall--Spring			
	Gardens	13 x 18-1/2	NYGS	7.50

ROX, HENRY

9679.	Vegetable World				
	(10)	9 x 7	AA	ea.	1.00
	Banana Chorale				
	Beauty Bath				
	Jumbo				
	Mardi-Gras				
	Over-Exposed				

Summer Romance
Sweet and Sour
Tears
Top Banana
Woman's Day

ROY, JAMINI (India, 1887-   )
9680.	Masquerade in			
	India	10 x 11	UNICEF	5. 00

ROYBOT, FERDINAND (French, 1840-1920)
9681.	Cavalier	30 x 24	CFA	7. 50

RUBENS, PETER PAUL (Flemish, 1577-1640)
9682.	The Alley	8 x 9	CFA	. 50
9683.	Archduke Albert of			
	Austria	15 x 8	IA	3. 00
9684.	The Artist's Son			
	Nicholas	12 x 9	CFA	3. 50
9685.	The Artist's Son			
	Nicholas, Age 2	10 x 8	CFA	3. 50
9686.	Castle Park	6 x 12	CFA	. 50
9687.	Chapeau de Paille	18 x 12-1/2	NYGS	5. 00
9688.	Christ Child, St.			
	John and Angels	21 x 34	NYGS	12. 00
9689.	Country Woman with			
	Cart	7 x 11	CFA	. 50
9690.	Dressing of Venus			
	c.	23 x 18	HNA	5. 95
9691.	Duke of Buckingham	15 x 10-1/2	AR	5. 00
9692.	Enfant au Bourelet	9 x 7	NYGS	4. 00
9693.	The Evening	8 x 9	CFA	. 50
9694.	Farm at Laeken	7 x 11	CFA	. 50
9695.	Four Philosophers	13 x 11	IA	3. 00
9696.	Fruitfulness	12 x 20	ESH	7. 50
9697.	Head of a Negro	24 x 18-1/2	PENN	1. 50
9698.	Helena Fourment and			
	her Children	24-1/2x17-1/2	PENN	1. 50
		12 x 9	CFA	2. 50
9699.	Herdsman	7 x 11	CFA	. 50
9700.	Holy Family	14 x 11	IA	3. 00
9701.	Horse Pond at Sun-			
	set	8 x 12	CFA	. 50
9702.	Isabelle Brant, First			
	Wife	14 x 11	IA	3. 00
9703.	Kermis	8 x 14	CFA	2. 50
9704.	Lady of the Court	14 x 11	AR	5. 00
9705.	Landscape with Rain-			
	bow	29 x 38	NYGS	30. 00
9706.	Maid of Honor	14 x 11	CFA	5. 00
9707.	Nativity	15 x 10	IA	3. 00
9708.	The Painter's Sons			
	c.	7 x 9	AP	. 25
9709.	Peasant and Cart	8 x 12	CFA	. 50
9710.	Peasant Girl	15 x 10	AR	4. 00

9711.	Praying Hands	18 x 15	NYGS		7. 50
	Details (2) of				
	No. 9711	10 x 15	NYGS	ea.	4. 00
9712.	Rainbow	9 x 12	CFA		. 50
9713.	Rubens and his First				
	Wife c.	10 x 8	NYGS		. 50
9714.	St. Catherine	15 x 9	AR		4. 00
9715.	St. Sebastian	15 x 11-1/2	AS		3. 25
9716.	St. Sebastian Succoured				
	by Angels	14 x 10	IA		3. 00
9717.	Self-Portrait	14 x 11	IA		3. 00
9718.	Summer	7 x 11	CFA		. 50
9719.	Susanna Fourment				
	c.	9 x 7	AP		. 50
9720.	Three Graces	15 x 11	AS		3. 25
9721.	Tiberius and Agrippina				
		26 x 22	NYGS		18. 00
9722.	Tribute Money c.	7 x 9	AP		. 50
9723.	Triumphal Entry				
	c.	7 x 9	AP		. 25
9724.	Venus and Adonis	10 x 15	IA		3. 00
	c.	8 x 10	NYGS		. 50
9725.	Virgin and Child	11 x 8	NYGS		. 50
9726.	Virgin and Child with				
	Forget-Me-Nots	21 x 15-1/2	NYGS		10. 00
9727.	Wreath of Fruit	20-1/2 x 35	NYGS		16. 00
9728.	Young Warrior	14 x 11	AR		6. 00
RUBIN,	REUVEN (Israeli, 1893-)				
9729.	Arabian Horses	22 x 36	NYGS		18. 00
9730.	Mother and Child	25-1/2 x 19	NYGS		15. 00
9731.	Springtime in Galilee				
		19-1/2 x 26	RL		10. 00
9732.	Women of Galilee	25-1/2 x 19	NYGS		15. 00
RUBINO,	MANFREDI (American Contemporary)				
9733.	Pompeiian Designs				
	(4)		NYGS	set	50. 00
9734.	Ceres	31 x 10			
9735.	Returning Victor	12 x 36			
9736.	Roman Parade	12 x 36			
9737.	Terpsichore	31 x 10			
RUBLEV					
9738.	Holy Trinity	27 x 22	NYGS		22. 00
RUFFINO					
9739.	Country Holiday				
	Scenes (4)	18 x 12	AK	ea.	5. 00
9740.	Little Dancer	12 x 8	AK	ea.	2. 50
9741.	Pastoral Frolic				
9742.	Rural Interlude				
9743.	Summer Ballad				
RUGH					
9744.	Burst of Flowers	20 x 48	AK		10. 00

RUISDAEL, JACOB VAN (Dutch, 1628-1682)
9745.   Castle at Bentheim   21 x 28   NYGS   16. 00
9746.   Country After the
        Storm   11 x 13   AS   3. 25
9747.   Flemish Landscape   25 x 35   CFA   20. 00
9748.   Forest Scene   c. 18 x 23   HNA   5. 95
9749.   Holland Landscape   25 x 35   IA   20. 00
9750.   Landscape   24 x 36-1/2   NYGS   20. 00
9751.   Landscape   11 x 14   IA   3. 00
9752.   Landscape, After the
        Rain   11 x 14   IA   3. 00
9753.   Landscape with a
        Foot Bridge   24 x 36-1/2   NYGS   20. 00
9754.   Landscape with Water-
        fall   24 x 34   ESH   18. 00
                              8 x 10-1/2   ESH   1. 00
9755.   Mill   c. 8 x 10   NYGS   . 50
9756.   Rocky Landscape   11 x 14   IA   3. 00
9757.   Rough Sea   c. 18 x 23   HNA   5. 95
9758.   Wheatfields   23 x 30   NYGS   16. 00
                              5 x 7   NYGS   . 50
9759.   Windmill at Wijk   28 x 34   NYGS   20. 00
                          c. 18 x 23   HNA   5. 95
                              16 x 20   NYGS   6. 00
                          c. 7 x 9   AP   . 50
RUMANIA
9760.   UWA Series (32)   11 x 14
                          or 14 x 11   NYGS   ea. 2. 00
RUNGE, JURGEN
9761.   Bay near Monaco   22 x 28   ESH   12. 00
9762.   Boats on Shore   18 x 24   ESH   10. 00
9763.   Calm Lake   23 x 31   CFA   15. 00
9764.   Landscape in Northern
        Germany   18 x 24   ESH   10. 00
9765.   Limone at Garda
        Lake   23-1/2 x 20   IA   12. 00
9766.   Limone near Garda
        See   23 x 19   CFA   12. 00
9767.   Mandello near Comer
        Sea   23-1/2 x 20   IA   12. 00
RUOPPOLO, GIOVANNI BATTISTA (Italian, 1620-1685)
9768.   Grapes and Fruit   26 x 32   CFA   15. 00
9769.   Still Life   11 x 13   IA   3. 00
RUSSELL, CHARLES MARION (American, 1865-1926)
9770.   Alarm   16 x 23-1/2   PENN   1. 00
9771.   Ambushed   14 x 11   CFA   1. 00
9772.   At Close-Quarters   10 x 11   CFA   1. 00
9773.   Bad One   16 x 24   AA   8. 00
9774.   Bell Mare   30 x 20   AA   12. 00
9775.   Bolter   14 x 10   CFA   1. 00
9776.   Broken Rope   17 x 26   AA   10. 00
9777.   Bronc to Breakfast   8 x 15   CFA   1. 00
9778.   Buffalo on the Move   11 x 16   CFA   1. 00

9779.	Call of the Law	9 x 13	CFA	1.00
9780.	Camp Cook's Troubles			
		13-1/2 x 20	AA	5.00
9781.	Capturing the Grizzly			
		8 x 15	CFA	1.00
9782.	Carson's Men	9 x 14	CFA	1.00
9783.	Cinch Ring	8 x 15	CFA	1.00
9784.	Cowboy Sport	9 x 13	CFA	1.00
9785.	Cowboy's Life	14 x 11	CFA	1.00
9786.	Deadline of the			
	Range	9 x 14	CFA	1.00
9787.	Desperate Stand	9 x 13	CFA	1.00
9788.	Discovery of Last			
	Chance Gulch	18 x 30	AA	12.00
9789.	Disputed Trail	14 x 11	CFA	1.00
9790.	Doubtful Visitor	13-1/2 x 20	AA	5.00
9791.	Fight between Black-			
	feet and Pigeons	16 x 23-1/2	PENN	1.00
9792.	Fire Boat	11 x 16	CFA	1.00
9793.	Heads or Tails	8 x 14	CFA	1.00
9794.	Hold-Up	8 x 13	CFA	1.00
9795.	Indians	18 x24	PENN	1.50
9796.	Indians Discovering			
	Lewis and Clark	18 x 24	PENN	1.00
9797.	Innocent Allies	14 x 21	AA	6.00
9798.	Intruders	16 x 23-1/2	PENN	1.00
9799.	Jerkline	24 x 36	IA	15.00
		9 x 13	CFA	1.00
9800.	Jerked Down	12-1/2 x 20	AA	5.00
		8 x 15	CFA	1.00
9801.	Land of Good			
	Hunting	11 x 16	CFA	1.00
9802.	Last Chance or			
	Bust	9 x 12	CFA	1.00
9803.	Laugh Kills Lonesome			
		18 x 30	AA	12.00
9804.	Lewis and Clark			
	Meeting the Flat-			
	heads	14 x 30	AA	10.00
9805.	Loops and Swift			
	Horses are Surer			
	than Lead	7 x 10	CFA	1.00
9806.	Mad Cow	8x 12	CFA	1.00
9807.	Meat's not Meat Till			
	It's in the Pan	14 x 21	AA	6.00
		9 x 13	CFA	1.00
9808.	Pipe of Peace	9 x 14	CFA	1.00
9809.	Pony Raid	11 x 16	CFA	1.00
9810.	Portfolio (6)	12 x 16	PENN ea.	1.00
9811.	Indians and Scouts Talking			
9812.	Intruders			
9813.	Letter to George W. Farr			

9814.	Squaw Travois			
9815.	Surprise Attack			
9816.	When Cows were Wild			
9817.	Prospectors	8 x 12	CFA	1. 00
9818.	Rainy Morning in a Cow Camp	8 x 11	CFA	1. 00
9819.	Rider of the Rough String	9 x 13	CFA	1. 00
9820.	Roping a Grizzly	8 x 11	CFA	1. 00
9821.	Roping a Wolf	8 x 11	CFA	1. 00
9822.	Roundup	14 x 30	AA	10. 00
9823.	Sagebrush Sport	8 x 14	CFA	1. 00
9824.	Salute of the Robe Trade	22-1/2 x 36	AA	15. 00
9825.	Scattering the Riders	8 x 11	CFA	1. 00
9826.	Serious Predicament	8 x 15	CFA	1. 00
9827.	Slick Ear	9 x 13	CFA	1. 00
9828.	Smoke of a Forty-Five	9 x 12	CFA	1. 00
9829.	Strenuous Life	16 x 24	AA	8. 00
		9 x 14	CFA	1. 00
9830.	Surprise Attack	16 x 22-1/2	PENN	1. 00
9831.	Tenderfoot	8 x 11	CFA	1. 00
9832.	Tight Dally and Loose Latgo	9 x 13	CFA	1. 00
9833.	Toll Collectors	20 x 30	AA	12. 00
		16-1/2x24-1/2	PENN	1. 50
9834.	Two of a Kind Win	9 x 13	CFA	1. 00
9835.	Wagon Boss	22-1/2 x 36	AA	15. 00
		10 x 16	CFA	1. 00
9836.	Warning Shadows	9 x 13	CFA	1. 00
9837.	When Cows were Wild	20 x 28	PENN	1. 50
9838.	When Horseflesh Comes High	8 x 15	CFA	1. 00
9839.	When Horses Turn Back	9 x 13	CFA	1. 00
9840.	When Mules Wear Diamonds	9 x 13	CFA	1. 00
9841.	When Nose of Horse Beats Eyes of Man	9 x 13	CFA	1. 00
9842.	When Sioux and Black-feet Meet	8 x 15	CFA	1. 00
9843.	When Tracks Spell Meat	9 x 13	CFA	1. 00
9844.	When Wagon Trails Were Dim	9 x 13	CFA	1. 00
9845.	Where Guns Were Their Passports	24 x 36	IA	15. 00
9846.	Who Killed the Bear, or "The Price of his Robe"	9 x 13	CFA	1. 00

9847.	Whose Meat?	9 x 13	CFA		1.00
9848.	Wild Horse Hunters	17 x 26	AA		10.00
		9 x 14	CFA		1.00
9849.	The World Was All				
	Before Them	24 x 36	NYGS		15.00

RUSSELL, GYRTH (English, 1892-)

9850.	Findochtie	10 x 15	ESH		2.00
9851.	St. Ives	10 x 15	ESH		2.00

RUSSELL, JOHN (English, 1745-1806)

9852.	Girl with Cherries	13-1/2 x 10	IA		3.00
		10 x 8	IA		1.75
		9-1/2 x 7	IA		1.75

RUSSELL, R. E.

9853.	Costa Brava View	24 x 30	PENN		1.95
9854.	Oriental Serenity				
	(4)	40 x 24	DAC	ea.	8.50
		20 x 12	DAC	ea.	3.50

RUTHS, VALENTIN (German, 1825-1905)

9855.	Morning	20 x 36	CFA		15.00

RUTLEDGE, WILLIAM

9856.	Les Bateaux	18 x 36	AS		12.00
9857.	Evening Reflections	16 x 29	ESH		8.00
9858.	Furioso	18 x 36	AS		12.00
9859.	Golden Day	18 x 36	AS		12.00
9860.	Sails at Daybreak	16 x 29	ESH		8.00
9861.	Sails at Sunset	18 x 36	AS		12.00
9862.	State Opening				
	Parliament	12-1/2 x 16	AS		6.00
9863.	Sundown	14-1/2 x 29	ESH		8.00

RUYSCH, RACHEL (Dutch, 1664-1750)

9864.	Basket of Flowers	11 x 15	IA		3.00
9865.	Flowers and Fruit	14 x 11	IA		3.00
9866.	Fruit	11 x 15	IA		3.00
9867.	Fruits and Flowers	4-1/2 x 15	AS		3.25
9868.	Fruits and Flowers	15 x 11	AS		3.25
9869.	Fruits, Flowers and				
	Insects	15 x 11	AS		3.25
		14 x 11	IA		3.00
9870.	In Full Bloom	20 x 16	NYGS		7.50
9871.	Summer Flowers	21-1/2x18-1/2	ESH		12.00

RUYSDAEL, G.

9872.	Paesaggio con Effeio				
	di Temporale	18-1/2 x 21	CFA		12.00

RUYSDAEL, JACOB VAN See RUISDAEL

RUYSDAEL, SALOMON VAN (Dutch, 1600-1670)

9873.	Landscape with River				
	and Fishermen	20 x 32-1/2	NYGS		15.00

RYDER, ALBERT PINKHAM (American, 1847-1917)

9874.	Moonlit Cove	13-1/2x16-1/2	NYGS		7.50
9875.	Toilers of the Sea	10 x 12	NYGS		12.00
		8-1/2x7-1/2	NYGS		.50

S

SAALBURG, ALLEN (American, 1899-)
9876. Wild Horses   12-1/2 x 18   NYGS   6.00
SAALBURG, LESLIE (American Contemporary)
9877. Autos (2)   15 x 30   AA   ea. 15.00
9878.   Country
9879.   Town
9880. Autos, Antique (6)   10 x 14   CFA   set 30.00
9881.   Ford, Model K,   1907   or ea. 6.00
9882.   Mercedes, 1909
9883.   Packard, 1912
9884.   Pierce Arrow, 1905
9885.   Seagrave, 1911 (Fire Engine)
9886.   Simplex, 1910
          Autos, Antique (10) 10 x 14   CFA   set 50.00
9887.   Columbia, 1905   or ea. 6.00
9888.   Knox, 1904
9889.   Locomobile, 1907
9890.   Maxwell, 1911
9891.   Mercer, 1911
9892.   Packard, 1916
9893.   Renault, 1908
9894.   Stanley, 1911
9895.   Welch, 1907
9896.   White, 1910
SAAR, F. (German) [Res. Austria]
9897. Lady in Orchid   11 x 9   NYGS   1.50
9898. Lilac Time   11 x 9   NYGS   1.50
SAAVEDRA, SANTOS
9899. Citando   15-1/2 x 23   IA   4.00
9900. Pase Ayudado Por
       Alto   15-1/2 x 23   IA   4.00
SADLER, WALTER DENDY (English, 1854-1923)
9901. Legal and Court
       Room Scenes (7)   14 x 19   CFA   ea. 12.00
9902.   Breach of Promise
9903.   Darby and Joan
9904.   End of Skein
9905.   For Fifty Years
9906.   Nearly Done
9907.   New Will
9908.   Plaintiff and Defendant
9909. Awakening   13 x 18   CAC   7.50
9910. Christening   22 x 15   CAC   7.50
9911. First of September   14 x 20   CAC   7.50
9912. For All my Fancy
       Dwells on Nancy   18 x 13   CAC   7.50
9913. Health to the Bride 18 x 24   CAC   7.50
9914. Hearts are Trumps   14 x 20   CAC   7.50
9915. Hunting Morn   15 x 20   CAC   7.50

9916.	A Little Mortgage	14 x 19	IA	12. 00
9917.	Marriage by Registrar	18 x 24	CAC	7. 50
9918.	Morning Gossip	15 x 20	CAC	7. 50
9919.	The Old and the Young	13 x 18	CAC	7. 50
9920.	Patience	11 x 15	CAC	6. 00
9921.	Rivals	12 x 17	CAC	7. 50
9922.	Scandal and Tea	12 x 17	CAC	7. 50
9923.	Squire's Song	15 x 19	CAC	7. 50
9924.	Uninvited Guests	13 x 19	CAC	7. 50
9925.	Whig and Tory	14 x 11	CAC	6. 00

SAFFORD, RUTH PERKINS (American, 1897-)
9926. Provincial Interiors
(4)   16 x 20   AK   ea. 5. 00
                9 x 12   AK   ea. 1. 50
SAITO, KYOSHI (Japanese Contemporary)
9927. Cat   21-1/2x12-1/2 AP   7. 50
          c. 9 x 7   AP   . 50
SAITO, YOSHISHIGE (Japanese, 1905-)
9928. Painting "E", 1958 24 x 19 NYGS   15. 00
SAKAI HOITSU (Japanese, 1761-1828)
9929. Chrysanthemums 29-1/2 x 10 NYGS   18. 00
9930. Peonies and
Chrysanthemums 29-1/2 x 10 NYGS   18. 00
SALIETTI, ALBERTO (Italian, 1892-)
9931. Collector's Still
Life   21-1/2x27-1/2 NYGS   12. 00
9932. Still Life: The Red
Table   23 x 27-1/2 NYGS   12. 00
9933. Still Life with Fruit
(6)   7-1/2x6-1/2 NYGS set   5. 00
          Apples   or ea.   1. 00
          Cherries
          Grapes
          Oranges
          Plums
          Strawberries
SALINAS, PORFIRIO (American, 1910-)
9934. Blue Bonnet Time 25-1/2x31-1/2 NYGS 12. 00
                17 x 21   NYGS   6. 00
                9 x 11   NYGS   1. 50
9935. Blue Bonnet Trail 25-1/2x31-1/2 NYGS 12. 00
                9 x 11   NYGS   1. 50
SALIS, PIETRO VON (Swiss, 1877-)
9936. Landscape in the
Alps   21 x 30   CAC   12. 00
SALISBURY, FRANK O. (English, 1874-1962)
9937. Franklin D. Roosevelt
                26 x 21   NYGS   12. 00
                17 x 13-1/2   NYGS   5. 00
                10-1/2x8-1/2 NYGS   1. 50

SALLMAN, WARNER E.

9938.	The Christ	20 x 16	DAC	3. 50
9939.	Christ our Pilot	20 x 16	IA	1. 50
		14 x 11	IA	1. 00
		10 x 8	IA	. 50
9940.	Crown of Thorns	14 x 11	IA	1. 00
9941.	Head of Christ	40 x 30	IA	10. 00
		28 x 22	IA	5. 00
	c.	24 x 20	PENN	1. 50
		20 x 16	IA	1. 50
		14 x 11	IA	1. 00
9942.	His Presence	40 x 26	IA	10. 00
		23-1/2 x 15	IA	1. 50
		15 x 10	IA	1. 00
		10 x 6-1/2	IA	. 50
9943.	Jesus, Light of the World	40 x 30	IA	10. 00
		20 x 16	IA	1. 50
		14 x 11	IA	1. 00
		10 x 8	IA	. 50
9944.	The Mother of Christ	20 x 16	IA	1. 50
		14 x 11	IA	1. 00

SALMON, J. M.

9945.	Pastoral	15 x 20	ESH	10. 00

SALVI, GIOVAN BATTISTA SEE SASSOFERRATO

SALVIATI (FRENCESCO DE' ROSSI) (Italian, 1510-1563)

9946.	Charity	14 x 11	AS	3. 25

SALVIATI, GINO

9947.	Rio S. Staes	24 x 48	DAC	10. 00
9948.	Rio S. Tomas	24 x 48	DAC	10. 00
		15 x 30	DAC	2. 00

SALVO, COSMO DE (American, 1894-)

9949.	Bali Beauties	24 x 20	NYGS	10. 00
		14 x 11	NYGS	3. 00
		7-1/2 x 6	NYGS	1. 00
9950.	Tropical Bounty	24 x 20	NYGS	10. 00
		14 x 11	NYGS	3. 00
		7-1/2 x 6	NYGS	1. 00

SALZBURG MASTER (German, c. 1516)

9951.	Portrait of a Boy	14-1/2x10-1/2	AR	6. 00

SAMMAN

9952.	Guardian of the Coast	23 x 29	CAC	12. 00

SAMPLE, PAUL (American, 1896-)

9953.	America--Its Soil (Map)	22 x 32-1/2	NYGS	6. 00
9954.	Boys' Ski Outing	26 x 36	NYGS	18. 00
9955.	Hunters	17-1/2 x 21	NYGS	10. 00
9956.	Maple Sugaring in Vermont	17 x 22	NYGS	10. 00
		6 x 7	NYGS	. 50

SANCHEZ Y COTAN, JUAN (Spanish, 1561-1627)
9957. Still Life: Quince,
       Cabbage, Melon and
       Cucumber   22 x 28   NYGS   16. 00
SANDBY, PAUL (English, 1725-1809)
9958. Ancient Beech Tree 17-1/2 x 26 ESH   15. 00
SANDERS, C.
9959. Little Little   20 x 24   AS   15. 00
SANDHAUS, E. KEATS
9960. Pineapple   19 x 10   CFA   7. 50
9961. Study in a Basket   15 x 19   CFA   7. 50
SANDROCK
9962. Blast Furnace   14 x 30   CAC   12. 00
SAN FRATELLO, MICHAEL
9963. Avocado   18 x 24   CFA   10. 00
SANGUINETTI, EDWARD PHINEAS (Italian, Ac. 1880)
9964. Great Metropolitan
       Stakes   14 x 22   NYGS   6. 00
SANJUAN, BERNARDO (Spanish Contemporary)
9965. Little Spanish Town 25 x 36   NYGS   16. 00
9966. Mediterranean
       Holiday   22-1/2 x 30 NYGS   12. 00
9967. Olive Trees,
       Mallorca   26 x 33   NYGS   16. 00
9968. Sailing off Costa
       Brava   22-1/2 x 30 NYGS   12. 00
9969. Still Life, 1964   22 x 30   NYGS   16. 00
SANO DI PIETRO (Italian, 1406-1481)
9970. Coronation of the
       Virgin   16 x 11   IA   3. 00
9971. Marriage of Count
       Sanseverino   15 x 10   IA   3. 00
9972. Virgin and Child
       (Siena)   15-1/2x11-1/2 AS   3. 25
9973. Virgin Annunciate   8" Diam.   IA   1. 50
SANTI, GIOVANNI (Italian, 1435-1494)
9974. St. Jerome   12 x 11   IA   3. 00
SANZIO See RAFFAELLO SANZIO
SARGENT, JOHN SINGER (American, 1856-1925)
9975. Black Brook   c.   20 x 24   PENN   1. 50
9976. Boats at Anchor   13 x 18   AJ   6. 00
9977. Burning Incense c. 23 x 18   HNA   5. 95
9978. Carnation, Lily,
       Lily, Rose   c.   9 x 7   AP   . 50
9979. Discouraged Prophets
                      c.   9 x 7   AP   . 50
9980. Hopeful Prophets
                      c.   9 x 7   AP   . 50
9981. El Jaleo   23-1/2 x 36 NYGS   18. 00
9982. James Whitcomb
       Riley   c.   9 x 7   AP   . 50
9983. Oyster Gatherers of

	Concale, 1878	22 x 23-1/2	NYGS	16.00
		c. 20 x 24	PENN	1.50
9984.	Robert de Civrieux	11 x 6	NYGS	.50
9985.	Simplon Pass, Green			
	Parasol c.	20 x 24	PENN	1.50
9986.	Street in Venice c.	18 x 23	HNA	5.95
9987.	White Ships	12 x 18	NYGS	7.50
9988.	William M. Chase	11 x 7	NYGS	.50

SARNOFF, ARTHUR

9989.	Body English	18 x 27	CFA	12.00
9990.	Oh! My New Ball	18 x 27	CFA	12.00
9991.	On Target	18 x 27	CFA	12.00
9992.	Pheasant Shoot	18 x 27	CFA	12.00

SARSONY, ROBERT

| 9993. | Pastoral Serenity | 24 x 60 | AK | 8.00 |
| 9994. | Rural Vista | 24 x 60 | AK | 8.00 |

SARTO, ANDREA DEL See ANDREA DEL SARTO

SARULLO, PASQUALE, O. P. M. (Italian, 1828-1893)

| 9995. | Immaculate Virgin | 15 x 11 | IA | 3.00 |
| 9996. | Madonna and Child | 15 x 11 | IA | 3.00 |

SASSETTA, STEFANO DI GIOVANNI (Italian, 1609-1685)

9997.	Journey of the Magi	8 x 11	NYGS	.50
		7 x 10	NYGS	.50
9998.	Legend of St. Francis			
		5 x 7	NYGS	.50
9999.	St. Anthony Leaving			
	his Monastery	18-1/2 x 14	NYGS	7.50
10,000.	St. George (Siena)	13 x 11	AS	3.25

SASSOFERATO (SALVI, GIOVAN BATTISTA) (Italian, 1609-1685)

10,001.	Blue Madonna	20 x 16	CAC	7.50
10,002.	Madonna of the			
	Rosary	14 x 10	IA	3.00
10,003.	Virgin and Child			
	(Venice)	14 x 11	AS	3.25
10,004.	Virgin and Child			
	(Rome)	14 x 11	AS	3.25
10,005.	Virgin and Child			
	with Angels	17 x 23	AS	7.50
		11 x 15	AS	3.25
10,006.	Virgin of Sorrow	23 x 19	AS	7.50
		14 x 11	AS	3.25
		13 x 10	IA	3.00
		10 x 8	IA	1.50
10,007.	Virgin with Folded			
	Hands	13-1/2 x 11	AS	3.25

SAVAGE, EDWARD (American, 1761-1817)

| 10,008. | The Washington Family, | | | |
| | 1796. | 21 x 18 | NYGS | 15.00 |

SAVARY, ROBERT (French Contemporary)

| 10,009. | Orchestra | 18 x 22 | ESH | 10.00 |

SAVIGNÉ

| 10,010. | Still Life Compositions | | | |

	(4)	24 x 12	DAC	ea.	3.50

SAVITT
10,011.	Horses, Thorough-				
	bred (6)	12 x 16	PENN	ea.	1.00
10,012.	Horses' Head, Facing Right				
10,013.	Horse's Head, Facing Left				
10,014.	Mare and Reclining Colt				
10,015.	Mare and Standing Colt				
10,016.	Thoroughbred, Facing Right				
10,017.	Thoroughbred, Facing Left				

SAVOLDO, GIOVANNI GIORLAMO (Italian, 1480-1548)
10,018.	Gaston de Foix	11 x 15	IA	3.00
10,019.	Raphael and Tobias	7 x 9	NYGS	.50
10,020.	Tobias and the			
	Archangel	11 x 14	IA	3.00

SAYRE, F. G.
| 10,021. | Carpet of Allah | 22 x 28 | CFA | 7.50 |

SCALCO, GIORGIO
| 10,022. | Still Life with | | | |
| | Clock | 24 x 30 | DAC | 7.50 |

SCHACHT, RUDOLF
| 10,023. | Galloping Horses | 20 x 31 | CFA | 18.00 |

SCHAFER, EMIL (Swiss, 1878-1959)
10,024.	In the Mountains near			
	Rome	29 x 22	CAC	12.00
10,025.	Moor and Bridge	13 x 18	CFA	5.00
10,026.	Moorland	13 x 18	CFA	6.00

SCHALDACH, WILLIAM J.
10,027.	Fish (2)	14 x 17	AA	ea.	5.00
10,028.	Black Bass				
10,029.	Brook Trout				

SCHALK, ERNST (German, 1827-1865)
| 10,030. | Toros Rojos | 18 x 24 | CFA | 15.00 |

SCHALKEN, GOFFREDO (Dutch, 1643-1706)
10,031.	Woman with Candle-			
	stick	15 x 11	AS	3.25
		14 x 11	IA	3.00

SCHALL
| 10,032. | Dancer | 10 x 8 | ESH | 1.00 |

SCHALTER
| 10,033. | Primitive Fruit | 20 x 25 | AA | 18.00 |

SCHATTE
| 10,034. | Autumn Day | 28 x 22 | CAC | 12.00 |

SCHEDONI, BARTOLOMEO (Italian, 1570-1615)
| 10,035. | Putto - Detail from | | | |
| | "Christian Charity" | 15 x 7 | IA | 3.00 |

SCHEFFER, ARY (Dutch, 1795-1858)
| 10,036. | Passers-By | 20 x 31 | RL | 10.00 |

SCHENK, ERIC
10,037.	Flower Paintings			
	(4)	22 x 28	CFA	ea.	10.00
	American Beauty Rose				

```
                Luscious Tea Rose
                Peach Hibiscus
                Sky Hibiscus
SCHIELE,  EGON (German, 1890-1918)
10, 038.    Field of Flowers    18 x 12         CFA         12. 00
SCHILBACH,  HEINRICH (German, 19th Century)
10, 039.    The Rhine at Ober
                Wesel           24 x 33         NYGS        18. 00
SCHINDLER
10, 040.    Park Landscape      16 x 21         AJ           7. 50
SCHLEIBNER,  KASPER (German, 1863-  )
10, 041.    Christ in the
                Wheatfields     26-1/2 x 38     IA          12. 00
10, 042.    Coena Domini        27-1/2x39-1/2   IA          12. 00
                                20 x 28         IA           6. 00
10, 043.    Immaculate Heart
                of Mary         13-1/2x9-1/2    IA           1. 50
10, 044.    Last Supper         27-1/2x39-1/2   IA          12. 00
                                19-1/2 x 28     IA           6. 00
10, 045.    Sacred Heart of
                Jesus           13-1/2 x9-1/2   IA           1. 50
SCHLEICH
10, 046.    Chremsulardsch      26 x 35         CFA         20. 00
SCHLEMMER,  FERDINAND LOUIS (American,  1893-  )
10, 047.    Firearms (4)         8 x 10         DAC    ea.   1. 00
                                 6 x 8          DAC    ea.    . 50
10, 048.    Locomotives,
                Famous (6)       8 x 10         DAC    ea.   1. 00
                                 6 x 8          DAC    ea.    . 50
10, 049.    Railways (2)         8 x 25-1/2     DAC    ea.   5. 00
                Railway,  1831
                Railway,  1833
SCHLEMMER,  OSKAR (German, 1888-1943)
10, 050.    Bauhaustreppe c.    7 x 9           AP            . 75
10, 051.    Concentric Group
                         c.     12 x 16         AP           2. 00
SCHLERETH,  HANS (German,  1897-  )
10, 052.    Sun Flowers         27-1/2 x 24     ESH         12. 00
SCHLÜTER,  CARL EBERHARD (Dutch,  1886-  )
10, 053.    Corn-Cobs           31-1/2 x 16     ESH          7. 00
10, 054.    Setting Sun         16 x 31-1/2     ESH          7. 00
SCHMALZ,  HERBERT (English,  1856-  )
10, 055.    Return from
                Calvary         16 x 24         IA           7. 50
                                8 x 12          IA     Gr.  10. 00
SCHMIDT,  ELMER G. (American Contemporary)
10, 056.    Sailing             16 x 12         CFA          3. 00
SCHMIDT,  PETER JO
10, 057.    In the Alps         23 x 28         ESH         10. 00
SCHMIDT-ROTTLUFF,  KARL (German,  1884-  )
10, 058.    Around a Hyacinth   28 x 26         NYGS        24. 00
10, 059.    Fishing Boats c.    20 x 24         PENN         1. 50
```

10, 060.	Landscape	c.	20 x 24	PENN	1. 50
10, 061.	Magnolias		30 x 22	ESH	10. 00
10, 062.	Sunny Window		23 x 30	AJ	15. 00

SCHNARS-ALQUIST, CARL WILHELM (German, 1885-)

10, 063.	Good Headway	17-1/2x26-1/2	CFA	10. 00
10, 064.	In the Tropics			
	(Eight Bells)	24 x 37	IA	15. 00
10, 065.	Weather Driven	17-1/2x26-1/2	CFA	10. 00

SCHNEID, OTTO (Czechoslovakian Contemporary)

10, 066.	David-Orpheus	15 x 11	IA	3. 00
10, 067.	Double Portrait	15 x 11	IA	3. 00
10, 068.	Ezekiel's Visions	11 x 13	IA	3. 00
10, 069.	Head	15 x 11	IA	3. 00
10, 070.	Head of Prophet	15 x 10	IA	3. 00
10, 071.	Jacob's Dream	13 x 11	IA	3. 00
10, 072.	Job	15 x 8	IA	3. 00
10, 073.	Prophet Ezekiel	15x 11	IA	3. 00
10, 074.	Self-Portrait with			
	Thorns	14 x 11	IA	3. 00

SCHOBER, W.

10, 075.	Evening Upon the			
	Mountains	23-1/2x31-1/2	ESH	Pr. 10. 00
10, 076.	Heathylands near			
	Lueneburg	23-1/2x31-1/2	ESH	Pr. 10. 00

SCHOLEI, WALTER (German, 1891-)

10, 077.	Bavarian Boy	12 x 8-1/2	ESH	Pr. 1. 50
10, 078.	Bavarian Girl	12 x 8-1/2	ESH	Pr. 1. 50
10, 079.	Late Summer Day	20 x 27-1/2	ESH	Pr. 8. 00
		16 x 20	ESH	Pr. 5. 00
10, 080.	Return from Fishing			
		16 x 20	ESH	Pr. 5. 00

SCHONEBERG, SHELDON CLYDE (American Contemporary)

10, 081.	Angel of Bleeker			
	Street, 1967	34 x 25	NYGS	16. 00

SCHONGAUER, MARTIN (German, c. 1430-1491)

10, 082.	Holy Family	10 x 7	NYGS	10. 00

SCHOOL OF THE UPPER RHINE (German, 15th Century)

10, 083.	The Princess	10-1/2 x 8	ESH	1. 00

SCHRAMM

10, 084.	Virgin of Mercy			
		c.	12-1/2x9-1/2	AP	1. 25
		c.	9 x 7	AP	1. 00

SCHREIBER, GEORGES (American, 1904-)

10, 085.	Center Ring	11 x 16	NYGS	7. 50
10, 086.	Haying	12 x 16	NYGS	5. 00
10, 087.	In Tennessee	12 x 16	NYGS	5. 00
10, 088.	Mississippi Moon	17 x 20-1/2	IA	7. 50

SCHREYVOGEL, CHARLES (American, 1861-1912)

10, 089.	Rough Riders	14-1/2x19-1/2	NYGS	5. 00

SCHRIMPF, GEORG (German, 1899-)

10, 090.	By the Lake	20 x 35	CFA	15. 00
10, 091.	Osterseen	22 x 31	CFA	12. 00

SCHUCH, K. (Austrian, 1846-1903)
10, 092. Apple Still Life with
          Pewter Mug   22 x 30   NYGS   20. 00
10, 093. Still Life   24-1/2 x 30   NYGS   22. 00
10, 094. Still Life of Apples 22 x 30   CFA   15. 00
SCHULZ
10, 095. Mother and Child
                    c.   9 x 7   AP   . 50
SCHULZE, E.
10, 096. Fextal (Engadin)   25-1/2 x 34   IA   12. 00
SCHUMACHER, ERNST
10, 097. French Church   23-1/2 x 28   ESH   10. 00
SCHURR, CLAUDE (French Contemporary)
10, 098. Fishing Boats   23 x 28   RL   12. 50
10, 099. Harbour Pattern   19 x 26   RL   12. 50
SCHUTZ, KARL (Austrian, 1745-1800)
10, 100. Vienna from the
          Belvedere   15 x 23   AR   10. 00
SCHWACHA, GEORGE (American, 1908-)
10, 101. Central Park   30 x 14   CFA   15. 00
10, 102. Fifth Avenue   30 x 14   CFA   15. 00
10, 103. Times Square   14 x 30   CFA   15. 00
SCHWARTZ, DAVIS F.
10, 104. California Landscapes
          (10)   16 x 20   IA   ea.   3. 00
10, 105.   Cypress Point
10, 106.   Early Autumn
10, 107.   Fisherman's Cabin
10, 108.   Lake Region
10, 109.   Mark Twain's Cabin
10, 110.   Mount Diablo, Cal. Ranch
10, 111.   Old Customs House, Monterey
10, 112.   San Juan Capistrano Mission
10, 113.   Sleepy Hollow Road
10, 114.   Tranquility
          California Landscapes
          (2)   20 x 16   IA   ea.   3. 00
10, 115.   Carmel Mission in Moonlight
10, 116.   San Carlos Church in Moonlight
          California Landscapes
          (6)   12 x 16   IA   ea.   2. 00
10, 117.   California Lake
10, 118.   Fisherman's Wharf, San Francisco
10, 119.   Mission near San Xavier del Bac, Tucson
10, 120.   Monterey Wharf
10, 121.   Santa Barbara Mission
10, 122.   Southern California Coast
          California Landscapes
          (4)   8 x 10   IA   ea.   1. 00
10, 123.   Coast near Monterey
10, 124.   Russian River, Cal.
10, 125.   San Francisco Harbor
10, 126.   San Francisco Wharf

10, 127.	Eucalyptus Trees	10 x 8	IA	1. 00
10, 128.	On the Road to			
	China Camp	15 x 20	IA	3. 00
10, 129.	Poplar Trees	10 x 8	IA	1. 00
SCHWARZER, L.				
10, 130.	On the Way to			
	Emmaus	20 x 40	AS	12. 00
		20 x 28	AS	12. 00
		14 x 31	AS	7. 50
10, 131.	Sermon on the			
	Mount	20 x 40	AS	12. 00
SCHWENINGER				
10, 132.	Duet	21 x 16	AA	7. 50
10, 133.	Language of			
	Flowers	21 x 16	AA	7. 50
SCHWIND				
10, 134.	Anna, Daughter of			
	the Artist	9 x 7	NYGS	10. 00
10, 135.	Bread Slicer	24 x 18	AJ	10. 00
10, 136.	Emperor Maximilian			
	in Prayer	18-1/2x13-1/2	AJ	6. 00
10, 137.	Ruebezahl	25 x 15	NYGS	20. 00
SCIARPELLONI, LORENZO See LORENZO DI CREDI				
SCILTIAN, GREGORIO (Armenian, 1900-)				
10, 138.	Philatelist	15 x 13	IA	3. 00
10, 139.	Studio Corner	15 x 12	IA	3. 00
10, 140.	Vagabonds	16 x 13	IA	3. 00
SCOTT, ANGUS				
10, 141.	Ploughman's Cat	22 x 28	AS	15. 00
SCOTT, HENRI (French, 1846-1884)				
10, 142.	Great Race from			
	China to London	24 x 40	AS	25. 00
SCOTT, PETER MARKHAM (English Contemporary)				
10, 143.	Bean Geese	7 x 10	ESH	2. 00
10, 144.	Brent Geese Flight-			
	ing	16 x 24	ESH	15. 00
		10 x 15	ESH	4. 00
		7 x 10-1/2	ESH	2. 00
10, 145.	Crowd on the			
	Dumbles	6-1/2 x 10	ESH	2. 00
10, 146.	Curlews	10 x 15	ESH	4. 00
10, 147.	First of Evening			
	Flight	11 x 15	ESH	12. 00
10, 148.	Flash by Two Trees			
		10 x 15	ESH	4. 00
10, 149.	Flight of Widgeon	8 x 10	ESH	2. 00
10, 150.	Floating on to			
	Merse	13 x 13	ESH	4. 00
10, 151.	Grey Geese over			
	Sea	11-1/2 x 15	ESH	4. 00
10, 152.	Greylags Rounding			
	Up	7 x 10	ESH	2. 00

10, 153.	Low Tide	12-1/2 x 15	ESH	4.00
10, 154.	Mallard, Stormy			
	Sky	11-1/2 x 15	ESH	4.00
		8 x 10	ESH	2.00
10, 155.	Mallard in a Quiet			
	Marsh	8 x 10	ESH	2.00
10, 156.	Pair of Teal	7 x 10	ESH	2.00
10, 157.	Pinkfeet Coming			
	Out	10 x 8	ESH	2.00
10, 158.	Pinkfeet Flighting	7 x 10	ESH	2.00
10, 159.	Pinkfeet, Stubble			
	Field	12-1/2 x 15	ESH	4.00
10, 160.	Promise of Frost	10-1/2 x 15	ESH	4.00
10, 161.	Shovelers on Windy			
	Dawn	8-1/2 x 10	ESH	2.00
10, 162.	Silhouettes	7 x 10	ESH	2.00
10, 163.	Taking to Wing	15 x 24	ESH	15.00
		14 x 22	ESH	6.00
		6-1/2 x 11	ESH	2.00
10, 164.	Teal, Grey			
	Morning	9 x 14	ESH	4.00
10, 165.	White Fronts	7-1/2 x 10	ESH	2.00
10, 166.	Widefens - Pinkfeet			
		12-1/2 x 15	ESH	4.00
10, 167.	Widgeon in the			
	Creek	7 x 10	ESH	2.00

SEAGO, EDWARD BRIAN (English Contemporary)

10, 168.	Anvil Cloud	19 x 24	ESH	15.00
10, 169.	Gondolas by the			
	Salute, Venice	20 x 28-1/2	RL	15.00
10, 170.	Her Chestnut Foal	17 x 22	ESH	10.00
10, 171.	Landmark	20 x 24	ESH	15.00
		16-1/2 x 20	ESH	6.00
10, 172.	Marshland Village	18-1/2 x 24	ESH	12.00
10, 173.	Saxon Church	9 x 11-1/2	ESH	2.00

SEASONWEIN

10, 174.	Augury	26-1/2x36-1/2	AA	20.00
10, 175.	Moonlight Sonata	36-1/2x26-1/2	AA	20.00
10, 176.	Whenever	26-1/2x36-1/2	AA	20.00

SEBASTIANO DEL PIOMBO See PIOMBO, SEBASTIANO DEL
SEDGWICK, P.

10, 177.	Bullfinches	10-1/2 x 15	ESH	4.00

SEGHERS, HERKULES (Dutch, 1589-1638)

10, 178.	Landscape	9 x 15	IA	3.00
10, 179.	Vase of Flowers	22-1/2 x 14	ESH	10.00

SEGNA DI BONAVENTURA (Italian, Fl. 1298-1327)

10, 180.	Crucifix	12-1/2x11-1/2	AS	3.25

SEGONZAC, ANDRÉ DUNOYER DE (French, 1884-)

10, 181.	Bay of St. Tropez	29-1/2 x 24	NYGS	18.00
10, 182.	Le Chenet de Notre			
	Dame	9 x 12	CFA	1.00
10, 183.	Garden Bouquet			
	c.	20 x 24	PENN	1.50

10, 184.	Hills Beyond the Bay	22-1/2x30-1/2	NYGS	16. 00
10, 185.	Landscape	17 x 22-1/2	NYGS	10. 00
10, 186.	Landscape with a Bridge	16 x 21	NYGS	10. 00
10, 187.	Landscape with River	17 x 23	NYGS	15. 00
10, 188.	Nature Morte a la Bouteille c.	17-1/2 x 22	AS	4. 00
10, 189.	Notre Dame, Paris c.	12-1/2x9-1/2	AP	1. 25
10, 190.	Paysage	23 x 17	NYGS	18. 00
10, 191.	Village Square	17 x 22-1/2	NYGS	15. 00
10, 192.	Village Street	22-1/2x16-1/2	ESH	10. 00

SELLAIO, JACOPO DEL (Italian, 1442-1493)

10, 193.	Banquet of Queen Vasti	11 x 15	IA	3. 00
10, 194.	Cavalcade	5-1/2 x15	AS	3. 25
10, 195.	Death of Lucretia	5-1/2 x 15	AS	3. 25

SEN, LALIT M. (American Contemporary)

10, 196.	Queen of the Hills	12 x 15	ESH	4. 00

SEPP

10, 197.	Crab Heron	15 x 11	ESH	8. 00
10, 198.	Goosander	17 x 22-1/2	ESH	10. 00
10, 199.	Green Woodpecker	15 x 11	ESH	8. 00
10, 200.	Hooded Merganser	17 x 22-1/2	ESH	10. 00

SERADOUR, GUY

10, 201.	Pom Pom	24 x 18-1/2	RL	10. 00

SERAPHINE

10, 202.	Ornamental Foliage	22-1/2 x 18	ESH	10. 00

SERPA, IVAN FERREIRA (Brazilian, 1923-   )

10, 203.	Construction No. 75	15-1/2x15-1/2	NYGS	10. 00

SERRIER, J. P.

10, 204.	Italians at Mont St. Michel	20 x 24	RL	10. 00

SESSIONS, JAMES M. (American, 1882-1962)

10, 205.	Fishing and Marine Subjects (2)	22 x 28	NYGS	ea.	12. 00
10, 206.	Fisherman's Wharf				
10, 207.	Ready to Sail				
	Fishing and Marine Subjects (4)	20 x 26-1/2	NYGS	ea.	12. 00
10, 208.	Fishermen				
10, 209.	Good Breeze				
10, 210.	Misty Morning				
10, 211.	Outward Bound				
	Fishing and Hunting Subjects (2)	20 x 26	NYGS	ea.	12. 00
10, 212.	Grouse Shooting				
10, 213.	Trout Stream				

		Marine and Landscape			
		Paintings (12)	17-1/2 x 24	IA	ea. 10. 00
10, 214.	After the Catch			
10, 215.	Backwater			
10, 216.	Blue Harbor			
10, 217.	Driving Home for Gloucester			
10, 218.	Geese Coming In			
10, 219.	Gloucester			
10, 220.	HerringBoats			
10, 221.	Pawtucket Inlet			
10, 222.	Pioneers			
10, 223.	Road to the Cove			
10, 224.	Strike of a Steelhead			
10, 225.	Vermont Farm			
10, 226.	Rounding the Horn	20 x 25	NYGS	12. 00

SEURAT, GEORGES PIERRE (French, 1859-1891)

10, 227.	Afternoon on the			
	Grande Jatte	22-1/2 x 33	AA	12. 00
	c.	8 x 10	ESH	1. 00
10, 228.	Back Part of a			
	Nude c.	16 x 12	AP	2. 00
10, 229.	Banks of the Seine			
	c.	20 x 24	PENN	1. 50
10, 230.	Circus	25 x 20	PENN	1. 50
10, 231.	Circus Parade c.	7 x 9	AP	. 50
10, 232.	Entrance to the Harbor,			
	Port-En-Bessin	21 x 25-1/2	MMA	16. 00
10, 233.	Fishing Fleet at			
	Port-En-Bessin	21 x 25-1/2	NYGS	16. 00
10, 234.	La Grande Jatte	11 x 8	NYGS	7. 50
10, 235.	Harbour at Honfleur			
		20 x 24	PENN	1. 50
		12 x 16	DAC	2. 50
10, 236.	Jeune Femme Se			
	Poudrant	28 x 23	NYGS	15. 00
10, 237.	Lady with a Muff			
	(B & W)	12 x 9	NYGS	3. 00
10, 238.	Landscape c.	8 x 10	ESH	1. 00
10, 239.	La Parade	10 x 8	NYGS	7. 50
10, 240.	Sea Coast	8 x 10	CFA	. 50
10, 241.	The Seine at			
	Courbevoie c.	23 x 18	HNA	5. 95
		22-1/2 x 18	ESH	10. 00
10, 242.	Side Show	22 x 33	NYGS	18. 00
10, 243.	Study for the			
	"Grande Jatte"			
	c.	8 x 10	ESH	1. 00
10, 244.	Sunday Afternoon on			
	the Island of La Grande			
	Jatte, 1884-86	24 x 36	IA	18. 00
		24 x 35-1/2	AJ	18. 00
		19 x 28	NYGS	12. 00

		18 x 27	PENN	1. 50
		7 x 11	NYGS	. 50
10, 245.	Sunday at Port-En-Bessin	17 x 21	AP	5. 00
10, 246.	Sunday on the Grande Jatte	24 x 35	CFA	18. 00
	c.	8 x 10	ESH	1. 00

SEVERINI, GINO (Italian, 1883-)

| 10, 247. | Still Life with Mandolin and Fruit | 17 x 21 | NYGS | 10. 00 |
| 10, 248. | Still Life with Pipe | 13 x 18 | NYGS | 12. 00 |

SHABNER

| 10, 248. | Nicola | 23 x 19 | IA | 7. 50 |
| 10, 249. | Sara | 23 x 19 | IA | 7. 50 |

SHACKETON, KEITH

10, 250.	Children of the Sun	20 x 25	AS	12. 00
10, 251.	Donkey, Mare and Foal	9 x 12	ESH	5. 00
10, 252.	Landfall	20 x 30	AS	10. 00
10, 253.	Nocturne	25 x 15	AS	10. 00
10, 254.	Nude	36 x 18	AS	15. 00
10, 255.	Thompson's Gazelles	25 x 15	AS	10. 00
10, 256.	Wild Swans	20 x 40	AS	20. 00

SHAHN, BEN (American, 1898-)

10, 257.	Ave, 1950 c.	8 x 10	NYGS	. 50
10, 258.	Laissez Faire	12 x 18	AR	5. 00
10, 259.	Ohio Magic c.	18 x 23	HNA	5. 95
10, 260.	Poster: Clown on Horse	28-1/2x22-1/2	PENN	1. 00
10, 261.	Poster: Studio Exhibit	28-1/2x22-1/2	PENN	1. 00
10, 262.	Silent Night (DR.)	28 x 22	AR	5. 00
10, 263.	Still Music	18 x 24	PENN	1. 50

SHAUNS, F.

| 10, 264. | Bouquet of Lilacs | 16 x 20 | IA | 3. 50 |

SHAW, B. K.

| 10, 265. | Flowerpiece | 11 x 9 | ESH | 2. 00 |

SHAW, BARBARA (English Contemporary)

| 10, 266. | Flower Piece, 1949 | 20 x 16 | RL | 10. 00 |
| 10, 267. | Flower Piece, 1951 | 20 x 16 | RL | 10. 00 |

SHAYER, WILLIAM J. (English, 1788-1879)

10, 268.	Half-Way House	24 x 36	AA	12. 00
10, 269.	Harvest Time	24 x 36	AA	12. 00
10, 270.	Lord William	20 x 26	AA	20. 00
10, 271.	Woodland Rest	28 x 36	NYGS	16. 00
		20 x 26	NYGS	10. 00

SHEELER, CHARLES (American, 1883-1965)

10, 272.	American Interior	18-1/2 x 17	NYGS	7. 50
10, 273.	American Landscape c.	7 x 9	AP	. 50
10, 274.	Architectural Cadences, 1954 c.	8 x 10	NYGS	. 50

10, 275.	Bucks County			
	Barn	18-1/2 x 24	NYGS	12. 00
10, 276.	City Interior c.	7 x 9	AP	. 25
10, 277.	Pertaining to Yachts			
	and Yachting	20 x 24	NYGS	12. 00
	c.	18 x 23	HNA	5. 95

SHEETS, MILLARD F. (American, 1907-)

10, 278.	First-Born	6 x 7	NYGS	. 50
10, 279.	Ho Ho Kane			
	(South Seas)	22 x 30	IA	12. 00
10, 280.	Road to the Sea	21-1/2x29-1/2	NYGS	15. 00
10, 281.	Toilers at Sunset	14 x 20	NYGS	7. 50

SHELTON

10, 282.	Home on the Range	24 x 48	AK	6. 00
		12 x 24	AK	2. 50

SHENG MOU (Chinese, 15th Century)

10, 283.	Landscape (Attrib.)	40 x 13-1/2	NYGS	18. 00

SHEPHERD, DAVID (English Contemporary)

10, 284.	Breath of Spring	14 x 18	AS	7. 50
10, 285.	Elephants at Amboseli			
		20 x 40	AS	20. 00
10, 286.	Elms in Winter	19-1/2 x 28	ESH	8. 00
10, 287.	Harbour, Mevagissey			
		20 x 30	AS	7. 50
10, 288.	Kynance Cove	20 x 30	AS	7. 50
10, 289.	Last Bales	20 x 30	AS	10. 00
10, 290.	London	20 x 30	AS	7. 50
10, 291.	Lords of the			
	Jungle	22-1/2 x 30	AS	12. 00
10, 292.	Low Tide, Polperro			
		20 x 30	AS	7. 50
10, 293.	March Sunlight	20 x 40	AS	20. 00
10, 294.	Melting Snow	20 x 31-1/2	AS	12. 00
10, 295.	Misty Morn	24 x 20	ESH	8. 00
10, 296.	Mukalla	19 x 30	AS	12. 00
10, 297.	Old Windsor Oak	20 x 30	AS	15. 00
10, 298.	Pride of Lions	20 x 30	AS	12. 00
10, 299.	Slave Island	20 x 30	AS	12. 00
10, 300.	Snow on the Equator			
		20 x 30	AS	15. 00
10, 301.	Storm over Amboseli			
		20 x 30	AS	12. 00
10, 302.	Summer Harvest	14 x 21	AS	7. 50
10, 303.	Winter Plough	20 x 30	AS	12. 00
10, 304.	Wise Old Elephant	20 x 30	AS	12. 00

SHEPHERD, P. D.

10, 305.	Boat-Yard at Salcombe			
		12 x 15	ESH	4. 00

SHEPLER, DWIGHT CLARK (American, 1905-)

10, 306.	Night Action Off			
	Savo	16 x 24	NYGS	6. 00
10, 307.	On the Glacier	14 x 20	NYGS	7. 50

10, 308.	Powder Snow	14 x 20	NYGS	7. 50
10, 309.	Task Force of Two			
	Navies	16 x 24	NYGS	6. 00
10, 310.	Tulagi Secured	16 x 24	NYGS	6. 00
10, 311.	Unloading Operations			
		12 x 18	NYGS	4. 00
SHERRIN,	DANIEL			
10, 312.	Harp of Trees	22 x 32	CFA	10. 00
10, 313.	In Full Sail	24 x 36	CFA	18. 00
10, 314.	Peaceful Evening	22 x 32	CFA	10. 00
SHERWIN,	FRANK (English,	1896-)		
10, 315.	Breton Hamlet	9-1/2x12-1/2	ESH	2. 00
10, 316.	Concarneau	14 x 18	CFA	5. 00
10, 317.	Coniston	14 x 18	CFA	5. 00
10, 318.	Country Lane	9-1/2x12-1/2	ESH	2. 00
10, 319.	Derwentwater	14 x 18	CFA	5. 00
10, 320.	Evening Light	12 x 16	ESH	3. 00
10, 321.	Harbour, Early			
	Morning	9 x 12	ESH	3. 00
10, 322.	Harbour Window	9 x 12	ESH	3. 00
10, 323.	Llanberris	14 x 18	CFA	5. 00
10, 324.	Little Harbour,			
	Majorca	9 x 12	ESH	3. 00
10, 325.	Loch Katrine	14 x 18	CFA	5. 00
10, 326.	Loch Lomond	14 x 18	CFA	5. 00
10, 327.	Low Tide, St. Ives	12 x 16	ESH	3. 00
10, 328.	Old Jetty, Newport	12 x 16	ESH	3. 00
10, 329.	Porloch Weir	9-1/2x12-1/2	ESH	2. 00
10, 330.	Tunny Boats	14 x 17-1/2	ESH	6. 00
10, 331.	Westcote's, St. Ives			
		12 x 16	ESH	3. 00
10, 332.	White Sails	9-1/2x12-1/2	ESH	2. 00
SHINN,	EVERETT (American,	1876-)		
10, 333.	Ballet c.	8 x 10	NYGS	. 50
10, 334.	Revue, 1908	18 x 24	PENN	1. 50
SHORTT,	ANGUS H. (Canadian Contemporary)			
10, 335.	Canada Geese	17 x 24-1/2	IA	5. 00
SHUMAKER,	PHILIP			
10, 336.	Autumn Reflections	24 x 36	DAC	7. 50
	c.	20 x 24	PENN	1. 50
10, 337.	Monhegan Gold			
	c.	20 x 24	PENN	1. 50
10, 338.	Mountain Retreat			
	c.	20 x 24	PENN	1. 50
10, 339.	Peaceful Valley			
	c.	20 x 24	PENN	1. 50
10, 340.	Sea in Splendor	24 x 48	DAC	10. 00
	c.	20 x 24	PENN	1. 50
SICKERT				
10, 341.	Summer Lightning	8 x 9	ESH	2. 00
SIDEMAN,	CAROL (American Contemporary)			
10, 342.	Young Artists	19 x 26	NYGS	10. 00

SIGNAC, PAUL (French, 1863-1935)

10, 343.	Antibes	9 x 11	CFA	. 50
10, 344.	Harbor, 1907	18 x 24	NYGS	10. 00
10, 345.	Harbour at Les			
	Sables d'Olonne	11 x 15-1/2	ESH	8. 00
10, 346.	Harbor of St. Tropez			
		22 x 18	CFA	12. 00
10, 347.	Paris	27 x 33	CFA	18. 00
10, 348.	Port of Paimpol	11-1/2 x 30	ESH	15. 00
10, 349.	Port of Saint-Cast	22 x 27	NYGS	7. 50
10, 350.	Quay at Clichy	17 x 24	PENN	1. 50
10, 351.	La Rochelle	11-1/2x16-1/2	NYGS	7. 50
10, 352.	Sea Breeze, Concarneau			
		18 x 22-1/2	ESH	10. 00
10, 353.	Venice--St. Maria			
	della Salute	26 x 32-1/2	NYGS	20. 00
10, 354.	Yellow Sails	24 x 30	ESH	15. 00

SIGNORELLI, LUCA (Italian, 1450-1523)

10, 355.	Anti-Christ	11 x 14	IA	3. 00
	Detail of No.			
	10, 355	15 x 11	IA	3. 00
10, 356.	Calling of the Elects			
		11 x 14	IA	3. 00
10, 357.	The Damned	11 x 14	IA	3. 00
	Detail of No.			
	10, 357	11 x 15	IA	3. 00
10, 358.	Dante, Portrait	15 x 12	IA	3. 00
10, 359.	Empidocles of			
	Agrigentum	15 x 11	IA	3. 00
10, 360.	End of World c.	8 x 10	NYGS	. 50
10, 361.	Flagellation			
	(Venice)	13-1/2x11-1/2	AS	3. 25
10, 362.	Holy Family	11" Diam.	AS	3. 25
10, 363.	Last Judgement	15 x 11	IA	3. 00
10, 364.	Madonna and Child	12" Diam.	IA	3. 00
10, 365.	Resurrection of the			
	Body	11 x 14	IA	3. 00
10, 366.	Sibyl and Prophet	11 x 15	IA	3. 00
10, 367.	Virgil	15 x 12	IA	3. 00

SIGNORINI, TELEMACO (Italian, 1835-1901)

10, 368.	Street in Settignano	10 x 15	IA	3. 00

SILVERMAN

10, 369.	Boats in Harbor	16-1/2 x 24	PENN	1. 50
10, 370.	The Cove c.	20 x 24	PENN	1. 50

SIMEONE, ADOLFO (Italian, 1885-)

10, 371.	Madonna of the			
	Rosary	19-1/2 x 28	IA	8. 00

SIMMON

10, 372.	Defiance c.	20 x 24	PENN	1. 50
10, 373.	Golden Charger			
	c.	20 x 24	PENN	1. 50

SIMON
| 10, 374. | Study (3) | 20 x 12 | DAC | ea. | 5. 00 |

SIMON-SCHAFER, HANS-ALBERT
| 10, 375. | In the Mountains |
| | near Rome | 23 x 29-1/2 | ESH | | 12. 00 |

SIMPSON, C.
| 10, 376. | President Kennedy | 24 x 20 | CAC | | 7. 50 |
| 10, 377. | The Straggler | 14-1/2x20-1/2 | ESH | | 12. 00 |

SINGER
| 10, 378. | Go-Go (12) | 15 x 6 | DAC | ea. | 1. 50 |

SINKO, LOUIS-ARMAND (French Contemporary)
| 10, 379. | Bouquet | 19-1/2 x 24 | NYGS | | 12. 00 |

SINTENIS, RENÉE (German, 1888-)
10, 380.	Donkey (Sculpture)
	c.	7 x 9	AP		. 25
10, 381.	Foal	9 x 11	CFA		3. 50
10, 382.	Gazelle	11 x 9	CFA		3. 50

SIRONI, MARIO (Italian, 1893-1961)
| 10, 383. | Return of the Mythe, |
| | 1956 | 20-1/2 x 24 | NYGS | | 12. 00 |

SISLEY, ALFRED (French, 1839-1899)
10, 384.	L'Abbrevoir	12 x 16	AR		3. 00
10, 385.	At Daybreak	11 x 13	IA		3. 00
10, 386.	Autumn Leaves
	c.	10 x 8	ESH		1. 00
10, 387.	Avenue	c.	8 x 10	ESH		1. 00
10, 388.	Banks of the Loing	20 x 25	CFA		15. 00
	c.	8 x 10	ESH		1. 00
10, 389.	Banks of the Oise	16 x 19-1/2	NYGS		10. 00
10, 390.	Banks of the Seine	19-1/2 x 25	AJ		12. 00
10, 391.	Barges at St. Mammes
		20 x 25	CFA		15. 00
10, 392.	Bell-Tower at Noise-
	le-Roi	18 x 24	NYGS		15. 00
10, 393.	Boat During
	Inundation	7 x 8	CFA		1. 00
10, 394.	Bridge in Moret
	(Pont de Moret)	20 x 25	CFA		18. 00
	c.	18 x 23	HNA		5. 95
		16 x 20	ESH		6. 00
10, 395.	Bridge at Sevres
	c.	18 x 23	HNA		5. 95
		15 x 18	AP		6. 00
10, 396.	Canal de L'Ourcq	24 x 30	PENN		1. 95
		12 x 16	DAC		2. 50
10, 397.	Canal St. Martin	19 x 25	AJ		12. 00
10, 398.	Covered Bridge	24 x 30	PENN		1. 95
10, 399.	La Croix-Blanche,
	St. Mammes c.	18 x 23	HNA		5. 95
10, 400.	Early Snow in
	Louveciennes c.	18 x 23	HNA		5. 95
10, 401.	Floods at Marly in
	1875	18-1/2x22-1/2	ESH		10. 00

10, 402.	Hampton Court			
	c.	17-1/2 x 22	AS	4. 00
10, 403.	High Road Seen from			
	the Way to Sevres	15 x 20	AP	5. 00
10, 404.	Innundation c.	9-1/2x12-1/2	AP	1. 25
10, 405.	L'Inondation a Port			
	Marly	18 x 20	PENN	1. 50
10, 406.	Landscape Near			
	Paris	14 x 21	NYGS	6. 00
10, 407.	Le Loing	20 x 25-1/2	NYGS	15. 00
10, 408.	Loing Canal	18 x 22	ESH	10. 00
10, 409.	Loing at Moret			
	c.	8 x 10	ESH	1. 00
10, 410.	Loing at Moret,			
	Sept. Afternoon			
	c.	8 x 10	ESH	1. 00
10, 411.	Molesey Weir	7 x 9	NYGS	. 50
10, 412.	Moret-Sur-Loing,			
	Morning Sunshine	18-1/2x22-1/2	ESH	10. 00
	c.	8 x 10	ESH	1. 00
10, 413.	Le Pont de Villenouve-			
	La-Garenne c.	17-1/2 x 22	AS	4. 00
10, 414.	Port Marly	15 x 24	AJ	10. 00
		11 x 18	CFA	5. 00
10, 415.	Prairie at By	21-1/2x27-1/2	ESH	15. 00
10, 416.	Regatta at Hampton			
	Court c.	8 x 10	ESH	1. 00
10, 417.	River Scene	17 x 22-1/2	ESH	10. 00
10, 418.	Road at Louveciennes			
		18 x 24	NYGS	10. 00
10, 419.	The Seine at Marly			
	c.	8 x 10	ESH	1. 00
10, 420.	The Seine at St.			
	Cloud	18-1/2x22-1/2	ESH	10. 00
10, 421.	September Afternoon			
	at Moret c.	8 x 10	ESH	1. 00
10, 422.	Small Square at			
	Argenteuil	19 x 28	PENN	1. 50
		15-1/2x22-1/2	ESH	10. 00
	c.	8x 10	ESH	1. 00
10, 423.	Snow at Louveciennes			
	c.	9-1/2x12-1/2	AP	1. 25
		8 x 6	CFA	1. 00
10, 424.	Springtime at Moret			
	c.	8 x 10	ESH	1. 00
10, 425.	Square at Argenteuil			
		8 x 12	CFA	. 50
10, 426.	Street at Louveciennes			
		18 x 24	NYGS	10. 00
10, 427.	Street in Marly	23 x 30	ESH	12. 00
		17-1/2x22-1/2	ESH	10. 00
10, 428.	Street in Moret	24 x 30	CFA	15. 00

10,429.	Tugboat	15-1/2 x 21	PENN	1.50
10,430.	View of St. Martin	19 x 25	CFA	12.00
10,431.	Village de Sablons	18 x 21-1/2	ESH	10.00

SITZMANN, EDWARD R. (American, 1874-)

10,432.	Happy Hollow	22 x 28	CFA	7.50

SKEAPING, JOHN R. (English, 1901-)

10,433.	Female Reed-Buck	13-1/2 x 11	ESH	5.00
10,434.	Group of Horses	19-1/2 x 27	ESH	10.00
10,435.	Leechwee Antelope	13-1/2 x 11	ESH	5.00
10,436.	Only Two In It	23 x 29	ESH	12.00
10,437.	Prancing Horse	19-1/2 x 27	ESH	10.00
10,438.	Reed Buck	11 x 13-1/2	ESH	5.00
10,439.	Rejoneador	17 x 18-1/2	RL	6.00

SKINNER, VIOLET (English Contemporary)

10,440.	Cooling Stream	18-1/2 x 32	RL	10.00
10,441.	High Spirits	18-1/2 x 32	RL	10.00
10,442.	Into the Happy Lands	18 x 32	RL	7.50
10,443.	Mares' Tails in the Sky	20 x 30	RL	7.50
10,444.	Wild White Horses	17 x 32	RL	7.50

SLATTER, MARY (English, 18th Century)

10,445.	Sampler, 1792	17 x 24	NYGS	12.00

SLAV-SLEPCEVIC See RAJKO

SLOAN, JOHN (American, 1871-1951)

10,446.	Hair-Dresser's Window	c. 8 x 10	NYGS	.50
10,447.	Haymarket	c. 20 x 24	PENN	1.50
10,448.	McSorley's Bar	c. 7 x 9	AP	.50
10,449.	Wake of the Ferry Boat II	18 x 22	NYGS	12.00

SLOANE, ERIC

10,450.	Autumn in New England	24 x 36	CFA	15.00
10,451.	Canvas Backs	18 x 24	AA	7.50
10,452.	End of Summer	24 x 36	CFA	15.00
10,453.	Landscapes (6)	24 x 48	AK	ea. 12.00
10,454.	Cloud Symphony	12 x 24	PENN	ea. 1.50
10,455.	First Snow			
10,456.	Nostalgic Autumn			
10,457.	Nostalgic Summer			
10,458.	October Gleaning			
10,459.	Old Spring House			
10,460.	Wagon Shed	24 x 36	CFA	15.00

SLUIS, VAN DER

10,461.	Fruit Baskets (2)	18 x 24	AK	ea. 6.00

SLUYTERMAN, GEORG

10,462.	Lueneburger Moorlands	23 x 30	ESH	10.00

SMALLWOOD, R. A.

10,463.	St. Paul's from Fleet Street	36 x 24	AS	15.00

SMITH, FRANK VINING (American Contemporary)

10,464.	Clipper Ship Red				
	Jacket	c.	7 x 9	AP	.50
10,465.	Sunlit Seas		25x 30	IA	10.00

SMITH, JESSIE WILLCOX (American)

10,466.	Morning Mist		24 x 30	CFA	10.00
10,467.	Seeing	c.	7 x 9	AP	.50
10,468.	We Give Thee				
	Thanks		16 x 15-1/2	NYGS	4.00

SMITH, LAWRENCE BEALL (American Contemporary)

10,469.	Frolic	17 x 22	NYGS	9.00
10,470.	Museum Visitor	24-1/2x18-1/2	NYGS	10.00

SMITH, MATTHEW (English, 1879-1959)

10,471.	Chrysanthemums	29-1/2 x 24	NYGS	18.00
10,472.	Landscape Near Aix			
		14 x 28	NYGS	15.00
10,473.	Still Life with Jug	18-1/2 x 22	NYGS	10.00
10,474.	Syringa, Peonies			
	and Pears	22 x 27	NYGS	18.00

SMITH, MINNA WALKER (American, 1883-)

10,475.	Purity	24 x 20	NYGS	10.00

SMITH, ROBERT J. (American Contemporary)

10,476.	Early American				
	Still Life (4)	c.	20 x 24	PENN	ea. 1.50
	Still Life: With				
	Lemons		16 x 20	DAC	ea. 5.00
	With Pumpkin				
	With Strawberries				
	With Watermelon				

SMITH, WALLACE H. (American Contemporary)

10,477.	Hell Gate Bridge,			
	New York	11 x 19	NYGS	6.00

SNAPPER, R.

10,478.	Bridge in Paris	24 x 48	DAC	10.00
10,479.	Chicago Views (4)	12 x 30	DAC	ea. 5.00
		8 x 17	DAC	ea. 1.50
10,480.	Continental Views			
	(8)	12 x 30	DAC	ea. 5.00
		8 x 17	DAC	ea. 1.50
10,481.	New York Views			
	(6)	30 x 12	DAC	ea. 5.00
		17 x 8	DAC	ea. 1.50

SNELL, OLIVE (Mrs. Pike) (English Contemporary)

10,482.	Florius	25 x 19	ESH	10.00

SNOW, EDWARD TAYLOR (American, 1844-1913)

10,483.	Meet at Blagdon	22 x 31	CFA	30.00

SNYDER

10,484.	Farm Landscapes			
	(4)	24 x 8	AK	ea. 2.50
		12 x 4	AK	ea. 1.00
	Farm Landscapes			
	(2)	8 x 24	AK	ea. 2.50
		4 x 12	AK	ea. 1.00

SODOMA (IL) (BAZZI, GIOVANNI ANTONIO) (Italian, 1477-1549)
10, 485.   Madonna and Child
           with Infant St. John 22 x 18   AA   7. 50
10, 486.   St. Sebastian   15 x 11   IA   3. 00
           Head--Detail of
           No. 10, 486   18 x 14   IA   3. 00
10, 487.   Scourging of Christ 15 x 11   IA   3. 00
10, 488.   Trance of St.
           Catherine   15 x 11   IA   3. 00
SOGLIANI, GIOVANNI ANTONIO (Italian, 1492-1544)
10, 489.   Crucifix   15 x 9-1/2   AS   3. 25
10, 490.   Virgin and Child
           and St. John   14 x 11-1/2   AS   3. 25
SOHL, WILL (German, 1906-)
10, 491.   The Cove   19 x 25   ESH   7. 50
SOLARIO, ANDREA DA (Italian, 1460-1527)
10, 492.   Charles D'Amboise   9 x 6   NYGS   . 50
10, 493.   Madonna with the
           Green Cushion   13 x 10   IA   3. 00
                          c.   10 x 8   ESH   1. 00
10, 494.   Virgin Nursing the
           Child   14 x 11   IA   3. 00
SOLDWEDEL
10, 495.   Xanadu   c. 20 x 24   PENN   1. 50
SONNTAG, WILLIAM (American, 1822-1900)
10, 496.   Mountain Lake Near
           Piedmont, Maryland,
           1860   26 x 40   NYGS   20. 00
SOORD, ALFRED (English, 1869-1915)
10, 497.   Lost Sheep   20 x 13   IA   4. 00
                               20 x 12-1/2   NYGS   6. 00
                               10 x 6-1/2   NYGS   1. 00
SORBI, RAFFAELE (Italian, 1844-1931)
10, 498.   Marriage of Beatrice
                               21 x 17   IA   10. 00
10, 499.   Promenade of Granduca
           Pietro Leopoldo   10 x 15   IA   3. 00
SOTTUNG
10, 500.   Childhood Days
                          c.   20 x 24   PENN   1. 50
10, 501.   Picnic   c.   20 x 24   PENN   1. 50
SOULAGES, PIERRE (French Contemporary)
10, 502.   Peinture, 1955   31-1/2x21-1/2 NYGS   20. 00
SOULET
10, 503.   Augustus   16 x 12   AS   6. 00
10, 504.   Emma   16 x 12   AS   6. 00
10, 505.   In Old Japan   10 x 30   AS   6. 00
10, 506.   Parasol Parade   10 x 30   AS   6. 00
SOUTER, J. B. (Scotch Contemporary)
10, 507.   Glory of the Garden
                               16 x 12   RL   3. 50
10, 508.   Summer's Pride   16 x 12   RL   3. 50

SOUTINE,	CHAIM (Russian, 1894-1943)			
10, 509.	Big Tree	24 x 19	PENN	1. 50
10, 510.	Chartres Cathedral	30 x 16-1/2	ESH	15. 00
10, 511.	Choir Boy	22-1/2 x 18	ESH	10. 00
10, 512.	Cook Boy c.	9 x 7	AP	. 50
10, 513.	Landscape, 1926	20 x 24	NYGS	12. 00
10, 514.	Portrait of a Boy	24 x 16-1/2	NYGS	12. 00
		22 x 15	PENN	1. 50
10, 515.	Woman in a Blue			
	Robe c.	10 x 8	ESH	1. 00
SOYER,	MOSES (Russian-American, 1899-)			
10, 516.	Blue Dancer	20 x 9	PENN	1. 50
10, 517.	Dancers c.	23 x 18	HNA	5. 95
		21 x 20	PENN	1. 50
10, 518.	Dancers at Rest			
	c.	24 x 20	PENN	1. 50
10, 519.	Dancers Reposed			
	c.	20 x 24	PENN	1. 50
10, 520.	Red Dancer	20 x 9	PENN	1. 50
10, 521.	Waiting for the			
	Audition c.	12 x 16	PENN	1. 00
SOYER,	RAPHAEL (American, 1899-)			
10, 522.	Farewell to Lincoln			
	Square c.	18 x 23	HNA	5. 95
10, 523.	Flower Vendor	18-1/2 x 20	NYGS	7. 50
10, 524.	Modern Tempo	20 x 15-1/2	NYGS	7. 50
10, 525.	Shop Girls c.	7 x 9	AP	. 50
SPAENDENCK,	GERADUS VAN (Dutch, 1746-1822)			
10, 526.	Rose a Cent			
	Feuilles	18 x 13	CFA	10. 00
10, 527.	Rose de Provins	17 x 13	CFA	10. 00
SPAGNA,	GIOVANNI DI PIETRO (Italian, 1480-1530)			
10, 528.	Study of a Nude Male			
	Model	10 x 6	AR	3. 50
SPAGNOLETTO,	LO See RIBERA, JOSE DE			
SPAGNUOLO,	LO See CRESPI, GIOVANNI MARIA			
SPAIN				
10, 529.	UWA Art Series			
	(32)	11 x 14		
	or	14 x 11	NYGS ea.	2. 00
SPEICHER,	EUGENE (American, 1883-)			
10, 530.	Jean Bellows	9 x 8	NYGS	. 50
10, 531.	Nude Back	16 x 20	NYGS	9. 00
SPEIER				
10, 532.	Miriam	23-1/2 x 20	ESH	10. 00
SPENCER				
10, 533.	Stallions, Celebrated			
	(6)	12 x 14	AA ea.	7. 50
SPENCER,	ROBERT (American, 1879-1931)			
10, 534.	Color Grandeur	24 x 40	DAC	8. 50
10, 535.	In Fairmone c.	8 x 10	NYGS	. 50
10, 536.	Roadside Dwellings	24 x 40	DAC	8. 50

10, 537.	Winter Wonder-land	24 x 40	DAC		8. 50
		24 x 30	PENN		1. 95
SPENCER,	STANLEY (English,	1891-1959)			
10, 538.	Magnolias	20 x 24	NYGS		9. 00
SPINELLI,	GAETANO (Italian,	1887-1945)			
10, 539.	Adoration	16 x 20	IA		7. 50
10, 540.	Expectation	25 x 17	IA		7. 50
	Detail of No. 10, 540	21 x 20	IA		7. 50
10, 541.	Marriage of Beatrice	21 x 17	IA		10. 00
10, 542.	Maternal Joys	13 x 11 Oval	IA		3. 00
10, 543.	Prelude	20 x 20	IA		7. 50
SPINOZA					
10, 544.	Rhapsody in Blue	20 x 48	AK		10. 00
10, 545.	Rhapsody in Brown	20 x 48	AK		10. 00
SPITZ					
10, 546.	Severe Judge	12 x 9-1/2	ESH	Pr.	2. 00
SPITZWEG,	KARL VON (German,	1808-1885)			
10, 547.	Art and Science	23-1/2 x 14	NYGS		18. 00
10, 548.	Bookworm	20 x 10-1/2	AJ		10. 00
		14 x 7	CFA		2. 50
10, 549.	Cactus' Friend	20 x 10-1/2	AJ		10. 00
		10-1/2x5-1/2	AJ		1. 75
10, 550.	Dreamer	14 x 11-1/2	AJ		5. 00
10, 551.	Girl with Kid	14 x 11	CFA		7. 50
10, 552.	The Hussar	23-1/2 x 14	NYGS		18. 00
10, 553.	Pensionists	10-1/2 x 6	AJ		2. 00
10, 554.	Perpetual Suitor	14 x 12	CFA		6. 00
10, 555.	Poor Poet	20 x 24	DAC		7. 50
		12 x 16	DAC		2. 50
10, 556.	Postman	14 x 12	CFA		6. 00
10, 557.	Stage Coach	14 x 12	CFA		6. 00
10, 558.	Sunday Morning	13 x 22	CFA		12. 00
10, 559.	Visit of the Sovereign	14 x 12	CFA		6. 00
SPRICK,	RICHARD (German,	1901-)			
10, 560.	In Mallorca	12 x 16	ESH		4. 00
SPRINGER					
10, 561.	Landscapes (4) c.	20 x 24	PENN	ea.	1. 50
10, 562.	Canal at Haarlem				
10, 563.	City Scene in Enkhuizen				
10, 564.	City View				
10, 565.	Town of Enkhuizen				
SPROTTE,	SIEGWARD (German Contemporary)				
10, 566.	Noon in Blue	22 x 31	CFA		15. 00
10, 567.	Northern Light	22 x 30	CFA		15. 00
10, 568.	Sands of Sylt	18 x 24	CFA		15. 00
SPY (SIR LESLIE WARD, KNOWN AS "SPY") (English, 1851-1922)					
10, 569.	Divorce	12-1/2x7-1/2	IA		2. 50
		9 x 5-1/2	IA		1. 50

10,570	Judges the				
	Claimant	12 x 8	IA		2.50
		9 x 6	IA		1.50
10,571.	Lord Chief Justice	12 x 7-1/2	IA		2.50
		9 x 5-1/2	IA		1.50
10,572.	Umpire	12 x 7-1/2	IA		2.50
		9 x 5-1/2	IA		1.50

SPUROPOULOS, JANNIS (Greek Contemporary)

10,573.	Oracle, 1960	35-1/2x23-1/2	NYGS		15.00

STABLI, ADOLPH (Swiss, 1843-1901)

10,574.	Stroll to the Lake	18 x 29	CFA		12.00

STAEL, DE See DE STAEL, NICHOLAS

STAHL, BEN (American Contemporary)

10,575.	Nativity	15 x 27	PENN		1.50

STANCIN

10,576.	Reverie I and II	24 x 48	AK	ea.	6.00

STANFIELD, C.

10,577.	Pisa	8 x 10	CFA		6.00

STANG

10,578.	Last Supper (After				
	DaVinci)	21-1/2 x 41	IA		10.00
		16 x 30	IA		5.00
		9 x 17	IA		2.00
		6-1/2 x 12	IA		1.00

STARECK, EDGAR

10,579.	Manhattan	15 x 40	DAC	10.00
10,580.	Metropolis	15 x 40	DAC	10.00
10,581.	New York View	24 x 48	DAC	10.00
10,582.	San Francisco View	24 x 48	DAC	10.00

STARK

10,583.	The Indian Trail			
	c.	7 x 9	AP	.50

STARKENBORGH, JACOBUS NICOLAS VAN (Dutch, 1822-)

10,584.	Crossing the River	24 x 36	DAC	7.50

STARNINA, GHERARDO (Italian, 1354-1403)

10,585.	The Thebaid	11 x 15	IA	3.00
		5-1/2x11-1/2	AS	3.25

STEARNS, FRED (American, 1885-1967)

10,586.	Chicago Scenes (2)				
	(DR.) (B & W)		NYGS	ea.	5.00
	Art Institute and				
	Michigan Ave.				
	Water Tower				

STEELE

10,587.	Haymakers c.	7 x 9	AP	.50

STEEN, JAN (Dutch, 1626-1679)

10,588.	Baptismal Party	6 x 7	NYGS	.50
10,589.	The Breakfast	11-1/2x14-1/2	AS	3.25
10,590.	Dancing Couple	22 x 30	AA	15.00
10,591.	Eve of St. Nicholas	9 x 8	NYGS	.50
10,592.	Family Concert	20 x 24	DAC	7.50
10,593.	Family Repast	13 x 11	IA	3.00

10, 594.	In the Bower	8 x 10	AR	3. 00
10, 595.	Young Woman at her Toilet	20 x 16	ESH	15. 00

STEER

10, 596.	Misty Morning on the Severn: Bridge North	9 x 13	NYGS	15. 00

STEFULA, GYORGY (German, 1913-)

10, 597.	Province Gate	18 x 21	CFA	10. 00
10, 598.	Provincial Basket	19 x 23	CFA	10. 00

STEIB

10, 599.	Moroccan Bazaar Street	27 x 22	CFA	12. 00

STEINHAUSER, WILHELM AUGUST (German, 1846-1924)

10, 600.	Christ Preaching	20 x 28-1/2	IA	7. 50
10, 601.	Return from Our Lord's Supper	23-1/2 x 22	IA	7. 50
		8 x 7-1/2	IA	. 75

STEINKE, BETTINA (American Contemporary)

10, 602.	Bringing Flowers Singing	16 x 12	IA	5. 00
10, 603.	Jumping Deer	16 x 12	IA	5. 00
10, 604.	Santa Clara Indian Girl	17-1/2x15-1/2	IA	6. 00
10, 605.	Taos Indian Boy	16 x 12	IA	5. 00
10, 606.	Taos Indian Girl	16 x 12	IA	5. 00

STEINLAUF

10, 607.	Doves	28 x 12	CFA	20. 00
10, 608.	Expression I	28 x 12	CFA	20. 00
10, 609.	Fishing Boats I and II	12 x 28	CFA	ea. 20. 00
10, 610.	Flower Vendor	28 x 12	CFA	20. 00
10, 611.	Girl with Dove	19 x 15	CFA	20. 00
10, 612.	Juanita	28 x 12	CFA	20. 00
10, 613.	Lolita	28 x 12	CFA	20. 00
10, 614.	Rosita	28 x 12	CFA	20. 00
10, 615.	Sisters	28 x 12	CFA	20. 00
10, 616.	Watermelon Boy	28 x 12	CFA	20. 00

STEINMANN, AUGUST (American Contemporary)

10, 617.	Pacific Surf	18 x 24	IA	7. 50

STELLA, JOSEPH (American, 1880-1946)

10, 618.	Brooklyn Bridge	26 x 15	PENN	1. 50
	c.	10 x 8	NYGS	. 50
10, 619.	Voice of the Nightingale	20 x 18-1/2	NYGS	10. 00

STENGEL, HANS (American, 1894-1928)

10, 620.	View of Pillnitz	15 x 19-1/2	AP	5. 00

STEVENS, ALFRED (Belgian, 1828-1906)

10, 621.	King Alfred and his Mother	14 x 13	AP	3. 00

STEVENS, SANFORD (American, 1897-)

10, 622.	Mexican Scenes (4)	16 x 20	CFA	ea. 5. 00

10,623.	El Cambo	7 x 9	CFA	ea.	1.50
10,624.	Flower Market				
10,625.	Siesta Time				
10,626.	Tropical Village				
	Mexican Scenes (2)	20 x 16	CFA	ea.	5.00
10,627.	Market Day	9 x 7	CFA	ea.	1.50
10,628.	Mexican Street Scene				

STEVENSON, BRUCE (American Contemporary)

10,629.	Treasure Island	18 x 24-1/2	RL		7.50

STEVENSON, ESTHER (American Contemporary)

10,630.	Children, Portraits				
	(2)	29 x 15	CFA	ea.	7.50
10,631.	April Showers				
10,632.	On the Beach				
	Children, Portraits				
	(8)	20 x 16	CFA	ea.	5.00
10,633.	Boy with Accordian				
10,634.	I Pledge Allegiance				
10,635.	John John				
10,636.	Little Girl				
10,637.	Little Leaguer				
10,638.	Spring Bonnets				
10,639.	We Give Thanks				
10,640.	Student				

STEWART

10,641.	Persian Pottery				
		c. 24 x 20	PENN		1.50
10,642.	Zinnias	c. 20 x 24	PENN		1.50

STEWART, ARTHUR (American)

10,643.	Big Sky	24 x 40	NYGS		16.00

STEWART, CHARLES EDWARD (Scotch Contemporary)

10,644.	Water Lilies	27 x 36	IA		15.00

STIELER

10,645.	Beethoven	c. 9 x 7	AP		.50

STOBART, JOHN (English Contemporary)

10,646.	Ariel and Taeping	20 x 29	ESH		10.00
10,647.	Cutty Sark	20 x 29	ESH		10.00
10,648.	Great Western Entering				
	New York Harbor	26 x 36	AA		15.00
10,649.	Heart of London	17-1/2 x 26	ESH		8.00
10,650.	Young America	26 x 36	AA		15.00

STOCKER, HANS (Swiss, 1896-)

10,651.	Creation	c. 18 x 23	HNA		5.95

STOKES, ADRIAN (English, 1854-)

10,652.	Autumn Near Locarno				
		14 x 22	ESH		15.00

STOKES, F. H.

10653.	Horses (2)	24 x 20	AA	ea.	7.50
10,654.	Stymie				
10,655.	War Knight				
	Horses (2)	16 x 20	AA	ea.	7.50
10,656.	Crusader				
10,657.	Hoop, Jr.				

STONE, W. B.
10, 658.   Hay Wagon   24 x 47-1/2   AA   15. 00
STOSKOPF, SEBASTIEN
10, 659.   Five Senses of
           Summer   15 x 25   CFA   10. 00
                        c.   9-1/2x12-1/2   AP   1. 25
STOSS, VEIT (German, 1447-1542)
10, 660.   Hands of St.
           Catherine   11 x 19   CFA   3. 50
STRANG, RAY (American, 1893-)
10, 661.   Curiosity   14 x 11   NYGS   3. 00
                             7-1/2 x 6   NYGS   1. 00
10, 662.   Double Trouble   24 x 28   NYGS   10. 00
                             11 x 14   NYGS   3. 00
10, 663.   Lazybones   14 x 11   NYGS   3. 00
                             7-1/2 x 6   NYGS   1. 00
10, 664.   Playmates   14 x 11   NYGS   3. 00
                             7-1/2 x 6   NYGS   1. 00
10, 665.   Slow Poke   24 x 28   NYGS   10. 00
                             11 x 14   NYGS   3. 00
10, 666.   Taffy   14 x 11   NYGS   3. 00
                             7-1/2 x 6   NYGS   1. 00
           Western Ranch Scenes
           (9)   7-1/2 x 10   NYGS   ea.   1. 00
10, 667.   Deer at Water Hole
10, 668.   Double Trouble
10, 669.   Lost and Found
10, 670.   Poppies and Mommies
10, 671.   Silver Creek
10, 672.   Slow Poke
10, 673.   Summer Storm
10, 674.   Taffy
10, 675.   Wild Horse Ranch
STRASSER, ROLAND (Austrian [Res. England] Contemporary)
10, 676.   Exotic Balinese
           Dancers (2)   19 x 10   AK   ea.   5. 00
STRATER, HENRY (American, 1896-)
10, 677.   Colts at Soda
           Springs   11-1/2 x 19   NYGS   6. 00
10, 678.   Winter in the Verde
           Valley   15 x 20   NYGS   6. 00
STRECKENBACH, MAX (German, 1867-1936)
10, 679.   Poppies and Larkspur
                             28 x 29-1/2   ESH   10. 00
STREV (English Contemporary)
10, 680.   Abstracts by Harriet
                             24 x 14-1/2   ESH   6. 00
                             11 x 7   ESH   1. 00
10, 681.   Amanda   17 x 15   ESH   5. 00
                             8-1/2 x 7   ESH   1. 00
10, 682.   Arabella   8-1/2 x 7   ESH   1. 00
10, 683.   Belinda   17 x 15   ESH   5. 00
                             8-1/2 x 7   ESH   1. 00

10, 684.	Bunny	8-1/2 x 7	ESH	1. 00
10, 685.	The Favourite	17 x 15	ESH	5. 00
		8-1/2 x 7	ESH	1. 00
10, 686.	First Aid	17 x 15	ESH	5. 00
		8-1/2 x 7	ESH	1. 00
10, 687.	Giggy	23 x 14-1/2	ESH	6. 00
		11 x 7	ESH	1. 00
10, 688.	Harriet	17 x 15	ESH	5. 00
		8-1/2 x 7	ESH	1. 00
10, 689.	Lucinda	17 x 15	ESH	5. 00
		8-1/2 x 7	ESH	1. 00
10, 690.	Senorita	24 x 19-1/2	ESH	8. 00
		8-1/2 x 7	ESH	1. 00
10, 691.	Topsy	17 x 15	ESH	5. 00
		8-1/2 x 7	ESH	1. 00
10, 692.	Young Satchmo	17 x 15	ESH	5. 00
		8-1/2 x 7	ESH	1. 00

STREVENS, JOHN L. (English Contemporary)

10, 693.	Among the Bracken	10 x 12	ESH	3. 00
10, 694.	Au Boulevard	20 x 25	AS	7. 50
10, 695.	Bouquet des Fleurs - Autumn	28 x 15	ESH	8. 00
10, 696.	Bouquet des Fleurs - Summer	28 x 15	ESH	8. 00
10, 697.	Bridget	29 x 19	ESH	10. 00
10, 698.	Children of the Ballet	20 x 24	ESH	10. 00
10, 699.	Les Deux Amies	18 x 22	ESH	10. 00
10, 700.	Fiesta in Valencia	20 x 24	ESH	12. 00
10, 701.	Fruits of Spain	15-1/2 x 31	ESH	12. 00
10, 702.	La Gitana	27-1/2x20-1/2	ESH	10. 00
10, 703.	In Old Granada	20 x 24	ESH	10. 00
		10 x 12	ESH	3. 00
10, 704.	Moment Musicale	20 x 25	AS	7. 50
10, 705.	Musicale	15-1/2 x 31	ESH	12. 00
10, 706.	La Rencontre	18-1/2 x 22	ESH	10. 00
10, 707.	Les Sevillanas	20 x 24	ESH	10. 00

STREYO

10, 708.	Madonna with Jesus			
		28 x 39-1/2	ESH	10. 00

STRIEGEL (OR STRIGEL), BERNHARD (German, 1460-1528)

10, 709.	Portrait	15 x 11	AS	3. 25
10, 710.	Portrait of Charles V	15 x 8	IA	3. 00

STRY, IRENE (American Contemporary)

10, 711.	First Love	24 x 30	DAC	7. 50

STUART, GILBERT (American, 1755-1828)

10, 712.	George Washington (U. S. Natl. Gall.)	24 x 19	NYGS	10. 00
		14 x 11	NYGS	3. 00
10, 713.	George Washington (Whiteside Coll.)	18 x 15	NYGS	5. 00
		9 x 7-1/2	NYGS	1. 50

10,714.	George Washington			
	(Met. Mus., N.Y.)	29 x 24	NYGS	15.00
		10 x 8	NYGS	.50
10,715.	George Washington	28 x 22	CFA	7.50
10,716.	George Washington	19 x 14-1/2	ESH	12.00
10,717.	George Washington			
	c.	24 x 20	PENN	1.50
10,718.	Mrs. Richard Yates,			
	1793	22 x 18	NYGS	12.00
10,719.	Skater c.	18 x 23	HNA	5.95

STUBBS, GEORGE TOWNLEY (English, 1756-1815)

10,720.	Lady and Gentleman			
	in a Carriage	21 x 25-1/2	NYGS	10.00
10,721.	Mares and Foals	14 x 24-1/2	NYGS	12.00
10,722.	Pumpkin and Stable			
	Lad	24-1/2 x 30	NYGS	15.00
10,723.	Three Brood Mares			
	at Grass	19 x 24	ESH	15.00

STUEMPFIG, WALTER (American, 1914-)

| 10,724. | West Wildwood | 15 x 20 | IA | 7.50 |

STUTZ, A.

10,725.	Chrysanthemums	23 x 28	IA	7.50
10,726.	Delphinium	28 x 22	IA	7.50
10,727.	Phlox	28 x 22	IA	7.50

SUARDI, BARTOLOMMEO (IL BRAMANTINO) (Italian, 1468-1535)

10,728.	Agony of Man	10-1/2 x 6	AR	3.00
10,729.	Holy Family	15 x 11	IA	3.00
10,730.	Putto Under a Vine	13 x 17	ESH	6.00
10,731.	Youthful Sforza	17 x 24	ESH	10.00

SULLY, THOMAS (American, 1783-1872)

10,732.	Anne W. Wain	20 x 16	AA	6.00
10,733.	Boy with a Torn			
	Hat c.	24 x 20	PENN	1.50
		18-1/2 x 14	ESH	12.00
	c.	9 x 7	AP	.50
10,734.	Lady with a Harp:			
	Eliza Ridgely c.	18 x 23	HNA	5.95
10,735.	Major John Biddle	27-1/2 x 23	NYGS	12.00
		11 x 9	NYGS	1.50
10,736.	Major Thomas			
	Biddle	20 x 16	NYGS	10.00
10,737.	Miss Pearce	28 x 23	AA	10.00
10,738.	Mrs. James			
	Montgomery	20 x 17	NYGS	10.00

SUSSMAYR, JOSEPH (ALSO CALLED "JOSY" AND "YOS")
(German Contemporary)

10,739.	Lake Starnberger			
	and Rose Island	23-1/2x31-1/2	NYGS	15.00
10,740.	Serenity	25 x 31	CFA	12.00

SUSTERMANNS, JUSTUS (Flemish, 1597-1681)

| 10,741. | Portrait of the Son | | | |
| | of Frederick III | 15-1/2 x 11 | AS | 3.25 |

10, 742.	Prince of Den-			
	mark	19 x 14	ESH	10. 00

SUTHERLAND, GRAHAM VIVIAN (English, 1903-)

10, 743.	Christ in Glory in the Tetramorph (Coventry Cathedral Tapestry)	23-1/2 x 12	NYGS	7. 50
10, 744.	Large Vine Pergola, 1948	28 x 17	NYGS	12. 00
10, 745.	Path in Wood II, 1958	24 x 20	NYGS	18. 00
10, 746.	Thorn Tree, 1954	30 x 13-1/2	NYGS	12. 00

SVET

10, 747.	Lilacs	c.	18 x 23	HNA	5. 95

SWABIAN SCHOOL (German, 15th Century)

10, 748.	Two Lovers	24 x 14	NYGS	12. 00

SWANN, A. M.

10, 749.	St. Gudule	13 x 8	ESH	2. 00

SWANSON, J. N.

10, 750.	Caught in the Open	25 x 40	IA	15. 00
10, 751.	Horse Thief Canyon			
		25 x 40	IA	15. 00

SWEBACH, BERNARD EDOUARD (French, 1800-1870)

10, 752.	The Ride	c.	10 x 8	ESH	1. 00

SWINNERTON, JAMES (American, 1875-)

10, 753.	Agathla Needle	26 x 20	IA	12. 00
10, 754.	Arizona Desert	30 x 40	IA	20. 00
10, 755.	Blooming Desert	16 x 21	NYGS	7. 50
10, 756.	Deep Canyon	24 x 36	IA	15. 00
10, 757.	Desert Cacti	21 x 47	DAC	10. 00
		14 x 22	DAC	3. 50
		11 x 24	DAC	3. 50
10, 758.	Desert End	28 x 34	IA	18. 00
10, 759.	Desert Horizon	24 x 40	DAC	8. 50
		14 x 22	DAC	3. 50
	Desert Paintings (3)	28 x 34	IA	Ea. 15. 00
10, 760.	Aspen Grove			
10, 761.	Blossoming Smoke Tree			
10, 762.	Palo Verde Tree in Bloom			
	Desert Paintings (4)	12 x16	IA	ea. 3. 50
10, 763.	Desert Smoke Tree in Bloom			
10, 764.	Field Sketch of Desert Ironwood Tree			
10, 765.	Field Sketch of Juniper Tree			
10, 766.	Smoke Tree in Corner of Desert			
	Desert Paintings (2)	16 x 12	IA	ea. 3. 50
10, 767.	Desert Smoke Tree			
10, 768.	Blossoming Palo Verde Tree			
	Desert Studies No. 1 to No. 4			
		16 x 20	IA	ea. 5. 00

10, 769.	No. 1 (Smoke Tree)			
10, 770.	No. 2 (Palo Verde)			
10, 771.	No. 3 (Saguaro and Palo Verde)			
10, 772.	No. 4 (Saguaro and Ironwood)			
10, 773.	Desert Valley	30 x 12	IA	10. 00
10, 774.	Grand Viewpoint, Grand Canyon, Arizona			
		28 x 34	IA	18. 00
10, 775.	Ironwood Tree	24 x 18	IA	10. 00
10, 776.	Palm Canyon	30 x 12	IA	10. 00
10, 777.	Salton Sea	24 x 40	DAC	8. 50
		14 x 22	DAC	3. 50
10, 778.	Salton Sea	24 x 18	IA	10. 00
10, 779.	Sunset in the Sand Country	30 x 40	IA	20. 00

SZYK, ARTHUR (Polish, 1894-)

10, 780.	Declaration of Independence	20 x 17	CFA	5. 00
		19 x 15-1/2	AP	5. 00

T

TADEMA See ALMA-TADEMA
TAKIS, NICHOLAS (American, 1903-)

	Air Transportation (3)	8 x 6	CFA	ea.	1. 50
10, 781.	Airship				
10, 782.	Blue Balloon				
10, 783.	Red Balloon				
10, 784.	Broadway	9 x 15	CFA		2. 00
10, 785.	Croquet	8 x 6	CFA		1. 50
10, 786.	Still Life (4)	8 x 6	CFA	ea.	1. 50

TALMAGE, ALGERNON (English, 1871-)

10, 787.	Country Road	17 x 20	ESH	6. 00

TALWINSKI, I.

10, 788.	Sylvia	25 x 20	RL	12. 50

TAMAYO, RUFINO (Mexican, 1899-)

10, 789.	Mandolins and Pineapples	19-1/2x27-1/2	NYGS	16. 00
10, 790.	Woman with Black Coif c.	24 x 20	PENN	1. 50

TAMM, FRANZ WERNER VON ("F. W. ") (German, 1658-1724)

10, 791.	Flower Still Life	30 x 23-1/2	NYGS	16. 00
10, 792.	Still Life with Flowers	30 x 24	CFA	12. 00

TAN AN CHIDEN (Japanese, 15th Century)

10, 793.	Night Heron	12-1/2 x 19	NYGS	20. 00

TANGUY, YVES (French, 1900-)

10, 794.	Five Strangers	28 x 28	CFA	15. 00
10, 795.	Rapidity of Sleep	20 x16	CFA	7. 50

TANSLEY, ERIC (English Contemporary)

10, 796.	Horses at Sunset	19-1/2x23-1/2	AS	6. 00

10, 797.	Moonlight Across the			
	Lake	28 x 20	ESH	8. 00
10, 798.	Moonlit Waters	17 x 29	ESH	8. 00
10, 799.	Oriental Waters	18 x 28	ESH	8. 00
TAPIES, ANTONIO (Spanish Contemporary)				
10, 800.	Pintura, 1958	22 x 26-1/2	NYGS	15. 00
TARRANT, MARGARET W.				
10, 801.	Adventure	9 x 12	ESH	2. 00
10, 802.	All Things Wise and			
	Wonderful	17-1/2 x 22	ESH	7. 50
		15 x 18	ESH	4. 50
		9-1/2 x 12	ESH	2. 00
10, 803.	Behold, I send			
	You Forth	18-1/2 x 22	ESH	7. 50
		13 x 16	ESH	4. 50
		9-1/2 x 12	ESH	2. 00
10, 804.	The Brook	14-1/2 x 19-1/2	ESH	4. 50
10, 805.	Divine Teacher	7-1/2x11-1/2	ESH	2. 00
10, 806.	An Elf to Tea	21 x 17-1/2	ESH	3. 50
10, 807.	Elfin Chorus	17-1/2 x 22	ESH	3. 50
10, 808.	Fairies'Oak	13-1/2 x 11	ESH	2. 00
10, 809.	First Flower			
	Service	9 x 12	ESH	2. 00
10, 810.	Good Friends	17-1/2 x 20	ESH	3. 50
10, 811.	He Prayeth Best Who			
	Loveth Best	23 x 18	ESH	7. 50
		16 x 13	ESH	4. 50
		12 x 9	ESH	2. 00
10, 812.	Heaven Sent Maid	12 x 8	ESH	2. 00
10, 813.	Homeward Bound	9 x 12	ESH	2. 00
10, 814.	How Beautiful	12 x 8-1/2	ESH	. 60
10, 815.	Kingdom of Heaven	5-1/2 x 12	ESH	2. 00
10, 816.	Lesser Brethren	16-1/2x12-1/2	ESH	4. 50
		12 x 9	ESH	2. 00
10, 817.	Lesson Time	17-1/2 x 21	ESH	3. 50
10, 818.	Lilies of the Field	11 x 8-1/2	ESH	2. 00
10, 819.	Loving Shepherd	18 x 23	ESH	7. 50
		13 x 16	ESH	4. 50
		9-1/2 x 12	ESH	2. 00
10, 820.	Magic Pipes	4-1/2 x 11	ESH	2. 00
10, 821.	Market Day	21 x 17-1/2	ESH	3. 50
10, 822.	Morning Carol	11-1/2 x 9	ESH	2. 00
		9 x 7	ESH	. 60
10, 823.	No Room at the			
	Inn	15-1/2x11-1/2	ESH	2. 00
10, 824.	O Come Let Us			
	Sing	18 x 28	ESH	5. 00
10, 825.	Peter's Friends	16 x 11	ESH	2. 00
10, 826.	Pleasure Trip	17-1/2 x 21	ESH	3. 50
10, 827.	The Race	17-1/2 x 21	ESH	3. 50
10, 828.	Spirit of Night	15 x 11-1/2	ESH	2. 00
10, 829.	Spring Gaiety	14 x 22	ESH	3. 50

10, 830.	Spring in Arcady	12 x 9	ESH	2. 00
10, 831.	Star of Bethlehem	17-1/2x23-1/2	IA	7. 50
		15 x 18	ESH	4. 50
		10 x 12	ESH	2. 00
10, 832.	Suffer Little Children			
		13 x 8	ESH	2. 00
10, 833.	Titania (The Fairy Way)	17-1/2 x 24	ESH	3. 50

TARRANT, P.

10, 834.	Welcome Spring	12 x 8	ESH	2. 00

TAUBER

10, 835.	Chrysanthemums	20 x 12	ESH	Pr. 4. 00
10, 836.	Cozy Gathering	12 x 9-1/2	ESH	Pr. 2. 00
10, 837.	Farm by the Lake	10 x 20	ESH	Pr. 4. 00
10, 838.	Gay Tipplers	23-1/2 x 20	ESH	Pr. 10. 00
		20 x 16	ESH	Pr. 5. 00
10, 839.	Lake in Bavaria	23-1/2x31-1/2	ESH	Pr. 10. 00
		16 x 20	ESH	5. 00
		12 x 16	ESH	3. 00
	Landscapes (4)	16 x 31-1/2	ESH	Pr. 8. 00
10, 840.	Boat in the Bay			ea.
10, 841.	Dutch Canal			
10, 842.	Evening Upon the Moor			
10, 843.	Heath			
10, 844.	Leave Off Work	12 x 9-1/2	ESH	Pr. 2. 00
10, 845.	Old Farm	10 x 20	ESH	Pr. 4. 00
10, 846.	Poppy	20 x 27-1/2	ESH	Pr. 8. 00
	Portraits (3)	9-1/2 x 7	ESH	Pr. 1. 50
10, 847.	Jolly Farmer			ea.
10, 848.	Old Forester			
10, 849.	Trade-Master			
10, 850.	Sunflowers	20 x 12	ESH	Pr. 4. 00
10, 851.	Sunny Autumn Day	23-1/2x31-1/2	ESH	Pr. 10. 00
10, 852.	View into Far Distance	12 x 16	ESH	Pr. 3. 00
10, 853.	Way in the Cornfield	20 x 27-1/2	ESH	Pr. 8. 00

TAUBES, FREDERIC (Austrian, 1900-)

10, 854.	Girl with a Finch	17-1/2 x 12	NYGS	7. 50
10, 855.	Rehearsal c.	7 x 9	AP	. 50

TAYLOR, A. (American Contemporary)

10, 856.	Light Seven	27-1/2 x 40	NYGS	20. 00

TAYLOR, L. CAMPBELL (English, 1874-)

10, 857.	Regency Days	21-1/2 x 18	RL	10. 00
10, 858.	Sampler	21 x 18	RL	10. 00
10, 859.	Spinning Wheel	22-1/2 x 18	ESH	12. 00
10, 860.	Summer Flowers	22 x 18-1/2	ESH	15. 00

TCHANG WOU (Chinese [Yuan Dynasty] 14th Century)

10, 861.	Mountain by the River	19 x 10	CFA	18. 00
10, 862.	Women by the River	9-1/2 x 22	CFA	30. 00

TCHEKHONINE, SERGE (Danish, 1898-)
10, 863.	Dignity	20 x 14-1/2	NYGS	12.00
10, 864.	Elegance	20 x 14-1/2	NYGS	12.00

TCHELICHEW, PAVEL (Russian, 1898-1957)
10, 865.	Balustrade	13-1/2 x 11	AR	6.00

TCHEN HONG CHEOU (Chinese [Ming Dynasty] 1599-1652)
10, 866.	Poetesse	22 x 14	CFA	30.00

TEAGUE, DONALD (American, 1897-)
Western Scenes
(4)		12 x 30	DAC	ea.	5.00
10, 867.	Good Company				
10, 868.	Packing In				
10, 869.	Sheriff's Posse				
10, 870.	Stage Coach Arrival				

TENIERS, DAVID (YOUNGER) (Flemish, 1610-1690)
10, 871.	Drinkers and			
	Gamblers	9 x 10	AR	3.00
10, 872.	Eaves-Dropped Tete-a-Tete			
		9 x 15	IA	3.00
10, 873.	Flemish Kermess	14 x 20	AP	5.00
10, 874.	Hockey Players	15-1/2x22-1/2	ESH	10.00
10, 875.	In a Country Inn	25-1/2 x 22	AJ	15.00
10, 876.	Kermesse	11 x 14	IA	3.00

TER BORCH, GERAERD (Dutch, 1617-1681)
10, 877.	Concert	26 x 21	NYGS	12.00
	c.	23 x 18	HNA	5.95
		20-1/2 x 16	NYGS	15.00
		20 x 16	AP	7.50
	c.	9 x 7	AP	.50
		7 x 6	CFA	1.00
10, 878.	Curiosity	20 x 18	PENN	1.50
10, 879.	Dutch Woman Drinking	12 x 11	IA	3.00
10, 880.	Gallant Soldier	14 x 11	IA	3.00
10, 881.	The Letter	21 x 18	ESH	15.00
	c.	10 x 8	AP	.50
10, 882.	The Lute c.	24 x 20	DAC	7.50
		16 x 12	DAC	2.50
10, 883.	The Lute Player	19-1/2 x 14	NYGS	15.00
10, 884.	Lute-Playing Woman			
	c.	24 x 20	PENN	1.50
10, 885.	The Suitor's Visit	18 x 17	NYGS	12.00
		10 x 9	CFA	2.00

TERBRUGGHEN, HENRIK (Dutch, 1588-1629)
10, 886.	Flute Player I	22 x 17	CFA	10.00
10, 887.	Flute Player II	22 x 17	NYGS	6.00

THAYER, ABBOT HENDERSON (American, 1849-1921)
10, 888.	Virgin c.	9 x 7	AP	.50
10, 889.	Young Woman c.	10 x 8	NYGS	.50

THELEN
10, 890.	Boats in the Shadows	23-1/2x31-1/2	NYGS	16.00

10,891.	Old Boats on the				
	Lagoon	23-1/2x31-1/2	NYGS		16.00

THEOTOCOPULI, DOMENICO See GRECO, EL
THIANT, GUY

10,892.	Horses of the Sea	18 x 26-1/2	ESH		12.00

THIEME, ANTHONY (American Contemporary)

10,893.	Blue Door	18 x 22	CFA		3.50
		12 x 15	CFA		3.00
10,894.	Blue Shutters	20 x 24	CFA		10.00
10,895.	Breaking Sunlight	25 x 30	CFA		15.00
10,896.	Bridge	25 x 30	CFA		12.00
		14 x 17	CFA		3.00
10,897.	Getting Ready	18 x 22	CFA		7.50
		12 x 15	CFA		3.00
10,898.	Lobsterman and				
	Gulls	25 x 30	IA		12.00
	Mexican Views (3)	12 x 15	CFA	ea.	3.00
10,899.	Mexican Village				
10,900.	Taxco Road				
10,901.	View of Taxco				
10,902.	New England Views				
	and Fishing Scenes				
	(6)	25 x 30	AA	ea.	10.00
10,903.	Autumn in New England				
10,904.	Bear Skin Neck				
10,905.	Going Out				
10,906.	In the Bahamas				
10,907.	Indian Summer				
10,908.	Village Street (Mass.)				
	New England Views and				
	Fishing Scenes (5)	25 x 30	CFA	ea.	12.00
10,909.	Aviles Street				
10,910.	Dreamy Lagoon				
10,911.	Fisherman's Haven				
10,912.	Morning by the River				
10,913.	North Easter				
	New England Views and				
	Fishing Scenes (4)	16 x 20	CFA	ea.	5.00
	Aviles Street				
	Dreamy Lagoon				
	Morning by the River				
	New England Landscapes				
	and Fishing Scenes				
	(20)	12 x 15	CFA	ea.	3.00
	Aviles Street				
	Dreamy Lagoon				
10,914.	Early Morning				
	Fisherman's Haven				
10,915.	Foggy Morning, Rockport				
10,916.	Going Out Fishing				
10,917.	Hauling Nets				
10,918.	In the Bahamas				

10, 919.	Late Afternoon			
	Morning by the River			
10, 920.	New England Street Scene			
10, 921.	New England Winter			
10, 922.	Rockport Wharf			
10, 923.	Silverlight			
10, 924.	Summer Morn			
10, 925.	Sunlit Surf			
10, 926.	Southern Waters			
10, 927.	North Easter	25 x 30	CFA	12. 00
		14 x 17	CFA	3. 00
10, 928.	Rainy Day in Rock-			
	port	25 x 30	CFA	15. 00
		12 x 15	CFA	3. 00
10, 929.	Southern Waters	25 x 30	IA	10. 00
		16 x 20	IA	5. 00
		12-1/2 x 15	IA	3. 00
		12 x 15	CFA	3. 00
10, 930.	Spanish Patio	20 x 24	CFA	10. 00

THOMA, HANS (German, 1839-1924)

10, 931.	At the Lake of			
	Garda c.	10 x 8	NYGS	. 50
10, 932.	Early Morning in			
	the Black Forest	20 x 29-1/2	NYGS	22. 00
10, 933.	Idylle at Bernau	30 x 25	CFA	18. 00
10, 934.	Landscape near			
	Main	22-1/2 x 28	AR	15. 00

THOMAS, ERNST (German, 1896-)

10, 935.	Field and Stream	24 x 48	DAC	10. 00
		12 x 30	DAC	5. 00
10, 936.	Homeward Bound	24 x 48	DAC	10. 00
		12 x 30	DAC	5. 00
10, 937.	Miller's Home	24 x 48	DAC	10. 00
		12 x 30	DAC	5. 00
10, 938.	Red Water Mill	24 x 48	DAC	10. 00
		12 x 30	DAC	5. 00

THOMAS: MICHEL (Yugoslavian [Res. France] Contemporary)

10, 939.	Fisherman	23 x 11-1/2	ESH	6. 00
10, 940.	Scholar	23 x 11-1/2	ESH	6. 00
10, 941.	Seafarers	21 x 47	DAC	10. 00

THOMPSON, JEROME B. (American, 1814-1886)

10, 942.	Old Oaken Bucket	24 x 38-1/2	AA	12. 00
		18 x 28	NYGS	12. 00
		16 x 21-1/2	AA	6. 00

THOMPSON, RALPH (American)

10, 943.	Chi-Chi	19-1/2 x 26	ESH	10. 00
10, 944.	Flamingoes	31-1/2 x 16	ESH	7. 00
10, 945.	Herons	31-1/2 x 16	ESH	7. 00
10, 946.	Lion Cub	15 x 23	NYGS	7. 50
10, 947.	Tiger Cub	15 x 23	NYGS	7. 50

THOMPSON, WORDSWORTH (American, 1840-1896)

10, 948.	Departing Guests	21-1/2 x 36	NYGS	16. 00

THOMSON, JOHN MURRAY (Scotch, 1885-)
10, 949.   Highland Ponies   14-1/2 x 24   ESH   10. 00
THON, WILLIAM (American Contemporary)
10, 950.   Light in Autumn   18 x 36   IA   18. 00
10, 951.   Moment in Venice   17-1/2 x 36   IA   18. 00
10, 952.   Twilight in Rome   24-1/2 x 40   NYGS   20. 00
THORNTON, (DR.) (English, Ac. c. 1800)
           Floral Paintings
           (4)   12 x 10   IA   ea.   1. 00
10, 953.   Group of Carnations
10, 954.   Pontic Rhododendron
10, 955.   Sacred Egyptian Bean
10, 956.   Tulips
THORP, W. E.
10, 957.   Thames, Late
           Afternoon   20 x 30   AS   10. 00
THURNER, GABRIEL EDOUARD (French, 1840-1907)
10. 958.   Ranunculus   11 x 11   CFA   2. 00
TIEPOLO, GIOVANNIA BATTISTA (Italian, 1696-1770)
10, 959.   Adoration of the
           Child Jesus   15 x 10   IA   3. 00
10, 960.   Alexander and the
           Daughters of Darius
                              13 x 11   IA   3. 00
10, 961.   Alexander and the
           Family of Darius   15 x 11   IA   3. 00
10, 962.   Apollo Pursuing
           Daphne   23-1/2 x 30   NYGS   18. 00
10, 963.   Baptism of
           Constantinus   15 x 8   IA   3. 00
10, 964.   Communion of St.
           Lucy   15 x 7   IA   3. 00
10, 965.   The Conception   15-1/2 x 9   AS   3. 25
10, 966.   Coronation with
           Thorns   11 x 12   IA   3. 00
10, 967.   Danae   11 x 15   IA   3. 00
10, 968.   Education of the
           Virgin   15 x 9   IA   3. 00
10, 969.   Fortitude and
           Wisdom   10 x 15   IA   3. 00
10, 970.   Heliodorus and
           Onias   11 x 13   IA   3. 00
10, 971.   Immaculate Virgin 15 x 8   IA   3. 00
10, 972.   Iphigenia's Sacrifice
                              8 x 15   IA   3. 00
10, 973.   Justice and Peace 11 x 13 oval   IA   3. 00
10, 974.   Madonna of the
           Goldfinch   20 x 16   NYGS   10. 00
10, 975.   Magnanimity of
           Scipio   15 x 11   IA   3. 00
10, 976.   Martyrdom of
           St. Agatha   15 x 11   IA   3. 00

10, 977.	Martyrdom of St. John of Bergamo	15 x 11		IA	3. 00
10, 978.	Minuet (Carnival Scene) c.	20 x 24		PENN	1. 50
		11 x 15		IA	3. 00
10, 979.	Netpune Offering Wealth to Venice	6 x 15		IA	3. 00
10, 980.	Oriental's Head	14 x 11		IA	3. 00
10, 981.	A Page	15 x 11		AS	3. 25
		14 x 11		IA	3. 00
10, 982.	Portrait of Antonio Riccobono	13 x 11		IA	3. 00
10, 983.	Procuratore Giovanni Guerini	15 x 11		IA	3. 00
10, 984.	Reynold in Armida's Garden	9 x 15		IA	3. 00
10, 985.	Road to Calvary	11 x 13		IA	3. 00
10, 986.	St. Catherine of Siena	15 x 11	Oval	IA	3. 00
10, 987.	St. Maximus and St. Oswald	16 x 9		IA	3. 00
10, 988.	Tarquinius and Lucretia	15 x 11	Oval	IA	3. 00
10, 989.	Temptations of St. Anthony	11 x 14		IA	3. 00
10, 990.	Timocleia and the Thracian	10" Diam.		NYGS	. 50
10, 991.	Trained Dogs	11 x 15		IA	3. 00
10, 992.	Transportation of the Holy House of Loreto	15 x 10		IA	3. 00
10, 993.	Triumph of Zephyr and Flora	16 x 11		IA	3. 00
10, 994.	Two Dying Warriors	15 x 10		IA	3. 00
10, 995.	Two Flying Putti	11 x 13		IA	3. 00

TINTORETTO (ROBUSTI, JACOPO) (Italian, 1518-1594)

10, 996.	Adam and Eve	10 x 14-1/2		AS	3. 25
10, 997.	Bacchus and Ariadne	11 x 13		AS	3. 25
	c.	8 x 10		NYGS	. 50
10, 998.	Battle Between the Turks and the Christians c.	20 x 24		PENN	1. 50
10, 999.	Christ at the Sea of Galilee	21 x 31		NYGS	18. 00
11, 000.	The Doge Mocenigo c.	8 x 10		AP	. 50
11, 001.	Marriage of Bacchus and Ariadne	11 x 13		IA	3. 00
11, 002.	Mercury and the Graces	18 x 19		ESH	10. 00

11, 003.   Miracle of St. Mark
                            11-1/2 x 15   AS   3. 25
                            11 x 14   IA   3. 00
                    c.   8 x 10   NYGS   . 50
11, 004.   Portrait of the
            Doge Mecenigo   15 x 11   AS   3. 25
11, 005.   Presentation of Maria
            in the Temple   11 x 13   IA   3. 00
11, 006.   Tarquin and Lucretia
                            9 x 7   NYGS   . 50
11, 007.   Trinity Adored by the
            Heavenly Choir   20 x 18   NYGS   10. 00
TIRATELLI, AURELIO
11, 008.   Pastorale   18 x 40   AS   20. 00
TISI, BENVENUTO DI PIETRO (KNOWN AS "GAROFALO") (Italian,
1481-1559)
11, 009.   Virgin and Child and
            Saints (Rome)   11-1/2 x 15   AS   3. 25
TITI, TIBERIO (Italian, 1573-1627)
11, 010.   Portrait of Leopold
            Medici as a Baby 11 x 15   IA   3. 00
TITIAN (TIZIANO VECELLIO) (Italian, 1477-1576)
11, 011.   Apollo and Daphne 7 x 15   IA   3. 00
11, 012.   Assumption of the
            Virgin   15 x 9   IA   7. 50
11, 013.   Cardinal de
            Granvella   c. 10x 8   NYGS   . 50
11, 014.   Caterina Comaro as
            St. Catherine of Al 15 x 10   IA   3. 00
11, 015.   Cavalier of Malta 14 x 11   AS   3. 25
11, 016.   The Concert   11 x 14-1/2   AS   3. 25
            Head - Detail of
            No. 11, 016.   15-1/2x11-1/2   AS   3. 25
11, 017.   Danae   10 x 15   IA   3. 00
11, 018.   Deposition   11 x 11   AS   3. 25
11, 019.   Doge Nicolo Marcello
                            13-1/2x11-1/2   AS   3. 25
                            13 x 11   IA   3. 00
11, 020.   Doge Soranzo   15 x 11   AS   3. 25
11, 021.   Duke of Norfolk
            (Supposed)   13 x 11   IA   3. 00
            Head - Detail of
            No. 11, 021.   15 x 11   IA   3. 00
11, 022.   Flora   c. 24 x 20   PENN   1. 50
                            14-1/2 x 11   AS   3. 25
                    c.   9 x 7   AP   . 50
            Head - Detail of
            No. 11, 022   16 x 11   IA   3. 00
11, 023.   Holy Family   11 x 15   AS   3. 25
11, 024.   Isabella of Portugal
                            20 x 16-1/2   AR   12. 00
11, 025.   Lavina, the Artist's

	Daughter	c.	23 x 18	HNA	5. 95
			20 x 16	NYGS	15. 00
			9 x 7	NYGS	. 50
11, 026.	Madonna and Child with St. John and St. Anthony		10 x 15	IA	3. 00
11, 027.	Magdalene		15 x 11	IA	3. 00
11, 028.	The Man with the Glove		19-1/2 x 17	IA	10. 00
			12 x 11	IA	3. 00
11, 029.	Paul III and his Grandsons, Alessandro and Ottavio		13 x 11	IA	3. 00
11, 030.	Pope Paul III		15 x 11	IA	3. 00
11, 031.	Portrait of a Gentleman		14 x 11	AS	3. 25
11, 032.	Portrait of a Lady known as "La Bella"		15 x 11	IA	3. 00
11, 033.	Portrait of a Man		8 x 10	CFA	1. 00
11, 034.	Portrait of a Young Woman at the Mirror		13 x 11	IA	3. 00
11, 035.	Presentation of Mary (Detail)		15 x 11	AS	3. 25
11, 036.	Queen Isabella		20 x 16	CFA	12. 00
11, 037.	Rape of Europa		8 x 9	NYGS	. 50
11, 038.	Reclining Venus (Venus of Urbino)		10 x 15	IA	3. 00
	Head - Detail of No. 11, 038		15 x 11	IA	3. 00
11, 039.	Sacred and Profane Love		11 x 27	IA	10. 00
			11 x 15	IA	3. 00
			6 x 15	AS	3. 25
	Nude - Detail of No. 11, 039		15 x 11-1/2	AS	3. 25
			14 x 11	IA	3. 00
	Dressed Figure - Detail of No. 11, 039		11 x 15	IA	3. 00
	Head of Nude - Detail of No. 11, 039		15 x 11	IA	3. 00
	Head of Dressed Figure - Detail of No. 11, 039		15 x 11	IA	3. 00
11, 040.	St. Christopher		15-1/2 x 10	AS	3. 25
11, 041.	St. John		15 x 10	AS	3. 25
11, 042.	St. Vincenzo of Ferrari		13 x 11	IA	3. 00
11, 043.	Salome		14-1/2x11-1/2	AS	3. 25

11,044.	The Saviour	15 x 11	AS	3.25
11,045.	Self-Portrait	14 x 11-1/2	AS	3.25
11,046.	Strozzi Child c.	8 x 10	AP	.50
11,047.	Tribute Money	26 x 19-1/2	NYGS	12.00
		25 x 18-1/2	NYGS	24.00
		18-1/2 x 14	NYGS	5.00
11,048.	Venus (Seated)	14-1/2 x 11	AS	3.25
11,049.	Venus and the Lute			
	Player	10 x 13	NYGS	.50
11,050.	Venus with the Little			
	Dog	10-1/2 x 15	AS	3.25

TOBEY, MARK (American, 1890-)

11,051.	Earth Circus	25 x 19	NYGS	15.00
11,052.	Edge of August			
	c.	8 x 10	NYGS	.50
11,053.	Golden City	20 x 30	ESH	15.00
11,054.	Homage to Rameau			
	c.	8 x 10	ESH	1.00

TODD, E.

11,055.	August Bouquet	20 x 16	RL	6.00
11,056.	Blossoms of May	20 x 16	RL	6.00

TOMA, GIOACCHINO (Italian, 1838-1891)

11,057.	Ashes Rain	9 x 15	IA	3.00

TOMANECK, JOSEPH (American, 1889-)

11,058.	Getting Acquainted	18 x 22	CFA	10.00

TOMASO, RICO (American, 1898-)

11,059.	Bull Fighters (4)	16 x 12	DAC	ea.	2.50
11,060.	Carmen	24 x 18	DAC		7.50
		12 x 9	DAC		1.50
11,061.	Clowns (4)	25 x 10	DAC	ea.	3.50
		15 x 6	DAC		1.50
11,062.	Country Boy	24 x 18	DAC		7.50
11,063.	Farol Passes c.	20 x 24	PENN		1.50
11,064.	Free as the Wind	24 x 40	DAC		8.50
		18 x 24	DAC		7.50
11,065.	Girl with Guitar				
	c.	24 x 20	PENN		1.50
		24 x 18	DAC		7.50
11,066.	Girl with Tambourine				
	c.	24 x 20	PENN		1.50
		24 x 18	DAC		7.50
11,067.	Lolita	24 x 18	DAC		7.50
		12 x 9	DAC		1.50
11,068.	Maria	24 x 18	DAC		7.50
		12 x 9	DAC		1.50
11,069.	Mustangs c.	20 x 24	PENN		1.50
		18 x 24	DAC		7.50
11,070.	Rainbow Trail	24 x 48	DAC		10.00
11,071.	Rosita	24 x 18	DAC		7.50
		12 x 9	DAC		1.50
11,072.	Toreros (2)	24 x 18	DAC	ea.	7.50
	Farol Passes				
	Pases de Castigo				

11, 073.	Water Sports (4)	25 x 10	DAC	ea.	3. 50
		15 x 6	DAC	ea.	1. 50

TOMLIN, BRADLEY (American, 1899-1953)

11, 074.	Number 11 c.	8 x 10	NYGS		. 50

TONELLI, SIRIO

11, 075.	Portrait of Christ	17 x 13	IA		3. 00
		13 x 10	IA		1. 00
		10 x 8	IA		. 50
		8 x 7	IA		. 20

TOPOLSKI, FELIKS (Polish [Res. England] Contemporary)

11, 076.	This England	19 x 30	CFA		5. 00

TORI, ANGELO See BRONZINO

TORINO

11, 077.	Anabella	12 x 9-1/2	ESH	Pr.	2. 00
11, 078.	Babsi	23-1/2x12	ESH	Pr.	6. 00
11, 079.	Bianca with Poodle	16 x 10	ESH	Pr.	4. 00
11, 080.	Billy	23-1/2 x 12	ESH	Pr.	6. 00
11, 081.	Britta	23-1/2 x 20	ESH	Pr.	10. 00
11, 082.	Colette-Cherie	20 x 12	ESH	Pr.	5. 00
11, 083.	Conny with Poppy	12 x 9-1/2	ESH	Pr.	2. 00
11, 084.	Eliza	16 x 10	ESH	Pr.	4. 00
11, 085.	Fred	16 x 10	ESH	Pr.	4. 00
11, 086.	Kirsten	20 x 12	ESH	Pr.	5. 00
11, 087.	Maona	20 x 12	ESH	Pr.	5. 00
11, 088.	Mario with Guitar	16 x 10	ESH	Pr.	4. 00
11, 089.	Natascha	23-1/2 x 20	ESH	Pr.	10. 00
11, 090.	Uschi with Teddy Bear	12 x 9-1/2	ESH	Pr.	2. 00
11, 091.	Youth	23-1/2x31-1/2	ESH	Pr.	10. 00

TOSA, MITSUOKI (Japanese, 1617-1691)

11, 092.	Quails and Flowers	16 x 16	NYGS		10. 00

TOULOUSE-LAUTREC, HENRI DE (French, 1864-1901)

11, 093.	Alfred La Guigne	14 x 11	NYGS		4. 00
11, 094.	Aristide Bruant	22 x 17	AR		5. 00
		12-1/2x9-1/2	AP		1. 25
		8 x 6	CFA		1. 00
11, 095.	Au Cirque	13 x 9	NYGS		7. 50
11, 096.	Au Moulin Rouge	14 x 16	IA		6. 00
11, 097.	Bar c.	23 x 18	HNA		5. 95
11, 098.	Cafe Concert	8 x 6	CFA		1. 00
11, 099.	Carmen c.	16 x 12	PENN		1. 00
11, 100.	La Chambre Separee	21-1/2x17-1/2	NYGS		12. 00
11, 101.	Le Chocolat Dancing c.	12-1/2x9-1/2	AP		1. 25
		8 x 6	CFA		1. 00
11, 102.	Clownesse c.	24 x 20	PENN		1. 50
11, 103.	The Clownesse Cha-U-Kao	23 x 17	NYGS		12. 00
		22-1/2x16-1/2	ESH		10. 00
	c.	10 x 8	ESH		1. 00
11, 104.	Les Coulisses	13 x 9	NYGS		7. 50

11, 105.	Country Drive	6 x 8	CFA	1. 00
11, 106.	The Country Party			
	c.	9-1/2x12-1/2	AP	1. 25
	c.	7 x 9	AP	1. 00
11, 107.	The Couple c.	20 x 24	PENN	1. 50
11, 108.	Danseuse	23 x 18-1/2	NYGS	12. 00
11, 109.	Desire Dihau	9 x 7	NYGS	. 50
11, 110.	Divan Japonais	22 x 17	AR	5. 00
	c.	12-1/2x9-1/2	AP	1. 25
	c.	9 x 7	AP	1. 00
11, 111.	Le Docteur Tapie			
	de Celeyran	15 x 7	IA	3. 00
11, 112.	Ecuyere	9 x 7	NYGS	7. 50
11, 113.	Englishman	8 x 6	CFA	1. 00
11, 114.	Equestrienne and her			
	Groom c.	8 x 10	ESH	1. 00
11, 115.	La Goulue c.	10 x 8	ESH	1. 00
11, 116.	The Goulue and her			
	Sister c.	12-1/2x9-1/2	AP	1. 25
		8 x 6	CFA	1. 00
11, 117.	La Grande Loge			
	c.	10 x 8	ESH	1. 00
11, 118.	Jane Avril	20 x 18	PENN	1. 50
	c.	12-1/2x9-1/2	AP	1. 25
		7 x 5	CFA	1. 00
11, 119.	Jane Avril Dancing			
	c.	24 x 20	PENN	1. 50
		23 x 12	ESH	10. 00
	c.	12-1/2x9-1/2	AP	1. 25
		9 x 6	CFA	1. 00
11, 120.	Jane Avril from the			
	Back	22 x 17-1/2	ESH	10. 00
11, 121.	Jane Avril Leaving			
	Moulin Rouge	32 x 24	CFA	15. 00
		28 x 15	NYGS	12. 00
	c.	12-1/2x9-1/2	AP	1. 25
		8 x 6	CFA	1. 00
11, 122.	A Jockey c.	12 x 16	PENN	1. 00
		6 x 8	CFA	1. 00
11, 123.	Leading-Rein c.	8 x 10	ESH	1. 00
11, 124.	Madame de Honorine			
		24 x 17	PENN	1. 00
11, 125.	Mlle. Eglantine			
	c.	9-1/2x12-1/2	AP	1. 25
11, 126.	Mlle. Lender c.	10 x 8	ESH	1. 00
11, 127.	Masked Ball c.	20 x 24	PENN	1. 50
11, 128.	Maxime Dethomas	14 x 11	NYGS	4. 00
11, 129.	May Belfort c.	12-1/2x9-1/2	AP	1. 25
11, 130.	Messalina	18 x 13	CFA	5. 00
11, 131.	Milliner	13 x 11	IA	3. 00
	c.	10 x 8	ESH	1. 00
11, 132.	Miss Eglantine's			
	Dance	6 x 8	CFA	1. 00

11, 133.	M. Bolleau au Cafe				
		20 x 16	PENN		1. 50
11, 134.	Mr. Warner at the				
	Moulin Rouge	10 x 8	ESH		1. 00
11, 135.	La Modiste	24 x 19	NYGS		12. 00
11, 136.	Moulin Rouge c.	24 x 20	PENN		1. 50
	c.	9 x 7	AP		1. 00
		9 x 5	CFA		1. 00
11, 137.	Moulin Rouge	14 x 16	AJ		6. 00
	c.	8 x 10	NYGS		. 50
11, 138.	Napoleon et ses				
	Generaux c.	22 x 17-1/2	AS		4. 00
11, 139.	Pony Trap c.	8 x 10	ESH		1. 00
11, 140.	Posters (10)	28-1/2 x 20	PENN	ea.	1. 00
	Aristide Bruant				
	Confetti				
	Divan Japonais				
	Galerie des Ponchettes				
	Gravures Rares				
	Jane Avril				
	Jane Avril Dansant				
	Moulin Rouge				
	La Revue Blanche				
	Troupe de Mlle. Eglantine				
11, 141.	Posters (3)	30 x 20	PENN	ea.	1. 00
	La Goulue				
	Lithographes				
	Theatre Antoine				
11, 142.	Profile of a Woman				
	c.	24 x 20	PENN		1. 50
11, 143.	Quadrille at the				
	Moulin Rouge c.	18 x 23	HNA		5. 95
11, 144.	Reine de Joie	22 x 17	AR		5. 00
11, 145.	La Revue Blanche				
	c.	12-1/2x9-1/2	AP		1. 25
11, 146.	Seated Clown	22 x 17	PENN		1. 50
11, 147.	Seated Girl, Profile				
	c.	16 x 12	PENN		1. 00
11, 148.	Sortie de Theatre	14-1/2x10-1/2	NYGS		7. 50
11, 149.	La Toilette	9 x 7	NYGS		. 50
11, 150.	Une Table au Moulin				
	Rouge c.	8 x 10	ESH		1. 00
11, 151.	Woman Combing her				
	Hair c.	9 x 7	AP		1. 00
11, 152.	Woman in a Wicker				
	Chair	26 x 19	DAC		7. 50
	c.	24 x 20	PENN		1. 50
11, 153.	Yvette Guilbert				
	c.	12-1/2x9-1/2	AP		1. 25
	c.	9 x 7	AP		1. 00
	2 Details of No.				
	11, 153	10 x 6	CFA		1. 00
		8 x 5	CFA		1. 00

TRAINI, FRANCESCO (Italian, 1320-1364)
11, 154. Triumph of Death   11 x 15   IA   3. 00
TRAVER, MARION GRAY (American, 1896-)
11, 155. Snow Bound   25 x 30   IA   7. 50
TRAVIS
11, 156. Street Scenes, Early
          U. S. (8)   11 x 14   AK   ea.   1. 50
                             8 x 10   AK   ea.   1. 00
                             6 x 8   AK   ea.   . 50
11, 157. Street Scenes, Southern
          U. S. (4)   12 x 15   AK   ea.   1. 75
                             8 x 10   AK   ea.   1. 00
                             6 x 8   AK   ea.   . 50
TRIER, HANN (German Contemporary)
11, 158. Back and Forth   19-1/2 x 31   NYGS   22. 00
TRILLITSCH, HANS PAUL (German, 1904-)
11, 159. Aquarium   16 x 33   ESH   Cv.   15. 00
11, 160. Fisher-Boats   19 x 28   ESH   Cv.   12. 00
11, 161. Sunflowers   28 x 19   ESH   Cv.   12. 00
TRIMPERT
11, 162. Martiques   16 x 31-1/2   ESH   Pr.   8. 00
                             8 x 16   ESH   Pr.   3. 00
11, 163. Paris, Notre Dame 16 x 31-1/2   ESH   Pr.   8. 00
                             8 x 16   ESH   Pr.   3. 00
11, 164. Sunflowers   16 x 31-1/2   ESH   Pr.   8. 00
TROYON, CONSTANT EMILE (French, 1810-1865)
11, 165. Farmyard   9 x 13   ESH   2. 00
11, 166. Game-Keeper and
          his Dogs   14 x 11   IA   3. 00
11, 167. Pasturage   c.   7 x 9   AP   . 50
TRUEBNER, WILHELM (German, 1851-1917)
11, 168. Housebuilders   17 x 27   NYGS   20. 00
TRUMBULL, JOHN (American, 1756-1843)
11, 169. Alexander Hamilton 18 x 14-1/2   NYGS   10. 00
11, 170. Declaration of
          Independence   20 x 30   NYGS   15. 00
                             9 x 14   NYGS   3. 00
                        c.   7 x 9   AP   . 50
11, 171. Battle of Bunker's
          Hill   22 x 30   NYGS   15. 00
                             9-1/2 x 13   NYGS   3. 00
TSAI CHENG-YI and CHING-YI (Chinese [K'ang Hsi Period] 1622-
1722)
11, 172. Flowers and Insects
                             11 x 40-1/2   NYGS   18. 00
TSENG YING PANG (Chinese Contemporary)
11, 173. Lone Tree, 1966   34-1/2 x 15   NYGS   15. 00
11, 174. Mountain in the
          Mist, 1966   34-1/2 x 15   NYGS   15. 00
TUNG LAI-CHEN
11, 175. Birds and Flowers
          (6)   c.   16 x 12   PENN   ea.   1. 00

```
                  Bird and:
                     Orange Flowers
                     Pomegranates
                     Red Berries
                     Red Flowers
                     Red Plums
                     Yellow Flowers
TUNG PANG-TA (Chinese, 1698-1769)
11, 176.    Chinese Landscapes
            (4)                 20 x 18       PENN   ea.   1. 50
TUNISIA
11, 177.    UWA Series (32)    11 x 14
                          or   14 x 11       NYGS   ea.   2. 00
TUNNICLIFFE, CHARLES (English Contemporary)
11, 178.    Mares and Foals   18 x 26        ESH         10. 00
11, 179.    Pony Foals        18 x 23-1/2    ESH         10. 00
11, 180.    Pony Group        13 x 28        ESH          6. 00
11, 181.    Secluded Pool     15 x 19        ESH         15. 00
11, 182.    Winter Estuary    24 x 16        ESH         12. 00
TURA, COSME (COSIMO) (Italian, 1430. 1495)
11, 133.    Member of the Este
            Family       c.   7 x 9          AP            . 50
11, 134.    Virgin and Child
            (Venice)         15 x 10         AS           3. 25
TURKEY
11, 135.    UWA Series (32)  11 x 14
                          or  14 x 11        NYGS   ea.   2. 00
TURNER, F. C. (English, 19th Century)
11, 136.    Horses:
11, 137.    Alice Hawthorne  19-1/2 x 24     AA          15. 00
11, 138.    Scott of Satirist 21 x 26        AA          15. 00
TURNER, JOSEPH MALLORD WILLIAM (English, 1775-1851)
11, 139.    Boats Carrying out
            Anchors      c.   20 x 24        PENN         1. 50
11, 140.    Bonneville, Savoy,
            c. 1812          26 x 34         NYGS        18. 00
11, 141.    Carthage     c.   8 x 10         NYGS          . 50
11, 142.    The Dogana and
            Santa Maria della
            Salute Venice, c.
            1843             23 x 36         NYGS        18. 00
11, 143.    Fighting Temeraire
                         c.   18 x 23        HNA          5. 95
                         c.   7 x 9          AP            . 50
11, 144.    Grand Canal,
            Venice           29-1/2 x 39     NYGS        20. 00
                             9 x 13          CFA          4. 00
                             8-1/2x12-1/2    AR           4. 00
11, 145.    Hastings c. 1835
                         c.   7 x 9          AP            . 25
11, 146.    Junction of the
            Thames           9 x 12          CFA          2. 00
```

11, 147.	Keelmen Heaving in			
	Coals by Moonlight	27 x 36	NYGS	20.00
		9 x 12	CFA	2.00
11, 148.	Lake from Petworth			
	House	16 x 36	NYGS	18.00
11, 149.	Lake Geneva	9 x 13	CFA	4.00
11, 150.	Lake Vierqaldstaetter			
		9-1/2 x 15	AR	4.00
11, 151.	Lake Von Bergen	9 x 13	CFA	4.00
		8-1/2 x 11	AR	4.00
11, 152.	Mortlake Terrace:			
	Early Summer Morning			
		17-1/2x23-1/2	NYGS	12.00
	c.	18 x 23	HNA	5.95
		8 x 11	CFA	2.00
11, 153.	Music Party, Pet-			
	worth	27 x 20	NYGS	18.00
11, 154.	Petworth Park	10 x 22-1/2	AP	6.00
11, 155.	Rockets and Blue			
	Lights	18 x 20	PENN	1.50
11, 156.	Sunset in Venice	8-1/2x12-1/2	AR	4.00
11, 157.	Sunset on the Grand			
	Canal	9 x 13	CFA	4.00
11, 158.	Venice	15 x 22-1/2	ESH	15.00
		9 x 13	CFA	4.00
	c.	7 x 9	AP	.60
11, 159.	Venice: Dogana and			
	San Giorgio Maggiore,			
	1834	22 x 30	NYGS	16.00
11, 160.	Venice, the Giudecca			
		8-1/2x12-1/2	AR	4.00
11, 161.	Venetian Scene - San			
	Benedetto, Looking			
	Toward Fusina	18-1/2 x 28	NYGS	12.00
TURNER,	MICHAEL			
11, 162.	Italian Grand Prix			
	Monza, 1965	15-1/2x19-1/2	ESH	6.00
TURTON,	W.			
11, 163.	Genoa	8 x 10	CFA	6.00
TUSCANY,	SCHOOL OF (Italian)			
11, 164.	Portrait of a Gentle-			
	woman, 15th Century			
		15-1/2x10-1/2	AS	3.25
11, 165.	Virgin and Child	15 x 8-1/2	AS	3.25
TWACHTMAN, JOHN HENRY (American, 1853-1902)				
11, 166.	Winter Harmony			
	c.	18 x 23	HNA	5.95
TWISTINTON-HIGGINS, E.				
11, 167.	Pas de Quatre	10 x 12	ESH	3.00
11, 168.	Pas de Trois	10 x 12	ESH	3.00
11, 169.	Sylphides	11-1/2x8-1/2	ESH	3.00
TYLER,	EARL			
11, 170.	Tutti-Frutti (2)	26 x 20	AK	Pair 10.00

U

UCCELLO, PAOLO (DONO, PAOLO DI) (Italian, 1397-1475)
11, 171.	The Battle (Florence)			
		8-1/2x15-1/2	AS	3. 25
11, 172.	Battle of San Romano			
	(Rout of San Romano)			
		19 x 34	CFA	20. 00
	c.	20 x 24	PENN	1. 50
	(2)	15 x 27	IA ea.	10. 00
11, 173.	Head of a Young			
	Man	9 x 7	AR	4. 00
11, 174.	The Hermits			
	(Florence)	10-1/2x14-1/2	AS	3. 25
11, 175.	Nativity (Stained			
	Glass)	11" Diam.	IA	3. 00
11, 176.	Portrait of Elizabeth			
	of Montefeltro	15 x 8	IA	3. 00
11, 177.	Portrait of a Young			
	Man (Chambery)	14-1/2x11-1/2	AS	3. 25
11, 178.	Resurrection of Christ			
	(Stained Glass)	11" Diam.	IA	3. 00
11, 179.	Selling of the Consecrated			
	Wafer	8 x 15	IA	3. 00

UCHERMANN, KARL (Norwegian, 1855-)
| 11, 180. | Playing Whelps | 14 x 19 | ESH | 7. 50 |

UFER, WALTER (American, 1876-)
| 11, 181. | Solemn Pledge c. | 7 x 9 | AP | . 50 |

UGOLINO DI VIERI (Italian, c. 1385)
| 11, 182. | Corporal Shrine | | | |
| | (2) | 15 x 12 | IA ea. | 3. 00 |

UHDE, KARL HERMANN FRITZ VON (German, 1848-1911)
11, 183.	The Children's			
	Friend	24 x 36-1/2	IA	15. 00
11, 184.	His Omnipresence	18-1/2x23-1/2	NYGS	10. 00

UNGEWITTER, INGE (CALLED "THE PAINTING AMAZON")
(German Contemporary)
11, 185.	Excurison on Horse-			
	back	24-1/2x31-1/2	ESH	Cv. 15. 00
11, 186.	Hunting with			
	Hounds	17 x 35	CFA	15. 00
11, 187.	Thoroughbred	22 x 19	CFA	15. 00

UNKNOWN ARTISTS - AMERICAN
11, 188.	Colonial America			
	(Mural)	38 x 96	PENN	5. 00
11, 189.	Colonial Portrait	11 x 9	NYGS	1. 50
11, 190.	Flowers and Fruit,			
	c. 1830	26 x 19-1/2	NYGS	12. 00
11, 191.	Girl in Blue	11 x 9	NYGS	1. 50
11, 192.	Grandmother's			
	Fruit	11 x 14	NYGS	3. 00
		6 x 7-1/2	NYGS	1. 00

11, 193.	Master Willoughby	20 x 16	NYGS	10. 00
11, 194.	Mr. R. T. Jones Putting			
	on the 18th Green	18 x 21-1/2	AP	7. 50
11, 195.	Mrs. Freake and			
	Baby Mary, c. 1674			
		21 x 18	NYGS	12. 00
	c.	10 x 8	AP	. 50
11, 196.	Portrait of a Boy			
	with Dog	23 x 18	PENN	1. 00
11, 197.	The Sargent Family			
	c.	18 x 23	HNA	5.9 5
11, 198.	Thanksgiving Fruit	11 x 14	NYGS	3. 00
		6 x 7-1/2	NYGS	1. 00
11, 199.	Velvet Paintings,			
	Early American			
11, 200.	Bountiful Harvest			
		11 x 14	NYGS	3. 00
		6 x 7-1/2	NYGS	1. 00
11, 201.	Farmer's Pride	11 x 14	NYGS	3. 00
		6 x 7-1/2	NYGS	1. 00
11, 202.	View on the Hudson,			
	c. 1850	16 x 21-1/2	AA	6. 00

UNKNOWN ARTISTS - AUSTRIAN

11, 203.	Mater Dolorosa			
	c.	9 x 7	AP	1. 00

UNKNOWN ARTISTS - BRITISH

11, 204.	Portrait of Queen			
	Elizabeth I of England			
		15 x 8	AS	3. 25
11, 205.	Prince of Wales,			
	1603 c.	24 x 20	PENN	1. 50
11, 206.	Sir John Harrington			
	c.	9 x 7	AP	. 25
11, 207.	Sir Thomas Gresham			
		19 x 14	ESH	7. 50

UNKNOWN ARTISTS - CHINESE

Five Dynasties Period 907-960

11, 208.	Deer in the Forest	20 x 16-1/2	NYGS	32. 00

Ming Period 1368-1644

11, 209.	Family Portrait	30 x 17	CFA	56. 00
11, 210.	Scroll of Eight Horses			
	(Detail)	13 x 30	ESH	15. 00

Sung Dynasty c. 1280 AD

11, 211.	Philosophers Comparing			
	Classic Texts			
	Part I	10 x 31	CFA	45. 00
	Part II	10 x 15	CFA	25. 00
11, 212.	Swans Under the			
	Trees	20 x 16-1/2	NYGS	32. 00
11, 213.	Tribute Horse	29 x 40	IA	24. 00

Tang Dynasty 618-907

11, 214.	Pottery Figure of a			
	Saddled Horse	21 x 28	NYGS	15. 00

11, 215.	Prancing Horse	21 x 28	NYGS		15. 00
11, 216.	Miscellaneous Periods Bloom Upon Bloom				
	c.	8 x 10	AP		. 50
11, 217.	Chinese Mandarin				
	Figures (12)	12-1/2 x 7	IA	ea.	2. 00
11, 218.	Deer in Woodland	6-1/2x9-1/2	CFA		2. 00
11, 219.	Fruits and Vegetables				
	(4)	18 x 24	CFA	ea.	7. 50
	Banana	17 x 14	CFA	ea.	7. 50
	Cucumber (8)	8 x 6	CFA	ea.	1. 00
	Gourd				
	Lotus				
	Orange				
	Pineapple				
	Pumpkin				
	Tangerine				
11, 220.	Magpie on Flower				
	Branch c.	8 x 10	AP		. 50
11, 221.	Mme. Wei i-Chien				
	c.	10 x 8	AP		. 50
11, 222.	Painted Tiles, Horses				
	and Flying Geese	10 x 31-1/2	ESH		15. 00

UNKNOWN ARTISTS - DUTCH

11, 223.	Landscape in the				
	Netherlands	12 x 22	ESH		6. 00

UNKNOWN ARTISTS - FLEMISH

11, 224.	Nativity	31 x 24-1/2	ESH		15. 00
11, 225.	Portrait of Mary				
	Bonciani-Baronelli	15 x 18	IA		3. 00
11, 226.	Vase of Flowers				
	(2)	34 x 25	IA	ea.	10. 00
		14 x 11	IA	ea.	3. 00

UNKNOWN ARTISTS - FRENCH

11, 227.	Annunciation, School				
	of Savoy	30 x 21	ESH		15. 00
11, 228.	French Harbor Scene				
	(Mural)	38 x 75	PENN		5. 00
11, 229.	Gabrielle D'Estrees				
	Bathing, 16th Century				
		14 x 11	IA		3. 00
11, 230.	Meal in the Forest				
	c.	8 x 10	ESH		1. 00
11, 231.	Nicholas Ferry, Called				
	Bébé, 18th Century	22-1/2 x 18	ESH		10. 00
11, 232.	Paris, La Seine,				
	Notre Dame	4 x 13	CFA		3. 00
11, 233.	Paris, La Seine,				
	La Concorde	4 x 14	CFA		3. 00
11, 234.	Park Phaeton c.	8 x 10	ESH		1. 00
11, 235.	Recits de la Vie				
	Anterieure du Bubba				
		17 x 13-1/2	CFA		10. 00

11, 236.	Tilling, 19th Century	c.	8 x 10	ESH	1. 00
11, 237.	Virgin and Child	c.	9 x 7	AP	1. 00

UNKNOWN ARTISTS - IRISH

11, 238.	Irish Miniature	11 x 8	CFA	5. 00

UNKNOWN ARTISTS - ITALIAN

11, 239.	Annunciation	11-1/2 x 11	AS	3. 25
11, 240.	Burning of Savonarola	11-1/2x13-1/2	AS	3. 25
11, 241.	Christ, the Virgin and St. John	14-1/2 x 10	AS	3. 25
11, 242.	Fountains of Rome (6)	9 x 12	CFA	ea. 10. 00
11, 243.	Fountains of Rome (B & W) (6)	9 x 12	CFA	ea. 7. 50
11, 244.	Portrait of Belluccia Caraffa	15 x 11-1/2	AS	3. 25
11, 245.	Portrait of Portia De'Rossi	15 x 11-1/2	AS	3. 25
11, 246.	Portrait of a Young Prince	15 x 11	AS	3. 25
11, 247.	Still Life, 17th Century	11 x 15	AS	3. 25

UNKNOWN ARTISTS - MISCELLANEOUS

11, 248.	Bust of Anonymous Man	10 x 7	AR	4. 00
11, 249.	Our Lady of Guadalupe	34 x 23	IA	4. 00

UPRKA, JOZA (Czechoslovakian, 1862-)

11, 250.	Moravian Peasants	c.	7 x 9	AP	. 50

URSZENYI, HELENA (Hungarian Contemporary)

11, 251.	Water Lilies	20 x 26	ESH	10. 00

USSI, STEFANO (Italian, 1822-1901)

11, 252.	Expulsion from Florence of the Duke of Athens	13 x 19	IA	7. 50
11, 253.	Maternal Joys Oval	15-1/2x11-1/2	AS	3. 25
	Oval	13 x 11	IA	3. 00

U. S. S. R.

11, 254.	UWA Series (32)	11 x 14		
	or	14 x 11	NYGS	ea. 2. 00

UTILI DA FAENZA (BERTUCCI, GIOVANNI BATTISTA, THE ELDER) (Italian, 1475-1516)

11, 255.	Madonna and Child with Angel	15 x 11	IA	3. 00
11, 256.	Madonna and Child with Two Saints	15 x 9	IA	3. 00

UTRILLO, MAURICE (French, 1883-1955)

11, 257.	Au Point de Vue	24 x 18	AR	12. 00
11, 258.	La Banlieue	24 x 30	DAC	7. 50
	c.	20 x 24	PENN	1. 50

11, 259.	La Basilique du Sacre-Coeur	22-1/2 x 18	ESH	10. 00
	c.	10 x 8	ESH	1. 00
11, 260.	Behind the Moulin de la Galette c.	8 x 10	ESH	1. 00
11, 261.	Berlioz House	5 x 9	CFA	1. 00
11, 262.	La Blanchisserie de la Bastille	12-1/2 x 10	NYGS	7. 50
11, 263.	La Butte de Momtmartre	15-1/2 x 19	NYGS	7. 50
	c.	8 x 10	ESH	1. 00
	Detail of No. 11, 263 c.	10 x 8	ESH	1. 00
11, 264.	Le Cabaret	14-1/2x17-1/2	AP	5. 00
11, 265.	Cafe du Nord	24 x 30	DAC	7. 50
11, 266.	La Caserne	20 x 24	CFA	15. 00
11, 267.	The Chateau c.	24 x 20	PENN	1. 50
11, 268.	Le Chateau Saint-Bernard	12-1/2 x 10	NYGS	7. 50
11, 269.	Christmas in Montmartre	18 x 26-1/2	NYGS	12. 00
		11 x 14	NYGS	3. 00
		6 x 7-1/2	NYGS	1. 00
11, 270.	Church of LaFerte-Milon	24 x 18	IA	7. 50
11, 271.	Church of Sacre-Coeur c.	18 x 23	HNA	5. 95
11, 272.	Church at St. Hilaire	14 x 18	AP	6. 00
11, 273.	Church at Saint-Severin	24 x 17-1/2	PENN	1. 50
	c.	23 x 18	HNA	5. 95
11, 274.	Un Coin du Village	12-1/2 x 10	NYGS	7. 50
11, 275.	Corsican Landscape	20 x 26	CFA	15. 00
11, 276.	Courtyard	20 x 24	NYGS	12. 00
11, 277.	Eglise de Banlieue c.	20 x 24	PENN	1. 50
11, 278.	Eglise de Banlieue Vers c.	16 x 12	PENN	1. 00
11, 279.	Eglise de Bourgogne	22 x 18-1/2	NYGS	10. 00
11, 280.	Eglise de Chatillon-Sur-Seine c.	12-1/2x9-1/2	AP	1. 25
	c.	9 x 7	AP	1. 00
11, 281.	Eglise de Couchey (Cher) France	18 x 21	AP	7. 50
		17-1/2 x 21	IA	7. 50
11, 282.	Eglise de Royan	31 x 11-1/2	NYGS	12. 00
		20 x 7-1/2	NYGS	5. 00
11, 283.	Eglise de St. Pierre	26 x 36	NYGS	15. 00

11, 284.	Eglise de St. Pierre			
		12-1/2 x 10	NYGS	7. 50
11, 285.	Eglise de Strins	24 x 30	DAC	7. 50
11, 286.	Faubourg Parisien	20 x 24	DAC	7. 50
11, 287.	Flowers in a Blue			
	Jug c.	10 x 8	ESH	1. 00
11, 288.	House with Bernot			
	Wall Poster	7 x 11	CFA	1. 00
11, 289.	House with Red			
	Door c.	20 x 24	PENN	1. 50
11, 290.	L'Impasse Cotlin			
	c.	9-1/2x12-1/2	AP	1. 25
	c.	7 x 9	AP	1. 00
11, 291.	In Front of the Chateau			
	of Chastelloux, 1932			
	c.	20 x 24	PENN	1. 50
11, 292.	Le Lapin-Agile	19-1/2 x 24	AR	12. 00
	c.	18 x 23	HNA	5. 95
		16 x 19-1/2	AP	7. 50
	c.	12 x 16	PENN	1. 00
	c.	7 x 9	AP	1. 00
		6 x 9	CFA	1. 00
11, 293.	Le-Lapin-Agile			
	c.	24 x 20	PENN	1. 50
		12-1/2 x 10	NYGS	7. 50
11, 294.	Lapin-Agile and Rue			
	St. Vincent c.	9-1/2x12-1/2	AP	1. 25
	c.	7 x 9	AP	1. 00
11, 295.	Lapin-Agile in the			
	Snow	19 x 30	ESH	15. 00
11, 296.	Lapin-Agile in			
	Winter	24 x 30	DAC	7. 50
11, 297.	Main Street in Anes			
	c.	8 x 10	NYGS	. 50
11, 298.	La Maison Bernot			
	c.	20 x 24	PENN	1. 50
11, 299.	Maison Mimi	19-1/2 x 24	NYGS	15. 00
		11 x 14	NYGS	3. 00
		6 x 7-1/2	NYGS	1. 00
11, 300.	Mimi Pinson's House			
	in the Snow c.	8 x 10	ESH	1. 00
11, 301.	Montmartre	24 x 30	DAC	7. 50
		22 x 30	AR	18. 00
		21 x 29	CFA	15. 00
	c.	20 x 24	PENN	1. 50
		15 x 20	AP	6. 00
		11 x 14	NYGS	3. 00
		6 x 7-1/2	NYGS	1. 00
11, 302.	Montmartre	12-1/2 x 10	NYGS	7. 50
11, 303.	Montmartre Corner			
	c.	20 x 24	PENN	1. 50
11, 304.	Montmartre in			
	Winter c.	24 x 30	PENN	1. 95

11, 305.	Montmartre, Moulin da la Galette	21 x 40	NYGS	18.00
11, 306.	Montmartre Theatre c.	8 x 10	NYGS	.50
11, 307.	Montmartre, Winter Scene c.	20 x 24	PENN	1.50
11, 308.	Le Motif a Montmartre	12-1/2 x 10	NYGS	7.50
11, 309.	Le Moulin de la Galette c.	30 x 24	PENN	1.95
		12-1/2 x 10	NYGS	7.50
	c.	10 x 8	NYGS	.50
11, 310.	Le Moulin da la Galette	24 x 30	DAC	7.50
		17 x 20	NYGS	10.00
		12 x 15	NYGS	16.00
11, 311.	Notre Dame de Paris	25 x 19	NYGS	12.00
	c.	12-1/2x9-1/2	AP	1.25
		12 x 9	CFA	1.00
	c.	10 x 8	ESH	1.00
11, 312.	Parisian Suburg	24 x 30	DAC	7.50
11, 313.	Petit Cafe, Montmartre	13 x 20	NYGS	7.50
		11 x 14	NYGS	3.00
		6 x 7-1/2	NYGS	1.00
11, 314.	Petite Rue de Montmartre	12-1/2 x 10	NYGS	7.50
11, 315.	La Place Ravignon	11 x 14	NYGS	16.00
11, 316.	La Place du Tertre c.	20 x 24	PENN	1.50
		18 x 26	NYGS	15.00
11, 317.	Porte St. Martin	21 x 24	NYGS	12.00
11, 318.	Poster: Galeria Petrides	35 x 23	PENN	1.00
11, 319.	Le Quartier St. Romain c.	20 x 24	PENN	1.50
11, 320.	Restaurant au Mont-Cenis	11 x 14	NYGS	3.00
		6 x 7-1/2	NYGS	1.00
11, 321.	Rheims Cathedral	35 x 24-1/2	ESH	18.00
11, 322.	Rue Artez	20 x 24	DAC	7.50
11, 323.	Rue Jeanne D'Arc	17 x 22-1/2	AP	10.00
	c.	9-1/2x12-1/2	AP	1.25
	c.	7 x 9	AP	1.00
11, 324.	Rue Jeanne D'Arc in the Snow	17 x 22-1/2	ESH	10.00
	c.	8 x 10	ESH	1.00
11, 325.	Rue de Montmartre c.	20 x 24	PENN	1.50
11, 326.	Rue du Mont-Cenis	26 x 36	NYGS	16.00
	c.	20 x 24	PENN	1.50
		18 x 22	ESH	10.00

	c.	9-1/2x12-1/2	AP	1. 25
	c.	8 x 10	ESH	1. 00
11, 327.	Rue Moulin Rouge	20 x 30	CFA	15. 00
11, 328.	Rue Ordener,			
	Montmartre	21-1/2 x 29	NYGS	16. 00
11, 329.	Rue a Pontoise	18 x 13	NYGS	18. 00
11, 330.	Rue St. -Rustique a			
	Montmartre	31 x 11-1/2	NYGS	12. 00
		20 x 7-1/2	NYGS	3. 00
		12-1/2 x 10	NYGS	7. 50
11, 331.	Rue St. Vincent	19 x 30	AA	15. 00
11, 332.	Rue a Sannois c.	20 x 24	PENN	1. 50
		13 x 20	NYGS	7. 50
		11 x 14	NYGS	3. 00
		6 x 7-1/2	NYGS	1. 00
11, 333.	Rue Seveste	17 x 21	NYGS	7. 50
11, 334.	Rue Tholoze c.	8 x 10	ESH	1. 00
11, 335.	Rue de Venice	23-1/2x16-1/2	AR	12. 00
11, 336.	Rue de Village	21 x 26	NYGS	15. 00
11, 337.	Rural France	18 x 22	NYGS	10. 00
		11 x 14	NYGS	3. 00
		6 x 7-1/2	NYGS	1. 00
11, 338.	Sacre-Coeur de			
	Montmartre	28 x 20	NYGS	15. 00
		25 x 20	PENN	1. 50
11, 339.	St. Severin c.	20 x 24	PENN	1. 50
11, 340.	St. Vincent Street	6 x 9	CFA	1. 00
11, 341.	Small Hostelry	24 x 30	DAC	7. 50
11, 342.	Snow in Montmartre			
	c.	20 x 24	PENN	1. 50
		17-1/2x23-1/2	NYGS	10. 00
		11 x 14	NYGS	3. 00
11, 343.	Snowy Street	6 x 9	CFA	1. 00
11, 344.	Spring in Montmartre			
		18 x 21-1/2	NYGS	10. 00
11, 345.	Square St. -Pierre	22 x 16-1/2	ESH	7. 50
	c.	10 x 8	ESH	1. 00
11, 346.	Steps	9 x 6	CFA	1. 00
11, 347.	The Street c.	20 x 24	PENN	1. 50
	c.	12 x 16	PENN	1. 00
11, 348.	Street in Anse	18 x 22-1/2	ESH	10. 00
11, 349.	Street in Asnieres			
	c.	8 x 10	NYGS	. 50
11, 350.	Street in Auteuil	18 x 22-1/2	ESH	10. 00
11, 351.	Street on Montmartre			
		13-1/2x19-1/2	AP	5. 00
11, 352.	Street in the Suburbs			
	c.	20 x 24	PENN	1. 50
11, 353.	Suburban Landscape			
	with Factory c.	12 x 16	PENN	1. 00
11, 354.	Suburban Street	18 x 22	NYGS	10. 00
		11 x 14	NYGS	3. 00
		6 x 7-1/2	NYGS	1. 00

11, 355.	La Tour Saint Jacques			
		31 x 11-1/2	NYGS	12. 00
		20 x 7-1/2	NYGS	5. 00
11, 356.	Varenne Castle			
	c.	8 x 10	NYGS	. 50
11, 357.	La Vielle Rue Saint-Vincent	12-1/2 x 10	NYGS	7. 50
11, 358.	Le Vieux College	12-1/2 x 10	NYGS	7. 50
11, 359.	Village Lane c.	9-1/2x12-1/2	AP	1. 25
		6 x 8	CFA	1. 00
11, 360.	Village Street	14 x 17	CFA	4. 00
11, 361.	Windmills of Montmartre c.	21 x 26	HNA	5. 95
11, 362.	Winter in Paris	24 x 30	DAC	7. 50
11, 363.	Winter Street Scene			
	c.	20 x 24	PENN	1. 50
	c.	12 x 16	PENN	1. 00

V

VAELTL, OTTO				
11, 364.	Summer Flowers	26 x 22-1/2	ESH	10. 00
VALADIÉ, JOHN (French Contemporary)				
11, 365.	Jeunesse	30-1/2x15	RL	10. 00
11, 366.	Laurette	30-1/2 x 15	RL	10. 00
11, 367.	Round-Up	22-1/2 x 28	RL	15. 00
11, 368.	St. Mark's Square	20 x 25	RL	10. 00
11, 369.	Solitude	25 x 20	RL	12. 50
11, 370.	What Next?	24-1/2 x 20	RL	15. 00
VALADON, SUSANNE (French, 1867-1938)				
11, 371.	Bouquet of Flowers in Front of a Window			
	c.	24 x 20	PENN	1. 50
11, 372.	Flowers c.	24 x 20	PENN	1. 50
11, 373.	Gladioli c.	10 x 8	ESH	1. 00
11, 374.	Village of St. Bernard	22-1/2 x 18	ESH	10. 00
VALCKENBORGH, LUK VAN (Flemish, 1540-1625)				
11, 375.	Harvest Time	27-1/2 x 47	AJ	20. 00
		21 x 36	AJ	12. 00
		12-1/2 x 21	AJ	7. 50
11, 376.	Summer Landscape	11 x 20	AJ	7. 50
VALLAYER-COSTER, ANNE (French, 1744-1818)				
11, 377.	Flowers and Fruit	15 x 13	ESH	5. 00
VALLET, MATH (French, 1901-1949)				
11, 378.	Baby in Cradle	13 x 11	CFA	3. 00
VAN, FRANS				
11, 379.	Casa Del Rio	15 x 40	DAC	10. 00
11, 380.	Casa Moreno	15 x 40	DAC	10. 00
11, 381.	Early American Scenes (4)	6 x 15	DAC ea.	1. 50

11, 382.	Egyptian Culture				
	(2)	22 x 10	DAC	ea.	5. 00
11, 383.	Engine Pumper	6 x 15	DAC		2. 50
11, 384.	Incan Culture (2)	10 x 22	DAC	ea.	5. 00
11, 385.	Iron Kettle	15 x 6	DAC		2. 50
11, 386.	Spinning Wheel	15 x 6	DAC		2. 50
11, 387.	Steam Train	6 x 15	DAC		2. 50

VAN ANTUM See ANTUM
VAN BLOEMAN See BLOEMAN
VANCE, JAMES

11, 388.	Mexico (4)	16 x 21 sheets	IA	ea.	3. 00
11, 389.	Floating Gardens				
11, 390.	Flower Pickers				
11, 391.	Market Day at Patzcuaro				
11, 392.	Shopping at Mercado				

VAN CLEVE See CLEVE, JOOS VAN
VAN DAEL See DAEL, JAN FRANS VAN
VAN DER GOES See GOES, HUGO VAN DER
VAND DER LECK

11, 393.	The Cat	16-1/2 x 13	AP	2. 00
		14 x 11	NYGS	3. 00

VAN DER LEUR, J.

11, 394.	Spring Splendor	24 x 30	CFA	10. 00

VANDERLYN, JOHN (American, 1775-1852)

11, 395.	George Washington	24 x 18	DAC	7. 50
		16 x 12	DAC	2. 50

VAN DER MEULEN, PIETER See MEULEN, PIETER VAN DER
VAN DER NEER, AERT See NEER, AERT VAN DER
VAN DER WEYDEN, ROGIER See WEYDEN, ROGIER VAN DER
VAN DONGEN See DONGEN, CORNELIUS VAN
VAN DYCK, (SIR) ANTHONY (OR ANTHONIS) (Flemish, 1599-1641)

11, 396.	Apostle Peter	22 x 17-1/2	ESH	7. 50
11, 397.	Apostle Thomas	22 x 17-1/2	ESH	7. 50
11, 398.	Armored Warrior	24 x 18	DAC	7. 50
11, 399.	Baby Stuart c.	9x 7	AP	. 50
11, 400.	Charles I and Henriette			
	of England	11 x 14	IA	3. 00
11, 401.	Children of Charles			
	First c.	7 x 9	AP	. 50
11, 402.	Count Henry Van Der			
	Bergh	35 x 21	AJ	15. 00
		20 x 17-1/2	NYGS	10. 00
11, 403.	Crucifix	15 x 10	IA	3. 00
11, 404.	Duke of Richmond	14 x 11	IA	3. 00
11, 405.	Filippo Cattaneo, Son			
	of Marchesa Elena			
	Grimaldi, 1623	24 x 16-1/2	NYGS	10. 00
11, 406.	Genoese Lady and			
	her Daughter	15 x 11	IA	3. 00
11, 407.	John of Montfort	15 x 11	IA	3. 00
11, 408.	Judgment of Paris	12 x 16-1/2	NYGS	12. 00
11, 409.	Madonna and Child			
	(Rome)	14-1/2x11-1/2	AS	3. 25

11, 410.	Madonna and Child with			
	St. Anthony	13 x 11	IA	3. 00
11, 411.	Man on Horseback	26 x 15	PENN	1. 50
11, 412.	Marchesa Elena			
	Grimaldi c.	10 x 8	NYGS	. 50
11, 413.	Maria with Jesus and			
	St. John	26-1/2x22-1/2	CFA	15. 00
11, 414.	Nativity	14 x 11	IA	3. 00
11, 415.	Nobleman	9 x 6-1/2	AR	3. 50
11, 416.	Philip, Lord Wharton			
		28 x 22	NYGS	16. 00
11, 417.	Portrait of Charles			
	First c.	9 x 7	AP	. 50
11, 418.	Portrait of Margaret			
	of Lorene	15 x 9	AS	3. 25
11, 419.	Portrait of a			
	Painter	10 x 8	AR	3. 00
11, 420.	Portrait of the Prince			
	Rodocanakis	14 x 10	IA	3. 00
11, 421.	Repose (or Rest) on the			
	Flight into Egypt	24 x 21	NYGS	15. 00
		20 x 17	CFA	5. 00
		13 x 11	IA	3. 00
	Angels - Detail of			
	No. 11, 421.	7 x 9	IA	1. 50
11, 422.	Self-Portrait	14 x 11	IA	3. 00
11, 423.	Son of Charles I	15 x 11	AS	3. 25
11, 424.	Viscount of Stafford	14 x 11	IA	3. 00
11, 425.	William II of Nassau			
	and Orange c.	10 x 8	NYGS	. 50
VAN EYCK, JAN (Flemish, 1390-1441)				
11, 426.	Angels Playing	24 x 11	AP	10. 00
11, 427.	Angels Singing	24 x 11	AP	10. 00
11, 428.	Annunciation	26 x 10	NYGS	12. 00
	c.	10 x 8	NYGS	. 50
11, 429.	Arnolfini and his Wife			
	(Marriage of Arnolfini)			
		25 x 18	CAC	12. 00
		21 x 15	ESH	15. 00
	c.	9 x 7	AP	. 60
11, 430.	Crucifixion	15 x 10	IA	3. 00
11, 431.	The Donors c.	7 x 9	AP	. 60
11, 432.	Ince Hall Madona			
	c.	24 x 20	PENN	1. 50
		24 x 18	DAC	7. 50
	c.	10 x 8	NYGS	. 50
11, 433.	Leal Souvenir	13-1/2 x 7	ESH	6. 00
11, 434.	Man with a Pink			
	c.	10 x 8	NYGS	. 50
11, 435.	Portrait of Cardinal			
	Albergati	13 x 10	IA	3. 00
11, 436.	Sainte Barbe	9 x 8	NYGS	4. 00

11,437.	St. Francis c.	10 x 8	NYGS	.50
11,438.	Virgin of Autun	20 x 18	ESH	10.00
		11 x 11	IA	3.00
11,439.	Virgin Worshipped by the Chancellor (Madonna and Chancellor Rolin)			
		11 x 10	CFA	2.50
	c.	9 x 7	AP	.50

VAN FALENS See FALENS, KAREL VAN
VAN GOGH, VINCENT (Dutch, 1853-1890)

11,440.	Les Alpiles	18 x 22-1/2	NYGS	10.00
11,441.	L'Arlesienne c.	16 x 12	PENN	1.50
	c.	9 x 7	AP	.50
11,442.	The Artist's Bedroom at Arles c.	20 x 24	PENN	1.50
		16-1/2 x 21	NYGS	5.00
	c.	8 x 10	NYGS	.50
11,443.	Autumn Landscape with Four Trees	16 x 20-1/2	NYGS	6.00
11,444.	Auvers	15 x 30	NYGS	12.00
	c.	7 x 9	AP	.50
11,445.	Auvers, Vue de Village	17-1/2 x 21	NYGS	7.50
11,446.	Basket of Fruit with Blue Gloves	19 x 24-1/2	NYGS	15.00
11,447.	Behind the Schenkweg (B & W)	12 x 19-1/2	NYGS	3.00
11,448.	Bell Lilies in a Copper Vase	30 x 24-1/2	ESH	15.00
		20 x 15-1/2	NYGS	5.00
11,449.	Bench	11 x 13	IA	3.00
11,450.	La Berceuse	26 x 20	PENN	1.50
		20-1/2 x 16	NYGS	5.00
11,451.	Blooming Apple Orchard	12 x 16	NYGS	4.00
11,452.	Blue Iris	6 x 8	CFA	1.00
11,453.	Boats, 1888	15 x 21	NYGS	18.00
11,454.	Boats Docked	6 x 8	CFA	1.00
11,455.	Boats of Saintes-Maries, 1888	25 x 31-1/2	NYGS	20.00
		22 x 28	NYGS	12.00
	c.	20 x 24	PENN	1.50
	c.	18 x 23	HNA	5.95
		16-1/2x20-1/2	NYGS	6.00
		16 x 20	CFA	6.00
	c.	8 x 10	ESH	1.00
11,456.	Boats on Beach	6 x 8	CFA	1.00
11,457.	Boy with Sickle	15-1/2x20-1/2	AP	3.50
11,458.	Breakfast Table	17-1/2 x 23	NYGS	12.00
11,459.	Bridge, 1889	23 x 28	CFA	18.00
		19 x 26	NYGS	18.00
		16 x 20	NYGS	6.00
		15 x 19-1/2	NYGS	6.00

		c.	8 x 10	NYGS	. 50
11, 460.	Bridge and Road		7 x 9	NYGS	. 50
11, 461.	Bridge at Arles		18 x 20	PENN	1. 50
			18 x 19-1/2	ESH	10. 00
		c.	8 x 10	ESH	1. 00
11, 462.	Bridge at Asnieres		16 x 22-1/2	ESH	10. 00
11, 463.	By the Riverside		16 x 21-1/2	CFA	10. 00
11, 464.	Café at Arles		17-1/2 x 25	AR	12. 00
			17 x 25	CFA	12. 00
11, 465.	Café at Night		22-1/2 x 18	ESH	10. 00
		c.	10 x 8	ESH	1. 00
			9 x 7	AP	. 50
			7 x 6	CFA	1. 00
11, 466.	Café de Nuit	c.	22 x 17-1/2	AS	4. 00
11, 467.	Café, Evening		22-1/2 x 18	NYGS	10. 00
11, 468.	Champs de Blé		8-1/2 x 11	NYGS	8. 00
11, 469.	Chestnut Blossoms		13 x 16	CFA	5. 00
11, 470.	Church at Auvers				
		c.	23 x 18	HNA	5. 95
			18 x 15	CFA	7. 50
		c.	10 x 8	ESH	1. 00
			8 x 7	CFA	1. 00
11, 471.	Cloister Garden		28-1/2 x 36	NYGS	28. 00
11, 472.	Cornfield		12 x 16	NYGS	4. 00
11, 473.	Cornfield near Arles				
			24 x 31	CFA	18. 00
11, 474.	Cornfield with				
	Cypresses		27 x 34-1/2	NYGS	20. 00
			15 x 19-1/2	AP	5. 00
		c.	8 x 10	ESH	· 1. 00
11, 475.	Cornfield with Rooks				
		c.	8 x 10	ESH	1. 00
11, 476.	Cornfields in				
	Provence		16 x 20-1/2	AP	5. 00
		c.	7 x 9	AP	. 50
11, 477.	Cottages	c.	18 x 23	HNA	5. 95
11, 478.	Cottages at Cordeville				
			18 x 22-1/2	ESH	10. 00
		c.	8 x 10	ESH	1. 00
11, 479.	La Crau		17-1/2x21-1/2	ESH	10. 00
		c.	8 x 10	ESH	1. 00
11, 480.	Cypres dans un Champ				
	de Blé		17-1/2 x 22	AS	4. 00
11, 481.	Cypress in the Field				
			25 x 32	CFA	18. 00
11, 482.	Cypress Landscape				
		c.	7 x 9	AP	. 50
11, 483.	Cypress Road		22-1/2x17-1/2	ESH	10. 00
11, 484.	Cypress Road with				
	Star		19 x 15	AP	5. 00
11, 485.	Cypresses, 1890		20 x 16	AJ	7. 50
			12 x 9	NYGS	2. 00

11,486.	Drawbridge	6 x 8	CFA	1.00
11,487.	Drawbridge at Arles			
		23-1/2x25-1/2	IA	18.00
		18-1/2 x 20	IA	10.00
		16 x 20	DAC	7.50
		15 x 15	NYGS	4.00
11,488.	Entrance to the Public Gardens at Arles	23-1/2 x 30	NYGS	18.00
11,489.	Evening Walk c.	9 x 7	AP	.60
11,490.	Farmer in the Field c.	24 x 20	PENN	1.50
11,491.	Farmhouses, Auvers, 1890	19 x 23	NYGS	7.50
11,492.	Field at Arles	19 x 24	PENN	1.50
11,493.	Field at Auvers	16 x 22	CFA	10.00
	c.	9-1/2x12-1/2	AP	1.25
		5 x 10	CFA	1.00
11,494.	Fishing Boats at Saintes-Maries			
	c.	18 x 23	HNA	5.95
		16 x 20	AP	5.00
11,495.	Fishing in the Spring	16 x 19-1/2	AP	5.00
	c.	7 x 9	AP	.60
11,496.	Flowering Almond Branch c.	10 x 8	ESH	1.00
11,497.	Flowering Chestnut Branch c.	8 x 10	ESH	1.00
11,498.	Flowering Garden	16 x 20	CFA	10.00
	c.	9-1/2x12-1/2	AP	1.25
11,499.	Flowering Tree	22 x 18	IA	10.00
11,500.	Flowers	12 x 8	AP	1.50
11,501.	Flowers in a Blue Vase	20-1/2 x 13	AP	4.00
		20-1/2x12-1/2	NYGS	5.00
		14 x 8-1/2	NYGS	2.00
11,502.	Flowers in a Copper Vase c.	24 x 20	PENN	1.50
	c.	10 x 8	ESH	1.00
11,503.	Garden at Daubigny	15 x 30	ESH	15.00
11,504.	Garden of Dr. Gachet			
	c.	8 x 10	ESH	1.00
11,505.	Girl with Shawl	17 x 9-1/2	NYGS	3.00
11,506.	Girl in a Straw Hat			
	c.	23 x 18	HNA	5.95
11,507.	Girl in White c.	23 x 18	HNA	5.95
11,508.	Les Glaieuls	22 x 12	NYGS	22.00
11,509.	Going to Work	18 x 16	NYGS	6.00
	c.	9 x 7	AP	.50
11,510.	Grass and Flowers under Trees	16-1/2 x 21	NYGS	7.50
11,511.	Green Corn	17-1/2 x 22	ESH	10.00
		14 x 17	CFA	7.50

		6 x 7	CFA	1.00
11,512.	Grinding Coffee	19-1/2 x 14	AP	3.50
11,513.	Gypsy Camp c.	20 x 24	PENN	1.50
		16-1/2 x 19	NYGS	5.00
11,514.	Gypsy Caravan	17-1/2 x 22	ESH	10.00
	c.	8 x 10	ESH	1.00
11,515.	Gypsy Encampment	14 x 16	CFA	4.00
		6 x 7	CFA	1.00
11,516.	Harvest	23 x 28	NYGS	26.00
11,517.	Haystacks in			
	Provence	19 x 23-1/2	NYGS	6.00
		15 x 30	CFA	15.00
	c.	7 x 9	AP	.50
11,518.	L'Homme a L'Oreille			
	Coupée c.	24 x 20	PENN	1.50
11,519.	Hospital, St. Remy			
	c.	12 x 16	PENN	1.00
11,520.	Hospital Garden of			
	St. Paul	20 x 16	NYGS	6.00
11,521.	Hospital Gardens			
	c.	9-1/2x12-1/2	AP	1.25
11,522.	Hospital Grounds at			
	St. Remy c.	12 x 16	PENN	1.00
11,523.	House at Auvers	23-1/2x19-1/2	PENN	1.50
11,524.	Houses at Auvers	23 x 28	IA	15.00
	c.	8 x 10	NYGS	.50
11,525.	Iris	20 x 16	PENN	1.50
11,526.	Irises	22-1/2 x 18	ESH	10.00
		19-1/2 x 16	AP	5.00
		9 x 7	NYGS	.50
11,527.	Le Jardin de			
	Daeigny	12 x 23	PENN	1.50
11,528.	Le Jardin de			
	l"Hopital	7 x 8	CFA	1.00
11,529.	Landscape at Auvers			
		25 x 31-1/2	NYGS	20.00
	c.	18 x 23	HNA	5.95
11,530.	Landscape with			
	Bridge	23 x 25	CFA	18.00
11,531.	Landscape with			
	Cypress	27 x 34-1/2	IA	18.00
		22 x 28	IA	18.00
		6 x 7	CFA	1.00
11,532.	Landscape with Green			
	Corn	24 x 30	DAC	7.50
		12 x 16	DAC	2.50
11,533.	The Lark c.	7 x 9	AP	.60
11,534.	Laurier Roses	23 x 28	NYGS	20.00
		18 x 22	CFA	10.00
11,535.	Little Gardens--			
	Montmartre c.	8 x 10	ESH	1.00
11,536.	Little Pear Tree in			
	Bloom	28-1/2 x 18	NYGS	15.00

11, 537.	Madame Roulin and			
	Child	16-1/2 x 14	AR	5. 00
11, 538.	Man Sowing	18 x 22-1/2	AJ	10. 00
11, 539.	La Meule	8-1/2 x 11	NYGS	7. 50
11, 540.	La Moisson en			
	Provence	19 x 23	NYGS	15. 00
11, 541.	Moulin de la			
	Galette c.	7 x 9	AP	. 60
11, 542.	La Mousme	24 x 18	PENN	1. 50
		20 x 16-1/2	NYGS	10. 00
		7-1/2x6-1/2	NYGS	. 50
11, 543.	The Mulberry Tree	22 x 25	NYGS	12. 00
11, 544.	Old Man Mourning	12 x 9-1/2	NYGS	1. 50
11, 545.	Olive Grove	16 x 20	NYGS	6. 00
	c.	8 x 10	ESH	1. 00
11, 546.	Olive Orchard,			
	1889	3-1/2 x 12	NYGS	1. 50
11, 547.	On Montmartre			
	c.	9-1/2x12-1/2	AP	1. 25
		8 x 6	CFA	1. 00
11, 548.	Open Air Cafe			
	(Outdoor Cafe)	22 x 18	CFA	10. 00
		19-1/2 x 16	AP	5. 00
11, 549.	Orchard	22 x 27	NYGS	12. 00
		8 x 10	ESH	1. 00
11, 550.	Painter	18 x 16	CFA	6. 00
11, 551.	Peasant	27-1/2 x 21	NYGS	26. 00
11, 552.	Peasant Reaping			
	Corn (DR.)	19-1/2x13-1/2	AP	3. 50
11, 553.	Peasant Walking	13 x 8	NYGS	1. 50
11, 554.	Peasant Working			
	(DR.)	19-1/2x14-1/2	NYGS	3. 50
11, 555.	Peasant Woman			
	Gleaning (Dr.)	19-1/2x13-1/2	NYGS	3. 50
11, 556.	Peasant Woman Home-			
	wards	19-1/2x12-1/2	NYGS	3. 00
11, 557.	Pere Tanguy	9 x 7	NYGS	. 50
11, 558.	Pink Peach Tree			
	c.	10 x 8	ESH	1. 00
11, 559.	Pink and White			
	Roses	23-1/2x30	NYGS	26. 00
	c.	20 x 24	PENN	1. 50
		16 x 20	NYGS	5. 00
11, 560.	Plain at Auvers-Sur-			
	Oise	16 x 22	CFA	10. 00
	c.	9-1/2x12-1/2	AP	1. 25
11, 561.	Plains at Auvers	16 x 32	AR	15. 00
		10 x 20	AR	5. 00
11, 562.	Poppy Field	25 x 31	CFA	18. 00
		24-1/2 x 31	NYGS	20. 00

11, 563.	Portrait of Armand Roulin	20 x 16	NYGS	5. 00
	c.	9 x 7	AP	. 60
11, 564.	Portrait of the Artist	24x 20	AJ	12. 00
11, 565.	Portrait of Dr. Gachet	22-1/2x18-1/2	NYGS	10. 00
11, 566.	Portrait of a Young Man	24 x 20	DAC	7. 50
		16 x 12	DAC	2. 50
11, 567.	Postman Roulin	28 x 22	NYGS	16. 00
11, 568.	Potato Field Behind Dunes	11 x 16-1/2	NYGS	3. 00
11, 569.	Railway Bridge			
	c.	20 x 24	PENN	1. 50
	c.	9-1/2x12-1/2	AP	1. 25
	c.	7 x 9	AP	1. 00
11, 570.	Restaurant de la Sirene	21 x 25	NYGS	12. 00
	c.	20 x 24	PENN	1. 50
11, 571.	River Boats c.	9-1/2x12-1/2	AP	1. 25
	c.	7 x 9	AP	1. 00
11, 572.	Roses and Anemones			
	c.	20 x 24	PENN	1. 50
		20 x 20	ESH	10. 00
		12 x 12	ESH	5. 00
11, 573.	Der Sämen c.	17-1/2 x 22	AS	4. 00
11, 574.	Schoolboy	12 x 11	IA	3. 00
11, 575.	Self-Portrait	24 x 20	NYGS	12. 00
		16 x 13	AJ	7. 50
11, 576.	Self-Portrait	17 x 14	NYGS	12. 00
		9 x 7	NYGS	. 50
11, 577.	Self-Portrait (Hat)			
	c.	10 x 8	ESH	1. 00
11, 578.	Self-Portrait (Man with a Pipe)	16-1/2x14-1/2	ESH	10. 00
	c.	10 x 8	ESH	1. 00
11, 579.	Sidewalk Cafe at Night	22 x 18	NYGS	10. 00
		20 x 15-1/2	NYGS	6. 00
11, 580.	Souvenir de Mauve	22 x 18	NYGS	10. 00
		21 x 17	NYGS	6. 00
11, 581.	The Sower	12-1/2 x 16	NYGS	12. 00
11, 582.	Sower in the Field	18 x 22-1/2	NYGS	10. 00
11, 583.	Stairway at Auvers	16 x 23	NYGS	10. 00
11, 584.	Starlight over the Rhone	20 x 25	NYGS	10. 00
11, 585.	Starry Night	20 x 26	AP	6. 50
		20 x 25	NYGS	10. 00
		18 x 22	ESH	10. 00
	c.	8 x 10	MMA	. 35
	c.	7 x 9	AP	. 50

11, 586.	Still Life with Bottle, Lemons and Oranges			
		16-1/2x19-1/2	NYGS	6. 00
11, 587.	Still Life, Flowers	16 x 19-1/2	AP	5. 00
11, 588.	Still Life, Fruit	16-1/2 x 20	IA	7. 50
		16 x 20	CFA	7. 50
11, 589.	Still Life with Gloves			
		12 x 16	NYGS	4. 00
11, 590.	Still Life with Onions			
		12 x 16	NYGS	4. 00
11, 591.	Still Life with Pears			
		18 x 23	NYGS	10. 00
11, 592.	Street in Auvers	28-1/2 x 36	NYGS	18. 00
		16 x 20	NYGS	6. 00
11, 593.	Street Pavers c.	20 x 24	PENN	1. 50
11, 594.	Street with Cypress			
	and Star c.	9 x 7	AP	. 60
11, 595.	Study of a Tree	14 x 19-1/2	NYGS	3. 00
11, 596.	Summer Evening near			
	Arles c.	18 x 23	HNA	5. 95
11, 597.	Sunflowers, 1888			
	(Philadelphia)	33-1/2x26-1/2	IA	18. 00
		30 x 23-1/2	NYGS	16. 00
		20-1/2 x 16	NYGS	6. 00
		20 x 15-1/2	IA	4. 00
11, 598	Sunflowers (Munich)			
		33-1/2 x 26	NYGS	18. 00
		32 x 24	CFA	18. 00
	c.	24 x 20	PENN	1. 50
		24 x 18	DAC	7. 50
	c.	23 x 18	HNA	5. 95
		16 x 12	DAC	2. 50
		15 x 12	AR	3. 00
	c.	9 x 7	AP	. 50
11, 599.	Sunflowers (London)			
		15 x 12	AP	3. 00
	c.	9 x 7	AP	. 50
		8 x 7	CFA	1. 00
11, 600.	Sunflowers (with Yellow Background) (Amsterdam)			
		32-1/2 x 25	IA	18. 00
		23 x 17	CFA	10. 00
		22 x 16-1/2	ESH	10. 00
		20-1/2x15-1/2	NYGS	6. 00
		20 x 15-1/2	IA	4. 00
	c.	10 x 8	ESH	1. 00
11, 601.	Sunny Midi, Arles	18 x 20	PENN	1. 50
		15-1/2 x 20	AJ	7. 50
11, 602.	Sunset at Arles			
	c.	8 x 10	ESH	1. 00
11, 603.	Thatched Cottages	14 x 21	CFA	7. 50
	c.	12 x 16	PENN	1. 00

		c.	9-1/2x12-1/2	AP	1.25
			6 x 9	CFA	1.00
11,604.	Three Trees		18 x 22	NYGS	10.00
11,605.	Tree in Bloom		22-1/2 x 18	AJ	10.00
11,606.	Tree Trunks	c.	9-1/2x12-1/2	AP	1.25
		c.	7 x 9	AP	1.00
11,607.	Vegetable Gardens		24-1/2 x 32	NYGS	18.00
			22 x 28	NYGS	12.00
			17-1/2 x 21	IA	10.00
			16 x 20	NYGS	5.00
11,608.	View of Arles		22 x 28	NYGS	20.00
			8 x 10-1/2	ESH	1.00
11,609.	View of Arles with Iris		20-1/2 x 25	IA	15.00
		c.	7 x 9	AP	.25
11,610.	View of Auvers				
		c.	8 x 10	ESH	1.00
11,611.	View of Les Stes. Maries-de-La Mer		22-1/2x18-1/2	NYGS	10.00
11,612.	Vincent's House at Arles		17 x 22-1/2	ESH	10.00
11,613.	Vineyard		17 x 22	CFA	10.00
11,614.	Walk at Twilight		20 x 17-1/2	NYGS	7.50
11,615.	Walk in Alyscamp Park		16 x 20	NYGS	6.00
11,616.	Walk in the Evening		12 x 11	IA	3.00
11,617.	Wheatfield		5 x 10	CFA	1.00
11,618.	Wheatfield with Crows	c.	9-1/2x12-1/2	AP	1.25
		c.	7 x 9	AP	1.00
11,619.	White Roses		30-1/2 x 24	NYGS	20.00
		c.	26 x 21	HNA	5.95
			26 x 20-1/2	IA	7.50
			26 x 20	PENN	1.50
			17 x 14	CFA	5.00
		c.	12-1/2x9-1/2	AP	1.25
		c.	9 x 7	AP	1.00
			7 x 6	CFA	1.00
11,620.	Willows at Sunset		12 x 13	NYGS	4.00
11,621.	Woman Binding Corn		17 x 21	NYGS	3.00
11,622.	Woman Chopping		14-1/2x16-1/2	NYGS	3.00
11,623.	Yellow Books	c.	9-1/2x12-1/2	AP	1.25
11,624.	Yellow Chair with Pipe		15 x 12	AP	3.00
		c.	10 x 8	ESH	1.00
11,625.	Zouave, 1888		14-1/2 x 12	NYGS	4.00
11,626.	Zouave Officer Milliet		19-1/2 x 16	NYGS	15.00
			14-1/2 x 12	NYGS	4.00

VAN HOLFT

11,627.	Dutch Fisher-Room	23-1/2 x 20	ESH	Pr. 10.00

VAN HUYSUM See HUYSUM, JAN VAN
VAN KESSEL See KESSEL, VAN
VAN LINT See LINT, E. VAN
VAN LOO, CARLE (French, 1705-1765)
11, 628. Virgin and Child   22-1/2x16-1/2   AS   7. 50
                              15 x 11   AS   3. 25
VAN MIERIS See MIERIS, FRANS VAN
VANNI, ANDREA (Italian, c. 1332-1414)
11, 629. St. Catherine of
          Siena (Siena)   15 x 8   AS   3. 25
VANNI, LIPPO (Italian, 1344-1372)
11, 630. Madonna and Child 15 x 10   IA   3. 00
VANNUCCI, PIETRO See PERUGINO
VAN OSTADE See OSTADE, ADRIAEN VAN
VAN SPAENDENCK See SPAENDENCK, GERADUS VAN
VANVITELLI, GASPAR (VAN WITTEL) (1655-1736)
11, 631. Castel Sant'Angelo,
          Rome   15 x 31   ESH   15. 00
11, 632. Piazza Del Quirinale
                             11 x 20   CFA   12. 00
11, 633. Ponte Roto   10 x 20   CFA   10. 00
11, 634. La Trineta Dei
          Monti   10 x 20   CFA   10. 00
11, 635. View on the
          Tevere   10 x 15-1/2   AS   3. 25
11, 636. Villa Medici   10 x 20   CFA   10. 00
VAN WITTEL See VANVITELLI, GASPAR
VARIN, RAOUL (French, 1893-)
11, 637. Baseball, 1865   17 x 23-1/2   PENN   1. 50
11, 638. Broadway, New York,
          1834   17 x 23   CFA   60. 00
11, 639. Chicago, 1865   17-1/2x22-1/2   PENN   1. 50
11, 640. New York, 1848   18 x 23   CFA   40. 00
11, 641. New York, 1852   18 x 29   CFA   75. 00
11, 642. New York from the
          East River   12 x 33   CFA   60. 00
11, 643. New York from the
          North River, 1839 12 x 33   CFA   60. 00
11, 644. Printing House Square,
          New York, 1864   17 x 22   CFA   40. 00
11, 645. St. Paul's Church,
          1831   18 x 23   CFA   40. 00
VAROTARI, ALESSANDRO See PADOVANINO, IL
VAS
11, 646. Clowns   24 x 20   CFA   35. 00
11, 647. Flowerpiece   24 x 20   CFA   35. 00
11, 648. Harbor Scene   24 x 24   CFA   35. 00
VASARI, GIORGIO (Italian, 1511-1574)
11, 649. Portrait of Lorenzo de'
          Medici, Il Magnifico
                             14 x 11   AS   3. 25
VASI, GIUSEPPE (Italian, 1710-1782)

11, 650.	Ancient Rome				
	(B & W) (4)	35-1/2x24-1/2	NYGS	ea. 60. 00
11, 651.	Monte Aventino				
11, 652.	Ruins of Ancient Rome				
11, 653.	Street of the Four Fountains				
11, 654.	View of Rome with Tiber Bridge				

VAYREDA, FRANCISCO (Spanish, 19th Century)

11, 655.	Place du Tertre	24 x 48	DAC	10. 00

VECELLIO, TIZIANO See TITIAN

VECCHIETTA, IL (LORENZO DI PIETRO) (Italian, 1412-1480)

11, 656.	Il Beato Andrea			
	Gallerani	16 x 10	IA	3. 00

VELASQUEZ, DIEGO RODRIGUEZ (Spanish, 1599-1660)

11, 657.	Alesandro Del Borro				
		c.	8 x 10	NYGS	. 50
11, 658.	Cardinal Gaspar				
		c.	9 x 7	AP	. 25
11, 659.	Christ on the Cross				
		c.	10 x 8	ESH	1. 00
11, 660.	Coronation of the				
	Virgin	c.	23 x 18	HNA	5. 95
		c.	10 x 8	ESH	1. 00
11, 661.	Don (Prince) Balthasar				
	Carlos		23-1/2x19-1/2	NYGS	10. 00
			19 x 16	PENN	1. 50
			14 x 12	NYGS	3. 00
			12-1/2 x 10	AS	3. 25
		c.	9 x 7	AP	. 60
11, 662.	Drinkers	c.	18 x 23	HNA	5. 95
			13 x 18	IA	3. 00
11, 663.	Immaculate Conception				
			28 x 21	NYGS	18. 00
11, 664.	Infanta		22 x 17	AR	12. 00
			7 x 6	CFA	1. 00
11, 665.	Infanta in White		22 x 17	CFA	12. 00
11, 666.	Infanta Margareta				
	Teresa		25 x 19	CFA	12. 00
			20 x 15	CFA	7. 50
11, 667.	Infanta Margarita		21 x 18	NYGS	10. 00
		c.	16 x 12	PENN	1. 00
			11 x 9	NYGS	1. 00
			8 x 6	CFA	1. 00
11, 668.	Infanta Margarita Teresa				
	in Red		24 x 18-1/2	ESH	15. 00
11, 669.	Infanta Marguerite		8 x 6	CFA	1. 00
11, 670.	Infanta Marguerite				
	en Rose	c.	12-1/2x9-1/2	AP	1. 25
11, 671.	Infanta Marguerita				
	Theresa		7 x 6	CFA	1. 00
11, 672.	Infanta Maria				
	Margarita		13 x 11	IA	3. 00
11, 673.	Infanta M. Therese				
		c.	12-1/2x9-1/2	AP	1. 25

11, 674.	Infanta Maria Theresa			
		31-1/2 x 24	NYGS	22. 00
11, 675.	Infante Philip Prosper			
		20 x 15	NYGS	10. 00
11, 676.	Maids of Honor	18 x 16	NYGS	5. 00
11, 677.	Les Meninas c.	7 x 9	AP	. 50
11, 678.	Merrymakers	13 x 18	NYGS	5. 00
11, 679.	Needlewoman	12 x 9	CFA	2. 00
11, 680.	Philip IV of Spain			
	c.	24 x 20	PENN	1. 50
		15-1/2x10-1/2	AS	3. 25
		15 x 11	IA	3. 00
	c.	10 x 8	NYGS	. 50
11, 681.	Pope Innocent X	14 x 11	IA	3. 00
	Head - Detail of			
	No. 11, 681	15 x 11-1/2	AS	3. 25
		15 x 11	IA	3. 00
11, 682.	Princess Margarita			
	Maria	16 x 13	NYGS	5. 00
11, 683.	Queen Mary Anne	13 x 11	IA	3. 00
11, 684.	Self-Portrait	15 x 10	IA	3. 00
11, 685.	Spinners c.	7 x 9	AP	. 60
11, 686.	Surrender of Breda	15 x 18	NYGS	5. 00
11, 687.	Tapestry Weavers	14 x 18	NYGS	5. 00
11, 688.	Venus and Cupid	19 x 27-1/2	AR	18. 00
		19 x 27	CFA	18. 00
11, 689.	Vulcan's Forge	11 x 14	AS	3. 25

VELDE, WILLEM VAN DE (Dutch, 1633-1707)

11, 690.	Calm Waters and			
	Warships	17 x 22	IA	10. 00
		11 x 14	IA	3. 00
11, 691.	Frigate in a Storm	22-1/2x18-1/2	ESH	10. 00
11, 692.	Harbour of Amsterdam			
		8 x 10-1/2	ESH	1. 00
11, 693.	Naval Battle in the			
	North Sea	20 x 31-1/2	ESH	15. 00
		8 x 10-1/2	ESH	1. 00
11, 694.	Passage of Charles II			
		17 x 22	IA	10. 00
		11 x 14	IA	3. 00

VENETO, (FRA) BARTOLOMEO (Italian, 1502-1530)

11, 695.	Portrait of a			
	Cavalier	15 x 11	AS	3. 25
11, 696.	Portrait of a			
	Gentleman	15 x 11	IA	3. 00
11, 697.	Portrait of a Man	10 x 8	NYGS	. 50
11, 698.	St. Catherine	14 x 11	ESH	6. 00

VENEZIANO, DOMENICO (Italian, 1390-1461)

11, 699.	The Florentine	20 x 13	AR	12. 00
11, 700.	Martyrdom of St.			
	Lucia	9 x 10	IA	3. 00
11, 701.	Portrait of a Girl	21 x 14	NYGS	15. 00

11, 702.	Portrait of a Young Woman c,	8 x 10	NYGS	. 50
11, 703.	Virgin Enthroned with Child and Saints	11 x 11	IA	3. 00
	St. Lucy - Detail of No. 11, 703	15 x 11	IA	3. 00
VENTOSA				
11, 704.	Ballerinas	28 x 22	DAC	12. 50
11, 705.	Maria Rooa	22 x 28	DAC	12. 50
11, 706.	Muchacha y Ukulele			
		28 x 22	DAC	12. 50
11, 707.	Nina del Canario	22 x 28	DAC	12. 50
11, 708.	Rincon de Bar	28 x 22	DAC	12. 50
11, 709.	Rosa Blanca	28 x 22	DAC	12. 50
	c.	24 x 20	PENN	1. 50
VERLINDE, CLAUDE (French Contemporary)				
11, 710.	La Danse	18 x 26	RL	12. 50
11, 711.	Vikings	16 x 40	RL	20. 00
VERMEER, JAN (VAN DELFT) (Dutch, 1632-1675)				
11, 712.	Artist in his Studio	22-1/2 x 19	ESH	10. 00
	c.	10 x 8	ESH	1. 00
11, 713.	Artist in the Studio			
	c.	23 x 18	HNA	5. 95
11, 714.	Artist's Studio	31 x 26	NYGS	18. 00
		25-1/2 x 21	ESH	15. 00
		24 x 20	CFA	7. 50
11, 715.	Concert	27 x 24	NYGS	18. 00
11, 716.	Cook c.	7 x 9	AP	. 50
11, 717.	Diana and the Nymphs			
		11 x 12	IA	3. 00
11, 718.	Girl Asleep	20 x 18	PENN	1. 50
	c.	9 x 7	AP	. 50
11, 719.	Girl at the Casement			
		17-1/2x15-1/2	ESH	15. 00
11, 720.	Girl Interrupted at her Music	15 x 17	NYGS	7. 50
11, 721.	Girl with a Turban	19 x 15-1/2	NYGS	7. 50
11, 722.	Girl with Yellow Turban	19 x 16	IA	12. 00
		18-1/2 x 16	IA	5. 00
11, 723.	Head of a Girl	20 x 17	PENN	1. 50
		19 x 16	ESH	15. 00
11, 724.	Kitchen Maid	17 x 15	CFA	10. 00
11, 725.	Lace Maker	24 x 18	DAC	7. 50
		17-1/2x15-1/2	NYGS	7. 50
	c.	10 x 8	ESH	1. 00
	c.	9 x 7	AP	. 60
11, 726.	Lace Makers c.	9-1/2x12-1/2	AP	1. 25
11, 727.	Lady at the Virginals	20 x 17	ESH	15. 00
		16 x 14	CFA	4. 00
11, 728.	Lady with a Lute			
	c.	7 x 9	AP	. 50

11, 729.	Lady and Gentleman			
	Drinking Wine	16-1/2 x 20	AP	5.00
	c.	8 x 10	NYGS	.50
11, 730.	The Letter c.	24 x 20	PENN	1.50
		22-1/2x17-1/2	DAC	7.50
		20 x 15	CFA	6.00
		19-1/2 x 16	NYGS	3.00
11, 731.	Little Street	20-1/2 x 17	PENN	1.50
11, 732.	The Love Letter	23-1/2 x 18	DAC	7.50
		16-1/2 x 14	NYGS	15.00
		16 x 13-1/2	PENN	1.50
		13 x 11	IA	3.00
11, 733.	Milkmaid	18 x 16	NYGS	10.00
		17-1/2 x 16	PENN	1.50
		10 x 8-1/2	NYGS	1.00
11, 734.	Mistress and			
	Maid	27 x 24	CFA	15.00
11, 735.	Music Lesson	20 x 16-1/2	ESH	6.00
11, 736.	Seamstress c.	24 x 20	PENN	1.50
11, 737.	Street in Delft c.	24 x 20	PENN	1.50
		22 x 17	ESH	15.00
		14 x 10	IA	3.00
		13 x 10-1/2	ESH	3.00
11, 738.	Tasting Wine	17 x 20	NYGS	15.00
		16 x 19	NYGS	6.00
11, 739.	View of Delft	21 x 25	ESH	15.00
	c.	7 x 9	AP	.50
11, 740.	Wester Church at			
	Amsterdam	7 x 12	AR	3.50
11, 741.	Wine Test	27 x 32	IA	15.00
		17 x 20	IA	10.00
11, 742.	Wine Tester	17 x 20	CFA	12.00
11, 743.	Woman in Blue	18 x 15	PENN	1.50
11, 744.	Woman at a Casement			
	c.	8 x 10	NYGS	.50
11, 745.	Woman Weighing			
	Gold	16 x 14-1/2	NYGS	7.50
11, 746.	Young Girl with a			
	Flute c.	8 x 10	NYGS	.50
11, 747.	Young Woman with a			
	Water Jug	18 x 16	NYGS	10.00
		10 x 9	NYGS	.50
VERNET,	CARLE (French, 1758-1836)			
11, 748.	Hunting Scene in			
	England	11 x 30-1/2	ESH	15.00
VERNET,	HORACE (French, 1789-1863)			
11, 749.	Barouche	13-1/2x22-1/2	ESH	10.00
VERNET,	CLAUDE-JOSEPH (French, 1712-1789)			
11, 750.	Alpine Shepherdess			
		36 x 23	NYGS	18.00
11, 751.	Bordeaux No. 9	21 x 29	CFA	30.00
11, 752.	Caleche c.	8 x 10	ESH	1.00

11,753.	Choix de Poisson	12 x 16	CFA	15.00
11,754.	Domino Francisco	12 x 16	CFA	15.00
11,755.	Game on the Tevere			
		9 x 12	DAC	2.00
11,756.	Marseille No. 4	18 x 29	CFA	30.00
11,757.	Les Pecheurs a la			
	Ligne	12 x 16	CFA	15.00
11,758.	Les Pecheurs Fortunes			
		12 x 16	CFA	15.00
11,759.	Stage-Coach c.	8 x 10	ESH	1.00
11,760.	Toulon No. 6	18 x 29	CFA	30.00
11,761.	Vue Proche de Genes			
		12 x 16	CFA	15.00
11,762.	Vue Proche de Mont			
		12 x 16	CFA	15.00

VERONESE, PAOLO (CALIARI, PAOLO) (Italian, 1528-1588)

11,763.	Annunciation (Venice)			
		7 x 11	AS	3.25
11,764.	Feast in the House of			
	Levi	10 x 22	IA	10.00
		11 x 15	AS	3.25
11,765.	Finding of Moses	24 x 18-1/2	PENN	1.50
11,766.	Marriage of St.			
	Catherine	15 x 11	IA	3.00
		15 x 9-1/2	AS	3.25
11,767.	Martyrdom of			
	St. Justine	10 x 12	IA	3.00
11,768.	St. Helena's Vision	22-1/2 x 13	ESH	10.00

VERROCCHIO, ANDREA DEL (Italian, 1435-1488)

11,769.	Baptism of Christ			
	(With Leonardo)	13 x 11	IA	3.00
	Heads of Angels -			
	Detail of No.			
	11,769	12 x 15	IA	3.00
11,770.	David (Sculpture)	15 x 10	IA	3.00

VERSPRONCK, JAN CORNELISZ (Dutch, 1597-1662)

11,771.	Girl in a Blue Dress			
	c.	20 x 24	PENN	1.50
11,772.	Little Girl in Blue			
	c.	7 x 9	AP	.25
11,773.	Portrait of a Young			
	Girl	20 x 16	NYGS	7.50

VERSTER

11,774.	Still Life with Bottles			
		20 x 14	NYGS	6.00

VERTES, MARCEL (Hungarian, 1895-)

11,775.	After the Performance			
		18 x 21-1/2	PENN	1.50
11,776.	Cheval au Cirque	19 x 14	NYGS	18.00
11,777.	Serenade	27 x 15	PENN	1.50
11,778.	Two Ballerinas	23 x 18	PENN	1.50
11,779.	Young Mother and			
	Child	24 x 18	PENN	1.50

VERVLOET, FRANZ (Belgian, 1795-1872)					
11, 780.	Canal Grande	9 x 12	DAC		2. 00
VICKERY, CHARLES					
11, 781.	Ocean Drama	24 x 36	RL		12. 50
VICTOR, LOUIS					
11, 782.	Country Towns				
	(2)	11 x 14	AK	ea.	1. 25
		8 x 10	AK	ea.	. 80
	Country Towns				
	(2)	16 x 9	AK	ea.	1. 50
		12 x 6	AK	ea.	1. 00
VIDAL, MARGARITA HAHN					
11, 783.	Enchanted Lotus	25 x 36	NYGS		15. 00
VIGEE-LEBRUN, ELISABETH See LEBRUN, ELISABETH VIGÉE					
VILLON, JACQUES (French, 1875-1963)					
11, 784.	Anger	18-1/2 x 22	ESH		10. 00
11, 785.	Portrait	13 x 10-1/2	NYGS		15. 00
11, 786.	Yellow Accent	19-1/2x23-1/2	NYGS		12. 00
VINCENT, HARRY AIKEN (American, 1867-1931)					
11, 787.	Lifting Fog	20 x 28	CFA		7. 50
11, 788.	New England Harbor				
		16 x 20	CFA		2. 50
VINCI, LEONARDO DA See LEONARDO DA VINCI					
VINCIATA (JOSEPH WALLACE KING) (20th Century)					
11, 789.	Claudio	14 x 10	IA		3. 00
11, 790.	Florence: Days of				
	Agony	15-1/2 x 21	IA		10. 00
11, 791.	Young Mother of				
	Tuscany	22 x 17	IA		10. 00
VINCIGUERRA, L.					
11, 792.	Landing Stage	15 x 30	RL		6. 00
11, 793.	Looking at the Day	23 x 28	RL		10. 00
11, 794.	River Boat	15 x 30	RL		6. 00
VIVANCOS					
11, 795.	Village Feast c.	20 x 24	PENN		1. 50
VIVARINI, BARTOLOMEO (Italian, 1432-1491)					
11, 796.	Madonna and Child	15 x 10	IA		3. 00
VIVES-ATSARA, J. (Spanish Contemporary)					
11, 797.	Pottery Vendor	25 x 20	RL		10. 00
VIVIN, LOUIS (French, 1861-1936)					
11, 798.	Notre Dame	6 x 8	CFA		1. 00
11, 799.	Quai de l'Horloge				
	c.	8 x 10	ESH		1. 00
VLAMINCK, MAURICE DE (French, 1876-)					
11, 800.	Les Arbres Rouges				
	(Red Trees)	24 x 30	ESH		15. 00
11, 801.	At Chatou c.	9-1/2x12-1/2	AP		1. 25
	c.	8 x 10	ESH		1. 00
		6 x 8	CFA		1. 00
11, 802.	Autumn Landscape				
	c.	20 x 24	PENN		1. 50
11, 803.	Auvers	27 x 33-1/2	NYGS		20. 00

11, 804.	Banks of the Seine near Chatou		18 x 22	ESH	10. 00
11, 805.	The Barn	c.	20 x 24	PENN	1. 50
11, 806.	The Barrier	c.	20 x 24	PENN	1. 50
11, 807.	Bateau à Voile		21-1/2 x 26	NYGS	18. 00
11, 808.	Blue Vase		21 x 25	NYGS	15. 00
11, 809.	Boats on the Seine		16 x 22	CFA	12. 00
11, 810.	Bougival	c.	9-1/2x12-1/2	AP	1. 25
			7 x 9	CFA	1. 00
11, 811.	Bouquet de Fleurs		7 x 8	CFA	1. 00
11, 812.	Bridge at Meulan		18-1/2 x 24	PENN	1. 50
11, 813.	Café	c.	20 x 24	PENN	1. 50
11, 814.	Le Carouge		20 x 25	ESH	15. 00
11, 815.	Chartres		16-1/2 x 19	NYGS	7. 50
11, 816.	Cottage		14 x 17	CFA	5. 00
11, 817.	Cottages	c.	18 x 23	HNA	5. 95
11, 818.	L'Etang de St. Cucufa				
		c.	17-1/2 x 22	AS	4. 00
11, 819.	Farm in Winter				
		c.	20 x 24	PENN	1. 50
11, 820.	Flowers		12-1/2x9-1/2	AP	1. 25
		c.	9 x 7	AP	1. 00
11, 821.	French Farmhouses		25 x 32	CFA	18. 00
			18 x 22	PENN	1. 50
11, 822.	Frigate		18 x 22-1/2	ESH	10. 00
11, 823.	Harvest	c.	20 x 24	PENN	1. 50
11, 824.	Hiver		13 x 16	NYGS	18. 00
11, 825.	Lake	c.	20 x 24	PENN	1. 50
11, 826.	Landscape, 1926		24 x 29	NYGS	20. 00
11, 827.	Landscape	c.	20 x 24	PENN	1. 50
			18 x 24	ESH	10. 00
11, 828.	Landscape in the Snow	c.	9-1/2x12-1/2	AP	1. 25
		c.	7 x 9	AP	1. 00
11, 829.	Lupins and Poppies		26 x 21	NYGS	16. 00
11, 830.	Old Port of Marseille				
			19-1/2 x 24	PENN	1. 50
11, 831.	Orage		16 x 18-1/2	NYGS	18. 00
11, 832.	Paysage		17 x 20-1/2	NYGS	22. 00
11, 833.	La Petite Gare		17-1/2 x 21	NYGS	22. 00
11, 834.	Pond	c.	8 x 10	ESH	1. 00
11, 835.	Red Field		17-1/2 x 22	ESH	10. 00
		c.	8 x 10	ESH	1. 00
11, 836.	River, 1910		23 x 28-1/2	NYGS	16. 00
		c.	12 x 16	PENN	1. 00
		c.	9-1/2x12-1/2	AP	1. 25
			7 x 8	CFA	1. 00
11, 837.	La Route		18 x 23	ESH	10. 00
11, 838.	La Route avec Peupliers		20-1/2 x 28	NYGS	15. 00
11, 839.	Rue de Village with Snow		14-1/2 x 18	AP	7. 50

11, 840.	Sailing Boats at Anchor			
		18 x 22-1/2	ESH	10. 00
11, 841.	St. Maurice-Les-			
	Charency	18 x 22-1/2	ESH	10. 00
	c.	8 x 10	ESH	1. 00
11, 842.	The Seine at Carrieres			
		18-1/2x22-1/2	ESH	10. 00
11, 843.	The Seine at Chatou			
		18 x 21-1/2	ESH	10. 00
11, 844.	Snow Scene c.	20 x 24	PENN	1. 50
11, 845.	Snowy Countryside	6 x 8	CFA	1. 00
11, 846.	Snowy Village	14 x 18	CFA	7. 50
11, 847.	Steeple Rising Through			
	Trees c.	9-1/2x12-1/2	AP	1. 25
		8 x 12	CFA	1. 00
11, 848.	Still Life with Flowers			
	and Fruits	18 x 23	HNA	5. 95
11, 849.	Still Life with Fruit			
		17 x 24	PENN	1. 50
11, 850.	Street Scene	21 x 25	NYGS	15. 00
11, 851.	Thatched Cottage	18 x 22	ESH	10. 00
11, 852.	Thatched Cottages	18 x 22	ESH	10. 00
	c.	9-1/2x12-1/2	AP	1. 25
	c.	8 x 10	ESH	1. 00
		7 x 8	CFA	1. 00
11, 853.	Through the Village			
		16-1/2x22-1/2	ESH	10. 00
11, 854.	Town on a River	22 x 27	NYGS	18. 00
11, 855.	Trees c.	20 x 24	PENN	1. 50
11, 856.	Vase of Flowers	20-1/2 x 16	PENN	1. 50
11, 857.	The Village c.	20 x 24	PENN	1. 50
11, 858.	Village Church c.	8 x 10	ESH	1. 00
11, 859.	Village in the Snow	24 x 30	CFA	18. 00
11, 860.	Village Landscape	19-1/2 x 24	PENN	1. 50
11, 861.	Village Lane	17-1/2x20-1/2	NYGS	10. 00
11, 862.	Village Street c.	20 x 24	PENN	1. 50
11, 863.	Village Street with			
	Church	20-1/2 x 25	NYGS	18. 00
11, 864.	Village Street in			
	Winter c.	8 x 10	ESH	1. 00
11, 865.	Wheat Landscape	19 x 24	PENN	1. 50
11, 866.	Winter Landscape	22 x 28	NYGS	16. 00
		18 x 24	PENN	1. 50
	c.	9-1/2x12-1/2	AP	1. 25
	c.	7 x 9	AP	1. 00
		6 x 8	CFA	1. 00

VO-DINH (Viet-Namese Contemporary)

11, 867.	Wind Play	14 x 20-1/2	UNICEF		10. 00

VOERMAN, JAN (Dutch, 1857-)

11, 868.	Florals (4)	12 x 9	DAC	ea.	1. 50

VOGEL VON VOGELSTEIN, KARL CHRISTIAN (German, 1788-1868)

11, 869.	Christ and the Children			
		15 x 11	AS	3. 25

11, 870.	The Master's Children			
		28 x 36	CAC	18. 00
11, 871.	Suffer Little Children			
		23-1/2 x 18	IA	7. 50
		14 x 10	IA	3. 00

VOGLER, KURT (German, 1893-)

11, 872.	Road in the Mountains			
		20 x 29	CFA	7. 50
11, 873.	Rocky Mountain Lake			
		20 x 29	CFA	7. 50

VOGT-VILSECK, MAX

11, 874.	Sheep in the Valley 23 x 35-1/2		IA	15. 00
11, 875.	View of the Zugspitze			
		27 x 33-1/2	NYGS	15. 00

VOLK, DOUGLAS (American, 1856-1935)

11, 876.	Abraham Lincoln	20 x 16	NYGS	9. 00
		14 x 11	NYGS	3. 00
	c.	9 x 7	AP	. 50
		8 x 6-1/2	NYGS	1. 00

VOLKAMER

11, 877.	Fruits, Antique			
	(4)	12 x 7	CFA set	20. 00
			or ea.	5. 00

VOLKMANN, HANS RICHARD VON (German, 1860-1927)

11, 878.	Ballet Dancers			
	(4)	14 x 11	IA ea.	2. 00
		8 x 6	IA ea.	1. 00
11, 879.	Little Princess	20 x 16	IA	6. 00
		14 x 11	IA	2. 50

VOLPI, ALFREDO (Brazilian Contemporary)

| 11, 880. | Casas | 25 x 12-1/2 | NYGS | 10. 00 |

VOLTERRANO, IL (FRANCESCHINI, BALDASSARE) (Italian, 1611-1689)

11, 881.	Cupid Sleeping	15 x 10	IA	3. 00
11, 882.	One of Arlotto's			
	Jokes	10 x 15	IA	3. 00

VON MUNCHHAUSEN See MUNCHHAUSEN, VON
VON SALIS, C.

| 11, 883. | Landscape in the | | | |
| | Alps | 21 x 30 | CFA | 12. 00 |

VOS, MARTIN DE (Flemish, 1531-1603)

11, 884.	Apollo and the			
	Muses	10 x 15	IA	3. 00
11, 885.	Little Girl with			
	Bell	13 x 9-1/2	ESH	2. 00
11, 886.	Portrait of a Lady 16 x 12		ESH	10. 00

VOYET, JACQUES (French Contemporary)

11, 887.	Across the River	24 x 40	RL	17. 50
11, 888.	Breton Coaster	22 x 27	RL	15. 00
11, 889.	Les Quatre Barques			
		22 x 26-1/2	RL	10. 00

VU-CAO-DAM (Viet-Namese Contemporary)

11,890.	Blue Madonna	21-1/2 x 16	RL	12.50
11,891.	Lotus Bowl	24 x 16-1/2	RL	15.00
11,892.	Yellow Madonna	21-1/2 x 16	RL	12.50

VUILLARD, JEAN EDOUARD (French, 1868-1940)

11,893.	Le Cargo a Quai	21 x 21	CFA	30.00
11,894.	Madame H. in her Salon	17 x 20	NYGS	20.00
11,895.	Madame Henreaux	8 x 9	CFA	.50
11,896.	Mother and Child c.	8 x 10	ESH	1.00
11,897.	Public Gardens, Tuileries c.	20 x 24	PENN	1.50
11,898.	Vase of Roses c.	10 x 8	ESH	1.00

W

WAAGEN, ADALBERT (German, 1834-)

11,899.	Loisach Valley	23-1/2 x 35	NYGS	15.00

WAGNER, HAROLD (American Contemporary)

11,900.	Antelope	18 x 24-1/2	IA	18.00
11,901.	Blue Bay	17 x 35	CFA	15.00
11,902.	Cranes	18 x 24-1/2	IA	18.00
11,903.	Horses on the Strand	23 x 31-1/2	IA	12.00
11,904.	Running Horses	18 x 24-1/2	IA	18.00
11,905.	Southern Harbor	18 x 35	CFA	15.00
11,906.	Two Horses	18 x 24-1/2	IA	18.00
11,907.	White Town by the Sea	18 x 35	CFA	15.00

WAGNER, PIERRE FREDERIC (French, 1897-)

11,908.	Harbour in Brittany	16 x 23	ESH	6.00

WAIDNER

11,909.	Good Shepherd	21 x 47	AS	12.00
		20 x 40	AS	12.00
		14 x 31	AS	7.50

WALCH, CHARLES (French, 1898-1948)

11,910.	Bird of Alps c.	20 x 24	PENN	1.50
11,911.	Cock	22-1/2 x 17	ESH	10.00
11,912.	Field Flowers	22-1/2 x 18	ESH	10.00
11,913.	The Little Snow	18 x 21-1/2	ESH	10.00
11,914.	Still Life c.	10 x 8	ESH	1.00

WALDMULLER, FERDINAND GEORGE (Austrian, 1793-1865)

11,915.	Almhutte	12 x 10	NYGS	10.00
11,916.	Beethoven	28 x 22-1/2	NYGS	26.00
11,917.	Lake Wolfgang	12 x 10	NYGS	10.00
11,918.	Vienna Woods	22 x 27	NYGS	20.00

WALKER, LESLEY

11,919.	Race	16 x 20	CFA	5.00
11,920.	Sovereign of the Seas	16 x 20	CFA	5.00
11,921.	With a Following Breeze	16 x 20	CFA	5.00

WALKOWITZ, ABRAHAM (American, 1880-)
11,922. Rest Day   7 x 21   AR   3.00
WALL-HILL, WILLIAM G. (American, 1792-1862)
          Views of Eastern U. S.
          (4)   14 x 21   IA   ea. 2.50
11,923.   Fort Edward
11,924.   New York from Governor's Island
11,925.   View near Fort Miller Bridge
11,926.   View near Hudson
WALSCAPELE, JACOB VAN (Dutch, Ac. 1667-1718)
11,927.   Flowerpiece   13 x 10-1/2   ESH   2.00
11,928.   Flowers, Insects and
          Strawberries   22 x 17-1/2   ESH   7.50
WALTER, H.
11,929.   Homeward   16 x 32   CFA   10.00
11,930.   Ilonka   23-1/2 x 20   ESH   Pr. 10.00
11,931.   Old Farm with
          Windmill   23-1/2x31-1/2 ESH   Pr. 10.00
WALTERS, H.
11,932.   On the Lake   16 x 31   CFA   12.00
WALTERS, SAMUEL (English, 1811-1882)
11,933.   Homeward Bound   12 x 14   AA   6.00
11,934.   The "Independence" 9 x 13   AA   2.00
11,935.   Outward Bound   12 x 14   AA   6.00
11,936.   The "Roscoe"   9 x 13   IA   2.00
WALTHER, CARL (German, 1880-1954)
11,937.   Birds (3)   8 x 10   ESH   ea. 1.00
          Avocet and Boatbill Heron
          Pochard
          Waxwing and Nutcracker
11,938.   Boats at Anchor 16 x 30   CFA   10.00
WANG HOUEI (Chinese, 1632-1720)
11,939.   Autumn Landscape 27 x 21   CFA   40.00
WANKLYN, J.
11,940.   Horses (6)   11 x 8   ESH   ea. 2.00
11,941.   Curious Foals
11,942.   Exit of the Fawns
11,943.   Four Calves
11,944.   Moonlight and her Foal
11,945.   Shetland Mare and Foal
11,946.   Young Donkeys
11,947.   Ponies in a Beech
          Wood   9-1/2 x 12   ESH   2.00
11,948.   Ponies on a Hill 9 x 12   ESH   2.00
WARD EDMOND F.
11,949.   Enter the Law   18 x 24   AA   10.00
WARD, VERNON D. (English, 1905-)
11,950.   Age of Innocence 20 x 24   ESH   7.50
11,951.   Anemones   11-1/2x15-1/2 ESH   4.00
11,952.   Anemones and
          Daisies   15 x 12-1/2   ESH   4.00
                           12 x 9-1/2   ESH   2.00

11,953.	Arrangement for July	26 x 22	AS	12.00
11,954.	August Beauty	15 x 29	ESH	7.50
11,955.	Autumn Harvest	18-1/2 x 22	ESH	7.50
		10 x 12	ESH	2.00
11,956.	Azaleas in May	18-1/2 x 22	ESH	7.50
		10 x 12	ESH	2.00
11,957.	Balmosal Castle	17 x 22	AS	5.00
11,958.	Barnagle Geese	20 x 16-1/2	AS	5.00
11,959.	Beauty Adorned	12 x 10	ESH	2.00
11,960.	Ben Slioch, Loch Maree, Scotland	12 x 15	ESH	3.00
11,961.	Blackcaps at Low Tide	13 x 20	AS	5.00
11,962.	Breaking Wave	11 x 15	ESH	3.00
11,963.	Cherry Blossom	18-1/2 x 22	ESH	7.50
11,964.	Cherry Blossom and Daffodils	32-1/2 x 14	ESH	10.00
11,965.	Clearing Day	13 x 20	CFA	7.50
11,966.	Clearing Day, Snowdon, North Wales	12 x 15	ESH	3.00
11,967.	Decor for a Rose	24 x 13	ESH	6.00
	Detail	12 x 10	ESH	2.00
11,968.	Decor for Two	30 x 10	AS	6.00
11,969.	Early Days	20 x 16	ESH	6.00
	Detail	12 x 10	ESH	2.00
11,970.	English Roses and French Pink Roses	17 x 22	AS	5.00
11,971.	English Roses and French Porcelain	17 x 22	IA	5.00
11,972.	Evening at Ullswater	24 x 30	AS	7.50
11,973.	Family in the Park	24 x 18-1/2	ESH	7.50
11,974.	Family Outing	20 x 26	AS	12.00
11,975.	Fawns in May	18 x 14	ESH	5.00
		12 x 10	ESH	2.00
11,976.	Flamingo Pink	30 x 10	AS	6.00
11,977.	Fleeting Shadows	12 x 16	ESH	4.00
11,978.	Forest Family	18 x 23-1/2	AS	12.00
11,979.	Freshening Winds	17 x 24	ESH	7.50
11,980.	Garden Beauty (Detail)	12 x 10	ESH	2.00
11,981.	Glade	18 x 14	ESH	5.00
		12 x 10	ESH	2.00
11,982.	Gladioli and Petunias	22 x 18-1/2	ESH	7.50
11,983.	Glory of June	18-1/2 x 22	ESH	7.50
11,984.	Gold for a Tortoise Shell	24 x 13	ESH	6.00
	Detail	12 x 10	ESH	2.00
11,985.	Gulls Alighting	17 x 24	ESH	7.50
11,986.	Harmony of Spring	20 x 24	ESH	7.50
		12-1/2 x 15	ESH	5.00

11, 987.	Harmony in White	30 x 10	AS	6. 00
11, 988.	Highland Spring	17 x 22	ESH	7. 50
11, 989.	June Bouquet	20 x 16	ESH	6. 00
11, 990.	June Roses	19-1/2x18-1/2	ESH	7. 50
11, 991.	Lakeside Beauty	20 x 16-1/2	AS	7. 50
11, 992.	Lakeside in Spring	20 x 24	ESH	7. 50
11, 993.	Land's End	25 x 36	AS	7. 50
11, 994.	Light of June	17 x 22	IA	5. 00
11, 995.	Light of Spring	30 x 10	AS	6. 00
11, 996.	Magic of Spring	18 x 24	ESH	7. 50
11, 997.	Mallard and Azaleas			
		30 x 10	AS	6. 00
11, 998.	May Flowering	18-1/2 x 22	ESH	7. 50
11. 999.	Mood of Spring	17 x 25	ESH	10. 00
12, 000.	Morning in September			
		16 x 12-1/2	ESH	5. 00
12, 001.	Mountains at Mourne			
		17 x 20	AS	3. 00
12, 002.	Nature's Mirror	20 x 24	ESH	7. 50
12, 003.	Old Cottages, Killarney			
		17 x 20	AS	3. 00
12, 004.	Old Harry Rocks,			
	Swanage, Dorset	12 x 15	ESH	3. 00
12, 005.	Oyster Catchers	11 x 15	ESH	4. 00
12, 006.	Peonies and Lupins			
		32-1/2 x 14	ESH	10. 00
12, 007.	Peonies and Porcelain			
		17 x 22	IA	5. 00
12, 008.	Pink Feet at Evening			
		13 x 20	AS	5. 00
12, 009.	Pintails Among			
	Daffodils	10-1/2 x 16	ESH	7. 50
12, 010.	Pintails Arriving	18-1/2 x 22	ESH	7. 50
12, 011.	Pintails in May	20 x 16-1/2	AS	5. 00
12, 012.	Prelude to Spring	15 x 12-1/2	ESH	4. 00
12, 013.	Rendezvous in Summer			
		29 x 12	ESH	6. 00
12, 014.	Rhythm in the Pool	30 x 10	AS	6. 00
12, 015.	Roses and Antirphinums			
		22 x 18-1/2	ESH	7. 50
12, 016.	Roses and Delphiniums			
		22 x 18-1/2	ESH	7. 50
		15 x 12-1/2	ESH	4. 00
12, 017.	Roses in July	22 x 16-1/2	ESH	10. 00
12, 018.	Scarlet for the			
	Garden	19-1/2x15-1/2	ESH	6. 00
	Detail	12 x 10	ESH	2. 00
12, 109.	Shovelers Coming			
	Inland	18 x 22	ESH	7. 50
		12 x 15	ESH	5. 00
12, 020.	Silverdee	17 x 22	AS	5. 00
12, 021.	Spring Babies	16 x 20	ESH	7. 50

12, 022.	Spring Bouquet	22 x 18-1/2	ESH		7. 50
		20 x 16	ESH		6. 00
12, 023.	Spring Colour	23 x 19	ESH		7. 50
12, 024.	Spring Flighting	20 x 24	ESH		7. 50
12, 025.	Spring Portrait	15-1/2 x 12	ESH		5. 00
12, 026.	Spring Preening	20 x 16-1/2	AS		5. 00
12, 027.	Spring Vista	22 x 18-1/2	ESH		7. 50
12, 028.	Spring's Heralds	15 x 13	ESH		5. 00
12, 029.	Springtime on the Lake	20-1/2 x 16	ESH		7. 50
12, 030.	Squall over Newlyn, Cornwall	12 x 15	ESH		3. 00
12, 031.	Street of the Black- smith	10-1/2 x 16	ESH		4. 00
12, 032.	Sudden Fears	19 x 24	ESH		7. 50
12. 033.	Summer Decor	25 x 19-1/2	ESH		7. 50
12, 034.	Summer Fragrance	18-1/2 x 22	ESH		7. 50
		12 x 15	ESH		4. 00
12, 035.	Summer Gold	17 x 22	IA		5. 00
12, 036.	Swan Lake (Birds)	20 x 16-1/2	AS		5. 00
12, 037.	Sweet September	14-1/2 x 29	ESH		7. 50
12, 038.	Teal on the Flats	20 x 16-1/2	AS		5. 00
12, 039.	Teal and Wistaria	30 x 10	AS		6. 00
12, 040.	Tones of Autumn	16 x 20	AS		7. 50
12, 041.	Tributes to Godesses: (6)	20 x 16	AS	ea.	2. 00
12, 042.	Ceres				
12, 043.	Diana				
12, 044.	Leda				
12, 045.	Persephone				
12, 046.	Psyche				
12, 047.	Venus				
12, 048.	Widgeon at Evening	20 x 16-1/2	AS		5. 00
12, 049.	Wings upon a Rose	29 x 12	ESH		6. 00
12, 050.	Wonder of Spring	30 x 10	AS		6. 00
12, 051.	Woodland Babies	16 x 20	AS		2. 00
WARFIELD, J. E.					
12, 052.	Landscapes and Street Scenes (4)	24 x 36	AK	ea.	6. 00
		12 x 16	AK	ea.	2. 50
		11 x 14	AK	ea.	1. 50
		8 x 10	AK	ea.	1. 00
	Landscapes and Street Scenes (4)	24 x 18	AK	ea.	2. 50
		16 x 9	AK	ea.	2. 00
		12 x 6	AK	ea.	1. 25
WARING, H. F.					
12, 053.	The Wren Front	10 x 15	ESH		2. 00
WARNER, J. H. (American, Ac. 1840)					
12, 054.	French Scenes (4)				
	c.	20 x 24	PENN	ea.	1. 50
12, 055.	Boats on the Seine				

12, 056.	Bridge over the Seine				
12, 057.	Springtime Along the Seine				
12, 058.	Street in Montmartre				

WARREN, EDMUND G. (English, d. 1909)

12, 059.	Toreador, No. 1 and				
	No. 2	20 x 9	AA	ea.	5. 00

WARSHAWSKY, ABEL GEORGE (American, 1883-)

12, 060.	La Belle Bretonne	20 x 16	IA		6. 00
12, 061.	La Fenetre Bleue				
	(Blue Window)	25 x 32	IA		7. 50

WATENPHUL, MAX P. (German)

12, 062.	Sailing Boats in				
	Venice	18 x 25	CFA		15. 00
12, 063.	Still Life	26 x 31	CFA		18. 00

WATERS, BILLIE (English, 1896-)

12, 064.	Baby Seal	16 x 11	ESH		12. 00
12, 065.	Innocence	14 x 16	ESH		12. 00
12, 066.	Little Fawn	14 x 16	ESH		12. 00
12, 067.	Lotus Pool	16 x 21	ESH		15. 00
12, 068.	Neptune's Horses	11-1/2 x 13	ESH		4. 00
12, 069.	White Doe	14 x 16	ESH		12. 00

WATSON, R. W. (American Contemporary)

12, 070.	Summer	16 x 20	CFA		2. 50
12, 071.	Winter	16 x 20	CFA		2. 50

WATTEAU, JEAN ANTOINE (French, 1684-1721)

12, 072.	After the Hunt	22 x 13	CAC		10. 00
12, 073.	The Art Gallery				
	(2 Parts) ea.	29-1/2x26-1/2	NYGS	ea.	28. 00
				pair	50. 00
12, 074.	Autumn	22 x 13	CAC		10. 00
12, 075.	Bird-Nesting	14 x 10	CAC		7. 50
12, 076.	Buffoon	9 x 12	CAC		2. 50
12, 077.	La Collation	12 x 9	IA		10. 00
12, 078.	The Concert	19 x 28	NYGS		12. 00
12, 079.	La Danse	28 x 33	NYGS		30. 00
		18 x 24	CAC		10. 00
12, 080.	La Danse en Plein				
	Aire	9 x 12	IA		10. 00
12, 081.	Deux Cousines	12 x 14	CFA		
12, 082.	Embarkation for				
	Cythera	21-1/2x31-1/2	NYGS		20. 00
		18 x 20	PENN		1. 50
		12 x 18	NYGS		5. 00
		10 x 15	IA		3. 00
		7 x 11	NYGS		. 50
12, 083.	L'Escarpolette				
	(The Swing)	14 x 11	CAC		7. 50
		12 x 10	IA		10. 00
12, 084.	Faux Pas	11 x 13-1/2	AJ		2. 50
12, 085.	Fete d'Amour	9 x 12	IA		10. 00
12, 086.	Fete Champetre	9 x 12	IA		10. 00
	c.	7 x 9	AP		. 50

12, 087.	"Finette"	9 x 7	IA	3. 00
12, 088.	Flute Player	11 x 14	IA	3. 00
		10 x 15	AS	3. 25
12, 089.	French Comedians	6 x 7	NYGS	. 50
12, 090.	Gallant	14 x 10	CAC	7. 50
12, 091.	La Gamme d'Amour			
	c.	8 x 10	ESH	1. 00
12, 092.	Gersaint's Signboard			
	c.	18 x 23	HNA	5. 95
12, 093.	Gilles, 1721 - Toile			
		13 x 11	IA	3. 00
	c.	9-1/2x12-1/2	AP	1. 25
		8 x 10	CFA	1. 00
12, 094.	Gilles and his			
	Family c.	7 x 9	AP	. 50
12, 095.	Girl Seated	9 x 7	CFA	4. 00
12, 096.	Guitarist	14 x 10	CAC	7. 50
12, 097.	Hunting Party	22 x 13	CAC	10. 00
12, 098.	Huntress	9 x 12	CAC	2. 50
12, 099.	L'Indifferent	12 x 9	CFA	2. 50
	c.	10 x 8	ESH	1. 00
		10 x 7	IA	3. 00
12, 100.	Lecon D'Amour	9 x 12	IA	10. 00
12, 101.	Lecon de Musique	9 x 12	IA	10. 00
12, 102.	Life in the Country	19-1/2 x 28	NYGS	20. 00
12, 103.	Little Musician	12 x 9	CFA	2. 50
12, 104.	Le Mezzetin	20-1/2 x 16	AP	5. 00
		8 x 6	NYGS	. 50
12, 105.	Mezzetins	9 x 7	NYGS	4. 00
12, 106.	Party in a Park	12 x 18	CAC	5. 00
12, 107.	Pastorale	22 x 18	NYGS	18. 00
		13 x 11	IA	3. 00
		10 x 9	NYGS	. 50
12, 108.	Pilgrim	14 x 10	CFA	4. 50
12, 109.	Pipe	14 x 10	CAC	7. 50
12, 110.	Shepherdess	9 x 12	CAC	2. 50
12, 111.	Spring	22 x 13	CAC	10. 00
12, 112.	Spring Song	14 x 10	CAC	7. 50
12, 113.	Summer	22 x 13	CAC	10. 00
		15-1/2 x 12	NYGS	14. 00
12, 114.	Trumpeter	11 x 14	CAC	7. 50
12, 115.	Two Cousins	14 x 12	CAC	7. 50
12, 116.	Winter	13 x 22	CAC	10. 00

WATTS, FREDERICK WATERS (English, 1800-1862)

12, 117.	Vale of Dedham	24 x 30	RL	15. 00

WATTS, GEORGE FREDERICK (English, 1817-1904)

12, 118.	Hope	20 x 16	CAC	5. 00
		14 x 11	CAC	3. 00
		12 x 9	CAC	2. 00
12, 119.	Sir Galahad	28 x 14	CAC	6. 00
		20 x 12	CAC	3. 50
	c.	9 x 7	AP	. 50

WAUGH, FREDERICK J. (American, 1861-1940)

12, 120.	A Bit of the Cape	30 x 36	NYGS	15. 00
		11 x 14	NYGS	3. 00
12, 121.	Breakers	26 x 36	IA	15. 00
12, 122.	Coast of Main	27 x 36	NYGS	15. 00
12, 123.	March--North			
	Atlantic	16 x 24	NYGS	7. 50
12, 124.	New Jersey Coast	15-1/2x21-1/2	IA	7. 50
12, 125.	Open Sea	27 x 36	NYGS	15. 00
12, 126.	Polar Bear c.	7 x 9	AP	. 50
12, 127.	Pounding Surf	22 x 28	NYGS	10. 00
		17 x 21	NYGS	7. 50
		11 x 14	NYGS	3. 00
12, 128.	Wild Weather	15 x 24	PENN	1. 50
12, 129.	Windward Shore	27 x 35-1/2	NYGS	15. 00
		11 x 14	NYGS	3. 00

WEBER, MAX (American, 1881-1961)

12, 130.	Flower Piece	24 x 20	AA	10. 00
12, 131.	In the Temple	21 x 14	AR	3. 00
12, 132.	Interior with Still			
	Life c.	9 x 7	NYGS	. 50
12, 133.	Still Life, 1950	19-1/2x23-1/2	PENN	1. 50
12, 134.	Still Life--Flowers	8 x 6	NYGS	. 50
12, 135.	Still Life with			
	Flowers	22-1/2 x 18	NYGS	10. 00
12, 136.	Summer	19 x 14-1/2	NYGS	7. 50
12, 137.	Three Literary			
	Gentlemen c.	8 x 10	NYGS	. 50

WEBER, ROY (American Contemporary)

12, 138.	Boogie Beat	11 x 14	AR	7. 50

WEBSTER, TOM (English, 1890-)

	Romantic Illustrations				
	(4)	14 x 10	CFA	ea.	1. 50
12, 139.	Love's Token				
12, 140.	Love's Young Dream				
12, 141.	Proposal				
12, 142.	Stolen Meeting				

WEBSTER, WALTER ERNEST (English, 1878-)

12, 143.	Heirlooms	22 x 18-1/2	ESH	15. 00
12, 144.	Sonata	22 x 21	ESH	15. 00

WECUS, WALTER VON (German, 1893-)

12, 145.	Ragusa	22 x 27-1/2	ESH	12. 00
12, 146.	Sailing the			
	Mediterranean	22 x 18	ESH	7. 50

WEHLE, JOHANNES (German, 1848-1930)

12, 147.	And They Followed			
	Him	19-1/2x31-1/2	IA	10. 00
		7 x 11	IA	1. 20

WEHN, R.

12, 148.	Sheepherd	20 x 16	ESH	Pr.	5. 00

WEIMANN, PAUL

12, 149.	Winter Landscape	20-1/2 x 29	ESH	10. 00

WEISGARD
      Nursery Rhymes
      (6)   11 x 14   PENN ea. 1. 50
12, 150.   Hey Diddle Diddle
12, 151.   Jumbo and Mouse
12, 152.   Kittens in Toyland
12, 153.   Mary Had a Little Lamb
12, 154.   Pups in Playland
12, 155.   Three Little Kittens
WEISSENBRUCH, JOHANNES HENDRIK (Dutch, 1824-1903)
12, 156.   Holland Landscape 19 x 31   CFA   12. 00
WELTERS, G.
12, 157.   Breaking Wave   20 x 40   IA   12. 00
12, 158.   Sunlit Sea   24 x 34-1/2 IA   12. 00
WENCK, PAUL (American, 1892-)
12, 159.   Grand Canyon,
           Arizona   27 x 36   CAC   12. 00
12, 160.   Rockies from Bear
           Lake   27 x 36   NYGS   16. 00
WENCKE
12, 161.   Mixed Flowers   17 x 14   CFA   3. 00
12, 162.   Sunflowers   14 x 17   CFA   3. 00
WESSON, EDWARD (English Contemporary)
12, 163.   Fishing Harbor in
           Cornwall   10 x 8   CFA   1. 00
WEST, BENJAMIN (American-English, 1738-1820)
12, 164.   Penn's Treaty c. 7 x 9   AP   . 50
WESTAL
12, 165.   Flying Home   24 x 48   DAC   10. 00
12, 166.   Golden Days   24 x 48   DAC   10. 00
12, 167.   Old Stone Bridge 24 x 60   DAC   15. 00
                        24 x 48   DAC   10. 00
12, 168.   Rustic Mill   15 x 30   DAC   2. 00
WESTALL, WILLIAM (English, 1765-1836)
12, 169.   Eton College   7 x 10   CFA   6. 00
12, 170.   Sion House   7 x 10   CFA   6. 00
WEYDEN, ROGIER VAN DER (ROGER DE LA PASTOURE) (Flemish,
1399-1464)
12, 171.   Adoration of the
           Three Kings   16-1/2 x 46 IA   24. 00
12, 172.   Annunciation   18-1/2x19-1/2 ESH   10. 00
                        8 x 5   IA   3. 00
12, 173.   Portrait of a Lady
                c.   16 x 12   PENN   1. 00
                      14 x 10   NYGS   7. 50
12, 174.   St. George and the
           Dragon   6 x 4   NYGS   6. 00
12, 175.   Still Life   c. 8 x 10   NYGS   . 50
12, 176.   Triptych Sforza   9 x 15   IA   3. 00
WEYTS, PAUWELS (Dutch, d. 1629)
12, 177.   The Saxony of
           Boston   20-1/2 x 26 AA   12. 00
                      10 x 13   AA   2. 00

WHEAT, JOHN
12, 178.	Good Old Winter			
	Time	18 x 26	PENN	1. 50
12, 179.	Red Bridge	13-1/2 x 35	NYGS	12. 00
12, 180.	September Harvest	13-1/2 x 35	NYGS	12. 00
12, 181.	Summer Winds	20 x 36	NYGS	12. 00

WHEATLEY, FRANCIS (English, 1747-1801)
| 12, 182. | Harvest Time | 28 x 36 | NYGS | 16. 00 |
| | | 20 x 26 | NYGS | 10. 00 |

WHISTLER, JAMES ABBOTT MC NEILL (American, 1834-1903)
12, 183.	At the Piano c.	7 x 9	AP	. 50
12, 184.	Battersea Beach	20 x 30	NYGS	16. 00
12, 185.	Battersea Bridge			
	c.	7 x 9	AP	. 50
12, 186.	Little Girl in			
	White	14 x 10	NYGS	7. 50
	c.	9 x 7	AP	. 50
12, 187.	Mother of the Artist			
	(Whistler's Mother)	20 x 24	NYGS	10. 00
		18 x 20	PENN	1. 50
		13-1/2x15-1/2	DAC	2. 50
		11 x 14	NYGS	3. 00
		8-1/2x9-1/2	NYGS	1. 00
12, 188.	Thomas Carlyle	19 x 16	ESH	12. 00
12, 189.	The White Girl	24 x 12	NYGS	12. 00

WHISTLER, REX JOHN (English, 1905-)
| 12, 190. | Caroline | 16 x 12 | ESH | 15. 00 |

WHITE, ETHELBERT (English, 1891-)
12, 191.	Deer-Park, Arundel			
		17-1/2 x 21	ESH	15. 00
12, 192.	Summer	16 x 19-1/2	ESH	6. 00

WHITNEY, E. A.
	New England Scenes			
	(4)	8 x 10	AA	ea. . 90
12, 193.	Fishing Village			
12, 194.	Lobsterman's Cove			
12, 195.	Saddle River			
12, 196.	Visitor			

WHORF, JOHN (American, 1903-1959)
12, 197.	Beachcombers	15 x 20	CAC	7. 50
12, 198.	Brightening Seine	13-1/2 x 19	NYGS	7. 50
12, 199.	Winter by the Sea	12-1/2 x 19	NYGS	6. 00

WICKHAM, PEGGY
12, 200.	Circus Comes to			
	Town	18 x 22	ESH	3. 50
12, 201.	Day in the Country	17 x 22	ESH	3. 50
12, 202.	Farm Scene	17-1/2 x 22	ESH	3. 50
12, 203.	Foals	17-1/2 x 22	ESH	3. 50
12, 204.	On the Beach	18 x 22	ESH	3. 50
12, 205.	Shasta Daisies	22 x 17	ESH	10. 00
12, 206.	Spanish Fishing			
	Village	17-1/2 x 22	ESH	3. 50

12, 207.	Village	17-1/2 x 22	ESH	3. 50

WIEGAND

12, 208.	Indian Summer	20 x 16	CAC	2. 50
12, 209.	Mother Earth	21 x 25	CAC	10. 00
12, 210.	November Glow	14 x 29	CAC	7. 50
12, 211.	Peonies	20 x 16	CAC	5. 00
12, 212.	Shimmering Fields	20 x 16	CAC	2. 50
12, 213.	Silvery Birches	14 x 29	CAC	7. 50

WIHAG

12, 214.	Venice	20 x 28	ESH	7. 00

WIJNANTS, JOHANNES (Dutch, 1620/5-1684)

12, 215.	Evening Landscape	29 x 37	NYGS	18. 00

WILA (Spanish Contemporary)

12, 216.	Animals (4)	16 x 12	IA	ea.	1. 50
12, 217.	Corzo (Fawn)				
12, 218.	Lucero (Foal)				
12, 219.	Pollino (Donkey)				
12, 220.	Platero (Donkey)				
	Dancers (2)	22-1/2x15-1/2	IA	ea.	5. 00
12, 221.	Piconera				
12, 222.	Revoltosa				

WILCOX, LESLIE A.

12, 223.	Eynsford, Kent	20 x 30	AS	7. 50
12, 224.	Mr Pepys' Navy	20 x 40-1/2	AS	22. 50

WILKE, PAUL ERNST (German, 1894-)

12, 225.	Going to Sea	20 x 29	CFA	7. 50
12, 226.	In the Harbor	20 x 29	CFA	7. 50

WILKINSON, NORMAN (English Contemporary(

12, 227.	White Cliffs of			
	Dover	15 x 21	ESH	6. 00

WILKS, BEN

12, 228.	Magic City No. 1			
	and No. 2	18 x 36 ea.	CFA	ea. 20. 00

WILLARD, ARCHIBALD M. (American, 1836-1918)

12, 229.	Spirity of '76	28 x 21	NYGS	12. 00
		26 x 20	CAC	7. 50
		21 x 16	AP	4. 00
		14 x 10-1/2	NYGS	3. 00
		12 x 9	CAC	2. 00
	c.	9 x 7	AP	. 50

WILLIAMS, A.

12, 230.	Glory of Summer	10 x 12	ESH	2. 00

WILLIAMS, GEORGE A. (American, 1875-)

12, 231.	In the Trossachs	24 x 30	AA	10. 00

WILLIAMS, WALTER (American Contemporary)

12, 232.	Peaceful Glade	24 x 48	AA	15. 00

WILMER, GEORGE (American Contemporary)

12, 233.	Mountain Lake	24 x 36	DAC	7. 50
		24 x 30	PENN	1. 95
12, 234.	Mountain Peaks	24 x 48	DAC	10. 00
12, 235.	Timberline Lake	24 x 36	DAC	7. 50
		24 x 30	PENN	1. 95

WILSON, MAURICE
12, 236.	Fallow Deer	19 x 22-1/2	ESH	7.50
12, 237.	Mallard Family	17-1/2 x 21	ESH	7.50
12, 238.	Norwegian Pony	15-1/2 x 21	ESH	4.00
12, 239.	Young Donkey	14-1/2 x 19	ESH	5.00

WINANTS, A. J. See WIJNANTS, JAN
WINDISCH-GRAETZ, F. J. N. (American Contemporary)
12, 240.	Spanish Riding School			
	(6)	12 x 8-1/2	NYGS	ea. 3.00 or
12, 241.	Capriole			set 15.00
12, 242.	Croupade			
12, 243.	Passage			
12, 244.	Piaffe			
12, 245.	Pirouette			
12, 246.	Volte			
	Spanish Riding School			
	(4)	12 x 18	NYGS	ea. 6.00
				set 20.00
12, 247.	Pas de Deux I			
12, 248.	Pas de Deux II			
12, 249.	Pas de Trois I			
12, 250.	Pas de Trois II			

WINKLER, HARRY
12, 251.	African Coast	16 x 31-1/2	ESH	7.00
12, 252.	Bosphorus	14 x 29-1/2	ESH	8.00
12, 253.	Bosphorus	31-1/2 x 16	ESH	7.00
12, 254.	Mallorca	14 x 39-1/2	ESH	8.00
12, 255.	Parrot	31-1/2 x 16	ESH	7.00
12, 256.	Venice	16 x 31-1/2	ESH	7.00

WINTER, FRITZ (German Contemporary)
12, 257.	Africana	28 x 30	NYGS	20.00
12, 258.	Before the Fire	12 x 13-1/2	AP	1.00
	c.	7 x 9	AP	1.00
12, 259.	Black Figurations	24 x 31-1/2	NYGS	20.00
12, 260.	Bright Yellow	20 x 21-1/2	NYGS	20.00
12, 261.	Grand Finale	18 x 31	CFA	20.00

WINTERHALTER, FRANZ XAVIER (German, 1806-1873)
12, 262.	Empress Eugenie and the Ladies of her Court	25 x 36	NYGS	18.00
		18 x 26	NYGS	10.00
	c.	8 x 10	ESH	1.00

WINTZ, RAYMOND (French, 1884-1956)
12, 263.	Blue Door	30 x 24	NYGS	12.00
		22 x 17-1/2	NYGS	7.50
		11 x 8	CFA	1.00
		10-1/2x8-1/2	NYGS	1.00
12, 264.	Breton Fishing Village	20 x 24	ESH	10.00
12, 265.	Breton Window	22 x 17-1/2	RL	6.00
12, 266.	Coast Scene in Brittany	20 x 24	ESH	10.00

12, 267.	Fishing Boats	21-1/2x17-1/2	NYGS		7. 50
12, 268.	Harbor Street	21-1/2 x 17	NYGS		7. 50
		10-1/2x8-1/2	NYGS		1. 00
		10 x 8	CFA		1. 00
12, 269.	Hydrangeas	20 x 24	ESH		10. 00
12, 270.	Joinville	23 x 28	NYGS		12. 00
12, 271.	Open Door	20 x 24	NYGS		10. 00
12, 272.	Return of the Tunny				
	Boat	7 x 11	CFA		1. 00
12, 273.	Road to the Sea	16 x 21	ESH		6. 00
		11 x 14-1/2	ESH		4. 00
12, 274.	Sunny Morning,				
	Ploumanach	19 x 25	RL		7. 50

WITTEL, VAN See VANVITELLI, GASPAR
WITZ, CONRAD (Swiss, 1398-1447)

12, 275.	Annunciation	28 x 28-1/2	NYGS		30. 00
12, 276.	Mourning Under the				
	Cross	10-1/2 x 14	NYGS		15. 00
12, 277.	St. Christopher				
		c. 23 x 18	HNA		5. 95

WOLSTENHOLME, DEAN (English, 1757-1837)

12, 278.	Essex Hunt Near				
	Epping	25 x 32-1/2	AA		12. 00

WOMACKA, WALTER (German Contemporary)

12, 279.	Landscape of the Isle				
	of Usedom c.	16 x 20	AP		5. 00
12, 280.	On the Shore	16 x 19	AP		5. 00

WONG, TYRUS (Chinese-American Contemporary)

12, 281.	Calligraphic Rhythm				
		12 x 39	IA		10. 00
12, 282.	Enchanted Isle				
	(2)	14 x 18	IA	ea.	7. 50
12, 283.	Fantasy (2)	14 x 18	IA	ea.	7. 50
12, 284.	Imaginary Landscape				
	(2)	14 x 18	IA	ea.	7. 50
12, 285.	Spring	12 x 35	IA		10. 00
12, 286.	Spring Eternal (2)	14 x 18	IA	ea.	7. 50
12, 287.	Tai-Ling in the				
	Rain	16 x 20-1/2	IA		5. 00
12, 288.	Three Friends of				
	Winter (3)	30 x 9-1/2	IA	ea.	7. 50
12, 289.	Bamboo				
12, 290.	Pine				
12, 291.	Plum				

WOOD, CARYL (MRS. ROBERT WOOD) (American Contemporary)

12, 292.	Still Life with				
	Melon	18 x 21	IA		6. 00

WOOD, CHRISTOPHER (English, 1901-1930)

12, 293.	Blue Boat	15-1/2 x 22	NYGS		12. 00
		13 x 22	CFA		10. 00
12, 294.	Market Cross,				
	Treboul	17 x 21	ESH		15. 00

12, 295.	Rug Seller	18 x 23	ESH	15. 00
12, 296.	Zebra and Parachute			
	c.	7 x 9	AP	. 50

WOOD, GRANT (American, 1892-1942)

12, 297.	American Gothic		24 x 20	DAC	7. 50
			24 x 19	PENN	1. 50
			20-1/2 x 17	NYGS	10. 00
			16 x 12	DAC	2. 50
			9-1/2x7-1/2	NYGS	1. 00
		c.	9 x 7	AP	. 50
12, 298.	Fall Plowing	c.	20 x 24	PENN	1. 50
			12 x 16	NYGS	5. 00
12, 299.	Midnight Ride of				
	Paul Revere		18 x 24	NYGS	10. 00
12, 300.	Spring in Town		20 x 18	NYGS	9. 00
12, 301.	Spring Landscape		18 x 21-1/2	NYGS	9. 00
			8-1/2 x 11	NYGS	1. 50
12, 302.	Stone City		21 x 27-1/2	NYGS	12. 00
		c.	20 x 24	PENN	1. 50
			16 x 21	NYGS	9. 00
		c.	7 x 9	AP	. 50
12, 303.	Woman with Plants		18 x 16	NYGS	7. 50
12, 304.	Young Corn		12 x 16	NYGS	5. 00
		c.	7 x 9	AP	. 50

WOOD, HUNTER

12, 305.	Ships (6)	12 x 16	DAC	ea.	2. 50
12, 306.	Blessing of the Bay				
12, 307.	Gertrude L. Thebaud				
12, 308.	Halifax				
12, 309.	Lightning				
12, 310.	S. S. Savanah				
12, 311.	Wing and Wind				

WOOD, ROBERT (American, 1889-)

12, 312.	Along the Pacific				
		c.	20 x 24	PENN	1. 50
12, 313.	Autumn Bronze		24 x 60	DAC	15. 00
			24 x 48	DAC	10. 00
			15 x 30	DAC	2. 00
12, 314.	Autumn Glade		24 x 36	IA	12. 00
			16 x 22	IA	3. 50
			12 x 16	IA	2. 00
12, 315.	Autumn Leaves		24 x 48	DAC	10. 00
			24 x 40	DAC	8. 50
12, 316.	Autumn Mood		16 x 20	IA	3. 00
12, 317.	Autumn Sunset		24 x 36	DAC	7. 50
			18 x 26	PENN	1. 50
			12 x 16	DAC	2. 50
12, 318.	Brook		16 x 20	IA	3. 00
12, 319.	California Desert		25 x 30	IA	10. 00
12, 320.	Carmel Coast		24 x 32	IA	10. 00
			16 x 20	IA	3. 00
12, 321.	Desert Grandeur		24 x 36	DAC	7. 50

12,322.	Desert in Spring	24 x 36	IA	12.00
		16 x 22	IA	3.50
12,323.	Desert Foliage	24 x 36	DAC	7.50
12,324.	Desert Vista	24 x 48	DAC	10.00
12,325.	Dreamer's Cove	25 x 30	IA	10.00
12,326.	Early Fall	24 x 36	IA	12.00
12,327.	Early Snow	24 x 36	IA	12.00
		12 x 16	IA	2.00
12,328.	Early Spring	24 x 36	DAC	7.50
	c.	20 x 24	PENN	1.50
		18 x 26	DAC	6.00
		12 x 16	DAC	2.50
12,329.	English Country- side	24 x 48	DAC	10.00
		15 x 30	DAC	2.00
12,330.	Evening in the Tetons	24 x 36	IA	12.00
		12 x 16	IA	2.00
12,331.	Fields of Blue	12 x 16	IA	2.00
12,332.	Golden Maples	26 x 36	IA	12.00
		16 x 22	IA	3.50
12,333.	Golden Shore	16 x 20	IA	3.00
12,334.	Golden West	24 x 36	IA	12.00
12,335.	Grand Teton	24 x 48	DAC	10.00
		24 x 36	DAC	7.50
	c.	24 x 30	PENN	1.95
		18 x 26	DAC	6.00
		12 x 16	DAC	2.50
12,336.	High Glory	25 x 30	IA	10.00
12,337.	In the Tetons, Wyoming	25 x 30	IA	10.00
		12 x 16	IA	2.00
12,338.	Lupines and Owl Clover	21 x 47	DAC	10.00
12,339.	Majestic Peaks	24 x 36	DAC	7.50
	c.	24 x 30	PENN	1.95
		18 x 26	DAC	6.00
		12 x 16	DAC	2.50
12,340.	Mill Stream	24 x 36	DAC	7.50
		12 x 16	DAC	2.50
12,341.	Montana Mountains	24 x 36	IA	12.00
12,342.	Mount Adams, Colorado	25 x 30	IA	10.00
12,343.	Mountain Home			
	c.	20 x 24	PENN	1.50
12,344.	Mountain Lake	24 x 36	IA	12.00
12,345.	Mountain Retreat			
	c.	24 x 30	PENN	1.95
12,346.	Mount Shasta	24 x 48	DAC	10.00
		24 x 36	IA	12.00
	c.	20 x 24	PENN	1.50
		12 x 30	DAC	5.00

12, 347.	Mountain Stream		24 x 36	DAC	7. 50
		c.	20 x 24	PENN	1. 50
			18 x 26	DAC	6. 00
			12 x 16	DAC	2. 50
12, 348.	North Country		24 x 36	IA	12. 00
12, 349.	Ocean Breeze		24 x 48	IA	12. 00
12, 350.	October Gold		24 x 48	DAC	10. 00
			24 x 36	IA	12. 00
		c.	20 x 24	PENN	1. 50
			12 x 30	DAC	5. 00
12, 351.	October Morn		24 x 48	DAC	10. 00
			24 x 36	DAC	7. 50
		c.	20 x 24	PENN	1. 50
			18 x 26	DAC	6. 00
			12 x 16	DAC	2. 50
12, 352.	Old Mill		24 x 48	DAC	10. 00
			24 x 36	DAC	7. 50
		c.	20 x 24	PENN	1. 50
			18 x 26	DAC	6. 00
			12 x 16	DAC	2. 50
12, 353.	Owens Valley		24 x 48	DAC	10. 00
12, 354.	Pacific Coast		24 x 36	IA	12. 00
			16 x 20	IA	3. 00
			12 x 16	IA	2. 00
12, 355.	Pacific Sunset c.		20 x 24	PENN	1. 50
			12 x 30	DAC	4. 00
			12 x 16	IA	2. 00
12, 356.	Palette of Autumn		28 x 36	IA	15. 00
12, 357.	Path of Gold		25 x 30	IA	10. 00
			12 x 16	IA	2. 00
12, 358.	Pine Grove Lake		24 x 48	DAC	10. 00
		c.	20 x 24	PENN	1. 50
			11 x 24	DAC	3. 50
12, 359.	Pine Lake		24 x 36	IA	12. 00
12, 360.	Point Lobos		12 x 16	IA	2. 00
12, 361.	Rocky Coast		24 x 48	DAC	10. 00
			11 x 24	DAC	3. 50
12, 362.	Rustic Homestead		24 x 36	DAC	7. 50
			18 x 26	PENN	1. 50
			12 x 16	DAC	2. 50
12, 363.	Sea and Sand		24 x 36	IA	12. 00
			16 x 22	IA	3. 50
12, 364.	Sea Splendor		16 x 20	IA	3. 00
12, 365.	Silver Sea		24 x 60	DAC	15. 00
			24 x 48	DAC	10. 00
			12 x 30	DAC	5. 00
12, 366.	Snow in the Catskills	c.	20 x 24	PENN	1. 50
12, 367.	Springtime		24 x 36	IA	12. 00
		c.	24 x 30	PENN	1. 95
			16 x 22	IA	3. 50
			12 x 16	IA	2. 00

12,368.	Sundown	24 x 36	IA	12.00
12,369.	Sunset, Dana Point	25 x 30	IA	10.00
12,370.	Sunset Shore	24 x 40	DAC	8.50
		12 x 30	DAC	5.00
12,371.	Texas Bluebonnets	25 x 30	AA	10.00
12,372.	Texas Spring	24 x 36	IA	12.00
12,373.	White Mountains and Aspens	24 x 60	DAC	15.00
12,374.	Winter in the Cascades	25 x 30	IA	10.00
		12 x 16	IA	2.00
12,375.	Winter's Arrival	25 x 30	IA	10.00
		12 x 16	IA	2.00
12,376.	Yosemite	24 x 48	DAC	10.00
	c.	20 x 24	PENN	1.50
		12 x 30	DAC	5.00

WOOD, THOMAS WATERMAN (American, 1823-1903)

12,377.	American Farmer	26 x 20	AK	7.50
		16 x 12	AK	2.50

WOODSON, JACK

12,378.	River Boats (4)	11 x 14	DAC	ea. 3.50
12,379.	Hapland			
12,380.	Hudson			
12,381.	Robert E. Lee			
12,382.	Whipporwill			

WOODVILLE, RICHARD C. (American, 1825-1855)

12,383.	First Step	25 x 27-1/2	NYGS	15.00

WOODY

12,384.	Sampans at Sunset	24 x 48	AK	6.00
		12 x 24	AK	2.50

WOOLF, SAMUEL JOHNSON ("S. J. ") (American, 1880-1965)

12,385.	Franklin Delano Roosevelt (DR.)	16 x 13	NYGS	4.00

WOOTTON, FRANK (English Contemporary)

12,386.	Coming Storm	22 x 36	RL	12.50
12,387.	Eastern Venture	20 x 24	AS	12.00
12,388.	In the Paddock	23 x 27-1/2	ESH	12.00
12,389.	Thundering Hooves	17 x 29	ESH	10.00
12,390.	Winding Lane	20 x 40	AS	20.00

WORTHINGTON, NETTER

12,391.	Italian Costume Figures (4)	14 x 8	DAC	ea. 2.40

WOUTCHEN (WU TCHEN) (Chinese, 1280-1350)

12,392.	Bamboo	23-1/2 x 11	CFA	25.00

WRIGHT, GEORGE

12,393.	Getting the Scent	17 x 25	CFA	5.00
12,394.	Tally-Ho	17 x 25	CFA	5.00

WUERMER, CARL (German-American, 1866-)

12,395.	Spring in the Valley	24 x 40	CFA	15.00

WYATT, HENRY (English, 1794-1840)

12,396.	Alfred Lord Tennyson	20 x 16-1/2	NYGS	10.00

WYETH, ANDREW (American Contemporary)

12,397.	Afternoon	27-1/2 x 18	AP	12.00
12,398.	Bradford House	18 x 30	AA	12.00
12,399.	Christina's World	16 x 24	MMA	7.50
	c.	8 x 10	NYGS	.50
12,400.	Coot Hunter	18 x 30	AA	12.00
12,401.	Ground Hog Day			
	c.	18 x 23	HNA	5.95
		18 x 18	AP	6.00
12,402.	Hunter c.	7 x 9	AP	.50
12,403.	Study for "April Wind"	19 x 24	PENN	1.50
12,404.	Young America	13-1/2 x 19	IA	7.50
WYNANTS See WIJNANTS				
WYNDHAM, R.				
12,405.	Fishing on the Medway	17-1/2 x 21	ESH	15.00
12,406.	Tickerage Mill	18 x 21	ESH	15.00

Y

YATRIDES				
12,407.	Bird of Paradise	25 x 30	AK	8.00
12,408.	Cactus and Melon	25 x 30	AK	8.00
YECKLEY, NORMAN				
12,409.	Arroyo Vista	24 x 36	DAC	7.50
12,410.	Spring Formal	24 x 36	DAC	7.50
YIN-TSO HSIUNG				
12,411.	Boats in a Misty Landscape	20 x 18	PENN	1.50
12,412.	Waterfall in the Pines	20 x 18	PENN	1.50
YOS (Ps. for SUSSMAYR, JOSEPH)				
12,413.	Amalfi	14 x 17-1/2	IA	3.00
12,414.	Autumn	24 x 32	IA	10.00
12,415.	Black Forest	14 x 18	IA	3.00
12,416.	Brook	14 x 17-1/2	IA	3.00
12,417.	By the Lake	24 x 36	IA	7.50
12,418.	Huron River	16 x 20	IA	2.50
12,419.	Konigsee	24 x 32	IA	10.00
		18 x 23-1/2	IA	6.00
12,420.	Lake Como	14 x 18	IA	3.00
12,421.	Lake Garda	14 x 18	IA	3.00
12,422.	Midsummer	24 x 36	IA	7.50
12,423.	Orchard Lake	16 x 20	IA	2.50
12,424.	Peaceful Valley	14 x 17-1/2	IA	3.00
12,425.	Portofino	14 x 17-1/2	IA	3.00
12,426.	Quiet Path Through the Woods	23 x 31	CFA	12.00
12,427.	Spring	19-1/2 x 39	IA	5.00
12,428.	Spring by the Lake	14 x 17-1/2	IA	3.00

12,429.	Spring in the				
	Forest	23 x 31	CFA		12.00
12,430.	Sunny Autumn	19-1/2 x 39	IA		5.00
12,431.	Sylvan Lake	16 x 20	IA		2.50
12,432.	Walnut Lake	16 x 20	IA		2.50

YOSA BUSON (Japanese, 1716-1783)

12,433.	Autumnal Landscape				
		24 x 10-1/2	IA		12.00

YOSHI, R.

12,434.	Docks	16 x 20-1/2	ESH		4.00

YOUNG, J.

12,435.	Chanticleer	24 x 20	AS		12.00

YOUNG-HUNTER, JOHN (Scotch-American, 1874-)

12,436.	The Santa Fe				
	Trail	26 x 47	CFA		24.00
		18 x 33	CFA		12.00
	c.	7 x 9	AP		.50

YUGOSLAVIA

12,437.	UWA Series (32)	11 x 14			
	or	14 x 11	NYGS	ea.	2.00

Z

ZABALETA, RAFAEL (Spanish, 1907-)

12,438.	Interior Y Paisaje	24 x 19	NYGS		12.00

ZABATERI

12,439.	Holy Heart of Jesus				
		39-1/2 x 28	ESH		10.00
		29 x 21-1/2	ESH		7.00
12,440.	Madonna with Jesus				
		21-1/2 x 29	ESH		7.00

ZAIS, GIUSEPPE (Italian, 1709-1784)

12,441.	Landscape (2)	10 x 15	AS	ea.	3.25

ZAMPIERI, DOMENICO See DOMENICHINO

ZAMPIGHI, EUGENIO

12,442.	Famous Hunting				
	Story	21 x 30	IA		10.00

ZARDO, ALBERTO (Italian, 1876-1959)

12,443.	Inundated Land	11 x 14-1/2	AS		3.25

ZARITSKY, JOSEPH (Israeli, 1891-)

12,444.	Tel Aviv, 1936	17 x 23-1/2	NYGS		12.00

ZATZKA, FRITZ (Austrian, Ac. 20th Century)

12,445.	Flight into Egypt	19-1/2x27-1/2	IA		7.50
12,446.	Holy Family	38-1/2x26	IA		12.00
12,447.	Holy Family	27x 38	IA		12.00

ZENDEL, GABRIEL (French, 1906-)

12,448.	Composition with				
	Fruit	18 x 24	NYGS		12.00

ZENDER

12,449.	Bassin a St. Denis	22 x 28	CFA		15.00

ZIEGLER, EUSTACE P.

12,449-a. Indian Mother and
           Child (Tanana)   24 x 36   AA   15.00
ZIMMERMAN, ERNST (German, 1856-1901)
12,450.   Christ and the
           Fisherman   21 x 26   IA   6.00
                                17 x 24   IA   2.50
ZINKEISEN, ANNA (Scotch, 1901-)
12,451.   Flowers of Spring   20 x 26   ESH   15.00
12,452.   Julia   30 x 22-1/2   AS   15.00
12,453.   High Summer   20 x 40   AS   16.00
12,454.   Morning Promenade 18 x 22   ESH   10.00
12,455.   Morning Ride   18 x 24   ESH   15.00
12,456.   Round Pond   11 x 9   ESH   2.00
12,457.   Spring Flowers   23 x 19   ESH   10.00
12,458.   Spring's Offering   21 x 24   ESH   12.00
12,459.   Werrington Azaleas
                                24 x 20   ESH   15.00
ZINKEISEN, DORIS CLARE (Scotch Contemporary)
12,460.   At Home   10-1/2x12-1/2 ESH   2.00
12,461.   Box at the Opera   18 x 22   ESH   10.00
12,462.   Elegance in the
           Paddock   10-1/2x12-1/2 ESH   2.00
12,463.   Fairy Queen   18-1/2x22-1/2 ESH   15.00
12,464.   Five Dancers   18 x 22   ESH   10.00
12,465.   From Back Stage   18 x 22   ESH   10.00
12,466.   Morning on the
           Esplanade   10-1/2x12-1/2 ESH   2.00
12,467.   Pat Smythe on
           Scorchin   18-1/2 x 24   RL   12.50
12,468.   Pavillon Dauphin   18 x 22   ESH   10.00
12,469.   Picnic   19 x 22   ESH   10.00
12,470.   Pleasure Boat   16 x 24   ESH   10.00
12,471.   Riverside Luncheon
           Party   10-1/2x12-1/2 ESH   2.00
12,472.   Rockers   21-1/2 x 30   RL   12.50
ZORACH, WILLIAM (American, 1887-)
12,473.   The Cove   15 x 22   NYGS   7.50
12,474.   Five Islands, Maine
                                12-1/2 x 19   NYGS   7.50
ZORN, ANDERS LEONARD (Swedish, 1860-1920)
12,475.   On the Stairs c.   7 x 9   AP   .60
ZUCCHERO, FEDERIGO (Italian, 1542-1609)
12,476.   King James VI   19 x 11-1/2   ESH   10.00
ZUCKERMANN (CIZEK SCHOOL, VIENNA) (Contemporary)
12,477.   Spring   19 x 18   AP   1.50
ZUND
12,478.   Farmer's House   12 x 9   CFA   4.00
12,479.   The Way to Emmaus
                                26-1/2 x 35   IA   15.00
                                19 x 25   IA   7.50
                                12 x 16   IA   4.00
                                8 x 11   IA   1.00

ZURBARAN, FRANCISCO DE (Spanish, 1598-1662)

12, 480.	Chestnuts in a Basket	6 x 7	CFA	1. 00
12, 481.	St. Francis	24 x 13	AP	10. 00
12, 482.	Still Life	24 x 32	NYGS	15. 00
12, 483.	Still Life	19 x 39	CFA	15. 00

Index to Titles

Alphabetical List of Titles followed by Artists' Names and Item Numbers

468

Avenue: Sisley 10, 387
Avenue deL'Opera in 1900:
Pissarro 8684
Avenue, Middleharnis, Holland:
Hobbema 5149
Avenue of Trees: Hobbema 5150
Aveyron: Lucas 6506
Avignon: Marc 6872
Aviles Street: Thieme 10, 909
Avocado: San Fratello 9963
Awaiting the Tide: Hankey
4643
Awakening: Keane 5702; Sadler
9909
Ayame (Iris): Gilroy 4066
Aylesbury Plain: Nash 7901
Azalea: Angelo 239
Azaleas: Chang Shu-Chi 1898
Azaleas in May: Ward 11, 956

B. von Hartenstein: Holbein 5202
Babies: Kroger 5981
Babies, Blue Ribbon: Deborah
2677
Babsi: Torino 11, 078
Baby in Cradel: Vallet 11, 378
Baby Seal: Waters 12, 064
Baby Show: Ross 9575
Baby Stuart: Van Dyck 11, 399
Baccarat Party: Dufy 3065
La Bacchanale: Corot 2200;
Dali 2502
Bacchanalia: Dali 2503
Bacchante: Pompeian 8757;
Roman 9518
Bacchic Festival of Cupids:
Pompeian 8770
Bacchus: Caravaggio 1560;
Reni 9162
Bacchus and Ariadne: Tintoretto
10, 997
Bacco Giovane: Caravaggio 1561
Bach: Pach 8081
Bachelor's Friends: Griffith 4401
Bachelor's Hall: Alken 72
Bacinio di San Marco from S.
Giorgio Maggiore: Canaletto
1470
Back and Forth: Trier 11, 158
Back Part of a Nude: Seurat
10, 228
Backgammon Players: Ostade 8056

The Backs, Cambridge: Petrie
8315
Backstage: Giralt Lerin 4172;
Keane 5718; Kuntz 6023
Backwater: Sessions 10, 215
Bad Kreuznach: Marc 6766, 6837
Bad One: Russell 9773
Bahama Chores: Johnson 5577
Bahama Morning: Johnson 5578
Bahamas: Hart 4703
Baie de Menton: Marc 6838
Baigneuse: Ingres 5446
Baigneuses: Cezanne 1723
Bailey's Beach: Hassam 4717
La Baiser a la Derobe:
Fragonard 3697
Bakery: Andre 133
Baking Day: Ross 9579
Le Bal: Lambert 6050
Bal a Bougival: Renoir 9181
Balancoire: Renoir 9182
Balcony: Manet 6693; Picasso
8351
Baldassare Monaco: Perugino
8282
Bali Beauties: Salvo 9949
Balinese Girl: Hoowij 5291
Balinesin: Dominique 2997
Ball Play Dance: Catlin 1690
Ballerina: Degas 2691; Keane
5726; Ludlum 6518; Picasso
8352
Ballerinas: Maio 6657; Medeiros
7264; Ventosa 11, 704
Ballet: Braque1096, 1097; Derain
2878; Knight 5890; Mosley
7793; Shinn 10, 333
Ballet Class: Degas 2692
Ballet Dancer: Degas 2693
Ballet Dancer: Fourth Position:
Degas 2694
Ballet Dancers: Cydney 2468;
Frederick 3758; Volkmann
11, 878
Ballet Elegante: Carina 1590
Ballet Encore: Degas 2695
Ballet Espagnol: Manet 6694
Ballet Figures: Golding 4209
Ballet Girl: Degas 2696
Ballet Girls: Degas 2697
Ballet Girls on Stage: Degas 2698
Ballet on Blue: Faust 3519

474

Ballet Practice: Edwards 3323
Ballet Scene: Degas 2699;
Klee 5804
Ballet School: Degas 2700;
Edwards 3324
Ballet Subjects: Munchhausen
7824
Ballet Teens: Maio 6658
Ballet Troupe: Degas 2701
Balloon: De Grazia 2816
Balloon No. 1: Haymson 4737
Balloon No. 2: Haymson 4738
Balloon with Horseman: Grose
4456
Balmosal Castle: Ward 11, 957
Balsano: Leitch 6249
Baltimore Butterfly: Peterson
8307
Baltimore, View: Garneray
3848; LeBreton 6189
Balustrade: Tchelichew
10, 865
Bambi Meets his Forest Friends:
Disney 2966
Bambina: Nicol 7966
Bambino: Robbia 9450
Bamboo: Chen-Chi 1953; Nguyen
7952; Wong 12, 289; Woutchen
12, 892
Bamboo Panel (Green Bird):
Chu 1995
Bamboo Panel (Yellow Bird):
Chu 1996
Bandilleros: Picasso 8353
Banjo: Haymson 4739
Banker's Table: Harnett 4679
Banks of the Loing: Sisley
10, 388
Banks of the Marne: Buffet
1319
Banks of the Oise: Daubigny
2560; Sisley 10, 389
Banks of the Seine: Buffet 1320;
Seurat 10, 229; Sisley 10, 390
Banks of the Seine near
Chatou: Vlaminck 11, 804
Banks of the Seine: Vetheuil:
Monet 7576
La Banlieue: Utrillo 11, 258
Banner at the Pavilion: Klee
5805
Banquet of Herod: Giotto 4100

Banquet of Jesus: Ghirlandaio
4028
Banquet of Queen Vasti: Jacopo
5497; Sellaio 10, 193
Baptism of Christ: Giotto 4101;
Leonardo 6264; Magnasco
6637; Verocchio 11, 769
Baptism of Constantine: Tiepolo
10, 963
Baptism of Jesus: Reni 9163
Baptismal Party: Steen 10, 588
Bar: Toulouse-Lautrec 11, 097
Bar at the Folies Bergere: Manet
6695
"Bar du Soleil" a Deauville:
Dongen 3002
Bar Lesperance: Kuntz 6024
Bara (Rose): Gilroy 4067
Barbados Pride: Gough 4240
Barbara: Pauli 8197
Barcarolle, Venezia: Montagu
7693
Barche Isola dei Pescatori: Marc
6767
Bard of Avon: Harnett 4680
Barefoot Church in Halle:
Feininger 3543
Barefoot Prodigy: Moore 7716
Bareford Mountains: Cropsey
2381
Bargaining for a Horse: Mount
7803
Barges at St. Mammes: Sisley
10, 391
Barges on the Seine: Martellini
7037
Barges on the Thames: Derain
2879
Baritone Sax: Pellerano
8246
Barn: Vlaminck 11, 805
Barnagle Geese: Ward 11, 958
Barney Oldfield Benz: Helck
4976
Barouche: Vernet 11, 749
La Barque Bleue: Monet 7577
Barque Orange a la Teste:
Palue 8115
Barque "Rosalie": Roux 9676
Barques a Gravelines: Derain
2880
Barques a La Rochelle: Marquet
6997

478

Black Knight: Munnings 7846
Black Label Bentley: Coulson
2298
Black Palette: Gris 4425
Black, White and Gray:
Kline 5873
Blackberries: Haymson 4775
Blackberry Patch: Grose 4457
Blackboard: Davies 2605
Blackcaps at Low Tide:
Ward 11, 961
Blackfriars: Derain 2881
Blacksmith at his Forge:
Le Nain 6255
Blacksmith Shop: Curtis 2456
La Blanchisserie de la
Bastille: Utrillo 11, 262
Blanket of Snow: Choultze 1991
Blast Furnace: Haymson 4740;
Sandrock 9962
Blenheim Leaving Star Hotel:
Havell 4725
The Blessing: Chardin 1922
Blessing of the Bay (Ship):
Wood 12, 306
The Blessing Strive: Hewes
5051
Blick ins Gartenhaus: Macke
6603
The Blind Leading the Blind:
Brueghel 1270
Blindman's Buff: Fragonard
3699; Goya 4248; Pater
8180
Blinky: Layton 6165
Blond Boy: Keane 5727
Blond Cocker Spaniel: Anderson
129
Bloom Upon Bloom: Unknown
11, 216
Blooming Apple Orchard:
Van Gogh 11, 451
Blooming Desert: Swinnerton
10, 755
Blooming Orchard: Jaques
5539
Blossom Time: Gamble 3837;
Oerder 8023; Ottema 8064
Blossom Time in England:
Hilder 5095
Blossom Valley: Graule 4314
Blossoming Garden: Matisse

7137
Blossoming Palo Verde Tree:
Swinnerton 10, 768
Blossoming Plum Tree:
Pissarro 8685
Blossoming Smoke Tree:
Swinnerton 10, 761
Blossoming Tree by the River:
Pechstein 8214
Blossoms in the Twilight: Klee
5808
Blossoms of May: Todd 11, 056
Blotter: Davies 2606
La Blouse Roumaine: Matisse
7138
Blue and White: Golding 4211;
Greer 4374
Blue Baloon: Takis 10, 782
Blue Basket: Leger 6224
Blue Bay: Wagner 11, 901
Blue Bird: Chu 1998; Rouault
9601
Blue Birds: Chu 1999; Pedersen
8222
Blue Boat: Monet 7577; Wood
12, 293
Blue Bonnet Time: Salinas 9934
Blue Bonnets: McGill 7235
Blue Bowl: Greene 4362; Reekie
9040
Blue Boy: Gainsborough 3805;
Picasso 8358, 8359
Blue Butterfly: Dawson 2641
Blue Cart: Hillier 5125
Blue Chrysanthemum: Mondrian
7562
Blue Clown: Kuhn 6012
Blue Coast: Feininger 3547
Blue Compote: Lowrie 6494
Blue Dancer: Soyer 10, 516
Blue Danube: Pearson 8202
Blue Door: Thieme 10, 893;
Wintz 12, 263
Blue Door, Newlyn: Harvey 4712
Blue Flask: Ensor 3433
Blue Fox: Marc 6889
Blue Girl Reading Book: Macke
6604
Blue Grosbeak: Audubon 317
Blue Gulf Stream: Andrews 166
Blue Harbor: Sessions 10, 216
Blue Harmony: Andrade 132

Blue Head: Klee 5809
Blue Horizon: Bruestle 1303;
  Chabanian 1848
Blue Horse: Marc 6890
Blue Horses: Marc 6891
Blue Iris: Van Gogh 11, 452
Blue Jay: Audubon 318
Blue Kimono: Pearson 8203
Blue Lake: Corinth 2182
Blue Lamp: Marque 6995
Blue Larkspur: Dobrowsky 2973
Blue Madonna: Sassoferato
  10, 001; Vu-Cao-Dam 11, 890
Blue Marine: Feininger 3548
Blue Mozart: Dufy 3069
Blue Night: Klee 5810
Blue Nude: Matisse 7139;
  Picasso 8360
Blue Poles: Pollock 8748
Blue Ribbon: Baptiste 437
Blue Ridge Mountains of
  Virginia: Makielski 6675
Blue Room: Graf 4296;
  Matisse 7140
Blue Rose: Mondrian 7563
Blue Sails: Feininger 3549
Blue Shutters: Thieme 10, 894
Blue Skyscrapers: Feininger
  3550
Blue Spruce: Rawson 8979
Blue Summer, Closed Blinds:
  Corneille 2195
Blue Tit and Pussy Willow:
  Ede 3313
Blue Titmouse: Flegel 3629
Blue Umber: Nay 7921
Blue Vase: Cezanne 1727; Haym-
  son 4741, 4759; Ibarz 5437;
  Vlaminck 11, 808
Blue Vase on Dark Back-
  ground: Redon 8998
Blue Waters: Adrion 14; Mac- ,
  Gregor 6587
Blue Window: Lamprecht 6058;
  Matisse 7141; Warshawsky
  12, 061
Blue Window in Cassis: Hassell
  4721
Blue-Winged Teal: Audubon 332;
  Jaques 5540
Bluebell and Convolvulus:
  Besler 657

Bluebell Time: Marston 7033
Blueberry Hill: Bruestle 1302
Blueroom Print: Campbell
  1465
The Boat: Blume 793; Manet
  6696
Boat at Sunrise: Pechstein
  8215
Boat Building at Flatford:
  Constable 2125
Boat During Inundation: Sisley
  10, 393
Boat in the Bay: Tauber 10, 840
Boat in Dogana, Venice:
  Kokoschka 5908
Boat Landing: Prendergast
  8855
Boat on the Pond: Hitchens
  5144
Boat Races at Argenteuil; Monet
  7582
Boat Scene: Marquet 6999
Boat Yard at Salcombe: Shepherd
  10, 305
Boathouse, Early Morning:
  Hitchens 5145
Boating: Manet 6697; Renoir
  9189
Boating Lake: Rendle 9154
Boating on the Epte: Monet
  7583
Boating Party: Cassatt 1655;
  Renoir 9190
Boating Party at Chatou:
  Renoir 9191
Boatman of Morte Fontaine:
  Corot 2202
Boats: Aynscomb-Harris 366;
  Bonny 898; Jurk 5615; Van
  Gogh 11, 453
Boats and Cliffs: Klee 5811
Boats and Regatta at Argenteuil:
  Monet 7584
Boats and Sea, Deer Island,
  Maine: Marin 6935
Boats and Seagulls: Dufy 3070
Boats Ashore: Albo 35
Boats at Anchor: Sargent 9976;
  Walther 11, 938
Boats at Argenteuil: Monet 7585
Boats at Deauville: Poucette
  8816

Brig "Prince de Neufchatel":
Cosgrave 2282
Brig "Solide": Roux 9677
Bright Cloud: Palmer 8112
Bright Yellow: Winter 12, 260
Brightening Seine: Whorf
12, 198
Bringing Flowers Singing:
Steinke 10, 602
Bristol Bulldog: Coulson
2299
Britania over Kilimanjaro:
Shepherd 10, 285
Britta: Torino 11, 081
Broadway: Takis 10, 784
Broadway, New York, 1834:
Varin 11, 638
Broadway Night: Marin 6936
Broken Jug: Greuze 4385
Broken Pitcher: Greuze 4386
Broken Rope: Russell 9776
Bronc to Breakfast: Russell
9777
Bronco Busters: Remington
9121
Bronze and Grey: Henry
5021
Bronze Skyline: Carter 1621
Brook: Marc 6857; Tarrant
10, 804;   Wood 12, 318;
Yos 12, 416
Brook in the Mountains:
Bachmann 389; Birkmann 707
Brook in the Woods: Bachmann
388; Kruger 5995
Brook Trout: Schaldach
10, 029
Brooklyn Bridge: Buffet 1326;
Gallais 3826; Gromaire
4446; Stella 10, 618
Brookside Mill: Hayward 4945
Brother and Sister: Padua 8093;
Roth 9588
Brother Leo Sees the Heavenly
Throne: Giotto 4102
Brown Beauties: Butterworth 1413
Brown Composition: Baumeister
516
Bucentaur at the Piazetta:
Canaletto 1472
Bucks County Barn: Sheeler
10, 275

Buckskins: Remington 9124
Buena Vista: Laycox 6163
Buffalo: Clapera 2055
Buffalo Bill: Bonheur 874
Buffalo Hunt: Catlin 1691;
Howland 5343
Buffalo Newsboy: Le Clear
6210
Buffalo on the Move: Russell
9778
Buffoon: Watteau 12, 076
Buffoonery: Klee 5813
Bull: Babylonia 375
Bull and Horses, Lascaux:
Prehistoric 8834
Bull Diving: Leigh 6239
Bull Dogging: Leigh 6240
Bull Fight: Ritter 9430
Bull Fight Day: Keane 5703
Bull Fighters: Boobis 900;
Tomaso 11, 059
Bull Ring: Picasso 8368
Bullfight: Dufy 3072; Goya 4249;
Groth 4500; Picasso 8369
Bullfighter: Buffet 1327
Bullfinches: Sedgwick 10, 177
Bulls, Horses and Stags,
Lascaux: Prehistoric 8835
Bulls of Loja: Durancamps
3181
Bunch of Anemones: Dufy 3073
Bunch of Apple-Blossoms:
Faust 3520
Bunch of Autumn Flowers:
Faust 3521
Bunch of Flowers: Dufy 3074;
Faistauer 3484; Manet 6702
Bunch of Violets: Durer 3195
Bunch of Wild Flowers:
Rousseau 9647
Bunches of Grape: Cerquozzi
1716
Bundlers: Millet 7442
Bunny: Strev 10, 684
Bunny Taxi: Barnes 451
The Burden: Daumier 2565
Burning Incense: Sargent 9977
Burning of Savonarola: Unknown
11, 240
Burning Prairies: Roloff 9513
Burst of Flowers: Rugh 9744
Bury Hunt: Agar 19

Rouault 9603
Christ and His Disciples:
Basaiti 494
Christ and the Little Children:
Komaroñ 5940
Christ and the Rich Young Ruler:
Hofmann 5187
Christ as Pilgrim: Angelico 188
Christ at the Sea of Galilee:
Tintoretto 10, 999
Christ at Thirty-Three: Hofmann
5188
Christ at Twelve: Hofmann
5189; Kroger 5986
Christ Before Pilate:
Mathauser 7127
Christ Blessing: Greco 4327;
Langlet 6092
Christ Blessing the Children:
Clementz 2086
Christ Child and Roe Deer:
Dawson 2672
Christ Child, St. John and
Angels: Rubens 9688
Christ the Comforter: O'Connell
8015
Christ Dead: Bronzino 1218
Christ Disputing with the
Doctors: Butinone 1410
Christ Driving the Traders from
the Temple: Greco 4328
The Christ Head: Barriviera
470; Bianchi 674
Christ Healing the Blind Man:
Greco 4329
Christ Healing the Sick Child:
Max 7220
Christ in Emmaus: Eichstaedt
3395
Christ in the Garden of
Gethsemane: Greco 4330;
Hofmann 5190
Christ in the Garden of Olives:
Mantegna 6752
Christ in Gethsemane: Goodman
4229
Christ in the Gethsemane
Garden: Ferrari 3591
Christ in Glory in the Tetra-
morph: Sutherland 10, 743
Christ in the Temple: Clementz
2087; Hofmann 5191

Christ in the Wheatfields:
Schleibner 10, 041
Christ the King: De Soto 2922
Christ Mocked by Soldiers:
Rouault 9604
Christ Mourning the City:
Flandrin 3627
Christ of St. John of the Cross:
Dali 2505, 2506
Christ of Sorrows: Marmion 6991
Christ on the Cross: Durer 3198;
Grunewald 4505; Reni 9166;
Velasquez 11, 659
Christ on Mount Olive: Albo 37
Christ on the Mount of Olives:
Giotto 4105; Hacker 4585;
Palma 8107
Christ our Pilot: Sallman 9939
Christ Preaching: Steinhausen
10, 600
Christ Preaching by the Sea:
Hofmann 5192
Christ Preaching on the Sea:
Golding 4212
Christ Rising from the Tomb:
Angelico 189
Christ Supporting the Cross:
Giorgione 4081
Christ Taking Leave of His
Disciples: Basaiti 495
Christ, the Virgin and St.
John: Unknown 11, 241
Christ Weeping over Jerusalem:
Hole 5218
Christ with the Children: Cizek
School 2043
Christening: Sadler 9910
Christian Intimacy: Rouault
9605
Christian Nocturne: Rouault
9606
Christina: Larsen 6097
Christina's World: Wyeth 12, 399
Christine: Edzard 3356
Christmas at Home: Moses 7779
Christmas at the Mill: Hilder
5097
Christmas in Montmartre:
Utrillo 11, 269
Christmas Party: Durrie 3248
Christopher Columbus: Piombo
8650

Classic Beauties: Cassandra
1653
Classic Figures: Raffaello 8914
Classical Head: Picasso 8380
Classical Landscape: Gellee
3982
Claude Desinant: Renoir 9199
Claudia: Dominique 2998
Claudine: Dyf 3265
Claudio Vinciata 11, 789
Clavadeleralp: Marc 6771
Clay, Henry: Brown 1243
Clearance in a Wood: Fromm-
hold 3779
Clearing Day: Ward 11, 965
Clearing Day, Snowdon, North
Wales: Ward 11, 966
Clearing Skies: Clausade 2060
Clematites: Dufy 3084
Cleopatra: Bronzino 1219;
Canlassi 1548; Reni 9167
Clinton, Dewitt: Brown 1244
Cliff of Etretat After Storm:
Courbet 2308
Clipper Nightingale: Grose 4469
Clipper Ship Challenge:
Cosgrave 2283
Clipper Ship Dreadnaught:
Currier and Ives 2427
Clipper Ship Flying Cloud:
Aylward 361; Cosgrave
2284
Clipper Ship Great Republic:
Currier and Ives 2445
Clipper Ship Red Jacket:
Smith 10, 464
Clipper Ship Sea Serpent:
Cosgrave 2285
Clipper Ship Sovereign of the
Seas: Cosgrave 2286
Clocks: Piranesi 8666
Cloister Garden: Van Gogh
11, 471
Clos de Mathurins: Pontoise:
Cezanne 1735
Close Ashore: Mitchell 7501
Cloud Symphony: Sloane
10, 454
Clown: Kutter 6034; Lignon 6331;
Patrick 8188; Rouault 9608;
9609
Clown Act: Martin 7051

Clown au Chapeau: Diaz 2953
Clown au Cheveux Rouges:
Diaz 2954
Clown and Dog: Kokoschka 5911
Clown avec Margeurite: Diaz
2955
Clown in Front of a Mirror:
Fiene 3610
Clown on a White Horse:
Chagall 1863
Clown with Accordian: Kutter
6035
Clown with Black Wig:
Kuhn 6013
Clownesse: Toulouse-Lautrec
11, 102
Clownesse Cha-U-Kao: Toulouse
Lautrec 11, 103
Clowns: Cydney 2470; Ritter
9431, 9432, 9433; Rouf 9642;
Tomaso 11, 061; Vas 11, 646
Coal Wagon: Gericault 4007
Coast Cottage: Crandall 2355
Coast in Italy: Betz 665
Coast Near Dieppe: Monet 7598
Coast Near Monterey: Schwartz
10, 123
Coast of East Lake: Heidingsfeld
4967
Coast of Etretat: Monet 7599
Coast of Italy: Marc 6858
Coast of Jugoslavia: Lorenz
6442
Coast of Lebanon: Harder 4664
Coast of Maine: Arentz 285;
Waugh 12, 122
Coast of Picardy: Benington 877
Coast of Spain: Medeiros 7269
Coast Scene in Brittany: Wintz
12, 266
Coastal Town in Spain: Mercade
7349
Coastline at Arcachon: Palue
8116
Coastline at Sete: Aigner 22
Cobblers: Jules 5608
Cochem: Marc 6772
The Cock: Buffet 1333; Chagall
1864; Picasso 8381; Reuther
9375; Walch 11, 911
Cock-Chaffinch and Japanese
Cherry: Ede 3314

Composition 1934: Kandinsky 5638
Composition 1942: Dali 2508
Composition No. 711: Kandinsky 5636
Composition in Bleu: Mondrian 7565
Composition in Blue: Lorjou 6481
Composition in Grey, Blue, Red and Yellow: Mondrian 7565-A
Composition in Orange: Lorjou 6482
Composition in Red: Appel 274
Composition, Peasants: Picasso 8382
Composition, Red and Grey: Bazas 523
Composition with Fruit: Zendel 12, 448
Compote Dish and Pitcher by the Window: Picasso 8383
Compote with Fruit and Guitar: Picasso 8384
Le Compotier: Gris 4428; Picasso 8385
Compotier d'Oranges: Henry 5023
La Comtesse D'Haussonville: Ingres 5447
Comtesse D'Orsay: Kobel 5899
Concarneau: Sherwin 10, 316
Concentric Group: Schlemmer 10, 051
Conception: Ciseri 2035; Tiepolo 10, 965
The Concert: Andreotti 164; Dufy 3085; Giorgione 4082; Ter Borch 10, 877; Titian 11, 016; Vermeer 11, 715
Le Concert Agreeable: Lavreince 6145
Concert Champetre: Giorgione 4083
Concert of the Angels: Grunewald 4506
Le Concerte Orange: Dufy 3086
Conch Boat: Mitchell 7507
Concours Hippique: Konrad 5946
Confectioner in Cairo: Kriesch 5973

Confidences: Renoir 9201
Confirmation: Crespi 2361
Coniston: Sherwin 10, 317
Conjuror: Bosch 947
Connecticut Hills: Kautzky 5680
Connemara: Craig 2339
Conny with Puppie: Torino 11, 083
Conquest of the Air: La Fresnaye 6042
Consolation: Nivert 7990
Construction No. 75: Serpa 10, 203
Consuelo: Hidalgo 5058
Contemplation: Picasso 8336
Continental Views: Snapper 10, 480
Conversation: Chang Ta T'Sien 1906; Pissarro 8694
Conversation Piece: Etruscan 3452; Matisse 7145
Conversion of Paul: Breughel 1275
Convoy at Rendezvous: Binning 695
Convoy Entering Mers-El-Kebir: Jamieson 5532
Conway: Dunlop 3176
The Cook: Aersten 17; Vermeer 11, 716
Cook Boy: Soutine 10, 512
Cooling Stream: Skinner 10, 440
Coombe Village, Oxfordshire: Hankey 4645
Coot Hunter: Wyeth 12, 400
Copper Glow: Blanchard 758
Copper Queen: Ray 8992
Copy Kittens: Hawley 4733
Coq Blanc: Lurcat 6546
Cordoba: Marc 6827
Cordon Bleu and Camelia: Eastman 3309
Corfe Castle: Marston 7034
Corn: Haymson 4755
Corn Ceremony: Couse 2328
Corn-Cobs: Schluter 10, 053
Corn Harvest: Brueghel 1276
Corn Pickers: Lee 6215
Corn Poppies: Monet 7600
Cornell Farm: Hicks 5054
Cornell U.: Haymson 4902
A Corner of Britain: Hilder 5098
Corner of the Pasture: Glannon 4189

Donkey Ride:Hermes 5026
La Donna Gravida: Raffaello
8919
La Donna Valata: Raffaello 8920
The Donors: Van Eyck 11, 431
Doorstep: Martin 7042
Doorway of S. Marco: Barratt
465
La Dore: Nino 7981
Dormeuse (Sleeper): Boucher 1020
Dormition of the Virgin:
Angelico 204
Douarnenez: Carpenter 1608
Double Crosser: Leigh 6241
Double Portrait: Giorgione
4084; Schneid 10, 067
Double Trouble: Strang 10, 662,
10, 668
Doubtful Visitor: Russell 9790
The Dove: Picasso 8396
Dove with Magnolias: Cheng-Wu-
Fei 1961
Dover Valley: Pelham 8232
Doves: Steinlauf 10, 607
Down to the Sea: Muris 7881
Down to the Valley: Frommhold
3780
Downland Farm: Rendle 9155
Downtown Rhythms, New York:
Franck 3750
Dragon: Babylonia 376; Baziotes
525
Dragon on Parade: Keane 5720
Drama: Daumier 2570
Drawbridge: Van Gogh 11, 486
Drawbridge at Arles: Van Gogh
11, 487
Drawing Cover: Alken 76
Drawing School: Campigli 1466
Drawings from the Lascaux
Caves: Prehistoric 8838
Dream: King 5786
Dream City: Moran 7724
Dream Improvization: Kandinsky
5639
Dream of Constantine: Piero
8603
Dream Ride: Glackens 4185
Dreamer: Gauguin 3889;
Spitzweg 10, 550
Dreamer's Cove: Hempfing 4983;
Wood 12, 325

Dreaming: Langlais 6091;
Parrish 8152
Dreaming Gypsy: Courbet 2312
Dreamy Corner: Marc 6860
Dreamy Lagoon: Thieme
10, 910
Dresden-Friedrich: Kirchner
5792
Dresden Neustadt: Kokoschka
5915
Dressing of Venus: Rubens
9690
Dressing Room: Huhn 6014
Drifter and Paddle Streamer:
Kelly 5746
Drifting: Hankey 4647
Driftwood: Haymson 4756
Drinkers: Velasquez 11, 662
Drinkers and Gamblers:
Teniers 10, 871
Driving Home for Gloucester:
Sessions 10, 217
Drop!: Blinks 777
Drummer: Klee 5821; Pellerano
8247
Drummond Children: Raeburn
8902
Dry River: Hurd 5419
Drying the Sails: Dufy 3090
Du Noir Qui Se Leve:
Riopelle 9428
Duc d'Orleans: Drouais 3026
Ducal Palace, Venice:
Canaletto 1483; Guardi 4521;
Lebreton 6191
Duchess of Devonshire:
Gainsborough 3807
Duchess of Maine as a Girl:
Mignard 7422
Duchess of Mazarin: Maes 6627
Duchess of Milan: Holbein 5203
Duchess of Urbino: Piero 8604
Duck Decoys: Kolman 5939
Duck Panel: Chu 2000, 2001,
Duck Pond: Barber 440; Nash
7898
Duck Resting: Graves 4318
Duckling: Graves 4319
Ducks: Fausett 3509-A; Fawsett
3540
Ducks at Dawn: Danchin 2526
Ducks in Flight: Danchin 2527

L'Etang: Letellier 6292
L'Etang de St. Cucufa: Vlaminck 11, 818
Ete, La Plage des Sables: Marquet 7003
Eternal City: Blume 794
Eternal East: Ross 9572
The Eternal Father: Dolci 2977
L'Eternite: Courbet 2313
Etienne Chevalier Adoring the Madonna: Fouquet 3687
Eton College: Canaletto 1484; Westall 12, 169
Etretat: Monet 7602
Etude: Fragonard 3702
Etude de Cavalier: Delacroix 2841
Etude d'Oiseaux: Pisano 8677
Eucalyptus Trees: Schwartz 10, 127
Eugene Manet a L'Ile de Wight: Morisot 7740
Evander and Aeneas: Giorgione 4085
Evangeliary: Byzantine 1436, 1437
Eve of St. Nicholas: Steen 10, 591
Evelone: Marc 6776
Evening: Parrish 8153; Rubens 9693
Evening at Ullswater: Ward 11, 972
Evening Calm: Manden 6681
Evening Enchantment: Chagall 1866
Evening Glow in Ireland: Bion 696
Evening Gold: Burton 1409
Evening in the Camargue: Quintane 8897
Evening in the Country: Nichols 7955
Evening in a Little Harbor: Manessier 6689
Evening in the Tetons: Wood 12, 330
Evening Landscape: Wijnants 12, 215
Evening Light: Sherwin 10, 320
Evening, Place du Chatelet: Herve 5042

Evening Reflections: Rutledge 9857
Evening, Spain: Ellis 3408
Evening Tide: Meyer 7384
Evening Upon the Moor: Tauber 10, 842
Evening Upon the Mountains: Schober 10, 075
Evening Walk: Van Gogh 11, 489
Evening's Comfort: Harnett 4683; Peto 8310
Evensong: Brett 1185
Eventails: Okada 8030
Eventide: Bonamici 854
Ewer - Lapis Lazuli: Medici 7288
Ewer - Silver Gilt: Medici 7289
Exaltation of the Flower: Greece 4345
Excursion on Horseback: Unge- witter 11, 185
Excursionist: Renoir 9205
Exit of the Fawns: Wanklyn 11, 942
Exotic Balinese Dancers: Strasser 10, 676
Expectation: Dawson 2668; Spinelli 10, 540
The Express: Bolstad 843
Expression I: Steinlauf 10, 608
Expulsion from Florence of the Duke of Athens: Ussi 11, 252
Expulsion from Paradise: Masaccio 7077
Eynsford: Hilder 5100
Eynsford, Kent: Wilcox 12, 223
Ezekiels Visions: Schneid 10, 068

Fabiola: Henner 5001
Fagot Attendu: Corot 2212
A Fair: Mostaert 7794
Fair Ground: Jones 5594
Fair Grounds: Marc 6869
Fair in Brittany: Boudin 1051
Fair Weather: Bloomster 792
Fairies' Oak: Tarrant 10, 808
The Fairman Brothers Four-in- Hand: Eakins 3297
Fairy Boat: Dawson 2644
Fairy Queen: Zinkeisen 12, 463
The Fairy Tale: Firle 3623

Flower Study on Green:
Machourek 6594
Flower Study on Red: Machourek
6595
Flower Vendor: Andre 136;
Paradise 8137; Rivera 9440;
Soyer 10, 523; Steinlauf 10, 610
Flower Vendors: Martinez
7056
Flowering Acaceas: Benezit 611
Flowering Almond Branch:
Van Gogh 11, 496
Flowering Chestnut Branch:
Van Gogh 11, 497
Flowering Dogwood: Golding
4214
Flowering Garden: Van Gogh
11, 498
Flowering Tree: Van Gogh
11, 499
Flowerpiece: Bosschaerts 951;
Brueghel 1254; Brussel 1305;
Cooper 2154; Hecke 4952;
Lenard 6259; Vas 11, 647
Flowers: Bonnard 887; Caselli
1646, 1647; Cezanne 1746;
DeMarco 2858; Guardi 4523;
Kutter 6036; Laessig 6039;
Lynn 6570; Niven 7984;
Picasso 8413; 8414; Pisis
8683; Pizzanelli 8730; Redon
9003; Rousseau 9653; Valadon
11, 372; Van Gogh 11, 500;
Vlaminck 11, 820
Flowers and Bowl of Fruit:
Gauguin 3897
Flower and Cat: Renoir 9211
Flowers and Fruit: Cezanne
1747; Fantin-Latour 3496;
Mario dei Fiori 6986; Rigoults
9424; Ruysch 9865; Unknown
11, 190; Vallayer 11, 377
Flowers and Fruits: Levier
6297; Matisse 7152
Flowers and Insects: Tsai
11, 172
Flowers and Lacquer: Flint
3639
Flowers and Lovers: Chagall
1867
Flowers and Music: Edzard
3359

Flowers and Music with Piano:
Edzard 3360
Flowers and Music with Violin:
Edzard 3361
Flowers and Pigeons: Llovet
6412
Flowers and Pineapple: Lorjou
6483
Flowers by an Open Window:
Levier 6298
Flowers for You: Jeudwine 5567
Flowers from my Garden: Dyf
3266
Flowers in Autumn: Kruger
5996
Flowers in a Blue Jug: Utrillo
11, 287
Flowers in a Blue Vase: Breug-
hel 1259; Redon 9004; Van
Gogh 11, 501
Flowers in a Brown Vase:
Brueghel 1260
Flowers in a Copper Vase: Van
Gogh 11, 502
Flowers in a Crystal Vase:
Manet 6707
Flowers in a Delft Vase: Brueg-
hel 1261
Flowers in a Jar: Redon 9005;
Rousseau 9654
Flowers in a Jug: Nicholson
7964
Flowers in a Landscape: Nigg
7975
Flowers in a Small Vase: Cezanne
1748
Flowers in a Vase: Brueghel
1262; Derain 2884; Gauguin
3898; Huysum 5429; Rivers
9448; Rouault 9614
Flowers, Insects and Strawberries:
Walscapele 11, 928
Flowers of the Hunt: Alken 73
Flowers of Spring: Zinkeisen
12, 451
Flowers on a Grey Background:
Bressler 1178
Flowers on a Marble Table:
Nigg 7976
Flowers on White: Padua 8094
Flowery Plum Trees: Pissarro
8696

Fruit Subjects: Haymson 4774
Fruitage of Autumn: Rawson
8983
Fruitfulness: Rubens 9696
Fruits: Deker 2834; Mignon 7425
Fruits Aglow: Harnett 4673
Fruits and Flowers: Caravaggio
1570; Desmoulins 2912; Fiori
3622; Huysum 5431; Porter
8795; Ruysch 9867, 9868
Fruits and Vegetables: Unknown
11, 219
Fruits, Antique: Volkamer
11, 877
Fruits of the Midi: Renoir
9212
Fruits of Spain: Strevens
10, 701
Full Cry: Alken 77; Herring
5033, 5035; Herring-Harris
5038; Jank 5535; Konrad 5948
Full River: Munnings 7847
Full Tide: Corbiere 2168
Fuller Family: Grose 4471
Fumagusta Harbour: Georghiou
4004
Fun on the Gate: Dawson 2673
Fun with the Chicks: Dawson
2648
Funeral Chorus: Etruscan
3462
Funeral of Phocion: Poussin
8824
Funeral of the Poet Panizza:
Grosz 4495
Fur Traders Descending the
Missouri: Bingham 690
Furioso: Hierer 5076; Rutledge
9858
Furnace: Merker 7353
Furstenau: Marc 6843
Future Ballerina: Cydney 2472
Future Scientist: Hidalgo 5059

Gabrielle and Coco: Renoir
9213
Gabrielle and Jean: Renoir
9214
Gabrielle and Rose: Renoir
9215
Gabrielle D'Estrees Bathing:
Unknown 11, 229
Gabrielle with Jean Renoir and

a Little Girl: Renoir 9216
Gallant: Watteau 12, 090
Gallant Soldier: TerBorch
10, 880
Galloping Horses: Roloff 9514;
Schacht 10, 023
Gamblers: Rombouts 9542
Game-Keeper and His Dogs:
Troyon 11, 166
Game of the Arrow: Catlin
1693
Game of Chess: Mai-Thu 6641
Game of Dice: Murillo 7862
A Game of Horse and Rider:
Fragonard 3705
A Game of Hot Cockles:
Fragonard 3706
Game on the Tevere: Vernet
11, 755
La Gamme d'Amour: Watteau
12, 091
Gandria: Marc 6844; Muscha
7892
Ganymede Pursued by Zeus:
Greece 4346
Garda Lake: Hanft 4635
Gardanne: Cezanne 1750
Garden at Brun: Friesz 3772
Garden at les Collettes: Renoir
9217
Garden at Daubigny: Van Gogh
11, 503
Garden Beauty: Ward 11, 980
Garden Bouquet: Bos 921;
Segonzac 10, 183
Garden Flowers: Dyf 3267;
Janch 5534; Niven 7987
Garden Gaiety: Huysum 5432
Garden Glory: Doring 3010
Garden in the Night: Lurcat
6547
Garden of Allah: Parrish 8154
Garden of Delights: Bosch 948
Garden of Dr. Gachet: Van Gogh
11, 504
Garden of Flowers: Montagu
7678
Garden of Love: Montagu 7679
Garden of Ministry: Menzel
7347
Garden of Romance: Montagu
7680

516

Hands of St. Catherine: Stoss
10, 660
Handsome Witch: Ray 8994
Hans Holbein, the Younger:
Hertenstein 5039
Hansel: Kaulbach 5677
Hapland (Boat): Woodson
12, 379
Happy Childhood: Dawson
2669
Happy Days: Detlefson 2942;
Iverd 5487
Happy Family: Cornell 2197
Happy Hollow: Sitzmann
10, 432
The Happy Hours: Postels 8800
Happy Reveller: Hals 4613
Happy Valley: Cornell 2197
Harbinger of Spring: Brown
1248
Harbor: Buffet 1337; Derain
2888; Dufy 3092; Signac
10, 344
Harbor at East Lake: Mollen-
hauer 7557
Harbor at Honfleur: Jongkind
5600; Seurat 10, 235
Harbor at Les Sables d'Olonne:
Signac 10, 345
Harbor at Rockport, Mass. :
Marc 6875
Harbor at Sete: Desnoyer
2916
Harbor at Trouville: Boudin
1053
Harbor by Night: Lucca 6507
Harbor, Early Morning:
Sherwin 10, 321
Harbor Entrance, Yarmough,
I. O. W. : Foster 3669
Harbor in Brittany: Buffet
1338; Marc 6861; Wagner
11, 908
Harbor, Mevagissey: Shepherd
10, 287
Harbor Night Scene: Franca
3733
Harbor of Algier: Desnoyer
2917
Harbor of Amsterdam: Velde
11, 692
Harbor of Barcelona: Barraud
468

Harbor of Joinville: Callot
1458
Harbor of Naples: Marquet
7004
Harbor of Saint-Tropez: Bonnard
888; Signac 10, 346
Harbor Pattern: Schurr 10, 099
Harbor Reflection: Holusa
5227
Harbor, St. Ives: Richmond
9414
Harbor Scene, Antwerp: Braque
1108
Harbor Scenes: Cooke 2152;
Gasser 3855; Vas 11, 648
Harbor Street: Boness 863;
Wintz 12, 268
Harbor Symphony: Marcel 6915
Harbor Towns: Johnson 5579
Harbor Traffic: Grant 4308
Harbor View--Phlox: Blenner
770
Harbor Window: Sherwin 10, 322
Hare: Durer 3203; Edwards 3348
Hark, Hark, the Lark: Nevinson
7946
Harlequin: Carreno de Miranda
1613; Derain 2889; Gris 4431;
Picasso 8433
Harlequin and a Dog: Rouault
9615
Harlequin and Mandolin:
Poucette 3817
Harlequin and Mirror: Picasso
8437
Harlequin on Horseback: Picasso
8438
Harlequin Sonata: Brass 1163
Harlequin with Guitar: Poucette
8818
Harlequin with Mask: Picasso
8439
Harlequinade: Hutton 5426
Harlequin's Carnival: Miro
7478
Harlequin's Family: Picasso
8440
Harlequins: Miro 6659
Harmony: Crowe 2406; Greene
4366
Harmony in Blue: Matisse 7161
Harmony in Pewter: Reekie
9041

Harmony in White: Ward 11, 987
Harmony in Yellow: Medeiros
7274
Harmony of Spring: Ward
11, 986
Harp of Trees: Sherrin 10, 312
Harp of the Winds: Martin
7053
Harriet: Strev 10, 688
Harvard, the Yard: Haymson
4903
Harvest: Bos 924; Generalic
3990; Lier 6323; Oudot 8070;
Van Gogh 11, 516; Vlaminck
11, 283
Harvest Bounty: Atherton 313
Harvest Time: Bachmann 396;
Glendening 4191; Hunt 5410;
Shayer 10, 269; Valckenborgh
11, 375; Wheatley 12, 182
Harvesters: Brueghel 1277;
Cizek School 2045
Harvesters' Meal: Brueghel
1278
Hastings, about 1835: Turner
11, 145
Hat Seller: Berman 647
Hauling Nets: Thieme 10, 917
Haus in Baumen: Jawlensky
5550
Hawaii: Rajko 9967
Hawaiian Girl: Brown 1250
Hawking: Blanchard 752
Hawking Party: Potter 8812
Hawthorne, New York: Picken
8592
Hay Harvest: Brueghel 1279
Hay Wagon: Stone 10, 658
Haydn: Bach 8084
Hayfield: Aldridge 66
Haying: Schreiber 10, 086
Haying Time: Fausett 3512
Haymakers: Dufy 3093; Green
4357; L'Hermitte; Steele
10, 587
Haymaking: Amiet 116; Brueghel
1280; Dufy 3094; L'Hermitte
6316
Haymarket: Sloan 10, 447
Haystack at Sunset: Monet 7609
Haystacks: Gauguin 3903
Haystacks in Provence: Van
Gogh 11, 517

Haywagon: Munter 7856
The Haywain: Constable 2134
He Prayeth Best Who Loveth
Best: Tarrant 10, 811
Head: Laurens 6137; Schneid
10, 069
Head of an Angel: Durer 3204
Head of an Apostle: Durer
3205
Head of the Artist's Mother:
Giacometti 4049
Head of a Boy: Rouault 9616
Head of a Carmelite: Masaccio
7084
Head of Cherub: Luti 6561
Head of a Child: Andrea del
Sarto 150; Robbia 9451
Head of Christ: Cimabue 2029;
Durer 3206; Greco 4331;
Sallman 9941
Head of a Clown: Buffet 1339
Head of a Girl: Cima de
Conegliano 2026; Greuze 4392;
Huber 5349; Martellini 7036;
Vermeer 11, 723
Head of Harlequin: Picasso 8441
Head of a Horse: Gericault 4010
Head of a Lion: Delacroix 2844
Head of Ludovica Tornabuoni:
Ghirlandaio 4033
Head of a Man: Klee 5832
Head of a Negro: Rubens 9697
Head of Prophet: Schneid 10, 070
Head of a Saint: Cavallino 1697
Head of St. Peter: Masaccio
7083
Head of Saturnis: Baldung 432
Head of Vengeance: Prud'hon
8874
Head of Venus: Botticelli 969
Head of the Virgin: Carli 1591;
Ghirlandaio 4035
Head of a Woman: Degas 2763;
Picasso 8442
Head of a Young Girl: Dobrowsky
2974; Maillol 6650
Head of a Young Man: Uccello
11, 173
Head with Open Eyes: Jawlensky
5551
Headed for Boston: Marin 6945
Heading for Home: Mason 7107

High Sea No. 2: Kalckreuth
5624
High Spirits: Skinner 10, 441
High Summer: Bezombes 672;
Zinkeisen 12, 453
High Tea: Gilroy 4069
High Yaller: Marsh 7027
Highland Loch: Breanski 1176
Highland Ponies: Thomson
10, 949
Highland Spring: Ward 11, 988
Hill Town: Cordoba 2177
Hille Bobbe: Hals 4614
Hillel: Levine 6302
Hills Beyond the Bay: Segonzac
10, 184
Hills of Donegal: Bion 697
Hillside Homes: Cardella 1586
Hillside in Etretat: Inness
5469
Hillside Stream: Pelham 8236
Hilltop: Parrish 8155
Hilltop Haven: Kautzky 5683
Himself: Henri 5004
Hireling Shepherd: Hunt 5411
Hiroshige: Mija 7426
Hirschjagd: Cranach 2344
His Madonna: Rosenthal 9569
His Omnipresence: Uhde 11, 184
His Presence: Sallman 9942
His Rose: Huldah 5379
Hispano-American Mural:
Orozco 8049
L'Hiver: Jacob 5490; Rouault
9618; Vlaminck 11, 824
Ho Ho Kane (South Seas):
Sheets 10, 279
Hockey Players: Teniers
10, 874
Hoic! Cover Hoic!: Gillet
4062
Holbein, Hans, the Younger:
Hertenstein 5039
Hold-Up: Russell 9794
Holiday: Campigli 1467;
Foujita 3676; Potthast 8815
Holiday in France: Jones 5593
Holiday Parade: Bolstad 829
Holiday with Grandfather:
Meyer 7383
Holland Landscape: Ruisdael
9749; Weissenbruch 12, 156

Hollywood Swing: Padua 8095
Holy Conversation: Palma 8108
The Holy Face: Byzantine 1438;
Rouault 9631
Holy Family: Baldung 433; Barto-
lommeo 485; Giotto 4116; Goes
4203; Greco 4332; Lorenzo di
Credi 6465; Luini 6520;
Maratta 6761; Michelangelo
7394; Pesaro 8303; Raffaello
8925; Reynolds 9384; Rubens
9700; Schongauer 10, 082;
Signorelli 10, 362; Suardi
10, 729; Titian 11, 023; Zatzka
12, 446, 12447
Holy Family on the Steps:
Poussin 8825
The Holy Heart: Batoni 506
Holy Heart of Christ: Batoni
507; Ciseri 2038
Holy Heart of Jesus: Zabateri
12, 439
Holy Mary: Giov. di Paolo 4164
Holy Mother: Albrecht 59
Holy Mountain III: Pippin 8661
Holy Night: Correggio 2268;
Dawson 2655; Ferrandiz
Castells 3588; Maratta 6762
The Holy One: Klee 5833
Holy Trinity: Rublev 9738
Homage to Mozart: Dufy 3095
Homage to Rameau: Tobey
11, 054
Homage to the Square: Albers
32
Home Again: Henry 5011
Home Camp in March: Gray
4324
Home Farm: Hilder 5104
Home for the Holidays: Claghorn
2051
The Home Lesson: Anker 244
Home on the Ranch: Megargee
7303
Home on the Range: Shelton
10, 282
Home Port: Amiot 121; Gasser
3856
Home Ranch: Eakins 3298
Home Sweet Home: Graf 4297;
Land 6079
Home to Thanksgiving: Durrie
3249

I and the Village: Chagall 1872
I Await the Letter: Gauguin 3904
I, Myself: Rousseau 9655
I Pledge Allegiance: Stevenson 10, 634
I raro Te Oviri: Gauguin 3905
I Saw the Figure Five in Gold: Demuth 2865
Ia Orana Maria: Gauguin 3906
Ibiza: Bueno 1316; Heidingsfeld 4969
Icarus' Fall: Roman 9526
Ice Bird and Seashells: Flegel 3634
Ice-Cream Man: Helps 4980
Ice Cream Vendor: Huldah 5380
Ice Glare: Burchfield 1389
Ice Landscape: Avercamp 356
Icebound: Metcalf 7364
Ichabod Verdure: Jaffe 5512
Ideas for Metal Sculpture Moore 7711
Idle Hours: Guba 4551
Idol: Matisse 7162
Idole: D'Altri 97
Idyle: Renoir 9240
Idylle at Bernau: Thoma 10, 933
Idyllic Landscape: Roman 9527
Ile de France: Marquet 7005
I'll Show the Way: Pike 8636
Ilonka: Walter 11, 930
I'm Tired: Kuniyoshi 6019
Imaginary Landscape: Poucette 8819; Wong 12, 284
The Immaculate Conception: Murillo 7865; Velasquez 11, 663
Immaculate Heart of May: Emery 3419; Schleibner 10, 043
Immaculate Virgin: Sarullo 9995; Tiepolo 10, 971
Immortal Indian: Mestrovic 7362
L'Impasse Cotlin: Utrillo 11, 290
Impenitent Thief: Durer 3207
Imperatrice Josephine: Prud'hon 8875
Imperia, Italy: Dzigurski 3282

Imperial Castle: Canaletto 1489
Imperial Castle, Schoenbrunn: Canaletto 1490
Imperial Chalet: Canaletto 1491
Imperial Mausoleum: Piranesi 8668
Impression at Sunrise: Monet 7612
Improvisation No. 10: Kandinsky 5642
Improvisation No. 30: Kandinsky 5644
Improvisation No. 35: Kandinsky 5645
Improvisation XIX: Kandinsky 5643
In Action: Osthaus 8061
In an Alpine Inn: Buri 1398
In the Alps: Erbsloh 3439; Schmidt 10, 057
In the Bahamas: Thieme 10, 906, 10, 918
In the Bavarian Moorland: Bachmann 398; Ehemann 3387
In Between: Keane 5698
In the Black Forest: Bachmann 399
In a Boat: Manet 6712
In the Bower: Steen 10, 594
In the Catskills: Cropsey 2386
In Central Park: Huldah 5381
In the Conservatory: Manet 6713
In the Country: Blommers 786
In a Country Inn: Teniers 10, 875
In the Days of Sail: Hilder 5105
In Egypt: Bartsch 491
In Fairmone: Spencer 10, 535
In the Fields: Ross 9581
In the Foothills: Legares 6221
In the Forest: Hofmann 5194; Rousseau 9656
In Front of the Chateau of Chastelloux: Utrillo 11, 291
In Full Bloom: Ruysch 9870
In Full Sail: Sherrin 10, 313
In a Garden: Persian 8276
In the Garden: Brush 1304; Cassatt 1656; Monet 7613; Pissarro 8700
In the Glittering Moonlight: Rehn 9047

531

Irish Setters: Danchin 2530; Hart 4701
Iron Kettle: Van 11,385
Iron Lady: Coulson 2301
The Ironer: Degas 2784; Picasso 8444
Ironers: Degas 2764
Ironwood Tree: Swinnerton 10,775
Isabella of Portugal: Titian 11,024
Isabelle Brant, First Wife: Rubens 9702
Isabelle D'Este: Leonardo 6269
Iserables: Marc 6785
Island of Geraniums: Gazzera 3972
The Isle: Eichhorn 3394
Isle de la Cité, Paris: De Presle 2875
Isle of Arran: Houston 5332
Isle of Bute: Houston 5333
Isle of Helgoland: Kalckreuth 5625
Isle of Istria: Montagu 7683
Isle of San Giorgio Maggiore: Guardi 4527
Isola Bella Sbocco Sul Lago: Marc 6786
Isola Dei Pescatori: Marc 6787
Isola Dei Pescatori Barche Alla Rivoca: Marc 6788
Isola San Giorgio: Buffet 1340
Israelites: Roberti 9481
It's Haying Time: Moses 7783
It's a Miss: Gilroy 4070
Italian Boy with Violin: Mancini 6679
Italian Cities: Korthals 5960
Italian Costume Figures: Worthington 12,391
Italian Fantasy: Cobelle 2099
Italian Grand Prix Monza, 1965: Turner 11,162
Italian Haven by Moonlight: Hackert 4587
Italian Harbor: Munnich 7841
Italian Landscape: Gair 3819; Hofer 5171; Peri 8265
Italian Landscape: Agnuzzo: Hofer 5172

Italian Landscape, the Apennines: Davies 2604
Italian Ruins: Piranesi 8669
Italian Square: Chirico 1985, 1986
Italian Views: Mapai 6759; Piranesi 8670, 8671
Italian Wharf: Medeiros 7271
Italian Woman: Picasso 8445
Italians at Mont St. Michel: Serrier 10,204
Die Italienerin: Rouault 9619
L'Italienne: Picasso 8445
Italy Romantic: Harnett 4674

Jack and the Beanstalk: Hencke 4988
Jackson, Andrew: Brown 1245
Jackson, General Stonewall: Cary 1628
Jackson, General T. J.: Elder 3403
Jacob Blessing His Children: Rembrandt 9070
Jacobea of Baden: Beham 560
Jacob's Dream: Bol 828; Rembrandt 9071; Schneid 10,071
Jacque Fray: Renoir 9244
Jade and China: Guion 4573
El Jaleo: Sargent 9981
Jamaica, B. W. I., Kingston: Haymson 4787
Jamaica, B. W. I., Street Scene: Haymson 4788
The James Baines: Knox 5896
James Stuart, Son of Charles I: Canevari 1545
James Whitcomb Riley: Sargent 9982
Jane: Ritter 9434
Jane Avril: Toulouse-Lautrec 11,118
Jane Avril Dancing: Toulouse-Lautrec 11,119
Jane Avril From the Back: Toulouse-Lautrec 11,120
Jane Avril Leaving Moulin Rouge: Toulouse-Lautrec 11,121
Jane Lumb: Johnson 5589
Jane Seymour: Holbein 5207
El Janguey: Ravenet 8977

534

535

538

Large Vase of Flowers: Renoir
9259
Large Vine Pergola: Sutherland
10, 744
The Large Way: Hundertwasser
5401
The Lark: Van Gogh 11, 533
Larkspur: Bille 683
Larkspur and Marguerites:
Hausen 4724
Larkspurs: Mai-Thu 6642
La Rochelle: Rosan 9562;
Signac 10, 351
Last Bales: Shepherd 10, 289
Last Barge Race: Foster 3670
Last Chance or Bust: Russell
9802
Last Communion: Bellechose
562
Last Journey on the Road:
Agasse 20
The Last Judgment: Angelico
209; Signorelli 10, 363
Last Ray of the Sun: Butinone
1412
Last Rays: Grant 4310
Last Snow: Cherepov 1967
The Last Supper: Andrea del
Sarto 151; Castagno 1668;
Fugel 3789; Ghirlandaio
4036; Leonardo 6270; 6271;
O'Connell 8016; Oswald
8062; Schleibner 10, 045;
Stang 10, 578
Late Afternoon: Thieme 10, 919
Late September: Cropsey 2390
Late Summer Day: Scholei
10, 079
Late Summer Day in the
Promontory: Gob 4199
Later Summer in Scotland:
Patrick 8192
Late Supper: Cordoba 2178
Latent Antagonism: Arikha 300
Latin Quarter Hotel: Kuntz
6026
Lattice Bridge: Murray 7890
Laugh Kills Lonesome: Russell
9803
Laughing Cavalier: Hals 4616
Laundress: Daumier 2582;
Degas 2770

Laundrymaid: Morland 7762
Laura: Giorgione 4088
Laurent Pony Cart: Karfoil
5666
Laurette: Valarie 11, 366
Laurier Roses: Van Gogh 11, 534
Lavender: Durer 3210
Lavender Harvest, Provence:
Clark 2058
Lavinia, the Artist's Daughter:
Titian 11, 025
The Lawn: Dufy 3103
Lazybones: Strang 10, 663
Leadbeaters Cockatoos: Botke
956
Leading-Rein: Toulouse-Lautrec
11, 123
Leal Souvenir: Van Eyck 11, 433
Leaping Horse: Constable 2135
Leave Off Work: Tauber 10, 844
Leave-Taking of Jesus: Lodi
6422
Leaving Honfleur: Jongkind 5601
Lecon d'Amour: Watteau 12, 100
Lecon de Musique: Watteau 12, 101
Leda: Pompeian 8766; Roman
9529; Ward 12, 044
Leda and the Swan: Leonardo
6272
Lee, Gen. Robert E. : Cary
1627; Elder 3404
Lee, Robert E. , Home, Arlington,
Va. : Haymson 4735
Leechwee Antelope: Skeaping
10, 435
Leeds to London: Henderson
4997
Leek Heads: Drawbell 3023
Legal and Court Room Scenes:
Sadler 9901
Legal Studies: Daumier 2574,
2581
Legend of the Nile: Klee 5839
Legend of St. Eligius and Gode-
berta: Christus 1992
Legend of St. Francis: Sassetta
9998
Legionnaires: Barth 475
Leila, Girl of Jerusalem:
Halewijn 4599
Leisure, Homage to Louis David:
Leger 6227

542

Loing Canal: Sisley 10, 408
Loire, Chateau d'Amboise:
Lloveras 6391
Loisach Valley: Waagen 11, 899
Lola de Valence: Manet 6715
Lolita: Steinlauf 10, 613; Tomaso
10, 067
London: Derain 2893; Shepherd
10, 290
London Bridge: Aldin 61;
Derain 2894
London, England, Changing
the Guard: Haymson 4790
London, England, Changing the
Guard at Buckingham Palace:
Haymson 4794
London, England, Houses of
Parliament: Haymson 4796
London, England, London Bridge:
Haymson 4795
London, England, Mansion
House: Haymson 4791
London, England, Old Curiosity
Shop: Haymson 4792
London, England, Tower Bridge:
Haymson 4793
London from Primrose Hill:
Hofer 5181
London from Richmond House:
Canaletto 1493
London, Houses of Parliament:
Lloveras 6392
London Morning: Folland 3650
London Parliament: Monet
7616
London Royal Mail: Henderson
4998
London, Tower Bridge: Buffet
1342; Kokoschka 5918
London Views: Korthals 5962
Lone Tenement: Bellows 600
Lone Tree: Tseng 11, 173
Lonely Tree: Friedrich 3769
Long Crendon: Neville 7941
Long-Horn Cattle Sign:
Remington 9139
Long Summer Days: Bordenave-
Aurous 907
Longhi Painting Portrait of a
Lady: Longhi 6432
Looking at the Day:
Vinciguerra 11, 793

Looking Forward: Iverd 5488
Looking Toward Chanctonbury
Ring: Gair 3818
Lookout: Keane 5723
Loops and Swift Horses are Surer
than Lead: Russell 9805
Lord Chief Justice: Spy 10, 571
The Lord's Image: Kroger 5987
Lords of the Jungle: Shepherd
10, 291
The Lord's Supper: Jambor
5524
The Lord Turned and Looked
Upon Peter: Beecroft 558
Lord William: Shayer 10, 270
Lorenzo de Medici: Gozzoli
4280, 4281, 4282
Losange: Fini 3615
Los Angeles, Cal., Civic Center:
Haymson 4797
Los Angeles, View: LeBreton
6194
Lost: Keane 5733
Lost and Found: Strang 10, 669
Lost Apache: DeGrazia 2804
Lost Scent: Hardy 4667
Lost Sheep: Soord 10, 497
Lotus: Chu Ta 2010
Lotus Bowl: Vu-Cao-Dam 11, 891
Lotus Flowers: Gough 4244;
Mei Feng 7305
Lotus Pool: Waters 12, 067
Louisiana Rice Fields: Benton
627
Love in May: Fujikawa 3792
Love, Labor and Leisure: Dehn
2526
Love Letter: Fragonard 3717;
Hidalgo 5069; Padua 8097;
Vermeer 11, 732
Love's Token: Webster 12, 139
Love's Young Dream: Webster
12, 140
Love Unto Death: Fragonard
3718
Lovers: Hutter 5425; Picasso
8458; Renoir 9268
Lovers Above the Town: Chagall
1873
Lovers in the Street: Picasso
8459
Lovers in the Tree Tops:
Chagall 1874

Madonna and Saints: Giov. del
Biondo 4161; Lorenzetti 6453;
Lorenzo Monaco 6476; Pin-
turicchio 8646
Madonna and Saints John and
Francis: Lorenzetti 6462
Madonna, Angels and St. Francis:
Lorenzetti 6462
Madonna, Angels and St. Francis:
Cimabue 2030
Madonna, Angels and Saints:
Ghirlandaio 4039
Madonna "La Belle Jardiniere":
Raffaello 8927
Madonna, Child and Angels:
Mainardi 6652
Madonna, Child, St. Anne and
St. John: Leonardo 6275
Madonna, Child and St. Francis:
Francia 3743
Madonna del Cardellino:
Raffaello 8928
Madonna del Dito: Dolci 2980
Madonna dei Francescani (The
Virgin Adored): Duccio 3037
Madonna del Granduca: Raffaello
8930
Madonna delle Grazie: Bellini
571
Madonna del Sacco: Andrea del
Sarto 156
Madonna della Scala: Correggio
2272
Madonna della Sedia (Madonna
of the Chair): Rafaello
8934
Madonna della Serra: Peri 8266
Madonna della Stella: Angelico
212
Madonna della Tenda: Raffaello
8937
Madonna Enthroned: Crivelli
2369
Madonna Enthroned and Saints:
Martini 7066; Memmi 7339
Madonna Immaculata: Giov. di
Paolo 4165
Madonna in the Meadow:
Raffaello 8932
Madonna in the Moonlight:
Giov. di Paolo 4166
Madonna in Red: Cuz 2467

Madonna in the Rose Garden:
Lochner 6416
Madonna of the Alberetti:
Bellini 570
Madonna of the Apple: Robbia
9453
Madonna of the Arbour: Cranach
2347
Madonna of the Carnation: Luini
6522
Madonna of the Chair: Raffaello
8934
Madonna of the Cherries:
Barocci 456
Madonna of the Childbirth:
Piero 8608
Madonna of the Finger: Dolci
2981
Madonna of Foligno: Raffaello
8929
Madonna of the Goldfinch: Tiepolo
10, 974
Madonna of the Grapes: Mignard
7423
Madonna of the Harpies: Andrea
del Sarto 157
Madonna of Humility: Angelico
213
Madonna of the Iris: Durer 3214
Madonna of the Lilies: Botticelli
981
Madonna of the Linaiuoli:
Angelico 214
Madonna of the Magnificat:
Botticelli 982
Madonna of Maison d'Orleans:
Raffaello 8931
Madonna of the Meadows: Bellini
572
Madonna of Mount Fileremo:
Byzantine 1440
Madonna of the Olives: Barabino
439
Madonna of Peace: Angelico 215
Madonna of the Pomgranate:
Botticelli 985
Madonna of Port Lligat: Dali
2512
Madonna of the Rosary: Sasso-
ferrato 10, 002; Simeone
10, 371
Madonna of the Rose Arbor:
Lochner 6417

Madonna of the Rose Bower:
Luini 6523
Madonna of the Rose Hedge:
Botticelli 988
Madonna of the Roses:
Botticelli 989
Madonna of San Sisto (Sistine):
Raffaello 8935
Madonna of the Sea: Botticelli
990
Madonna of Senigallia: Piero
869
Madonna of the Seraphim:
Botticelli 991
Madonna of the Street: Ferruzzi
3593
Madonna of the Trees: Bellini
573
Madonna of the Veil: Dolci
2982
Madonna Orans: Bartoli 480
Madonna Tempi: Raffaello 8936
Madonna with the Canopy:
Botticelli 992
Madonna with Child: Martini
7065
Madonna with the Green Cushion:
Solario 10, 493
Madonna with Jesus: Streyo
10, 708; Zabateri 12, 440
Madonna with the Lilies:
Robbia 9454
Madonna with the Pomegranate:
Raffaello 8933
Madonna with Sleeping Child:
Mantegna 6754
Madonna with the Soup: David
2596
Madonna with Sweet Pea:
Master 7117
Madonnina: Ferruzzi 3593
Madrid, Puente di Segovia:
Lloveras 6393
Maenads, Attic Vase: Greece
4348
La Maesta: Martini 7067
Magdalena: Piero 8610
The Magdalene: Dolci 2983;
Perugino 8292; Piombo 8651;
Titian 11, 027
Magic City: Wilks 12, 228
Magic of Spring: Ward 11, 996

Magic Pipes: Tarrant 10, 820
Magna Carta: Flint 3642
Magnanimity of Scipio: Tiepolo
10, 975
Magnolia: Berten 655; Gent
3994; Greene 4367
Magnolia Blossoms: Hall 4602
Magnolias: Boness 860; Bos
925; Jurk 5617; King 5787;
Oerder 8024; Schmidt-Rottluff
10, 061; Spencer 10, 538
Magpie on Flower Branch:
Unknown 11, 220
Maid of Honor: Rubens 9706
Maid with a Tray of Fruit:
Chirlandaio 4040
Maids from Avignon: Picasso
8392
Maids of Honor: Velasquez
11, 676
Maimonides: Levine 6306
Main Street in Anes: Utrillo
11, 297
Main Street Trolley: Grose
4476
Maine Islands: Marin 6947
Maison Bernot: Utrillo 11, 298
La Maison Blanche: Brayer
1169
Maison Dubois: Layton 6168
La Maison du Pendu: Cezanne
1779
Maison Mimi: Utrillo 11, 299
The Maize God: Aztec 370
Maja Dressed: Goya 4256
Maja Nude: Goya 4257
Majestic Peaks: Wood 12, 339
Majestic Tetons: Dzigursky
Majesty of the Mountains: Muller
7813
Major John Biddle: Sully 10, 735
Major T. Bouch, MFH, with the
Belvoir Hounds 7849
Major Thomas Biddle: Sully
10, 736
Maker of Preserves: Gris 4432
Male Figure: Masaccio 7086
Mallard and Azaleas: Ward
11, 997
Mallard, Anglesay: Monahan
7561
Mallard Duck: Audubon 334

Mallard Family: Dawson 2656;
Wilson 12, 237
Mallard in a Quiet Marsh:
Scott 10, 155
Mallard Rising: Harrison 4696
Mallard, Stormy Sky: Scott
10, 154
Mallards: Bailey 424
Mallorca: Ehemann 3388;
Marc 6794; Munoz 7855;
Winkler 12, 254
Mallorca Harbor: Lloveras
6394
Maloja: Marc 6795
Mal's Restaurant: Layton 6169
Malvern Hall: Constable 2136
Man: Lurcat 6549
Man and Beast: Orovida 8047
Man and Machinery: Rivera
9442
Man and the Star: Lurcat 6550
Man at a Door: Rembrandt
9075
Man of Opinion: Grosz 4496
Man of the Twentieth Centruy:
O'Higgins 8029
Man of War Cutter: Knell
5884
Man on Horseback: Van Dyck
11, 411
Man on a Tight Rope: Klee
5841
Man O'War: Amick 108; Morris
7773
Man Resting: Buffet 1343
Man Sowing: Van Gogh 11, 538
Man with an Axe: Gauguin 3913
Man with Flowers: Alex 70
The Man with the Glove:
Titian 11, 028
Man with a Golden Helmet:
Rembrandt 9076
Man with Guitar: Picasso 8463
Man with a Hoe: Millet 7449
Man with a Medal: Botticelli
993
Man with a Pink: Van Eyck
11, 434
Man with Two Horses on a Shore:
Chirico 1988
Man, Woman and Child: Miro
7479

Manchester Valley: Pickett
8596
Mandello Near Comer Sea:
Runge 9767
Mandolin: Beecher 555;
Haymson 4798
Mandolin and Guitar: Picasso
8464
La Mandoline: Braque 1115
Mandolins and Pineapples:
Tamayo 10, 789
Mandrill and Mangabeys:
Feibush 3541
Manhattan: Grosz 4497; Mac
Iver 6599; Stareck 10, 579
Manhattan Harbor: Grosz 4498
Manhattan Nocturne: Franck
3752
Mannequins at the Races: Dufy
3105
Manor House: Munch 7818
Manton from La Pausa:
Churchill 2017
Many Friends: Dawson 2657
Many Views: Keane 5709
Maona: Torino 11, 087
Maple Family: Jaffe 5515
Maple Sugaring in Vermont:
Sample 9956
Mara: Hindu 5134
Marble Table: Braque 1116
March 14-47 (Still Life on a
Table): Nicholson 7959
March 1960 (Grey and White with
Ochre): Hilton 5130
March Gallery: Layton 6170
March - North Atlantic: Waugh
12, 123
March of the Kings: Jones 5595
March on Lower Rhine: Perfall
8264
March Sunlight: Shepherd 10, 293
Les Marchandes des Modes:
Boucher 1025
Marche St. Medard, Paris:
Darche 2552
Marchesa Elena Grimaldi:
Van Dyck 11, 412
Marcus Aurelius: Panini 8125
Mardi Gras: Bassford 501;
Cezanne 1780; Maio 6661
Mare and Foal in the Paddock:
Konrad 5950

Marriage of St. Catherine:
Correggio 2274; Gozzoli 4285;
Lorenzo Veneziano 6478;
Michelino 7415; Murillo 7872;
Parmigianino 8147; Veronese
11, 766
Marriage of St. Ursula:
Carpaccio 1601
Marriage of the Virgin: Angelico
216; Fouquet 3690; Giotto
4125; Raffaello 8938
Mars Jealous of Adonis: Albani
30
Mars, Orange and Green:
Dove 3021
Marseille: Dufy 3108
Marseille No. 4: Vernet
11, 756
Marseille, Notre Dame de la
Garde: Dufy 3109
Marseilles, the Old Port:
Dufy 3110
Marsh Grasses: Barker 444
Marshall, John: Brown 1246
Marshall's House: Hopper 5139
Marshland Village: Seago 10, 172
Marshy Country: Bachmann 407
Marten Stalking Bird: Ghiberti
4023
Martha: Hundertwasser 5402
Martin Luther: Cranach 2348
La Martinique: Gauguin 3915
Les Martigues: Barle 447;
Marc 6877; Monticelli 7702;
Trimpert 11, 162
Martyrdom of St. Agatha:
Tiepolo 10, 976
Martyrdom of St. Justine:
Veronese 11, 767
Martyrdom of St. Lucia:
Veneziano 11, 700
Martyrdom of St. Matthew:
Caravaggio 1572
Martyrdom of Saints: Correggio
2275
Martyrdom of Saints Cosmas and
Damian into the Fire:
Angelico 217
Mary: Kroger 5989
Mary and Her Little Lamb:
Hencke 4992
Mary Eliza: Eurich 3474

Mary Had a Little Lamb:
Weisgard 12, 153
Mary Magdalen: Caravaggio
1573; Greco 4334
Maryland and Pennsylvania:
Blair 728
Mask: Crepet 2359; Klee 5842
Masked Ball: Toulouse-
Lautrec 11, 127
Masks: Baumeister 520; Ensor
3435
Masquerade: Bassford 502
Masquerade Children: Boobis
903
Masquerade in India: Jamini
9680
Massacre des Innocents (Mass-
acre of the Innocents):
Angelico 218; Brueghel 1286;
Matteo 7210; Reni 9169
Master Hare: Reynolds 9390
Master Lambton: Lawrence
6156
Master of Life, Health and
Happiness: Anderson 125
Master Simpson: Devis 2952
Master Willoughby: Unknown
11, 193
The Master's Children: Vogel
11, 870
Masters of the Cloth Guild:
Rembrandt 9077
Matador: Buffet 1344; Freund
3767; Machourek 6567; Picasso
8465; Rojas 9506
Matador I: Feuerborn 3604
Matador II: Feuerborn 3605
Mater Dolorosa: Cleve 2090;
Greco 4335; Michelangelo
7400; Unknown 11, 203
Mater Dulce: Giov. di Paolo
4167
Mater Purissima: Morelli 7734
Maternal Duty: Hooch 5280
Maternal Joys: Spinelli 10, 542;
Ussi 11, 253
Maternité: Picasso 8466, 8467
Maternity: Canlassi 1546;
Gauguin 3916; Miro 7480;
Picasso 8468; Preti 8862;
Robert 9455
Le Matin: Huet 5365

Matterhorn: Kokoschka 5920; Le Cervin 6209; Marc 6796; Mazetti 7227
Max Schmitt in a Single Scull: Eakins 3300
Maxine Dethomas: Toulouse-Lautrec 11, 128
Maxwell 1911: Saalburg 9890
May Belfort: Toulouse-Lautrec 11, 129
May Blossoms: Greer 4376
May Bud: Huldah 5384
May Day Frolic: Brueghel 1267
May Flowering: Ward 11, 998
May 4th and 5th, 1961: Bissier 713
Maya: Gilroy 4072
Mayan Goddess: Aztec 371
Mayan Prince: Dusso 3255
Mayan Princess: Dusso 3256
Mayflower Yacht: Lever 6294
Maytime: Huldah 5385
McSorley's Bar: Sloan 10, 448
Meadow: Renoir 9276
Meadow at Mont Foucauld: Pissarro 8702
Meadow Stream: Frankl 3754
Meal in the Forest: Unknown 11, 230
Meat's not Meat Till it's in the Pan: Russell 9807
Medea Before Murdering Her Children: Pompeian 8767
Medical Studies: Daumier 2583
Medici, Lorenzo de: Gozzoli 4280, 4281
Medici, Piero de: Gozzoli 4282
Medici, Giuliano de: Gozzoli 4283, 4284
Meditation: Bowers 1076; Hodler 5169
Meditation I, II, III: Jawlensky 5554
Meditation of the Passion: Carpaccio 1602
Meditterranean at Marseilles: Jawlensky 5555
Mediterranean Harbour: Muris 7883
Mediterranean Holiday: Sanjuan 9966

Mediterranean Scene: Dufy 3051
Mediterranean Street: Hann 4659
Mediterraneé: Huberger 5356
Medley of Spring: Greene 4370
The Meet: Herring 5034, 5035, 5036; Konrad 5951
Meet at Blagdon: Snow 10, 483
Meet at the Lodge: Bennett 617
Meet of the Vine Hounds: Calvert 1461
The Meeting: Konrad 5952
Meeting at the Golden Gate: Giotto 4126
Meeting in a Park: Pater 8185
Meeting of Frederic III with Eleanor of Portugal: Pinturicchio 8647
Meeting Outside a Park: Pater 8186
Meeting Place: Kosa 5964
Melancholie: Chaput 1918
Melita: Fini 3616
Melody in Pink: Medeiros 7275
Le Melon d'Eau: Bezombes 673
Melton Hunt: Dalby 2501
Member of the Este Family: Tura 11, 133
Memories: Detlefson 2944
Memories of Strauss: Edwards 3336
Memory Lane: Cherepov 1968
Men on the Dock: Bellows 601
Menagerie: Miro 7481
Les Meninas: Velasquez 11, 677
Menton: Marc 6797
Mentone: Hankey 4651
Menuett: Lancret 6071
Meo mit Pferochen: Lasard 6101
La Mer: Philippe 8331
La Mer a L'Estaque: Cezanne 1781
Mer au Havre: Dufy 3111
Mercedes 1909: Saalburg 9882
Mercer 1911: Saalburg 9891
Merchant George Gisze: Holbein 5209
Mercury and the Graces: Tintoretto 11, 002
The Mermaid and the Sailboats: Dufy 3112

New Born: La Tour 6105
New England: Blanch 738
New England Barn: Grose 4477
New England Church: Grose 4478
New England Dock: Levi 6295
New England Farm: Fiene 3611
New England Harbor: Vincent 11, 788
New England Harbors: Haymson 4808
New England Harbors, Boothbay: Haymson 4809
New England Harbors, Gloucester: Haymson 4810
New England Harbors, Rockport: Haymson 4811
New England Homestead: Gerry 4017
New England Scenes: Grose 4479; Whitney 12, 193
New England Street Scene: Thieme 10, 920
New England Views and Fishing Scenes: Thieme 10, 902
New England Winter: Thieme 10, 921
New-Fangled Engine: Bolstad 846
New Horizons: Capuletti 1556
New Jersey Coast: Waugh 12, 124
New Lazarus: Evergood 3481
New Mexico No. 2, Area near Taos: Marin 6951
New Orleans: Drummond 3034; Garneray 3850; Le Breton 6195; Lloveras 6396
New Orleans, La. , Lace Balconies: Haymson 4812
New Orleans, La. , Old Residence: Haymson 4813
New Orleans, La. , Prete House: Haymson 4814
New Orleans, La. , Vieux Carré: Haymson 4815
New Orleans Panels: Hamilton 4627
New Orleans Square: Kuntz 6027
New Quay: Richardson 9409
New Scholar: Brownscombe 1252

New Will: Sadler 9907
New Yacht: Dawson 2659
New Year on the Cimarron: Remington 9152
New York: Buffet 1345; Garneray 3851
New York 1848: Varin 11, 640
New York 1852: Varin 11, 641
New York, Brooklyn Bridge Arch: Haymson 4816
New York, Brooklyn Bridge Harbor: Haymson 4853
New York, Brooklyn View: Le Breton 6196
New York, Central Park: Haymson 4817
New York, Central Park Lake: Haymson 4832
New York, Central Park Skating: Haymson 4818
New York, Central Park Skyline: Haymson 4854
New York, Central Park, Winter Night: Haymson 4819
New York City Nos. 1 and 2: Haymson 4860, 4861
New York City Scenes: Gallais 3825, 3830
New York, Downtown Skyline: Haymson 4826
New York, East River Harbor: Haymson 4855
New York, Empire State Building: Haymson 4856
New York, Fifth Avenue: Haymson 4851
New York from Brooklyn: Haymson 4828
New York from the East River: Varin 11, 642
New York from Governor's Island: Wall-Hill 11, 924
New York from the North River 1839: Varin 11, 643
New York, Fulton Market: Haymson 4833
New York, George Washington Bridge: Haymson 4827
New York, George Washington Bridge, Night: Haymson 4857
New York, Grand Central Terminal: Haymson 4820, 4852

558

New York, Harbor: Mariani 6931
New York, Hudson River Skyline:
Haymson 4834
New York Landmarks: Meek
7297
New York, Lever House:
Haymson 4837
New York, Little Church Around
the Corner: Haymson 4838
New York, Lower Manhattan:
Lloveras 6397
New York, Lower New York Bay:
Haymson 4858
New York, Lower Park Avenue:
Haymson 4839
New York, Manhattan: Huberger
5357
New York, Metropolitan Museum:
Haymson 4840
New York, Mid-Town Water-
front: Haymson 4859
New York, Pan-Am. Building:
Haymson 4821
New York, Philharmonic Hall,
Lincoln Center: Haymson
4835
New York, the Plaza: Haymson
4836
New York, Public Library:
Haymson 4829, 4849
New York, Queensborough Bridge,
Night: Haymson 4862
New York, Rockefeller Center:
Haymson 4822, 4841
New York, Rockefeller Plaza:
Haymson 4850
New York, St. Patrick's
Cathedral, Nos. 1 and 2:
Haymson 4842, 4843
New York Skyline: Buffet 1346;
Haymson 4844
New York Skyline, Lower New
York from Brooklyn: Haym-
son 4830
New York, Statue of Liberty:
Haymson 4823
New York Stock Exchange:
Haymson 4824, 4845
New York, Tugs at Work:
Haymson 4863
New York, U. S. Treasury Build-
ing: Haymson 4846

New York United Nations
Secretariat: Haymson 4825
New York, United Nations
Panorama: Haymson 4864
New York, United Nations Sky-
line: Haymson 4831
New York, Vanderbilt Avenue:
Haymson 4847
New York Views: Snapper
10, 481; Stareck 10, 581
New York, Wall Street:
Lloveras 6398
New York, Washington Square:
Haymson 4848
New York, Washington Square
Park: Haymson 4865
New York Yacht Club Trophy
Race, Cowes Regatta: Jarvis
5547
Newfound Gap: Byrum 1423
Newlyweds of the Eiffel Tower:
Chagall 1876
Newport, Rhode Island in 1730:
Newell 7948
News Vendor: Andre 138
Newsboy: Bowers 1077
Niccolini-Cowper Madonna:
Raffaello 8940
Nice: Rodewald 9492
Niche, Fruit and Flowers:
Golding 4218
Nicholas Ferry, Called Bebe:
Unknown 11, 231
Nickel Plate Road: Harbart
4663
Nicola: Shabner 10, 248
Nicole: Eisendieck 3399
Nicole et Nicolette: Eisendieck
3400
Nicolo da Uzzano: Donatello
3000
Night: Candell 1542; Manessier
6691
Night Action off Savo: Shepler
10, 306
Night Fishing at Antibes: Picasso
8484
Night Hawks: Hopper 5320
Night Heron: Tan 10, 793
Night Patrol: Aldin 62
Night Watch: Rembrandt 9079
Nightfall: Montez 7699

Nude Woman Lifting Her Arm:
Picasso 8488
Number 1, 1967: Pelham 8240
Number 11: Tomlin 11, 074
Number 27, 1950: Pollock
8750
Nuptial Allegory: Botticelli
996
Nurnberg from the West:
Durer 3216
Nurnberg Wife in Ball Dress:
Durer 3217
Nurnberg Wife in Church Dress:
Durer 3218
Nurnberg Wife in House Dress:
Durer 3219
Nursery Decorations: Miro 7484
Nursery Rhymes: Weisgard
12, 150
Nursery Stories: Hencke 4985
Nurseryland: Bell 561
Nut Cracker: Edwards 3338
Nuthatch and Silver Birch:
Ede 3317
Nymph Pursued by a Satyr:
Dossi 3013
Nymphenburg Castle: Canaletto
1495
Les Nymphes: Renoir 9291

The Oaks: Rousseau 9674
Oarsmen at Chatou: Renoir
9292
Oast Cottage: Cundall 2409
Oath of the Horatii: David
2601
Oath of Love: Fragonard 3720
Oaxaca: Rivera 9446
Obelisk: Robert 9460
Ober-Reissen: Feininger 3568
Oblique Progression: Pereira
8261
Ocean Avenue, Carmel:
Cascella 1638
Ocean Breeze: Wood 12, 349
Ocean Drama: Vickery 11, 781
Ocean Racers: Dawson 2633
Ocean Racing: Cribb 2365
October Gleaning: Sloane
10, 458
October Gold: Wood 12, 350
October Meeting: Munnings
7851

October Morn: Wood 12, 351
October Morning: Kent 5763
October Sunshine: Kautzky
5685
Odalisque: Boucher 1032;
Delacroix 2849; Matisse
7173
Odalisque with Raised Arms:
Matisse 7174
Odd Birds Bathing: Minami
7455
Odd Birds in a Tree: Minami
7456
Ode to a Summer Floral:
Moskowitz 7792
Odysseus: Beckmann 540
Off the Coast of Arran:
McGregor 7249
Off Concarneau: Eschbach 3443
Off the Highlands: Mitchell
7503
Off the Main Road: Henry 5013
Off San Francisco: Dunbar 3175
Off the Western Land: Olsson
8039
Off to Market: De Grazia 2813
The Offering: Etruscan 3466;
Gauguin 3922
Offshore Wind: Dawson 8984
Oh! My New Ball!: Sarnoff 9990
Ohio Magic: Shahn 10, 259
Oil Splatters on Leaves:
MacIver 6600
L'Oise near Pontoise: Pissarro
8705
L'Oiseau Lyre: Picart 8338
Old and New: Iverd 5489
The Old and the Young: Sadler
9919
Old Archway: John 5574
Old Banjo: Keane 5742
Old Boats on the Lagoon:
Thelen 10, 891
Old Bridge: Derain 2897;
Robert 9461
Old Bridge, Venice: John 5575
Old Bruton Church (Williamsburg,
Va.): Claghorn 2053
Old Canal Bridge: Marc 6863
Old Checkered House: Moses
7785
Old Church and Steps: Lowry
6502

On the Costa Brava: Fessler
3595
On the Glacier: Shepler 10, 307
On the Havelsee: Kruger 6000
On the Heath: Gob 4200
On Horseback at the Seashore:
Gauguin 3923
On Lago-Maggiore: Luschner
6555-A
On the Lake: Morisot 7746;
Walters 11, 932
On the Lake in the Bois de
Boulogne: Morisot 7747
On Lake Maggiore: Bradshaw
1084
On Montmartre: Van Gogh
11, 547
On Morse Mountain: Marin
6952
On the Range: Arenys 295
On the River: Rousseau 9663
On the Road: Otter 8066
On the Road to China Camp:
Schwartz 10, 128
On the Sands, Berwick on Tweed:
Lowry 6503
On the Seine: Monet 7619
On the Shore: Womacka 12, 280
On Stage: Gropper 4450
On the Stairs: Zorn 12, 475
On Target: Sarnoff 9991
On the Terrace: Morisot 7748;
Renoir 9293
On the Threshold: Keane 5701
On the Vibes: Pellerano 8249
On the Way to Emmaus:
Schwarzer 10, 130
On the Way to Market: Crocker
2376
On the Way to Sevres: Corot
2236
On a Wind: Briscoe 1215
Once from the Gray of Night
Emerged: Klee 5844
Once Upon a Time: Albo 50
One Hundred Horses in Pasture:
Langshih-Ning 6093
One of Arlotto's Jokes:
Volterrano 11, 882
Onions and Bottle: Cezanne
1797
Only Two in It: Skeaping
10, 436

Open Air Cafe: Van Gogh 11, 548
Open Door: Wintz 12, 271
Open Sea: Waugh 12, 125
Open Season: Mason 7103
Open Unto Me: Beecroft 559
Open Window, Collioure:
Matisse 7175
Open Window in Nice: Dufy 3116
Opening Night: Feuerborn 3606
The Opera: Dufy 3117
Ophilie: Redon 9008
Opposition of Lines, Red and
Yellow: Mondrian 7568
O'Prevetariello: Mancini 6678
Optimist: Lane 6089
Oracle: Spuropoulos 10, 573
Orage: Vlaminck 11, 831
Orange Girl: Obstner 8011
Orange Sails: Feininger 3569
Orange Vendor: Renoir 9294
Oranges and Crystal: Blanchard
759
Oranges: Land of Plenty: Bove
1069
Orchard: Dyf 3270; Pissarro
8706; Van Gogh 11, 549
Orchard Lake: Yos 12, 423
Orchestra: Dufy 3118; Savary
10, 009
Orchid and White: Greene 4372
Orchid Still Life: Buffet 1347
Orchids: Boness 861; Cochran
2105; Philpot 8332
Oregon Trail: Bierstadt 679
Orestes and Pylades: Roman
9530
Oriental Birds and Flowers:
Honda 5265
Oriental Castle: Klee 5845
Oriental Garden: Gazzera 3973
Oriental Girls: Litt 6376
Oriental/Pansy: Gazzera 3974
Oriental Rider: Ross 9573
Oriental Serenity: Russell 9854
Oriental Simplicity: Ross 9574
Oriental Splendor: Nelson 7932
Oriental Sunset: Le Ba Dang
6185
Oriental Waters: Tansley 10, 799
Orientalische Szene: Lasard
6102
Oriental's Head: Tiepolo 10, 980

564

Pont Neuf au Soleil: Marquet
7013
Pont St. Marie: Kelly 5750
Pont St. Michel: Marquet
7014
Ponte della Paglia: Prendergast
8857
Ponte, Molle, Rome: Poussin
8829
Ponte Roto: Vanvitelli 11, 633
Ponte Vecchio, Florence:
Brandeis 1089; Hoowij 5292
Pontic Rhododendron: Thornton
10, 954
Pontoise: Pissarro 8710
Pony Chaise: Montpezat 7707
Pony Foals: Tunnicliffe 11, 179
Pony Group: Tunnicliffe 11, 180
Pony Raid: Russell 9809
Pony Trap: Toulouse-Lautrec
11, 139
Poodle: Meyer-Eberhardt 7386
Pool of London: Derain 2898
Pool with Nympheas: Monet
7622
Poor Fisher: Gauguin 3926
Poor Man's Store: Peto
8314
Poor Poet: Spitzweg 10, 555
Pope Innocent X: Velasquez
11, 681
Pope Julius II: Raffaello
8941
Pope Paul III: Titian 11, 030
Poplar Trees: Schwartz 10, 129
Poplars: Cezanne 1806
Poplars, Jura Valley:
Hamilton 4629
Poppies: Buffet 1355; Epstein
3438; Monet 7623
Poppies and Cornflowers:
Desnoyer 2918
Poppies and Larkspur:
Streckenbach 10, 679
Poppies and Mommies: Strang
10, 670
Poppy: Tauber 10, 846
Poppy Field: Van Gogh 11, 562
Poppy Girl: Piot 8654
Pork Butcher's Wife: Mazzon
7232
Porloch Weir: Sherwin 10, 329

The Port: Metzinger 7378
Port at Douellan: Puy 8887
Port Breton: Buffet 1357
Port D'Audierne: Marquet 7016
Port de Cannes: Deschamps
2909
Port de Dieppe: Friesz 3773
Port D'Eyrac: Palue 8118
Port du Havre: Marquet 7017
Port de Strasbourg: Gantner
3840
Port Majean: Marc 6811
Port Marly: Sisley 10, 414
Port Noyo: Kelsey 5758
Port of Algiers: Desnoyer 2919;
Marquet 7015
Port of Beaulieu: Buffet 1356
Port of Bordeaux: Manet 6730
Port of Collioure: Derain 2899
Port of Croisic: Chauleur 1949
Port of Dieppe: Friesz 3773
Port of Duisburg: Macke 6618
Port of Honfleur: Dufy 3127
Port of La Rochelle: Buffet
1358
Port of Paimpol: Signac 10, 348
Port of Saint-Cast: Signac
10, 349
Port of St. Mandrier: Baboulene
374
Port of St. Tropez: Manguin
6749
Port of Toulon: Friesz 3774
Portage: Homer 5250
Porte de la Tournelle: De Potvin
2869
Porte St. Denis: Berger 642;
Blondin 788
Porte St. Martin: Utrillo 11, 317
Portello and the Brenta Canal:
Canaletto 1500
Portfolio: Audubon 326, 331,
336; Currier and Ives 2423;
Moses 7788; Russell 9810
Portico, Fruit and Flowers:
Golding 4219
Portico with Lantern: Canaletto
1501
Portinari Triptych: Goes 4204
Porto Ferraio: Marcel 6916
Porto d'Jochia: Purrmann 8879
Portofino: Caselli 1651, 1652;
Monti 7701; Yos 12, 425

Portrait of Don Biagio Milanesi:
Perugino 8294
Portrait of Don Garcia De'Medici:
Bronzino 1221
Portrait of Dora Maar:
Picasso 8501
Portrait of El Conde de Teba:
Goya 4261
Portrait of an Elderly Man:
Holbein 5210
Portrait of Eleanor of Toledo
with her Son John: Bronzino
1222
Portrait of Eleanora of Toledo:
Bronzino 1223
Portrait of Elisabeth of
Montefeltro: Uccello 11, 176
Portrait of Elisabetta Gonzaga:
Mantegna 6756
Portrait of Emperor Maximilian
I: Durer 3227
Portrait of Erasmus: Holbein
5211
Portrait of Estelle: Degas
2778
Portrait of Evangelista Scappi:
Francia: 3744
Portrait of Ferdinand VII:
Goya 4262
Portrait of Florentine Lady
(The Magdalene): Pietro
8627
Portrait of Francesco Maria della
Rovere, Duke of Urbino:
Raffaello 8942
Portrait of Francesco Sforza
as a Child: Conti 2149
Portrait of Gabrielle: Renoir
9302
Portrait of Galeazzo Sforza:
Pollaiuolo 8746
Portrait of a Gentleman:
Maratta 6763; Titian
11, 031; Veneto 11, 696
Portrait of a Gentlewoman:
Pietro 8628; Tuscany 11, 164
Portrait of a German Officer:
Hartley 4706
Portrait of Gertrude Stein:
Picasso 8502
Portrait of a Girl: Audubon 337;

Mainardi 6653; Piero 8613;
Veneziano 11, 701
Portrait of Giuliano de'Medici:
Pontormo 8790
Portrait of Henry VIII: Holbein
5212
Portrait of Irma Brunner:
Manet 6733
Portrait of Jaime Sabartes:
Picasso 8504
Portrait of Jasper Schade von
Westrum: Hals 4617
Portrait of Jeanne Hebuterne:
Modigliani 7532
Portrait of Jeune Femme:
Nattier 7916
Portrait of Jeune Fille: Renoir
9303
Portrait of a Lady: Bugiardini
1382; Chen Yang 1956;
Cranach 2353; Holbein 5213;
Liotard 6344; Luini 6524;
Master 7120; Pollaiuolo 8743;
Reynolds 9396; Vos 11, 886;
Weyden 12, 173
Portrait of a Lady, Known as
"La Bella": Titian 11, 032
Portrait of Lady Van Muyden:
Modigliani 7533
Portrait of a Lady with an
Ostriche-Feather Fan:
Rembrandt 9089
Portrait of Leopold Medici as
a Baby: Titi 11, 010
Portrait of Lord Seaham as a
Boy: Lawrence 6162
Portrait of Lorenzo de'Medici,
Il Magnifico: Vasari 11, 649
Portrait of Louis XIV: Nanteuil
7896
Portrait of Lucie Berard:
Renoir 9304
Portrait of Lucrezla Panciatichi:
Bronzini 1224
Portrait of Maddalena Strozzi-
Doni: Raffaello 8943
Portrait of M. G. Coquiot:
Picasso 8503
Portrait of M. Seriziat: David
2602
Portrait of Mme. Blumer:
Manet 6734

574

Portrait of Mme. Hayden:
Modigliani 7534
Portrait of Mme. Le Brun:
Le Brun 6204
Portrait of Mme. Seriziat and
Her Son: David 2603
Portrait of Mme. Zborowska:
Modigliani 7535
Portrait of Madame "Z":
Picasso 8505
Portrait of Madamoiselle Chanel:
Laurencin 6130
Portrait of Madamoiselle Rinieri:
Ingres 5455
Portrait of a Man: Antonello da
Messina 265; Bronzino 1225;
Cranach 2354; Ghirlandaio
4047; Holbein 5214; Mainardi
6654; Maratta 6764; Memling
7330; Pourbus 8820; Titian
11, 033; Veneto 11, 697
Portrait of Margaret of Lorene:
Van Dyck 11, 418
Portrait of Maria De'Medici,
Daughter of Cosimo I:
Bronzini 1226
Portrait of Mary Bonciani-
Baronelli: Unknown 11, 225
Portrait of Michelangelo:
Bugiardini 1383
Portrait of a Model: Renoir
9305
Portrait of N. Machiavelli:
Crostofano 2366
Portrait of a Negro: Derain
2900
Portrait of a Nobleman:
Ausuino da Forli 261
Portrait of an Officer: Hals
4618
Portrait of an Old Man: Lippi
6356; Rembrandt 9090
Portrait of an Old Woman:
Kessel 5783
Portrait of a Painter: Van Dyck
11, 419
Portrait of Perugino: Raffaello
8944
Portrait of Pippo Spano:
Castagno 1670
Portrait of Portia de'Rossi:
Unknown 11, 245

Portrait of the Prince Rodoxana-
kis: Van Dyck 11, 420
Portrait of Princess of Este:
Carriera 1618
Portrait of Queen Elisabeth I of
England: Unknown 11, 204
Portrait of a Rabbi: Rembrandt
9091
Portrait of Rembrandt and
Saskia: Rembrandt 9092
Portrait of Rene de Gas:
Degas 2779
Portrait of Richard Southwell:
Holbein 5215
Portrait of a Saint in Prayer:
Grunewald 4510
Portrait of Sir Winston
Churchill: Birley 709
Portrait of the Son of Frederick
III: Sustermanns 10, 741
Portrait of Sonia: Fantin-Latour
3497
Portrait of Stefano Colonna:
Bronzino 1227
Portrait of Tommaso Inghirami:
Raffaello 8945
Portrait of Ulrich Varnbuhler:
Durer 3228
Portrait of Unknown Man:
Memling 7331, 7332
Portrait of Unknown Woman:
Bronzino 1228; Counis 2303;
Leonardo 6277
Portrait of Venetian Woman:
Derain 2901
Portrait of Verrocchio: Lorenzo
di Credi 6471
Portrait of a Woman: Botticelli
998; Cranach 2349; Chirlandaio
4048; Hals 4619; Modigliani
7536; Padovanino 8091
Pisano 8678
Portrait of a Woman Called
"The Fair": Parmigianino
8148
Portrait of a Young Girl: Lorenzo
di Credi 6468; Morisot 7749;
Renoir 9306; Verspronck
11, 773
Portrait of a Young Lady:
Gauguin 3927; Ghirlandaio
4043

Portrait of a Young Man:
Botticelli 999; Bronzino 1229;
Lippi 6357; Memling 7333;
Perugino 8295; Uccello
11, 177; Van Gogh 11, 566
Portrait of a Young Nobleman:
Raffaello 8946
Portrait of a Young Prince:
Unknown 11, 246
Portrait of a Young Roman Lady:
Piombo 8653
Portrait of a Young Woman:
Breu 1200; Degas 2780;
Modigliani 7537; Veneziano
11, 702
Portrait of a Young Woman,
Version XIII: Picasso 8506
Portrait of a Young Woman at
the Mirror: Titian 11, 034
Portrait of a Youth: Bellini
594; Beltraffio 608;
Botticelli 1000; Lotto 6490;
Predis 8832
Portrait of a Youth in a Black
Cap: Lorenzo di Credi 6469
Portrait of a Youth in a Red
Cap: Lorenzo di Credi
6470
Portraits: De Grazia 2814;
Gentilini 4003; Haymson
4887; Igor 5441; Ingwersen
5461; Munch 7815
Portraits, Mexican Children:
Haymson 4888
Portraits of Children: Blacky
720; Dekoning 2836; Medeiros
7280
Portraits of Girls: Grisot 4443
Portraits, Spanish: Maio 6662
Pose, Classique: Munchhausen
7829
Positano, Italy: Dzigurski 3291
Posters: Buffet 1359, 1360;
Calder 1457; Cezanne 1808;
Chagall 1879, 1880; Dufy
3128, 3129, 3130; Etruscan
3469; Gris 4434; Kandinsky
5652 to 5655; Klee 5849 to
5851; Leger 6228; Matisse
7179, 7180; Miro 7490;
Mondrian 7570; Motherwell
7796; Picasso 8507; Pollock
8751; Rouault 9629, 9630;

Shahn 10, 260, 10, 261;
Toulouse-Lautrec 11, 140,
11, 141; Utrillo 11, 318
Postman: Spitzweg 10, 556
Postman Roulin: Van Gogh
11, 567
Pot de Fleurs: Cezanne 1809
Pot of Flowers with Pears:
Cezanne 1810
Potato Field Behind Dunes:
Van Gogh 11, 568
Potipher's Wife: Morelli 7735
Potter's Son: Dallas-Simpson
2519
Pottery Figure of a Saddled
Horse: Unknown 11, 214
Pottery Vendor: Vives 11, 797
Poultry Market: Beuckelaer 670
Poultry Yard: Anker 248
Pounding Surf: Waugh 12, 127
Powder Snow: Shepler 10, 308
Pragser Wildsee: Bachman 412
Prairie at By: Sisley 10, 415
Prancing Horse: Skeaping
10, 437; Unknown 11, 215
The Prayer: Maes 6630
Praying Hands (Hands of a Pray-
ing Apostle): Durer 3229;
Rubens 9711
Prelude: Spinelli 10, 543
Le Prelude de Nina: Boilly 825
Prelude to Spring: Ward 12, 012
Premiere au Rendezvous:
Huldah 5392
La Premiere Sortie: Renoir
9307
Preparation for the Festival:
Berentz 632
Preparing for Church: Blommers
787
Preparing to Sail: Greig 4378
The Presence: Borthwick 917
The Presentation in the Temple:
Angelico 222; Carpaccio 1604;
Giov. da Milano 4160
Presentation of Maria in the
Temple: Tintoretto 11, 005
Presentation of Mary: Titian
11, 035
Presentation of the Virgin:
Giotto 4130
President Kennedy: Simpson
10, 376

Le Preteur sur Gages: Metsys 7375
Pride of Lions: Shepherd 10, 298
Primavera: Botticelli 1001; Pradier 8831
Primitive Fruit: Schalter 10, 033
Primitive Portraits: Cary 1630
Primitive Sculptor: Couse 2331
The Prince: Montagu 7692; Parrish 8159
Prince Balthazar Carlos: Velasquez 11, 661
Prince of Denmark: Sustermanns 10, 742
Prince of Wales: Munnings 7852
Prince of Wales 1603: Unknown 11, 205
Prince Philip, Duke of Edinburgh: Halliday 4603
Prince Riding an Elephant: Mughal 7811
The Princess: School 10, 083
Princess and Her Attendant: Hindu 5135
La Princesse de Cleves: Laurencin 6131
Princess of Este: Pisano 8679; Pollaiuolo 8744
Princess Isabella Maria: Moro 7765
Princess Margarita Maria: Velasquez 11, 682
Princess Mary Anne: Nattier 7917
Princess Mary Louise: Nattier 7918
Princess Metternich: Daffinger 2498
Princess White Stripe: Grimm 4409
Princeton, Nassau Hall: Haymson 4904
Print Collector: Daumier 2587
Printemps: Huldah 5393; Jacob 5491; Lancret 6075
Printemps a Chatou: Renoir 9308
Printemps a Vienne: Edwards 3339

Printing House Square, New York 1864: Varin 11, 644
Prisoner: Latour 6111
Prize Boy: Currier and Ives 2436
Procession: Picasso 8508
Procession of the Cross: Bellini 563
Procession of the Kings: Memling 7334
Procession to Calvary: Brueghel 1292
Procuratore Giovanni Guerini: Tiepolo 10, 983
Prodigal Son: Feti 3596
Profile of a Woman: Toulouse-Lautrec 11, 142
Profusion of Beauty: Huygens 5427
Promenade: Burchfield 1392; Lavreince 6147; Nerfin 7934
Promenade at Nice: Beckmann 542
Promenade of Granduca Pietro Leopoldo: Sorbi 10, 499
Promise of Frost: Scott 10, 160
Promise of Rain: Birch 704
Promised Land: Amick 110
Promontory in Austria: Gaston 3870
Prophet Daniel: Michelangelo 7401
Prophet Ezekiel: Michelangelo 7402; Schneid 10, 073
Prophet Isiah: Michelangelo 7403
Prophet Jeremiah: Michelangelo 7404
Prophet Joel: Michelangelo 7405
Prophet Jonah: Michelangelo 7406
Prophet Zacharias: Michelangelo 7407
Proposal: Webster 12, 141
Prospecting for Cattle Range: Remington 9142
Prospectors: Russell 9817
Prothonatary Swamp Warbler: Audubon 329
The Proud'hon Family: Courbet 2321
Provencal Caprice: Flint 3643
Provencal Jug: Bonnard 894

Quiet Estuary: Breton 1180;
Folland 3651
Quiet Harbor: Faust 3531;
Richardson 9411
Quiet Haven: Cerny 1710
Quiet Inlet: Kautzky 5688
Quiet Moment: Miller 7437
Quiet Mooring: Bordenave-
Aurous 908
Quiet Path Through the Woods:
Yos 12, 426
Quiet River: Pasmore 8175
Quiet Solitude: Parrish 8160
Quiet Waters: Freitag 3762
Quintet: Meiersdorf 7310
Quintette: Dufy 3131
El Quitasol: Goya 4264
Quorn Hounds: Grant 4305

Rabbi of Vitebsk: Chagall 1881
Rabbi with Book: Chagall 1882
Rabbi with Torah: Chagall 1883
Rabbit and Red Casserole:
Buffet 1341
Rabbits: Dawson 2660; Koninck
5944
The Race: Cahoon 1454; Tarrant
10, 827; Walker 11, 919
Race at Epsom: Dufy 3132
Race Horses: Degas 2781
Race Horses at Longchamps:
Degas 2782
Race Track: Dufy 3133
Racecourse at Deauville: Dufy
3134
Races: Gropper 4451
Races at Deauville: Dufy 3135
Races at Goodwood: Dufy 3136
Rachmaninoff: Lupas 6540
Racing Home the Cutty Sark:
Dawson 2634
Racing Wings: Dawson 2635
Raftsmen Playing Cards:
Bingham 691
Ragga-Moppets: Eden 3321
Raggedy Romeo: Livingston
6381
Ragusa: Wecus 12, 145
Railway Bridge: Van Gogh
11, 569
Railway Cut: Cezanne 1812
Railways: Schlemmer 10, 049

Rain Forest: Jaffe 5517
Rain on the Way: Ghilchik 4024
Rainbow: Beckmann 543; Dawson
2666; Rubens 9712
Rainbow Over the Exe: Girtin
4178
Rainbow Trail: Tomaso 11, 070
Rainy Day in Rockport: Thieme
10, 928
Rainy Morning in a Cow Camp:
Russell 9818
Rainy Season: Hurd 5421
Rake's Progress: Hogarth 5198
Ram in the Night: Lurcat 6553
Ramapo River Near Suffern,
New York: Marin 6962
Ram's Head with Hollyhock and
Little Hills: O'Keeffe 8035
Ramsau Near Berchtesgaden:
Bachmann 413
Rancheria: Hurd 5422
Ranger's Farm, Richmond Park:
Bateman 505
Ranunculus: Thurner 10, 958
Raoul Rochette: Ingres 5456
Rape of Europa: Titian 11, 037
Raphael and Tobias: Savoldo
10, 019
Rapid Transit: Bolstad 848
Rapidity of Sleep: Tanguy
10, 795
Rapids, Hudson River: Homer
5251
Ras Casse: Buffet 1362
The "Rattlesnake": Phelan
8323
The Ray: Oxtoby 8078
Rays of the Sun: Miro 7491
The Reader: Corot 2241; Henner
5002; Renoir 9309
The Reading: Hilair 5084, 5085;
Manet 6735
Reading From Homer: Alma-
Tadema 86
Reading Girl: Corot 2242
Reading Girl in White: Renoir
9310
Reading Girl with Straw Bonnet:
Renoir 9311
Reading Lady: Padua 8099
Reading Little Girl: Pizzanelli
8732

583

Salton Sea: Swinnerton 10, 778
Salute of the Robe Trade:
  Russell 9824
Der Samen: Van Gogh 11, 573
Sampans: Le Ba Dang 6186
Sampans at Sunset: Woody
  12, 384
Sampler: Slatter 10, 445; Taylor
  10, 858
Samplers: Mariana 6927
San Carlos Church in Moonlight:
  Schwartz 10, 116
San Cipriano, Corsica: Peri
  8267
San Francisco: Meryon 7359
San Francisco, Cal.: LeBreton
  6197
San Francisco, Cal., Cable Cars:
  Haymson 4896
San Francisco, Cal., Fisherman's
  Wharf: Haymson 4897
San Francisco, Cal., Skyline:
  Haymson 4898
San Francisco Harbor: Schwartz
  10, 125
San Francisco-Oakland Bridge:
  Lloveras 6405
San Francisco View: Stareck
  10, 582
San Francisco Wharf: Schwartz
  10, 126
San Giorgio from the Riva
  Schiavoni: John 5576
San Giorgio Maggiore: Dufy
  3152; Guardi 4537
San Juan Capistrano Mission:
  Schwartz 10, 112
San Marco, Venezia: Lloveras
  6406
San Pietro: Chandos 1894
San Salvatore: Marc 6818
San Vigilio, Lake of Garda:
  Hopf 5297
Sanary sur Mer: Cardella 1588
Sand Cart: Bellows 602
Sand Dunes: Arentz 288
Sand Dunes and Crescent Moon:
  Feininger 3573
Sand Team: Bellows 602
Sand of Sylt: Sprotte 10, 568
Sannox Bridge: Houston 5334
Sant Angelo Bridge and Castle,
  View: Piranesi 8674

Sant Antioco: Chandos 1895
Santa Barbara Mission:
  Schwartz 10, 121
Santa Clara Indian Girl: Steinke
  10, 604
Santa Fe Trail: Young-Hunter
  12, 436
Santa Maria della Salute:
  Guardi 4538; Marieschi 6934
Santa Maria della Salute,
  Venice: Canaletto 1513
Santa Maria from San Giorgio:
  Fontanarosa 3653
Santa Maria Maggiore: Piranesi
  8675
Santa Maria Trastavere: Meek
  7302
Santa Trinita Bridge at Florence:
  Fontanesi 3656
Santiago Madonna: Murillo 7876
Sapho: Roman 9536
Les Sapins: Bardone 443
Sara: Shabner 10, 249
The Sargent Family: Unknown
  11, 197
Sarlat: Marc 6853
Saskia: Rembrandt 9096
Saskia at Toilet Table:
  Rembrandt 9097
Satin Gown: Greene 4359
Saturday Night on the Ranch:
  Megargee 7304
Satyr and Peasant: Jordaens
  5606
Sauvetage: Lipchitz 6347
The Saviour: Coleman 2116;
  Leonardo 6283; Munkacsy
  7837; O'Connell 8020; Titian
  11, 044
Savonarola: Bartolommeo 488
Savoyard Boy: Johnson 5587
Sax Man: Pellerano 8252
Saxon Church: Seago 10, 173
The Saxony of Boston: Weyts
  12, 177
Scandal and Tea: Sadler 9922
Scarlet for the Garden: Ward
  12, 018
Scarlet Ibis: Audubon 340
Scarlet Ribbons: Dallas-
  Simpson 2521
Scattering the Riders: Russell
  9825

593

594

Still Life with Pitcher: Bille
684; Bos 935; Protic 8873
Still Life with Plate: Bille
685
Still Life with Playing Cards:
Braque 1152
Still Life with Plums: Bos 936
Still Life with Pottery Jug:
Bos 937
Still Life with Red Apple:
Braque 1153
Still Life with Red Shawl:
Picasso 8540
Still Life with Statue: Cezanne
1835
Still Life with Storm Lantern:
Bos 938
Still Life with Strawberries:
Bos 939
Still Life with Sunflowers:
Bos 940
Still Life with Tangerines:
Bos 941
Still Life with Tankard: Bos
942; Chardin 1939
Still Life with Thunder:
MacDonald 6581
Still Life with Violin: Newton
7950
Still Life with Wallpaper:
Picasso 8541
Still Life with White Plate:
Buffet 1370
Still Life with Yellow Jug:
Picasso 8542
Still Life with Yellow Orchids:
Beckmann 548
Still Music: Shahn 10, 263
Still Waters: Peri 8268
Stilles Moor: Bocker 804
Stillness of Eternity: Montlack
7706
Stockade: Cezanne 1836
Stoke by Nayland: Constable
2140
Stolen Kiss: Fragonard 3726
Stolen Meeting: Webster
12, 142
Stone-Breakers: Courbet 2324
Stone City: Wood 12, 302
Stone Mason's Yard: Canaletto
1518

Stone Pines, Antibes: Monet
7644
Storage Room: Hooch 5285
Storm: Boilly 826; Bordi 912;
Giorgione 4092; Keane 5712
Storm at Sea: Bakhuyzen 427
Storm Clears: Ashley 308
Storm Clouds: Bordi 913
Storm Over Amboseli: Shepherd
10, 301
Storm Over Taos: Marin 6965
Storm Queen: Ray 8995
Storming the Citadel: Fragonard
3727
Stormy Day in Connemara:
Henry 5024
Stormy Landscape: Rembrandt
9104
Stormy Ocean: Pechstein 8220
Stormy Waters: Cohran 2112
Story Hour: Caraud 1558
Story of a Candle: Ardon 281
Story Teller: Hyams 5435
Stowing the Sail, Bahamas:
Homer 5257
Straggler: Simpson 10, 377
Strand and Casino of Nizza:
Dufy 3158
Strand of Guernsey: Renoir
9336
Stranded Boat: Braque 1154
Strandweg: Burkhard 1401
Strauss Waltz: Albo 54
Strawberries: Haymson 4778
Strawberry Girl: Anker 254
Stray: Keane 5740
Stray Cur, Eucalyptus Grove
1961: Okamura 8031
Stream of Life: Deman 2856
The Street: Utrillo 11, 347
Street at Louveciennes:
Sisley 10, 426
Street Cafes: Amadio 101
Street Dancing, Seville: Bove
1074
Street in Anse: Utrillo 11, 348
Street in Asnieres: Utrillo
11, 349
Street in Auteuil: Utrillo
11, 350
Street in Auvers: Van Gogh
11, 592

601

Study, St. Jerome: Cesare da
Sisto 1718
Stummer Schmerz: Jawlensky
5561
Stump Speaking: Bingham 693
Stuppach Madonna: Grunewald
4511
Sturdy Landmark: Detlefson
2949
Sturmische Einfart: Feininger
3579
Stymie: Stokes 10, 654
Submarine Garden: Cerny 1713
Suburban Landscape with
Factory: Utrillo 11, 353
Suburban Street: Buffet 371;
Utrillo 11, 354
Suburbs of Paris: Chin 1979
Such a Devoted Husband:
Daumier 2578
Sudden Fears: Ward 12, 032
Suffer Little Children: Tarrant
10, 832; Vogel 11, 871
Sugar Bowl with Fruit: Braque
1156
Sugar Maples: Jaffe 5521
Sugaring Off: Moses 7789
Suite Byzantine: Music 7893
Suitor's Visit: Ter Borch
10, 885
Sultan's Favorite: Guardi 4542
Summer: Blanchard 756;
Boucher 1040; Cathelin 1683;
Keisecki 5744; Lancret 6076;
Miro 7494; Monet 7647;
Roberti 9474; Rousseau 9668;
Rubens 9718; Watson 12, 070;
Watteau 12, 113; Weber 12, 136;
White 12, 192
Summer Afternoon: Durand
3186
Summer Ballad: Ruffino 9743
Summer Beauties: Bartning
479
Summer Blooms: Bove 1075
Summer Bounty: Nichols 7957
Summer Bouquet: Fromhold
3779; Picasso 8544
Summer Breezes--Off the
Needles: Dawson 2637
Summer City: Bellows 604
Summer Clouds: Clausade
2063

Summer Day: Kraus 5969
Summer Day by the Sea:
Beckmann 549
Summer Day in the Palace
Garden: Guardi 4543
Summer Day in Rome: Dill
2965
Summer Days: Falter 3492
Summer Decor: Ward 12, 033
Summer (or Wood) Duck:
Audubon 342
Summer Evening near Arles:
Van Gogh 11, 596
Summer Flowers: Bartel 472;
James 5529; Niven 7988;
Ruysch 9871; Taylor 10, 860;
Vaeltl 11, 364
Summer Fragrance: Ward
12, 034
Summer Glory: Blenner 775;
Cooper 2155; Hilder 5090
Summer Gold: Ward 12, 035
Summer Harvest: Shepherd
10, 302
Summer Harvesters: Brueghel
1294
Summer Holiday: Carson 1620
Summer Idyll: Ottema 8065
Summer in Angus: Patrick
8194
Summer in Devonshire: Hankey
4656
Summer in Italy: Rohricht 9504
Summer in Venice: Deschamps
2910
Summer Inlet: Gasser 3861
Summer Landscape: Davis
2623; Friedrich 3770; Kruger
6006; Laufman 6115; Noro
8003; Valckenborgh 11, 376
Summer Lightning: Sickert
10, 341
Summer Morn: Thieme 10, 924
Summer Palace: Kano 5665
Summer Redbird: Audubon 330
Summer Reflections: Dekay
2833
Summer Seas: Ninnes 7980
Summer--Le Soir: Huet 5367
Summer Spice: Blanchard 760
Summer Splendour: Cooper
2156

604

605

608

Trotting Horses: Faust 3537
Trousseau: Hawthorne 4734
Trout River: March 6918
Trout Stream: Sessions 10, 213
Trumpet Player: Medeiros
7279
Trumpeter: Watteau 12, 114
Trumpeter of the Hussars:
Gericault 4014
Le Tub: Degas 2791
Tugboat: Sisley 10, 429
Les Tuileries: Claver 2073
Tulagi Secured: Shepler 10, 310
Tulip Field: Monet 7651
Tulip Fields at Sassenheim:
Monet 7652
Tulips: Beckmann 550; Besler
661; Dongen 3007; Dufy 3163;
Golding 4221; Thornton
10, 956
Tulips and Anemones: Dufy
3164
Tulips in Holland: Monet 7653
Tumblers: Picasso 8552
Tumbling Waves: Mandon 6685
Tuna Fleet: Callot 1459
Tunk Mountains, Autumn, Maine:
Marin 6968
Tunny Boats: Sherwin 10, 330
Turkey Buzzard: Homer 5260
Turkish Bath: Ingres 5459
Turkish Shawl: Picasso 8553
Turkish Women: Ingres 5460;
Picasso 8554
Turning Point: Arkle 301
Turning Stake Boat: Eakins
3305
Turquoise Vase with Flowers:
Redon 9013
Tuscan Landscape: Ceccone
1703
Tutti-Frutti: Tyler 11, 170
Twelfth of August: Blinks 782
Twelfth Step Cafe: Layton 6172
Twilight: Clavé 2070; Ende
3423; Parrish 8167
Twilight in Rome: Thon 10, 952
Twilight on the Lake: Corot
2252
Twin Pines: Pelham 8237
Twittering Machine: Klee 5866
Two Angels: Andrea del Sarto
163

Two Ballerinas: Vertes 11, 778
Two Bathers: Renoir 9341
Two Birds: Ma Lin 6573
Two Birds and Apples: Chieng-
Ying Chang 1977
Two Brothers: Picasso 8555
Two Budgerigars: Chieng-Ying
Chang 1978
Two Bulls: Prehistoric 8843
Two Carmelites: Masaccio
7085
Two Children: Morisot 7753;
Picasso 8556
Two Children in White: Renoir
9342
Two Cousins: Watteau 12, 115
Two Cranes: Hindu Art 5137
Two Dancers on Stage: Degas
2792
Two Dancers with Fan: Degas
2793
Two Dancing Girls: Feinrich
3585
Two Deer: Marc 6909
Two Dying Warriors: Tiepolo
10, 994
Two Fawns: Hopking 5300
Two Figures: Pieper 8599
Two Figures on a Tahitian
Beach: Gauguin 3950
Two Fish: Clavé 2069
Two Flying Putti: Tiepolo 10, 995
Two Girls at the Piano: Renoir
9343
Two Girls in Blue: Renoir 9344
Two Girls in a Meadow: Renoir
9345
Two Girls Nude: Gauguin 3951
Two Girls on Yellow: Grimm
4410
Two Harlequins: Picasso 8557
Two Heads: Appel 277; Miller
7435
Two Horses: Erni 3440; Koshang
Lan 5965; Wagner 11, 906
Two Ladies in a Theatre Box:
Guys 4583
Two Little Girls: Mai-Thu 6645
Two Lovers: Modigliani 7541;
Swabian 10, 748
Two-Masters Becalmed: Marin
6969
Two Noblemen: Masolino 7098

Two of a Kind Win: Russell 9834
Two Peasants: Kirchner 5797
Two Riders: Marini 6985
Two Sheep: Marc 6910
Two Sisters: Fini 3617; Picasso 8558; Renoir 9346
Two Squirrels: Hopking 5301
Two Tahitian Women with Mangoes: Gauguin 3952
Two Women Seated: Moore 7715
Two Women with Umbrellas: Renoir 9347
Two Yachts: Feininger 9581
Two Young Girls: Matisse 7204; Renoir 9348
Tyrolese Landscape: Corinth 2191

U. S. Mail Boat: Bauman 512
U. S. Marshall's Revolver: Clayton 2079
U. S. S. Constitution: Aylward 364; Grose 4488
U. W. A.: Australia 353; Austria 354; Bulgaria 1384; Cyprus 2482; Czechoslovakia 2483; Egypt 3381; Ethiopia 3447; Greece 4354; India 5444; Iran 5474; Israel 5481; Japan 5538; Mexico 7382; Norway 8004; Poland 8740; Rumania 9760; Spain 10, 529; Tunisia 11, 177; Turkey 11, 135; U. S. S. R. 11, 254; Yugoslavia 12, 437
Ulanova in Giselle: Edwards 3344
Ullswater: Cooper 2160
Ulysses and the Sirens: Picasso 8559
Umpire: Spy 10, 572
Uncle Dominic: Cezanne 1839
Under Summer Skies: Parrish 8168
Understanding One: Klee 5867
UNESCO World Art Series: See U. W. A.
Uninvited Guests: Sadler 9924
United Nations Headquarters, New York: Dufy 3165
Unity: Blinks 783

Unknown Beauty: Baschenis 497
Unloading Operations: Shepler 10, 311
Unwelcome Intruders: Flint 3644
Up in Central Park: Hahn 4595
Upland Breezes: Dawson 2667
Upper Grand Canal: Canaletto 1521
Upper Hudson: Cropsey 2400
Uprising: Daumier 2591
Urbino: Montagu 7689
Urchins: Murillo 7878
Urnersee: Marc 6823
Uschi with Teddy Bear: Torino 11, 090

Vagabonds: Sciltian 10, 140
Vairumati: Gauguin 3953
Vale of Dedham: Watts 12, 117
Valley Farm: Constable 2141; Hurd 5424
Valley Forge, Pa.: Haymson 4921
Valley Stream: Pelham 8244
La Valse: Edwards 3345
Vanity: Chang Shu-Chi 1903; Dyf 3278
Varenne Castle: Utrillo 11, 356
Variation: Jawlensky 5562
Variation Classique: Munchhausen 7830
Variation--Swan Lake: Munchhausen 7834
Vase: Haymson 4762
Le Vase Blanc: Cathelin 1684; Lignon 6332
Vase de Fleurs: Redon 9014
Vase of Anemones: Dufy 3166
Vase of Canna: Margotton 6925
Vase of Chrysanthemums: Monet 7654
Vase of Flowers: Cezanne 1840 to 1842; Heem 4960; Melatti 7317; Redon 9015 to 9017; Rousseau 9671; Seghers 10, 179; Unknown 11, 226; Vlaminck 11, 856
Vase of Mixed Flowers: Os 8055
Vase of Peonies: Manet 6742
Vase of Roses: Renoir 9349; Vuillard 11, 898
Vase of Tulips: Cezanne 1843

Vase with Flowers: Picasso
8560
Vaudeville Artist No. 1: Grau-
Sala 4313
Vaumarcus: Marc 6855-A
Vegetable Gardens: Van Gogh
11, 607
Vegetable Market: Metsu 7372
Vegetable World: Rox 9679
Veil of Veronica: Feti 3597
Veiled Goldfish: Chater 1947
Veiled Lady: Raffaello 8957
Veluti in Speculum: Hofmann
5186
Velvet Paintings, Early
American: Unknown 11, 199
Venetian Courtesan: Forabosco
3659
Venetian Fantasy: Cobelle 2102
Venetian Lady: Longhi 6435
Venetian Lovers: Bordone 914
Venetian Masquerade: Marrucci
7026
Venetian Scene, San Benedetto
Looking Toward Fusina:
Turner 11, 158
Venetian Vista: Massa 7110
Venezia, Bacinio de San Marco:
Marc 6881
Venezia, Canale della Giudecca:
Marc 6882
Venice: Benali 610; Brockedon
1216; Buffet 1375; Canaletto
1522; Desnoyer 2920; Ehemann
3393; James 5531; Lloveras
6409; Mac Iver 6601; Turner
11, 158; Wihag 12, 214; Winkler
12, 256
Venice, Bacino di San Marco:
Kokoschka 5927
Venice, Canal Grande:
Canaletto 1523
Venice, Dogana and San Giorgio
Maggiore: Turner 11, 160
Venice, Giudecca: Turner
11, 161
Venice--Gondola: Renoir 9350
Venice in Blue Light:
Mouly 7801
Venice, Italy, Canal: Haymson
4922
Venice, Italy, Doge's Palace:
Haymson 4923

Venice, Italy, Gondolas:
Haymson 4924
Venice, Italy, St. Marks:
Haymson 4925
Venice, Piazza San Marco:
Canaletto 1524
Venice, St. Marks Square:
Renoir 9351
Venice, San Giorgio Maggiore:
Guardi 4544; Monet 7655
Venice, San Marco Harbor:
Canaletto 1525
Venice, St. Maria della Salute:
Kokoschka 5928; Signac 10, 353
Venice Vert et Gris: Mouly
7802
Venice with Campanile:
Luschner 6558
Venise: Carzou 1633; Guardi
4545
Venise, Vue de Torcello:
Hambourg 4624
Venus: Botticelli 968, 1005;
Franciabigio 3747; Golding
4222; Lorenzo di Credi
6472; Modigliani 7542; Titian
11, 048; Ward 12, 047
Venus and Adonis: Rubens 9724
Venus and Cupid: Bronzino
1230; Medici 7296; Velasquez
11, 688
Venus and the Lute Player:
Titian 11, 049
Venus and Mars: Pompeian 8784
Venus at the Mirror: Lys 6571
Venus of Urbino: Titian 11, 038
Venus with the Little Dog:
Titian 11, 050
Verdict of the People: Bingham
694
Verity: Grose 4489
Vermont Farm: Sessions 10, 225
Vermont Landscape: Lucioni
6515
Vermont Pastorale: Faucett
3518; Lucioni 6516
Vernissage: Dufy 3167
Vers le Pacifique: Ambraseth
102
Versailles: Dongen 3008
The Viaduct: Cezanne 1844
Victor Guye: Goya 4267

Victorian Interior: Pippin 8662
Victorian Portraits: Howard
5342
Victorious Cupid: Caravaggio
1583
Victory Dance: Remington 9146
Victory of Constantine Over
Maxentius: Piero 8620
Victory of DeNain: Mathieu
7132
Victory of Samothrace: Greece
4355
La Vie en Rose: Dufy 3168
Le Vielle Rue Saint-Vincent:
Utrillo 11, 357
Vienna from the Belvedere:
Canaletto 1526; Schutz 10, 100
Vienna Woods: Waldmuller
11, 918
La Vierge aux Animaux: Durer
3243
Le Vieux College: Utrillo
11, 358
View at Hampstead Heath:
Constable 2142
View from the Forest: Hopf
5299
View from Hyde Park: Bartlett
476
View from Louveciennes:
Pissarro 8723
View from the Study Window:
Bratby 1165
View in the Black Forest:
Munding 7836
View in Perspective of a
Perfect Sunset: Berman 648
View in the Rhone Valley:
Kokoschka 5930
View into Far Distance: Tauber
10, 852
View into Mountains: Grimm
4421
View near Fort Miller Bridge:
Wall-Hill 11, 925
View near Hudson: Wall-Hill
11, 926
View near King's Bromley-on-
Trent: Gainsborough 3816
View near Volterra: Corot 2254
View of Amsterdam, West
Church Tower: Monet 7656

View of the Arc Valley:
Cezanne 1845
View of Arles: Van Gogh 11, 608
View of Arles with Iris:
Van Gogh 11, 609
View of Auvers: Van Gogh
11, 610
View of a Bay: Rosa 9557
View of Cagnes: Renoir 9352
View of the Canale di Brenta:
Guardi 4546
View of a City: Lorenzetti 6457
View of Clerval: Bombois 853
View of Dedham: Gainsborough
3817
View of Delft: Vermeer 11, 739
View of Dresden: Canaletto
1527; Kokoschka 5929
View of the Ducal Palace and
the Piazzetta: Canaletto
1528
View of Florence: Corot 2253
View of the Gazzada: Canaletto
1529
View of the Grand Canal in
Venice: Canaletto 1530
View of Grenoble: Jongkind
5603
View of Innsbruck: Durer 3240
View of Ischia: Pitloo 8727
View of the Laguna at Venice:
Guardi 4547
View of London: Canaletto 1531
View of London with the Thames:
Canaletto 1532
View of Mount Vernon: Bartlett
477; Grailly 4300
View of Munich: Canaletto 1533
View of Murano Canal: Canaletto
1534
View of Ossining: Havell 4731
View of Paris: Dufy 3060
View of Pillnitz: Stengel 10, 620
View of Pirna: Canaletto 1535
View of Pirna with the Fortress
of Sonnenschein: Canaletto
1536
View of the Post Office: Renoir
9353
View of the Roman Forum:
Panini 8133
View of Rome: Canaletto 1537

614

Village Wedding: Brueghel 1296
Village with Watermill: Hobbema 5161
Ville d'Avray: Corot 2255
Villefranche: Barle 449
Villendry: Haymson 4773
Villeneuve-les-Avignon: Corot 2256
Vincent's House at Arles: Van Gogh 11, 612
Vineyard: Van Gogh 11, 613
Vintage: Goya 4268
Violin: Beecher 557; Crepet 2360; Picasso 8562
Violin and Glasses: Gris 4441
Violin and Pipe with the Word Polka: Braque 1159
Violin et Verres: Gris 4441
Violinist: Chagall 1888
Violinist Seated: Degas 2794
Violoncello Player: Metsu 7373
Virgil: Signorelli 10, 367
The Virgin: Angelico 209; Daddi 2489, 2490; Duccio 3040; Luini 6526; Perugino 8301; Raffaello 8958; Thayer 10, 888
Virgin Adoring: Correggio 2277; Lippi 6367, 6368; Pinturicchio 8649
Virgin Adoring the Child: Baldovinetti 430; Botticini 1010; Correggio 2278; Dolci 2989; Lippi 6360, 6361, 6369; Neri 7935; Perugino 8298
Virgin Adoring the Child, and Angels: Botticini 1011
Virgin and Child: Angelico 234; Antoniazzo Romano 269; Baldovinetti 429; Bartolo di Fredi 481; Batoni 510; Bellini 583; Catalonian 1677; Cignani 2020; Crivelli 2370 to 2372; Dolci 2990, 2991; Duccio 3041; Florence School 3648; Fouquet 3693; Fuhric 3791; Gaddi 3801; Gentile 4000; Giambono 4050; Giotto 4155; Lambertini 6051; Lippi 6371 to 6373; Lorenzetti 6458, 6459, 6463; Lorenzo Veneziano 6479; Luini 6527; Maestro 6635; Matteo 7214; Metsys 7327; Murillo 7879;

Neroccio 7939; Novolone 8010; Rico 9418: Rubens 9725; Sano 9972; Sassoferrato 10, 003, 10, 004; Tura 11, 134; Tuscany 11, 165; Unknown 11, 237; Van Loo 11, 628
Virgin and Child and Sacred History: Lippi 6374
Virgin and Child and St. John: Sogliani 10, 490
Virgin and Child and Saints: Tisi 11, 009
Virgin and Child Enthroned and Saints: Perugino 8299
Virgin and Child in Glory: Altdorfer 96
Virgin and Child with Angels: Angelico 235; Sassoferrato 10, 005
Virgin and Child with Forget-Me-Nots: Rubens 9726
Virgin and Child with St. Anne and John the Baptist: Leonardo 6285
Virgin and Child with St. George and St. Paul: Bellini 585
Virgin and Child with Saints: Bellini 584
Virgin and St. Anne: Lorenzo da Sanseverino 6477
Virgin and St. John: Grunewald 4512
Virgin and Saints: Angelico 236
Virgin Annunciate: Bonfigli 371; Botticini 1012; Lippi 6362, 6370; Sano 9973
Virgin, Child and St. Anne: Leonardo 6286
Virgin, Child, Magdalene and St. Catherine: Bellini 586
Virgin Enthroned: Angelico 237; Guido 4567
Virgin Enthroned and Two Angels: Memling 7336
Virgin Enthroned with Angel Musicians: Boccati 798
Virgin Enthroned with Angels: Boccati 799
Virgin Enthroned with Child: Crivelli 2373
Virgin Enthroned with Child and Saints: Veneziano 11, 703

615

Virgin Enthroned with Saints:
Mantegna 6758
Virgin Enthroned with Saints and
Federico da Montefeltro:
Piero 8621
Virgin Forest at Sunset: Rousseau
9672
Virgin Nursing the Child:
Solario 10, 494
Virgin of Autun: Van Eyck
11, 438
Virgin of the Bowl: Correggio
2279
Virgin of the Chaplet: Murillo
7880
Virgin of Divine Love: Raffaello
8960
Virgin of Humility: Giov. di
Paolo 4171
Virgin of the Impannata:
Raffaello 8961
Virgin of Lourdes: Ciseri 2040
Virgin of Mercy: Schramm
10, 084
Virgin of the Misericordia:
Parri 8149; Piero 8622
Virgin of the Red Cherubs:
Bellini 587
Virgin of the Rocks: Leonardo
6287
Virgin of St. Jerome: Correggio
2280
Virgin of Sorrow: Sassoferrato
10, 006
Virgin of Sorrows: Marmion
6992
Virgin of Succour: Daddi 2491
Virgin of the Throne: Memling
7337
Virgin of the Veil: Castello 1673
Virgin Surrounded by Animals:
Durer 3243
Virgin with the Blue Diadem:
Raffaello 8959
Virgin with the Child and St.
John: Raffaello 8962
Virgin with Child and Saints:
Perugino 8300
Virgin with Folded Hands:
Sassoferrato 10, 007
Virgin with St. Ines and St.
Thecla: Greco 4340

Virgin with Sleeping Child:
Bellini 588
The Virgin Worshipped by the
Chancellor: Van Eyck 11, 439
Visa: Davis 2624
Viscount of Stafford: Van Dyck
11, 424
Vision of a Brother and of the
Bishop: Giotto 4156
Vision of Ezechiel: Raffaello
8963
Vision of St. Eustace: Pisano
8680
Vision of St. Hubert: Master
7115
Vision of Santa Pina: Ghirlandaio
4044
Visit of the Sovereign: Spitzweg
10, 559
Visit to the Temple: Chang
Shu-Chi 1904
The Visitation: Albertinelli 34
Visitation of the Virgin:
Ghirlandaio 4045
Visitor: Whitney 12, 196
Vitellini Bianchi: Palizzi 8105
Voice of the Nightingale: Stella
10, 619
Voiles: Bessil 663
Volte: Windisch-Graetz 12, 246
Volubilis: Dufy 3170
La Vue Difficile: Boilly 827
Vue de la Place San Marc:
Cachard 1451
Vue Proche de Genes: Vernet
11, 761
Vue de la Salute from La
Piazzetta: Cachard 1452
Vue Proche de Mont: Vernet
11, 762
Vulcan's Forge: Velasquez
11, 689

W. Van Haythuysen: Hals 4623
Wachtung Scene: Bross 1238
Wade Gallery: Layton 6174
Wagner: Pach 8088
Wagon Boss: Russell 9835
Wagon in the Dunes: Corot 2257
Wagon Shed: Sloane 10, 460
Wagon Trail: Frommhold 3784
Waif: Dallas-Simpson 2523;
Keane 5741

616

Waterfall in the Pines: Yin-Tso
12, 412
Waterfowl: Roman 9539
Watermelon: Lowrie 6496
Watermelon Boy: Steinlauf
10, 616
Watermill with a Red Roof:
Hobbema 5162
The Wave: Hokusai 5200
Waves: Kalckreuth 5627
Way in the Cornfield: Tauber
10, 853
Way in the Heathyland:
Bachmann 417
Way in the Park: Bachmann
418
The Way to Emmaus: Zung
12, 479
Way to the Quarry: Morado
7723
Way to the Village Church:
Leader 6179
Wayside Barn: Pelham 8238
Wayside Inn: Grose 4490
We Give Thanks: Stevenson
10, 639
We Give Thee Thanks: Smith
10, 468
We Greet Thee: Gauguin 3955
We Three: Lier 6329
The Weald: Hilder 5118
Weaning the Calf: Homer
5262
Weary Sportsman: Morland
7764
Weather Beaten: Homer 5263
Weather Driven: Schnars
10, 065
Weathervane Crane: Minami
7457
Weber: Pach 8089
Webster, Daniel: Brown 1247
Wedding Bells: Meunier 7381
Wedding D nce: Brueghel 1297
Wedding Feast: Brueghel 1299
Wedding Feast in Holland:
Oomeling 8044
Wedding in the Thirties: Henry
5018
Weeping Willow: Monet 7659
Welch 1907: Saalburg 9895
Welcome Spring: Tarrant 10, 834

Well Fleet: Johnson 5583
Welsh Estuary: Bradshaw 1086
Welsh Farm: Bradshaw 1087
Werdenberg: Marc 6885
Werrington Azaleas: Zinkeisen
12, 459
The West: Gropper 4454
West Country Harbour: Greig
4381
West Country Mails: Pollard
8747
West Highlands Landscape:
Clark 2059
West Park: Beckmann 551
West Point: Haymson 4905
West Side: Maile 6648
West Springfield: Moore 7717
West Wildwood: Stuempfig
10, 724
Westchester Hills: Hays 4943
Wester Church in Amsterdam:
Vermeer 11, 740
Westerham Mill: Hilder 5119
Western Scenes: Teague 10, 867
Western Sea: Feininger 3583
Western Vista: Dzigurski 3287
Westcote's, St. Ives: Sherwin
10, 331
Westminster Bridge: Aldin 64
Westminster Bridge and the
Houses of Parliament: Klitz
5876
Westminster from Somerset
House: Canaletto 1540
Westward: Blashfield 762
Wet Sands, Bamburgh: Flint
3645
Wet Season Seascape: Australia
352
Wettersteingebirge: Bachmann
419
Whadden Chase at Waterloo:
Lyne 6569
What Happened to Your Hand:
Anderson 126
What Next: Valadie 11, 370
What's O'Clock: Hemsley 4984
Wheat Landscape: Vlaminck
11, 865
Wheatfield: Van Gogh 11, 617
Wheatfield with Crows: Van Gogh
11, 618

Wheatfields: Ruisdael 9758
When Autumn Comes: Rawson 9896
When Autumn is Here: Pushman 8882
When Cows Were Wild: Russell 9816, 9837
When Evening Comes: Froot 3786
When Horseflesh Comes High: Russell 9838
When Horses Turn Back: Russell 9839
When the Leaves Begin to Fall: Freitag 3764; Kruger 6009
When Mules Wear Diamonds: Russell 9840
When Nose of Horse Beats Eyes of Man: Russell 9841
When Sioux and Blackfeet Meet: Russell 9842
When Tracks Spell Meat: Russell 9843
When Wagon Trails Were Dim: Russell 9844
Whenever: Seasonwein 10, 176
Where Do We Come From: Gauguin 3956
Where the Fisherfolk Live: Rawson 8987
Where Guns Were Their Passports: Russell 9845
Where the Sun Goes: Amick 112
Whig and Tory: Sadler 9925
Whipporwill: Woodson 12, 382
Whirlaway: Amick 113; Morris 7775, 7776
Whirling: Kandinsky 5661
Whispering: Cydney 2480
Whispering Breeze: Newton 7949
Whistler's Mother: Whistler 12, 187
Whistling Boy: Duveneck 3262
White 1910: Saalburg 9896
White and Brown Mums: DeMarco 2859
White and Gold Peonies: Carrier 1615
White and Purple Water Lilies: Monet 7660

White Begonias: Booth 905
White Birch: Parrish 8169
White Birches in Vermont: Lucioni 6517
White Canadian Barn No. 2 1932: O'Keeffe 8036
White Caps: Dzigurski 3293
White Cliffs of Dover: Wilkinson 12, 227
White Cloth: Braque 1160
White Clown: Picasso 8564
White Doe: Waters 12, 069
White Dress: Matisse 7205
White Flower: O'Keeffe 8037
White Fluted Vase: Clayton 2075
White Fronts: Scott 10, 165
White Girl: Whistler 12, 189
White Gloves: Dyf 3279
The White Horse: Bellows 605; Constable 2145; Gauguin 3957; Potter 8813
White Horses: Arenys 298
White House in Dangast: Heckel 4955
White Houses in Brittany: Buffet 1376
White Hydrangeas: Helstrom 4982
White Kitten: Armour 304
White Lilac: Manet 6745
White Mallows: Back 382
White Mill: Lancaster 6062
White Mountain Scenery: Durand 3188
White Mountains and Aspens: Wood 12, 373
White Navajo Pinto: Leigh 6244
White Roses: Huldah 5397; Renoir 9354; Van Gogh 11, 619
White Sails: Arco 280; Sherwin 10, 332
White Ships: Sargent 9987
White Thoroughbreds: Arenys 299
White Town by the Sea: Wagner 11, 907
White Vase: Haymson 4763
Whitehall from Richmond House: Canaletto 1541
Who Killed the Bear, or "The Price of his Robe": Russell 9846

The Window: Delauney 2853;
Picasso 8565
Window in Bucks: Nash 7900
The Winds: Botticelli 970
Windsor Castle: Lloveras 6411
Windsor from the River:
Hilder 5121
Windswept Palms: Hayward
4948
Windward Shore: Waugh 12, 129
Wine Glass: Braque 1161
Wine Press: Puvis 8885
Wine Test: Vermeer 11, 741
Wine Tester: Vermeer 11, 742
Wing and Wind: Wood 12, 311
Wing of a Roller: Durer 3244
Winged Balloon: Grose 4491
Wings on Water: Hodgkins 5163
Wings Upon a Rose: Ward
12, 049
Winky: Layton 6175
Winning Tack: Dawson 2639
Winter: Blanchard 757; Boucher
1043; Cathelin 1685; Lancret
6077; Morganthuler 7736;
Rawson 8988; Rosai 9561;
Watson 12, 071; Watteau
12, 116
Winter by the Sea: Whorf 12, 199
Winter Estuary: Tunnicliffe
11, 182
Winter Games: Brett 1196
Winter Harbor: Gasser 3864
Winter Harmony: Twachtman
11, 166
Winter: Hunters in the Snow:
Brueghel 1300
Winter Idyl: Crane 2356
Winter in Angus: Patrick 8195
Winter in the Cascades:
Wood 12, 374
Winter in the Catskills: Lee
6218
Winter in the Marshes: Jacob
5493
Winter in New England: Blake
733; Kautzky 5692
Winter in Paris: Utrillo 11, 362
Winter in the Verde Valley:
Strater 10, 678
Winter Landscape: Brueghel 1268;
Grant 4312; McKnight 7260;
Neer 7929; Vlaminck 11, 866;

Weimann 12, 149
Winter Landscape near Dam-
martin: Cathelin 1686
Winter Morning: Ganso 3839
Winter Nightfall in the City:
Hassam 4720
Winter Plough: Shepherd
10, 303
Winter Scene: Avercamp 357;
Pissarro 8726
Winter Scene, Evening: Aver-
camp 357; Currier and Ives
2449
Winter Sea: Kerr 5774
Winter Silence: Ogden 8026
Winter, the Skaters: Lancret
6078
Winter Sport, Cortina D'Ampezzo:
Cascella 1643
Winter Sports: Hugo 5372
Winter Street Scene: Utrillo
11, 363
Winter Sun: Jacob 5494
Winter Sunshine: Eschbach
3444
Winter Teals: Danchin 2534
Winter Twilight: Moses 7791
Winter, a View of Monhegan,
Maine: Kent 5767
Winter Wonderland: Spencer
10, 537
Winter Worries: Meyer-
Eberhardt 7387
Winter's Arrival: Wood 12, 375
Winter's Glory: Aldrich 65
Winter's Mirror: Andre-Petit
141
Wintry Landscape: Nokina 7998
Wire-Haired Terrier: Anderson
131
Wisconsin Landscape: Curry
2455
Wise and Foolish Virgins:
Blake 736
Wise Old Elephant: Shepherd
10, 304
Wisteria: Monet 7662
With a Follwing Breeze: Walker
11, 921
With Grandma: MacEwen 6583
Wivenhoe Park, Essex:
Constable 2147
Wolfs in Hunting: Faust 3539

623

Xanadu: Soldwedel 10, 495

Yacht: Buffet 1377
Yacht America: Brierly 1204
Yacht at LeHavre: Dufy 3171
Yacht Basin: Dufy 3172
Yacht Basin, Geneva: Jaques
5546
Yachting Panorama: Greig
4382
Yachts at Deauville: Dufy 3173
Yale: Haymson 4907
Yealm River, Newton Ferrers:
Goodwin 4231
Yehudah: Levine 6307
Yellow Accent: Davies 2613;
Villon 11, 786
Yellow and Pink Roses: Redoute
9038
Yellow and Red Still Life:
Bonnard 897
Yellow Bird: Adler 13
Yellow Boat: Palue 8120
Yellow Books: Van Gogh 11, 623
Yellow-Breasted Chat: Audubon
345
Yellow Cactus: Luschner 6559
Yellow Chair with Pipe:
Van Gogh 11, 624
The Yellow Christ: Gauguin
3966
Yellow Cloud: Kohlstadt 5905
Yellow Coat: Macke 6621
Yellow Dahlias: Cathelin 1687
Yellow Flowers in a Blue Vase:
Leger 6234
Yellow Harlequin: Degas 2800
Yellow Horses: Marc 6911
Yellow Iris: Monet 7666
Yellow Iris with Pink Cloud:
Monet 7667
Yellow Irises: Morris 7772
Yellow Lily: Didot 2964
Yellow Madonna: Vu-Cao-Dam
11, 892
Yellow Mums: De Marco 2860
Yellow Roses: Beckmann 553
Yellow Sails: Signac 10, 354
Yellow Ships: Hundertwasser
5405
Yellow Tamein: Kelly 5753
Yellow Tulips: Booth 906

Yellow Vermilion: Nay 7927
Yosemite: Wood 12, 376
Yosemite Falls: Daniels 2537
Young America: Stobart
10, 650; Wyeth 12, 404
Young Apprentice: Modigliani
7550
Young Artists: Sideman
10, 342
Young Boy: Greuze 4399
Young Corn: Wood 12, 304
Young Dignity: Dawson 2662
Young Donkey: Wilson 12, 239
Young Donkeys: Wanklyn 11, 946
Young Field Hare, Study:
Durer 3247
Young Flute Player and a Man:
Etruscan 3472
Young Girl: Anker 257; Heem-
skerck 4962; Pippal 8660;
Renoir 9362
Young Girl at an Open Half-Door:
Rembrandt 9113
Young Girl at an Open Half-
Window: Rembrandt 9115
Young Girl at Piano: Renoir
9363
Young Girl at a Window:
Rembrandt 9114
Young Girl Bathing: Renoir 9364
Young Girl Combing her Hair:
Renoir 9365
Young Girl Holding Kitten:
Baptiste 438
Young Girl in White Dress:
Matisse 7208
Young Girl Knitting: Anker 258
Young Girl Peeling Apples:
Maes 6632
Young Girl Reading: Fragonard
3730
Young Girl Reading a Letter:
Raoux 8974
Young Girl Seated: Picasso
8590
Young Girl Singing into a Mirror:
Liotard 6346
Young Girl Waiting: Morisot
7754
Young Girl with Arm Upraised:
Picasso 8591
Young Girl with a Bird: Greuze
4400